Entrepreneurial Strategies for the Internationalization and Digitalization of SMEs

Ahmad Rafiki
Universitas Medan Area, Indonesia

Sylvia Nabila Azwa Ambad
Universiti Teknologi MARA, Malaysia

Nor Farradila Abdul Aziz
Universiti Teknologi MARA, Malaysia

A volume in the Advances in Business Strategy and Competitive Advantage (ABSCA) Book Series

Published in the United States of America by
IGI Global
Business Science Reference (an imprint of IGI Global)
701 E. Chocolate Avenue
Hershey PA, USA 17033
Tel: 717-533-8845
Fax: 717-533-8661
E-mail: cust@igi-global.com
Web site: http://www.igi-global.com

Copyright © 2024 by IGI Global. All rights reserved. No part of this publication may be reproduced, stored or distributed in any form or by any means, electronic or mechanical, including photocopying, without written permission from the publisher.
Product or company names used in this set are for identification purposes only. Inclusion of the names of the products or companies does not indicate a claim of ownership by IGI Global of the trademark or registered trademark.

Library of Congress Cataloging-in-Publication Data

CIP DATA PROCESSING

2024 Business Science Reference
ISBN(hc): 9798369335185
ISBN(sc): 9798369349410
eISBN: 9798369335192

British Cataloguing in Publication Data
A Cataloguing in Publication record for this book is available from the British Library.

All work contributed to this book is new, previously-unpublished material.
The views expressed in this book are those of the authors, but not necessarily of the publisher.

For electronic access to this publication, please contact: eresources@igi-global.com.

Advances in Business Strategy and Competitive Advantage (ABSCA) Book Series

Patricia Ordóñez de Pablos
Universidad de Oviedo, Spain

ISSN:2327-3429
EISSN:2327-3437

MISSION

Business entities are constantly seeking new ways through which to gain advantage over their competitors and strengthen their position within the business environment. With competition at an all-time high due to technological advancements allowing for competition on a global scale, firms continue to seek new ways through which to improve and strengthen their business processes, procedures, and profitability.

The **Advances in Business Strategy and Competitive Advantage (ABSCA) Book Series** is a timely series responding to the high demand for state-of-the-art research on how business strategies are created, implemented and re-designed to meet the demands of globalized competitive markets. With a focus on local and global challenges, business opportunities and the needs of society, the **ABSCA** encourages scientific discourse on doing business and managing information technologies for the creation of sustainable competitive advantage.

Coverage

- Joint Ventures
- Competitive Strategy
- International Business Strategy
- Resource-Based Competition
- Globalization

IGI Global is currently accepting manuscripts for publication within this series. To submit a proposal for a volume in this series, please contact our Acquisition Editors at Acquisitions@igi-global.com or visit: http://www.igi-global.com/publish/.

The (ISSN) is published by IGI Global, 701 E. Chocolate Avenue, Hershey, PA 17033-1240, USA, www.igi-global.com. This series is composed of titles available for purchase individually; each title is edited to be contextually exclusive from any other title within the series. For pricing and ordering information please visit http://www.igi-global.com/book-series/advances-business-strategy-competitive-advantage/73672. Postmaster: Send all address changes to above address. Copyright © IGI Global. All rights, including translation in other languages reserved by the publisher. No part of this series may be reproduced or used in any form or by any means – graphics, electronic, or mechanical, including photocopying, recording, taping, or information and retrieval systems – without written permission from the publisher, except for non commercial, educational use, including classroom teaching purposes. The views expressed in this series are those of the authors, but not necessarily of IGI Global.

Titles in this Series

For a list of additional titles in this series, please visit:
http://www.igi-global.com/book-series/advances-business-strategy-competitive-advantage/73672

Organizational Paradigms of Global Business Fusion of Technology and Cultural Diversity
Alessandra Ricciardelli (University of Naples "Federico II", Italy) and Maurizio Decastri (University of Rome Tor Vergata, Italy)
Business Science Reference • copyright 2024 • 330pp • H/C (ISBN: 9798369334829) • US $285.00 (our price)

Impact of New Technology on Next-Generation Leadership
Alka Agnihotri (Galgotias University, India) Renu Agarwal (UTS Business School, Australia) Alka Maurya (Amity University, Noida, India) Manasi Sinha (Galgotias University, India) and Balamurugan Balusamy (Shiv Nadar Institution of Eminence, India)
Business Science Reference • copyright 2024 • 337pp • H/C (ISBN: 9798369319468) • US $395.00 (our price)

Economics and Environmental Responsibility in the Global Beverage Industry
Cristina Raluca Gh. Popescu (University of Bucharest, Romania & The Bucharest University of Economic Studies, Romania) Javier Martínez-Falcó (University of Alicante, Spain & University of Stellenbosch, South Africa) Bartolomé Marco-Lajara (University of Alicante, Spain) Eduardo Sánchez-García (University of Alicante, Spain) and Luis A. Millán-Tudela (University of Alicante, Spain)
Business Science Reference • copyright 2024 • 439pp • H/C (ISBN: 9798369321492) • US $285.00 (our price)

Building Organizational Resilience With Neuroleadership
Shefali Saluja (Chitkara Business School, Chitkara University, India) Jyoti Kukreja (Jagannath International Management School, India) and Sandhir Sharma (Chitkara Business School, Chitkara University, India)
Business Science Reference • copyright 2024 • 352pp • H/C (ISBN: 9798369317853) • US $275.00 (our price)

701 East Chocolate Avenue, Hershey, PA 17033, USA
Tel: 717-533-8845 x100 • Fax: 717-533-8661
E-Mail: cust@igi-global.com • www.igi-global.com

Table of Contents

Preface xxv

Chapter 1
A Conceptual Study on Entrepreneurship and Digital Innovation 1

    Hasan Huseyin Uzunbacak, Suleyman Demirel University, Turkey
    Şerife Karagöz, Süleyman Demirel University, Turkey
    Tuğba Erhan, Süleyman Demirel University, Turkey

Chapter 2
A Paradigm Shift Among Indian SMEs Towards Adoption of Affiliate Marketing and Social Media 21

    Raj Kumar Singh, Graphic Era Hill University, India
    Bhanupriya Khatri, Chandigarh University, India
    Nidhi Sharma, Chandigarh University, India
    Shad Ahmad Khan, University of Buraimi, Oman

Chapter 3
A Systematic Literature Review on Strategies for Enhancing International SMEs' Performance in Malaysia and Future Research Agenda 49

    Sylvia Nabila Azwa Ambad, Universiti Teknologi MARA, Malaysia
    Mazurina Mohd Ali, Universiti Teknologi MARA, Malaysia & Kampus
        Puncak Alam, Malaysia

Chapter 4
Digital Financial Capability and Entrepreneurial Performance in MSMEs 77

    Sari Nuzullina Ramadhani, Universitas Medan Area, Indonesia
    Rana Fathinah Ananda, Universitas Medan Area, Indonesia
    Dyah Setyaningrum, Universitas indonesia, Indonesia
    Nur Azizah Siregar, Universitas Medan Area, Indonesia

Chapter 5
Elevating SME Success: A Comprehensive Exploration of Source Credibility in Shaping Consumer Attitudes Toward TikTok Advertisements 89

    Bernadine Adel Sitorus, Universiti Teknologi MARA, Malaysia
    Sylvia Nabila Azwa Ambad, Universiti Teknologi MARA, Malaysia
    Cynthia Robert Dawayan, Universiti Teknologi MARA, Malaysia

Chapter 6
Enhancing SME Internationalization and Digitalization Through Candidate Elimination Algorithms: A Strategic Approach 110

    C. V. Suresh Babu, Hindustan Institute of Technology and Science, India
    Barath Kumar S., Hindustan Institute of Technology and Science, India
    Nithesh Kumar C., Hindustan Institute of Technology and Science, India
    Dhineshwaren M., Hindustan Institute of Technology and Science, India
    Abbas S., Hindustan Institute of Technology and Science, India

Chapter 7
Entrepreneurial Strategies for Business Intelligence and Blockchain 137

    Kathirvel Ayyaswamy, Department of Computer Science and
        Engineering, Panimalar Engineering College, Chennai, India
    Naren Kathirvel, Anand Institute of Higher Technology, India
    Subramanian C., Eswari Engineering College, India
    Maheswaran C. P., Sri Krishna College of Technology, India

Chapter 8
Entrepreneurial Strategies for Sustainable Performance of Small and Medium Enterprises in Unprecedent Times 164

    Mugove Mashingaidze, Great Zimbabwe University, Zimbabwe
    Segolame Kalayakgosi, Department of Business Management, BA
        ISAGO University, Botswana
    Ephraim Govere, Department of Business Management, BA ISAGO
        University, Botswana

Chapter 9
Factors Affecting Green Purchase Behaviors for Small and Medium
Enterprises (SMEs) in Uganda ....
198
> *Wasswa Shafik, School of Digital Science, Universiti Brunei
>   Darussalam, Gadong, Brunei & Dig Connectivity Research
>   Laboratory, Kampala, Uganda*

Chapter 10
Evaluating the Impact of Crowdfunding on Emerging Markets: Legal
Frameworks, Investment Potential, and Financial Reporting within IFRS in
the Entrepreneurial Ecosystem ....
225
> *Betül Açikgöz, Yozgat Bozok University, Turkey*

Chapter 11
How Does Rural Entrepreneurship Contribute to the Resilience and
Sustainability of Rural Communities? ....
255
> *Onan Marakali Siregar, Faculty of Social and Political Sciences,
>   Universitas Sumatera Utara, Indonesia*
> *Hatta Ridho, Faculty of Social and Political Sciences, Universitas
>   Sumatera Utara, Indonesia*
> *Muhammad Arifin Nasution, Faculty of Social and Political Sciences,
>   Universitas Sumatera Utara, Indonesia*
> *Muhammad Dharma Tuah Putra Nasution, Universitas Pembangunan
>   Panca Budi, Indonesia*

Chapter 12
Innovation Dynamics in Family Firms: A Content Analysis Study..................
273
> *Muhammad Dharma Tuah Putra Nasution, Universitas Pembangunan
>   Panca Budi, Indonesia*
> *Muhammad Chaerul Rizky, Universitas Pembangunan Panca Budi,
>   Indonesia*
> *Maya Macia, Universitas Pembangunan Panca Budi, Indonesia*
> *Noni Ardian, Universitas Pembangunan Panca Budi, Indonesia*
> *Suwarno Suwarno, Universitas Pembangunan Panca Budi, Indonesia*
> *Husni Muharram Ritonga, Universitas Pembangunan Panca Budi,
>   Indonesia*

Chapter 13
Internationalisation of Family SMEs: A Bibliometric Analysis of Recent Trends and Future Research Direction.. 294

Maulidar Agustina, Universitas Syiah Kuala, Indonesia
M. Shabri Abd. Majid, Universitas Syiah Kuala, Indonesia
Hafasnuddin Hafasnuddin, Universitas Syiah Kuala, Indonesia
Yahya Yahya, Sekolah Tinggi Ilmu Ekonomi Sabang, Indonesia

Chapter 14
Internationalization Strategies: A Complementary Perspective Using the Resource Dependency Theory 316

António Carrizo Moreira, University of Aveiro, Portugal
Adriana Simões, University of Aveiro, Portugal
Ana Sofia Sousa, University of Aveiro, Portugal
João Gonçalo Martins, University of Aveiro, Portugal

Chapter 15
Synergizing Fashion Design and Entrepreneurship Education: Pathways and Implications... 343

Zhang Xiaohan, Shandong Vocational College of Science and Technology, China
Rohana Zur, College of Creative Arts, University Technology MARA, Malaysia

Chapter 16
The Impact of Value Co-Creation of the NAIFEST Exhibition on the Perceived Value of INDOBUILDTECH 2022 Exhibitors: The Dynamic Interaction of DART Model on Value Co-Creation Towards Customer Perceived Value.. 371

Sakanti Sasri, University of Indonesia, Indonesia
Retno Kusumastuti, University of Indonesia, Indonesia

Chapter 17
Modeling Service Quality and Religiosity Towards the Implementation of the Principles of Trust and Customer Satisfaction 406

    Nilam Sari, State Islamic University of Ar-Raniry, Indonesia
    Winny Dian Winny Safitri, State Islamic University of Ar-Raniry, Indonesia
    Riski Rinaldi, State Islamic University of Ar-Raniry, Indonesia
    Nevi Hasnita, State Islamic University of Ar-Raniry, Indonesia
    Maisya Auliandhana, State Islamic University of Ar-Raniry, Indonesia

Compilation of References 417

About the Contributors 489

Index 493

Detailed Table of Contents

Preface xxv

Chapter 1
A Conceptual Study on Entrepreneurship and Digital Innovation 1

    Hasan Huseyin Uzunbacak, Suleyman Demirel University, Turkey
    Şerife Karagöz, Süleyman Demirel University, Turkey
    Tuğba Erhan, Süleyman Demirel University, Turkey

In the contemporary business landscape, digital innovation and entrepreneurship mutually reinforce and enhance one another as crucial elements. The interrelation between these concepts becomes evident as technological advancements become integrated into the realm of business. While digital innovation involves the creation of new technologies and business models, entrepreneurship symbolizes the effort to transform these innovative ideas into commercial value. Entrepreneurs can develop new and competitive advantage ventures by embracing digital innovation and evaluating technologically compatible business opportunities. This paradigm, in which digital innovation is intertwined with entrepreneurship, can create a basis on which businesses focus on constantly producing innovative solutions to achieve success in the rapidly changing digital ecosystem. In this context, the main objective of this study is to provide a fresh viewpoint for comprehending the relationship between digital innovation and entrepreneurship, with the intention of steering subsequent research endeavors in this area.

Chapter 2
A Paradigm Shift Among Indian SMEs Towards Adoption of Affiliate
Marketing and Social Media ....
21

    Raj Kumar Singh, Graphic Era Hill University, India
    Bhanupriya Khatri, Chandigarh University, India
    Nidhi Sharma, Chandigarh University, India
    Shad Ahmad Khan, University of Buraimi, Oman

The purpose of this study was to evaluate how likely small and medium enterprises (SMEs) are to adopt affiliate marketing and social media to improve their customer base, profitability, and sustainable growth. Data was collected from 523 entrepreneurs in India, using a purposive sampling method. The results revealed that affiliate marketing has a significant impact on social media and consumer buying intention. Additionally, there are considerable connections between producer's intent and affiliate marketing, producer's intent and social media, and producer's intent and consumer buying intention. This study highlights the critical role of social media and affiliate marketing in enhancing consumer purchasing intentions in SMEs. Based on the results, marketers are recommended to effectively engage with customers on social media platforms to improve their purchasing intentions. This research is groundbreaking as it provides valuable insights into the relationship between social media, affiliate marketing, and consumer behavior in the SME sector.

Chapter 3
A Systematic Literature Review on Strategies for Enhancing International SMEs' Performance in Malaysia and Future Research Agenda 49

   Sylvia Nabila Azwa Ambad, Universiti Teknologi MARA, Malaysia
   Mazurina Mohd Ali, Universiti Teknologi MARA, Malaysia & Kampus
     Puncak Alam, Malaysia

SMEs face more intimidating obstacles in international expansion than their larger counterparts. These challenges arise from resource limitations, innovation, and globalisation. Nonetheless, there exists a scarcity of SLRs targeting international business strategies for SMEs, with the majority focused on global growth challenges. This chapter aims to bridge this gap by conducting a systematic analysis of strategies for enhancing international SMEs' performance, mapping intellectual territories, and proposing future research directions. Utilising the Scopus database, 22 relevant articles were selected. Applying thematic analysis techniques, the study uncovered seven main themes that contributed to the enhancement of international SME performance in Malaysia. The main themes are; Strategic Orientation, Digital Transformation and E-Commerce, Intellectual Capital, Sustainability and Environmental Practices, Managerial Capabilities, Risk and Markert Uncertainty and Business Culture. These themes encapsulate the 19 sub-themes that contribute to SME success in the global marketplace. Despite an improving trend in SME international performance, the analysis shows a fragmented environment. This highlights the need for a complete, systematic study to help academics, SMEs, and policymakers reach the global market.

Chapter 4
Digital Financial Capability and Entrepreneurial Performance in MSMEs 77

    Sari Nuzullina Ramadhani, Universitas Medan Area, Indonesia
    Rana Fathinah Ananda, Universitas Medan Area, Indonesia
    Dyah Setyaningrum, Universitas indonesia, Indonesia
    Nur Azizah Siregar, Universitas Medan Area, Indonesia

This chapter aims to describe and discuss digital financial capabilities and entrepreneurial performance in currently developing MSMEs. This study, using content analysis tools, refers to a number of sources, including reports, government documents, research publications, and a research database called Scopus. The study on digital financial capabilities and entrepreneurial performance in MSMEs is also covered in this chapter, with active nations and affiliates publishing research publications. Improving digital financial skills and entrepreneurial performance faces a number of obstacles in different nations. It is crucial that practitioners, researchers, and other stakeholders examine specific research on the relationship between digital financial capabilities and entrepreneurial performance in order to find effective solutions for the nation.

Chapter 5
Elevating SME Success: A Comprehensive Exploration of Source Credibility in Shaping Consumer Attitudes Toward TikTok Advertisements 89

    Bernadine Adel Sitorus, Universiti Teknologi MARA, Malaysia
    Sylvia Nabila Azwa Ambad, Universiti Teknologi MARA, Malaysia
    Cynthia Robert Dawayan, Universiti Teknologi MARA, Malaysia

This study examines the impact of TikTok influencers on the Malaysian cosmetic industry, focusing on source credibility dimensions (trustworthiness, expertise, attractiveness) and their effect on consumers' attitudes toward advertisement. The data was gathered via a Google Form survey, targeting 18-34 year old active TikTok users, analysed using SmartPLS 4.0. Findings show that trustworthiness and attractiveness of influencers positively influence attitudes toward advertisements for local cosmetics, but expertise does not. The implications of this study include insights for influencer marketing dynamics on TikTok, especially for SMEs in utilising influencers to advertise their cosmetic products.

Chapter 6
Enhancing SME Internationalization and Digitalization Through Candidate Elimination Algorithms: A Strategic Approach 110

    C. V. Suresh Babu, Hindustan Institute of Technology and Science, India
    Barath Kumar S., Hindustan Institute of Technology and Science, India
    Nithesh Kumar C., Hindustan Institute of Technology and Science, India
    Dhineshwaren M., Hindustan Institute of Technology and Science, India
    Abbas S., Hindustan Institute of Technology and Science, India

This chapter explores the potential of candidate elimination algorithms in facilitating the internationalization and digitalization of small and medium-sized enterprises (SMEs). By focusing on their application in real-time marketing on social media platforms, SMEs can gain valuable direction for optimizing their marketing campaigns. Leveraging advanced algorithms becomes imperative for SMEs to remain competitive in today's digital age. The chapter delves into the integration of candidate elimination algorithms into the overarching rule base governing marketing strategies. Through an in-depth analysis of existing literature and empirical studies, the efficacy of these algorithms in enhancing SME marketing performance and global expansion is evaluated. The research aims to provide SMEs with actionable insights on utilizing candidate elimination algorithms to improve their internationalization and digitalization endeavors, thereby contributing to the literature on SME transformation and digital marketing strategies.

Chapter 7
Entrepreneurial Strategies for Business Intelligence and Blockchain 137

    Kathirvel Ayyaswamy, Department of Computer Science and
        Engineering, Panimalar Engineering College, Chennai, India
    Naren Kathirvel, Anand Institute of Higher Technology, India
    Subramanian C., Eswari Engineering College, India
    Maheswaran C. P., Sri Krishna College of Technology, India

Blockchain is a distributed database that is shared by multiple system nodes. The reason it is named blockchain is that it gathers data in encrypted blocks that are connected to other sets of blocks to create a virtual chain. The development of numerous cryptocurrencies, dApp monetization, smart personal contracts, decentralized finance apps (Defi), and non-fungible tokens (NFTs), preceded general adoption of the blockchain concept. Blockchain technology (BT) is digital money, which increases in value every hour by a factor of bigger than its previous worth. Even though blockchain's widespread appeal has been confined to its role in the development of bitcoin and other cryptocurrencies, a number of other applications are currently being developed steadily. This demonstrates the promise of decentralized technology and the undeniable influence of blockchain on business across many industries.

Chapter 8
Entrepreneurial Strategies for Sustainable Performance of Small and Medium Enterprises in Unprecedent Times 164

    Mugove Mashingaidze, Great Zimbabwe University, Zimbabwe
    Segolame Kalayakgosi, Department of Business Management, BA
        ISAGO University, Botswana
    Ephraim Govere, Department of Business Management, BA ISAGO
        University, Botswana

This chapter aims at examining the effect of entrepreneurial strategies on the sustainable performance of SMEs in Harare, Zimbabwe. The target population of the study was 3000 manufacturing SMEs in Harare. Data were drawn from a sample of 302 manufacturing SMEs using cross-sectional primary data collected from Harare. The chapter employed both descriptive and inferential statistics to estimate the effect of entrepreneurial strategies on sustainable performance. The results revealed that entrepreneurial marketing strategy, strategic partnerships, technological innovation, and business model innovation are positively and significantly related to sustainable performance. Hence, the chapter concludes that SMEs need to employ sustainable entrepreneurial strategies to enhance their survival in a rapidly changing marketing environment. SMEs with a strong orientation towards entrepreneurial orientation have better sustainable performance in developing countries. The major limitation of the chapter is that it focuses only on manufacturing SMEs in Harare, Zimbabwe.

Chapter 9
Factors Affecting Green Purchase Behaviors for Small and Medium
Enterprises (SMEs) in Uganda ....
198
> *Wasswa Shafik, School of Digital Science, Universiti Brunei Darussalam, Gadong, Brunei & Dig Connectivity Research Laboratory, Kampala, Uganda*

This study examines the environmentally conscious purchasing patterns of small and medium-sized enterprises (SMEs) in Uganda through several approaches. This research offers a critical analysis of the definition and significance of the term, emphasizing the worldwide importance and relevance of environmentally conscious consumption to small and medium-sized enterprises in Uganda. This study examines the viability of Uganda's SMEs in terms of sustainability. The study found that economic, environmental, regulatory, and customer variables influence small and medium-sized enterprises' green purchasing. This study employs the ideas of planned behavior and the diffusion of innovation to predict these acts. The study acknowledges the limitations in its sample size and data-gathering methods despite conducting a thorough examination. Finally, considering the limitations imposed by SME constraints, the study suggests conducting further research on green procurement and learning from the experiences and insights gained.

Chapter 10
Evaluating the Impact of Crowdfunding on Emerging Markets: Legal
Frameworks, Investment Potential, and Financial Reporting within IFRS in
the Entrepreneurial Ecosystem ....
225
> *Betül Açikgöz, Yozgat Bozok University, Turkey*

The study examines the impact of crowdfunding on E7 countries, highlighting its ongoing legal construction and potential for new investments and economic growth. Traditional financial institutions are hesitant to invest in innovative ventures due to risk perception. Crowdfunding, a non-conventional financial tool, has gained popularity in US and Europe, but its adoption in emerging markets is relatively recent. Study also discusses the financial reporting mechanism of crowdfunding activities, which are explained within the framework of IFRS. Crowdfunding transactions' accounting treatment depends on the campaign's nature and financial reporting requirements. Entities must determine appropriate treatment for funds received, such as revenue, liability, or equity. Equity crowdfunding may involve recognizing financial instruments like IFRS 9, while revenue recognition principles under IFRS 15 may apply for campaigns in exchange for goods or services. Disclosures about crowdfunding activities, contingent liabilities, and fair value measurement may be required in accordance with IFRS 13.

Chapter 11
How Does Rural Entrepreneurship Contribute to the Resilience and Sustainability of Rural Communities? 255

 Onan Marakali Siregar, Faculty of Social and Political Sciences,
  Universitas Sumatera Utara, Indonesia
 Hatta Ridho, Faculty of Social and Political Sciences, Universitas
  Sumatera Utara, Indonesia
 Muhammad Arifin Nasution, Faculty of Social and Political Sciences,
  Universitas Sumatera Utara, Indonesia
 Muhammad Dharma Tuah Putra Nasution, Universitas Pembangunan
  Panca Budi, Indonesia

Research on rural entrepreneurship is essential for fostering economic advancement, generating employment opportunities, and reducing poverty in rural areas. This chapter explores the unique characteristics and challenges of rural entrepreneurship compared to urban settings, highlighting the need for tailored policies and support systems. Additionally, it examines how rural entrepreneurship contributes to the resilience and sustainability of rural communities through innovative business models and economic diversification. Despite its significance, several issues remain unaddressed, prompting this study to investigate the role of rural entrepreneurship in driving economic growth, overcoming challenges, and fostering innovation for sustainable development.

Chapter 12
Innovation Dynamics in Family Firms: A Content Analysis Study.................. 273

    Muhammad Dharma Tuah Putra Nasution, Universitas Pembangunan Panca Budi, Indonesia
    Muhammad Chaerul Rizky, Universitas Pembangunan Panca Budi, Indonesia
    Maya Macia, Universitas Pembangunan Panca Budi, Indonesia
    Noni Ardian, Universitas Pembangunan Panca Budi, Indonesia
    Suwarno Suwarno, Universitas Pembangunan Panca Budi, Indonesia
    Husni Muharram Ritonga, Universitas Pembangunan Panca Budi, Indonesia

This chapter explores the significance of incremental innovation in family-owned businesses, examining their engagement, the factors shaping their innovation behavior, and the practical implications for stakeholders. Content analysis delves into various facets of entrepreneurial activities within these businesses, offering insights into their innovation processes and challenges. The findings highlight the pivotal role of existing and new knowledge in driving incremental innovation. Despite challenges such as risk aversion and succession planning, family firms leverage their unique resources to maintain a competitive edge. This chapter contributes to understanding how family-owned businesses engage in incremental innovation and its implications for long-term success and sustainability. Future research could explore wealth creation dynamics and the influence of organizational culture on innovation within these firms.

Chapter 13
Internationalisation of Family SMEs: A Bibliometric Analysis of Recent Trends and Future Research Direction..
294
    Maulidar Agustina, Universitas Syiah Kuala, Indonesia
    M. Shabri Abd. Majid, Universitas Syiah Kuala, Indonesia
    Hafasnuddin Hafasnuddin, Universitas Syiah Kuala, Indonesia
    Yahya Yahya, Sekolah Tinggi Ilmu Ekonomi Sabang, Indonesia

The global business landscape is undergoing a transformative shift, with small and medium-sized enterprises (SMEs) gaining prominence. Among them, family-owned SMEs uniquely blend familial ties with entrepreneurship, playing a pivotal role in the international market. This study conducts a bibliometric analysis of 1,355 scholarly articles within the Scopus database, revealing nine thematic clusters related to the internationalization of family SMEs. Key areas include SMEs, family business, family firms, small and medium sized enterprises, and innovation. The analysis highlights a growing scholarly interest in this field, with the *Family Business Review* originating from the United States, indexed Q1, emerging as a significant contributor. The insights not only contribute to academic discourse but also offer guidance for practitioners and policymakers aiming to support the sustainable growth and competitiveness of family SMEs globally. This study lays a foundation for future research, directing scholars towards unexplored areas in the dynamic realm of family SME internationalization.

Chapter 14

Internationalization Strategies: A Complementary Perspective Using the Resource Dependency Theory 316

 António Carrizo Moreira, University of Aveiro, Portugal
 Adriana Simões, University of Aveiro, Portugal
 Ana Sofia Sousa, University of Aveiro, Portugal
 João Gonçalo Martins, University of Aveiro, Portugal

This chapter explores the internationalization path of ALPHA, a family-owned, medium-sized Portuguese company. The analysis reveals a two-stage process. Initially, ALPHA's gradual market entry aligns with the Uppsala model, prioritizing geographically close markets and leveraging accumulated experience. However, later stages demonstrate network-based theory influences. While lacking formal networks, ALPHA prioritizes strong B2B relationships with large international clients, mirroring network bridges for market access. The case highlights the importance of trust-based B2B relationships for success. ALPHA leverages these partnerships to gain market knowledge and access new opportunities. Exporting plays a vital role, keeping ALPHA updated on technological trends and fostering innovation through diverse client projects. The company prioritizes a pragmatic approach focused on strong client relationships and win-win partnerships, emphasizing trust as a key resource. While the RBV perspective highlights investment in internal resources, reliance on intermediaries introduces limitations.

Chapter 15
Synergizing Fashion Design and Entrepreneurship Education: Pathways and Implications... 343

    Zhang Xiaohan, Shandong Vocational College of Science and
        Technology, China
    Rohana Zur, College of Creative Arts, University Technology MARA,
        Malaysia

This chapter examines the integration of fashion design education with innovative entrepreneurship education in response to the contemporary socio-economic demands of the global fashion industry. By interweaving different theories, it articulates a theoretical foundation for a cohesive approach that aims to enhance the entrepreneurial capacities of fashion design students. The first section introduces the evolving landscape of the fashion industry, marked by technological advancements, shifting market dynamics, and sustainable practices. Subsequent analysis reveals the impact of an integrated curriculum on cultivating entrepreneurial intentions, as evidenced by a longitudinal study in Shandong. Strategies for implementing this integrated approach emphasize the creation of a curriculum that mirrors the symbiotic relationship of a DNA double helix, with fashion design and entrepreneurship education as inseparable strands. The innovative educational model is posited as essential for developing the multifaceted skill set required for aspiring fashion entrepreneurs to thrive in industry.

Chapter 16
The Impact of Value Co-Creation of the NAIFEST Exhibition on the Perceived Value of INDOBUILDTECH 2022 Exhibitors: The Dynamic Interaction of DART Model on Value Co-Creation Towards Customer Perceived Value... 371

Sakanti Sasri, University of Indonesia, Indonesia
Retno Kusumastuti, University of Indonesia, Indonesia

This research study discusses the impact of NAIFEST exhibition co-creation value on the perceived value of IndoBuildTech 2022 exhibitors. Co-creation is a strategy made to provide easy access for IndoBuildTech exhibitors to meet and interact with SME architects who are one of the main targets of IndoBuildTech expo visitors. Authors use the concept of the DART framework (dialogue, access, risk assessment, and transparency) as a dimension of value co-creation to determine the factors that affect the perceived value of IndoBuildTech 2022 exhibitors with price and quality dimensions. The findings in this study prove that there is an impact of the DART dimension that affects the value of the co-creation of the NAIFEST exhibition on the perceived quality of IndoBuildTech 2022 exhibitors. Meanwhile, the risk assessment dimension consistently does not affect the co-creation value of the NAIFEST exhibition on the perceived price and quality of IndoBuildTech 2022 exhibitors.

Chapter 17
Modeling Service Quality and Religiosity Towards the Implementation of the Principles of Trust and Customer Satisfaction 406

> Nilam Sari, State Islamic University of Ar-Raniry, Indonesia
> Winny Dian Winny Safitri, State Islamic University of Ar-Raniry, Indonesia
> Riski Rinaldi, State Islamic University of Ar-Raniry, Indonesia
> Nevi Hasnita, State Islamic University of Ar-Raniry, Indonesia
> Maisya Auliandhana, State Islamic University of Ar-Raniry, Indonesia

Satisfaction is a feeling that arises, happy or disappointed, after seeing the results of a product that meets expectations. Basically, consumers will choose goods that are cheap and of good quality. Then there are other things that influence this, namely service quality and religiosity. In the practice of buying and selling, the principle of trust is also applied. When carrying out the practice of buying and selling, both traders and consumers must have the same nature of trust. This research aims to analyze the influence of service quality and religiosity on the application of the principles of trust and customer satisfaction with a case study at the electronic store using probability sampling techniques. The analytical method in this research uses structural equation modeling (SEM) PLS. The customer satisfaction model shows that the service variable influences the implementation of trust and satisfaction, while the trust variable influences customer satisfaction.

Compilation of References 417

About the Contributors 489

Index 493

Preface

In the rapidly evolving landscape of global commerce, the twin forces of internationalization and digitalization have emerged as critical determinants of success for Small and Medium-sized Enterprises (SMEs). The decision to expand beyond domestic borders and integrate digital technologies into business operations is not merely a strategic choice but a necessity for survival and growth in today's interconnected and technologically advanced world.

This edited reference book, *Entrepreneurial Strategies for the Internationalization and Digitalization of SMEs*, brings together a wealth of knowledge and insights from leading experts in the fields of entrepreneurship, innovation, and business strategy. Our primary aim is to provide a comprehensive guide that addresses the myriad challenges and opportunities associated with internationalizing and digitalizing SMEs.

Internationalization requires SMEs to navigate complex and often unpredictable environments. These include diverse regulatory landscapes, cultural differences, and competitive pressures that demand a nuanced understanding and strategic foresight. Digitalization, on the other hand, necessitates significant investment in technology, as well as the development of new capabilities and business models to harness the potential of digital tools effectively.

Our book delves into the concepts, methods, strategies, approaches, and models essential for SMEs embarking on these transformative journeys. We explore how entrepreneurial mindsets and strategies can drive efficient and effective business operations, facilitating both international expansion and digital transformation.

An essential consideration highlighted in this book is the need for sustainable business practices. While the primary goal of digitalization and internationalization is often profit maximization, it is imperative to balance this with environmentally-conscious strategies that contribute to long-term sustainability. Achieving green outcomes is not just a societal expectation but a critical factor for future prosperity. The internationalization and digitalization of SMEs should therefore be aligned with sustainable development goals, ensuring that business growth does not come at the expense of our planet.

The content of this book is structured to serve as a practical reference for a diverse audience, including practitioners, academicians, students, businessmen, entrepreneurs, and policymakers. Each chapter is meticulously crafted to offer valuable insights into various aspects such as entrepreneurship, innovation, digitalization, human capital, and business models. The book also addresses the interplay between organizational culture and sustainability, providing solutions and strategies that are both effective and environmentally responsible.

We believe that this book will not only enhance the understanding of the complexities involved in the internationalization and digitalization of SMEs but also inspire actionable strategies that contribute to sustainable business practices. Through the insights provided, we hope to equip our readers with the knowledge to drive meaningful change and achieve long-term success in the global marketplace.

We extend our heartfelt thanks to all the contributors, reviewers, and supporters who have made this book possible. It is our sincere hope that this compilation of expertise will serve as a valuable resource for all those dedicated to advancing the field of SME management and entrepreneurship.

Chapter 1: A Conceptual Study on Entrepreneurship and Digital Innovation

In this foundational chapter, Hasan Huseyin Uzunbacak, Serife Karagöz, and Tugba Erhan from Suleyman Demirel University, Turkey, explore the symbiotic relationship between entrepreneurship and digital innovation. They argue that the integration of technological advancements into business practices not only fosters the creation of new technologies and business models but also catalyzes entrepreneurial endeavors to transform these innovations into commercial successes. This chapter sets the stage for understanding how digital innovation can be leveraged by entrepreneurs to develop competitive ventures, emphasizing the need for continuous innovation in a rapidly evolving digital ecosystem. The authors aim to provide a fresh perspective that will guide future research in this dynamic field.

Chapter 2: A Paradigm Shift Among Indian SMEs Towards Adoption of Affiliate Marketing and Social Media

Raj Kumar Singh, Bhanupriya Khatri, Nidhi Sharma, and Shad Khan present a compelling analysis of the growing adoption of affiliate marketing and social media by Indian SMEs. Based on data from 523 entrepreneurs, the study reveals significant impacts of affiliate marketing on consumer buying intentions and highlights the critical role of social media in enhancing these effects. The chapter underscores the importance of engaging effectively with customers on social media platforms

Preface

to boost purchasing intentions, offering valuable insights for marketers and entrepreneurs aiming to leverage these tools for sustainable growth.

Chapter 3: A Systematic Literature Review on Strategies for Enhancing International SMEs' Performance in Malaysia and Future Research Agenda

Sylvia Nabila Azwa Ambad and Mazurina Mohd Ali conduct a systematic literature review to identify strategies that enhance the performance of international SMEs in Malaysia. Utilizing thematic analysis of 22 articles from the Scopus database, they identify seven main themes and 19 sub-themes that contribute to SME success in the global market. This chapter highlights the fragmented nature of current research and calls for a more comprehensive, systematic approach to guide academics, SMEs, and policymakers in navigating international expansion challenges.

Chapter 4: Digital Financial Capability and Entrepreneurial Performance in MSMEs

Sari Nuzullina Ramadhani, Rana Ananda, Dyah Setyaningrum, and Nur Siregar delve into the relationship between digital financial capabilities and entrepreneurial performance in MSMEs. Using content analysis of various sources, they identify key challenges and propose solutions for enhancing digital financial skills to improve business performance. This chapter serves as a critical resource for practitioners, researchers, and stakeholders aiming to foster entrepreneurial growth through improved financial capabilities.

Chapter 5: Elevating SME Success: A Comprehensive Exploration of Source Credibility in Shaping Consumer Attitudes Toward TikTok Advertisements

Bernadine Adel Sitorus, Sylvia Nabila Azwa Ambad, and Cynthia Robert Dawayan investigate the influence of TikTok influencers on consumer attitudes towards advertisements in the Malaysian cosmetic industry. Their study finds that trustworthiness and attractiveness significantly impact consumer attitudes, while expertise does not. The chapter provides actionable insights for SMEs on leveraging influencer marketing to enhance brand perception and consumer engagement on TikTok.

Chapter 6: Enhancing SME Internationalization and Digitalization Through Candidate Elimination Algorithms: A Strategic Approach

C.V. Suresh Babu, Barath Kumar S, Nithesh Kumar C, Dhineshwaren M, and Abbas S explore the use of candidate elimination algorithms to support the internationalization and digitalization of SMEs. By analyzing their application in social media marketing, the authors demonstrate how these advanced algorithms can optimize marketing campaigns and improve SME performance in global markets. The chapter offers practical strategies for SMEs to integrate these technologies into their business operations.

Chapter 7: Entrepreneurial Strategies for Business Intelligence and Blockchain

Kathirvel Ayyaswamy, Naren Kathirvel, and Subramanian C discuss the transformative potential of blockchain technology and its applications beyond cryptocurrencies. They highlight the role of blockchain in developing decentralized applications, smart contracts, and digital finance. This chapter provides a comprehensive overview of how blockchain can drive innovation and efficiency across various business sectors, offering strategic insights for entrepreneurs.

Chapter 8: Entrepreneurial Strategies for Sustainable Performance of Small and Medium Enterprises in Unprecedented Times

Mugove Mashingaidze examines the impact of entrepreneurial strategies on the sustainable performance of manufacturing SMEs in Harare, Zimbabwe. Using structural equation modeling, the study identifies key strategies such as entrepreneurial marketing, strategic partnerships, and technological innovation that contribute to sustainable performance. The chapter emphasizes the importance of adopting sustainable entrepreneurial practices to ensure business resilience in volatile markets.

Chapter 9: Factors Affecting Green Purchase Behaviors for Small and Medium Enterprises (SMEs) in Uganda

Wasswa Shafik investigates the factors influencing green purchasing behaviors among Ugandan SMEs. The study uses theories of planned behavior and diffusion of innovation to analyze economic, environmental, regulatory, and customer influences on green procurement. Despite limitations in sample size, the chapter provides critical insights into promoting sustainable practices within SMEs and calls for further research in this area.

Chapter 10: Financial Reporting Mechanism of Crowdfunding Experiences: Evidence From the Emerging Markets

Betül AÇIKGÖZ explores the financial reporting mechanisms of crowdfunding in E7 countries, highlighting its potential for economic growth and new investments. The chapter discusses the accounting treatment of crowdfunding transactions within the framework of IFRS, emphasizing the importance of accurate financial reporting for equity crowdfunding and other campaigns. This study provides essential guidance for entities navigating the complexities of crowdfunding in emerging markets.

Chapter 11: How Does Rural Entrepreneurship Contribute to the Resilience and Sustainability of Rural Communities?

Onan Siregar, Hatta Ridho, Muhammad Arifin Nasution, and Muhammad Dharma Tuah Putra Nasution explore the role of rural entrepreneurship in fostering economic development, job creation, and poverty reduction in rural areas. The chapter highlights the unique challenges and opportunities of rural entrepreneurship and its contribution to community resilience and sustainability. The authors call for tailored policies and support systems to enhance the impact of rural entrepreneurial initiatives.

Chapter 12: Innovation Dynamics in Family Firms. A Content Analysis Study

Muhammad Dharma Tuah Putra Nasution, Muhammad Rizky, Maya Macia, Noni Ardian, and Suwarno Suwarno examine the innovation processes within family-owned businesses through content analysis. They highlight the importance of incremental innovation driven by existing and new knowledge, despite challenges such as risk aversion and succession planning. This chapter provides insights into how family firms leverage their unique resources for sustained competitive advantage and suggests avenues for future research.

Chapter 13: Internationalisation of Family SMEs: A Bibliometric Analysis of Recent Trends and Future Research Direction

Maulidar Agustina, M. Shabri Abd. Majid, Hafasnuddin Hafasnuddin, and Yahya Yahya conduct a bibliometric analysis of scholarly articles on the internationalization of family SMEs. The study identifies nine thematic clusters and highlights the growing interest in this field. The chapter offers valuable insights for academics, practitioners, and policymakers on supporting the global expansion of family-owned SMEs and suggests future research directions.

Chapter 14: Internationalization Strategies: A Complementary Perspective Using the Resource Dependency Theory

António Moreira, Adriana Simões, Ana Sousa, and João Martins analyze the internationalization strategies of ALPHA, a Portuguese family-owned company. They reveal a two-stage process involving the Uppsala model and network-based theory, emphasizing the importance of trust-based B2B relationships. The chapter highlights the role of strong client partnerships in gaining market knowledge and fostering innovation, providing practical lessons for SMEs pursuing international expansion.

Chapter 15: Synergizing Fashion Design and Entrepreneurship Education: Pathways and Implications

Xiaohan Zhang and Rohana Zur explore the integration of fashion design and entrepreneurship education to meet the evolving demands of the global fashion industry. They propose an innovative curriculum that combines these fields, enhancing entrepreneurial capacities among fashion design students. The chapter presents a theoretical foundation and practical strategies for implementing this integrated approach, emphasizing the need for multifaceted skills in aspiring fashion entrepreneurs.

Chapter 16: The Impact of Value Co-Creation of the NAIFEST Exhibition on the Perceived Value of INDOBUILDTECH 2022 Exhibitors: The Dynamic Interaction of DART Model on Value Co-Creation Towards Customer Perceived Value

Sakanti Sasri and Retno Kusumastuti investigate the impact of co-creation value at the NAIFEST exhibition on the perceived value of IndoBuildTech 2022 exhibitors. Using the DART framework, they analyze factors such as dialogue, access, risk assessment, and transparency that influence perceived quality and price. The

Preface

chapter provides insights into how co-creation strategies can enhance exhibitor value, offering practical implications for organizing successful trade shows and exhibitions.

Chapter 17: Modeling Service Quality and Religiosity Towards the Implementation of the Principles of Trust and Customer Satisfaction

In this chapter, Nilam Sari, Winny Dian Winny Safitri, Riski Rinaldi, Nevi Hasnita and Maisya Auliandhana explore the interplay between service quality, religiosity, and their impact on trust and customer satisfaction within the context of an electronic store. Utilizing probability sampling techniques and structural equation modeling (SEM) PLS, the research demonstrates how service quality directly influences the implementation of trust and satisfaction, while trust itself significantly affects overall customer satisfaction. Through this study, the chapter highlights the importance of integrating both service excellence and religious principles to foster trust and enhance customer satisfaction in commercial transactions.

In conclusion, this edited reference book, *Entrepreneurial Strategies for the Internationalization and Digitalization of SMEs*, offers a thorough exploration of the critical elements driving the success of small and medium-sized enterprises in today's global and digital marketplace. The contributions from esteemed experts in entrepreneurship, innovation, and business strategy provide a rich tapestry of knowledge and practical insights that are indispensable for SMEs navigating the complexities of internationalization and digitalization.

The chapters collectively underscore the necessity for SMEs to adapt and innovate continually. By delving into various dimensions such as digital innovation, strategic marketing, resilience during crises, financial capability, and sustainable practices, this book equips entrepreneurs and business leaders with the tools needed to thrive in an ever-evolving business environment. Moreover, the emphasis on sustainable practices aligns with the global imperative for environmentally responsible growth, ensuring that business success does not compromise our planet's future.

This book is designed to serve as a valuable resource for a broad audience, including practitioners, academicians, students, entrepreneurs, and policymakers. Each chapter is meticulously crafted to offer actionable strategies and solutions that address the unique challenges faced by SMEs. Whether it is understanding the impact of digital technologies, navigating international markets, or fostering innovation within family firms, the insights provided herein will undoubtedly inspire and guide readers towards achieving long-term success.

We extend our deepest gratitude to all contributors, reviewers, and supporters who have made this book a reality. It is our sincere hope that this compilation of expertise will not only enhance the understanding of SME internationalization and digitalization but also inspire the implementation of sustainable and innovative business practices worldwide. Through this work, we aim to contribute to the advancement of SME management and entrepreneurship, fostering a future where small and medium-sized enterprises can thrive and drive global economic growth.

Ahmad Rafiki
Universitas Medan Area, Indonesia

Sylvia Nabila Azwa Ambad
Universiti Teknologi MARA, Malaysia

Nor Farradila Abdul Aziz
Universiti Teknologi MARA, Malaysia

Chapter 1
A Conceptual Study on Entrepreneurship and Digital Innovation

Hasan Huseyin Uzunbacak
https://orcid.org/0000-0002-3297-1659
Suleyman Demirel University, Turkey

Şerife Karagöz
Süleyman Demirel University, Turkey

Tuğba Erhan
https://orcid.org/0000-0002-5697-490X
Süleyman Demirel University, Turkey

ABSTRACT

In the contemporary business landscape, digital innovation and entrepreneurship mutually reinforce and enhance one another as crucial elements. The interrelation between these concepts becomes evident as technological advancements become integrated into the realm of business. While digital innovation involves the creation of new technologies and business models, entrepreneurship symbolizes the effort to transform these innovative ideas into commercial value. Entrepreneurs can develop new and competitive advantage ventures by embracing digital innovation and evaluating technologically compatible business opportunities. This paradigm, in which digital innovation is intertwined with entrepreneurship, can create a basis on which businesses focus on constantly producing innovative solutions to achieve success in the rapidly changing digital ecosystem. In this context, the main objective of this study is to provide a fresh viewpoint for comprehending the relationship between digital innovation and entrepreneurship, with the intention of steering subsequent

DOI: 10.4018/979-8-3693-3518-5.ch001

research endeavors in this area.

INTRODUCTION

Digitalization embodies a paradigm shift focused on contemporary technologies, encompassing artificial intelligence, the Internet of Things, big data, and digital transformation. These technological advancements fundamentally alter innovation ecosystems and impact competitiveness and economic growth processes by transforming conventional management models (Tomizawa et al., 2020). Besides, digital technologies are radically changing individuals' and organizations' lives and business processes, and this change is progressing rapidly. Hence, it is crucial to embrace digital transformation and proactively seize the opportunities it offers (Berger et al., 2021: 2).

Numerous studies propose that the digitalization of businesses, along with enhanced capabilities for data collection and analysis, can bolster innovation efforts (Lee et al., 2014: 290). Plus, innovation refers to the implementation of novel products, services, processes, or marketing strategies. This entails either the inception of entirely new creations or the substantial enhancement and advancement of existing ones. It involves transforming creative ideas into value-producing outputs. As the use of digital technologies in the innovation process is stated as "digital innovation" (Nam, 2023: 207) that refers to the implementation of a new or significantly improved product, good, service, process, or marketing method. In other words, the use of digital technologies in the innovation process is called "digital innovation" that requires technological processes and applications to be carried out in a digital environment, the infrastructure to be suitable for digital transformation, and the dissemination of digital experiences (Nambisan et al., 2017). Moreover, digital innovation refers to the concept of an innovation ecosystem in the digital domain with a complex network of heterogeneous social and technical elements developed together over time and used to refer to technological environments, methodologies, concepts, business application areas, organizations, and contexts (Purbasari et al., 2023:5). Furthermore, the swift proliferation of digital technology is fundamentally reshaping the economy and questioning existing beliefs regarding entrepreneurship (Lee et al., 2014: 290). This phenomenon also highlights the potential to generate entrepreneurial opportunities (von Briel et al., 2018).

Digital technology is reshaping the business world by offering new opportunities for entrepreneurship and questioning traditional business models. Entrepreneurs can design innovative products and services and reach a wider customer base by taking advantage of the opportunities offered by digital technology. Therefore, the interaction between digital technology and entrepreneurship triggers a rapid and continuous change in the business world, providing entrepreneurs with a competitive advantage.

Entrepreneurship is defined as "the capacity and willingness to develop, organize, and manage a business venture with all its risks to make a profit." Entrepreneurs not only seek profit but they are also considered as creative designers of innovative thinking and business processes (Iwueke et al., 2019: 48). Entrepreneurs are considered as being the primary source of economic growth and sustainability, and they contribute to the economy by creating new sources of wealth or adding innovation to existing resources. Therefore, researchers are increasingly focusing on entrepreneurship due to its relevance to critical concerns such as bolstering employment, fostering economic expansion, promoting innovation, alleviating unemployment, enhancing the quality of products and services, navigating economic downturns, enhancing competitiveness by enhancing economic adaptability (Dogrusoz et al., 2023: 148).

Innovation is an essential component and a necessary condition of entrepreneurship. Entrepreneurs seize market opportunities and gain competitive advantage by developing innovative ideas and approaches. Without innovation, entrepreneurs remain stuck with existing business models and cannot adapt to changing market conditions. Therefore, encouraging and supporting innovation is critical for the sustainability and success of entrepreneurship (Stam, 2008).

Innovation and entrepreneurship must be strongly framed together with digitalization. Digitalization offers entrepreneurs opportunities to develop new business models, optimize processes and improve customer experience. It also helps entrepreneurs gain competitive advantage by increasing the speed of innovation. This interaction enables the adoption of new technologies and promotes digital transformation, while giving entrepreneurs the flexibility to develop innovative products and services. Therefore, this connection between digitalisation, innovation and entrepreneurship supports continuous development and change in business.

On the other hand, the impact of digital innovation and entrepreneurship on employment is a multifaceted issue that requires careful attention and consideration (Kreiterling, 2023: 9). While entrepreneurs create new business opportunities using digital technologies, digital innovation also allows entrepreneurs to transform their business models and processes. Thus, using digital innovation, entrepreneurs can solve existing problems, create new opportunities, and grow their businesses. Combining digital innovation and entrepreneurship enables organizations to adapt to environmental changes and gain competitive advantage quickly. This review study focuses on original research that conceptually addresses the concepts of digital innovation and entrepreneurship in the national literature. As a result of the current literature review, no study was found in the national literature discussing these two concepts. It is assumed that this gap will ensure the study's originality and the potential for an in-depth understanding of the relationship between these two concepts. In this context, this study offers a new perspective better to understand the connection between digital innovation and entrepreneurship and to guide future research on this topic.

DIGITAL INNOVATION AND ENTREPRENEURSHIP: BASIC CONCEPTS AND RELATIONSHIPS

Entrepreneurship

Amidst globalization, entrepreneurial endeavors and the significance of individual entrepreneurs are growing in prominence. In the current competitive landscape, it has become essential for entrepreneurial individuals to transition into successful business ventures. Entrepreneurial individuals, called human capital, are the key to factors such as increasing competitiveness in international markets by contributing to the economic development of a country, developing high-value-added products, generating employment opportunities, and augmenting production and exports (Denli, 2023: 62). The term "entrepreneur" originates from the French word "entrepreneur" and is commonly employed both in everyday conversations and within economic contexts. Entrepreneur refers to people appointed to undertake a specific business project. Concepts such as entrepreneurship and entrepreneurial process have been derived from the idea of entrepreneur. An entrepreneur is typically viewed as an individual who oversees particular projects and possesses a comprehension of entrepreneurship principles. In other words, undertaking certain projects means performing certain tasks and taking responsibility for the project to achieve certain results (Workie et al., 2019).

Entrepreneurship is a concept of great importance that has gained a firm place in numerous fields in modern times. Rather than diminishing over time, this interest has instead surged with remarkable momentum from the past to the present (Kaya and Girgin, 2023: 22). In the early 1800s, the French economist J. B. Say defined an entrepreneur as "an individual who reallocates economic resources from an area with lower productivity and returns to one with higher productivity and returns" (Drucker and Maciariello, 2014: 21).

Entrepreneurship is a complex and multifaceted concept that has been the focal point of numerous discussions, often defined in diverse ways by various authors. While some individuals perceive entrepreneurship primarily as a "risk-bearing" endeavor, others characterize it as a pursuit driven by "innovation" or a propensity for "excitement-seeking." (Havinal et al., 2009). In contemporary times, the entrepreneurial endeavors of individuals have garnered significant importance. Entrepreneurship covers a process that produces goods or services by combining labor, technology, capital, and natural resources (Yılmaz and Sünbül, 2016: 195). According to an alternative definition, entrepreneurship is characterized as a process whereby an individual or a collective group utilizes their capabilities and seizes opportunities through innovation to address needs, thereby generating value and fostering growth, irrespective of available resources (Robbins and Coulter, 2012: 537). The entrepreneur transfers organizational resources to a new project to develop new products and decides to expand his organization globally to gain new customers (George and Jones, 2012: 12). However, reaching out to new customers and meeting the dynamic changes of consumption require several strategies in order to implement novel approaches with multiple innovations toward the market (Markard et al., 2020). Otherwise, it can be challenging to handle the emergence of the new products, marketing campaigns with strategic approaches. Therefore, to successfully and effectively navigate these challenges, organizations need successful entrepreneurs to obtain organizational goals within the digital era. According to Lambing and Kuehl (2000), successful entrepreneurs have desire for success with high motivation, also they are willing to pursue goals, they are determined with a high sense of confidence, they are good at clarifying and overcoming potential risks; also they have creative approaches to evaluate changes, and they primarily focus on success paying attention to details doing their best to fulfill the goals.

Successful entrepreneurship does not happen by accident. There are certain processes and stages that ensure success. While some entrepreneurs succeed, some fail. There are various reasons for this. There are many reasons why people fail to start a business: factors such as being too young or too old to start a business, insufficient financial capital, not having enough social network, lack of time, lack of skills or experience (Setia, 2018: 14).

These features represent critical elements to the overall profile of successful entrepreneurs. Each of them plays an important role in overcoming challenges and achieving success in the entrepreneurial journey. Entrepreneurs distinguish themselves through their independent mindset, innovative thinking abilities, and knack for translating their aspirations into tangible accomplishments. They take bold steps by going beyond mediocrity's limits and participating in continuous development, transformation and breakthrough. Entrepreneurship is a dynamic process that includes not only courage and originality but also the ability to adapt to constantly changing conditions, create new opportunities and stimulate innovation (Tarhan, 2021: 75). To achieve success, entrepreneurs must possess fundamental skills including innovation, the ability to identify opportunities, perseverance, knowledge, a commitment to quality, strategic planning, and adept problem-solving capabilities (Havinal, 2009).

According to Hatala's (2005: 61-64) study, the challenges in the path of entrepreneurship are lack of self-confidence, personal problems, lack of talent, logistical difficulties, financial requirements and time constraints.

Table 1. Challenges of Entrepreneurship

Lack of Self-confidence	The individual's ability to cope with self-confidence problems and ability to start a business is considered essential as these may have effects in entrepreneurship. Lack of self-confidence may lead to consequences such as not trusting the business idea and hesitancy in the decision to start a business, which may affect the chance of success.
Personal Problems	Lack of family support may negatively affect the business process, and the entrepreneur may be forced to create his or her own support network, depriving from the traditional support systems. This is a source of fear that personal life problems may affect work performance and the business may fail.
Lack of Talent	This factor is when a person has the capacity to run a successful business, his capacity to start a business increases. Lack of experience of the business owner, amount of knowledge required for entrepreneurship.
Logistical Difficulties	This factor is critical in evaluating the business idea and collecting appropriate logistics information during the business start-up process. However, this process can sometimes be challenging depending on the type of business and this can cause entrepreneurs to be passive about legal remedies.
Financial Requirements	This factor includes both personal and business finances, which can be challenging to start a business.
Time Constraints	This factor relates to the ability to obtain the time required to develop the business idea encompassing the individual's ability to balance the process of starting a business with family and personal life. However, individuals who are busy with other social life events or activities may not have enough time to develop their business ideas, which may cause a delay to initiate the business.

Digital Innovation

Innovation emerges from the evolving needs of society, and it is essential for many organizations to enhance their chances of success, gain competitive advantage, foster prosperity, and even ensure survival (Queiroz et al., 2020: 37). Innovation has become the key driver of business success in today's competitive markets (Kreiterling, 2023) and it is considered a critical capability to gain competitive advantage and provide value to customers (Baláž et al., 2023: 1).

The utilization of digital technologies in the process of innovation constitutes digital innovation. (Nambisan et al., 2017: 223). In the digital era, effectively managing digital innovations is crucial for organizations striving to enhance growth, sustainability, and competitiveness (Aksoy, 2023). Schumpeter (1934) defined digital innovation as using new combinations of digital and physical components in the process of developing new products (Yoo, 2010: 725). In this context, digital innovation not only defines an outcome of innovation but also radically changes the fundamental nature of new products and services. Digital innovation enables innovation collectives that include dynamic groups of actors with various goals and capabilities, encourages others to innovate by producing new types of innovation processes, and generally affects many sectors (Nambisan et al., 2017: 223). Digital innovation includes creating new digital business models using digital technologies, launching social media initiatives, integrating customer experience into business processes, increasing efficiency, maximizing personalization, and benefiting from the creative power of an ecosystem (Satı, 2023).

Ecosystem of Digital Innovation

Businesses leverage digital innovation to generate value from their operations and interactions with stakeholders. These interactions occur within the digital innovation ecosystems of the specific markets, regulatory institutions, and environmental conditions in which businesses operate. The concept of an "innovation ecosystem" refers to a natural ecosystem consisting of elements that function together and refers to a structure consisting of elements that work together to maintain a state of balance (Suseno and Standing, 2017). The digital innovation ecosystem is a complex network that evolves over time and includes technological environments, methodologies, concepts and business practices. This network brings together different social and technical elements that contribute to innovation in the digital field (Chae, 2019). Indeed, the digital innovation ecosystem can serve as an analytical framework that links digital entrepreneurs with the broader innovation ecosystem.

This framework focuses on the more networked nature of digital entrepreneurship and analyzes this feature within the entire innovation ecosystem. In this way, it provides a deeper understanding of how innovation occurs by providing a comprehensive and versatile perspective (Beliaeva et al., 2020). Digital innovation ecosystems are complex systems that are connected and interact with each other and create new products and value through digital technologies (Suseno and Standing, 2017). In general, a digital innovation ecosystem is a structure in which digital technologies, business applications, entrepreneurship, and other elements interact and promote innovation in the digital field. This structure enables the integration of information from different disciplines and an understanding of digital development.

Digital Innovation and Sustainability

In highly competitive environments, sustainability holds significant importance both economically and environmentally. Research by Melane-Lavado et al. (2018) indicates that creating innovative products that prioritize environmental considerations plays a crucial role in tackling economic and ecological challenges. In this context, the relationship between innovation and sustainability is often summarized with "sustainable innovation." Veloso et al. (2020) state that digital innovation plays a vital role in the field of sustainability, and there is a strong interaction between these two concepts. Digital innovation can offer solutions to reduce environmental impacts and use resources more efficiently. For example, digital technologies such as smart grids, energy efficiency, and recycling management can be used to achieve sustainability goals.

Additionally, tools such as digital platforms and data analytics play an essential role in collecting, tracking, and analyzing sustainability-related data. This way, businesses can make better decisions and implement sustainability strategies more effectively (Veloso et al., 2020). Digital sustainability can be defined as the perfect combination of sustainability and digital requirements (George et al., 2021).

Interaction Between Digital Innovation and Entrepreneurship

The fundamental role of information and technology characterizes an information society. Entrepreneurship plays a vital role in such a society by injecting knowledge and skills into the economy, thereby contributing to societal advancement. Entrepreneurship based on individual talents has become one of the fundamental dynamics of this society. For this reason, the importance of entrepreneurship is increasing in the information society (Arslan, 2002: 2). Digitalization and innovation have been among the primary focus points of businesses in recent years, and both concepts are factors that significantly affect the success factors of businesses (Karaçuha and Pado, 2018: 118). Digital innovation has emerged as an essential catalyst for entrepreneurial success in today's increasingly competitive markets. The widespread adoption of digital technology significantly affects economic growth and social transformation in businesses of different sizes and operating in various sectors (Kreiterling, 2023: 1).Upon reviewing the literature, it becomes evident that several studies explore a relationship between digital innovation and entrepreneurship. For example, in a policy document prepared by Calvino and Criscuolo (2019) for the Organization for Economic Co-operation and Development (OECD), they examined the effects of digital technologies on business dynamics, especially job entry and reallocation rates. The research concluded that, according to the OECD, the determining factors of employment have an essential relationship between digitalization and government policies. The study indicates that digitalization contributes 35-40% of business innovation and approximately 40% of cross-country diversity. The authors suggested that this highlights the substantial impact of national regulations and policies on the overall economic growth of a region, including the success of entrepreneurship and digital innovation.

Galindo-Martín et al. (2019) analyzed 29 European countries to determine the overall effects of digital innovation on societies. Their research has affirmed the significance of the relationship between value creation, digital transformations, digital profits, and entrepreneurship. They observed that heightened incentives for entrepreneurship, new opportunities and increased competition across relevant markets, could foster additional innovations and subsequent digital transformations.

Kreiterling (2023) reviewed seven studies evaluating the effects and consequences of digital innovation on entrepreneurship in various sociopolitical contexts. Research results demonstrate that increasing innovation output scores and the ability to adopt innovative models are associated with higher GNP growth rates. Studies have shown that technological changes contribute to 35-40% of these dynamics, while regional factors account for the remaining 40%. The findings that internet use provides excellent benefits for businesses are also remarkable. This effect, which reduces operational costs, increases sales and improves customer interaction, has allowed 83% of companies to expand their markets and 78% to work more effectively with suppliers. Digitalization has created a positive feedback loop between these two variables, encouraging the expansion of entrepreneurship into new markets. These findings highlight the positive effects of digital innovation on entrepreneurship and the importance of digitalization in business.

Dávila et al. (2023) conducted a study involving 310 students to examine the impact of innovation competencies on the entrepreneurship of university students. Their research revealed that 53.2% of the students exhibited a high level of innovation competence, while 56.9% demonstrated a high level of entrepreneurship competence.

The Impact of Digital Transformation on Entrepreneurship

In the context of the industrial revolution, digital transformation signifies a shift that enhances businesses' capacity to improve their effectiveness and competitiveness across all economic sectors. While this digital transformation offers a variety of opportunities for businesses, large and small, many businesses still need help to make significant headway in implementing digital transformation. Simultaneously, enterprises encounter challenges in comprehending the full extent of this transformation and discerning which technologies will yield tangible benefits for their operational processes (Queiroz et al., 2020: 32). Digital transformation encompasses the integration of digital technology into all facets of businesses, instigating fundamental changes in their operational paradigms (Aksoy, 2023).

Li et al. (2018) emphasize the significance of investigating how entrepreneurs can actively propel digital transformation efforts. Also, several diverse factors impact a business's capacity to embrace its digital transformation strategy. As highlighted by Hamburg (2019), these factors may pertain to the work environment. For instance, aspects such as the industry's competition level, the organization's readiness for technology adoption, and the regulatory landscape can collectively influence the business's or industry's capability to embrace a digital transformation strategy (Scott, 2007).

Entrepreneurship has undergone significant transformation in recent years, largely driven by digital technologies, platforms, and infrastructures dynamics. These elements fundamentally reshape how value is created in entrepreneurial endeavors (Jafari-Sadeghi et al., 2021). Kraus et al. (2019) claim that digital transformation has led to significant changes in how entrepreneurs conduct business activities. It's noted that these changes are occurring across various domains, including "digital business models, digital entrepreneurship process, platform strategies, digital ecosystems, entrepreneurship education, and social, digital entrepreneurship." The research conducted by Jafari-Sadeghi et al. (2021) shows that the relationships between digital transformation, entrepreneurship, and digital technology use have significant consequences. Research findings reveal that technology entrepreneurship positively impacts the number of patent and trademark applications in a country.

Use of Digital Technologies in Entrepreneurship

In recent years, businesses have increasingly embraced digital technology with greater intensity. Digital technology is becoming increasingly vital in assisting companies in achieving their objectives. By using digital technology as a strategic advantage, businesses achieve improved performance in many areas, from decision processes to production processes, from various product designs to high-quality service delivery and time, cost, and risk management. These new perspectives can cause significant changes, especially by transforming the innovation processes, product and service portfolios, and resource environments of businesses (Karacuha and Pado, 2018: 118).

Digital technology is "the combination of information, computing, communication, and connection technologies" (Bharadwaj et al., 2013: 471). According to another definition, "digital technology" is a broad concept that includes various technological fields such as social media, the internet of Things, big data, mobile, and cloud computing (Legner et al., 2017).

Digital technology facilitates social, economic, and cultural transformation by serving as both the outcome and the foundation of innovation. From this standpoint, it fosters increased interaction, participation, and innovation within businesses and society (Yoo et al., 2010). In this digitalization process, developing new digital technologies such as Big Data, blockchain, and artificial intelligence plays an important role. The application of these technologies offers flexible regulation and adequate support opportunities for small and medium-sized businesses (Shafigullina et al., 2020). The swift advancement of digital technologies, the proliferation of financing options, and the growing enthusiasm for the sector have collectively started to significantly influence innovation and entrepreneurship endeavors. This means that digitalization and digital innovations form the basis of the entrepreneurship ecosystem. As Chae and Gog (2020) state, digital technologies not only accelerate the development of products and services but also significantly contribute to creating new business opportunities. In this context, entrepreneurs and businesses must focus on digital transformation to gain a competitive advantage and achieve sustainable growth.

Nambisan (2017) emphasizes that new digital technologies are critical to improving entrepreneurial processes and outcomes. New digital platforms, mainly social media technologies, have been adopted more entrepreneurially. However, various actors must have the necessary competencies to use these new technologies effectively. In this context, participation in an influential network of relationships can support making the most of new technologies and creating practical innovations.

Challenges of Entrepreneurship and Digital Innovation

Entrepreneurship is a process that results in creativity, innovation, and business growth. It refers to the ability of individuals to turn these ideas into action, which involves creating wealth that provides social benefit through innovative thinking and application to meet consumer needs by using their efforts, time, and thoughts (Workie et al., 2019). Entrepreneurs encounter various entrepreneurial barriers, which encompass the challenges in launching a new venture or scaling up an existing one. These hurdles can pose significant challenges to entrepreneurial success and entail potential risks. Especially in small businesses, many entrepreneurs fail due to various problems and obstacles. The biggest obstacle to entrepreneurship is considered a "failure." Karl H. Vesper stated the obstacles to entrepreneurship as follows (Havinal, 2009):

- Lack of a workable concept
- Lack of market knowledge
- Lack of technical skills
- Insufficient starting capital
- Lack of job knowledge
- Lack of motivation or apathy
- Social stigma
- Time constraints and distractions
- Legal restrictions and regulations
- Monopoly and protectionism
- Obstacles related to patents

Digital innovation is becoming an inevitable necessity in today's business world. However, the obstacles encountered in transitioning to these new technologies are quite evident for many businesses. Digital innovation is increasingly becoming an unavoidable requirement in the contemporary business landscape. Yet, numerous businesses need more support when transitioning to these new technologies. Overcoming these obstacles and completing an effective digital transformation is of great importance for companies to gain a competitive advantage in the future.

According to Ramilo (2016) and Holmström (2018: 107), the obstacles to digital innovation are stated as follows:

- Difficulties in concretizing the roles and impacts of digital innovation actors
- Difficulties in explaining digital innovation, regardless of the characteristics of digital technology,
- Difficulties in explaining digital innovation overly specifically

The Impact of Entrepreneurship on Digital Innovation

Entrepreneurship and innovation are positively related to each other and interact to contribute to the development of organizations. These two concepts complement each other and are vital for corporate success and sustainability in today's dynamic and changing business environment. Entrepreneurship and innovation represent dynamic and holistic processes in entrepreneurial and innovative organizations (Zhao, 2006). Innovation, the process of doing something new or different, is a goal that entrepreneurs constantly seek to meet the changing demands of customers. Even if entrepreneurs are not the creators of new products or production/service methods, they must be able to use these inventions in their businesses (Havinal, 2009).

The impact of entrepreneurship on innovation constantly supports the creation of new ideas in the business world and questions existing business models. According to Peter Drucker (2006), while digitalization undoubtedly emerges as an essential driver of entrepreneurship and innovation, it also gives rise to obscure technologies that appeal only to a specific market or are overshadowed by new alternatives. It should be taken into account that all entrepreneurs mayneed help adapting to the rapid change of digital innovation or may not be interested in working with unknown technologies (Kreiterling, 2023).

Entrepreneurship and innovation are positively related to each other and interact to contribute to the development of organizations. These two concepts are complementary to each other and are vital for corporate success and sustainability in today's dynamic and changing business environment. Entrepreneurship and innovation represent dynamic and holistic processes in entrepreneurial and innovative organizations (Zhao, 2006). Innovation, the process of doing something new or different, is a goal that entrepreneurs constantly seek to meet the changing demands of customers. Even if entrepreneurs are not the creators of new products or production/service methods, they must have the ability to use these inventions in their businesses (Havinal, 2009).

The impact of entrepreneurship on innovation constantly supports the creation of new ideas in the business world and questions existing business models. According to Peter Drucker (2006), while digitalization undoubtedly emerges as an important driver of entrepreneurship and innovation, it also gives rise to obscure technologies that appeal only to a specific market or are overshadowed by new alternatives. It should be taken into account that all entrepreneurs may experience difficulties in adapting to the rapid change of digital innovation or may not be interested in working with unknown technologies (Kreiterling, 2023).

The Role of Digital Innovation in the Business World

In the contemporary business landscape, digital innovation management holds significant importance, particularly due to factors such as technological convergence, accelerated development cycles, and increasing market opportunities significantly affecting the business environment (Aksoy, 2023). Digital technologies put great pressure on businesses to innovate and transform their business models. It requires businesses to transform their business models using digital technologies, innovate to increase operational efficiency, increase customer engagement, and launch successful new products. Solving existing business problems and improving organizational practices through the application of new digital technologies is called digital innovation. This is critical for the long-term sustainability and growth of businesses. Therefore, every company aiming for long-term success must embrace digital innovation to remain competitive (Tiwari, 2022).

Digital innovation management has emerged as a critical element today. The fundamentals of traditional innovation management now include elements such as optimized processes and product development together with the complex world of digital technologies (Yoo et al., 2010). This broad scope shows businesses a range of challenges and new opportunities brought by the digital age. As Aksoy (2023) states, this situation highlights the important issues that businesses face and need to evaluate. Digital innovation is an innovation that leads to the transformation of traditional business models and involves the development of new business practices and processes using the opportunities provided by digital technologies. This process enables entrepreneurs, businesses, and societies to find creative solutions using digital tools to respond to the new requirements brought by digitalization and gain a competitive advantage. As stated by Yoo et al., (2010), digital innovation encourages transformation in the business world and society by fully utilizing the potential offered by digital technologies. The effects of digital innovation include productivity, profitability, risk reduction, and customer loyalty. This process results in the redesign and simplification of business processes by increasing productivity, resulting in increased sales and higher margins to increase profitability. In addition, internal results such as reducing errors and minimizing risks are also measured. Since innovation provides new approaches to business processes, results such as time to market, product features, and consumer access are also important in evaluating the effects of innovation (Kohli and Melville, 2018).

Future Trends in Digital Innovation and Entrepreneurship

Today advances in technology lead to changes in individuals' lifestyles and compel organizations to adapt accordingly to these developments. Business managers and those responsible for the information technology department need to assess the prevailing trends in innovation and determine how they can improve their business, create new business models, and increase their competitiveness. Technological progress, including advancements like the Internet of Things, blockchain, artificial intelligence, and the enhancement of cognitive capabilities, along with factors such as the globalized economy, the transformation of markets, and developments in communication technologies, have the potential to change the world radically. Hence, it's crucial for businesses to embrace and execute process innovation in the constantly evolving digital era (Guarda et al., 2021).

Entrepreneurship trends are the changing tendencies that emerge for entrepreneurs to seize business opportunities and achieve success. Often, the greatest opportunities for starting a new venture arise, especially when the entrepreneur is at the beginning of a trend that will continue for a long time. Hirsch et al. (2017) defined seven entrepreneurship trends in areas such as wearable technologies, environmentally friendly applications, changes in payment systems, making hobby products known as the maker trend, mobile technologies, innovations in the health sector, and the Internet of things (Hirsch et al., 2017).

CONCLUSION

In a destructive competitive environment, the importance of digital technologies for the survival and sustainability of businesses is increasing day by day. Businesses through leveraging digital technology across various domains, spanning decision-making and production processes, as well as diverse product designs, ultimately enhancing the delivery of quality products and services. This situation increases the digital innovation capacity of businesses (Nam, 2023: 206). Digital innovation provides a competitive advantage for businesses that embrace the changes brought about by technological advances and successfully implement these changes (Nambisan et al., 2017: 223). It is argued that digital innovation and entrepreneurship will have a significant impact on employment (Cunningham et al., 2015). Entrepreneurship is characterized by its dynamic nature and plays a crucial role in sustaining the dynamism of contemporary economies while generating employment opportunities. Entrepreneurship is characterized by its dynamic nature (Tarhan, 2021: 75) and plays a crucial role in sustaining the dynamism of contemporary economies while generating employment opportunities (Klapper, 2006). In this context, creative thinking and producing practical solutions requires focusing on energy and passion. In addition, entrepreneurship includes features such as taking risks, using time effectively, having knowledge and skills in the field of business, and team coordination skills (cooperation, working together, team building) (Tarhan, 2021: 75).

Limitations and Suggestions for Future Studies

This study has some limitations. For instance, it attempts to establish a theoretical foundation for future research on the concepts of digital innovation and entrepreneurship, which greatly influence the success of organizations where individuals are employed. Future research can be supported by empirical studies, and the practical effects of these concepts can be examined in more detail. In order to progress in the field of digital innovation and entrepreneurship, it is essential for businesses to adopt a flexible and open culture. Encouraging innovative ideas, providing training opportunities to employees, and encouraging flexibility in business processes can support developments in this area. In terms of entrepreneurship, it is assumed that businesses invest more in venture capital, mentoring programs and entrepreneurial ecosystems, which can help new entrepreneurs develop their skills and become more effective in the business world.

REFERENCES

Aksoy, C. (2023). Digital Innovation Management: Frameworks, Strategies, and Future Perspectives. *Uluslararası İşletme Bilimi ve Uygulamaları Dergisi*, 3(2), 1–19.

Arslan, K. (2002). Üniversiteli Gençlerde Mesleki Tercihler ve Girişimcilik Eğitimleri. *Doğuş Üniversitesi Dergisi*, 6, 1–11.

Baláž, V., Jeck, T., & Balog, M. (2023). Firm performance over innovation cycle: Evidence from a small European economy. *Journal of Innovation and Entrepreneurship*, 12(40).

Beliaeva, T., Ferasso, M., Kraus, S., & Damke, E. J. (2020). Dynamics of digital entrepreneurship and the innovation ecosystem: A multilevel perspective. *International Journal of Entrepreneurial Behaviour & Research*, 26(2), 266–284. 10.1108/IJEBR-06-2019-0397

Berger, E. S., Von Briel, F., Davidsson, P., & Kuckertz, A. (2021). Digital or not–The future of entrepreneurship and innovation: Introduction to the special issue. *Journal of Business Research*, 125, 436–442. 10.1016/j.jbusres.2019.12.020

Bharadwaj, A., El Sawy, O. A., Pavlou, P. A., & Venkatraman, N. (2013). Digital business strategy: Toward a next generation of insights. MIS Quarterly: Management. *Information Systems*, 37(2), 471–482.

Calvino, F., & Criscuolo, C. (2019). Business dynamics and digitalisation. OECD STI Policy Papers, 62. https:// www. oecd- ilibrary. org/ scien ce- and- techn ology/ busin ess- dynam ics- and- digit alisa tion_ 6e0b0 11a- en

Chae, B. (2019). A general framework for studying the evolution of the digital innovation ecosystem: The case of big data. *International Journal of Information Management*, 45, 83–94. 10.1016/j.ijinfomgt.2018.10.023

Cunningham, P., Cunningham, M., & Ekenberg, L. (2015). Assessment of potential ICT-related collaboration and innovation capacity in east Africa [Paper presentation]. *2015 IEEE Global Humanitarian Technology Conference (GHTC)*, Seattle, WA, USA. 10.1109/GHTC.2015.7343961

Dávila, M. A. M., Pantaleón, A. J. S., Caro, O. C., Bueloth, M. R., & Rios, I. D. M. (2023). Innovation and Entrepreneurship Skills in University Students, Amazonas, Peru, 2023. *Migration Letters : An International Journal of Migration Studies*, 20(7), 557–575.

Denli, İ. (2023). Girişimci Adaylarının Girişimcilik Profillerinin Belirlenmesi: Üniversite Öğrencileri Örneği. *Girişimcilik ve Kalkınma Dergisi*, 18(1), 49–63.

Doğrusöz, L. A., & Uluçay, A. P. (2023). Kültürün Girişimcilik Niyeti Üzerindeki Etkisinde Algılanan İsteğin Moderatör Rolü: İstanbul Örneği. *İşletme Araştırmaları Dergisi*, 15(1), 147-161.

Drucker, P., & Maciariello, J. (2014). *Innovation and entrepreneurship*. Routledge. 10.4324/9781315747453

Drucker, P. F. (2006). *Innovation and entre-preneurship: practice and principles*. HarperCollins Publishers.

Galindo-Martín, M., Castaño-Martinez, M. S., & Méndez-Picazo, M. T. (2019). Digital transformation, digital dividends and entrepreneurship: A quantitative analysis. *Journal of Business Research*, 101, 522–527. 10.1016/j.jbusres.2018.12.014

George, G., Merrill, R. K., & Schillebeeckx, S. J. (2021). Digital sustainability and entrepreneurship: How digital innovations are helping tackle climate change and sustainable development. *Entrepreneurship Theory and Practice*, 45(5), 999–1027. 10.1177/1042258719899425

George, J. M., & Jones, G. R. (2012). *Understanding and managing organizational behavior* (6th ed.). Pearson Prentice Hall.

Guarda, T., Balseca, J., García, K., González, J., Yagual, F., & Castillo-Beltran, H. (2021, March). Digital transformation trends and innovation. *IOP Conference Series. Materials Science and Engineering*, 1099(1), 012062. 10.1088/1757-899X/1099/1/012062

Hamburg, I. (2019). Implementation of a digital workplace strategy to drive behaviour change and 19 improve competencies. In *Strategy and Behaviors in the Digital Economy*. IntechOpen.

Hatala, J. P. (2005). Identifying barriers to self-employment: The development and validation of the barriers to entrepreneurship success tool. *Performance Improvement Quarterly*, 18(4), 50-70.

Havinal, V. (2009). *Management and Entrepreneurship*. New Age International.

Holmström, J. (2018). Recombination in digital innovation: Challenges, opportunities, and the importance of a theoretical framework. *Information and Organization*, 28(2), 107–110. 10.1016/j.infoandorg.2018.04.002

Iwueke, E. L., Anyarum, G. O., Fagorite, V. I., Okeke, O. C., & Ehujuo, N. N. (2019). Entrepreneurship: Characteristics, practices and impacts on Nigeria economy in relation to geosciences. *IIARD Int J Econ Bus Manage*, 5, 48–63.

Jafari-Sadeghi, V., Garcia-Perez, A., Candelo, E., & Couturier, J. (2021). Exploring the impact of digital transformation on technology entrepreneurship and technological market expansion: The role of technology readiness, exploration and exploitation. *Journal of Business Research*, 124, 100–111. 10.1016/j.jbusres.2020.11.020

Karaçuha, E., & Güven, P. A. D. O. (2018). Dijital inovasyon stratejisi yönetimi. *Uluslararası Bilimsel Araştırmalar Dergisi*, 3(1), 118–130.

Kaya, A., & Girgin, D. (2023). Sınıf Öğretmeni Adaylarının Girişimcilik Becerilerinin İncelenmesi: Bir Karma Yöntem Araştırması. *Pamukkale Üniversitesi Sosyal Bilimler Enstitüsü Dergisi*, (55), 21–42.

Klapper, L. (2006). Entrepreneurship: how much does the business environment matter? Viewpoint series. note 313. Financial and Private Sector Development Vice Presidency, World Bank Group.

Kohli, R., & Melville, N. P. (2018). Digital innovation: A review and synthesis. *Information Systems Journal*, 29(1), 200–223. 10.1111/isj.12193

Kraus, S., Palmer, C., Kailer, N., Kallinger, F. L., & Spitzer, J. (2019). Digital entrepreneurship. *International Journal of Entrepreneurial Behaviour & Research*. Advance online publication. 10.1108/IJEBR-06-2018-0425

Kreiterling, C. (2023). Digital innovation and entrepreneurship: A review of challenges in competitive markets. *Journal of Innovation and Entrepreneurship*, 12(1), 49. 10.1186/s13731-023-00320-0

Lambing, P., & Kuehl, C. R. (2000). *Entrepreneurship*. Prentice Hall.

Lazazzara, A., Nacamulli, R. C., Rossignoli, C., & Za, S. (2019). *Organizing for Digital Innovation*. Springer. 10.1007/978-3-319-90500-6

Lee, G., Park, G., & Yoon, B. (2014). Open innovation in SMEs-An intermediated network model. *Research Policy*, 43(5), 865–874.

Legner, C., Eymann, T., Hess, T., Matt, C., Böhmann, T., Drews, P., Mädche, A., Urbach, N., & Ahle-mann, F. (2017). Digitalization: Opportunity and Challenge for the Business and Information Systems Engineering Community. *Business & Information Systems Engineering*, 59(4), 301–308. 10.1007/s12599-017-0484-2

Li, L., Su, F., Zhang, W., & Mao, J. Y. (2018). Digital transformation by SME entrepreneurs: A capability perspective. *Information Systems Journal*, 28(6), 1129–1157. 10.1111/isj.12153

Markard, J., Geels, F. W., & Raven, R. (2020). Challenges in the acceleration of sustainability transitions. *Environmental Research Letters*, 15(8), 081001. 10.1088/1748-9326/ab9468

Melane-Lavado, A., Álvarez-Herranz, A., & González-González, I. (2018). Foreign direct investment as a way to guide the innovative process towards sustainability. *Journal of Cleaner Production*, 172, 3578–3590. 10.1016/j.jclepro.2017.03.131

Nambisan, S., Lyytinen, K., Majchrzak, A., & Song, M. (2017). Digital innovation management. *Management Information Systems Quarterly*, 41(1), 223–238. 10.25300/MISQ/2017/41:1.03

Purbasari, R., Munajat, E., & Fauzan, F. (2023). Digital Innovation Ecosystem on Digital Entrepreneur: Social Network Analysis Approach. *International Journal of E-Entrepreneurship and Innovation*, 13(1), 1–21. 10.4018/IJEEI.319040

Queiroz, J., Leitão, P., Pontes, J., Chaves, A., Parra, J., & Perez-Pons, M. E. (2020). A quality innovation strategy for an inter-regional digital innovation hub. *ADCAIJ: Advances in Distributed Computing and Artificial Intelligence Journal*, 9(4), 31–45. 10.14201/ADCAIJ2020943145

Ramilo, R. D. (2016). *Key Determinants and Barriers to Digital Innovation Adaptation Among Architectural Practices* (Doctoral dissertation, Universiti Teknologi Malaysia).

Robbins, S. P., & Coulter, M. A. (2012). *Management* (11th ed.). Pearson Education.

Satı, Z. (2023). Yeni Dijital Teknolojiler ve Dijital İnovasyon Yönetimi. Academic Press.

Scott, J. E. (2007). An e-transformation study using the technology-organization-environment framework. *BLED 2007 Proceedings*, 55.

Setia, S. (2018). Personality profile of successful entrepreneurs. Journal of Economics. *Business & Accountancy Ventura*, 21(1), 13–23. 10.14414/jebav.v21i1.1004

Shafigullina, A. V., Akhmetshin, R. M., Martynova, O. V., Vorontsova, L. V., & Sergienko, E. S. (2020). Analysis of entrepreneurial activity and digital technologies in business. *Advances in Intelligent Systems and Computing*, 908, 183–188. 10.1007/978-3-030-11367-4_17

Stam, E. (2008). Entrepreneurship and innovation. In Nooteboom, B., & Stam, E. (Eds.), *Micro-foundations for innovation policy*. Amsterdam University Press.

Suseno, Y., & Standing, C. (2017). The systems perspective of national innovation ecosystems. *Systems Research and Behavioral Science*, 35(3), 282–307. 10.1002/sres.2494

Tarhan, M. (2021). Girişimcilik becerisinin kazandırılması bağlamında girişimcilerin öz yaşam öykülerine yönelik bir değerlendirme. *Bolu Abant İzzet Baysal Üniversitesi Eğitim Fakültesi Dergisi*, 21(1), 74–86. 10.17240/aibuefd.2021.21.60703-815358

Tiwari, S. (2022). Supply chain innovation in the era of industry 4.0. In *Handbook of Research on Supply Chain Resiliency, Efficiency, and Visibility in the Post-Pandemic Era* (pp. 40–60). IGI Global. 10.4018/978-1-7998-9506-0.ch003

Tomizawa, R., Dolan, K. A., & Englis, B. G. (2020). Digitalization and business model innovation: A review and synthesis. *Journal of Business Research*, 122, 860–869.

Veloso, E., da Silva, R. C., Trevisan, L., & Dutra, J. (2020). Technological innovations in the work environment and the career of the millennium generation. *Innovation & Management Review*, 17(4), 379–394. 10.1108/INMR-05-2019-0070

von Briel, F., Davidsson, P., & Recker, J. (2018). Digital technologies as external enablers of new venture creation in the IT hardware sector. *Entrepreneurship Theory and Practice*, 42(4), 553–576. 10.1177/1042258717732779

Workie, B., Chane, M., Mohammed, M., & Birhanu, T. (2019). Enteepreneurship. Addis Ababa, Ethiopia: Ministry of Science and Higher Education.

Yoo, Y., Henfridsson, O., & Lyytinen, K. (2010). Research commentary-the new organizing logic of digital innovation: An agenda for information systems research. *Information Systems Research*, 21(4), 724–735. 10.1287/isre.1100.0322

Zhao, F. (2006). Entrepreneurship and innovation in e-business: An integrative perspective. In Zhao, F. (Ed.), *Entrepreneurship and Innovations in EBusiness: An Integrative Perspective* (pp. 1–17). Igi Global.

Chapter 2
A Paradigm Shift Among Indian SMEs Towards Adoption of Affiliate Marketing and Social Media

Raj Kumar Singh
 http://orcid.org/0000-0003-2113-8677
Graphic Era Hill University, India

Bhanupriya Khatri
Chandigarh University, India

Nidhi Sharma
 http://orcid.org/0000-0002-3014-2312
Chandigarh University, India

Shad Ahmad Khan
 http://orcid.org/0000-0001-7593-3487
University of Buraimi, Oman

ABSTRACT

The purpose of this study was to evaluate how likely small and medium enterprises (SMEs) are to adopt affiliate marketing and social media to improve their customer base, profitability, and sustainable growth. Data was collected from 523 entrepreneurs in India, using a purposive sampling method. The results revealed that affiliate marketing has a significant impact on social media and consumer buying intention.

DOI: 10.4018/979-8-3693-3518-5.ch002

Additionally, there are considerable connections between producer's intent and affiliate marketing, producer's intent and social media, and producer's intent and consumer buying intention. This study highlights the critical role of social media and affiliate marketing in enhancing consumer purchasing intentions in SMEs. Based on the results, marketers are recommended to effectively engage with customers on social media platforms to improve their purchasing intentions. This research is groundbreaking as it provides valuable insights into the relationship between social media, affiliate marketing, and consumer behavior in the SME sector.

1. INTRODUCTION

The widespread use of the internet nowadays has led to various deviations in the commercial sector, by this application being able to connect individuals through telecommunication device usage and enabling its operators to contact up-to-date data in period (Maksimovic, 2018). The advancement of the internet, telecommunication, and information technology has resulted in major changes in all aspects of the company, with the marketing function being the most impacted (Eid & El-Gohary, 2013) (Krishnamurthy & Singh, 2005). Businesses are working hard to reap the benefits of the digital revolution (Ramanathan et al., 2012). As we live in the digital era and are progressing towards society 5.0 (Magd et al., 2023a; Karyamsetty et al., 2023), digitalization of business activities irrespective of size, type, and operation is becoming inevitable (Magd et al., 2023b).

Social media (SM) is the rapidly expanding marketing platform in the whole world (Coremetrics, 2010). SM usage is rapidly increasing among organizations (Chatterjee & Kumar Kar, 2020) and is now observed as a critical technique (Iankova et al., 2019), although companies are using an assortment of SM stages (Ainin et al., 2015). SM is a good fit for Small and Medium Enterprises (SMEs) because of its simplicity to use, technological management, and capacity to connect with a large no. of prospective customers (Tajudeen et al., 2018; Khan, 2023). SM is a popular option for SMEs (Alford & Page, 2015; Khan, 2023) as it allows more transparent communication and helps businesses understand and respond to consumer demands professionally and effectively (Parveen et al., 2016). As experts highly favor the benefits of social networking marketing, SMEs must decide whether to implement this innovative marketing technology because of lack of verifiable outcomes, as well as difficulty creating measuring criteria to evaluate efficacy, are among the hurdles.

When a business recruits trustworthy affiliate marketers to publicize its goods and services on its own website is referred to as affiliate marketing (AM) (Duffy, 2005) (Mazurek & Kucia, 2011). AM is rapidly becoming one of the most popular online advertisings as well as e-commerce techniques for increasing sales (Fox &

Wareham, 2012). It appears to have more ability than preceding online marketing pains (Duffy, 2005). Establishments are attractive additional concerns in affiliate marketing, as the greatest are trying to locate themselves in e-commerce manufacturing with the help of associates (Newton & Ojo, 2018).

SMEs have traditionally been the foundation of national economies. Most govt. views the SME sector as a key economic engine and provider of job opportunities (MacGregor & Vrazalic, 2007). In most countries, SMEs play a significant role in economic activity (Simpson & Docherty, 2004). Marketing is a strategic instrument for business development that aids in the appropriate growth and long-term viability of micro, small, and medium-sized businesses. It is critical for the success of any business, and although major corporations have hired people to handle the marketing of their products or services, micro (handicraft) as well as other small businesses lack the financial resources to invest in promoting crafts items.

Many studies have been conducted which examined the influence of SM on customer buying decisions (Vithayathil et al., 2020), brand recognition, and buy intention (Wang et al., 2019; Kamal et al., 2022), retaining customers and buying decision engagement (Alalwan, 2018). Even though the literature suggests that entrepreneurs are frequently utilizing social media and affiliate marketing there seems to be little systematic study on the topic of social media, affiliate marketing, producers' intent, and consumer buying intention case of SMEs of handicraft industries. Such a study is necessary to fill the gap of existing studies by determining how much has been learned about SM, AM, and producers' intent to use these types of marketing which can impact consumer buying decisions as well as well. The goal of the research study is to measure the producer's intent to adopt affiliate marketing and social media to increase customer base, profitability, and sustainable growth. To understand the role played by AM or SM.

The rest of the paper is prepared as follows: The literature study and conceptual model are presented in Section 2. In section 3, the research methodology is explained. The study's data analysis and results are accessible in section 4. Discussion is carried out in section 5. Conclusions are presented in section 5, followed by theoretical and practical consequences, and finally, the study's findings are explained.

2. LITERATURE REVIEW

2.1. Affiliate Marketing (AM)

AM is one of the significant devices of internet marketing and is accepted to be more practical, increment an association's item perceived, just as the ROI (Iwashita et al., 2018). Accordingly, a superior comprehension of AM ideas and the variables that impact the goal to utilize AM is fundamental for all specialists, associations, and businesses (Patrick & Hee, 2019). Affiliate marketing can be seen as a customer channel in which customers (as opposed to products) are passed along the channel. In this "affiliate channel," the shipper pays the affiliate for alluded customers and afterward benefits by selling them items and administrations (Libai et al., 2003). Affiliate marketing is likewise straightforwardly connected to a solid execution, new consumer securing, and higher profitability which are firmly identified with an association's cost effectiveness for promoting (Patrick & Hee, 2019). AM is characterized as a commission-based online organization, whereby its partners advance and sells included products as well as administrations through extra dissemination sources (Patrick & Hee, 2019). Affiliate marketing includes three significant partners: merchants, trying to arrive at their intended interest groups on the web; affiliates, giving traffic to vendors; and intermediary agencies, liable for encouraging trades among dealers and affiliates (Mariussen, 2011).

Affiliate marketing implies association recruited confided in affiliate advertisers (outsider distributers) to advance the products and enterprises of an association through its site (Journal & Movement, 2018). Along these lines, AM can likewise be characterized as a strategy for an association to reevaluate the selling of its items (Patrick & Hee, 2019).

Affiliate marketing keeps on being seen as a worth wrecking circulation channel, more reasonable for mass-market products, affiliate marketing can offer extra dispersion sources, using a compelling minimal effort deals power, and can upgrade brand strength through suitable openness (Mariussen et al., 2010).

The impeding effect on the support's image from contrarily seen or unlawful practices concerning the affiliate can be critical also (Janssen & van Heck, 2007). Furthermore, there can be a negative effect on a support's image when the affiliate items and administrations are conflicting with the support's image (Fox & Wareham, 2007).

2.2. Social Media (SM)

Social media offer various qualities to associations by improving brand popularity (Umair Manzoor et al., 2020; Saleem et al., 2023). The credibility of social media promoting efforts should be remembered by marketers (Arora et al., 2020; Saleem et al., 2022). Credibility emphatically impacts the disposition of Indian millennials toward social media advertisements (Arora et al., 2020; Sharma et al., 2023a). Social media is a useful asset for promoting and publicizing efforts. Organizations can utilize social media to target and impact client perspectives (Ebrahim, 2020; Sharma 2023b). SM advertisements are portrayed by a few properties, including intuitiveness, assumptions, and hedonic motivation (Umair Manzoor et al., 2020).

These properties may influence consumer buying behavior. However, it is particularly challenging to plan social media advertisements such as alluring people to purchase something (Reza et al., 2020; Naim & Khan, 2023).

In marketing, the customer's trust is for the most part characterized as the eagerness of a customer to return to a brand. (Umair Manzoor et al., 2020). Trust and social media impact altogether influence shoppers' buying expectations. Improving sites' quality upgrades customers' trust (Arora et al., 2020). Thus, trust plays a significant part in online business by straightforwardly affecting the buying aims of customers. (Umair Manzoor et al., 2020). Qualities of social media advertising straightforwardly impact brand loyalty and in a roundabout way impact brand value mediated by brand trust (Ebrahim, 2020). Brand attitude also has critical intermediation in the connection between customer buying aims and SM marketing. Individuals interface with brands and organizations on social media (Latif & Calicioglu, 2020). Brand trust (BT) plays an intermediary part in the connection between social media promotions and buying expectations (Latif & Calicioglu, 2020).

2.3. Customer Buying Intention (CBI)

The term consumer buying behavior is characterized as the examination of when, where, why, and how individuals buy an item (Anjana, 2018). Consumer buying behavior is a decision process just as the mentality of individuals associated with buying and utilizing items. Consumers settle on buy choices for buying little as well as huge items (Adam, 2020; Naim & Khan, 2023). After perceiving a need or a want, consumers start looking for items or administrations that fit their necessities (Anjana, 2018). Consumer Buying Behavior builds the web-based business and coordinated digital platform (Nowsin et al., 2020; Khan & Magd, 2021; Magd & Khan, 2022; Magd et al., 2022). CBI is essentially controlled by cost, execution, and govt. activities measurements (Master & Master, 2020). However, measurements, for example, eco-accommodating products, data concerning company and friends, ecological concern, and social impact were discovered immaterial (Kumar et al., 2019).

Consumer buying behavior is for the most part impacted by family, peers, colleagues, assessment pioneers, and the associations of the public which the consumer sees for settling on his choice for buying an item (Kumar et al., 2019). Clients have an instinct that items that are mostly secret, low cost, and basic bundling have a high possibility of danger because the quality and estimation of these items aren't trustable (Anjana, 2018). The fulfillment of the consumers turns into the central objective of a business endeavor (Dangi et al., 2020). The work to guarantee consumer fulfillment lies in understanding the consumer's preferences, assumptions, and inspiration (Deng et al., 2010). A consumer's inspirational disposition should be framed more emphatically to create consumer buying goals (Yadav & Mahara,

2019). Understanding consumer buying goals is significant because their last buying behavior can be anticipated from their expectations (Meitiana et al., 2019). Price reduction is intentionally utilized in various businesses to advance the purchase decision to buy an item since a value decrease may diminish customers' apparent danger related to trying another, less-known item unexpectedly (Ashraf et al., 2014).

2.4. Producer's Intent (PI)

The producers or firms supply different merchandise and enterprises in the market as indicated by the request of the purchasers (Staake et al., 2009; Khan et al., 2022). Henceforth, if the quantity of producer builds, at that point the aggregate supply of products and enterprises will likewise increment. Producers sit in the center between the "Imaginative Types" (otherwise called "Creation") and the Merchants/Finance individuals. It is difficult to work, as one needs to adjust one's enthusiasm for the task with the quantifiable profit for the business. Producers are additionally business visionaries. They are the principal facilitators of the relative multitude of components of creation like land, work, capital, and so on. They ordinarily take the duty to distribute the components of creation for leading smooth business exercises. Producers are the main people, who take the activities to use all the monetary assets, like wood assets, land assets, mineral assets, water assets, human or work assets, and so on ideally or effectively for the creation exercises.

2.5. Paradigm Shift in Indian SMEs Embracing Affiliate Marketing and Social Media

In the contemporary world, where digitalization is paving its way in almost every activity a business in involved (Yadav et al., 2025; Naim et al., 2024a; Naim et al., 2024b; Khatri et al., 2024; Zareen & Khan, 2023; Khatri et al., 2024), the landscape of the marketing and consumer acquisition too has undergone a major shift in the recent years (Khan, 2023). The emergence of digital technology, including social media and affiliate marketing, has provided businesses including SMEs with unprecedented opportunities to expand their customer base, establish beneficial alliances, and spur growth (Fahim, 2020; Khan, 2024; Naim et al., 2023; Khan & Naim, 2024). The affiliate marketing through digital platform has appeared as a potential tool for the Indian SMEs seeking to expand the reach of their products and the customer base.

In the present times, one of the important considerations for the SMEs is the access to finance and financial prudence (Saxena et al., 2023), the affiliate marketing through social media comes as a cost effective option for the SMEs. Through collaborating with affiliates, entities that endorse goods or services in return for a fee, these organizations can access extensive and highly focused networks of prospective clients. The affordability and quantifiability of affiliate marketing are its greatest features. SMEs only give affiliates money when a specific goal is met, like generating leads or a sale. This pay-for-performance strategy reduces financial risk and guarantees that marketing initiatives result in measurable outcomes (Olbrich et al., 2019). One of the important pillars of the of the affiliate marketing is public relations, where most of the affiliates are related to the SMEs not only because of the fees or payments made to them but also because of the relationship system they are with such SMEs, as endorsing a business or products also puts on stake the individual rapport of such affiliate individuals, such public relations plays an important role (Khan et al. 2023a; Khan et al., 2023b). Affiliate marketing allows SMEs to leverage the credibility and influence of their partners, who often have established audiences and high levels of trust within their respective niches. This symbiotic relationship not only amplifies brand visibility but also fosters a sense of authenticity and trustworthiness among potential customers (Olbrich et al., 2019; Saleem et al., 2022; Saleem et al., 2023).

As we live in the digital age, social media has become an indispensable component of any successful marketing strategy, and Indian SMEs are no exception. For SMEs with limited marketing budgets, social media provides a cost-effective way to reach a vast and engaged audience. By creating compelling content, engaging with followers, and leveraging influencer partnerships, these businesses can effectively promote their products or services and foster a loyal customer base (Saleem et al., 2023; Khan et al., 2023a). Moreover, social media serves as a powerful tool for customer engagement and feedback (Khan et al., 2023b; Khan & Rena, 2023). SMEs can leverage these platforms to gather valuable insights, address concerns, and tailor their offerings to better meet the evolving needs and preferences of their target markets.

In a study by Khan et al. (2024), the normal Indian SMEs were found to be less involved in the digital marketing practices, however the growth in the transition was found to be good. With the advent of AI in digital marketing, it has become relatively easier and faster to create content and push to the digital marketing platform (Masoom et al., 2024). Indian SMEs may become a powerful marketing force by fusing the engagement and community-building capabilities of social media with the reach and influence of affiliates (Khan et al., 2024; Sharma et al., 2023a). By interacting with their followers on social media and directing traffic to the SME's website or online store, affiliates can use their online presence to market goods and services (Iwashita & Tanimoto, 2016; 2018). On the other hand, SMEs can work with influencers and content producers on SM channels, utilizing their pre-existing following and trust to increase brand awareness and encourage sales. In addition to boosting marketing efforts, this synergy exposes potential buyers to goods and services through reliable sources and active communities, which in turn builds authenticity and trust. Those who can successfully leverage the mutual benefits of SM and affiliate marketing will surely become trailblazers in the rapidly evolving field of digital marketing, redefining the standards of success for SMEs in India.

2.6. Hypothesis Development

2.6.1. PI, AM, SM, and CBI

Affiliate Marketing originates as an enormously stimulating impression for individuals who request to effort with Internet auctions, also being an inordinate instrument for Creators who request to upsurge raise of their products on Cyberspace. Producers get several distribution channels, thus impacting more customers and, therefore, making more sales. There are different formats for affiliate programs. It's up to the Producer to decide which one best fits her product and her business goals. There are many studies conducted on entrepreneurship and social media (Olanrewaju et al., 2020; Durkin et al., 2013; McCann & Barlow, 2015). Also, a study has been conducted on entrepreneurship intention in manufacturing SMEs (Ahadi & Kasraie, 2020). So we hypothesize -

H1: PI significantly influences AM in case of SMEs.
H2: PI significantly influences SM in case of SMEs.
H3: PI significantly influences CBI in case of SMEs.

2.6.2. AM and SM

Performance criteria and indicators used in emerging marketing channels like affiliate marketing and social media, on the other hand, are mainly practitioner-driven and controlled by that of the Information Technology sector (IT) (Mariussen, 2011). During such a marketing campaign, many channels, such as advertisements, AM, direct e-mail, SM marketing, and so on, are available. As a result, businesses may reach the greatest number of new consumers while still maintaining relationships with existing customers (Nowsin et al., 2020). With the rise of social networking platforms on the internet, AM g has become increasingly popular. Given the character of persons who are engaged in SM, the authors claim that SM is viewed as a fruitful environment with the capacity to thrive and generate marketing outcomes (Haikal et al., 2020). SM based AM positively influence the demand of e-commerce (Haikal et al., 2020). The advanced usage of Affiliate marketing and additional comparative expertise extensively examined. The connection of affiliate through social media advertising also growing the quantity of lead (Ghosal et al., 2020). The affiliate system makes a connection or webpage to uphold a association between customers and sellers in directive to produce recompence for the associates who performances as a distributer using SM sites such as blogs, Facebook, and YouTube. AM eases the customer's acquisition of a creation through the affiliate system (Trend buy) (V et al., 2018). So we hypothesize –

H4: AM significantly influences SM in case of SMEs.

2.6.3. AM and CBI

Affiliate marketing might be an imminent system of web marketing and online business, which quintessence exists in the move of obligation regarding deals onto an outsider, specifically, on customers (Fahim, 2020). Affiliate marketing is turning into a significant wellspring of customer securing. Numerous shippers pay affiliates a reference expense for each reference that is changed over into a consumer (pay-per conversion) (Libai et al., 2003). The AM is more advantages to the merchant to keep up the drawn out relationship with consumer for increment the business powers (V et al., 2018). The consumer pays a charge to the holder for the administrations, applications, or products. Since AM is click-based publicizing, a holder compensates an affiliate through the ASP (Affiliate Service Provider) (Iwashita & Tanimoto, 2016). As one organization embodies, working together vendors and affiliates are regularly offers "customized" interfaces, including various pointers – more commission-centered for affiliates, and more customer-and execution arranged for merchants (Mariussen et al., 2010). So, we hypothesize -

H5: AM significantly influences CBI in case of SMEs.

2.6.4. SM and CBI

Social media is rapidly being utilized for commercial reasons (Aral et al., 2013) (Baethge et al., 2016), and its widespread adoption has an impact on customer behaviour (X. Wang et al., 2019) (Daugherty & Hoffman, 2014). There is a significant connection between SM, customers, and promotions of product and service (Hajli, 2014) (Hamidi et al., 2019) (Kwahk & Kim, 2017). Customers may compare items and services offered by different merchants via social media, as well as consult with one another through direct conversation, comments, suggestions, and other means of sharing knowledge and experiences (Christodoulides et al., 2011). So, we hypothesize –

H6: SM significantly influences CBI in case of SMEs.

Figure 1. Conceptual Framework

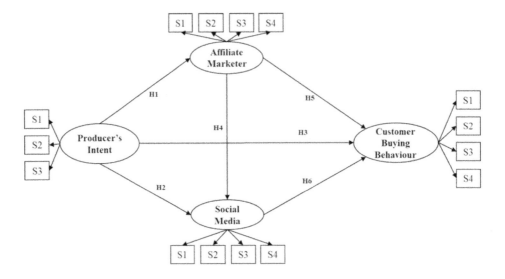

3. RESEARCH METHODOLOGY

This research was conducted on the SMEs of Moradabad and Shambhal, Uttar Pradesh, India. Primary data was collected from the entrepreneurs of the selected locations through an online questionnaire. Online data collection was done by using purposive sampling (non- probability) method. The questionnaire was consisting of fifteen items explored from the literature. Items of the constructs were measured on a 7-point Likert scale (strongly agree to strongly disagree i.e., 7 to 1). In total, 523 responses were received as complete in all respect for final analysis. The final data was analyzed by Partial Least Square Structural Equational Modelling in SmartPLS Software 3.3.3 version. The sample size was estimated by using software named G*Power version 3.1.9.7 (Faul et al., 2009). The minimum sample size by the software was 165 respondents reported in Figure 2 but we have collected data from 523 respondents to get more precise results.

Figure 2. G*Power Analysis

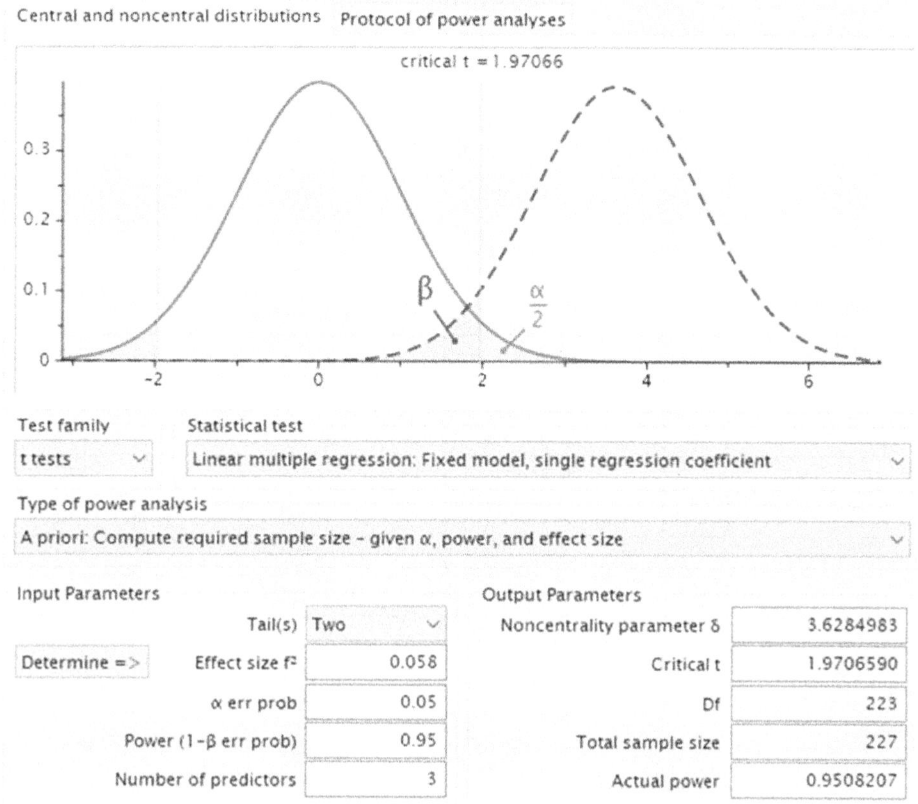

4. DATA ANALYSIS

The below table 1 depicts a descriptive analysis of the respondents. The primary data was collected from 523 entrepreneurs of handicraft units in Moradabad, Uttar Pradesh, popularly known as brass city of India. According to Export Council of India (EPCH), there are more than 9000 registered units in Moradabad producing handicraft products. In this study, majority of the respondents i.e., 419 (80.11%) are male; however, 104 (19.89%) respondents are female. This demographic profile of the respondents in this study reveals that the majority of the entrepreneurs are young, 291 respondents were having an age group of 36 to 45 years (55.64%)

and 135 respondents were into the age group of 25-35 (25.81%). Majority of the respondents are graduate i.e. 271 (51.82%) and post graduate i.e. 63 (12.05%). The age of the SSI units is also very important to consider which reflects the tendency towards adoption of affiliate marketing and social media. The data reveals that majority of the units are quite young like 203 (38.81%) units are up to 5 years old and 197 (37.67%) units are having age between 5 to 10 years which reflect good composition of the respondent for this study.

Table 1. Demographics of the Respondents

Demographics	Category	Frequency (Total no. of Respondents)	Percentage (%)
Gender	Male	419	80.11%
	Female	104	19.89%
Age (in years)	25–35	135	25.81%
	36–45	291	55.64%
	46 and above	97	18.55%
Qualification	Under-graduation	189	36.14%
	Graduation	271	51.82%
	Post-graduation and above	63	12.05%
Age of the SSE Unit (in years)	0–5	106	20.27%
	5–10	203	38.81%
	10–15	197	37.67%
	15 and above	17	3.25%
Type of SSE	Handicraft Units - SSI	523	100.00%

Table 2 depicts results of measurement model assessment which includes Factor loading (FL), Cronbach alpha, Henseler's rho_A, Composite reliability (CR) and Average variance extracted (AVE). The Cronbach alpha value of each construct is above the threshold limit i.e., 0.70 (Hair et al., 2019). Even the rho_A value of the construct is ranging from 0.764 to 0.912 which is above the threshold limit 0.70 (Hair et al., 2019) to establish the constructs' reliability. To measure the internal reliability, we have analyzed AVE score and the calculated AVE score is found above the threshold value 0.50 (Hair et al., 2019). The CR of all the constructs is ranging from 0.842 to 0.938, which means the internal consistency reliability of the constructs is good.

Table 2. Measurement Model Assessment

Latent Construct	Measured Variables	Factor Loading	Cronbach Alpha	rho_A	CR	AVE
Affiliate Marketing	Brand awareness (AffMar1)	0.834	0.904	0.907	0.933	0.778
	Product promotion (AffMar2)	0.892				
	Value creation (AffMar3)	0.926				
	Customer relationships (AffMar4)	0.874				
Customer Buying Intention	Perceived value (Cust1)	0768	0.758	0.764	0.842	0.572
	Perceived quality (Cust2)	0.742				
	Perceived trust (Cust3)	0.803				
	Perceived risk (Cust4)	0.707				
Producers Intent	Market expansion (Prod1)	0.797	0.812	0.829	0.888	0.726
	Return on Investment (Prod2)	0.87				
	Sustainability growth (Prod3)	0.886				
Social Media	Brand Recognition (SM1)	0.884	0.912	0.912	0.938	0.79
	Brand reputation (SM2)	0.877				
	High credibility (SM3)	0.889				
	Trust building (SM4)	0.906				

The investigation of the discriminant validity by considering Farnell and Larcker's Criterion (F&L Criterion) (1981) whereby the calculated value i.e., the under root of AVE of the constructs on the diagonal is higher than the constructs' inter-items correlation values. Since there is no similarity between the values of the constructs so the requirement of F&L Criterion method is fulfilled. Table 3 depicts the results.

Table 3. Discriminant Validity (F&L Criterion)

	AM	CBI	PI	SM
AM	**0.882**			
CBI	0.498	**0.756**		
PI	0.428	0.607	**0.852**	
SM	0.374	0.657	0.388	**0.889**

The new criterion of Heterotrait-Monotrait ratio of correlations (HTMT) is also one method which is used to investigate the discriminant validity of constructs. Table 4 shows the result of HTMT analysis and found that the values of HTMT are less than the suggested limit (Henseler et al., 2015) of HTMT is less than 0.85.

Table 4. Discriminant Validity Assessment (HTMT Ratio)

	AM	CBI	PI	SM
AM				
CBI	0.593			
PI	0.493	0.773		
SM	0.412	0.704	0.444	

Figure 2 depicts the structural path model of dependent and independent constructs and variables. During the literature review, we have identified six major hypotheses (Figure 1) and developed paths model.

Figure 3. Structure Equation Model Results

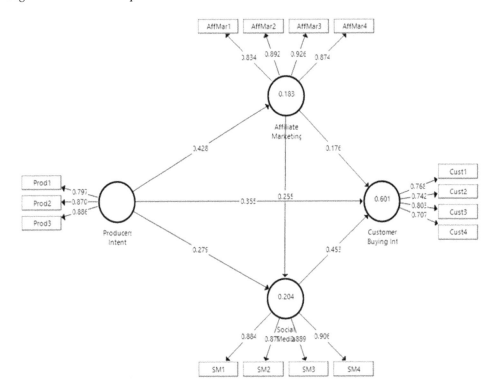

Table 5 shows the result of structural model assessments. To find out the required p-values of the hypotheses bootstrapping process was done with the suggested 5000 bootstraps that too without changing the signs (Hair et al., 2020). The results revealed that AM significantly influences CBI, AM with Std. Beta (β) 0.176 and 0.255 respectively. It is also evident that PI has a significant impact on AM, CBI, and SM with Std. Beta (β) 0.428, 0.355, and 0.279 respectively. The influence of SM on CBI is also significant with Std. Beta (β) 0.453. The R2 (R Square) of the endogenous construct CBI is significantly high 60.1%. The t-values of all the relationships lie between 3.11 to 9.588. There are some indirect relationships also in the conceptual framework of this study. PI significantly influences CBI when AM is the mediator between the two. There is also a significant relationship between AM and CBI with SM as a mediator. AM and SM also act as mediators in a significant relationship of PI and CBI. PI significantly influences CBI when SM is the mediator between the two. PI also influences SM with AM as a mediator.

Table 5. Structural Model Assessments

Hypothesis	Relationship	Std. Beta (β)	Std. Error	t-value	P-value	CI 97.50%	CI 2.50%	Decision
H1	AM -> CBI	0.176	0.042	4.164	0.000	0.261	0.093	Accepted
H2	AM -> SM	0.255	0.05	5.145	0.000	0.356	0.162	Accepted
H3	PI -> AM	0.428	0.061	7.034	0.000	0.538	0.301	Accepted
H4	PI -> CBI	0.355	0.044	8.053	0.000	0.445	0.271	Accepted
H5	PI -> SM	0.279	0.053	5.279	0.000	0.382	0.177	Accepted
H6	SM -> CBI	0.453	0.047	9.588	0.000	0.544	0.359	Accepted
	PI -> AM -> CBI	0.076	0.024	3.11	0.020	0.131	0.036	Supported
	AM -> SM -> CBI	0.115	0.023	4.981	0.000	0.167	0.075	Supported
	PI -> AM -> SM -> CBI	0.049	0.013	3.69	0.000	0.008	0.027	Supported
	PI -> SM -> CBI	0.126	0.027	4.739	0.000	0.183	0.078	Supported
	PI -> AM -> SM	0.109	0.031	3.533	0.000	0.178	0.056	Supported

5. DISCUSSION

The true potential for Indian SMEs lies in the seamless integration of affiliate marketing and social media tactics. By combining these complementary approaches, businesses can harness the collective reach, influence, and engagement potential of their affiliates and social media communities to amplify their marketing efforts exponentially. On the one hand, affiliates can leverage their established social media presence and credibility to promote the SME's products or services authentically. Through engaging content, personalized recommendations, and leveraging the trust they have cultivated with their followers, affiliates can drive targeted traffic to the business's website or online store. This approach not only expands the SME's reach but also fosters a sense of confidence and trustworthiness among potential customers, as recommendations come from trusted sources within their sphere of influence. On the other hand, SMEs can collaborate with influential creators and thought leaders on various social media platforms, tapping into their engaged audiences and leveraging their expertise and credibility. By partnering with industry influencers, businesses can benefit from their established communities, amplifying brand visibility and fostering authentic connections with potential customers. This approach allows SMEs to piggyback on the influencer's existing rapport with their followers, increasing the likelihood of resonating with their target market and driving conversions.

Moreover, the synergy between affiliate marketing and social media extends beyond mere promotion and awareness. SMEs can leverage social media as a powerful tool for customer engagement, gathering valuable insights, addressing concerns, and fostering a loyal community. By actively listening to their audience and responding to feedback, businesses can tailor their offerings, refine their strategies, and cultivate long-lasting relationships with their customers. Affiliates, too, can leverage social media to engage with their audiences, share their experiences, and provide authentic endorsements, further solidifying the trust and credibility that underpins successful affiliate marketing campaigns. This two-way communication not only strengthens brand loyalty but also empowers affiliates to become brand advocates, amplifying the reach and impact of marketing efforts. Furthermore, the data-driven nature of both affiliate marketing and social media strategies allows SMEs to measure and optimize their campaigns with precision. By tracking performance metrics, analyzing audience engagement, and monitoring conversions, businesses can continually refine their approaches, allocate resources more effectively, and maximize their return on investment.

The synergy between affiliate marketing and social media creates a virtuous cycle, where the collective reach, influence, and engagement potential of these strategies reinforce and amplify one another. By leveraging this powerful combination, Indian SMEs can effectively navigate the ever-evolving digital landscape, forge authentic connections with their target audiences, and drive sustainable growth in an increasingly competitive market.

6. CONCLUSION

The major aim of this study was to analyze the SMEs' intent towards adoption of SM & AM and to measure the producer's intent to adopt affiliate marketing and social media to increase customer base, profitability, and sustainable growth. The results of the study revealed that AM significantly influences SM and CBI. The results also show that there is a significant relationship between PI and AM, PI and SM, PI and CBI. This study helps clarify the concept of SM and AM for SMEs that can influence consumer buying intention and determine the relationships between SM, AM and CBI in SMEs.

Thus, it can be said that Indian SMEs can amplify their marketing efforts by integrating affiliate marketing and social media tactics. Affiliates can use their social media presence to promote SMEs' products or services, while businesses can partner with influential creators to tap into their audiences. Social media is also a powerful tool for customer engagement, allowing SMEs to tailor their offerings and cultivate long-lasting relationships. The data-driven nature of both strategies allows businesses to measure and optimize their campaigns with precision. By leveraging this powerful combination, Indian SMEs can forge authentic connections with their target audiences and drive sustainable growth in a competitive market.

6.1 Theoretical Implications

This research study has broad academic inferences on how SM and AM can be used by SMEs to influence consumer buying intentions. With the increase of social networking platforms on cyberspace, AM has become increasingly popular. Given the character of persons who are engaged in SM, the authors claimed that SM is regarded as a fertile environment with the potential to thrive and generate marketing outcomes.

6.2 Practical Implications

Based on the prevalence of SM site as critical platforms, this study indicates that marketers should grasp the finest approaches for developing social communication with customers over all these websites. The most dependable indicators that demonstrate a link between a customer's desire and the purchase itself are indeed the consumer's purchasing intentions. Consumer buying behavior is for the most part impacted by family, peers, colleagues, assessment pioneers, and the associations of the general public which the consumer sees as settling on his choice for buying an item. Consumer buying behavior is essentially controlled by cost, execution, and government activities measurements. Businesses will be able to ensure improved online customer purchasing behavior. Companies may build exclusive e-commerce in the corporate sector by applying SM and AM. It will be possible if SM technologies and AM techniques are used successfully. Consumers will purchase improved matters consequently, and extra chances for future study will be discovered.

6.3 Limitations of the study

The limitations of this study are first, this is cross cross-sectional study and data was gathered in the period of 3 months, so future studies can adopt the longitudinal method. Secondly, this study included only one cluster of entrepreneurs of small-scale industries producing handicraft products located in Moradabad and Shambhal (Uttar Pradesh) so as a result of the various cross-cultural aspects, it is strenuous to simplify the responses of this study to various nations and circumstances. Future research might provide intriguing findings if more data from other clusters or countries are collected, and a cross-cluster differentiation is performed. Thirdly, according to the Export Council of India (EPCH), there are more than 9000 registered units in Moradabad producing handicraft products and the sample size is 523 for this study which means future studies can be done with a larger sample size.

REFERENCES

Adam, A. I. (2020). Impact of Visual Merchandising on Customer Impulse buying behavior in retail stores in Sudan. *Asian Journal of Management*, 11(1), 29. 10.5958/2321-5763.2020.00006.2

Ahadi, S., & Kasraie, S. (2020). Contextual factors of entrepreneurship intention in manufacturing SMEs: The case study of Iran. *Journal of Small Business and Enterprise Development*, 27(4), 633–657. 10.1108/JSBED-02-2019-0074

Ainin, S., Parveen, F., Moghavvemi, S., Jaafar, N. I., & Mohd Shuib, N. L. (2015). Factors influencing the use of social media by SMEs and its performance outcomes. *Industrial Management & Data Systems*, 115(3), 570–588. 10.1108/IMDS-07-2014-0205

Akçura, M. T. (2010). Affiliated marketing. *Information Systems and e-Business Management*, 8(4), 379–394. 10.1007/s10257-009-0118-4

Alalwan, A. A. (2018). Investigating the impact of social media advertising features on customer purchase intention. *International Journal of Information Management*, 42, 65–77. 10.1016/j.ijinfomgt.2018.06.001

Alford, P., & Page, S. J. (2015). Marketing technology for adoption by small business. *Service Industries Journal*, 35(11–12), 655–669. 10.1080/02642069.2015.1062884

Anjana, S. S. (2018). A study on factors influencing cosmetic buying behavior of consumers. *International Journal of Pure and Applied Mathematics*, 118(9), 453–459.

Aral, S., Dellarocas, C., & Godes, D. (2013). Introduction to the Special Issue —Social Media and Business Transformation: A Framework for Research. *Information Systems Research*, 24(1), 3–13. 10.1287/isre.1120.0470

Arora, T., Kumar, A., & Agarwal, B. (2020). Impact of social media advertising on millennials buying behaviour. *International Journal of Intelligent Enterprise*, 7(4), 481–500. 10.1504/IJIE.2020.110795

Ashraf, M. G., Rizwan, M., Iqbal, A., & Khan, M. A. (2014). The promotional tools and situational factors' impact on consumer buying behaviour and sales promotion. *Journal of Public Administration and Governance*, 4(2), 179. 10.5296/jpag.v4i2.5844

Baethge, C., Klier, J., & Klier, M. (2016). Social commerce—State-of-the-art and future research directions. *Electronic Markets*, 26(3), 269–290. 10.1007/s12525-016-0225-2

Chatterjee, S., & Kumar Kar, A. (2020). Why do small and medium enterprises use social media marketing and what is the impact: Empirical insights from India. *International Journal of Information Management*, 53, 102103. 10.1016/j.ijinfomgt.2020.102103

Christodoulides, G., Jevons, C., & Blackshaw, P. (2011). The Voice of the Consumer Speaks Forcefully in Brand Identity. *Journal of Advertising Research, 51*(1), 101–111. 10.2501/JAR-51-1-101-111

Dangi, N., Gupta, S. K., & Narula, S. A. (2020). Consumer buying behaviour and purchase intention of organic food: A conceptual framework. *Management of Environmental Quality*, 31(6), 1515–1530. 10.1108/MEQ-01-2020-0014

Daugherty, T., & Hoffman, E. (2014). eWOM and the importance of capturing consumer attention within social media. *Journal of Marketing Communications*, 20(1–2), 82–102. 10.1080/13527266.2013.797764

Deng, X., Hui, S. K., & Hutchinson, J. W. (2010). Consumer preferences for color combinations: An empirical analysis of similarity-based color relationships. *Journal of Consumer Psychology*, 20(4), 476–484. 10.1016/j.jcps.2010.07.005

Duffy, D. L. (2005). Affiliate marketing and its impact on e-commerce. *Journal of Consumer Marketing*, 22(3), 161–163. 10.1108/07363760510595986

Durkin, M., McGowan, P., & McKeown, N. (2013). Exploring social media adoption in small to medium-sized enterprises in Ireland. *Journal of Small Business and Enterprise Development*, 20(4), 716–734. 10.1108/JSBED-08-2012-0094

Ebrahim, R. S. (2020). The Role of Trust in Understanding the Impact of Social Media Marketing on Brand Equity and Brand Loyalty. *Journal of Relationship Marketing*, 19(4), 287–308. 10.1080/15332667.2019.1705742

Eid, R., & El-Gohary, H. (2013). The impact of E-marketing use on small business enterprises' marketing success. *Service Industries Journal*, 33(1), 31–50. 10.1080/02642069.2011.594878

Fahim, T. (2020). *A Study on Consumer Attitude towards Affiliate Marketing for E-Business*. Academic Press.

Faul, F., Erdfelder, E., Buchner, A., & Lang, A. G. (2009). Statistical power analyses using G*Power 3.1: Tests for correlation and regression analyses. *Behavior Research Methods*, 41(4), 1149–1160. 10.3758/BRM.41.4.114919897823

Fox, P., & Wareham, J. (2007). Controlling your brand: Contractual restrictions placed by Internet retailers on affiliate marketing activities in Spain. *20th Bled EConference - EMergence: Merging and Emerging Technologies, Processes, and Institutions - Conference Proceedings*, 125–142.

Fox, P. B., & Wareham, J. D. (2012). Governance mechanisms in internet-based affiliate marketing programs in Spain. In *Transformations in E-Business Technologies and Commerce: Emerging Impacts* (pp. 222-239). IGI Global. 10.4018/978-1-61350-462-8.ch014

Ghosal, I., Prasad, B., & Behera, M. (2020). Impact of Affiliate Marketing on E-Buying Behavior of Millennial – A TAM Based Approach With Text Analysis. SSRN *Electronic Journal*. 10.2139/ssrn.3638929

Haikal, E. K., Freihat, S. M., Homsi, D., Joudeh, J. M. M., & Hashem, T. N. (2020). The role of supply chain strategy and affiliate marketing in increasing the demand for ecommerce-Social media POV. *International Journal of Supply Chain Management*, 9(1), 832–844.

Hair, J. F.Jr, Howard, M. C., & Nitzl, C. (2020). Assessing measurement model quality in PLS-SEM using confirmatory composite analysis. *Journal of Business Research*, 109, 101–110. 10.1016/j.jbusres.2019.11.069

Hair, J. F., Risher, J. J., Sarstedt, M., & Ringle, C. M. (2019). When to use and how to report the results of PLS-SEM. *European Business Review*, 31(1), 2–24. 10.1108/EBR-11-2018-0203

Hajli, M. N. (2014). A study of the impact of social media on consumers. *International Journal of Market Research*, 56(3), 387–404. 10.2501/IJMR-2014-025

Hamidi, F., Shams Gharneh, N., & Khajeheian, D. (2019). A Conceptual Framework for Value Co-Creation in Service Enterprises (Case of Tourism Agencies). *Sustainability (Basel)*, 12(1), 213. 10.3390/su12010213

Henseler, J., Ringle, C. M., & Sarstedt, M. (2015). A new criterion for assessing discriminant validity in variance-based structural equation modeling. *Journal of the Academy of Marketing Science*, 43(1), 115–135. 10.1007/s11747-014-0403-8

Iankova, S., Davies, I., Archer-Brown, C., Marder, B., & Yau, A. (2019). A comparison of social media marketing between B2B, B2C and mixed business models. *Industrial Marketing Management*, 81, 169–179. 10.1016/j.indmarman.2018.01.001

Iwashita, M., & Tanimoto, S. (2016). Highly secure transaction system for affiliate marketing. *2016 IEEE 5th Global Conference on Consumer Electronics, GCCE 2016*, 1–3. 10.1109/GCCE.2016.7800492

Iwashita, M., Tanimoto, S., & Tsuchiya, K. (2018). Framework of highly secure transaction management for affiliate Services of video advertising. *Procedia Computer Science*, 126, 1802–1809. 10.1016/j.procs.2018.08.097

Janssen, D., & van Heck, E. (2007). How Will Online Affiliate Marketing Networks Impact Search Engine Rankings? *ERIM Report Series Reference No. ERS-2007-042-LIS*.

Journal, I., & Movement, I. (2018). Affiliate Marketing : Meaning. *Working and Challenges.*, 2(X), 199–203.

Kamal, S., Naim, A., Magd, H., Khan, S. A., & Khan, F. M. (2022). The Relationship Between E-Service Quality, Ease of Use, and E-CRM Performance Referred by Brand Image. In Naim, A., & Kautish, S. (Eds.), *Building a Brand Image Through Electronic Customer Relationship Management* (pp. 84–108). IGI Global. 10.4018/978-1-6684-5386-5.ch005

Karyamsetty, H. J., Khan, S. A., & Nayyar, A. (2023). Envisioning Towards Modernization of Society 5.0- A Prospective Glimpse on Status, Opportunities, and Challenges With XAI. In Al-Turjman, F., Nayyar, A., Naved, M., Singh, A. K., & Bilal, M. (Eds.), *XAI Based Intelligent Systems for Society 5.0* (pp. 223–267). Elsevier. 10.1016/B978-0-323-95315-3.00005-X

Khan, S. A. (2023). E-Marketing, E-Commerce, E-Business, and Internet of Things: An Overview of Terms in the Context of Small and Medium Enterprises (SMEs). In Naim, A., & Devi, V. (Eds.), *Global Applications of the Internet of Things in Digital Marketing* (pp. 332–348). IGI Global. 10.4018/978-1-6684-8166-0.ch017

Khan, S. A., & Magd, H. (2021). Empirical Examination of MS Teams in Conducting Webinar: Evidence from International Online Program conducted in Oman. *Journal of Content. Community and Communication*, 14(8), 159–175. 10.31620/JCCC.12.21/13

Khan, S. A., Magd, H., Bhuyan, U., Jonathan, H., & Naim, A. (2024). Digital Marketing (DM): How are Small Business Enterprises (SBEs) of Bhutan and Sikkim (India) Responding to it? In *Digital Influence on Consumer Habits: Marketing Challenges and Opportunities* (pp. 135-145). Emerald Publishing Limited. 10.1108/978-1-80455-342-820241008

Khan, S. A., Magd, H., & Epoc, F. (2022). Application of Data Management System in Business to Business Electronic Commerce. In Naim, A., & Malik, P. K. (Eds.), *Competitive Trends and Technologies in Business Management* (pp. 109–124). Nova Science Publishers.

Khan, S. A., Magd, H., Khatri, B., Arora, S., & Sharma, N. (2023a). Critical Success Factors of Internet of Things and Digital Marketing. In Naim, A., & Devi, V. (Eds.), *Global Applications of the Internet of Things in Digital Marketing* (pp. 233–253). IGI Global. 10.4018/978-1-6684-8166-0.ch012

Khan, S. A., & Naim, A. (2024). XAI in Society 5.0 through the lens of Marketing and HRM. In Al-Turjman, F., Nayyar, A., Naved, M., Singh, A. K., & Bilal, M. (Eds.), *XAI Based Intelligent Systems for Society 5.0* (pp. 327–363). Elsevier. 10.1016/B978-0-323-95315-3.00004-8

Khan, S. A., Narula, S., Kansra, P., Naim, A., & Kalra, D. (2023b). Should Marketing and Public Relations be Part of the Institutional Accreditation Criterion of Business Schools? An Appraisal of Accreditation Criterion of Selected Accreditation Agencies. In Naim, A. (Ed.), *Accreditation Processes and Frameworks in Higher Education* (pp. 349–375). Nova Science Publishers. 10.52305/QUVJ6658

Khan, S. A., & Rena, R. (2023). Emerging Green Practices, Internet of Things, and Digital Marketing: A Response to the Global Economic and Climate Crises. In Naim, A., & Devi, V. (Eds.), *Global Applications of the Internet of Things in Digital Marketing* (pp. 1–16). IGI Global. 10.4018/978-1-6684-8166-0.ch001

Khatri, B., Shrimali, H., Khan, S. A., & Naim, A. (2023). Role of HR Analytics in Ensuring Psychological Wellbeing and Job Security: Learnings From COVID-19. In Yadav, R., Sinha, M., & Kureethara, J. (Eds.), *HR Analytics in an Era of Rapid Automation* (pp. 36–53). IGI Global. 10.4018/978-1-6684-8942-0.ch003

Khatri, B., Singh, R. K., Arora, S., Khan, S. A., & Naim, A. (2024). Optimizing Supply Chain Management Indicators for Sustainable Supply Chain Integration and Customer Loyalty: Potential Role of Environmentally Responsible Practices. In Ramakrishna, Y., & Srivastava, B. (Eds.), *Strategies for Environmentally Responsible Supply Chain and Production Management* (pp. 156–181). IGI Global. 10.4018/979-8-3693-0669-7.ch008

Krishnamurthy, S., & Singh, N. (2005). The international e-marketing framework (IEMF). *International Marketing Review*, 22(6), 605–610. 10.1108/02651330510630230

Kumar, V., Hundal, B. S., & Kaur, K. (2019). Factors affecting consumer buying behaviour of solar water pumping system. *Smart and Sustainable Built Environment*, 8(4), 351–364. 10.1108/SASBE-10-2018-0052

Kwahk, K.-Y., & Kim, B. (2017). Effects of social media on consumers' purchase decisions: Evidence from Taobao. *Service Business*, 11(4), 803–829. 10.1007/s11628-016-0331-4

Latif, S., & Calicioglu, C. (2020). Impact of social media advertisement on consumer purchase intention with the intermediary effect of brand attitude. *International Journal of Innovation. Creativity and Change*, 11(12), 602–619.

Libai, B., Biyalogorsky, E., & Gerstner, E. (2003). Setting Referral Fees in Affiliate Marketing. *Journal of Service Research*, 5(4), 303–315. 10.1177/1094670503005004003

MacGregor, R., & Vrazalic, L. (2007). The Role of Small Business Strategic Alliances in the Adoption of E-Commerce in Small/Medium Enterprises (SMEs). In *Small Business Clustering Technologies* (pp. 242–280). IGI Global. 10.4018/978-1-59904-126-1.ch012

Magd, H., Ansari, M. S. A., & Khan, S. A. (2023a). Need for Explainable Artificial Intelligence Ethnic Decision Making in Society 5.0. In Al-Turjman, F., Nayyar, A., Naved, M., Singh, A. K., & Bilal, M. (Eds.), *XAI Based Intelligent Systems for Society 5.0* (pp. 103–127). Elsevier. 10.1016/B978-0-323-95315-3.00010-3

Magd, H., & Khan, S. A. (2022). Effectiveness of using online teaching platforms as communication tools in higher education institutions in Oman: Stakeholders perspectives. *Journal of Content. Community and Communication*, 16, 148–160. 10.31620/JCCC.12.22/13

Magd, H., Khan, S. A., & Bhuyan, U. (2022). Social Entrepreneurship Intentions Among Business Students in Oman. In Magd, H., Singh, D., Syed, R., & Spicer, D. (Eds.), *International Perspectives on Value Creation and Sustainability Through Social Entrepreneurship* (pp. 76–93). IGI Global. 10.4018/978-1-6684-4666-9.ch005

Magd, H., Khan, S. A., Khatri, B., Sharma, N., & Arora, S. (2023b). Understanding the Relationship Between IoT and Digital Marketing: A Bibliometric Analysis. In Naim, A., & Devi, V. (Eds.), *Global Applications of the Internet of Things in Digital Marketing* (pp. 123–140). IGI Global. 10.4018/978-1-6684-8166-0.ch007

Maksimovic, M. (2018). *Greening the Future: Green Internet of Things (G-IoT) as a Key Technological Enabler of Sustainable Development*. 10.1007/978-3-319-60435-0_12

Manzoor, U., Baig, S. A., Hashim, M., & Sami, A. (2020). Impact of Social Media Marketing on Consumer's Purchase Intentions: The Mediating role of Customer Trust. *International Journal of Entrepreneurial Research*, 3(2), 41–48. 10.31580/ijer.v3i2.1386

Mariussen, A. (2011). Rethinking marketing performance measurement: Justification and operationalisation of an alternative approach to affiliate marketing performance measurement in Tourism. *Ereview of Tourism Research*, 9(3), 65–87.

Mariussen, A., Bowie, D., & Paraskevas, A. (2010). Affiliate Marketing Optimisation in Hospitality and Tourism: A Multiple Stakeholder Perspective. *Service Industries Journal*, 30(10), 1707–1722. 10.1080/02642060903580714

Masoom, K., Rastogi, A., & Khan, S. A. (2024). Impact of AI on Knowledge-based Marketing: A Study of B2B Markets. In Singh, N., Kansra, P., & Gupta, S. L. (Eds.), *Digital Influence on Consumer Habits: Marketing Challenges and Opportunities* (pp. 147–158). Emerald Publishing Limited. 10.1108/978-1-80455-342-820241009

Master, O., & Master, O. (2020). *Four Consumer Behavior Theories Every Marketer Should Know Theory of Reasoned Action Engel, Kollet, Blackwell (EKB) Model*. Academic Press.

Mazurek, G., & Kucia, M. (2011). Potential of affiliate marketing. *The 7th International Conference Management of Technological Changes – MTC 2011*, 1–4.

McCann, M., & Barlow, A. (2015). Use and measurement of social media for SMEs. *Journal of Small Business and Enterprise Development*, 22(2), 273–287. 10.1108/JSBED-08-2012-0096

Meitiana, M., Setiawan, M., Rohman, F., & Irawanto, D. W. (2019). Factors affecting souvenir purchase behavior: Valuable insight for tourism marketers and industry. *The Journal of Business and Retail Management Research*, 13(03), 248–255. 10.24052/JBRMR/V13IS03/ART-22

Naim, A., & Khan, S. A. (2023). Impact and Assessment of Electronic Commerce on Consumer Buying Behaviour. In Naim, A., & Devi, V. (Eds.), *Global Applications of the Internet of Things in Digital Marketing* (pp. 264–289). IGI Global. 10.4018/978-1-6684-8166-0.ch014

Naim, A., Khan, S. A., Malik, P. K., Hussain, M. R., & Dildar, M. S. (2023). Internet of things support for Marketing Sports and Fitness Products. *2023 3rd International Conference on Advancement in Electronics & Communication Engineering (AECE)*, 215-219. 10.1109/AECE59614.2023.10428323

Naim, A., Khan, S. A., Mohammed, A. B., & Malik, P. K. (2024a). Applications of High Performance Computing and AI in Green Digital Marketing. In Naim, A. (Ed.), *AI Applications for Business, Medical, and Agricultural Sustainability* (pp. 47–67). IGI Global. 10.4018/979-8-3693-5266-3.ch003

Naim, A., Mohammed, A. B., Fatima, N., Khan, S. A., Alnfiai, M. M., & Malik, P. K. (2024b). Applications of Artificial Intelligence in Environmental Resource Business Management and Sustainability. In Naim, A. (Ed.), *AI Applications for Business, Medical, and Agricultural Sustainability* (pp. 1–22). IGI Global. 10.4018/979-8-3693-5266-3.ch001

Newton, S., & Ojo, M. (2018). *Driving Traffic and Customer Activity Through Affiliate Marketing.* 10.4018/978-1-5225-2656-8.ch007

Nowsin, N., Hossain, I., & Bala, T. (2020). *Impact of Social Media on Consumer Buying Behavior through Online Value Proposition: A Study on E-Commerce Business in Bangladesh.* Academic Press.

Olanrewaju, A. S. T., Hossain, M. A., Whiteside, N., & Mercieca, P. (2020). Social media and entrepreneurship research: A literature review. *International Journal of Information Management, 50*, 90–110. 10.1016/j.ijinfomgt.2019.05.011

Olbrich, R., Schultz, C. D., & Bormann, P. M. (2019). The effect of social media and advertising activities on affiliate marketing. *International Journal of Internet Marketing and Advertising*, 13(1), 47–72. 10.1504/IJIMA.2019.097896

Parveen, F., Jaafar, N. I., & Ainin, S. (2016). Social media's impact on organizational performance and entrepreneurial orientation in organizations. *Management Decision*, 54(9), 2208–2234. 10.1108/MD-08-2015-0336

Patrick, Z., & Hee, O. C. (2019). Factors Influencing the Intention to Use Affiliate Marketing: A Conceptual Analysis. *International Journal of Academic Research in Business & Social Sciences*, 9(2), 701–710. 10.6007/IJARBSS/v9-i2/5608

Ramanathan, R., Ramanathan, U., & Hsiao, H.-L. (2012). The impact of e-commerce on Taiwanese SMEs: Marketing and operations effects. *International Journal of Production Economics*, 140(2), 934–943. 10.1016/j.ijpe.2012.07.017

Reza, A., Sarraf, A., & Teshnizi, H. (2020). The Effect of Social Media Advertising Properties on Customer Buying Intention (Case Study: Consumers of Cosmetic Products). *International Journal of Research in Business Studies and Management*, 7(5), 10–17.

Saleem, M., Khan, S. A., Al Shamsi, I. R., & Magd, H. (2023). Digital Marketing Through Social Media Best Practices: A Case Study of HEIs in the GCC Region. In Naim, A., & Devi, V. (Eds.), *Global Applications of the Internet of Things in Digital Marketing* (pp. 17–30). IGI Global. 10.4018/978-1-6684-8166-0.ch002

Saleem, M., Khan, S. A., & Magd, H. (2022). Content Marketing Framework for Building Brand Image: A Case Study of Sohar International School, Oman. In Naim, A., & Kautish, S. (Eds.), *Building a Brand Image Through Electronic Customer Relationship Management* (pp. 64–83). IGI Global. 10.4018/978-1-6684-5386-5.ch004

Saxena, C., Khatri, B., & Khan, S. A. (2023). Factors Hindering Women Entrepreneurs' Access to Institutional Finance: An Empirical Study From the Banker Perspective. In Gupta, V. (Ed.), *Fostering Global Entrepreneurship Through Business Model Innovation* (pp. 101–114). IGI Global. 10.4018/978-1-6684-6975-0.ch004

Sharma, N., Khatri, B., & Khan, S. A. (2023a). Do e-WOM Persuade Travelers Destination Visit Intentions? An investigation on how Travelers Adopt the Information from the Social Media Channels. *Journal of Content. Community and Communication*, 17(9), 147–161. 10.31620/JCCC.06.23/11

Sharma, N., Khatri, B., Khan, S. A., & Shamsi, M. S. (2023b). Extending the UTAUT Model to Examine the Influence of social media on Tourists' Destination Selection. *Indian Journal of Marketing*, 53(4), 47–64. 10.17010/ijom/2023/v53/i4/172689

Simpson, M., & Docherty, A. J. (2004). E-commerce adoption support and advice for UK SMEs. *Journal of Small Business and Enterprise Development*, 11(3), 315–328. 10.1108/14626000410551573

Staake, T., Thiesse, F., & Fleisch, E. (2009). The emergence of counterfeit trade: A literature review. *European Journal of Marketing*, 43(3/4), 320–349. 10.1108/03090560910935451

Tajudeen, F. P., Jaafar, N. I., & Ainin, S. (2018). Understanding the impact of social media usage among organizations. *Information & Management*, 55(3), 308–321. 10.1016/j.im.2017.08.004

V, S., M, V. S., K, M., & Priya, A. R. S. (2018). A study on impact of an affiliate marketing in e-business for consumers' perspective. *International Journal of Engineering and Technology, 10*(2), 471–475. 10.21817/ijet/2018/v10i2/181002050

Vithayathil, J., Dadgar, M., & Osiri, J. K. (2020). Social media use and consumer shopping preferences. *International Journal of Information Management*, 54, 102117. 10.1016/j.ijinfomgt.2020.102117

Wang, X., Lin, X., & Spencer, M. K. (2019). Exploring the effects of extrinsic motivation on consumer behaviors in social commerce: Revealing consumers' perceptions of social commerce benefits. *International Journal of Information Management*, 45, 163–175. 10.1016/j.ijinfomgt.2018.11.010

Wang, X.-W., Cao, Y.-M., & Park, C. (2019). The relationships among community experience, community commitment, brand attitude, and purchase intention in social media. *International Journal of Information Management*, 49, 475–488. 10.1016/j.ijinfomgt.2019.07.018

Yadav, R., & Mahara, T. (2019). An Empirical Study of Consumers Intention to Purchase Wooden Handicraft Items Online: Using Extended Technology Acceptance Model. *Global Business Review*, 20(2), 479–497. 10.1177/0972150917713899

Yadav, U. S., Tripathi, R., Rena, R., Khan, S. A., & Ghosal, I. (2025). Use and Effect of Fintech Awareness in Women for Sustainable Development in Small Industry during COVID-19 Pandemic: An Empirical Analysis with UTUAT model. *International Journal of Electronic Finance.* Advance online publication. 10.1504/IJEF.2025.10062118

Zareen, S., & Khan, S. A. (2023). Exploring Dependence of Human Resource Management (HRM) on Internet of Things (IoT) and Digital Marketing in the Digital Era. In Naim, A., & Devi, V. (Eds.), *Global Applications of the Internet of Things in Digital Marketing* (pp. 51–66). IGI Global. 10.4018/978-1-6684-8166-0.ch004

Chapter 3
A Systematic Literature Review on Strategies for Enhancing International SMEs' Performance in Malaysia and Future Research Agenda

Sylvia Nabila Azwa Ambad
http://orcid.org/0000-0003-1693-8514
Universiti Teknologi MARA, Malaysia

Mazurina Mohd Ali
Universiti Teknologi MARA, Malaysia & Kampus Puncak Alam, Malaysia

ABSTRACT

SMEs face more intimidating obstacles in international expansion than their larger counterparts. These challenges arise from resource limitations, innovation, and globalisation. Nonetheless, there exists a scarcity of SLRs targeting international business strategies for SMEs, with the majority focused on global growth challenges. This chapter aims to bridge this gap by conducting a systematic analysis of strategies for enhancing international SMEs' performance, mapping intellectual territories, and proposing future research directions. Utilising the Scopus database, 22 relevant articles were selected. Applying thematic analysis techniques, the study uncovered seven main themes that contributed to the enhancement of international SME performance in Malaysia. The main themes are; Strategic Orientation, Digital Transformation and E-Commerce, Intellectual Capital, Sustainability and

DOI: 10.4018/979-8-3693-3518-5.ch003

Copyright © 2024, IGI Global. Copying or distributing in print or electronic forms without written permission of IGI Global is prohibited.

Environmental Practices, Managerial Capabilities, Risk and Markert Uncertainty and Business Culture. These themes encapsulate the 19 sub-themes that contribute to SME success in the global marketplace. Despite an improving trend in SME international performance, the analysis shows a fragmented environment. This highlights the need for a complete, systematic study to help academics, SMEs, and policymakers reach the global market.

1. INTRODUCTION

Small and Medium-sized Enterprises (SMEs) play a pivotal role in various aspects, including job provision, GDP contribution, wealth creation, innovation promotion, and export drive. Globally, SMEs constitute the majority of businesses and serve as crucial contributors to job creation and overall economic progress. They represent approximately 90% of businesses and contribute to over 50% of global employment. In emerging economies, formal SMEs contribute significantly to national income (GDP), accounting for up to 40% (World Bank, 2020). SMEs are crucial to Malaysia's economic expansion since they employ 47.8% of the workforce, generate 11.7% of the nation's total exports, and grow the nation's GDP (NST Business, 2023). The labor-intensive nature of SMEs positions them as significant job generators, expected to play a crucial role in technology advancement, organizational innovation, and economic competitiveness (Singh, 2022). With their entrepreneurial spirit, flexibility, and adaptability, SMEs act as catalysts for economic growth, making substantial contributions to employment and economic development in both developed and developing nations (Gherghina et al., 2020).

However, small and medium-sized enterprises (SMEs) frequently encounter barriers that hinder their participation in global trade. These barriers include insufficient financial resources, lack of familiarity with foreign markets, intricate regulatory frameworks, and the requirement for specialized knowledge in domains like logistics and export compliance (Andres et al., 2022; Rahman et al., 2020). Frequently, larger, more established companies with higher resources and brand recognition compete fiercely with SMEs. Yet, small and medium-sized enterprises (SMEs) also exhibit distinct benefits, including agility, flexibility, and its capacity to swiftly adjust to evolving market dynamics. Their smaller sizes enable them to engage in more individualized customer interactions and make quick decisions, which can be beneficial in niche markets or when addressing particular customer requirements (Yusuf et al., 2022). Furthermore, small and medium-sized enterprises (SMEs) frequently possess a robust entrepreneurial drive and a propensity for innovation, which empowers them to identify unexplored prospects and separate themselves apart from more sizable rivals (Anwar et al., 2022). SME expansion into international markets is possible with the utilization of their competitive advantages and provision of networks and resources, as well as the proper assistance, strategic planning, and support (Falahat et al., 2022).

Hence, it is critical to undertake a more comprehensive investigation into the factors that influence the drivers of the performance of international small and medium-sized enterprises (SMEs). The structure of this chapter is outlined as follows: following the introduction (Section 1), Sections 2 and 3 detail the materials and methodology. In Section 4, the findings from thematic analysis are presented, followed by Section 5, which addresses limitations and suggests future research directions. Section 6 serves as the concluding part of this chapter.

2. LITERATURE REVIEW

2.1 SMEs and Internationalization

In the 1960s, the initial research on international business focused predominantly on multinational corporations. The emergence of research on smaller firms did not begin until the late 1980s (Steinhauser et al., 2021). This is due to the fact that a number of nations, especially those with balance of payment deficits, have attempted to increase the international activities of their small and SMEs to stimulate economic development and reduce unemployment (Ruzzier et al., 2006). Additionally, globalization has made it essential for small and medium-sized enterprises to explore opportunities in foreign markets to remain competitive. As more businesses expand internationally, competition increases as a result of technological advancements and the removal of trade barriers. Rapid globalization facilitates the international expansion of SMEs in a more timely and effective manner (Osano, 2019).

International business has been defined as the activities of a company that conducts economic transactions across national borders. Additionally, it may include conducting business overseas (Peng, 2018). Globalization superseded this phrase starting in the early 1970s (Gjellerup, 2000). Globalization entails overseeing a company's operations on a global scale, extending beyond limited geographical boundaries. It involves the integration of competitive markets worldwide, which in turn challenges conventional export practices and necessitates adaptability to swiftly evolving marketing and production landscapes. This is one of the reasons why SMEs must adapt to globalization more quickly (Ruzzier et al., 2006).

Globalization of the economy has presented SMEs with numerous obstacles as a result of the escalating level of competition. Consequently, shortly after their inception, the rate of failure for SMEs is comparatively high. SMEs must therefore implement survival strategies and strategic approaches in order to effectively confront the numerous global challenges that the SME sector faces (Gamage et al., 2020). Therefore, this study aims to systemically review the factors affecting international SMEs' Performance in Malaysia.

3. METHODOLOGY

This chapter employed the systematic literature review (SLR) methodology as suggested by Tranfield et al. (2003). It consists of three major stages: 1) planning the review, 2) conducting the review, and 3) reporting and dissemination. This review aims to answer the research question: How do Malaysia's Small and Medium Enterprises (SMEs) implement strategies to enhance their international business performance? This research question is chosen due to the limited review focused on the international SMEs' performance, especially in Malaysia. In this era of globalization, it is essential for SMEs to enter the global market and establish a competitive edge.

To answer the research question, the Scopus database was chosen for its extensive and profound content, frequently selected by scholars. Additionally, it is the foremost meticulously curated repository of abstracts and citations in global research literature at present (Schotten et al., 2017). The search began in February 2024. The keywords used in this SLR are for articles with titles containing the terms "small" or "medium" or "micro" or "SME," in combination with "international" and "global." To be more accurate, the search is limited to the subject area of Business, Management, and Accounting. There were 957 documents found. For more updated information, articles published within three years from 2021 to 2023 were chosen. Additionally, to ensure quality and standardization, only papers published as articles in English and empirical research are included in this SLR. After this exclusion, only 123 documents were processed to the next stage. These documents were scrutinized to determine if they could be used in the thematic analysis on the strategies used for international SMEs performance and whether they were conducted among Malaysia's SMEs. After thorough examination of the abstracts and full papers, only 24 articles that fulfilled the inclusion criteria and were usable for the review. By utilizing the final list of articles, the analysis incorporated insights into the leading themes, trends, and patterns of the respective research. Following this, a comprehensive analysis of each paper was conducted with the intention of addressing the research questions initially presented. The list of articles utilized in this SLR is presented in Table 1. The final stage involves reporting and dissemination concerning the thematic analysis of the strategies used by Malaysia's SMEs in enhancing their international business performance.

Table 1. List of Review Articles

	Authors	Title	
1	Mah P.Y.; Chuah F.; E-Vahdati S.	Corporate Sustainability Orientation, Sustainable Development Practices, and Firm Performance of MSMEs in Malaysia.	Q2
2	Ismail M.; Mohamad N.; Ahamat A.	Managerial Capabilities, Learning Orientation and Performance Of International Halal Industry Using Upper Echelon Theory	Q3
3	Pertheban T.R.; Thurasamy R.; Marimuthu A.; Venkatachalam K.R.; Annamalah S.; Paraman P.; Hoo W.C.	The Impact of Proactive Resilience Strategies on Organizational Performance: Role of Ambidextrous and Dynamic Capabilities of SMEs in Manufacturing Sector	Q1
4	Sharfaei S.; Ong J.W.; Ojo A.O.	The effects of dynamic capabilities on international SMEs' performance	Q4
5	Sharfaei S.; Wei Ong J.; Ojo A.O.	The impact of market uncertainty on international SME performance	Q2
6	Ahmad N.; Imm N.S.; Basha N.K.; Aziz Y.A.	Exploring The Driving Factors of International Performance: Evidence from Business Service SMEs In Malaysia	Q4
7	Akpan I.J.; Effiom L.; Akpanobong A.C.	Towards developing a knowledge base for small business survival techniques during COVID-19 and sustainable growth strategies for the post-pandemic era	Q2
8	Annamalah S.; Paraman P.; Ahmed S.; Pertheban T.R.; Marimuthu A.; Venkatachalam K.R.; T R.	Exploitation, exploration and ambidextrous strategies of SMES in accelerating organisational effectiveness	Q2
9	Ismail M.B.; Mohamad N.B.; Ahamat A.	Learning Orientation as Mediator between International Entrepreneurial Orientation and International Firm Performance in Global Halal Industry	Q2
	Falahat M.; Soto-Acosta P.; Ramayah T.	Analysing the importance of international knowledge, orientation, networking and commitment as entrepreneurial culture and market orientation in gaining competitive advantage and international performance	Q1
	Waqas A.; Halim H.; Ahmad N.	Design leadership and SMEs Sustainability; Role of Frugal Innovation and Technology Turbulence	Q4
	Tze San O.; Latif B.; Di Vaio A.	GEO and sustainable performance: the moderating role of GTD and environmental consciousness	Q1
	Hu M.K.; Kee D.M.H.	Fostering sustainability: reinventing SME strategy in the new normal	Q2
	Qalati S.A.; Ostic D.; Sulaiman M.A.B.A.; Gopang A.A.; Khan A.	Social Media and SMEs' Performance in Developing Countries: Effects of Technological-Organizational-Environmental Factors on the Adoption of Social Media	Q2
	Aljuboori Z.M.; Singh H.; Haddad H.; Al-Ramahi N.M.; Ali M.A.	Intellectual Capital and Firm Performance Correlation: The Mediation Role of Innovation Capability in Malaysian Manufacturing SMEs Perspective	Q1
	Ahmad N.; Ng S.I.; Basha N.K.; Aziz Y.A.	Why knowledge-based human resource management matters for business service SMEs?	Q3

continued on following page

Table 1. Continued

	Authors	Title		
	Mohamad A.; Mohd Rizal A.; Kamarudin S.; Sahimi M.	Exploring the Co-Creation of Small and Medium Enterprises, and Service Providers Enabled by Digital Interactive Platforms for Internationalization: A Case Study in Malaysia		Q1
	Reza S.; Mubarik M.S.; Naghavi N.; Nawaz R.R.	Internationalisation challenges of SMEs: Role of intellectual capital		Q3
	Falahat M.; Lee Y.-Y.; Soto-Acosta P.; Ramayah T.	Entrepreneurial, market, learning and networking orientations as determinants of business capability and international performance: the contingent role of government support		Q1
	Ismail A.; Majid A.H.A.; Rahman M.A.; Jamaluddin N.A.; Susantiy A.I.; Setiawati C.I.	Aligning Malaysian SMEs with the Megatrends: The Roles of HPWPs and Employee Creativity in Enhancing Malaysian SME Performance		Q2
	Ahmad N.; Imm N.S.; Basha N.K.; Aziz Y.A.	How do the dynamic capabilities of Malaysian service small and medium-sized enterprises (SMEs) translate into international performance? Uncovering the mechanism and conditional factors		Q3
	Zulkiffli S.N.A.; Padlee S.F.	Sustainable Outsourcing Decisions, Competitive Capabilities and Business Performance Of Malaysian Manufacturing SMEs A Confirmatory Factor Analysis Approach		Q3

4. THEMATIC ANALYSIS: FACTORS INFLUENCING SMES' INTERNATIONAL BUSINESS PERFORMANCE

Analyzing the content of the papers revealed recurring themes that were subsequently investigated. At this point, strategies to enhance international business performance were identified. As illustrated in Table 1, seven major themes were determined.

Table 2. Themes and Sub-themes

Item	Themes	Sub-themes
1.	Strategic Orientation	1. Learning Orientation 2. Entrepreneurial Orientation 3. Marketing Orientation
2.	Digital Transformation and E-Commerce	1. Digital Technologies 2. Business Model Modifications
3.	Intellectual Capital	1. Human Capital 2. Relational Capital 3. Structural Capital
4.	Sustainability and Environmental Practices	1. Corporate Sustainability orientation 2. Green Entrepreneurial Orientation 3. Outsourcing Orientation

continued on following page

Table 2. Continued

Item	Themes	Sub-themes
5.	Managerial Capabilities	1. Dynamic Capabilities 2. Ambidextrous Capabilities 3. Top Management Capabilities 4. Crisis Management Techniques
6.	Risk and Markert Uncertainty	-
7.	Business Culture	1. Organizational culture 2. Entrepreneurial Culture

4.1 Strategic Orientation

In today's competitive landscape, organizations need strategic orientation to achieve superior performance and long-term viability This entails substituting pandemonium with logical and predictive approaches in management. Strategic orientation is crucial for success, setting organizations apart and impacting all aspects of their achievements. It's about modern thinking, leadership, and enhancing competitiveness and performance (AlQersh et al., 2022). It refers to the strategic direction a company takes to encourage behaviors that lead to sustained success and a competitive advantage. Strategic orientation consist of various dimensions such as market orientation, entrepreneurial orientation, and learning orientation. Strategic orientation is widely used in research on strategy, entrepreneurship, and marketing, reflecting the importance of aligning business practices with long-term success (Uzoamaka et al., 2020). In this review, four studies found that strategic orientation positively influence the international business performance (Ismail et al., 2023a; Ismail et al., 2023b; Falahat et al., 2022; Falahat et al., 2021).

4.1.1 Learning Orientation

The learning orientation (LO) of an organization influences its approach to knowledge creation and learning. It resembles the organization's approach to learning. A high level of LO necessitates the constant reevaluation of one's relationship with the environment and the appreciation of learning as a means of adapting to environmental changes. LO is dependent on market orientation, or the efficiency with which an organization processes market data. Firms that possess a robust LO recognize the significance of gaining knowledge from their surroundings and hold the conviction that innovation does not spontaneously emerge in reaction to alterations. This approach has a constructive impact on the organization's innovation and performance (Frank et al., 2012). Organizational learning in SMEs differs significantly from that of larger organizations, with notable variations in organizational structure, formalization, management, communication, and cultural inclinations towards innovation and market orientation (Michna, 2009). Despite these distinctions, limited attention has been given to studying the unique learning dynamics of SMEs.

In this systematic literature review (SLR), a study conducted by Ismail et al. (2023a; 2023b) found that learning orientation (LO) has the strongest effect on the international firm performance of small and medium halal export manufacturers in Malaysia. In other words, the higher the level of LO—commitment to learning, shared vision, open-mindedness, facilitated leadership, and decentralized strategic planning—the better the international business performance. They measured international performance using overseas sales volume, overseas sales growth, and overseas profitability. Similarly, a study conducted by Falahat et al. (2021) revealed that LO impacts the financial and strategic performance of small and medium-sized enterprises (SMEs), accelerates and expands the scope of internationalization, and promotes the growth of business capability. A total of 251 small and medium enterprises (SMEs) encompassing various industries were included in the sample for this research.

4.1.2 Entrepreneurial Orientation (EO)

The concept of entrepreneurial orientation originated from the research of Mintzberg (1973) and Khandwalla (1977), which revealed that entrepreneurial firms were more proactive in their pursuit of new business opportunities and tended to undertake greater risks than other types of firms. Nevertheless, it was likely Miller's (1983) research that gave rise to the construct in its current usage. Entrepreneurship, according to Miller (1983), is a multidimensional concept that encompasses the proactiveness, risk-taking, and innovation-related actions of the firm. Furthermore, Lumpkin and Dess (1996) have argued that EO should include two additional dimensions, autonomy and competitive aggressiveness. Currently, there are five EO dimensions that are widely used and treated as formative second order construct; innovativeness, proactiveness, risk taking, autonomy and competitive aggressiveness (George, 2011). EO has been emphasized as crucial for enhancing company success. In this current SLR, a study conducted among SMEs in Malaysia found that EO has a positive effect on international firm performance (Falahat et al., 2021).

4.1.3 Market Orientation

Having a good grasp of market information processing (MO) is valuable for the firm's sustainability and competitive advantage (Wang et al., 2022). MO involves how much a company gathers, shares, and responds to market intelligence about current and future customer needs, competitor strategies, channel requirements, and the overall business environment. According to resource-based theory, companies with strong MO tend to perform better because they understand their customers' needs and desires, competitor strategies, channel requirements, and the market environment better than their competitors. Similarly, among all strategic dimensions, MO has the strongest effect on firm performance (Wang et al., 2022). However, Falahat et al. (2022) found that market orientation is positively related to competitive advantage but not to international performance of SMEs in Malaysia.

4.2 Digital Transformation and E-Commerce

The convergence of digital transformation with e-commerce provides significant synergies for Malaysia's international SMEs, allowing them to use digital technologies to boost e-commerce growth and competitiveness. Lee and Park (2020) claim that digital transformation is essential for SMEs to effectively implement e-commerce strategies and overcome challenges such as digital literacy, cybersecurity, and logistics infrastructure. According to Ahmad et al. (2019), the seamless integration of digital technologies along with e-commerce platforms allows SMEs to achieve operational excellence, client intimacy, and product innovation.

4.2.1 Digital Technologies

Digital technologies play a critical role in enhancing SMEs' performance, especially in the context of overcoming challenges such as the COVID-19 pandemic. By identifying and evaluating strategies that SMEs can employ to survive the challenges posed by the COVID-19 pandemic, Akpan et al (2023) emphasize the importance of internal resources, digital technologies, funding for digitization, and social entrepreneurship in helping SMEs survive challenges and achieve sustainable growth post-pandemic. These strategies could lead SMEs to achieve competitive advantage and sustainable growth in the global market. Mohamad et al. (2022) suggest using digital interactive platforms to promote collaboration between SMEs and service providers. The study highlights the revolutionary potential of digital technologies and their capacity to overcome various challenges, including limited resources and limits in internationalisation efforts. The emphasis is on the transformative influence of digital platforms, which allow SMEs to overcome obstacles and improve overall performance.

Insights for SMEs looking to enhance sustainability practises can be gained from Waqas et al (2022)'s investigation of how technological turbulence moderates the relationship between frugal innovation and design leadership. Technology turbulence is a term used to describe how much an industry has changed technologically. It emphasises how quickly technology advances cause it to become outdated, and how businesses can leverage their own internal resources to adjust. The fourth industrial revolution has sped up technical advancement, creating new avenues for creativity. Technology turbulence stimulates firms to adopt new technologies and enhance employee abilities, which may have an impact on organisational goals and innovation processes, according to a Malaysian study. But SMEs can find it difficult to keep up with the quick changes in technology, which could hinder their capacity for innovation and sustainability.

4.2.2 Business Model Modification

A key factor in improving SMEs' effectiveness in an international setting is business model adaptation. SMEs may increase consumer involvement, attract a wider audience, and become more competitive in the digital economy by incorporating social media into their business strategies. The effect of social media adoption on organisational, technological, and environmental elements of SME performance was highlighted by Qalati et al. (2022). According to this study, social media use significantly improves SMEs' company performance. The study also showed that, after environmental factors, organisational considerations have the biggest beneficial impact on social media usage. Thus, by incorporating social media into their business plans, SMEs can take advantage of enhanced performance and obtain a competitive edge in global markets.

4.3 Intellectual Capital

Intellectual capital encompasses intangible assets and resources within an organisation that enhance its value creation and competitive advantage. It consists of three primary components: human capital, structural capital, and relational capital (Aljuboori et al., 2021). According to Reza et al. (2021), intellectual capital refers to a company's employees' knowledge, skills, and abilities (human capital), its relationships with different stakeholders (relational capital), and its business processes (structural capital).

4.3.1 Human Capital (Knowledge-Based Human Resource Management, High-Performance Work Practices (HPWPs), Employee Creativity)

Human capital refers to employees' knowledge, expertise, and professional skills, as well as their experience, education level, and creativeness in an organization (Mubarik, 2015). A study by Reza et al. (2021), which looks at how SMEs are affected by internationalisation challenges and how intellectual capital plays a part in the relationship between these challenges and a firm's internalisation, found that human capital has a direct and significant impact on a firm's performance and that it mitigates (neutralises) the negative effects of these challenges by giving businesses the tools they need to overcome them. Human capital development is an essential component of intellectual capital as it can have a significant impact on transforming current export-related assets or resources within an organisation.

In their study, Ismail et al. (2018) explored the mediating role of employee creativity in high-performance work practices. They found that employee creativity influences the relationship between job design and SME financial performance, which in turn leads to higher performance in Malaysian firms. This highlights the important role of employees in improving high performance within companies. Similarly, Aljuboori et al. (2023), studied intellectual capital's influence on firm performance, also discovered that investing in human capital could enhance firm performance in Malaysian manufacturing SMEs. This indicates that human capital can serve as a valuable resource for companies, resulting in increased competitive advantages and greater performance. Highly competent and experienced employees have a greater capacity to generate innovative ideas, resulting in improved firm performance. For instance, human resource practices such as job design and training that emphasise the development of creative problem-solving skills, may enhanced employees' abilities to generate different solutions (creativity-relevant skills) and enhance their knowledge of products and customer service skills (domain-relevant skills), which are essential for fostering creativity within the organisation (Ismail et al., 2018).

4.3.2 Relational Capital (Access to Financing, Government Facilitation)

This is the value that is derived from the relationships that an organization has with its stakeholders, such as customers, suppliers, partners, and the community. It includes the organization's reputation, brand image, and customer loyalty. Relational capital is important because it helps to build trust and enhance the organization's competitive position. As highlighted by Reza et al. (2021), relational capital can facilitate organisations to improve interaction, sharing of knowledge, and consideration of win-win situations with its supply chain partners. By doing this, it assists the organisation in minimising the detrimental impacts of challenges, both internal and external.

4.3.3 Structural Capital

This refers to the supportive infrastructure within an organization that helps to facilitate knowledge sharing, innovation, and decision-making. It includes systems, processes, patents, trademarks, and databases. Structural capital is important because it enables the organization to leverage its knowledge effectively. Furthermore, it enabled the storage of information in a database system and facilitated its accessibility to users, benefiting decision-makers.

Aljuboori et al. (2023), in their study on intellectual capital's influence on firm performance, clearly confirmed that structural capital enhances innovation capability. Hence, the firms' high level of innovation capability generates higher firm performance in manufacturing SMEs in Malaysia. The result also supports the assumption of resource-based view theory, where the effective utilisation of internal resources enhances competitive advantages for higher performance.

In conclusion, intellectual capital is vital for SMEs to innovate, adapt, and compete effectively in the constantly evolving business environment. By efficiently managing and utilising human, relational, and structural capital, SMEs can improve their performance, foster innovation, and achieve sustainable growth.

4.4 Sustainability and Environmental Practices

Sustainability and environmental practices have become widely recognised as essential elements of business strategy, impacting both organisational performance and the well-being of society. Multiple studies have investigated various aspects of sustainability initiatives and their impact on businesses, society, and the environment.

4.4.1 Corporate Sustainability Orientation

Corporate sustainability orientation refers to the commitment of organisations to integrate environmental, social, and economic considerations into their business operations. Mah et al. (2023), in their study, emphasise the significance of understanding how corporate sustainability orientation and environmental practices impact firm performance, especially in the context of SMEs. The study highlights that in order to create value for the company and ultimately result in successful firm performance, corporate sustainability orientation reflects the strategy and orientation of the company with respect to sustainability, taking into account all sustainability dimensions as well as its stakeholders. Furthermore, the focus on corporate sustainability and environmental practices is important. A firm's perspective on sustainability-related issues is linked to its actions, which reflect the firm's environmental practices and lead it to move in the direction of its stakeholders' interests. The findings also revealed the environmental practices had a significant influence on the SMEs' success. This demonstrates that organisations' environmental consciousness will enhance their environmental practices as part of their business care. Finally, the findings of this study indicate that environmental practices could improve the relationship between corporate sustainability orientation and firm performance. This might indicate that the corporate sustainability orientation of a firm will lead to environmental practices and the success of the firm.

Meanwhile, another study by Waqas et al. (2022) highlights the importance of design leadership and frugal innovation in enhancing SME sustainability, especially in the context of addressing global issues like climate change and poverty. The study emphasizes how these factors can help SMEs adopt business practices that are less harmful to society and align with the United Nations' Sustainable Development Goals (SDGs). Additionally, the study explores the moderation of technology turbulence in the relationship between design leadership and frugal innovation, providing valuable insights for SMEs aiming to improve their sustainability practices. The findings of this study indicate that design leadership is positively and significantly correlated with the sustainability of SMEs. Frugal innovation plays a crucial role in mediating the connection between design leadership and the sustainability of SMEs. Likewise, technology turbulence also plays a significant but antagonistic role in moderating the relationship between design leadership and frugal innovation.

Therefore, managers of SMEs should focus on designing leadership strategies to provide cost-effective and affordable innovative products to cater to the needs of customers in emerging markets. This will not only maintain their business but also contribute to its overall sustainability. Moreover, manufacturing businesses' innovation processes might be affected by technological advancements, and SME management should be ready to deal with these external uncertainties by improving their skills or developing new production capabilities.

4.4.2 Green Entrepreneurial Orientation

Green entrepreneurial orientation emphasises utilising environmentally friendly technologies and practices to promote innovation and sustainability. SMEs can achieve sustainable growth and capitalise on emerging green markets by adopting green innovation and production processes.

In their study, Tse Zan et al. (2022) investigate the relationship between intellectual capital (IC) manifested as green entrepreneurial orientation (GEO) and the sustainable performance of manufacturing SMEs in Pakistan and Malaysia. This study is significant as it addresses the global call to combat climate change by effectively managing IC to promote green initiatives. Despite previous research linking GEO to firm performance, the role of GEO in leveraging sustainable performance has been underexplored, making your study novel and valuable. Despite earlier studies linking GEO to firm performance, the exact role of GEO in leveraging sustainable performance is relatively unknown, making this analysis both innovative and informative. Using a three-wave research methodology and data from 296 respondents, the authors conclude that IC as GEO has a considerable impact on sustainable performance, with green technology dynamism (GTD) and environmental consciousness functioning as moderating role. The results of this study possess practical implications for managers of Pakistani and Malaysian SMEs, indicating that fostering GEO, GTD, and environmental consciousness may enhance sustainable performance and contribute to the United Nations SDG-2030 agenda. Overall, this study contributes to the literature by broadening our understanding of GEO as a form of IC that promotes long-term performance, particularly in developing nations such as Pakistan and Malaysia.

4.4.3 Outsourcing Orientation

Outsourcing orientation refers to SMEs' strategic decision to outsource non-core functions to specialized partners, which has an impact on environmental practices and sustainability. Zulkiffli & Padlee (2021) explore the role of outsourcing in supporting sustainability efforts and enhancing competitive advantage in Malaysian manufacturing SMEs. The theme of the study emphasises the growing importance of environmental and social responsibility issues in developing sustainable outsourcing strategies and influencing business performance. Zulkiffli & Padlee (2021) also highlight that outsourcing is important to ensure competitive advantages for SMEs. The suggest that strategic outsourcing of certain functions enables firms to enhance business performance and sharpen competitive capabilities by focusing on core competencies. Furthermore, outsourcing can be a strategic tool for improving SMEs' operational efficiency and effectiveness in achieving company objectives. SMEs should improve their outsourcing skills to expand SMEs' overall performance, including cost savings, enhanced organisational focus, and access to higher capabilities.

4.5 Managerial Capabilities

Managerial capabilities are the skills, competencies, and strategic acumen possessed by organisational leaders and managers that are important in driving organisational performance and accomplishing strategic objectives. Studies in this field explore various aspects of managerial capabilities and their impact on organizational success especially in the context of SMEs.

4.5.1 Dynamic Capabilities

According to Pertheban et al., (2023), dynamic capabilities refer to the regular utilisation of organisational processes that utilise resources, especially those procedures focused on integrating, reconfiguration, obtaining, and releasing resources to align with changes in the market. An organization's dynamic capabilities are a set of actions that explain its functioning and operations. Using the dynamic capabilities perspective, they looked at the link between proactive resilience strategies, ambidextrous skills, and the performance of small businesses in the manufacturing sector. The results support the dynamic capabilities theory (DCT) by seeing resilience strategies as dynamic skills that help small businesses develop ambidextrous skills. This can impact supply chain stability and enhance organisational performance.

Moreover, Sharfaei et al. (2023), which focus on understanding how international SMEs in developing countries, such as Iran, can overcome challenges and improve their performance, highlight the importance of developing dynamic capabilities and leveraging competitive advantage in achieving high performance. Despite the findings that dynamic capabilities may not directly impact performance and competitive advantage may not mediate this relationship in the context of the study, the findings provide valuable insights and recommendations for international SMEs seeking to enhance their performance in developing markets.

4.5.2 Ambidextrous Capabilities

Ambidextrous capabilities enhance an organization's ability to explore new opportunities and effectively use current resources. According to Pertheban et al. (2023), SMEs in the manufacturing industry can improve their performance by using ambidextrous strategies to strengthen organisational capabilities. Their research highlights the need of proactive resilience strategies and ambidextrous capabilities in navigating the complexities of the global business landscape while ensuring sustainable operations during abrupt changes. The results suggest that when SMEs combine proactive resilience strategies with ambidextrous capabilities, they can achieve synergistic effects. Combining visibility and predetermined decision plans with ambidextrous capabilities can establish a reinforcing cycle, which in turn strengthen the effectiveness of proactive resilience strategies. This synergy enables SMEs to navigate uncertainties, capitalise on opportunities, and achieve better organisational performance.

Similarly, a study by Annamalah et al. (2023) that focus on how SMEs in the manufacturing sector can develop resilience strategies to adapt to dynamic and challenging market conditions. The study highlights that ambidexterity could assist SMEs strengthen their competencies, allowing them to deal more effectively with uncertainty in their surroundings. According to the findings, ambidexterity has been proposed as a potential connection between proactive resilience and performance. These findings show that SMEs are more likely to encounter the shocks provided by a changing business environment. SMEs should never cease investigating and seizing opportunities that lead to better performance.Top of Form

4.5.3 Top Management Capability

Top management capability refers to the talents and skills acquired by an organization's senior leadership team, which play an important role in influencing strategic direction, decision-making, and overall organisational performance.

Ismail et al. (2023) highlight the unique focus of the study on applying Upper Echelon Theory (UET) in the context of the halal industry, an area that has received little academic attention previously. Their research emphasises the importance of the top-management team's (TMT) knowledge and international experience in shaping corporate strategy and performance. Furthermore, the study proposes the concept of learning orientation as a critical mediator in transmitting tacit knowledge within organisations, hence influencing their global performance.

On a similar note, Ahmad et al. (2021) investigate the significance of top management competence within Malaysian SMEs, particularly in terms of aligning with global megatrends to promote economic development and competitiveness. Their findings emphasise the importance of using employee creativity as a key driver for enhancing SME performance and adapting to transformational global forces.

These studies highlight the strategic importance of top management capability in leading organisations to success, whether it's overcoming industry-specific problems like those in the halal sector or responding to larger global trends. Ultimately, they emphasise the significance of effective leadership and management techniques in promoting organisational growth and sustainability.

4.5.4 Crisis Management Techniques

Crisis management techniques refer to the strategies and practices that organisations use to respond to and reduce the impact of unexpected occurrences on their operations and stakeholders.

A study by Hu and Kee (2021) investigated crisis management techniques, focusing on their use in small and medium-sized firms (SMEs) against the backdrop of the "new normal" era. Their findings highlight the importance for SMEs to create a sustained competitive edge by using internal resources and realigning their business strategies. The study emphasises the importance of SMEs showing dynamism, foresight, and adaptability, as well as the opportunity for these businesses to capitalise on emerging opportunities in both regional and global markets. Since the internationalisation process is complex, the study suggests that SMEs that are not yet ready should begin developing their resources and capabilities so that they can explore future international markets. They may begin the internationalisation process by venturing into indirect export activities. By doing so, SMEs will have to improve the consistency and quality of their products in order to achieve their objectives. Therefore, by strategically developing and implementing efficient business strategies, small and medium-sized enterprises (SMEs) can capitalise on the significant business opportunities in global marketplaces and expand their firm to new levels of success.

4.6 Risk and Market Uncertainty

Risk and market uncertainty are used to describe the challenges and unpredictability that organisations encounter in their operating environments, including factors such as economic fluctuations, regulatory changes, and technological disruptions. For instance, Sharfaei et al. (2023) examine the strategies used by multinational SMEs in Iran to navigate market volatility and achieve their performance goals. Their study highlights the significance of understanding how market uncertainty affects performance and the role of competitive advantage in moderating this relationship. For instance, economic uncertainty caused by the COVID-19 epidemic and subsequent lockdowns has been clearly evident. Many companies faced uncertainty in this environment, especially those unable to operate totally remotely by utilising various technologies. Hence, technological adoption reduces the uncertainty of the COVID-19 pandemic and lessens its impact on businesses. The results indicate that market uncertainty impacts the performance of multinational SMEs, consistent with prior research. A such, multinational SMEs need to consider the impact of uncertainty to accomplish their objectives. This is especially crucial in developing markets, which are more ambiguous. The multinational SMEs could gain more by selecting markets with lower uncertainty to optimise their profits.

4.7 Business Culture

4.7.1 Organizational Culture

Organisational culture encompasses the shared values, beliefs, and norms that shape the behavior and interactions within an organization. It significantly influences employee attitudes, behaviours, and performance, eventually affecting organisational effectiveness and success.

Ismail et al. (2023) conducted a study highlighting the importance of learning orientation as a key aspect of organizational culture, particularly within SMEs operating in the halal industry. They emphasize how a strong learning orientation can prepare SMEs to navigate uncertain global environments effectively. The study also reveals that learning orientation mediates the relationship between international entrepreneurial orientation and international firm performance. By fostering a culture of continuous learning and adaptation, SMEs can enhance their sustainability and competitiveness in the global halal market. The finding also indicates that found that learning orientation is a source of competitive advantage that positively affects the performance of SMEs and also essential for boosting corporate success.

4.7.2 Entrepreneurial Culture

Entrepreneurial culture relates to the values, attitudes, and behaviours that promote entrepreneurship and innovation within an organisation. It encourages risk-taking, inventiveness, and a proactive approach to recognising and exploiting business opportunities.

Falahat et al. (2022) conducted a study that highlighted the critical requirements of entrepreneurial culture and market orientation for young companies seeking to gain a competitive advantage and superior global performance. Their research indicates how these cultural factors help young entrepreneurial firms expand rapidly into foreign markets, despite obstacles such as insufficient resources and experience. Furthermore, the study sheds insight on the function of government intervention in reinforcing the relationship between competitive advantage and international achievement. The findings indicate that SMEs may compete in global marketplaces and achieve sustainable growth by fostering an entrepreneurial culture and adapting to market needs. Furthermore, the findings also confirm that entrepreneurial culture and market orientation are key sources of competitive advantage in a rising economy.

Based on the studies, both emphasise the importance of organisational and entrepreneurial cultures in influencing the success and performance of SMEs. Organisations may enhance their long-term sustainability and growth prospects by understanding and leveraging these cultural factors to promote innovation, adaptation, and competitiveness.

5. LIMITATION AND FUTURE RESEARCH DIRECTIONS

Similar to other studies, this research also has limitations, thus suggesting avenues for future research directions. First, this SLR is limited to the performance of international SMEs in Malaysia within the period of three years from 2021 until 2023. Further research ought to encompass a more extensive temporal and geographical scope. Furthermore, it is recommended that forthcoming research endeavors incorporate a comparative analysis that spans multiple countries. This would yield significant insights into the ways in which the determinants of SME business performance differ depending on the context. For instance, an exploration of the variations in strategic orientation among small and medium-sized enterprises (SMEs) in emergent markets such as Malaysia, as compared to other nations, may yield valuable insights for mutual learning and improvement. Furthermore, it is critical to investigate emerging trends, particularly in light of swift technological progress and shifting market dynamics, in order to comprehend the ways in which trends such as remote work and the circular economy, in addition to artificial intelligence and blockchain, influence the international business performance of SMEs. The adoption and integration of these emerging trends into the strategies of SMEs as well as their implications for internationalization and competitiveness, could be the subject of future research.

6. CONCLUSION

6.1 Summary of Findings

This study examines the strategies for enhancing international SMEs' performance in Malaysia provides valuable insights into various factors influencing SMEs' success in the global market. The study identifies key strategies such as optimizing international strategic orientation, improving corporate governance, developing key employee capabilities, leveraging dynamic capabilities, emphasizing innovation, and fostering collaborations in production and distribution as critical for enhancing SME internationalization and performance.

By optimizing international strategic orientation, SMEs could encompass the management of the organization's objectives and assets with the requirements and prospects presented by global markets. SMEs can prepare successful strategies for entering and expanding into markets, which play a focal role in expanding their performance in the global arena. Additionally, good corporate governance practices are essential for SMEs operating internationally. This holds the establishment of transparent decision-making procedures, the assurance of accountability, and the continuation of ethical standards. By enhancing corporate governance, SMEs can bolster their credibility and reputation, both of which are vital for fostering trust with international partners and stakeholders.

It is utmost important for SMEs to invest in the enhancement of key employee capabilities and innovation. Through the education of key employee capabilities, SMEs can construct a competent and driven workforce capable of driving international expansion and achieving prosperity. SMEs also should give emphasis to innovation, as they can set themselves apart from their competitors, allure new customers, and stimulate growth in international markets. By capitalizing on the capabilities and innovation, SMEs can succeed in the extremely competitive global market and seize a plethora of unprecedented growth opportunities.

It is also important for SMEs to collaborate with other firms or partners can in expanding their production and distribution networks on a global scale. By encouraging these collaborations in production and distribution, SMEs are able to strengthen their international presence and effectiveness, ultimately resulting in enhanced performance.

6.2 Contributions of the Study

This research enhances knowledge regarding the determinants that impact the international business performance of Malaysian SMEs through an exhaustive examination of main themes and subthemes. Through the identification and examination of these factors, the study provides significant insights into the intricate dynamics that influence the operations of small and medium-sized enterprises (SMEs) on a global level. Furthermore, the research emphasizes the significance of business culture, strategic orientation, digital transformation, intellectual capital, sustainability practices, managerial capabilities, and risk management in facilitating the success of SMEs. Moreover, through the synthesis of prior research discoveries, this study not only elevates theoretical comprehension but also offers pragmatic ramifications for policymakers, researchers, and stakeholders who aim to bolster the expansion and competitiveness of SMEs. In its entirety, this study contributes to the body of knowledge in the subject and establishes a foundation for subsequent investigations and interventions that seek to promote the sustainable development of SMEs not only in Malaysia but also in other regions.

6.3 Implications for Practice

The practical implications of the study's findings for SMEs and practitioners engaged in international business operations are manifold. To begin with, recognizing the significance of strategic orientation emphasizes the necessity for small and medium-sized enterprises (SMEs) to synchronize their operating strategies with long-term viability through the promotion of knowledge acquisition, entrepreneurial spirit, and market adaptability. Furthermore, the importance placed on digital transformation and electronic commerce underscores the criticality of harnessing digital technologies to bolster operational efficiency, innovation, and competitiveness in the worldwide market. Furthermore, acknowledging the significance of intellectual capital emphasizes the necessity of allocating resources towards human, relational, and structural assets in order to foster innovation, adaptation, and long-term expansion.

Moreover, the significance of incorporating environmental, social, and economic factors into the operations of SME businesses is highlighted by the emphasis on sustainability and environmental practices. These strategies encompass the implementation of green entrepreneurial practices, corporate sustainability orientation, and outsourcing approaches that advocate for stakeholder engagement and environmental accountability. In today's highly informed customer environment, with a heightened awareness of sustainability, firms that fail to address social, environmental, and economic sustainability will be outcompeted in the market. Furthermore, in order to navigate market uncertainties and propel organizational performance, organizational leaders and managers must cultivate dynamic, ambidextrous, and crisis management abilities, as this highlights the significance of managerial capabilities.

In addition, it is crucial for SMEs to cultivate proactive resilience strategies and exploit competitive advantages in order to minimize risks and seize opportunities in ever-changing business environments, as this highlights the significance of risk and market uncertainty. Furthermore, in order to enhance performance and competitiveness, SMEs must cultivate organizational cultures that encourage learning, innovation, and entrepreneurship, as highlighted by the significance of business culture. In general, these ramifications offer practical advice for professionals aiming to improve the performance and competitiveness of SMEs in the global marketplace, both in Malaysia and other regions.

6.4 Concluding Remarks

Overall, this study provides valuable insights for researchers, SMEs, and policymakers, highlighting the importance of adopting strategies that enhance international SMEs' performance and suggesting future research directions in this area. By understanding and implementing these strategies, SMEs in Malaysia can improve their competitiveness in global markets. The thematic analysis of factors influencing SME international business performance in Malaysia reveals a multifaceted landscape shaped by strategic orientation, digital transformation, intellectual capital, sustainability practices, managerial capabilities, risk management, and business culture. Each of these factors plays a crucial role in determining SME success in the global marketplace. This study holds significant value as a guideline for policymakers to implement policies supporting SMEs in expanding into global markets. It addresses a notable gap in existing research in this area. Additionally, the study illuminates the limited research on identifying international business performance. Its findings will be invaluable for future research, offering a comprehensive understanding of the determinants of international business performance over the past three years.

REFERENCES

Ahmad, N., Ng, S. I., Basha, N. K., & Aziz, Y. A. (2021). How do the dynamic capabilities of Malaysian service small and medium-sized enterprises (SMEs) translate into international performance? Uncovering the mechanism and conditional factors. *International Journal of Business Science and Applied Management*, 16(1), 1–27.

Ahmad, N., Ng, S. I., Basha, N. K., & Aziz, Y. A. (2022). Why knowledge-based human resource management matters for business service SMEs? *International Journal of Management Practice*, 15(5), 549–585. 10.1504/IJMP.2022.125470

Ahmad, N., Ng, S. I., Kamal Basha, N., & Abdul Aziz, Y. (2023). Exploring The Driving Factors of International Performance: Evidence from Business Service SMEs in Malaysia. *Journal of International Students*, 19(2), 119–159. 10.32890/jis2023.19.2.5

Ahmad, N. H., Ismail, H., & Wok, S. (2019). High-performance work practices, human capital and performance of SMEs in Malaysia. *Journal of Small Business and Enterprise Development*, 26(2), 298–315.

Akpan, I. J., Effiom, L., & Akpanobong, A. C. (2023). Towards developing a knowledge base for small business survival techniques during COVID-19 and sustainable growth strategies for the post-pandemic era. *Journal of Small Business and Entrepreneurship*, 1–23. 10.1080/08276331.2023.2232649

Aljuboori, Z. M., Singh, H., Haddad, H., Al-Ramahi, N. M., & Ali, M. A. (2021). Intellectual capital and firm performance correlation: The mediation role of innovation capability in Malaysian manufacturing SMEs perspective. *Sustainability (Basel)*, 14(1), 154. 10.3390/su14010154

AlQershi, N. A., Saufi, R. B. A., Mokhtar, S. S. M., Muhammad, N. M. N., & Yusoff, M. N. H. B. (2022). Is strategic orientation always beneficial? A meta-analysis of the relationship between innovation and business sustainability: A dynamic capabilities perspective from Malaysian insurance companies. *Sustainable Futures : An Applied Journal of Technology, Environment and Society*, 4, 100075. 10.1016/j.sftr.2022.100075

Andres, B., Poler, R., & Guzman, E. (2022). The influence of collaboration on enterprises internationalization process. *Sustainability (Basel)*, 14(5), 2843. 10.3390/su14052843

Annamalah, S., Paraman, P., Ahmed, S., Pertheban, T. R., Marimuthu, A., Venkatachalam, K. R., & Ramayah, T. (2023). Exploitation, exploration and ambidextrous strategies of SMES in accelerating organisational effectiveness. *Journal of Global Operations and Strategic Sourcing*.

Anwar, M., Clauss, T., & Issah, W. B. (2022). Entrepreneurial orientation and new venture performance in emerging markets: The mediating role of opportunity recognition. *Review of Managerial Science*, 16(3), 769–796. 10.1007/s11846-021-00457-w

Business, N. S. T. (2023, February 10). *Malaysian MSMEs post higher revenue in 2022*. New Straits Times. https://www.nst.com.my/business/2023/02/878451/malaysian-msmes-post-higher-revenue-2022

Ensari, M. Ş., & Karabay, M. E. (2014). What helps to make SMEs successful in global markets? *Procedia: Social and Behavioral Sciences*, 150, 192–201. 10.1016/j.sbspro.2014.09.030

Falahat, M., Lee, Y. Y., Soto-Acosta, P., & Ramayah, T. (2021). Entrepreneurial, market, learning and networking orientations as determinants of business capability and international performance: The contingent role of government support. *The International Entrepreneurship and Management Journal*, 17(4), 1–22. 10.1007/s11365-020-00738-y

Falahat, M., Soto-Acosta, P., & Ramayah, T. (2022). Analysing the importance of international knowledge, orientation, networking and commitment as entrepreneurial culture and market orientation in gaining competitive advantage and international performance. *International Marketing Review*, 39(3), 463–481. 10.1108/IMR-02-2021-0053

Frank, H., Kessler, A., Mitterer, G., & Weismeier-Sammer, D. (2012). Learning orientation of SMEs and its impact on firm performance. *Journal of Marketing Development and Competitiveness*, 6(3), 29–41.

Gamage, S. K. N., Ekanayake, E. M. S., Abeyrathne, G. A. K. N. J., Prasanna, R. P. I. R., Jayasundara, J. M. S. B., & Rajapakshe, P. S. K. (2020). A review of global challenges and survival strategies of small and medium enterprises (SMEs). *Economies*, 8(4), 79. 10.3390/economies8040079

George, B. A. (2011). Entrepreneurial orientation: A theoretical and empirical examination of the consequences of differing construct representations. *Journal of Management Studies*, 48(6), 1291–1313. 10.1111/j.1467-6486.2010.01004.x

Gherghina, . C., Botezatu, M. A., Hosszu, A., & Simionescu, L. N. (2020). Small and medium-sized enterprises (SMEs): The engine of economic growth through investments and innovation. *Sustainability (Basel)*, 12(1), 347. 10.3390/su12010347

Gjellerup, P. (2000). SME support services in the face of globalisation. Concerted action seminar, Opening address. In *Conference Proceedings, Danish Agency for Trade and Industry, Copenhagen* (pp. 16-28). Academic Press.

Hu, M. K., & Kee, D. M. H. (2022). Fostering sustainability: reinventing SME strategy in the new normal. *Foresight, 24*(3/4), 301-318.

Ismail, A., Majid, A. H. A., Rahman, M. A., Jamaluddin, N. A., Susantiy, A. I., & Setiawati, C. I. (2021). Aligning Malaysian SMEs with the megatrends: The roles of HPWPs and employee creativity in enhancing Malaysian SME performance. *Global Business Review*, 22(2), 364–380. 10.1177/0972150918811236

Ismail, M., Mohamad, N., & Ahamat, A. (2023). Learning Orientation as Mediator between International Entrepreneurial Orientation and International Firm Performance in Global Halal Industry. Academic Press.

Ismail, M., Mohamad, N., & Ahamat, A. (2023). Managerial Capabilities, Learning Orientation And Performance Of International Halal Industry Using Upper Echelon Theory. *International Journal of Business and Society*, 24(1), 119–140. 10.33736/ijbs.5608.2023

Khandwalla, P. N. (1977). Some top management styles, their context and performance. *Organization and Administrative Sciences, 7*(4), 21-51.

Lee, C. Y., & Park, S. (2020). The impact of digital technology on the internationalization of SMEs: Evidence from developing countries. *Journal of International Business Studies*, 51(6), 1005–1024.

Mah, P. Y., Chuah, F., & Sahar, E. (2023). Corporate Sustainability Orientation, Sustainable Development Practices, and Firm Performance of MSMEs in Malaysia. *Asian Journal of Business Research*, 13(2), 107–127. 10.14707/ajbr.230152

Michna, A. (2009). The relationship between organizational learning and SME performance in Poland. *Journal of European Industrial Training*, 33(4), 356–370. 10.1108/03090590910959308

Miller, D. (1983). The correlates of entrepreneurship in three types of firms. *Management Science*, 29(7), 770–791. 10.1287/mnsc.29.7.770

Mintzberg, H. (1973). Strategy-making in three modes. *California Management Review*, 16(2), 44–53. 10.2307/41164491

Mohamad, A., Mohd Rizal, A., Kamarudin, S., & Sahimi, M. (2022). Exploring the Co-Creation of Small and Medium Enterprises, and Service Providers Enabled by Digital Interactive Platforms for Internationalization: A Case Study in Malaysia. *Sustainability (Basel)*, 14(23), 16119. 10.3390/su142316119

Morgan, N. A., Vorhies, D. W., & Mason, C. H. (2009). Market orientation, marketing capabilities, and firm performance. *Strategic Management Journal*, 30(8), 909–920. 10.1002/smj.764

Mubarik, M. S. (2015) Human Capital and Performance of Small & Medium Manufacturing Enterprises: A Study of Pakistan, University of Malaya, Malaysia, PhD thesis.

Nguyen, P. V., Huynh, H. T. N., Lam, L. N. H., Le, T. B., & Nguyen, N. H. X. (2021). The impact of entrepreneurial leadership on SMEs' performance: The mediating effects of organizational factors. *Heliyon*, 7(6), e07326. 10.1016/j.heliyon.2021.e0732634195431

Osano, H. M. (2019). Global expansion of SMEs: Role of global market strategy for Kenyan SMEs. *Journal of Innovation and Entrepreneurship*, 8(1), 13. 10.1186/s13731-019-0109-8

Peng, M. W. (2018). *Global 4: global business*. Cengage Learning.

Pertheban, T. R., Thurasamy, R., Marimuthu, A., Venkatachalam, K. R., Annamalah, S., Paraman, P., & Hoo, W. C. (2023). The Impact of Proactive Resilience Strategies on Organizational Performance: Role of Ambidextrous and Dynamic Capabilities of SMEs in Manufacturing Sector. *Sustainability (Basel)*, 15(16), 12665. 10.3390/su151612665

Qalati, S. A., Ostic, D., Sulaiman, M. A. B. A., Gopang, A. A., & Khan, A. (2022). Social media and SMEs' performance in developing countries: Effects of technological-organizational-environmental factors on the adoption of social media. *SAGE Open*, 12(2). 10.1177/21582440221094594

Rahman, M., Akter, M., Odunukan, K., & Haque, S. E. (2020). Examining economic and technology-related barriers of small-and medium-sized enterprises internationalisation: An emerging economy context. *Business Strategy & Development*, 3(1), 16–27. 10.1002/bsd2.71

Reza, S., Mubarik, M. S., Naghavi, N., & Nawaz, R. R. (2021). Internationalisation challenges of SMEs: Role of intellectual capital. *International Journal of Learning and Intellectual Capital*, 18(3), 252–277. 10.1504/IJLIC.2021.116468

Ruzzier, M., Hisrich, R. D., & Antoncic, B. (2006). SME internationalization research: Past, present, and future. *Journal of Small Business and Enterprise Development*, 13(4), 476–497. 10.1108/14626000610705705

Schotten, M., Meester, W. J., Steiginga, S., & Ross, C. A. (2017). A brief history of Scopus: The world's largest abstract and citation database of scientific literature. In *Research analytics* (pp. 31–58). Auerbach Publications. 10.1201/9781315155890-3

Sharfaei, S., Ong, J. W., & Ojo, A. O. (2023). The effects of dynamic capabilities on international SMEs' performance. *International Journal of Globalisation and Small Business*, 13(3), 247–267. 10.1504/IJGSB.2023.130321

Singh, A.K. (2022). A study on the growth and role of SMES in Indian economy. International journal of financial management and economics. 10.33545/26179210.2022.v5.i2.158

Steinhäuser, V. P. S., Paula, F. D. O., & de Macedo-Soares, T. D. L. V. A. (2021). Internationalization of SMEs: A systematic review of 20 years of research. *Journal of International Entrepreneurship*, 19(2), 164–195. 10.1007/s10843-020-00271-7

Tranfield, D., Denyer, D., & Smart, P. (2003). Towards a methodology for developing evidence-informed management knowledge by means of systematic review. *British Journal of Management*, 14(3), 207–222. 10.1111/1467-8551.00375

Tze San, O., Latif, B., & Di Vaio, A. (2022). GEO and sustainable performance: The moderating role of GTD and environmental consciousness. *Journal of Intellectual Capital*, 23(7), 38–67. 10.1108/JIC-10-2021-0290

Uzoamaka, N. O. P., Ifeoma, A. R., & Nosike, C. J. (2020). Strategic orientation dimensions: A critical review. *Int J Res Innov Soc Sci*, 4(9), 609–612.

Wang, Y., Xue, X., & Guo, H. (2022). The sustainability of market orientation from a dynamic perspective: The mediation of dynamic capability and the moderation of error management climate. *Sustainability (Basel)*, 14(7), 3763. 10.3390/su14073763

Wang, Y., Xue, X., & Guo, H. (2022). The sustainability of market orientation from a dynamic perspective: The mediation of dynamic capability and the moderation of error management climate. *Sustainability (Basel)*, 14(7), 3763. 10.3390/su14073763

Waqas, A., Halim, H. A., & Ahmad, N. H. (2022). Design leadership and SMEs Sustainability; Role of Frugal Innovation and Technology Turbulence. *International Journal of Systematic Innovation*, 7(4), 1–17.

World Bank. (2020). World Bank SME Finance. Author.

Yusuf, M., Surya, B., Menne, F., Ruslan, M., Suriani, S., & Iskandar, I. (2022). Business agility and competitive advantage of SMEs in Makassar City, Indonesia. *Sustainability (Basel)*, 15(1), 627. 10.3390/su15010627

Zulkiffli, N. A., & Padlee, F. (2021). Sustainable outsourcing decisions, competitive capabilities and business performance of Malaysian manufacturing SMEs: A confirmatory factor analysis approach. *Journal of Sustainability Science and Management*, 16(1), 158–173. 10.46754/jssm.2021.01.014

Chapter 4
Digital Financial Capability and Entrepreneurial Performance in MSMEs

Sari Nuzullina Ramadhani
Universitas Medan Area, Indonesia

Rana Fathinah Ananda
Universitas Medan Area, Indonesia

Dyah Setyaningrum
Universitas indonesia, Indonesia

Nur Azizah Siregar
Universitas Medan Area, Indonesia

ABSTRACT

This chapter aims to describe and discuss digital financial capabilities and entrepreneurial performance in currently developing MSMEs. This study, using content analysis tools, refers to a number of sources, including reports, government documents, research publications, and a research database called Scopus. The study on digital financial capabilities and entrepreneurial performance in MSMEs is also covered in this chapter, with active nations and affiliates publishing research publications. Improving digital financial skills and entrepreneurial performance faces a number of obstacles in different nations. It is crucial that practitioners, researchers, and other stakeholders examine specific research on the relationship between digital financial capabilities and entrepreneurial performance in order to

DOI: 10.4018/979-8-3693-3518-5.ch004

Copyright © 2024, IGI Global. Copying or distributing in print or electronic forms without written permission of IGI Global is prohibited.

find effective solutions for the nation.

1. INTRODUCTION

SMEs in Indonesia take a very important role as support for the economy. SMEs are the main driver of the economy with the main function of SMEs being able to provide employment opportunities for millions of people who are absorbed in the formal and informal sectors. More than 95% of businesses in all economic sectors are MSMEs, and they employ more than 95% of the workforce (Bellefleur, 2012). SMEs have contributed to the formation of Gross Domestic Product (GDP) and play an important role in increasing national productivity, generating high-quality jobs, and encouraging inclusive growth (Shinozaki, 2022,).

Asia's strong expansion in recent decades, fueled primarily by the private sector and particularly by micro, small, and medium-sized firms (MSMEs), has undoubtedly benefited the global economy. MSMEs, for instance, made up 97.6% of all businesses in Southeast Asia between 2010 and 2020, employed 67.0% of the labor force, and generated an average of 40.5% of GDP per nation (Southeast Asia comprises Brunei Darussalam, Cambodia, Indonesia, Lao People's Democratic Republic, Malaysia, Myanmar, the Philippines, Singapore, Thailand, and Viet Nam). The MSME influence in Indonesia is significantly higher than the average for Southeast Asia. For almost ten years, the number of MSMEs has steadily expanded, growing by about 2% annually.

The total of 99.9% of all businesses, or 65 million MSMEs, existed as of the end of 2019. 120 million people, or 97% of Indonesia's workforce, were employed by MSMEs. Additionally, they made up Rp9,581 trillion, or 60.5%, of the GDP, which is 20% more than the average for Southeast Asia. As a result, MSME development is essential for Indonesia to achieve inclusive and resilient growth (Asian Development Bank, 2021).

In 2019, there were 64.2 million MSMEs spread throughout Indonesia. The numbers continue to increase; in 2020, the number of MSMEs reached 65.3 million (UMKM, 2020). In 2022 the number of SMEs will be 64 million spread throughout Indonesia (UMKM, 2022). MSMEs contribute to national GDP (Gross Domestic Product) by 61% and 16.65% to national export earnings; MSMEs are able to absorb up to 97% of the total workforce in Indonesia.

2. LITERATURE REVIEW

2.1 The Development of MSMEs in Indonesia

MSMEs in Indonesia have an important contribution to support the economy. These days, the main driver of the economy in Indonesia is the MSME sector. In addition to playing a role in national economic growth and employment, MSMEs also play a role in the distribution of development results and are the driving force for the growth of national economic activity. In short, it can be concluded that MSMEs are the main pillars of the Indonesian economy. The main characteristic of MSMEs is their ability to develop flexible business processes with relatively low costs. The presence of MSMEs is not only in the context of increasing income but also in the context of income distribution. This is understandable because the MSME sector involves many people with various businesses.

The scope of MSMEs product development includes volatile food, local economic development and Entrepreneurs. In terms of increasing access, development focuses on increasing access to finance, markets, knowledge, networks, innovation and digitalisation. Infrastructure and institutional support also impact the formation of an optimal MSME ecosystem through regulatory and policy support, financial inclusion, consumer protection, education/literacy, business models, monitoring and evaluation, as well as strengthening the institutional arrangements and information systems. In addition, stronger corporatisation, more accurate granular information and data, optimal and intensive coordination between government ministries/agencies, greater use of innovation and technology and the creation of a supporting ecosystem are also key determinants of successful MSME development in Indonesia.

2.2 Digitalization Transformation for MSMEs

Digital transformation is the main driver of growth and competitiveness of MSMEs in Indonesia. By utilizing digital technology, MSMEs can increase efficiency, reach new markets and increase customer satisfaction. Government support, increased digital literacy, and strong infrastructure are critical to facilitating this transformation and ensuring sustainable development in the MSME sector.

Digitalization increases the range of entrepreneurial prospects and encourages experimentation, which drives higher levels of discovery, this has a major impact on entrepreneurial performance. It has been found that the use of digital technology by entrepreneurs in Southeast Asian countries has a significant beneficial impact on the company's likelihood of success, product innovation, and anticipated future job creation. Additionally, digitalization increases profitability and drives sustainability for business owners (Asian Development Bank, 2022).

The United Nations has proposed the 2030 Agenda for Sustainable Development, which aims to promote inclusive and sustainable economic growth. This will be achieved by offering financial services to micro, small and medium enterprises (MSMEs) to help them formalize and grow. This means that people and small businesses will get maximum benefits from digital finance (Johri et al., 2024). MSMEs can overcome several obstacles and increase their financial stability and growth possibilities by providing them access to digital financial services and technologies. MSMEs may have access to insurance products through digital platforms that protect against unforeseen circumstances including illness, theft and natural disasters. This maintains the continuity of MSME businesses. Apart from that, safe and private MSME financial data is very important when they use digital financial services.

Apart from digital payments, social media and e-commerce also have a major impact on microeconomic entrepreneurial efforts that change the situation (Chen, 2016). Hard evidence on how digitalization has given rise to and supported micro-enterprises or individuals is scarce, although there is research on the digital transformation of companies from a management perspective. Undoubtedly, digital payments serve as a foundation for business model development, which in turn gives rise to a number of other Digital Finance Capabilities, including digital credit and digital investments (Bansal, Bruno, Denecker, Goparaju, & Niederkorn, 2018). According to research, digital payments have a significant and beneficial impact on all phases of entrepreneurship, including financial performance, innovation, and business start-up (Sekabira & Qaim, 2017; Yin, Gong, & Guo, 2019).

2.3 The Importance of Digital Financial Capability for MSMEs

Digital financial capabilities are essential for MSMEs to thrive in the modern economy. This improves financial management, reduces costs, increases operational efficiency and opens up new market opportunities. By adopting digital financial tools, MSMEs can improve their resilience, competitiveness and overall business performance, thereby contributing significantly to their long-term success and sustainability. At the same time, as financial services become increasingly digitally sophisticated, consumers using financial services must be more tech-savvy than ever before to avoid issues related to fraud prevention and accessibility of financial services (Morgan et al., 2019).

Therefore, it's important to understand the new requirements for having financial competence in the digital age and to give careful consideration to the growing significance of digital financial capability. Though they may not be exactly explicit, scholarly insights into DFC have already been made, and the issues have been made apparent. To help consumers and small businesses take full advantage of the increasingly digital financial landscape, for instance, the OECD highlights the crucial role that financial literacy plays (OECD, 2017b). According to Lyons et al. (2020), there is a need to redefine traditional financial literacy to incorporate digital literacy because of the substantial effects that both digital literacy and financial literacy have on financial inclusion.

The first relatively comprehensive dimensions of digital financial literacy, such as awareness of risks associated with digital finance, knowledge of risk control strategies, and knowledge of consumer rights and redress procedures, were proposed by Morgan et al. (2019), to the best of our knowledge. The definition's structure makes it clear that Morgan et al. (2019) only covers the essential knowledge for utilizing DFS; pertinent behaviors are not covered. There isn't much material available right now on the definition of DFC. In conclusion, effects of some financial capability components on entrepreneurial performance have been discovered prior to the definition of DFC. Detailed analyses are still required to determine whether and how those elements affect entrepreneurial performance. Furthermore, although some observations have been made on the changes that digitization has brought about, there hasn't been much thorough research done up to this point on the important relationships surrounding entrepreneurial activity. Furthermore, research on the origins and significance of DFC in the commercial and microeconomic spheres is still in its infancy.

2.4 Entrepreneurial Performance

Entrepreneurship is a methodical process that involves making decisions about investments, financing, and risk management, the success of an entrepreneur's ventures depends on their knowledge of and aptitude for managing their financial resources, or financial capability (Su & Kong, 2019). Previous research has mostly concentrated on the beneficial impact of financial literacy on entrepreneurial activities when it comes to the relationship between financial capacity and entrepreneurial performance. According to these research, entrepreneurs who possess the necessary financial knowledge and abilities can access formal credit and other financial resources, which can help them mitigate liquidity issues and boost sales and profitability. As an idea Financial competence, which goes beyond financial literacy to cover financial behavior and financial environment, can help entrepreneurs make better decisions when making financial decisions in addition to ensuring that they have more favorable access to financial resources.

Thus, rather than financial literacy, financial aptitude may theoretically contribute more to this rise in entrepreneurial performance. Thus, investigating the relationship between financial capacity and entrepreneurial performance is crucial (Yi, Meng, at all, 2023). The entrepreneurial decisions made by households are significantly and favorably impacted by financial knowledge and abilities (Yin et al., 2015; Cumurovic & Hyll, 2019). The claim is that families would be better able to take advantage of borrowing possibilities, their risk tolerance would shift, and they would be more able to request and obtain formal credit, all of which would support their decision to become entrepreneurs, if they had the necessary financial knowledge and expertise. There is, however, little detailed discussion of how financial expertise and knowledge affect business innovation, which we believe undervalues this aspect of company success. Although there aren't many studies examining the connection between financial views and entrepreneurship, we assume that there may be one through financial actions, as Atkinson and Messy's (2012) research indicates a favorable correlation between the two.

Financial literate people are more adept at obtaining and processing basic financial information, have better opportunities to finance their ventures, and are more willing to take risks, according to research by Cumurovi and Hyll (2019) and Li and Qian (2020) on the impact of financial literacy on entrepreneurial decisions and outcomes. Furthermore, a number of academics have made the case that financial literacy is an intangible human resource that improves entrepreneurial success by assisting in the management of corporate finances and the acquisition of tangible financial resources (Yin et al., 2015). Therefore, financial capability—a concept that stems from financial literacy—could enhance entrepreneurs' choice of borrowing channels, raise effective credit demand, and reduce liquidity constraints. It could also foster entrepreneurial decision-making and management, which is crucial for the success of business operations. Thus, potentially, financial acumen rather than financial literacy may have a bigger impact on entrepreneurial achievement.

3. METHODS

This study was conducted using descriptive qualitative method and content analysis based on literature review from journals or academic research articles, websites, electronic databases (secondary data) and other relevant sources. From the sources of previous research sources, this argumentation and discussion is created.

4. DISCUSSION

4.1 Factors Influence the Digital Financial Capabilities and Entrepreneurial Performance of MSMEs

The factors that influence the digital financial capabilities and entrepreneurial performance of Micro, Small, and Medium Enterprises (MSMEs) include:

a) Financial Literacy:

Understanding financial concepts related to business, debt, savings, insurance, and investment in the digital era is crucial for MSMEs to achieve good performance.

b) Digital Financial Services Adoption:

The adoption of digital financial services, such as digital payment systems and online banking, can streamline financial transactions and improve efficiency.

c) Government Support:

Government support through digital technology-based policies and resources is essential for MSMEs to adopt digital financial services and improve their financial performance.

d) Financial Inclusion:

Financial inclusion, which involves access to financial services and products, is a significant determinant of MSME financial performance.

e) Digital Literacy:

While digital literacy is not a determining factor in improving MSME financial performance, it is still important for MSMEs to develop digital capabilities to remain competitive.

f) Resource Development:

MSMEs should focus on developing their resources, particularly in information technology and human resources, to enhance their competitiveness.

g) External Factors:

External factors such as market trends, consumer behavior, and technological advancements can also influence MSME performance and the adoption of digital financial services

4.2 Strategy to improve Digital Financial Capabilities and Entrepreneurial Performance for MSMEs

To improve digital financial capabilities and entrepreneurial performance for Micro, Small, and Medium Enterprises (MSMEs), several strategies can be employed:

a) Financial Literacy Training:
   - Provide comprehensive financial literacy training to MSME owners and managers, focusing on digital financial concepts such as debt, savings, insurance, and investment in the digital era.
   - This training should emphasize the importance of financial literacy in improving business performance and profitability.

b) Digital Financial Services Adoption:
   - Encourage MSMEs to adopt digital financial services, such as digital payment systems, online banking, and mobile wallets, to streamline financial transactions and improve efficiency.

-This can be achieved through government support, financial inclusion initiatives, and digital literacy programs.

c) Government Support and Policies:
-The government should actively guide and assist MSMEs in adopting digital financial services by formulating digital technology-based policies and providing necessary resources.
-This support should be aligned with the strategic direction of the Financial Services Authority (OJK) regarding financial inclusion for the MSME sector.

d) Digital Business Transformation:
-MSMEs should continually enhance their digital literacy, along with their conventional and technological literacies, to remain competitive in the Industry 4.0 era.
-This involves developing digital capabilities, such as acquiring digital technology, identifying new digital opportunities, and mastering the latest digital technology.

e) Digitalization and Innovation:
-Encourage MSMEs to innovate and utilize digitalization to improve their performance. This can include utilizing web media, social media, and digital marketplaces to promote products and reach a wider customer base.
-Innovation and technology can help MSMEs adapt to changes in consumer behavior and market trends, ultimately improving their performance.

f) Resource Development:
-MSMEs should focus on developing their resources, particularly in information technology and human resources, to enhance their competitiveness.
-This includes building digital capabilities and ensuring that MSMEs have access to the necessary digital infrastructure and skilled personnel.

CONCLUSION

MSMEs need to grasp entrepreneurial performance and possess digital finance skills since digitalization enables MSME participants to leverage digital technology for product and service marketing, boosting operational effectiveness, and enhancing customer communication. MSMEs may more efficiently monitor business performance and manage finances thanks to digital financial capabilities. Furthermore, financial literacy enhances the ability of MSME players to manage financial risks, make better financial decisions, and increase their capacity for investment. In the meanwhile, MSME actors can enhance their capacity for innovation and enhance their capacity for digital technology adaptation through entrepreneurial performance. The connection between digital and financial literacy enables MSME players to enhance their consumer communication and digital financial skills. Digital and financial literacy also help MSME actors become more innovative and better able to adjust to changing technological environments.

Furthermore, those strategies above could give impacts of programs for MSMEs, such as training and empowerment of basic financial literacy, strengthen the cooperation with regional government and decentralization of MSMEs digital requirement, Knowledge-sharing for MSMEs. By implementing these strategies, MSMEs can improve their digital financial capabilities and entrepreneurial performance, ultimately enhancing their competitiveness and sustainability in the market.

REFERENCES

Asian Development Bank. (2022). *Asian Development Outlook 2022 Update: Entrepreneurship in the Digital Age*. Author.

Atkinson, A., McKay, S., Collard, S., & Kempson, E. (2007). Levels of financial capability in the UK. *Public Money & Management*, 27(1), 29–36. 10.1111/j.1467-9302.2007.00552.x

Atkinson, A., & Messy, F. (2012). Measuring financial literacy: Results of the OECD/international network on financial education (INFE) pilot study. In OECD working Papers on finance, Insurance and private pensions, No. 15. OECD Publishing. https://www.oecd-ilibrary.org/finance-and-investment/measuring-financial-literacy_5k9csfs90fr4-en

Bansal, S., Bruno, P., Denecker, O., Goparaju, M., & Niederkorn, M. (2018). Global payments 2018: A dynamic industry continues to break new ground. McKinsey Global Banking Report. https://www.mckinsey.com/~/media/McKinsey/Industries/Financial%20Services/Our%20Insights/Global%20payments%20Expansive%20growth%20targeted%20opportunities/Global-payments-map-2018.ashx

Bellefleur, D., Murad, Z., & Tangkau, P. (2012). *and Micro, Small, and Medium Sized Enterprise Development*. United States Agency International Development From The American People.

Chen, L. (2016). From Fintech to Finlife: The case of Fintech Development in China. *China Economic Journal*, 9(3), 225–239. 10.1080/17538963.2016.1215057

Cumurovic, A., & Hyll, W. (2019). Financial literacy and self-employment. *The Journal of Consumer Affairs*, 53(2), 455–487. 10.1111/joca.12198

Cunningham, J. A., Damij, N., Modic, D., & Olan, F. (2023). MSME technology adoption, entrepreneurial mindset and value creation: A configurational approach. *The Journal of Technology Transfer*, 48(5), 1574–1598. 10.1007/s10961-023-10022-0

Johnson, E., & Sherraden, M. S. (2007). From financial literacy to financial capability among youth. *Journal of Sociology and Social Welfare*, 34(3), 119. 10.15453/0191-5096.3276

Johri, A., Asif, M., Tarkar, P., Khan, W., Rahisha, , & Wasiq, M. (2024). Digital financial inclusion in micro enterprises: Understanding the determinants and impact on ease of doing business from World Bank survey. *Humanities & Social Sciences Communications*, 11(1), 361. 10.1057/s41599-024-02856-2

Kojo Oseifuah, E. (2010). Financial literacy and youth entrepreneurship in South Africa. *African Journal of Economic and Management Studies*, 1(2), 164–182. 10.1108/20400701011073473

Li, R., & Qian, Y. (2020). Entrepreneurial participation and performance: The role of financial literacy. *Management Decision*, 58(3), 583–599. 10.1108/MD-11-2018-1283

Luo, Y., Peng, Y., & Zeng, L. (2021). Digital financial capability and entrepreneurial performance. International Review of Economics & Finance, 76, 55–74. https://doi.org/. 2021.05.01010.1016/j.iref

Lyons, A. C., Kass-Hanna, J., Liu, F., Greenlee, A. J., & Zeng, L. (2020). Building financial resilience through financial and digital literacy in South Asia and Sub-Saharan Africa. In *ADBI working paper 1098*. Asian Development Bank Institute.

Morgan, P. J., Huang, B., & Trinh, L. Q. (2019). The need to promote digital financial literacy for the digital age. In Realizing education for all in the digital age. T20 Report (pp. 40–46). https://www.adb.org/sites/default/files/publication/503706/adbi-realizing-education-all-digital-age.pdf#page=56

OECD. (2017a). Financial education for micro, small and medium-sized enterprises in asia. https://www.oecd.org/finance/Financial-education-for-MSMEs-in-Asia.pdf

OECD. (2017b). G20/OECD INFE report on adult financial literacy in G20 countries. Paris: OECD. https://www.oecd.org/daf/fin/financial-education/G20-OECD-INFE

OECD. (2021). *The Digital Transformation of SMEs*. OECD.

Perotti, V., Zottel, S., Iarossi, G., & Bolaji-Adio, A. (2013). *Making sense of financial capability surveys around the world: A review of existing financial capability and literacy measurement instruments*. The World Bank.

Sekabira, H., & Qaim, M. (2017). Can mobile phones improve gender equality and nutrition? Panel data evidence from farm households in Uganda. *Food Policy*, 73, 95–103. 10.1016/j.foodpol.2017.10.004

Shinozaki, S. (2022). Informal Micro, Small, and Medium-Sized Enterprises and Digitalization: Evidence from Surveys in Indonesia. ADBI Working Paper 1310. Tokyo: Asian Development Bank Institute

Su, L. L., & Kong, R. (2019). Financial literacy, entrepreneurial training and farmers' entrepreneurial decision-making. *Journal of South China Agricultural University*, 18(03), 53–66.

Sun, J., & Zhang, J. (2024). Digital Financial Inclusion and Innovation of MSMEs. *Sustainability (Basel)*, 16(4), 1404. 10.3390/su16041404

Yi, H., Meng, X., Linghu, Y., & Zhang, Z. (2023). Can financial capability improve entrepreneurial performance? Evidence from rural China, Economic Research-. *Ekonomska Istrazivanja*, 36(1), 1631–1650. 10.1080/1331677X.2022.2091631

Yin, Z., Gong, X., & Guo, P. (2019). The impact of mobile payment on entrepreneurship——micro evidence from China household finance survey. *China Industrial Economics*, (3), 119–137.

Yin, Z., Song, Q., Wu, Y., & Peng, C. (2015). Financial knowledge, entrepreneurial decision and motivation. *Guanli Shijie*, (1), 87–98.

Chapter 5
Elevating SME Success:
A Comprehensive Exploration of Source Credibility in Shaping Consumer Attitudes Toward TikTok Advertisements

Bernadine Adel Sitorus
http://orcid.org/0009-0001-4979-8987
Universiti Teknologi MARA, Malaysia

Sylvia Nabila Azwa Ambad
http://orcid.org/0000-0003-1693-8514
Universiti Teknologi MARA, Malaysia

Cynthia Robert Dawayan
http://orcid.org/0000-0001-9127-4442
Universiti Teknologi MARA, Malaysia

ABSTRACT

This study examines the impact of TikTok influencers on the Malaysian cosmetic industry, focusing on source credibility dimensions (trustworthiness, expertise, attractiveness) and their effect on consumers' attitudes toward advertisement. The data was gathered via a Google Form survey, targeting 18-34 year old active TikTok users, analysed using SmartPLS 4.0. Findings show that trustworthiness and attractiveness of influencers positively influence attitudes toward advertisements for local cosmetics, but expertise does not. The implications of this study include insights for influencer marketing dynamics on TikTok, especially for SMEs in utilising influencers to advertise their cosmetic products.

DOI: 10.4018/979-8-3693-3518-5.ch005

1. INTRODUCTION

In the evolving realm of digital communication, social media had played an important role in the emergence of Social Media Influencers (SMIs). They are renowned to amass a substantial following and exert a notable influence over consumer' decision making processes (Hudders et al., 2021), which inherently position them at the core of influencer marketing (Vrontis et al., 2021). Notably, their recommendations have gone beyond traditional advertising methods, creating a higher level of trust that increases product credibility and motivates consumers to make purchases (Schouten et al., 2020; Ye et al., 2021). This change is due to their effective communication and the development of meaningful connections with audiences through genuine and relatable personalities. By sharing insights about their personal lives and recommending products that fit their lifestyle, they make influencer marketing more effective for increasing brand visibility and impact in the digital landscape (Audrezet et al., 2020).

Over the past decade, influencer marketing has undergone substantial growth, assuming a strategic significance in brand promotion that surpasses the impact of traditional marketing (Shoukat et al., 2023). Currently, the influencer marketing industry is valued at 21.1 billion USD in 2023, marking a 29% increase from 2022, with over 80% of marketers allocating dedicated budgets (Santora, 2023). In addition to that, while Instagram, Facebook and YouTube have long been pillars of influencer marketing, Kepios Digital Global Report recently revealed that TikTok has emerged as a dominant platform, with a substantial potential advertisement reach of 1.09 billion users, which is equivalent to 21.1% of the internet user base (Geyser, 2023). Additionally, this trend shows no difference than in Malaysia, especially when Malaysia was revealed to reach 95% of TikTok penetration, which is the third highest in the world, according to a report by (Statista, 2023c) on TikTok penetration on selected country in territory as of October 2023. On this basis, directing the marketing efforts towards Malaysian consumers through the influence of social media influencers on TikTok would yield great results.

Among various sectors, the cosmetic industry in Malaysia is primed to capitalize significantly on this evolving trend. The confidence of this stems from a survey that was revealed by (Statista, 2023b), where it was found that 53% of the respondents thought that influencers were the most effective at promoting beauty or personal care products. Furthermore, the cosmetic industry is a highly profitable industry in Malaysia, with 2.68 billion USD revenue in 2022 (Statista, 2023a), however, the market share is highly dominated by established international cosmetic companies (Masood et al., 2023). Hence, this calls a need for Malaysian cosmetic industry players, specifically SMEs to elevate their marketing strategies and actively promote their products because if the trend of favouring foreign cosmetic products among

Malaysians continue to persist, the local cosmetic industry will risk a continual erosion of market share, and this will ultimately pose a threat towards the local economic resilience.

Given the proven effectiveness of integrating social media influencers into marketing strategies (e.g., Fan et al., 2023; Tiwari et al., 2023; Li and Peng, 2021), we believe that exploring the impact of incorporating TikTok influencers in marketing efforts will be able to contribute valuable insights into the enhancement of local cosmetic products competitiveness against international cosmetic products. In the realm of social media influencers, their credibility characteristics play a key role in shaping consumers' attitude (Belanche et al., 2021; Nafees et al., 2021; Sokolova & Kefi, 2020). Following this, a burgeoning amount of research has been conducted in the pursuit of understanding how credibility traits of SMIs can affect consumers' attitude towards advertisements, with most of it utilizing the seminal three-dimensional source credibility model by Ohanian (1990). The model was originally developed for accessing the credibility of celebrities, encompassing dimensions such as trustworthiness, expertise, and attractiveness. It has undergone validation and is widely recognized as a reliable tool for evaluating consumers' perceptions of advertisements, brand attitudes, and purchase decisions (Halder et al., 2021).

Despite the increasing focus on Social Media Influencers (SMIs), the literature on influencer marketing remains limited, particularly in relation to TikTok influencers. Existing studies predominantly focuses on Instagram (e.g., Duh and Thabethe, 2021; De Veirman and Hudders, 2020; Herrando and Martín-De Hoyos, 2022; Nafees et al., 2021), and YouTube (Le & Hancer, 2021; Miranda et al., 2021; Muda, 2019; Muda & Hamzah, 2021; Xiao et al., 2018), with minimal attention given to TikTok. Furthermore, in the context of cosmetic studies among Malaysian consumers, research has mainly concentrated on specific products like halal, green or Korean cosmetics, while the study on Malaysian local cosmetic products remained scarce. Therefore, aiming to fill these gaps, this study seeks to investigate the impact of TikTok influencers' credibility traits (trustworthiness, expertise, and attractiveness) on consumers' attitude towards advertisement.

2. LITERATURE REVIEW

Underpinning Theory

Social Identity Theory (SIT), first proposed by Tajfel (1978), is a theory that posits that the group plays a crucial role in shaping individual identities, emphasizing the importance of one's sense of self being intertwined with their belonging to a social group (Hogg & Abrams, 1988). This social categorization is a fundamental aspect on an individual's self-concept, as highlighted by Haslam and Ellemers (2005). SIT suggests that people internalize group affiliations to develop a positive social identity, contributing to enhanced self-esteem (Trepte, 2013). The theory introduces the concept of self-categorization, wherein individuals evaluate and compare the worth of their in-groups (similar others) and out-groups (dissimilar others), a process that influences social identity and self-esteem (Trepte & Loy, 2017).

SMIs are individuals who have garnered a sizable and devoted following on social media platforms by sharing their opinions and personal experiences (Vrontis et al., 2021). They were often regarded as peers or role models by their followers, and they wield influence, with their followers valuing their recommendations and trusting their judgements. This concept is very close and aligned with SIT, which suggests that people tend to favour those within their own group or category. Building on this theory, this research proposes that when SMIs features and endorse a local cosmetic in their TikTok videos, their followers are more likely to have positive attitude towards the influencers' TikTok video.

Consumers' Attitude Towards Advertisement

In the realm of advertising, MacKenzie et al. (1986) defined attitude toward the advertisement as the inclination to react favourably or unfavourably to a specific advertising stimulus within a defined exposure situation, representing their evaluative stance. Additionally, it was described as the thoughts and feelings of consumers toward a particular advertisement (Kirmani & Campbell, 2009). This concept has garnered substantial research interest among marketers (Gaber et al., 2019) due to its predictive relevance to behaviours, making it a commonly used determinant of advertising effectiveness (Oumlil & Balloun, 2020).

In addition to that, Muda and Hamzah (2021) underscored the importance of understanding consumers' attitude as it influences behavioural intentions, such as purchase intention. Established theories like the Theory of Reasoned Action (TRA), Theory of Planned Behaviour (TPB), and Technology Acceptance Model (TAM) have consistently positioned attitude as definitive antecedent of behavioural intentions (Ing & Ming, 2018). In alignment with Ajzen's (1991) perspective, a more favourable attitude toward a particular behaviour is believed to result in a stronger intention to perform that behaviour.

In the Malaysian cosmetic industry, the prevailing preference among consumers for foreign cosmetic products is notable. Malaysians have grown accustomed to encountering advertisements from globally recognized companies and international brands, fostering the perception that foreign cosmetics are of higher quality thank local ones (Lew & Sulaiman, 2014; Rani & Krishnan, 2018). This discrepancy in perception poses a challenge within the local cosmetic market, emphasizing the

Trustworthiness and Attitude Towards Advertisement

According to Hovland et al. (1953), trustworthiness can be referred as the degree to which an audience perceives the assertions made by a communicator to be ones that the speaker considers valid. It is a crucial factor in persuasion, as research consistently found that trustworthiness exerts a positive impact on message persuasiveness, surpassing the influence of less trustworthy sources (Ohanian, 1990). Individuals generally resist accepting information from an untrustworthy source, as opposed to a trustworthy one, hence, there is a tendency to quickly adopt information without meticulous scrutiny, relying on the perceived trustworthiness of the source (Hovland & Weiss, 1951; Priester & Petty, 2003; Sparkman, Jr. & Locander, 1980).

This study refers to advertisement as TikTok videos posted by influencers. In the context of influencer marketing, studies have been conducted to examine the effects of trustworthiness towards consumers' attitude towards advertisement. Accordingly, trustworthiness, particularly in influencer-generated branded posts, significantly shapes social media users' attitude toward branded content, with a stronger impact on purchase intentions compared to content and source-related factors (Lou & Yuan, 2019). This notion has proven to be true according to several recent studies (e.g., Jin and Muqaddam, 2019; Schouten et al., 2020; Gomes et al., 2022). On this basis, we propose that when SMIs are perceived as trustworthy, their followers are more likely to act favourably towards the promotional content on TikTok. Hence, based on the literature, we propose the following hypothesis:

H1: SMIs' trustworthiness positively influences consumers' attitude towards advertisement.

Expertise and Attitude Towards Advertisement

Expertise, in the context of source credibility, can be referred as the perceived level of competence or authority of a communicator (Ohanian, 1990). Expertise involves possessing advanced knowledge, extensive experience, and proficient problem-solving skills in a specific domain, as well as substantial understanding in particular area, exceeding that of ordinary people (Ismagilova et al., 2020; Muda & Hamzah, 2021; Verma & Dewani, 2021; Wiedmann & von Mettenheim, 2020). The pivotal role of expertise in shaping the level of conviction for consumers decisions underscores the paramount importance of credible sources, as messages backed by expertise not only instil confidence but also elevate the overall credibility of the source in the eyes of the audience (Masuda et al., 2022).

In commercial settings, a heightened perception of expertise in a source, as opposed to a less expert source, correlates with favourable attitudes toward both the endorser and the advertisement (Pornpitakpan, 2004). This pattern extends to the realm of influencer marketing, where the expertise of influencers holds the potential to elevate credibility, enrich message processing and cultivate a positive influence on consumer attitudes and behaviour. This, in turn, leads to a heightened persuasion and stronger inclination towards products endorsed by credible influencers (Hughes et al., 2019). Accordingly, SMIs that possesses significant expertise are inclined to share professional and intricate content, thereby offering consumers valuable professional services, and enhancing their interpersonal communication efficiency (Li & Peng, 2021). Due to this, consumers will have higher tendency to accept the contents of recommendations offered by influencers perceived as experts in the areas of interest (Chetioui et al., 2020). Previous research had also confirmed that people often rely on source expertise when forming attitude (e.g., Chetioui et al., 2020; Choi & Lee, 2019a; Miranda et al., 2021). For these reasons we believe that:

H2: SMIs' expertise positively influences consumers' attitude towards advertisement.

Attractiveness and Attitude Towards Advertisement

The persistent stereotype encapsulated by the saying "What is beautiful, is good "has garnered extensive scholarly attention, particularly in the domain of celebrity endorsements. The concept of attractiveness, often synonymous with an individual's physical appearance, assumes paramount significance in shaping perceptions of credibility (Amos et al., 2008; Ohanian, 1990). Within the context of celebrity endorsements, the persuasiveness of messages conveyed by celebrity endorsers, as perceived by consumers, is significantly influenced by the perceived attractiveness of the endorser. Accordingly, it was generally agreed that consumers are more likely to be persuaded by celebrity endorser who is physically attractive, as they may associate endorsers' attractiveness with positive attributes such as likability, popularity, and social status (Halder et al., 2021). Moreover, Schimmelpfennig and Hunt (2020) highlighted that that physically attractive endorsers are consistently liked more than neutral and less attractive endorsers and are evaluated more favourably.

This phenomenon extends its influence into the realm of marketing, where empirical evidence consistently indicates a positive association between the attractiveness of endorsers and the perceived credibility of advertising, especially then the promoted products are closely tied to considerations of physical appearance (Munnukka et al., 2016). Moreover, the importance of beauty and attractiveness in the selection of models, endorsers, and spokespeople is emphasized in industries such as cosmetics (Muda and Hamzah, 2021). In the context of SMIs, studies underscore the pivotal role of attractiveness in shaping attitudes towards advertising conducted by influencers (Balaban & Mustătea, 2019). Based on this discussion, we posit that when the SMI is physically attractive, their followers are more likely to respond favourably towards their advertising content on TikTok. Hence, we postulate the following hypothesis:

H3: SMIs' attractiveness positively influences consumers' attitude towards advertisement.

Research Framework

This study utilizes Ohanian's (1990) source credibility model to examine the effects of source credibility traits (i.e., trustworthiness, expertise, and attractiveness) towards consumers' attitude toward advertisements. Figure 1.0 illustrates the research framework of this study.

Figure 1. Research Framework

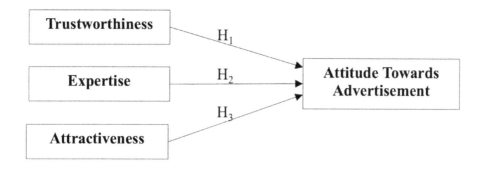

3. METHODOLOGY

Participants and Procedures

This research utilizes a quantitative research design to validate the proposed hypotheses. Data were gathered through self-administered online survey conducted on Google Form. The selection of this method was predicated on the prerequisite that respondents have internet access. To ensure the reliability and validity of the measurement items, we executed questionnaire pretesting which includes experts' review from Universiti Teknologi MARA, as well as a debriefing session with respondents before conducting the actual data collection.

Through purposive sampling method, the respondents were chosen based on whether they follow a TikTok influencer that features local cosmetic products on their TikTok videos, and whether they have not purchased local cosmetic products through the recommendations of a TikTok influencer before. The sample size of this study was determined through G*Power estimation. Based on F test for multiple linear regression via a fixed mode of R2 deviation from zero, with a medium effect size of .15 Cohen (1992), a power level of .95 and three predictor variables, the minimum calculated sample size was 119. The usable data collected is 164, exceeding the minimum required sample.

Accordingly, majority of the respondents are female, constituting 87.2% of the sample. Additionally, most of the respondents fell within the 18 to 24 age brackets, comprising 79.9% of the total. Students represented the largest segments of respondents, accounting for 72.6% (n=119), and a significant proportion of them reported having no access to monthly income (66.5%). Furthermore, a substantial number of respondents indicated that their highest educational level was at the STPM/Diploma or equivalent (48.8%).

Measurements

The measurement items used in this study were adapted from established research, then modified to align with the current study settings. The measurement items for source credibility dimensions, namely, trustworthiness, expertise, and attractiveness encompass five measurement items for each construct were derived from Muda and Hamzah (2021). Meanwhile, for the construct attitude towards advertisement is derived from Belanche et al. (2021), it encompasses a total of four items and was modified to fit into the study's current context. All items in this study were assessed on a seven-point Likert scale, ranging from one (strongly disagree) to seven (strongly agree).

4. DATA ANALYSIS

The data analyses were performed using the SmartPLS 4.0 software application (Ringle et al., 2022). It is chosen as the analytical tool for this study due to its compatibility with the structural equation modelling (PLS-SEM) framework, which is designed to offer causal explanations, making it particularly suitable for research focused on prediction (Hair et al., 2019). Essentially, the objective of this study involves investigating the relationships among trustworthiness, expertise, and attractiveness (as causes), and consumers' attitude towards advertisement (as the effect), hence why it is suitable to be employed in this study.

Common Method Variance

Assessing common method bias is imperative for a robust data analysis in research. In this study, we followed Kock et al.'s (2021) guidelines to address common method bias (CMB) through a combination of procedural and statistical controls. Procedurally, confidentiality of respondents was rigorously maintained, and participants were explicitly informed that there were not inherently correct or incorrect responses. Additionally, marker variables were strategically integrated into the questionnaire to further mitigate potential CMB.

To address common method variance (CMV), this study employed the statistical marker variable technique. This method involves using marker variables as covariates in statistical analysis to account for assumed sources of method variance. Marker variables, chosen based on low correlations with study variables, ideally include scales unrelated to the research context. According to Simmering et al. (2015), despite not directly measuring CMV, markers should exhibit minimal or insignificant variance compared to the study variables. By following established procedures, this study adopted marker variable developed by Miller and Chiodo (2008), which is known as "attitude towards blue colour", comprising on three unrelated items, mainly on preferences for the colour blue.

The Beta (β) values showed negligible variance (ranging from 0.000 to 0.002), and there were no alterations in R^2 upon introducing the marker variables. This finding further suggests the lack of significance of CMV, indicating that it was not a prominent concern in this study.

Measurement Model

This study utilized the Partial Least Squares Structural Equation Modelling (PLS-SEM) technique through SmartPLS 4.0 software, following the recommendation of Ringle et al. (2022). Furthermore, to ensure the robustness of the measurement model, we evaluated its validity and reliability based on established criteria outlined by Hair et al. (2019). The assessment involved item loadings, Average Variance Extracted, and Composite Reliability (CR). In line with the criteria, it is advisable for items loadings of reflective constructs to surpass 0.708, indicating that the constructs account for more than 70% of the variance in the indicator. Such loading levels suggest a satisfactory level of item reliability. Additionally, acceptable AVE values are above 0.5, and the CR should be a minimum of 0.7.

As depicted in Table 1, all loadings were deemed acceptable, with values exceeding 0.708 for each item, except for ATT3. Moreover, the AVE and CR values consistently exceeded the recommended thresholds of 0.5 and 0.7, respectively, affirming the reliability and internal consistency of all measurements within the model. Additionally, the Cronbach Alpha values in this study ranged from 0.901 to 0.943, surpassing the 0.7 threshold, indicative of high reliability. This underscores the effectiveness of the constructs in precisely assessing the intended theoretical constructs.

Table 1. Measurement Model Analysis

Construct/Items	Loadings	α	CR	AVE
Trustworthiness		0.934	0.950	0.791
TR1	0.905			
TR2	0.885			
TR3	0.864			
TR4	0.923			
TR5	0.868			
Expertise		0.943	0.956	0.814
EX1	0.892			
EX2	0.915			
EX3	0.921			
EX4	0.904			
EX5	0.877			
Attractiveness		0.901	0.930	0.770
ATT1	0.850			
ATT2	0.924			
ATT3	Deleted			
ATT4	0.850			
ATT5	0.884			
Attitude towards Advertisement		0.926	0.948	0.820
AAD1	0.895			
AAD2	0.931			
AAD3	0.926			
AAD4	0.868			

Subsequently, we conducted discriminant validity assessment through HTMT analysis. Following the threshold set by Franke and Sarstedt (2019) and Henseler et al. (2015), HTMT values should not surpass 0.85. Additionally, employing a more stringent criterion and a lenient mode criterion, the values should be equal or less than 0.90. As illustrated in Table 2, the highest recorded value is 0.752, indicating that respondents were able to differentiate between variables. To sum up, both validity assessments confirm the reliability and validity of the measurement items.

Table 2. HTMT

	TR	EX	ATT	AAD
TR				
EX	0.752			
ATT	0.522	0.469		
AAD	0.722	0.611	0.653	

Structural Model

Following the guidelines outlined by Hair et al. (2019), this study presents the path coefficients, standard errors, t-values, and p-values for the structural model in Table 3. These statistical measures were computed using a 5,000-sample-resample bootstrapping technique, as detailed by (Ramayah et al., 2018). In addition to that, Hahn and Ang (2017) emphasized that relying solely on p-values is insufficient for determining the significance of hypothesis. Instead, a comprehensive evaluation incorporating multiple criteria, such as p-values, confidence intervals and effect sizes, is recommended. Table 3 offers a concise overview of these criteria for assessing the proposed hypotheses.

The direct impact of the source credibility dimensions, encompassing trustworthiness, expertise, and attractiveness) resulted in R^2 of 0.565 (with Q^2=0.453). This suggests that all three predictors collectively accounted for 56.5% of the variance in consumers' attitude towards advertisements. Trustworthiness (H1: β=0.412, p=0.000) and attractiveness (H3: β=0.352, p=0.000) were found to have a positive relationship with consumers' attitude towards advertisements. Conversely, expertise (H2: β=0.129, p=0.067) displayed no significant relationship with consumers' attitude towards advertisement.

Table 3. Path-Coefficient Assessment

Relationship	Std Beta	Std Dev	t-value	p-value	BCILL	BCIUL	f^2	Result
TR -> AAD	0.412	0.087	4.735	0.000	0.262	0.559	0.182	Supported
EX -> AAD	0.129	0.086	1.500	0.067	-0.005	0.281	0.019	Not Supported
ATT -> AAD	0.352	0.068	5.125	0.000	0.235	0.459	0.212	Supported

5. DISCUSSION

Our research findings support H1, which proposed that SMIs' trustworthiness positively influencers consumers' attitudes towards advertisements. This finding aligns with existing literature, which underscores the critical role of trustworthiness in persuasion. According to Hovland et al. (1953), trustworthiness is the degree to which an audience believes that the communicator's assertions are valid. This attribute has consistently been shown to enhance message persuasiveness (Ohanian, 1990). Our result suggests that when followers perceive SMIs as trustworthy, they are more likely to adopt the information provided without doubt, resulting in favorable attitude towards the advertising content. This is consistent with previous studies indicating that trustworthiness of SMIs significantly shapes social media users' attitudes and impacts their purchase intention.

In contrast, our findings do not support H2, which posited that SMIs' expertise positively influences consumers' attitudes towards advertisements. While expertise is generally acknowledged as an important factor in shaping consumer attitude and decision-making (Ismagilova et al., 2020; Muda & Hamzah, 2021; Ohanian, 1990), our study did not find significant evidence to support this in the context of TikTok influencers. The insignificance of SMIs' expertise in this study may be related to the study's focus on cosmetic products. Most respondents in this study are females, who are typically knowledgeable and experienced in using cosmetic products. Therefore, SMIs' expertise might not be as appealing or influential to the consumers in this context.

Conversely, the empirical evidence from this study substantiates H3, indicating that SMIs' attractiveness positively influences consumers' attitudes toward SMIs' advertising content on TikTok. This finding aligns with the "What is beautiful is good" stereotype, which suggests that individuals associate physical attractiveness with positive attributes such as "likability, popularity, and social status (Amos et al., 2008; Halder et al., 2021; Ohanian, 1990). The results are consistent with prior research indicating that physically attractive endorsers are more likely to elicit positive responses from consumers (Schimmelpfennig & Hunt, 2020). In the realm of influencer marketing, the attractiveness of SMIs plays a crucial role in shaping consumer attitudes toward advertisements. This is particularly relevant on platforms like TikTok, where visual appeal is a significant component of content engagement. Our findings support previous studies that have highlighted the importance of attractiveness in the selection of models, endorsers, and spokespeople, especially in industries related to physical appearance, such as cosmetics (Balaban & Muståtea, 2019; Muda & Hamzah, 2021; Munnukka et al., 2016).

Theoretical and Managerial Implications

This study offers a significant theoretical contribution by integrating Social Identity Theory (SIT) and Ohanian's (1990) source credibility model to investigate the impact of social media influencers' (SMIs) source credibility traits (i.e., trustworthiness, expertise, and attractiveness) on consumer attitudes towards advertisements. Aligned with Vrontis et al.'s (2021) recommendation, the research extends the application of SIT to relatively unexplored domain of SMIs, enriching the theoretical foundation of SIT and showcasing its adaptability in contemporary communication channels. Furthermore, this research not only affirm the relevance of SIT in comprehending consumer responses to SMIs' advertisement content on TikTok, but also contribute to a deeper understanding of the specific components of source credibility under the light of SMIs, which is represented by a limited amount of study.

Furthermore, from the viewpoints of managerial implications, this study underscores the pivotal importance of prioritizing trustworthiness and physical attractiveness in the selection of influencers for local cosmetic products on TikTok. Firstly, to emphasize and effectively utilize the trustworthiness of SMIs, SMEs can start by scrutinizing track record of the influencer, ensuring a history of genuine and transparent engagements as well as evaluating the consistency of their messaging. In the efforts of promoting local cosmetic products, managers in SMEs should encourage influencers to authentically integrate local cosmetic products into their content, fostering a sense of reliability and transparency. Eventually, cultivating long-term relationship with trustworthy influencers can strengthen the association between the influencers' credibility and the endorsed cosmetic brand. By transparently communicating the brand's values and commitments through trustworthy SMIs, SMEs can instil confidence in consumers, ultimately contributing to positive attitudes and perceptions towards TikTok advertisements featuring local cosmetic products.

Additionally, in the cosmetic industry, physical attractiveness has long been considered to play a crucial role (Muda & Hamzah, 2021; Munnukka et al., 2016). The finding from this study implies that SMEs should prioritize influencers who exhibit physical attractiveness when promoting cosmetic products. This can involve selecting influencers with facial features, grooming styles, and overall presentation that align with prevalent beauty standards and resonate with the target audience's perceptions of attractiveness. The influencers' physical appearance should complement the cosmetic products being promoted, creating a seamless and visually appealing connection. Conclusively, SMEs should aim to leverage the influencers' physical attractiveness as a powerful tool to capture the attention of the audience, enhance the perceived desirability of the endorsed cosmetic products, and ultimately contribute to positive consumer attitudes toward TikTok influencer advertisements for local cosmetic products.

Limitations and Future Research Suggestions

While this research has made undeniable and significant contributions both theoretically and managerially, it is not without limitations. Firstly, the generalizability of the findings is constrained by the focus on Malaysian consumers and TikTok influencers. To enhance the robustness of future research, we recommend conducting comparative studies across diverse cultural contexts. Exploring the dynamics in different regions could unveil cross-cultural variations in social identity and shed light on the impact of influencer marketing on consumer attitudes.

Addressing another limitation, this study exhibits a sampling bias, with most respondents being female students. Future research could strive for a more balanced demographic spectrum, considering factors such as age, occupation, and socio-economic status. This inclusive approach would contribute to a more comprehensive understanding of how source credibility influences attitudes among different population segments.

Furthermore, the study faces a limitation due to its cross-sectional design, preventing the establishment of causality between variables. To address this, future studies could adopt a longitudinal research design. This approach allows researchers to capture the dynamic nature of consumer attitudes over time and explore the long-term effects of source credibility on attitudes towards advertisements.

Notably, this research solely focuses on the effects of source credibility, overlooking various other factors that could contribute to consumers' attitudes toward advertisements. We propose future research to delve deeper into the uniqueness of Social Media Influencers (SMIs) compared to celebrity endorsers. Factors such as their perception of ordinariness, authenticity, or similarity could be incorporated into future studies. Furthermore, considering SMIs' distinct engagement with followers, future research could explore factors like online engagement in the research framework.

ACKNOWLEDGMENT

We would like to acknowledge the financial support from Universiti Teknologi MARA through the *Geran Insentif Penyeliaan (GIP)* 2023, grant number 600-RMC/GIP 5/3 (025/2023), which has been instrumental in supporting this research.

REFERENCES

Ajzen, I. (1991). The theory of planned behavior. *Organizational Behavior and Human Decision Processes*, 50(2), 179–211. 10.1016/0749-5978(91)90020-T

Amos, C., Holmes, G., & Strutton, D. (2008). Exploring the relationship between celebrity endorser effects and advertising effectiveness: A quantitative synthesis of effect size. *International Journal of Advertising*, 27(2), 209–234. 10.1080/02650487.2008.11073052

Audrezet, A., de Kerviler, G., & Guidry Moulard, J. (2020). Authenticity under threat: When social media influencers need to go beyond self-presentation. *Journal of Business Research*, 117, 557–569. 10.1016/j.jbusres.2018.07.008

Balaban, D., & Mustățea, M. (2019). Users' perspective on the credibility of social media influencers in Romania and Germany. *Romanian Journal of Communication and Public Relations*, 21(1), 31–46. 10.21018/rjcpr.2019.1.269

Belanche, D., Casaló, L. V., Flavián, M., & Ibáñez-Sánchez, S. (2021). Building influencers' credibility on Instagram: Effects on followers' attitudes and behavioral responses toward the influencer. *Journal of Retailing and Consumer Services*, 61, 102585. Advance online publication. 10.1016/j.jretconser.2021.102585

Ben Oumlil, A., & Balloun, J. L. (2020). Millennials' attitude toward advertising: An international exploratory study. *Young Consumers*, 21(1), 17–34. 10.1108/YC-10-2018-0865

Chetioui, Y., Benlafqih, H., & Lebdaoui, H. (2020). How fashion influencers contribute to consumers' purchase intention. *Journal of Fashion Marketing and Management*, 24(3), 361–380. 10.1108/JFMM-08-2019-0157

Choi, W., & Lee, Y. (2019). Effects of fashion vlogger attributes on product attitude and content sharing. *Fashion and Textiles*, 6(1), 6. Advance online publication. 10.1186/s40691-018-0161-1

Cohen, J. (1992). Statistical power analysis. *Current Directions in Psychological Science*, 1(3), 98–101. 10.1111/1467-8721.ep10768783

De Veirman, M., & Hudders, L. (2020). Disclosing sponsored Instagram posts: The role of material connection with the brand and message-sidedness when disclosing covert advertising. *International Journal of Advertising*, 39(1), 94–130. 10.1080/02650487.2019.1575108

Duh, H. I., & Thabethe, T. (2021). Attributes of Instagram influencers impacting consumer brand engagement. *International Journal of Internet Marketing and Advertising*, 15(5), 1. 10.1504/IJIMA.2021.118261

Fan, F., Chan, K., Wang, Y., Li, Y., & Prieler, M. (2023). How influencers' social media posts have an influence on audience engagement among young consumers. *Young Consumers*, 24(4), 427–444. 10.1108/YC-08-2022-1588

Franke, G., & Sarstedt, M. (2019). Heuristics versus statistics in discriminant validity testing: A comparison of four procedures. *Internet Research*, 29(3), 430–447. 10.1108/IntR-12-2017-0515

Gaber, H. R., Wright, L. T., & Kooli, K. (2019). Consumer attitudes towards Instagram advertisements in Egypt: The role of the perceived advertising value and personalization. *Cogent Business and Management*, 6(1), 1618431. Advance online publication. 10.1080/23311975.2019.1618431

Geyser, W. (2023). *36 Vital TikTok Stats to Inform Your Marketing Strategy*. https://influencermarketinghub.com/tiktok-stats/#toc-2

Gomes, M. A., Marques, S., & Dias, Á. (2022). The impact of digital influencers' characteristics on purchase intention of fashion products. *Journal of Global Fashion Marketing*, 13(3), 187–204. 10.1080/20932685.2022.2039263

Hahn, E. D., & Ang, S. H. (2017). From the editors: New directions in the reporting of statistical results in the Journal of World Business. In *Journal of World Business* (Vol. 52, Issue 2, pp. 125–126). Elsevier.

Hair, J. F., Risher, J. J., Sarstedt, M., & Ringle, C. M. (2019). When to use and how to report the results of PLS-SEM. *European Business Review*, 31(1), 2–24. 10.1108/EBR-11-2018-0203

Halder, D., Pradhan, D., & Roy Chaudhuri, H. (2021). Forty-five years of celebrity credibility and endorsement literature: Review and learnings. In *Journal of Business Research* (Vol. 125, pp. 397–415). Elsevier Inc. 10.1016/j.jbusres.2020.12.031

Haslam, S. A., & Ellemers, N. (2005). Social identity in industrial and organizational psychology: Concepts, controversies and contributions. *International Review of Industrial and Organizational Psychology*, 2005(20), 39–118. 10.1002/0470029307.ch2

Henseler, J., Ringle, C. M., & Sarstedt, M. (2015). A new criterion for assessing discriminant validity in variance-based structural equation modeling. *Journal of the Academy of Marketing Science*, 43(1), 115–135. 10.1007/s11747-014-0403-8

Herrando, C., & Martín-De Hoyos, M. J. (2022). Influencer endorsement posts and their effects on advertising attitudes and purchase intentions. *International Journal of Consumer Studies*, 46(6), 2288–2299. 10.1111/ijcs.12785

Hogg, M. A., & Abrams, D. (1988). Social identifications: A social psychology of intergroup relations and group processes. In *Social identifications: A social psychology of intergroup relations and group processes*. Taylor & Frances/Routledge.

Hovland, C. I., Janis, I. L., & Kelley, H. H. (1953). Communication and persuasion. In *Communication and persuasion*. Yale University Press.

Hovland, C. I., & Weiss, W. (1951). The influence of source credibility on communication effectiveness. *Public Opinion Quarterly*, 15(4), 635–650. 10.1086/266350

Hudders, L., De Jans, S., & De Veirman, M. (2021). The commercialization of social media stars: A literature review and conceptual framework on the strategic use of social media influencers. *International Journal of Advertising*, 40(3), 327–375. 10.1080/02650487.2020.1836925

Hughes, C., Swaminathan, V., & Brooks, G. (2019). Driving Brand Engagement Through Online Social Influencers: An Empirical Investigation of Sponsored Blogging Campaigns. *Journal of Marketing*, 83(5), 78–96. 10.1177/0022242919854374

Ing, G. P., & Ming, T. (2018). Antecedents of consumer attitude towards blogger recommendations and its impact on purchase intention. *Asian Journal of Business and Accounting*, 11(1), 293–323.

Ismagilova, E., Slade, E., Rana, N. P., & Dwivedi, Y. K. (2020). The effect of characteristics of source credibility on consumer behaviour: A meta-analysis. *Journal of Retailing and Consumer Services*, 53, 101736. Advance online publication. 10.1016/j.jretconser.2019.01.005

Jin, S. V., & Muqaddam, A. (2019). Product placement 2.0: "Do Brands Need Influencers, or Do Influencers Need Brands?" *Journal of Brand Management*, 26(5), 522–537. 10.1057/s41262-019-00151-z

Kirmani, A., & Campbell, M. C. (2009). Taking the target's perspective: The persuasion knowledge model. *Social Psychology of Consumer Behavior*, 297–316.

Kock, F., Berbekova, A., & Assaf, A. G. (2021). Understanding and managing the threat of common method bias: Detection, prevention and control. *Tourism Management*, 86, 104330. 10.1016/j.tourman.2021.104330

Le, L. H., & Hancer, M. (2021). Using social learning theory in examining YouTube viewers' desire to imitate travel vloggers. *Journal of Hospitality and Tourism Technology*, 12(3), 512–532. 10.1108/JHTT-08-2020-0200

Lew, S., & Sulaiman, Z. (2014). Consumer Purchase Intention toward Products Made in Malaysia vs. Made in China: A Conceptual Paper. *Procedia: Social and Behavioral Sciences*, 130, 37–45. 10.1016/j.sbspro.2014.04.005

Li, Y., & Peng, Y. (2021). Influencer marketing: Purchase intention and its antecedents. *Marketing Intelligence & Planning*, 39(7), 960–978. 10.1108/MIP-04-2021-0104

Lou, C., & Yuan, S. (2019). Influencer Marketing: How Message Value and Credibility Affect Consumer Trust of Branded Content on Social Media. *Journal of Interactive Advertising*, 19(1), 58–73. 10.1080/15252019.2018.1533501

MacKenzie, S. B., Lutz, R. J., & Belch, G. E. (1986). The Role of Attitude toward the Ad as a Mediator of Advertising Effectiveness: A Test of Competing Explanations. *JMR, Journal of Marketing Research*, 23(2), 130–143. 10.1177/002224378602300205

Masood, A., Hati, S. R. H., & Rahim, A. A. (2023). Halal cosmetics industry for sustainable development: A systematic literature review. In *International Journal of Business and Society* (Vol. 24, Issue 1, pp. 141–163). Universiti Malaysia Sarawak. 10.33736/ijbs.5609.2023

Masuda, H., Han, S. H., & Lee, J. (2022). Impacts of influencer attributes on purchase intentions in social media influencer marketing: Mediating roles of characterizations. *Technological Forecasting and Social Change*, 174, 121246. Advance online publication. 10.1016/j.techfore.2021.121246

Miller, B. K., & Chiodo, B. (2008). Academic entitlement: Adapting the equity preference questionnaire for a university setting. *Southern Management Association Meeting*.

Miranda, S., Cunha, P., & Duarte, M. (2021). An integrated model of factors affecting consumer attitudes and intentions towards youtuber-generated product content. *Review of Managerial Science*, 15(1), 55–73. 10.1007/s11846-019-00370-3

Muda, M. (2019). Examining the source credibility of user-generated beauty contents (UGBC) on youtube in influencing consumers' purchase intention. *Malaysian Journal of Consumer and Family Economics, 22*(2), 167–184. https://www.scopus.com/inward/record.uri?eid=2-s2.0-85074890363&partnerID=40&md5=d35167bbab9a46d50f11a80a7e15c7fa

Muda, M., & Hamzah, M. I. (2021). Should I suggest this YouTube clip? The impact of UGC source credibility on eWOM and purchase intention. *Journal of Research in Interactive Marketing, 15*(3), 441–459. 10.1108/JRIM-04-2020-0072

Munnukka, J., Uusitalo, O., & Toivonen, H. (2016). Credibility of a peer endorser and advertising effectiveness. *Journal of Consumer Marketing, 33*(3), 182–192. 10.1108/JCM-11-2014-1221

Nafees, L., Cook, C. M., Nikolov, A. N., & Stoddard, J. E. (2021). Can social media influencer (SMI) power influence consumer brand attitudes? The mediating role of perceived SMI credibility. *Digital Business, 1*(2), 100008. Advance online publication. 10.1016/j.digbus.2021.100008

Ohanian, R. (1990). Construction and validation of a scale to measure celebrity endorsers' perceived expertise, trustworthiness, and attractiveness. *Journal of Advertising, 19*(3), 39–52. 10.1080/00913367.1990.10673191

Pornpitakpan, C. (2004). The Persuasiveness of Source Credibility: A Critical Review of Five Decades' Evidence. *Journal of Applied Social Psychology, 34*(2), 243–281. 10.1111/j.1559-1816.2004.tb02547.x

Priester, J. R., & Petty, R. E. (2003). The Influence of Spokesperson Trustworthiness on Message Elaboration, Attitude Strength, and Advertising Effectiveness. *Journal of Consumer Psychology, 13*(4), 408–421. 10.1207/S15327663JCP1304_08

Ramayah, T., Cheah, J., Chuah, F., Ting, H., & Memon, M. A. (2018). Partial least squares structural equation modeling (PLS-SEM) using smartPLS 3.0. *An Updated Guide and Practical Guide to Statistical Analysis*.

Rani, N. S. A., & Krishnan, K. S. D. (2018). Factors that influence Malay students in purchasing skincare products in Malaysia. *The Journal of Business and Retail Management Research, 13*(01). Advance online publication. 10.24052/JBRMR/V13IS01/ART-02

Ringle, C. M., Wende, S., & Becker, J.-M. (2022). SmartPLS 4. Oststeinbek: SmartPLS GmbH. *J. Appl. Struct. Equ. Model.*

Santora, J. (2023). *17 Key Influencer Marketing Statistics to Fuel Your Strategy*. https://influencermarketinghub.com/influencer-marketing-statistics/

Schimmelpfennig, C., & Hunt, J. B. (2020). Fifty years of celebrity endorser research: Support for a comprehensive celebrity endorsement strategy framework. *Psychology and Marketing*, 37(3), 488–505. 10.1002/mar.21315

Schouten, A. P., Janssen, L., & Verspaget, M. (2020). Celebrity vs. Influencer endorsements in advertising: The role of identification, credibility, and Product-Endorser fit. *International Journal of Advertising*, 39(2), 258–281. 10.1080/02650487.2019.1634898

Shoukat, M. H., Selem, K. M., & Asim Shah, S. (2023). How Does Social Media Influencer Credibility Blow the Promotional Horn? A Dual Mediation Model. *Journal of Relationship Marketing*, 22(3), 172–201. 10.1080/15332667.2023.2197767

Simmering, M. J., Fuller, C. M., Richardson, H. A., Ocal, Y., & Atinc, G. M. (2015). Marker variable choice, reporting, and interpretation in the detection of common method variance: A review and demonstration. *Organizational Research Methods*, 18(3), 473–511. 10.1177/1094428114560023

Sokolova, K., & Kefi, H. (2020). Instagram and YouTube bloggers promote it, why should I buy? How credibility and parasocial interaction influence purchase intentions. *Journal of Retailing and Consumer Services*, 53, 101742. Advance online publication. 10.1016/j.jretconser.2019.01.011

Sparkman, R. M. Jr, & Locander, W. B. (1980). Attribution Theory and Advertising Effectiveness. *The Journal of Consumer Research*, 7(3), 219. 10.1086/208810

Statista. (2023a). *Beauty and personal care industry in Malaysia - statistics & facts*. https://www.statista.com/topics/11070/beauty-and-personal-care-industry-in-malaysia/#topicOverview

Statista. (2023b). *Effectiveness of influencers worldwide 2021*. https://www.statista.com/statistics/1275239/effectiveness-influencers-worldwide/

Statista. (2023c). *TikTok penetration in selected countries and territories 2023*. https://www.statista.com/statistics/1299829/tiktok-penetration-worldwide-by-country/

Tajfel, H. E. (1978). *Differentiation between social groups: Studies in the social psychology of intergroup relations*. Academic Press.

Tiwari, A., Kumar, A., Kant, R., & Jaiswal, D. (2023). Impact of fashion influencers on consumers' purchase intentions: Theory of planned behaviour and mediation of attitude. *Journal of Fashion Marketing and Management*. Advance online publication. 10.1108/JFMM-11-2022-0253

Trepte, S. (2013). Social Identity Theory. In *Psychology of Entertainment* (pp. 255–271). Routledge.

Trepte, S., & Loy, L. S. (2017). Social identity theory and self-categorization theory. *The International Encyclopedia of Media Effects*, 1–13.

Verma, D., & Dewani, P. P. (2021). eWOM credibility: A comprehensive framework and literature review. *Online Information Review*, 45(3), 481–500. 10.1108/OIR-06-2020-0263

Vrontis, D., Makrides, A., Christofi, M., & Thrassou, A. (2021). Social media influencer marketing: A systematic review, integrative framework and future research agenda. *International Journal of Consumer Studies*, 45(4), 617–644. 10.1111/ijcs.12647

Wiedmann, K.-P., & von Mettenheim, W. (2020). Attractiveness, trustworthiness and expertise – social influencers' winning formula? *Journal of Product and Brand Management*, 30(5), 707–725. 10.1108/JPBM-06-2019-2442

Xiao, M., Wang, R., & Chan-Olmsted, S. (2018). Factors affecting YouTube influencer marketing credibility: A heuristic-systematic model. *Journal of Media Business Studies*, 15(3), 188–213. 10.1080/16522354.2018.1501146

Ye, G., Hudders, L., De Jans, S., & De Veirman, M. (2021). The Value of Influencer Marketing for Business: A Bibliometric Analysis and Managerial Implications. *Journal of Advertising*, 50(2), 160–178. 10.1080/00913367.2020.1857888

Chapter 6
Enhancing SME Internationalization and Digitalization Through Candidate Elimination Algorithms:
A Strategic Approach

C. V. Suresh Babu
 http://orcid.org/0000-0002-8474-2882
Hindustan Institute of Technology and Science, India

Barath Kumar S.
 http://orcid.org/0009-0007-6607-3455
Hindustan Institute of Technology and Science, India

Nithesh Kumar C.
Hindustan Institute of Technology and Science, India

Dhineshwaren M.
Hindustan Institute of Technology and Science, India

Abbas S.
Hindustan Institute of Technology and Science, India

ABSTRACT

This chapter explores the potential of candidate elimination algorithms in facilitating the internationalization and digitalization of small and medium-sized enterprises

DOI: 10.4018/979-8-3693-3518-5.ch006

(SMEs). *By focusing on their application in real-time marketing on social media platforms, SMEs can gain valuable direction for optimizing their marketing campaigns. Leveraging advanced algorithms becomes imperative for SMEs to remain competitive in today's digital age. The chapter delves into the integration of candidate elimination algorithms into the overarching rule base governing marketing strategies. Through an in-depth analysis of existing literature and empirical studies, the efficacy of these algorithms in enhancing SME marketing performance and global expansion is evaluated. The research aims to provide SMEs with actionable insights on utilizing candidate elimination algorithms to improve their internationalization and digitalization endeavors, thereby contributing to the literature on SME transformation and digital marketing strategies.*

1. INTRODUCTION

The goal of this study is to see whether candidate elimination algorithms could help small, medium-sized businesses (SMEs) internationalize and digitize their operations. This study focuses on the method of applying such algorithms for real-time marketing in social media networks, giving SMEs direction in what they should do during their marketing campaign.

Small and medium-sized businesses (SMEs) are critical components of today's global economy. However, numerous hurdles impede their smooth transition to digitization. To remain competitive in the digital age, SMEs must successfully use complex algorithms. Candidate elimination algorithms are well-known for their speed in decision-making processes, and they hold great promise for SMEs looking to streamline their internationalisation efforts (Xu, Q., et al 2024). This study focuses on incorporating candidate elimination algorithms into the larger rule base that governs diverse decision-making processes. Specifically, it investigates its use in real-time marketing on social media sites (Suresh Babu, C. V., Mahalashmi, et. al 2023). SMEs can use these algorithms to improve their social media marketing efforts, thereby achieving their overall digitization and internationalisation aims. The study's goal is to equip SMEs with insights on how to successfully use these algorithms to produce better results and stay competitive in today's dynamic business world.

1.1 Scope and Methodology

This research project seeks to explore thoroughly into candidate elimination methods and their application in the context of SME internationalisation and digitization. It will conduct a thorough assessment of the existing literature, including candidate elimination algorithms, SME internationalisation plans, digital marketing methodologies, and social media platform optimisation techniques. This holistic approach ensures a thorough understanding of the issue by combining insights from several fields. Also, the research will advance from theory exploration to practical inquiry. Furthermore, it will evaluate the efficiency of integrating candidate elimination algorithms into real-time marketing efforts on social media networks through the use of case studies, surveys and demanding data analytics (Hervé, A., et al., 2020). This stage of actual data collection is important because it helps us gather real-life examples on how algorithms operate within small and medium sized enterprises. For a firm grounding in the results, a methodology will go for an equal mix of qualitative and quantitative approaches. Qualitative techniques will enable an in-depth appreciation of the root causes and situational constraints that promote the uptake of candidate elimination algorithms in SMEs. Conversely, quantitative methods will give statistical verifications and quantify the empirical trends and results, leading to an exhaustive comprehension of the research topic. This paper seeks to help small businesses attract more customers through the internet by looking at what previous studies have said and doing research.

1.2 Goal of Research

The main goal of this research is to give small and medium-sized companies (SMEs) a hands-on approach on how candidate elimination algorithms can be used to enhance their globalization and computerization initiatives. SMEs will also be able to receive hands-on tools on how they can improve their digital marketing by weighing the pros and cons of incorporating candidate elimination algorithms into their social media advertising. In addition, this study aims towards contributing to the already existing body of research concerning SME internationalization and digital transformation by developing an innovative concept that fuses algorithmic decision-making with real-time marketing strategies. This study aims at connecting these two fields with the hope of providing fresh insights as well as new ways of doing things that can help small-medium enterprises (SMEs) navigate the intricacies of global markets and tap into opportunities offered by online platforms when it comes to company advancement. Moreover, the study seeks to bridge a gap in the literature by offering empirical data and actionable hints on the efficacy of including candidate elimination algorithms in operational marketing techniques. Using thorough investigations and examples, the investigation is intended to check the suggested model and stake out a position for small- to mid-sized businesses seeking to enhance their e-commerce strategies amid the current fierce competition (Pereira, C. S., et al 2022).

2. LITERATURE REVIEW

2.1 Scope

The literature analysis will include a thorough examination of key concepts and theories in three major areas: candidate elimination algorithms, SME internationalisation and digitalization, and real-time marketing on social media platforms.

I. Candidate elimination algorithms: A discussion of several candidate elimination techniques (such as nearest neighbour, Naive Bayes, and decision trees). Exploration of the ideas and procedures that underpin candidate elimination methods. A review of the applications of candidate elimination methods in machine learning, data mining, and decision-making.

II. SME internationalisation and digitization: Examining digital transformation trends and the value of digitization for SMEs. An examination of methods and tactics for SME internationalisation and digitization, including market access modes, international marketing, and digitalization activities. Identifying the elements that influence SMEs' decisions on internationalisation and digitization.

III. Real-time marketing via social media platforms: Definition and importance of real-time marketing in the digital age. Exploration of real-time marketing strategies and approaches used on social media platforms. Examining the problems and prospects of real-time social media marketing

2.2 Literature Synthesis

Various scholarly sources across three key domains have contributed in the literature synthesis, namely: candidate elimination algorithms, SME internationalization and digitalization, and real-time marketing on social media platforms. In candidate elimination algorithms, diverse forms, such as closest neighbour and decision trees, which have practical applications in decision-making processes across disciplines, are examined. These studies showcase how adaptable and useful candidate elimination algorithms are, although they recognize that they may have some limits and difficulties. Although digitalization can be a growth and expansion opportunity for SMEs, it also poses multiple challenges as well as complexities at the same time. If they are to be able navigate global marketplace successfully, it is critical that SMEs comprehend these dynamics. It has also been revealed through literature review just how vital SME internationalization and digitalization are as they illuminate how intricate these concepts can get. At the same time, literature underlines how important it is that real-time marketing plays a significant role when it comes to social media platforms in today's digital environment. To boost SME presence and involvement as observed in the online world, there are ways of achieving this. In this same context, it has been noted that incorporating date served with algorithms into real-time marketing becomes an imperative. The primary purpose of these tools is to help SMEs take advantage of global growth and penetrate international markets through focused marketing campaigns. In general, bringing together literature emphasizes a candidate elimination method, the internationalization and digitalization of SME and the marketing strategies that are in real time are interrelated. Through using what is learned from these areas, small and medium enterprises are enabled come up with well thought out measures to improve their online visibility, widen their customer base, and ensure consistent expansion within the contemporary business environment that is full of competition.

3. THEORETICAL FRAMEWORK

3.1 Introduction

The conceptual structure for this study is based on fundamental concepts and theories from decision-making, marketing, and digital transformation. At its foundation is the incorporation of candidate elimination algorithms into Small and Medium-sized Enterprises (SMEs)' strategic efforts for internationalization and digitization, notably in the context of real-time marketing on social media platforms. This paradigm seeks to give a structured perspective through which to examine the interactions of algorithmic decision-making, SME strategy, and digital marketing methods.

3.2 Conceptual Definition

Candidate elimination algorithms are a class of computational techniques used in decision-making frameworks to systematically reduce prospective options or candidates based on certain criteria or parameters. These algorithms use iterative methods to gradually eliminate fewer desirable options until they arrive at a final conclusion or pick. In the framework of this study, candidate elimination algorithms are used as a strategic tool by small and medium-sized firms (SMEs) looking to improve their internationalisation and digitization efforts. SMEs can improve their marketing strategies and decision-making processes by incorporating these algorithms into real-time marketing applications on social media platforms, giving them a competitive advantage in the global market. The conceptual framework includes the use of candidate elimination algorithms to help SMEs navigate the complexity of foreign markets while also using the promise of digital platforms for business expansion and growth. To elaborate, these algorithms help SMEs sift through massive amounts of data and discover the most attractive opportunities or prospects for international expansion. By carefully removing less viable choices, SMEs may concentrate their resources and efforts on the pathways with the greatest chance of success. Furthermore, including candidate elimination algorithms into real-time marketing software enables SMEs to adapt and respond quickly to shifting market dynamics and consumer preferences. Furthermore, these algorithms can help SMEs optimise their marketing initiatives by focusing on specific demographic segments or geographical regions with a high probability of success. This tailored strategy not only improves marketing effectiveness, but also increases ROI and overall business performance.

3.3 Application Theory

Candidate elimination algorithms represent a class of computational techniques strategically employed in decision-making frameworks to systematically narrow down prospective options or candidates based on specific criteria or parameters. These algorithms leverage iterative methods, progressively eliminating less desirable options until reaching a final decision or selection. Candidate elimination algorithms have a value function that can be used to improve global expansion as well as digital integration initiatives in small and medium-size companies. They are derived from computational intelligence (CI) and decision theory which are based on the principles of systematic decision-making as well as data-driven optimization, especially by using big data analytics techniques – something similar to what applies in math where you have arrays representing various positions within a crossword puzzle game!

3.4 Illustrative Example

Let's imagine an e-commerce company, let's say it's called "Tech gen", and it's looking to grow its market presence internationally while improving its digital marketing strategy. Tech Trend sells high-tech gadgets and accessories online.

Figure 1. Barnstorming on Digital Marketing Strategy

Source: created in https://designer.microsoft.com/image-creator

International Expansion: Tech gen decides to expand its reach beyond its home market and targets several European and Asian countries for expansion. But entering new markets comes with its own set of challenges

Digitization Initiatives: Understanding local consumer preferences Navigating regulatory requirements Optimizing logistics at the same time, Tech gen understands the need for digitization in order to scale its operations and connect with its customers. It wants to use digital platforms, especially social media to increase brand awareness, engage customers, and boost sales.

Integration of Candidate Elimination Algorithms: To streamline its internationalization and digitalization activities, Tech gen intends to incorporate candidate removal algorithms into its marketing strategy. These algorithms assist Tech gen in making data-driven decisions by analysing customer behaviour, market trends, and demographic information in real-time.

Real-Time Marketing on social media: Tech gen conducts targeted marketing strategies on social media platforms such as Facebook, Instagram, and Twitter. Tech gen can optimize these efforts by using candidate elimination algorithms to discover and target the most potential client segments based on criteria such as geography, interests, and purchase behaviour.

Iterative Optimisation: Tech gen marketing strategies are continuously refined over time employing candidate elimination algorithms. It analyses performance measurements, identifies trends, and iteratively modifies targeted settings to maximise ROI while also achieving internationalisation and digitization objectives.

3.5 Limitations and Assumptions

Data Availability and Quality: One constraint of this study is its reliance on publicly available data for analysis and empirical research. The correctness, completeness, and reliability of the collected data may differ, thereby affecting the validity of the conclusions.

Applicability: Another drawback concerns the study's findings' generalizability. The research may concentrate on certain industries, geographical regions, or market situations, restricting the applicability of the findings to broader settings.

Algorithm Complexity and Implementation Challenges: The study assumes that SMEs have access to and can effectively execute candidate elimination methods. However, the intricacy of these algorithms and the technical skills necessary for execution may provide difficulties for some SMEs.

Market Dynamics and External Factors: The study assumes that market circumstances stay reasonably steady during the research period. However, external factors such as economic fluctuations, regulatory changes, and technological disruptions might have an impact on the effectiveness of SME internationalisation and digitization plans.

Ethical and Privacy Considerations: The study assumes that the employment of candidate elimination algorithms in marketing operations complies with ethical norms and protects user privacy. However, there may be ethical consequences for algorithmic decision-making, such as data privacy, algorithmic bias, and transparency.

Resource restrictions: According to the study, SMEs may suffer resource restrictions such as financial limitations, limited access to technology, and labour shortages. These limits could affect the practicality and scalability of applying candidate elimination algorithms in SME marketing strategies.

3.6 Key Components

- **Candidate Elimination techniques:** This component serves as the research's foundation and includes techniques such as nearest neighbour, decision trees, and Naive Bayes. Understanding the ideas and mechanics of candidate elimination algorithms is critical for successfully incorporating them into SMEs' marketing strategy (Nithya, C. L., et al., 2019).

- **SME Internationalisation and Digitization:** Key components include an assessment of the obstacles and opportunities that SMEs encounter while growing abroad and implementing digital technology (Gaweł, A., et al., 2022). This includes market entry options, international marketing strategies, and the significance of digital transformation for SME competitiveness.
- **Real-Time Marketing on Social Media Platforms:** This section discusses the role of social media platforms in current marketing strategies, especially the importance of real-time marketing tactics and procedures. Understanding user engagement dynamics, data analytics, and algorithmic optimisation for social media platforms
- **Consider the following scenario:** Tech gen announces a new smartwatch device and initiates a sponsored Instagram post. The marketing team uses candidate elimination algorithms to measure user engagement data in real-time, such as likes, comments, and click-through rates. As the campaign develops, the algorithm determines which demographic segments are more positive about the product, allowing Tech gen to change its targeting strategy accordingly.

Iterative Optimisation: Tech gen marketing strategies are continually refined utilizing candidate elimination algorithms. It examines performance metrics, recognizes trends, and iteratively modifies targeting settings to maximize ROI and full fill internationalization and digitization objectives.

In this illustrative example, Tech gen can increase its internationalization and digitization efforts through the optimization of real-time marketing campaigns on social media platforms as a result of integrating candidate elimination algorithms. This Strategic Approach provides SMEs with the opportunity to make sound choices, efficiently reach their target audience and drive business growth both domestically and internationally. In this illustrative example, Tech gen can increase its internationalization and digitization efforts through the optimization of real-time marketing campaigns on social media platforms as a result of integrating candidate elimination algorithms (Suresh Babu, C. V, Swapna et al., 2023). This Strategic Approach provides SMEs with the opportunity to make sound choices, efficiently reach their target audience and drive business growth in both domestic and foreign markets.

4. RESEARCH METHODOLOGY

4.1 Introduction

The research approach used to investigate the integration of candidate elimination algorithms for SME internationalisation and digitalization via real-time marketing on social media platforms is critical to assuring the study's rigour and validity. This section describes the approaches and procedures utilised to gather, analyse, and interpret data in order to effectively address the research objectives (Wu, G., Hashemi, M., et al., 2022).

4.1.2 Defining the Problem

Small and medium-sized enterprises (SMEs) are increasingly recognising the value of internationalisation and digitalization in order to remain competitive in today's global economy. However, many SMEs struggle to properly use social media marketing methods to increase their international presence and digital reach. The goal of this project is to create a social media marketing optimisation framework that utilises the Candidate Elimination Algorithm to help SMEs improve their internationalisation and digitalization efforts through targeted and data-driven marketing tactics.

4.1.3 Data Collection and Analysis

- Collect social media data from multiple sites related to the target overseas markets.
- using the Candidate Elimination Algorithm to uncover patterns, trends, and preferences across demographic groupings and geographic regions.
- Consider language, culture, interests, and purchasing behaviour while developing marketing strategy.

4.1.4 Segmenting and Targeting

- Divide the international audience into segments depending on the Candidate Elimination Algorithm results.
- Create personalised marketing campaigns for each category, concentrating on content and message that speaks to their unique preferences and interests.

- Use the algorithm to constantly fine-tune and update these segments based on real-time feedback and engagement data.

4.1.5 Content Localization

Use the Candidate Elimination Algorithm's findings to identify potential content localization opportunities.

- Translate and adjust social media content to reflect the cultural subtleties and language preferences of various global markets.
- Test and iterate on several content versions to discover the most effective strategy for each target demographic.

4.1.6 Influencer Identification and Engagement

Use the Candidate Elimination Algorithm to find influencers with a significant presence and impact in the target overseas markets.

- Collaborate with these influencers to market SME products or services to their audience, using their authority and reach.

Monitor and analyse the impact of influencer relationships in order to optimise future partnership initiatives.

4.1.7 Ad Campaign Optimisation

- Set up sponsored advertising campaigns on social media networks aimed at international audiences.
- Use the Candidate Elimination Algorithm to optimise ad targeting criteria including demographics, interests, and geographic area.
- Continuously monitor ad performance metrics such as click-through rates, conversion rates, and return on investment (ROI), and alter campaign parameters in accordance with the algorithm's suggestions.

4.1.8 Engagement and community-building

Encourage involvement with international audiences by actively participating in discussions, replying to comments, and promptly responding to customer inquiries.

- Use the Candidate Elimination Algorithm to uncover hot themes and conversations that are relevant to your target markets, then modify your content and interaction strategy accordingly.
- Create a sense of community among your international followers by sharing user-generated content, hosting contests or giveaways, and creating interactive experiences.

Figure 2. Flow Chart

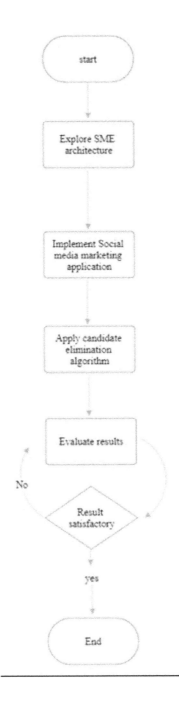

The steps of which it guides SMEs entail collecting and analyzing data from overseas markets, segmenting and targeting international audiences' localizing content, identifying and engaging with influencers optimizing ad campaigns, fostering engagement as well community building in social media platforms Thereby, the flowchart acts as a roadmap for SMEs to employ the Candidate Elimination Algorithm and other techniques for enhancing their digital marketing GCC_markup performance.

4.2 Ethical Consideration

- **Transparency and Informed Consent:** Before engaging SMEs or individuals in research, it is critical to provide clear and full information about the study's objectives, procedures, potential risks, and benefits. Obtaining informed consent from all participants, including SME owners, managers, and employees, ensures that they understand the study's objective and ramifications. Furthermore, participants should be notified of their freedom to withdraw from the study at any time without consequence.
- **Data Privacy and Confidentiality:** Handling sensitive data pertaining to SME operations and marketing plans necessitates rigorous respect to data privacy rules and ethical principles. To prevent unauthorised access or breaches, researchers must anonymize and securely store all obtained data, including sensitive business information and consumer data. Respecting confidentiality is critical for maintaining confidence with SME participants and protecting their competitive interests.
- **Fairness and Equity:** To avoid bias and discrimination, candidate removal algorithms must be implemented in a fair and equitable manner. Researchers should be aware of algorithmic biases that may disproportionately affect specific demographic groups or areas. Algorithmic decision-making procedures that are fair and transparent should be prioritised in order to promote inclusion and reduce potential harm.
- **Accountability and Responsibility**: Researchers are responsible for seriously evaluating the ethical implications of their research and accepting responsibility for any potential hazards or unexpected repercussions. This entails routinely analyzing the ethical implications of algorithmic tactics used in SME internationalization and digitization activities, as well as making required revisions to minimize harm and respect ethical norms.
- **Continuous Ethical Oversight**: Throughout the study process, continual ethical oversight and evaluation are required to guarantee that ethical concerns are followed and that any new ethical difficulties are addressed swiftly.

Creating an independent ethics committee or interacting with ethical experts can provide significant insight and help when negotiating complicated ethical quandaries associated to SME internationalisation, digitization, and algorithmic decision making.

4.3 Block Diagram

This block diagram provides a high-level overview of the project's flow, beginning with defining the project objective, conducting a literature review, outlining the research methodology, collecting and analysing data, integrating candidate elimination algorithms into SME internationalisation and digitization efforts, implementing real-time marketing on social media, optimising marketing strategies, evaluating algorithmic strategies for SMEs, and concluding with recommend

Figure 3. Block Diagram

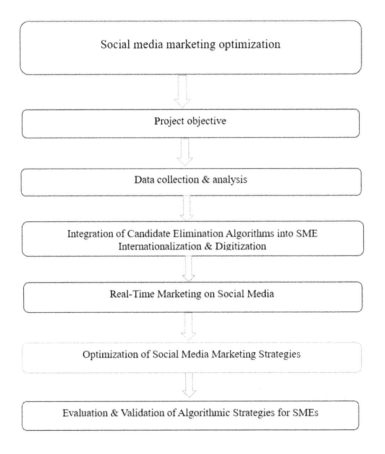

5. DISCUSSION

5.1 Existing Methodologies

- Mixed-Methods Approach: Many existing methodologies take a mixed-methods approach, integrating qualitative and quantitative techniques to examine the use of candidate elimination algorithms in SME internationalisation and digitization activities. This approach enables researchers to obtain both qualitative insights from case studies and interviews, as well as quantitative data from surveys and analytics tools, in order to provide a holistic knowledge of the phenomenon.
- Case Study Analysis: Case study analysis is a popular tool for investigating how SMEs use candidate elimination algorithms for internationalisation and digitization. Researchers examine real-world examples of SMEs using algorithmic marketing methods on social media sites. Researchers examine these situations in depth to find best practices, obstacles, and outcomes connected with algorithmic decision-making in SME contexts.
- Surveys and Interviews: Surveys and interviews are commonly used to collect empirical data on SMEs' experiences, perspectives, and attitudes concerning candidate elimination algorithms, as well as their impact on internationalisation and digitization initiatives. Surveys can provide quantitative insights on the prevalence and effectiveness of algorithmic tactics, whereas interviews provide qualitative insights into SMEs' underlying motives, problems, and decision-making processes (Basuki, C., et al 2023).
- Data Analytics and Experimentation: Data analytics techniques such as statistical analysis and machine learning algorithms are used to analyse enormous datasets gathered from SMEs' real-time marketing activity on social media platforms (Suresh Babu, C. V. & Praveen, S. 2023). Researchers can evaluate the efficacy of algorithmic optimisation approaches and discover areas for development by looking at measures like engagement rates, conversion rates, and ROI. Furthermore, experimentation approaches like A/B testing enable academics to assess the efficacy of various algorithmic strategies and discover the best solution for SMEs.
- Simulation and modelling approaches are used to test the impact of candidate elimination algorithms on SME internationalisation and digitization processes. Researchers create computational models that simulate SMEs' behaviour, market dynamics, and algorithmic decision-making processes (Rahman, M., et al 2023 and Suresh Babu, C. V. & Rahul. A., 2024). Researchers can use

simulation studies to investigate diverse scenarios, test theories, and forecast the consequences of different algorithmic solutions in a controlled setting

5.2 Implementation

```
class CandidateElimination:

    def __init__(self, n_features):

        # Initialize specific and general hypotheses

        self.specific_hypothesis = ['0']  n_features

        self.general_hypothesis = ['?']  n_features

    def fit(self, X, y):

        for i, x in enumerate(X):

            if y[i] == 'Y':

                # Update specific hypothesis

                for j, feature in enumerate(x):

                    if self.specific_hypothesis[j] == '0':
```

```
                        self.specific_hypothesis[j] = feature

                    elif self.specific_hypothesis[j] != feature:

                        self.specific_hypothesis[j] = '?'


                # Remove inconsistent general hypotheses

                for j, feature in enumerate(x):

                    if self.specific_hypothesis[j] != feature:

                        self.general_hypothesis[j] = self.specific_hypothesis[j]

            else:

                # Update general hypothesis

                for j, feature in enumerate(x):

                    if self.specific_hypothesis[j] != feature and self.specific_hypothesis[j] != '?':
```

```
                    self.general_hypothesis[j] = self.specific_hypothesis[j]



    def predict(self, X):

        predictions = []

        for x in X:

            if self.is_consistent(x):

                predictions.append('Y')

            else:

                predictions.append('N')

        return predictions



    def is_consistent(self, x):

        for i, feature in enumerate(x):
```

```python
                if self.specific_hypothesis[i] != '?' and self.specific_hypothesis[i] != feature:

                    return False

                if self.general_hypothesis[i] != '?' and self.general_hypothesis[i] == feature:

                    return False

        return True


# Example usage:

X = [

    ['Male', '25-34', 'High', 'Positive'],

    ['Female', '18-24', 'Medium', 'Neutral'],

    ['Male', '25-34', 'Low', 'Negative']

]

y = ['Y', 'Y', 'N']
```

```python
ce = CandidateElimination(n_features=len(X[0]))

ce.fit(X, y)


test_data = [

    ['Male', '18-24', 'High', 'Positive'],

    ['Female', '25-34', 'Medium', 'Neutral']

]

predictions = ce.predict(test_data)

print(predictions)   # Output: ['Y', 'N']
```

```
# Example dataset

X = [

    ['Male', '25-34', 'High', 'Positive'],

    ['Female', '18-24', 'Medium', 'Neutral'],

    ['Male', '25-34', 'Low', 'Negative']

]

y = ['Y', 'Y', 'N']
```

In this dataset:

Each row represents an instance.

The columns represent features, such as gender, age range, income level, and sentiment.

The X variable contains the feature values for each instance.

```
The y variable contains the corresponding labels for each
instance, where 'Y' indicates a positive instance and 'N' indi-
cates a negative instance.
```

Consider the following scenario: a SME (Small and Medium-sized Enterprise) wants to target consumers on social media platforms based on demographic information and content sentiment. In this example, the SME wants to improve its social media marketing strategy by identifying consumers who are likely to respond positively to its advertisements. The Candidate Elimination technique can assist with this by iteratively refining hypotheses based on observed results. The predictions can then be used to target individuals who are more likely to respond positively to the SME's social media marketing initiatives, allowing it to improve its marketing strategy and digital reach.

6. CONCLUSION

To summarise, the incorporation of candidate elimination algorithms is a promising route for improving Small and Medium-sized Enterprises (SMEs) internationalisation and digitization initiatives, notably in the arena of real-time marketing on social media platforms. This study shed light on the possible benefits and drawbacks of using candidate elimination algorithms in SME situations by conducting a thorough evaluation of existing literature and methodology. Businesses that strategically integrate these algorithms into their SME marketing strategies may make data-driven decisions, optimise their real-time marketing efforts, and increase their worldwide competitiveness. Case studies and empirical research have shown that algorithmic approaches improve SME visibility, engagement, and sales on social media platforms.

However, it is critical to recognise the limitations and ethical implications of applying candidate removal methods. Privacy considerations, data security, algorithmic biases, and resource limits must all be addressed to guarantee that algorithmic decision-making is used responsibly and ethically in SME environments.

7. FUTURE SCOPE

- Further study is needed to investigate sophisticated algorithmic optimisation strategies designed specifically for SMEs, taking into account variables such as resource restrictions, scalability, and interpretability.

- Comparative studies across cultural contexts can provide useful insights into the effectiveness of algorithmic tactics in a variety of market environments, as well as help to shape the development of culturally sensitive approaches (H. A. Rozak., et al 2023)
- Longitudinal studies that monitor the long-term influence of candidate elimination algorithms on SME performance and sustainability can provide useful information about the scalability and durability of algorithmic strategies across time.
- Exploring the integration of candidate elimination algorithms with emerging technologies such as artificial intelligence, machine learning, and blockchain might provide SMEs with additional opportunities to innovate and differentiate themselves in the digital arena.

REFERENCES

Aghazadeh, H., Zandi, F., Amoozad Mahdiraji, H. & Sadraei, R. (2023). Digital transformation and SME internationalisation: unravelling the moderated-mediation role of digital capabilities, digital resilience and digital maturity. *Journal of Enterprise Information Management.* 10.1108/JEIM-02-2023-0092

Basuki, C., Pratiwi, C. P., & Rahmatika, R. A. (2023). Implementation Search Engine Optimization (SEO) to Improve Marketing F&B Industry. *Bit-Tech: Binary Digital - Technology, 6*(1), 87–94. 10.32877/bt.v6i1.904

Cui, T. H., Ghose, A., Halaburda, H., Iyengar, R., Pauwels, K., Sriram, S., Tucker, C., & Venkataraman, S. (2021). Informational Challenges in Omnichannel Marketing: Remedies and Future Research. *Journal of Marketing, 85*(1), 103-120. 10.1177/0022242920968810

Gaweł, A., Mroczek-Dąbrowska, K., & Pietrzykowski, M. (2022). Digitalization and Its Impact on the Internationalization Models of SMEs. doi:10.1007/978-3-03 1-11371-0_210.1007/978-3-031-11371-0_2

Hervé, A., Schmitt, C., & Baldegger, R. (2020). Internationalization and Digitalization: Applying digital technologies to the internationalization process of small and medium-sized enterprises. *Technology Innovation Management Review, 10*(7), 29-41. doi:10.22215/timreview/137310.22215/timreview/1373

Hervé, A., Schmitt, C., & Rico, B. (2020). Internationalization and Digitalization: Applying digital technologies to the internationalization process of small and medium-sized enterprises. *Technology Innovation Management Review, 10*, 28-40. doi:10.22215/timreview/137310.22215/timreview/1373

Lemon, K. N., & Verhoef, P. C. (2016). Understanding Customer Experience Throughout the Customer Journey. *Journal of Marketing, 80*(6), 69-96. doi:10.1509/jm.15.042010.1509/jm.15.0420

Martínez-Peláez, R., Ochoa-Brust, A., Rivera, S., Félix, V. G., Ostos, R., Brito, H., Félix, R. A., & Mena, L. J. (2023). Role of Digital Transformation for Achieving Sustainability: Mediated Role of Stakeholders, Key Capabilities, and Technology. *Sustainability, 15*(14), 11221. doi:10.3390/su15141122110.3390/su151411221

Nithya, C. L., Dixit, S., & Khodhanpur, B. I. (2019). Prediction of breast cancer using Find-S and Candidate elimination algorithm. In *2019 4th International Conference on Computational Systems and Information Technology for Sustainable Solution (CSITSS)* (pp. 1-4). Bengaluru, India: IEEE. doi:10.1109/CSITSS47250.2019.903104610.1109/CSITSS47250.2019.9031046

Pereira, C. S., Durão, N., Moreira, F., & Veloso, B. (2022). The Importance of Digital Transformation in International Business. *Sustainability, 14*(2), 834. doi:10.3390/su1402083410.3390/su14020834

Rahman, M., Hack-Polay, D., Shafique, S., & Igwe, P. A. (2023). Dynamic capability of the firm: Analysis of the impact of internationalisation on SME performance in an emerging economy. *International Journal of Emerging Markets*, 18(9), 2383–2401. 10.1108/IJOEM-02-2021-0236

Rao, P., Kumar, S., Chavan, M., & Lim, W. M. (2023). A systematic literature review on SME financing: Trends and future directions. *Journal of Small Business Management*, 61(3), 1247–1277. 10.1080/00472778.2021.1955123

Reim, W., Yli-Viitala, P., Arrasvuori, J., & Parida, V. (2022). Tackling business model challenges in SME internationalization through digitalization. *Journal of Innovation & Knowledge, 7*, 100199. doi:10.1016/j.jik.2022.10019910.1016/j.jik.2022.100199

Rozak, H. A., Adhiatma, A., Fachrunnisa, O., & Rahayu, T. (2023, November). Social Media Engagement, Organizational Agility and Digitalization Strategic Plan to Improve SMEs' Performance. *IEEE Transactions on Engineering Management*, 70(11), 3766–3775. 10.1109/TEM.2021.3085977

Suresh Babu, C. V. (2023). *Artificial Intelligence and Expert Systems*. Anniyappa Publications.

Suresh Babu, C. V., Mahalashmi, J., Vidhya, A., Nila Devagi, S., & Bowshith, G. (2023). Save Soil Through Machine Learning. In Habib, M. (Ed.), *Global Perspectives on Robotics and Autonomous Systems: Development and Applications* (pp. 345–362). IGI Global. 10.4018/978-1-6684-7791-5.ch016

Suresh Babu, C. V., & Praveen, S. (2023). Swarm Intelligence and Evolutionary Machine Learning Algorithms for COVID-19: Pandemic and Epidemic Review. In Suresh Kumar, A., Kose, U., Sharma, S., & Jerald Nirmal Kumar, S. (Eds.), *Dynamics of Swarm Intelligence Health Analysis for the Next Generation* (pp. 83–103). IGI Global. 10.4018/978-1-6684-6894-4.ch005

Suresh Babu, C. V., & Rahul, A. (2024). Securing the Future: Unveiling Risks and Safeguarding Strategies in Machine Learning-Powered Cybersecurity. In Almaiah, M., Maleh, Y., & Alkhassawneh, A. (Eds.), *Risk Assessment and Countermeasures for Cybersecurity* (pp. 80–95). IGI Global. 10.4018/979-8-3693-2691-6.ch005

Suresh Babu, C. V., Swapna, A., Chowdary, D. S., Vardhan, B. S., & Imran, M. (2023). Leaf Disease Detection Using Machine Learning (ML). In Khang, A. (Ed.), *Handbook of Research on AI-Equipped IoT Applications in High-Tech Agriculture* (pp. 188–199). IGI Global. 10.4018/978-1-6684-9231-4.ch010

Wibawa, B. M., Baihaqi, I., Nareswari, N., Mardhotillah, R. R., & Pramesti, F. (2022). Utilization of social media and its impact on marketing performance: A case study of SMEs in Indonesia. *International Journal of Business and Society*, 23(1), 19–34. 10.33736/ijbs.4596.2022

Wu, G., Hashemi, M., & Srinivasa, C. (2022). PUMA: Performance Unchanged Model Augmentation for Training Data Removal. *Proceedings of the AAAI Conference on Artificial Intelligence*, 36(8), 8675–8682. 10.1609/aaai.v36i8.20846

Xu, Q., Chen, W., Dang, B., & Shi, Y. (2024, February 28). (2024). Employee protection and innovation in small and medium-sized enterprises: The moderating effect of regional digitalization. *Journal of Small Business and Entrepreneurship*, 1–21. Advance online publication. 10.1080/08276331.2024.2315541

Chapter 7
Entrepreneurial Strategies for Business Intelligence and Blockchain

Kathirvel Ayyaswamy
  http://orcid.org/0000-0002-5347-9110
Department of Computer Science and Engineering, Panimalar Engineering College, Chennai, India

Naren Kathirvel
Anand Institute of Higher Technology, India

Subramanian C.
  http://orcid.org/0000-0003-2629-3182
Eswari Engineering College, India

Maheswaran C. P.
  http://orcid.org/0000-0001-5985-2564
Sri Krishna College of Technology, India

ABSTRACT

Blockchain is a distributed database that is shared by multiple system nodes. The reason it is named blockchain is that it gathers data in encrypted blocks that are connected to other sets of blocks to create a virtual chain. The development of numerous cryptocurrencies, dApp monetization, smart personal contracts, decentralized finance apps (Defi), and non-fungible tokens (NFTs), preceded general adoption of the blockchain concept. Blockchain technology (BT) is digital money, which increases in value every hour by a factor of bigger than its previous worth. Even though blockchain's widespread appeal has been confined to its role in the development of bitcoin and other cryptocurrencies, a number of other applications are currently being developed steadily. This demonstrates the promise of decentralized technology and the undeniable influence of blockchain on business across many industries.

1. INTRODUCTION

We are aware that BT extends beyond transactions and cryptocurrencies, let's examine the technologies that serve as the foundation for blockchain technology and how it advances technological advancement. The Four Elements of Blockchain Technology's Foundation (Sudha, & Kathirvel, 2023a)

A. ICO

Initial Coin Offerings (ICO) are a type of fundraising used by businesses and startups that incorporate Blockchain technology into their operations (Sudha, & Kathirvel, 2023b). This is how it functions:

Prior to announcement making the necessary preparations for the ICO is the first step in the process. At this point (Sudha, & Kathirvel, 2022), digital advertising promotions are launched on Internet that ICO investors frequently visit, and the white paper—which contains the project's details—is being produced.

Supplying: It consists of the written policy terms and environments of the agreement that are given to potential investors are given in Figure 1.

Figure 1. ICO Token System

Shareholders are offered an investment vehicle known as a crypto coin in exchange for their capital. Each crypto coin has a unique toe given to it.

Strategy for Advertising: This is the phase in which the real work is done. The target audience for the campaign is small investors and institutions, and it usually lasts up to one month. The demand is far more than that of the other well-liked fundraising strategy.

B. Smart Contract

Smart Contracts are the other technology that has become well-known in the realm of blockchain-powered businesses, after ICOs. With BT based Smart Contracts as shown in Figure 2, you can accomplish the same goals as their equivalents in the physical world: no party may violate the terms of the agreement.

When using BT based smart contracts, party is required to contribute a guaranteed amount to a separate account that is outside of their mechanism and is only free when the contract's terms and situations are met. Many essential features are promised by the design of smart contracts, including inherent trust, high transactional speed, accuracy, and zero conflicts.

Figure 2. Smart Contracts

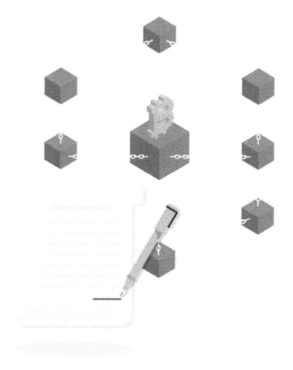

C. Cryptocurrency Wallets

Figure 3. Cryptocurrency Wallet

The second blockchain component we'll examine is cryptocurrency wallet apps as shown in the Figure 3, which are what got the decentralization movement started. In the state that bitcoin has made for itself, there are currently over 1,600 cryptocurrencies in circulation worldwide, and more are being introduced practically every day. No matter what use you choose to give your cryptocurrency wallet, you have a lot of alternatives, especially in terms of development. Options include hardware wallets, paper wallets, hot/cold wallets, mobile banking wallets, Internet web online wallets, and personal desktop computer wallets.

D. Blockchain NFTs

NFTs are the most widely used investing method in 2022 and are a relatively new addition to the Blockchain family. What makes NFTs so unique? To begin with, they aren't tradable. For instance, Bitcoin may be exchanged for other bitcoins with no loss in value because it is fungible. NFTs, however, cannot be traded.

Fundamentally, everything digital that is original to you—like music, drawings, pictures, etc.—can be considered an NFT. They are most likely trending on all social media platforms now a days everyone wants to secure digital moneys (Kathirvel, 2024a). NFTs are a component of powered moneys on the Ethereum Blockchain that are enabled by smart contracts (Kathirvel, 2024b). You should look into the development if this is something that interests you for your startup or established company.

2. LITERATURE REVIEW

There are countless uses and applications for blockchain as a service across different industrial areas. Now let's examine the leading sectors that have integrated decentralization into their everyday operations (Kathirvel et al., 2022a).

2.1 Blockchain in Healthcare

The fact that blockchain is transforming the medical field and ready to solve many of the problems that impede effective care and medical across the world, despite the numerous debates surrounding the impact of BT on the healthcare sector and whether or not it is a realistic possibility (Kathirvel et al., 2022b). The decentralized spaces left by blockchain are those where healthcare is lacking. Blockchain facilitates:

- **Fast Data Access:** Dispersed and safe access to patient health data is made possible by the distributed ledger that is included in the Blockchain and Healthcare Mix package. Real-time changes are also made to the patient's shared data (Kathirvel et al., 2024e).
- **System Interoperability:** Cryptocurrency provides an international decentralized computer network and internet.
- **Security of Data:** Only those who require access to the patient's data can access it, as it is entirely decentralized and unchangeable.

Blockchain technology in healthcare enables the centralization of user-generated IoT data and medical organization data in one location.

2.2 Blockchain in FinTech

Figure 4. Blockchain in Finance Sector

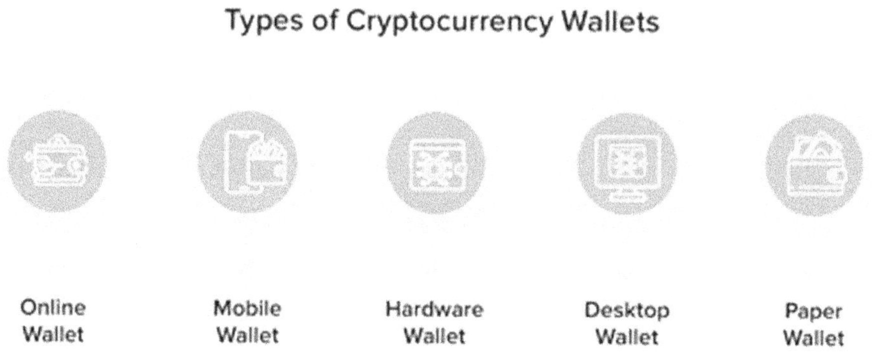

Types of Cryptocurrency Wallets

Online Wallet | Mobile Wallet | Hardware Wallet | Desktop Wallet | Paper Wallet

Technological innovation entered the globe through the merger of FinTech (refer Figure 4) and Blockchain. Blockchain will undoubtedly bring about a digital revolution in the banking sector overall, affecting all other financial areas as well. This

Entrepreneurial Strategies for Business Intelligence and Blockchain

includes KYC procedure, credit and debit transactions, and reduced costs. Take a look at how Asian Bank used Appinventiv's assistance to adopt a blockchain-based, cryptocurrency-focused banking solution through its app. The customer recognition system, electronic payment methods, insurance, loans, and credits are the monetary services that will begin to exhibit symbols of simplification and speedier, reliable procedures.

2.3 Blockchain in Real Estate

Probably the only real estate industry has successfully proposed and use BT in real estate is the industry real estate sector. The industry's very definition is made up of procedures that Blockchain for Real Estate may simplify and decentralize as shown in Figure 5.

Figure 5. BT in Real Estate Sector

If you examine the current state of adoption of BT in real estate, you will discover that governments in multiple countries are utilizing decentralization and BT to promote more efficient real estate practices in their respective countries, in addition to individual property developers, real estate brokers, and insurance providers.

Entrepreneurial Strategies for Business Intelligence and Blockchain

2.4 Blockchain in Manufacturing

The Internet of Things is present in every technological trend that you look at. BT and IoT (Industrial IoT) (Kathirvel and Maheswaran, 2023a), two technological phenomena, it is combined to save industrial and supply chain companies from using manual labor.

Figure 6. Supply chain and Manufacturing Industry

Uses of Blockchain in Supply chain and Manufacturing

- Supply chain auditing
- 3D printing design rights
- Lowering barriers to entry
- Reducing systemic failures
- Improving trust in products
- IoT device authentication
- Better tracking of maintenance
- Securing critical DataLogs
- Local, direct-to-consumer platforms
- Production part approval process (PPAP) & sourcing of materials

Blockchain technology can assist in tracking the history of all linked devices for manufacturing and operations problems if it is directly connected to IoT devices. The global decentralized ledger in the supply chain can prevent collusion and tampering with any machinery data, hence eliminating a single source of error in the world of IoT. In order to prevent risks, IoT and BT can also offer harmony and contract models in digital bonds.

By serving as a safe, scalable, and transparent energy transaction ecosystem, blockchain technology is completely changing the energy industry. For a detailed understanding of blockchain's influence, read our blog post on How It's Disrupting the Energy Sector.

3. METHODOLOGY USED IN RECENT STARTUPS AND INITIATIVES

There's no denying that the efficiency and profitability generated by incorporating blockchain technology into their processes makes it too important for BT companies to ignore. However, the majority of organizations that have implemented blockchain for business are still outweighed by those who haven't.

3.1 Research Methodology in Blockchain

The presence of legacy technologies that have greatly improved a business is a contributing factor to the challenge of implementing any new technology. It's time for businesses to release their worries, but still proceed with caution. They should start using enterprise blockchain solutions in certain areas of their operations and only scale up if they see tangible benefits from the technology (refer Figure 7).

Figure 7. Enterprises BT

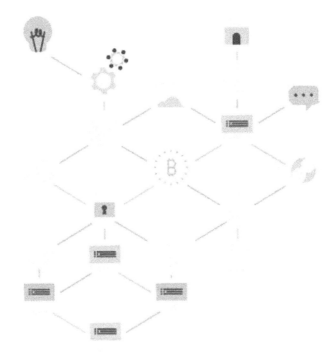

You too can join the ranks of businesses benefiting from decentralized technology by using platforms like Ethereum, Hyperledger Fabric, R3 Corda, Ripple, and Quorum.

3.2 Blockchain in Startups

Like Businesses, Startups do not face legacy system issues that could delay the integration of BT into their daily operations. Therefore, when you are a startup, you've got an advantage over established players in the market by using technology that addresses nearly all of the issues that prevent businesses from providing genuine value to both internal and external stakeholders.

With all of its parts, Blockchain for New companies can do more than just build a fence around all of the processes that a startup needs to handle more frequently than an established organization, such as managing a decentralized team and creating contracts between various stakeholders given in Fig. 6.

There is seldom a procedure that is not affected by decentralization when discussing the integration of BT inside a startup ecosystem. This is a great opportunity for entrepreneurs who want to attract capital or just make a name for themselves as industry innovators.

Figure 8. BT Startup

3.3 Blockchain Solutions to Digital Business

The business world is entering the most revolutionary era thanks to BT, as forward-thinking companies, inventors, and investors embrace blockchain (Kathirvel et al., 2021a) solutions to promote transparency and trust. Let us determine which Blockchain solution is most suitable for your organization, ranging from developing mobile applications to facilitating international transactions.

3.3.1 Blockchain in Business Transactions

Transactions are at the heart of every industry you examine because they are the most fundamental business operation. In addition to its widespread use, the problems with transactions are also industry-wide: a lack of safety (Subramaniam et al., 2021b), a lack of clearness, and a lack of subsidiarity. For each of these problems, BT offers a standard solution. These are the various ways that Blockchain for Transactions can make a difference, regardless of the industry that is being closely examined.

a. **Enhanced Openness and Security of Data.** Virtual distributed ledgers, or blockchains, are devoid of all these drawbacks. Transactions are kept in a structured manner, encrypted, and unchangeable. All nodes can access them, but they cannot be changed.
b. **Getting Rid of Middlemen.** Miners work tirelessly to solve mathematical puzzles (Kathirvel et al., 2021c) and confirm blockchain transactions, with no involvement from third parties for mediation or verification. Once the calculations are finished, the transaction is validated and then added to the distributed ledger.
c. **Effectiveness in Communities.** One of the biggest advantages of BT is the speed at which settlements can be finalized.

3.3.2 Blockchain in Mobile Business Apps

BT mobile application manufacturing is changing and being disrupted in many ways as a result of new technologies and use cases, but there are (Kathirvel et al., 2021d) still a number of areas where the sector is still behind, including high advertising costs, inconsistent in-app purchase procedures, and the app approval process (Khalaf et al., 2022). Let's shed a little illumination about the way BT is applied in apps to address these enduring problems facing the mobile app market (Selvaraj Naveneethan et al., 2022).

3.3. App Approval Process

By putting approval policies and apps on a public ledger that is accessible for public scrutiny, the integration of BT into app creation breaks the dominance of the Play Store and App Store.

3.3.1 In-App Acquisition

When it comes to in-app purchases, consumers are initially charged by the app store for permitting in-app transactions on their platform (Kathirvel et al., 2021e). After that, they incur additional costs from the debit or credit card they use to make the purchase, such as transaction fees and processing fees. All of these reductions in a user's in-app purchases typically total more than thirty percent; this is something that can be easily averted by using cryptocurrency payments with no transaction costs.

3.3.2 Expensiveness of Advertising

Decentralizing the ad platforms allows one to cut out the middlemen and lower transaction costs by increasing transparency throughout the entire process (Kathirvel et al., 2021f). These are just a few instances of how Blockchain technology (Kathirvel et al., 2021g). can be used to further streamline the mobile app market.

4. THEORETICAL FINDING IN BLOCKCHAIN SECURITY SOLUTIONS

Blockchain security can protect and render tamper-proof a variety of corporate operations because to its decentralization, encryption, and immutability features. The combination of blockchain technology (Kathirvel et al., 2024h) with security will significantly influence and contribute to the protection of data protection, data transparency, infrastructure security (Kathirvel et al., 2021h), and the password-free economy (Kathirvel et al., 2024c). This is just a summary of the various ways blockchain technology may help secure your company; to learn more about how blockchain (Kathirvel et al., 2024g) can protect your mobile app company.

All in all, what matters most is how much it will cost you to use Blockchain technology, which has the potential to make you a disruptive force in the industry (Kathirvel et al., 2024f). Services related to the development of blockchain (Kathirvel et al., 2024i) are most frequently obtained by startups and large companies from reputable development firms (Kathirvel and Naren, 2024d), whose staff of professionals may assist in connecting your company with a decentralized ecosystem.

4.1 Factors Affecting Blockchain App Development

The following factors affecting the BT app development Cost are

Blockchain App Category

A. Cryptocurrency Based Solution
B. Non-Cryptocurrency Based Solutions

4.2 App Services for Blockchain

4.2.1 Digital-Wallet

A distributed decentralized ledger capable of removing a single point of failure in the Internet of Things ecosystem and safeguarding all device data against manipulation and collusion ICO Development of Smart Contracts Distributed Ledger Technology

4.2.2. Crypto-Market

These thus are the variables that affect the price of developing a blockchain app. As promised, let us now introduce you to the Blockchain App Development Cost Estimate's numerical values. The sort of Blockchain service you use will also affect the cost factor (Yongcong Fang et al., 2022).

5. DISCUSSION OF CASE STUDIES: 3D BIOPRINTING

By making it possible to create biological tissues and organs that function (Andreas et al., 2022), 3D bioprinting, a rapidly developing technology, has the potential to transform the field of tissue engineering (Weiping et al., 2021). Living cells and biomaterials are layer-by-layer deposited during the procedure to produce intricate 3D structures that resemble the architecture of natural tissue. It is essential for tissue regeneration and organ transplantation to be able to accurately control the spatial distribution of cells and extracellular matrix (ECM) elements to create structures with certain mechanical and biological qualities.

5.1 3D Bioprinting

The bioprinter itself, the bio-inks (materials used to print the cells and ECM), and the living cells are three important elements in the 3D bioprinting process (Murphy et al., 2014). Inkjet-based and extrusion-based bioprinters are the two primary categories into which they can be divided (Earnest et al., 2021). Although extrusion-based printers utilize pneumatic or mechanical pressure to extrude bio-ink through a tiny nozzle, ink jet-based printers use thermal or piezoelectric technologies to expel droplets of bio-ink onto a substrate. Depending on the application, both types of printers offer advantages and disadvantages (Ibrahim et al., 2015).

Natural polymers like collagen and hyaluronic acid, synthetic polymers like polycaprolactone and polyethylene glycol, and mixtures of these materials can all be used to create bio-inks (Kang et al., 2016). The final tissue construct's desirable mechanical and biological qualities (Kathirvel et al., 2023b), as well as the bio ink's suitability for printing with living cells, all influence the choice of bio-ink.

Living cells are essential to the 3D bioprinting process because they give the tissue construct its useful qualities. Stem cells, primary cells, immortalized cell lines, and other sources can all be used to create new cells. Because different cell types have varied qualities and functions, the selection of cell type relies on the particular application. For instance, (Barron et al., 2004) stem cells are valuable in regenerative medicine applications because they can develop into many cell types. Primary cells, which are separated straight from tissues, are more faithful to the original tissue and are capable of producing physiological responses that are more precise. Although immortalized cell lines, which are produced from cancer cells, are frequently employed in research (Kathirvel & Naren, 2024), they may not be acceptable for use in therapeutic settings because of tumorigenic potential

Cell separation and preparation, bio-ink preparation, the printing of the tissue construct, and post-printing processing are typical processes in the 3D bioprinting process. Incubation, which encourages cell division and tissue growth, as well as mechanical and/or chemical treatments to enhance the construct's mechanical qualities, are all examples of post-printing processing (Francoise Marga & Karoly Jakab, 2012).

While 3D bioprinting technology has made significant progress in recent years, there are still many challenges that need to be addressed before it can be widely adopted for clinical applications. These include improving the resolution and speed of printing, optimizing the choice and composition of bio-inks, and ensuring the viability and functionality of printed cells. Additionally, ethical and regulatory considerations must be taken into account when developing 3D bio-printed tissues and organs for transplantation.

5.2 Techniques and Materials Used in 3D Bioprinting

Due to its potential to completely change tissue engineering and regenerative medicine, the topic of 3D bioprinting (Andreas et al., 2022) is s still in its infancy but has recently attracted a lot of interest. By layer-by-layer depositing cells, biomaterials, and growth factors, this method produces intricate three-dimensional (3D) structures that closely resemble the structure and functionality of natural tissues and organs. Here are the various methods and supplies utilized in 3D bioprinting.

5.2.1 Techniques

A. Inkjet bioprinting: This method uses a customized inkjet printer to precisely deposit cells and biomaterials onto a substrate. To produce a 3D structure, the printer produces cell and biomaterial droplets that are ejected onto the substrate layer by layer (Andreas et al., 2022). Because of its capacity to generate high-resolution structures with exact control over cell arrangement, this approach is widely employed (Vivian et al., 2020).

B. Extrusion-based bioprinting: This method extrudes a bio-ink made of cells, a hydrogel, or another biomaterial through a nozzle to create a three-dimensional structure. To build complicated structures, the nozzle has three-dimensional movement capabilities. This method is frequently employed because it can print substantial structures with high cell densities (Michael et al., 2022).

Bioprinting with a laser concentrates energy into a small area of a substrate that has been covered in cells and biomaterials. A 3D structure is produced as a result of the energy fusing and solidifying the cells and biomaterials. This method is very helpful for printing highly cell-viable, high-resolution structures (Chung et al., 2020) (see Fig. 1).

5.2.2 Materials

5.2.2.1 Hydrogels: Due to their capacity to offer cells a 3D environment in which to grow and develop, hydrogels are frequently employed as bio-inks in 3D bioprinting. Hydrogels can be made to support particular cell types (Earnest et al., 2021) and can imitate the mechanical characteristics of natural tissues (Wang et al., 2020).

5.2.2.2 Decellularized extracellular matrix (DECM): is produced by eliminating cells from tissues and organs and leaving the extracellular matrix in its place (ECM). To provide a scaffold for cells to grow and differentiate, this ECM can be employed as a bio-ink. Cell attachment, proliferation, and differentiation have all been demonstrated to be supported by ECM (Yiwei Wang et al., 2021).

5.2.2.3 Synthetic polymers: In 3D bioprinting, synthetic polymers like poly (lactic-co-glycolic acid) (PLGA) and polycaprolactone (PCL) are frequently utilized as biomaterials. To construct hybrid scaffolds, these materials can be mixed with different biomaterials and tailored to imitate the mechanical characteristics of native tissues (Pengfei Liu et al., 2022).

3D bioprinting is an intriguing field that is fast developing and has exciting potential in a wide range of applications, including regenerative medicine, drug screening, and disease modeling. The functionality, accuracy, and resolution of 3D bioprinted structures are being actively improved by researchers through the development of novel materials and methods. With further development, 3D bioprinting might be essential in solving some of the biggest problems in biology and medicine.

5.3 Current Applications of 3D Bioprinting

The creation of tailored medicine is a promising area for 3D bioprinting (Qing Gao & Zhenjie Liu, 2017). Patient-specific tissues and organs that can be utilized for drug testing and other medical procedures can be made via 3D bioprinting. Researchers showed the possibility of 3D bio-printing for producing liver and heart tissue models that may be used to assess drug toxicity and efficacy (Advincula et al., 2021).

In the area of regenerative medicine, 3D bioprinting (Qing Gao & Zhenjie Liu, 2017) has vital uses as well. Researchers can produce intricate tissues and organs using 3D bioprinting that can be utilized to treat or replace diseased or damaged tissues. Researchers created a 3D bio-printed scaffold that could support the development of cartilage tissue (Xu et al., 2020). The potential for treating a wide range of medical diseases with the ability to build such sophisticated tissues is great.

Personalized medicine, regenerative medicine, and 3D bio-printing (Qing Gao & Zhenjie Liu, 2017) have all been applied to the planning and practice of surgical procedures. Surgeons can plan surgeries and create plans for reducing risks and maximizing outcomes using 3D-printed replicas of patient-specific organs. Researchers showed the value of 3D (Zhaoguo Xue et al., 2022) bio-printed models for preoperative planning in heart surgery (Cyrus et al., 2021).

3D bioprinting offers a lot of potential for the future of medicine as its applications continue to grow. 3D bioprinting has the potential to completely alter how we approach medical care and treatment with further research and development.

Figure 9. 3D Bioprinting

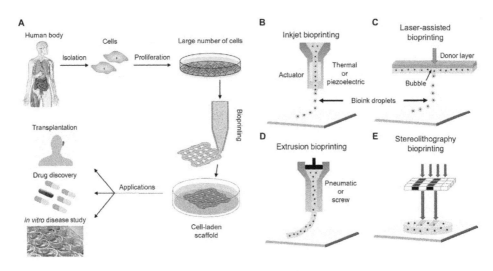

5.4 Quality Control in 3D Bioprinting

A crucial component of 3D bioprinting is quality control, which makes sure that the printed tissues or organs have the appropriate structural and functional characteristics. The difficulties of quality control in 3D bioprinting (Qing Gao & Zhenjie Liu, 2017) have been addressed in recent years using a variety of strategies, from improved imaging techniques to machine learning algorithms explained in Figure 8.

The requirement to maintain high printing accuracy and precision are one of the fundamental problems in 3D bioprinting (Qing Gao & Zhenjie Liu, 2017). To do this, several researchers have looked into the use of real-time monitoring and feedback systems to change the printing parametrial- time based on the results seen. For instance, (Mahyar Alimian et al., 2020) suggested a vision-based monitoring system in a recent study that employs machine learning algorithms to analyze the printed structures (Gobinath, 2024g) in real time and modify the printing parameters as necessary. To achieve high printing accuracy and precision, (Shukla et al., 2022) presented an intelligent quality control system that combines computer vision, machine learning, and robots.

The requirement to guarantee the biological functionality of the printed tissues or organs is a crucial component of quality control in 3D bioprinting. This necessitates evaluating the printed cells' and tissues' vitality, morphology, and functionality. A non-invasive imaging method based on multi-photon microscopy was suggested

(Yu et al., 2020) in recent work to evaluate the extracellular matrix and cellular components of printed tissues. According to the study, the method could accurately determine whether printed cells and tissues were viable and what shape they took (Zhaoguo et al., 2022).

Several studies have looked into the use of quality control standards and guidelines for 3D bioprinting in addition to these methods. For instance, (Kangning Wang, 2021) emphasized the necessity for standardized protocols and guidelines for 3D bioprinting to ensure uniform and trustworthy results in a recent study. The assessment put up a set of criteria, including structural integrity, cellular organization, and biological functionality, that may be used to gauge the quality of printed tissues and organs.

To ensure that the printed tissues and organs satisfy the required standards in terms of structural and functional features, quality control is an essential component of 3D bioprinting. The accuracy, precision, and functioning of tissues and organs created by 3D bioprinting have recently increased because of developments in imaging methods, machine learning algorithms, and quality control standards (Gobinath, 2024).

Figure 10. Flowchart of 3D Bioprinting

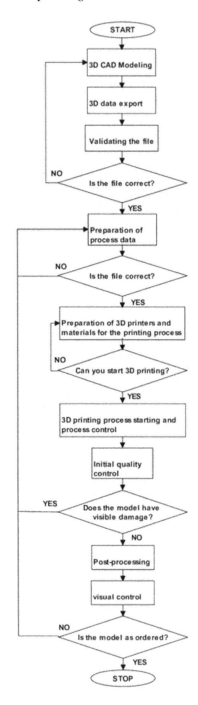

6. ADVANTAGES OF BT USING STARTUPS

Blockchain technology has been a game-changer for entrepreneurship, offering several advantages to startups and small businesses:

- **Decentralization:** Blockchain enables decentralized systems, removing the need for intermediaries. This allows entrepreneurs to create innovative business models without relying on centralized authorities.
- **Transparency and Security:** The immutable nature of blockchain ensures transparency and security in transactions. This fosters trust among customers and partners, which is crucial for startups aiming to establish credibility.
- **Smart Contracts:** These self-executing contracts automate and enforce agreements without intermediaries, reducing costs and potential disputes for entrepreneurs.
- **Funding through ICOs and STOs**: Initial Coin Offerings (ICOs) and Security Token Offerings (STOs) provide alternative fundraising methods for startups, allowing them to access global investment opportunities.
- **Supply Chain Management:** Blockchain (Yongcong et al., 2022) enhances traceability, reducing fraud and ensuring the authenticity of products, which is especially beneficial for startups dealing with supply chains.
- **Tokenization and Asset Management:** Entrepreneurs can tokenize assets, enabling fractional ownership and making traditionally illiquid assets more accessible to investors.
- **Data Security and Privacy:** Blockchain offers enhanced data security and privacy controls, enabling entrepreneurs to protect sensitive information effectively.

Despite these benefits, entrepreneurs should consider challenges such as scalability, regulatory uncertainties, and the need for technical expertise when implementing blockchain solutions. However, when integrated thoughtfully, blockchain can offer tremendous opportunities for entrepreneurial ventures.

Importance of Customer Engagement in Modern Marketing

Customer engagement is a crucial aspect of modern marketing strategies, as it helps build brand loyalty, drive sales, and foster long-term customer relationships. In today's competitive marketplace, businesses must go beyond traditional advertising to connect with their audience on a deeper level. Customer engagement is directly linked to brand loyalty and advocacy, as engaged customers develop a strong affinity for a brand, leading to repeat purchases and positive word-of-mouth referrals.

By cultivating meaningful interactions, businesses can create brand ambassadors who champion their products or services, amplifying their reach and influence. Customer engagement is also closely tied to customer satisfaction and retention, as when customers feel valued and appreciated, they are more likely to remain loyal and continue doing business with the brand (Kathirvel et al., 2024a).

Customer engagement is a crucial tool for businesses to improve their products, services, and customer experience. Engaged customers provide valuable feedback through surveys, reviews, and social media interactions, which can inform strategic decision-making and product development. By listening to their audience and acting on their feedback, businesses can demonstrate commitment to continuous improvement and customer-centricity, strengthening their competitive position. Additionally, customer engagement drives sales and revenue growth, as engaged customers are more likely to make purchases, upgrade to premium offerings, and participate in upsell and cross-sell opportunities (Khan & Iqbal, 2020).

7. FUTURE RESEARCH DIRECTION

A gap analysis is vital for identifying opportunities and enhancing a company's customer engagement efforts, with important objectives outlining specific areas to focus on.

- Evaluate existing engagement metrics, such as social media interactions, email open rates, and customer satisfaction scores, to understand the current state of customer engagement.
- Compare engagement metrics against industry benchmarks and competitors to identify areas of strength and weakness.
- Conduct market research and customer surveys to gain insights into the preferences, behaviors, and expectations of the target audience regarding engagement strategies and channels.
- Assess the effectiveness of existing technology and tools for customer engagement, such as CRM systems, marketing automation platforms, and social media management tools, to identify gaps and opportunities for improvement.
- Analyze the effectiveness of current content strategies in driving engagement, including the type, format, and distribution channels of content, to identify areas for optimization and refinement.
- Evaluate the quality and responsiveness of customer service and support channels, such as live chat, phone support, and self-service portals, to ensure they meet customer expectations for engagement and satisfaction.

- Assess the level of employee engagement and empowerment in delivering exceptional customer experiences, as engaged employees are more likely to drive positive customer interactions and outcomes.
- Explore emerging trends and technologies in customer engagement, such as artificial intelligence, chatbots, and personalized experiences, to identify opportunities for innovation and differentiation.

A gap analysis helps businesses understand their customer engagement state, identify improvement opportunities, and develop targeted strategies to enhance engagement and drive business growth in the modern marketing landscape. This comprehensive understanding informs the development of effective marketing initiatives.

8. CONCLUSION

Blockchain is a distributed database that is shared by multiple system nodes. The reason it is named Blockchain is that it gathers data in encrypted blocks that are connected to other sets of blocks to create a virtual chain. These days, businesses use blockchain technology and its various features, like as ICOs and smart contracts, for a variety of objectives that are related to their daily operations. Because of these built-in characteristics, blockchain is now used in a number of sectors, including Real Estate, Finance, Agriculture field, Healthcare sector, Education Institutions, Design and Manufacturing unit, and Retail shopping, etc. The article titled Blockchain Beyond Cryptocurrencies provides a thorough explanation of the various use cases and areas of BT. A promising innovation, 3D bioprinting has the potential to completely change the landscape of regenerative medicine. Yet, there are possible concerns linked with its use, such as problems with quality control, just like with any technology. Artificial intelligence (AI) has become a potent tool for enhancing 3D bioprinting quality control in recent years. To guarantee the security and effectiveness of produced tissues and organs, AI quality control plays a crucial role in 3D bioprinting. AI is going to play an increasingly significant role in advancing the caliber and dependability of 3D bioprinting technology as the field of regenerative medicine develops.

REFERENCES

Advincula, R. C., Dizon, J. R. C., Caldona, E. B., Viers, R. A., Siacor, F. D. C., Maalihan, R. D., & Espera, A. H.Jr. (2021). On the progress of 3D-printed hydrogels for tissue engineering. *MRS Communications*, 11(5), 539–553. 10.1557/s43579-021-00069-134367725

Alimian, M., Ghezavati, V., & Reza, T.-M. (2020). New integration of preventive maintenance and production planning with cell formation and group scheduling for dynamic cellular manufacturing systems. *Journal of Manufacturing Systems*, 56, 341–358. Advance online publication. 10.1016/j.jmsy.2020.06.011

Andreas, I. (2022). Three-dimensional bioprinting in medical surgery, 3D Printing: Applications in Medicine and Surgery. https://science.sciencemag.org/content/338/6109/921

Ayyaswamy, K. (2024b). Enhancing Digital Technology Planning, Leadership, and Management to Transform Education. In Bhatia, M., & Mushtaq, M. T. (Eds.), *Navigating Innovative Technologies and Intelligent Systems in Modern Education* (pp. 1–9). IGI Global. 10.4018/979-8-3693-5370-7.ch001

Barron, J. A., Wu, P., Ladouceur, H. D., & Ringeisen, B. R. (2004). Biological laser printing: a novel technique for creating heterogeneous 3-dimensional cell patterns. Biomed Microdevices. https://pubmed.ncbi.nlm.nih.gov/15320636/

Chung, J. J., Im, H., Kim, S. H., Park, J. W., & Jung, Y. (2020). Toward Biomimetic Scaffolds for Tissue Engineering: 3D Printing Techniques in Regenerative Medicine. Front. Bioeng. Biotechnol. https://www.frontiersin.org/articles/10.3389/fbioe.2020.586406/full

Cyrus, W. (2021). A fluid-supported 3D hydrogel bioprinting method. *Biomaterials*, 276, 121034. Advance online publication. 10.1016/j.biomaterials.2021.121034

Earnest, P. (2021). 3D Bioprinting of Vascularized Tissues for in vitro and in vivo Applications. Front Bioeng Biotechnol. https://www.ncbi.nlm.nih.gov/pmc/articles/PMC8158943/

Fang, Guo, Liu, Xu, Mao, Mo, Zhang, Ouyang, Xiong, & Sun. (2022). Advances in 3D Bioprinting. *Chinese Journal of Mechanical Engineering: Additive Manufacturing Frontiers*. 10.1016/j.cjmeam.2022.100011

Gao, Q., Liu, Z., Lin, Z., Qiu, J., Liu, Y., Liu, A., Wang, Y., Xiang, M., Chen, B., Fu, J., & He, Y. (2017). 3D Bioprinting of Vessel-like Structures with Multilevel Fluidic. *ACS Biomaterials Science & Engineering*, 3(3), 399–408. Advance online publication. 10.1021/acsbiomaterials.6b00064333465937

Gobinath, V., Ayyaswamy, K., & Kathirvel, N. (2024). Information Communication Technology and Intelligent Manufacturing Industries Perspective: An Insight. *Asian Science Bulletin*, 2(1), 36–45. 10.3923/asb.2024.36.45

Gobinath, V. M., Kathirvel, A., Rajesh Kanna, S. K., & Annamalai, K. (2024). Chapter 5: Smart Technology in Management Industries: A Useful Perspective. Artificial Intelligence Applied to Industry 4.0. Wiley Publisher. https://www.wiley.com/en-us/Topics+in+Artificial+Intelligence+Applied+to+Industry+4+0-p-978139421611610.1002/9781394216147.ch5

Ibrahim & Hospodiuk. (2015). Current advances and future perspectives in extrusion-based bioprinting. 10.1016/j.biomaterials.2015.10.076

Kang, H. W., Lee, S., Ko, I., Kengla, C., Yoo, J. J., & Atala, A. (2016). A 3D bioprinting system to produce human-scale tissue constructs with structural integrity. *Nature Biotechnology*, 34(3), 312–319. Advance online publication. 10.1038/nbt.341326878319

Kathirvel, A. (2024a). Applications of Serverless Computing: Systematic Overview. In Aluvalu, R., & Maheswari, U. (Eds.), *Serverless Computing Concepts, Technology and Architecture* (Vol. 221-233). IGI Global. 10.4018/979-8-3693-1682-5.ch014

Kathirvel, A. (2024b). Innovation and Industry Application: IoT-Based Robotics Frontier of Automation in Industry Application. In Satishkumar, D., & Sivaraja, M. (Eds.), *Internet of Things and AI for Natural Disaster Management and Prediction* (pp. 83–105). IGI Global. 10.4018/979-8-3693-4284-8.ch004

Kathirvel, A., & Gobinath, V. M. (2024). Chapter 1: A Review on Additive Manufactuing in Industrial. *Modern Hybird Machince and Super Finishing Process: Technology and Application*. CRC Publiser/Chapman and Hall. https://books.google.co.in/books/about/Modern_Hybrid_Machining_and_Super_Finish.html?id=I_VW0AEACAAJ&source=kp_book_description&redir_esc=y

Kathirvel, A., Gopinath, V. M., Naren, K., Nithyanand, D., & Nirmaladevi, K. (2024). Manufacturing Smart Industry Perspective an Overview. *American Journal of Engineering and Applied Sciences*, 17(1), 33–39. 10.3844/ajeassp.2024.33.39

Kathirvel, A., & Maheswaran, C. P. (2023). Chapter 8: Enhanced AI-Based Intrusion Detection and Response System for WSN. Artificial Intelligence for Intrusion Detection Systems. CRC Publiser/Chapman and Hall. https://www.taylorfrancis.com/chapters/edit/10.1201/9781003346340-8/enhanced-ai-based-intrusion-detection-response-system-wsn-kathirvel-maheswaran10.1201/9781003346340-8

Kathirvel, Maheswaran, Subramaniam, & Naren. (2023). Chapter 25: Quantum Computers Based on Distributed Computing Systems for the Next Generation: Overview and Applications. Quantum Computers Based on Distributed Computing Systems for the Next Generation, Handbook of Research on Quantum Computing for Smart Environments. IGI Global. 10.4018/978-1-6684-6697-1.ch025

Kathirvel, A., & Naren, A. K. (2024a). Critical Approaches to Data Engineering Systems Innovation and Industry Application Using IoT. In *Critical Approaches to Data Engineering Systems and Analysis*. IGI Global. 10.4018/979-8-3693-2260-4.ch005

Kathirvel, A., & Naren, A. K. (2024b). Diabetes and Pre-Diabetes Prediction by AI Using Tuned XGB Classifier. In Khang, A. (Ed.), *Medical Robotics and AI-Assisted Diagnostics for a High-Tech Healthcare Industry* (pp. 52–64). IGI Global., 10.4018/979-8-3693-2105-8.ch004

Kathirvel, A., Naren, K., Nithyanand, D., & Santhoshi, B. (2024). Overview of 5G Technology: Streamlined Virtual Event Experiences. *Advances of Robotic Technology*, 2(1), 1–8. 10.23880/art-16000109

Kathirvel, A., Rithik, G., & Naren, A. K. (2024). Chapter 11: Automation of IOT Robotics. In *Predicting Natural Disasters with AI and Machine Learning*. IGI Global. 10.4018/979-8-3693-2280-2.ch011

Kathirvel, A., Subramaniam, M., Navaneethan, S., & Sabarinath, C. (2021). Improved IDR Response System for Sensor Network. Journal of Web Engineering, 20(1), 53–88. 10.13052/jwe1540-9589.2013

Kathirvel, A., Sudha, D., Naveneethan, S., Subramaniam, M., Das, D., & Kirubakaran, S. (2022). AI Based Mobile Bill Payment System using Biometric Fingerprint. *American Journal of Engineering and Applied Sciences*, 15(1), 23–31. 10.3844/ajeassp.2022.23.31

Khalaf, A. T., Wei, Y., Wan, J., Zhu, J., Peng, Y., Abdul Kadir, S. Y., Zainol, J., Oglah, Z., Cheng, L., & Shi, Z. (2022). Bone Tissue Engineering through 3D Bioprinting of Bioceramic Scaffolds: A Review and Update. *Life (Chicago, Ill.)*, 12(6), 903. Advance online publication. 10.3390/life1206090335743934

Liu, P., Zhao, R., Li, H., Zhu, T., Li, Y., Wang, H., & Zhang, X.-D. (2022). Near-infrared-II deep tissue fluorescence microscopy and application. Nano Research. https://www.ncbi.nlm.nih.gov/pmc/articles/PMC8126817/

Marga & Jakab. (2012). Toward engineering functional organ modules by additive manufacturing. 10.1088/1758-5082/4/2/022001

Michael, Pramanik, Basak, Prakash, & Shankar. (2022). Progress and challenges on extrusion based three-dimensional (3D) printing of biomaterials. 10.1016/j.bprint.2022.e00223

Murphy, S., & Atala, A. (2014). 3D bioprinting of tissues and organs. *Nature Biotechnology*, 32(8), 773–785. 10.1038/nbt.295825093879

Naveneethan, Madhan, & Kathirvel. (2022). Identifying and Eliminating the Misbehavior Nodes in the Wireless Sensor Network. In Soft Computing and Signal Processing. ICSCSP 2021. Advances in Intelligent Systems and Computing, vol 1413. Springer International Publishing. 10.1007/978-981-16-7088-6_36

Shukla, A. K., Gao, G., & Kim, B. S. (2022). Applications of 3D Bioprinting Technology in Induced Pluripotent Stem Cells-Based Tissue Engineering. Micromachines. https://www.ncbi.nlm.nih.gov/pmc/articles/PMC8876961/

Subramaniam, M., Kathirvel, A., Sabitha, E., & Anwar Basha, H. (2021). Modified Firefly Algorithm and Fuzzy C-Mean Clustering Based Semantic Information Retrieval. Journal of Web Engineering, 20(1), 33–52. 10.13052/jwe1540-9589.2012

Sudha, D., & Kathirvel, A. (2022). An Intrusion Detection System to Detect and Mitigating Attacks Using Hidden Markov Model (HMM) Energy Monitoring Technique. Stochastic Modeling an Applications, 26(3), 467-476.

Sudha, D., & Kathirvel, A. (2023a). The performance enhancement of Aodv protocol using GETUS. International Journal of Early Childhood Special Education, 15(2), 115-125. DOI:10.48047/INTJECSE/V15I2.11

Sudha, D., & Kathirvel, A. (2023b). The effect of ETUS in various generic attacks in mobile ad hoc networks to improve the performance of Aodv protocol. International Journal of Humanities, Law, and Social Sciences, 9(1), 467-476.

Vivian, Real, & Palma. (2020). A new method for 3D printing drugs: melting solidification printing process. 10.2217/3dp-2020-0024

Wang, C., Zhang, L., Qin, T., Xi, Z., Sun, L., Wu, H., & Li, D. (2020). 3D printing in adult cardiovascular surgery and interventions: a systematic review. J Thorac Dis. https://www.ncbi.nlm.nih.gov/pmc/articles/PMC7330795/

Wang, K. (2021). Unified distributed robust regression and variable selection framework for massive data. *Expert Systems with Applications*, 186, 115701. Advance online publication. 10.1016/j.eswa.2021.115701

Wang, Y., Deng, L., Zheng, L., & Robert, X. (2021). Temporal convolutional network with soft thresholding and attention mechanism for machinery prognostics. *Journal of Manufacturing Systems*, 60, 512–526. Advance online publication. 10.1016/j.jmsy.2021.07.008

Xu, S., Jiang, M., Lu, Q., Gao, S., Feng, J., Wang, X., He, X., Chen, K., Li, Y., & Ouyang, P. (2020). Properties of Polyvinyl Alcohol Films Composited With Hemicellulose and Nanocellulose Extracted From Artemisia selengensis Straw. *Frontiers in Bioengineering and Biotechnology*, 8, 980. Advance online publication. 10.3389/fbioe.2020.0098032984277

Xue, Z., Jin, T., Xu, S., Bai, K., He, Q., Zhang, F., Cheng, X., Ji, Z., Pang, W., Shen, Z., Song, H., Shuai, Y., & Zhang, Y. (2022). Assembly of complex 3D structures and electronics on curved surfaces. *Science Advances*, 8(32), 32. 10.1126/sciadv.abm692235947653

Yu, C. (2020). A Perspective on Using Machine Learning in 3D Bioprinting. *International Journal of Bioprinting*, 253. https://www.ncbi.nlm.nih.gov/pmc/articles/PMC7415853/32782987

Zhou, W., Li, X., Duan, H., & Pengyu, L. (2021). Multi-Material Integrated Three-Dimensional Printing of Cylindrical Li-Ion Battery. Journal of Manufacturing Science and Engineering. https://www.sciencedirect.com/science/article/pii/S1226086X17301559

KEY TERMS AND DEFINITIONS

Blockchain: A blockchain is a public ledger that is digitally distributed and decentralized via a network.

Consensus: The fundamental goal of the consensus algorithm, which is to come to a consensus and guarantee the network's dependability, can be created with a variety of features. a mechanism that certifies a transaction as genuine.

Ethereum: With smart contract features, Ethereum is a decentralized blockchain. The platform's native coin is called ether. Bitcoin has a larger market capitalization than ether among cryptocurrencies. Open-source software is what it is. 2013. Programmer Vitalik Buterin came up with the idea for Ethereum.

Ledger: A distributed ledger that uses blocks of data connected in a chain using encryption, making it difficult to change.

Scalability: Scalability refers to the capacity of a system to maintain or improve its performance under increasing operational demands.

Security: In order to ensure confidentiality, integrity, and availability, security refers to the use of procedures and policies to protect systems, data, and information against damage, interruption, or unauthorized access. It is an all-encompassing strategy to guard against possible dangers and weaknesses across a range of sectors.

Sharding: A single dataset can be sharded and distributed among several databases, allowing it to be kept on several servers.

Chapter 8
Entrepreneurial Strategies for Sustainable Performance of Small and Medium Enterprises in Unprecedent Times

Mugove Mashingaidze
Great Zimbabwe University, Zimbabwe

Segolame Kalayakgosi
Department of Business Management, BA ISAGO University, Botswana

Ephraim Govere
Department of Business Management, BA ISAGO University, Botswana

ABSTRACT

This chapter aims at examining the effect of entrepreneurial strategies on the sustainable performance of SMEs in Harare, Zimbabwe. The target population of the study was 3000 manufacturing SMEs in Harare. Data were drawn from a sample of 302 manufacturing SMEs using cross-sectional primary data collected from Harare. The chapter employed both descriptive and inferential statistics to estimate the effect of entrepreneurial strategies on sustainable performance. The results revealed that entrepreneurial marketing strategy, strategic partnerships, technological innovation, and business model innovation are positively and significantly related to sustainable performance. Hence, the chapter concludes that SMEs need to employ sustainable entrepreneurial strategies to enhance their survival in a rapidly changing marketing environment. SMEs with a strong orientation towards entrepreneurial orientation

DOI: 10.4018/979-8-3693-3518-5.ch008

have better sustainable performance in developing countries. The major limitation of the chapter is that it focuses only on manufacturing SMEs in Harare, Zimbabwe.

BACKGROUND, AIM AND, RATIONALE

Small and medium companies (SMEs) have play a crucial role in driving economic growth, generating employment opportunities, reducing poverty, and promoting social integration worldwide (Makanyeza et al, 2023; Mashingaidze et al, 2021a). Mabenge et al. (2020) assert that a (SME) sector is a crucial indicator of a prosperous and resilient economy. According to Bushe et al. (2018), the majority of developed countries account their growth and wealth on SMEs. These enterprises are recognized for their ability to solve socio-economic challenges (Makanyeza et al., 2023; Bomani et al., 2022). Despite their critical role in socio-economic development, SMEs face challenges due to insufficient financial, technical, and managerial resources, which can adversely affect their performance (Suchek et al., 2023; Lew et al., 2023). Santoro et al. (2018) encourage SME owner/managers to adopt strategies to consistently navigate change and uncertainty to achieve growth and a competitive edge. The rise in environmental turbulence is primarily caused by market instability, shifts in client demands, and rapid technical advancements (Ferraris et al., 2019). The unstable operating environment provides a plethora of opportunities and dangers to small enterprises (Gathungu & Baariu, 2018).

An increasing corpus of study has attempted to examine how SMEs might improve their performance in this situation. Entrepreneurship experts propose that the performance of SMEs is influenced by entrepreneurial strategies (Arzubiaga et al., 2018; Ferreira et al., 2021). According to the contingency management theory, this chapter suggests that when faced with new and unfavourable business situations, SMEs should respond effectively and be capable of adapting to the situation (Kusa et al., 2022). Additionally, the capacity to adapt their entrepreneurial strategies may be necessary due to shifts in market conditions (Suder et al., 2022). Prior research suggests that SMEs have the option to implement many strategies, such as entrepreneurial orientation (EO) (Covin & Wales, 2019), strategic alliances (Suchek and Franco, 2023), business model innovation (Lew et al., 2023), and technology innovation (Mabenge et al., 2020). These strategies demonstrate the capacity of SMEs to proactively navigate an uncertain environment by employing decision-making, strategic planning, management philosophy, and entrepreneurial behaviour (Zighan et al., 2022). Nevertheless, Bocken and Short (2021) emphasize the importance for SMEs to incorporate sustainability into their entrepreneurial strategies. SMEs have a significant role in the advancement of society, the economy, and the generation of environmental benefits (Bocken & Short, 2021). Therefore, it is imperative for SMEs to strategically incorporate and practically execute the Sustainable Development Goals (SDGs) in their business operations. This will establish them as advocates for sustainability (Dana et al. 2022).

This chapter aims to examine the impact of entrepreneurial techniques on the sustainable performance of SMEs in Zimbabwe. The United Nations' 2030 Agenda for Sustainable Development, introduced in 2015, acknowledges the significant role that private organizations play in addressing global development and environmental issues by accomplishing the (SDGs). The SMEs sector possesses specialized skills, knowledge, managerial capabilities, financial resources, and a willingness to take on high-risk endeavours, all of which can contribute significantly to achieving this global objective (Musabayana et al. 2020). Therefore, the present interest lies in examining how SMEs enhance their ability to achieve the SDGs. Considering that SMEs constitute the foundation of many global economies (Bomani et al., 2018), it is crucial to ensure their long-term viability in order to promote job creation and foster economic growth (Mabenge et al., 2020). In the past five years, multiple academic studies have been done to investigate the challenges faced by SMEs in attaining the SDGs (Oppong, 2022; Govindan et al., 2020). This chapter assesses the strategic options available to SMEs in developing nations to improve their sustainability in the midst of several problems. This chapter acknowledges that SMEs are the backbone of most national economies. It also recognizes that while individual SMEs may have limited economic, social, and environmental influence, their collective impact can surpass that of large enterprises when considered together.

LITERATURE REVIEW

Small and Medium Enterprises in Developing Countries

The importance of SMEs in the developing African countries cannot be emphasized. Small and medium-sized enterprises in Africa account for more than 90% of all businesses and make up more than 50% of the Gross National Product (GDP) (Mabenge et al., 2020). The significance of SMEs in the development process of developing nations continues to be a significant subject in policy discussions (Bushe, 2019). African nations undergoing growth have implemented policies that support the advancement of SMEs (Mashingaidze et al., 2021b). SMEs constitute the bulk of firms in these countries, therefore exerting a substantial influence on the economy. Musabayana et al. (2022) note that SMEs in developing countries are encountering difficult and unsuitable conditions, which impede their performance (Mabenge et al., 2020). Lukhele and Soumonni (2020) add that SMEs face several obstacles that hamper their long-term viability notwithstanding their positive impact on development.

The high percentage of business failure in emerging nations, particularly in Africa, is alarming, as only a minority of firms are able to endure beyond a few months to one year (Mashingaidze et al., 2021b). Bhorat et al. (2018) claims that the mortality rate of SMEs in African countries is still unacceptably high, with a failure rate of five out of seven new businesses during their first year. Based on data from the World Bank in 2012, Chad has a failure rate of 65% and is regarded as one of the most difficult countries to do business in due to inadequate regulatory frameworks. In Uganda, over 33% of newly established businesses cease operations within the first year, while in South Africa, the failure rate varies between 50% and 95% depending on the particular industry (Bushe, 2019). Bowmaker-Falconer and Herrington (2020) conducted a study in 2015 which found that 75% of SMEs in South Africa do not succeed in becoming established businesses. This failure rate is the highest in the world for the country.

This position provides the Zimbabwean government with an extra chance to acknowledge that the success of SMEs requires both significant support and the encouragement of their entrepreneurial ability. SMEs in developing countries need the ability to identify and carry out entrepreneurial activities in order to take advantage of new opportunities (Lew et al., 2023). By adopting this strategy, they are able to create new enterprises, leading to a lasting competitive edge (Covin & Wales, 2019). SME owners/managers should adopt sustainable entrepreneurial strategies that efficiently address the social, economic, and environmental impacts in order to guarantee the continued success of their enterprises beyond a five-year period.

Unprecedented Times and Uncertainty

In an uncertain economic environment, the future growth and stability of enterprises may be jeopardized by an increased probability of conflicts among managers (Covin & Wales, 2019). In addition, the existence of uncertainty in the operating environment increases the financial and operational risks that firms encounter (Gilchrist et al., 2014). According to the real-option theory, when an investment is irreversible, the heightened uncertainty in the business environment increases the value and attractiveness of the firm's choice to delay. Enterprises are compelled to either halt or reduce their investments (Hambrick, 1983). Therefore, it is essential to consider the influence of the interaction between environmental unpredictability and entrepreneurial strategy on the long-term sustainability of a business. Economic or political shocks can have a detrimental impact on the long-term sustainability of SMEs by increasing uncertainty. This could potentially increase the likelihood of strategic failures. Xu et al. (2021) established that heightened uncertainty leads to a decrease in the overall economic activity of firms. Zimbabwe is a developing nation that regularly revises its economic policies in accordance with shifting economic circumstances and political objectives (Musabayana et al., 2020). Hence, businesses in Zimbabwe, including SMEs are much more worried about their future financial viability (Mashingaidze et al., 2022). Consequently, individuals are growing more prudent and increases their inclination to engage in risky entrepreneurial behaviours. In addition, they are augmenting the quantity of cash they retain as a precautionary measure. Based on real options theory, this chapter contends that in the face of increasing economic uncertainty, corporations that initially embarked on high-risk expansion strategies are more inclined to decrease their investments.

Entrepreneurial Strategies

The ability of a firm to survive in a critical scenario is heavily reliant on the promptness with which its management and owners react to the problem and implement corrective measures (Storey, 2016). This could involve modifying the company's business strategy to align with the shifts in the external or internal organizational environment and integrating novel solutions and activities (Thorgren & Williams, 2020). The subsequent sections delineate the four entrepreneurial strategies that small and medium-sized enterprises (SMEs) might embrace within a crisis.

Technological Innovations

In the current business environment, it is essential for all business organizations to prioritize innovation in order to succeed (Haddoud et al., 2023). From a SME perspective, innovation often refers to the creation of novel products or processes that can more effectively and profitably fulfil client demands compared to existing ones (Radicic & Petković, 2023). SMEs must establish and strengthen their internal digital skills. (Makanyeza et al, 2023).) In order to effectively adapt to market changes and enhance their innovation performance and growth. In today's highly competitive and disruptive business landscape, SMEs need to employ big data, the Internet of Things (IoT), artificial intelligence (AI), and digital twins to improve their capacity to endure and bounce back from crises (Scoutto et al., 2021). SMEs can gain numerous advantages by adopting business cloud solutions, with the most significant one being the ability to access comprehensive platforms that can potentially provide enough advantage to compete with larger businesses (Coleman et al., 2016; Giotopoulos et al., 2022). Big Data analytics empower small and medium-sized enterprises (SMEs) to utilize large volumes of data to get valuable insights, enhance operational efficiency, and improve their marketing strategies (Haddoud et al., 2023). The Internet of Things (IoT) enables the continuous monitoring of data, the ability to foresee maintenance needs, and the efficient allocation of resources. This leads to enhanced productivity and reduced costs for SMEs (Radicic & Petković, 2023). Generative pre-trained transformers (GPT) technology enables chatbots to provide scalable customer support solutions and enhance engagement for SMEs (Haddoud et al., 2023; Cordero et al., 2022). Data analysis algorithms can assist SMEs in extracting important insights from their data, hence facilitating improved decision-making and fostering innovation (Davenport & Harris, 2018; Liu et al., 2020).

Entrepreneurial Marketing

Entrepreneurial marketing (EM) is the integration of entrepreneurship with marketing (Zahara et al., 2023). EM relates to the marketing efforts carried out by entrepreneurs or owners/managers of entrepreneurial enterprises (Stokes, 2000). Small and micro enterprises with an entrepreneurial mind-set require a marketing approach that is tailored to their limited resources and lack of operational infrastructure (Al-Weshah et al., 2022). Therefore, implementing effective EM strategy can give SMEs a competitive advantage in the market, despite their limited resources (Al-Shaikh & Hanaysha, 2023; Ferreira et al., 2019; Sadiku-Dushi et al., 2019). Entrepreneurial businesses prioritize innovative marketing tactics due to limited resources that may prevent them from meeting industry norms (Alqahtani & Uslay, 2020). Therefore, SMEs can improve their digital marketing strategies and stay ahead in an uncertain environment by swiftly responding to customer input and adjusting to evolving market trends (Al-Shaikh & Hanaysha, 2023; Sia et al., 2016).

EM is increasingly being recognized as a strategic approach for businesses functioning in uncertain conditions (Rezvani & Fathollahzadeh, 2020; Whalen et al., 2015). However, EM in small entrepreneurial firms faces several problems, including constraints on internal resources, high business costs, challenges in dealing with government entities, limited credibility and reputation (Al-Weshah, 2019), uncertainty in demand (Kakeesh et al., 2024), resource limitations and limited customer loyalty or market share (Rezvani & Fathollahzadeh, 2020), a shortage of management skills coupled with unprofessional management practices (Al-Shaikh & Hanaysha, 2023).

Strategic Networks and Partnerships

Strategic alliances are long-term partnerships between two or more organizations that work together to share resources, expertise, and knowledge in order to strengthen their positions in the market (Kiprotich et al., 2015). Strategic partnerships are increasingly crucial in the strategic blueprints of both prominent and lesser-known firms (Nwokocha & Madu, 2020). In order to gain a competitive advantage, SMEs need to actively develop and nurture connections with their supply chain partners, consumers, and competitors. It is important for SMEs to acknowledge the essential role of strategic alliances in this process (Audretsch et al., 2023). McDowell et al. (2016) establish a comparison between this association and marriage, in which the connected parties maintain separate identities but work together towards a common goal in response to technical and/or market-related factors.

The longevity of an alliance is contingent upon the contentment, proficiency, commitment, and harmony among the parties involved (Widjajanti et al., 2023). Strategic alliances offer a flexible solution when the circumstances are uncertain (Prabhudesai & Prasad, 2017). SMEs heavily rely on external networks to obtain crucial resources including knowledge, technology, funding, and skills. These networks are essential for SMEs to innovate and expand their operations (Suchek & Franco, 2023). Networks can serve as a means of enhancing resilience and sustainability (Wikaningrum et al. 2020). SMEs can establish several types of partnerships outside the traditional buyer-supplier dynamic, which demonstrate the connections they build with their ecosystem through the exchange of products, services, assets, as well as through open innovation and collaboration. These networks include production networks, knowledge and innovation networks (including universities and providers of knowledge-intensive commercial services), and strategic partnerships (OECD, 2022). These kinds of cooperation are significant for facilitating the access of SMEs to strategic resources. They share both unique but common characteristics with production and innovation networks (Andrenelli, et al., 2019).

Business Model Innovations

Enterprises have the ability to obtain valuable new technologies by adopting suitable business strategies (Foss & Saebi, 2017). A business model (BM) is a theoretical structure that delineates the core principles upon which a business functions (Massa et al., 2017). In order to maintain competitiveness and long-term viability, organizations must enhance their business model and efficiently oversee it through performance management (Shao et al., 2019). Clauss (2017) asserts that business model innovations (BMI) involves the act of altering and restructuring a company's value proposition, value generation, and value capture. Each firm possesses a BMI that comprises three interrelated elements: value proposition, value generation, and value capture (Clauss, 2017; Clauss et al., 2019). The dimension of value proposition pertains to the breadth of solutions that a company provides and the manner in which it communicates those solutions to clients (Lew et al., 2023). Value creation is the act of a corporation generating value by utilizing its resources and competencies along its value chain (Albats et al., 2023). Value capture refers to the process by which a corporation translates its value offer into revenue (Clauss, 2017). Kim and Min (2015) suggest that using a new business model to restructure assets can potentially result in opportunities to achieve a competitive edge.

Sustainable Performance

Business sustainability encompasses the ability to efficiently manage and incorporate economic, social, and environmental practices and issues in order to safeguard the growth and longevity of an organization (Sun et al., 2018). In order to achieve sustainable performance, SMEs should match their objectives with the changes in both their internal operations and the external business environment. They should also aim for a state of dynamic equilibrium, where they can adapt and respond effectively to these fluctuations (Moore & Manring, 2008). In order to attain corporate sustainability, business practitioners must give priority to the execution of socially and ecologically acceptable activities (Rezaee, 2016).

Establishing effective and practical metrics is crucial for evaluating and overseeing sustainable performance in SMEs (Shuaib et al., 2014). Utilizing appropriate metrics to assess sustainable performance in SMEs aims to enhance the decision-making process (Sartal et al., 2020). This chapter employs both absolute and relative measurements to assess the sustainable performance of SMEs. Absolute metrics assess the entire sustainability performance of a company, while relative metrics evaluate the sustainability performance in a specific area (such as water usage) relative to the performance in another area (such as total production) (Ahi & Searcy, 2015). Modern small and medium-sized enterprises (SMEs) must enhance their economic, environmental, and social sustainability in order to thrive. In this chapter, indicators related to financial benefits (such as profit and revenue), costs (including labour cost and material cost), and market competitiveness (such as R&D spending, on-time delivery, lead time, and product quality) were utilized to assess and control the economic sustainability performance of SMEs.

Khan et al. (2015) argue that there is a lack of research that has attempted to map the global study of sustainable performance. Empirical research on the social, economic, and environmental dimensions of sustainability is scarce, as indicated by the small number of studies conducted (Malesios et al., 2018; Rezaee, 2016). Further empirical evidence is necessary to establish the association between sustainability and the improvement of a company's value and performance, while considering its core components. Existing research indicates a scarcity of adequate empirical studies that have investigated the whole concept of business sustainability in SMEs (Malesios et al., 2018).

Hypotheses Development

This chapter explores the impact of business strategy on the sustainable performance of SMEs in an unstable environment, specifically in Zimbabwe. In this regard four entrepreneurial strategies are examined, the adoption of entrepreneurial marketing strategy, strategic partnerships, technological innovation, and business model innovation.

Technological Innovations and Sustainable Performance

In today's highly competitive and rapidly changing world, innovation has become an essential requirement for all modern businesses aiming to survive and thrive, especially in the face of repeating crises (Radicic & Petković, 2023). Experts concur that the adoption and execution of particular innovative strategies, in line with a certain level of entrepreneurial skill, can contribute to the survival and durability of numerous SMEs (Parrilli et al., 2023; Galvan-Martínez et al., 2019; Mabenge et al., 2023). In their study Abdilahi et al. (2017) found that innovation has a substantial impact on the performance and growth of SMEs. Kijkasiwat and Phuensane (2020) discovered that the performance of SMEs in Eastern Europe and Central Asia may be enhanced by implementing both product and process innovation, which leads to an expansion in market share. Nevertheless, the correlation is contingent upon the magnitude of the company and its ability to get financial resources. According to Guo et al. (2018), research and development (R&D) expenditure improves the performance of Chinese manufacturing enterprises that employ product differentiation. The study conducted by Carrasco-Carvajal et al. (2022) shows that SMEs benefit from technological innovation because it enables them to adapt and succeed in highly volatile and constantly evolving competitive settings. In their study, Muharam et al. (2020) discovered a clear and direct relationship between process innovation, market innovation, and the financial performance of organizations. Bodlaj and Čater (2019) found that promoting higher levels of innovation enables SMEs to achieve better financial performance. Consequently,

H_1: Technological innovation is positively related to the sustainable performance of SMEs.

Entrepreneurial Marketing and Sustainable Performance

The increased uncertainty in the marketplace renders conventional marketing methods ineffectual in enhancing organizations' success. Prior studies indicate that incorporating an entrepreneurial mind-set in the formulation of marketing strategies enables organizations to recognize and exploit profitable opportunities, while effectively managing their marketing initiatives and operations (Fard & Amiri, 2018; Al-Weshah, 2019; Whalen et al., 2015). Several scholars argue that EM has the capacity to improve organizational performance more effectively in uncertain situations (e.g., Eggers, Hansen, & Davis, 2012; Rezvani & Fathollahzadeh, 2020; Sadiku-Dushi et al., 2019;; Al-Shaikh & Hanaysha, 2023; Sia et al., 2016; Whalen et al. 2015; Al-Weshah, 2019). Kakeesh et al. (2024) examined the interplay between entrepreneurial marketing orientation and business performance among SMEs in the services sector. The results underscore a significant positive relationship between entrepreneurial marketing orientation and business performance among service-based SMEs in Jordan. Alqahtani and Uslay (2020) established that EM is one of the critical determinants of growth and survival of the SME sector. Hence,

H_2: Entrepreneurial marketing is positively related to the sustainable performance of SMEs.

Strategic Networks and Partnership and Sustainable Performance

The significance of both domestic and international connections for the functioning of SMEs is extensively demonstrated (OECD, 2019). Competing necessitates SMEs to acquire strategic resources such as financing, skills, and innovation assets. Due to their limited size, SMEs typically have to seek these resources outside rather than relying on internal pooling and internalization (OECD, 2021). The extent and calibre of connections also play a crucial role in generating external economies of scale (Wikaningrum et al., 2020). Recent evidence indicates that SMEs that achieve sustained high growth and improved performance and productivity have used strategies to invest in expanding their network (OECD, 2022). According to the study conducted by Wikaningrum et al. (2020), it was shown that strategic partnerships have a beneficial and substantial impact on the productivity of companies. Adam et al. (2021) found that forming partnerships has a positive impact on a corporation's ability to get resources and improve performance. Onoshakpor et al. (2020) argue that increased collaboration among entrepreneurs offers various benefits, including enhanced access to information, funding, social and financial support, and knowledge exchange, which is substantiated by empirical research. Ghauri et al. (2023) show that cooperatives provide opportunities for SMEs to share information and knowledge through social and community events. Consequently,

H$_3$: Strategic partnership is positively related to the sustainable performance of SMEs.

Business Model Innovation and Sustainable Performance

There is a growing consensus among scholars on the correlation between BMI and firm performance (Salfore et al., 2023). In their study, Chen et al. (2019) discovered that BMI has a more significant influence on enhancing a company's success when compared to innovation in product and process. Cucculelli and Bettinelli (2015) emphasized that implementing innovative changes to a company's business strategy is associated with favourable results in terms of venture success. Clauss et al. (2019) found that using creative approaches in BMI improves firm performance, leading to better economic outcomes. Hagiu and Wright (2015) argue that two organizations with identical resources, assets, and digital technologies might exhibit vastly different business performance due to variations in their business models. According to Wirtz (2019), numerous distinguished experts have acknowledged and emphasized the correlation between BMI and a company's business performance. Thus,

H$_4$: Business model innovation is positively related to the sustainable performance of SMEs.

METHODOLOGY

The objective of the chapter is to investigate the relationship between entrepreneurial strategies and the sustainable performance of SMEs. The chapter adopted a positivist philosophy and employed a quantitative research approach. In addition, the study employed a cross-sectional survey methodology. In order to achieve this, the researcher employed primary data acquired from owner/managers of SMEs in Harare, Zimbabwe. The study targeted a cohort of 3000 SMEs situated in Harare. The study sample consisted of 341 manufacturing SMEs, which were selected using simple random sampling method, as determined by the Krejcie & Morgan (1970) table. The study excluded start-ups since they did not have a well-developed and sustainable strategy in place (Mashingaidze et al., 2021). In this study, a manufacturing SME is defined as a legally registered, non-subsidiary, autonomous business that transforms raw materials and components into products with greater worth. These businesses hire between 6 and 75 employees, generate an annual revenue of little more than US$1,000,000, and have assets valued at no more than US$1,000,000. The segmentation of SMEs into distinct sub-sectors in this chapter was determined based on the categorization system created by the Zimbabwean government.

Data was collected using standardized questionnaires. The questionnaire consisted of three separate sections: background information, entrepreneurial strategy, and sustainable performance. The background information portion included characteristics such as gender, respondents' position in the company, level of education, age of the enterprise, manufacturing sub-sector, and the number of employees. Information on entrepreneurial techniques was acquired by employing particular constructs from proven instruments. The questionnaire comprises of 6 modified items from Clauss (2017) for assessing Business Model Innovation (BMI), 6 items from Makanyeza and Dzvuke (2015) for evaluating technological innovations, 6 items from Morrish et al. (2010) for assessing entrepreneurial marketing, and 6 items from Nwokocha and Madu (2020) for assessing strategic network and partnership. The rating for each item is measured on a scale ranging from 1 (representing strongly disagreement) to 5 (representing strong agreement). Khan et al. (2015) recommended using social, environmental, and economic variables to collect data on the sustainable performance of SMEs. The sustainable performance statistics were evaluated using a Likert-type scale, which consisted of response alternatives ranging from 1 (strongly disagree) to 5 (strongly agree). The evaluation of SME performance relied on subjective views due to the proprietors' general unwillingness to disclose their company's financial information to other parties (Mashingaidze et al., 2021). Therefore, owners/managers were asked to assess their company's performance relative to prominent competitors in the industry for the previous two years.

Prior to collecting data, we obtained informed consent from all individuals included in our research. The consent form clearly outlined the purpose of the study and guaranteed that all collected data would be kept confidential and used solely for academic purposes. The questionnaire contained a cover page that offered a thorough explanation of the study's goals and assured the confidentiality of data collection. After two weeks, follow-up actions were taken to remind the beneficiaries. A total of 302 fully completed questionnaires were collected, resulting in an effective response rate of 88.6%.

FINDINGS AND DISCUSSION

Descriptive Statistics

This section presents and analyses demographic data, reliability data and the description of the construct.

Demographic Data

The demographic information of the study participants is presented in Table 1 below.

Table 1. Sample Description (n=302)

Item	Distribution	Frequency (f)	Percentage (%)
Gender	Male	271	89.7
	Female	31	10.3
	Total	302	100.0
Age	18-31	71	23.6
	31-41	119	39.4
	42-52	81	26.9
	Above 52	31	10.3
	Total	302	100.0
Responsibility	Owner	207	68.5
	Manager	95	31.5
	Total	302	100.0
Level of education	High school and below	108	35.8
	Diploma	97	32.1
	Degree	70	23.2
	Postgraduate degree	27	8.9
	Total	302	100.0
Manufacturing sector	Food products	72	23.8
	Chemical & petroleum	43	14.2
	Wood & Furniture	93	30.8
	Clothing & footwear	36	12.0
	Metals	58	19.2
	Total	302	100.0
Age of firm	3-9	88	29.1
	10-15	91	30.2
	16-20	80	26.5
	21 and above	43	14.2
	Total	302	100.0
No. of employees	1-5	74	24.5
	6-20	153	50.7
	21-40	59	19.5

continued on following page

Table 1. Continued

Item	Distribution	Frequency (f)	Percentage (%)
	41-75	31	10.3
	Total	302	100.0

Source: SPSS Output (2024)

According to Table 1, SMEs that were managed by hired managers made up 68.5% of all the respondents, slightly above the percentage of SMEs led by their owners, which was 31.5%. The study participants consisted of 89.7% males and 10.3% females. Out of all the participants, 64.2% had completed tertiary education. Just 40.7% of them had been in business for over 16 years. SMEs were dispersed evenly throughout different sectors, with the furniture sector having the highest number of SMEs and the clothes and footwear sector having the lowest number.

Reliability Analysis

The results of the dependability analysis are presented in Table 2. Cronbach's alpha index was used to assess the reliability of the questionnaire. Moreover, the Cronbach's alpha test assesses the feasibility of conducting more advanced tests on the data (Saunders et al., 2019).

Table 2. Reliability Test Results

Measure	Number of Items	Alpha	Comment
Technological innovation	6	0.826	Very reliable
Entrepreneurial marketing	6	0.950	Very reliable
Strategic networks and partnerships	6	0.733	Reliable
Business model innovations	6	0.809	Very reliable
Sustainable performance	5	0.834	Very reliable
Total	**29**	**0.830**	**29**

Source: SPSS Output (2024)

Creswell (2016) states that a coefficient with a value above 0.7 is regarded as reliable. Each of the five constructs in this investigation had an Alpha value ranging from 0.733 to 0.950. The alpha index values indicate the highest level of internal consistency for entrepreneurial marketing (0.950), followed by business model innovations (0.809), sustainable performance (0.833), technological innovations (0.846), and strategic networks and partnerships (0.733). Furthermore, these findings illustrate that researchers were able to do further studies on the data due to the average alpha index of 0.8406.

Construct Description

Participants were instructed to indicate their level of agreement or disagreement with the statement using a rating scale ranging from 1 (indicating strong disagreement) to 5 (indicating strong agreement). Table 3 below presents the mean, average mean, and standard deviation for the Entrepreneurial strategies (ES) and Sustainable Performance (SP) constructs.

Table 3. Descriptive Statistics

Construct	Population	MN	Std Dev.	Avg Mean
Technological innovation	302	4.352	.791	
Entrepreneurial marketing	302	4.823	.832	
Strategic Partnerships	302	4.031	.861	
Business model innovations	302	4.336	.792	
Sustainable performance	302	4.763	.681	
The overall mean of all the constructs				4.461

Source: SPSS Output (2024)

A mean of 4.763 was found for sustainable performance, indicating that respondents strongly agreed that their enterprises have sustainable performance. The average mean for technological innovation produced a result of 4.352, indicating a high level of agreement. The mean for entrepreneurial marketing was 4.823, which leans toward very "certain" in terms of opinions about the respondent's entrepreneurial marketing behaviour. In regards to strategic partnerships, respondents concurred (mean of 4.031) that strong business alliances are crucial for their industry. Last but not least, a mean score of 4.336 for business model innovations was reported, indicating a very high tendency to innovate the business models. Despite displaying high levels of agreement, further analysis of the predictive effect of entrepreneurial strategy constructs on sustainable performance is crucial since overall sustainable performance and its predictors produced a mean of 4.461. The sections that follow evaluate the specific contributions made by each independent factor to the sustainable performance of SMEs in Zimbabwe.

HYPOTHESES TESTING

Technological Innovations and Sustainable Performance

Table 4 indicates an R-value of .692 implying that there is an above average strong and positive relationship between technological innovations and the sustainable performance of SMEs in Zimbabwe. Additionally, Table 4 displays an R^2 of .479, demonstrating that 47.9% of the sustainable performance of SMEs in Zimbabwe is due to technological innovations.

Table 4. Technological Innovations and Sustainable Performance Model Summary

Model	R	R Square	Adjusted R Square	Std. Error of the Estimate
1	.692[a]	.479	.432	.304

Source: SPSS Output (2024)

Table 5 shows the ANOVA results for regression coefficient. The results showed that technological innovations are statistically weighty in accounting for the sustainable performance of SMEs in Zimbabwe.

Table 5. Analysis of Variance for Technological Innovations and Sustainable Performance

Model		Sum of Squares	df	Mean Square	F	Sig.
1	Regression	77.910	1	3.268	231.472	.000[b]
	Residual	9.657	301	.102		
	Total	85.567	302			

a. Predictors: (Constant), Technological innovations
b. Dependent Variable: Sustainable performance
Source: SPSS Output (2024)

The Analysis of Variance shows that the model was a good fit for the data; ANOVA ($F(1, 301) = 231.472$, $p = .000$). The significance value 0.000 is less than 0.05 indicating that the model is statistically significant in forecasting of the sustainable performance. The predictor with low value <0.05 is a meaningful addition to a model. This study shows an $F_{(cal)} = 231.472 > F_{(critical)} = 1.96$ hence, the influence of technological innovations on the sustainable performance of SMEs was positive. These findings confirms the first hypothesis, which suggests a positive connection between technical innovation and the sustainable performance of SMEs, as evidenced by a significantly positive path coefficient. The findings imply that technological innovations play a crucial role in determining the success of a corporation in today's rapidly changing environment (Minhas & Sindakis, 2022). The study conducted by

Carrasco-Carvajal et al. (2022) demonstrates that SMEs derive advantages from technological innovation, as it allows them to adjust and thrive in highly turbulent and rapidly changing competitive environments. Therefore, these findings confirm previous empirical research on the impact of technology innovations on corporate success (Muharam et al., 2020; Minhas & Sindakis, 2022; Laidoune et al., 2022; Haudi et al., 2021; Liu et al., 2019).

Entrepreneurial Marketing and Sustainable Performance

Table 7 shows the regression results of the connection between entrepreneurial marketing and the sustainable performance of SMEs. The table displays an R-value of .802 confirming a strong and positive relationship between the independent and dependent variable. The study findings also showed that a coefficient of determination of .634, illustrates that 63.4% of the sustainable performance of SMEs can be explained entrepreneurial marketing. The adjusted R^2 was .784 indicates that 21.6% of sustainable performance is due to other external variables.

Table 7. Entrepreneurial Marketing and Sustainable Performance Model Summary

Model	R	R Square	Adjusted R Square	Std. Error of the Estimate
1	.802ª	.643	.784	.191

Source: SPSS Output (2024)

Table 8 below illustrates the ANOVA results for regression analysis coefficient. The findings show that entrepreneurial marketing is also statistically significant predictor of the sustainable performance of SMEs in Zimbabwe.

Table 8. Analysis of Variance for Entrepreneurial Marketing and Sustainable Performance

Model		Sum of Squares	df	Mean Square	F	Sig.
1	Regression	136.905	1	43.732	632.103	.000ᵇ
	Residual	8.420	301	2.057		
	Total	145.325	302			

a. Predictors: (Constant), Entrepreneurial marketing
b. Dependent Variable: Sustainable performance
Source: SPSS Output (2024)

Table 8 highlights that there is a significant link between entrepreneurial marketing and sustainable performance. The Analysis of Variance shows that the model was a good fit for the data; ANOVA (F (1, 301) = 632.103, p =.000.) The significance value 0.000 is less than 0.05 indicating that the model is statistically significant in forecasting the sustainable performance of SMEs in Zimbabwe. The study uncovered a positive correlation between entrepreneurial marketing and the long-term viability of SMEs in Zimbabwe. Therefore, the second hypothesis stating that "there is a positive correlation between entrepreneurial marketing and the sustainable performance of SMEs in Zimbabwe" is confirmed. This discovery is consistent with the viewpoint of Sadiku-Dushi et al. (2019), who contend that in dynamic markets, business professionals employ efficient entrepreneurial marketing strategies and techniques to enhance the worth of their companies by concentrating on client attraction, value generation, and innovation. Similarly, Morrish et al. (2010) believe that when there is greater uncertainty in the marketplace, traditional marketing strategies become less effective in improving the performance of organisations. Therefore, to improve their long-term effectiveness, SMEs require more innovative entrepreneurial marketing strategies (Rezvani & Fathollahzadeh, 2020; Sadiku-Dushi et al., 2019; Alqahtani & Uslay, 2020; Al-Shaikh & Hanaysha, 2023; Sia et al., 2016; Whalen et al. 2015; Al-Weshah, 2019).

Strategic Networks and Partnership and Sustainable Performance

Table 9 indicates an R-value of .402 implying that there is an above average strong and positive relationship between strategic networks and partnership and sustainable performance of SMEs in Zimbabwe. Additionally, Table 9 displays an R^2 of .162, demonstrating that 16.2% of the sustainable performance of SMEs in Zimbabwe is due to strategic networks and partnership. The adjusted R^2 was .354 indicates that 64.6% of sustainable performance is due to other external variables.

Table 9. Strategic Networks and Partnership and Sustainable Performance Model Summary

Model	R	R Square	Adjusted R Square	Std. Error of the Estimate
1	.402ª	.162	.354	.334

Source: SPSS Output (2024)

Table 9 shows the ANOVA results for regression coefficient. The results showed that strategic networks and partnership are statistically weighty in accounting for the sustainable performance of SMEs in Zimbabwe.

Table 9. Analysis of Variance for Strategic Networks and Partnership and Sustainable Performance

Model		Sum of Squares	df	Mean Square	F	Sig.
1	Regression	127.321	1	25.373	283.019	.000[b]
	Residual	9.732	301	.393		
	Total	137.053	302			

a. Predictors: (Constant), Strategic networks and partnership
b. Dependent Variable: Sustainable performance
Source: SPSS Output (2024)

Table 9 shows that strategic networks and partnership is significant in influencing the sustainable performance of SMEs. The Analysis of Variance shows that the model was a good fit for the data; ANOVA $(F (1, 301) = 283.019, p =.000.)$. The significance value 0.000 is less than 0.05 indicating that the model is statistically significant in forecasting the sustainable performance of SMEs. These findings donate support for the claim that strategic partnerships have a favourable impact on enhancing sustainable performance. Suchek and Franc (2023) assert that SMEs are particularly dependent from external networks to access strategic resources, such as knowledge, technology, finance or skills, and to innovate and grow. Prior research has confirmed the present findings, as exemplified by the study conducted by Wikaningrum et al. (2020), which demonstrated that strategic partnerships have a considerable influence on business productivity. Similarly, Adam et al. (2021) argue that forming partnerships results in the acquisition of technology and resources, which in turn enhances business performance. According to theory, stronger partnerships provide several advantages, including financial assistance and the exchange of expertise (Ghauri et al., 2023; Onoshakpor et al., 2020).

Business Model Innovation and Sustainable Performance

Table 10 shows the regression results of the connection between business model innovation and the sustainable performance of SMEs. The table displays an R-value of .764 confirming a strong and positive relationship between the independent and dependent variable. The study findings also showed that a coefficient of determination of .584, illustrates that 58.4% of the sustainable performance of SMEs can be explained business model innovation. The adjusted R^2 was .603 indicates that 39.7% of sustainable performance is due to other external variables.

Table 10. Business Model Innovation and Sustainable Performance Model Summary

Model	R	R Square	Adjusted R Square	Std. Error of the Estimate
1	.764[a]	.584	.603	.301

Source: SPSS Output (2024)

Table 11 below illustrates the ANOVA results for regression analysis coefficient. The findings show that business model innovation is also statistically significant predictor of the sustainable performance of SMEs in Zimbabwe.

Table 11. Analysis of Variance for Business Model Innovation and Sustainable Performance

Model		Sum of Squares	df	Mean Square	F	Sig.
1	Regression	89.076	1	31.425	534.392	.000[b]
	Residual	11.056	301	.091		
	Total	100.132	302			

a. Predictors: (Constant), Business model innovation
b. Dependent Variable: Sustainable performance
Source: SPSS Output (2024)

The Analysis of Variance shows that the model was a good fit for the data; ANOVA (F (1, 301) = 534.392, p =.000.) The significance value 0.000 is less than 0.05 indicating that the model is statistically significant in forecasting of the sustainable performance. The predictor with low value <0.05 is a meaningful addition to a model. This study shows an $F_{(cal)}$ = 534.392 > $F_{(critical)}$ = 1.96 hence, the influence of business model innovation on the sustainable performance of SMEs was positive.

Findings indicate that a BMI has a substantial and positive impact on the sustainable performance of SMEs. Thus, H_4 was confirmed. The study's findings confirm that innovating the BMI has a favorable impact on the sustainable performance of SMEs. Prior research has identified a direct correlation between BMI and the performance of companies (Salfore et al., 2023; Chen et al., 2019). Cucculelli and Bettinelli (2015) argue that making creative modifications to a company's business strategy is linked to beneficial outcomes in terms of venture performance.

CONCLUSIONS AND IMPLICATIONS

The study sought to investigate the influence of entrepreneurial methods on the long-term effectiveness of SMEs. This study was conducted due to the little and inconclusive empirical evidence about the relationship between entrepreneurial strategies and the sustainable performance of SMEs, particularly in developing countries such as Zimbabwe. Therefore, it was essential to conduct this study to enhance understanding of the relationship between specific strategies and the long-term success of SMEs. Acquiring this understanding is essential as it enables the formulation of efficient business strategies to prolong the survival of small and medium enterprises in volatile marketplaces.

The study found that technical innovation played a key role in explaining the sustainable performance of SMEs, based on the empirical investigation. The results suggest that SMEs with a significant focus on technical innovation exhibit superior long-term success in the manufacturing sector within the study area. This study makes a theoretical contribution to the existing literature by examining the impact of technical innovations on the sustainable performance of SMEs in Zimbabwe, with a specific focus on Harare. Previous research in this area has been insufficient. These findings are significant because they provide policymakers and SME owners with practical knowledge about the impact of technical innovation on the success of enterprises. Effective collaboration, communication, and Open Innovation (OI) among SMEs, government entities, and education and research institutions, is critical to sustainable performance of SMEs during an economic crisis. Thus, SMEs should enhance their proficiency in utilising digital technology. This includes enhancing their capacity to seamlessly integrate all customer channels digitally, optimising their ability to establish networks, and effectively managing clients in the digital realm. SMEs in Zimbabwe may benefit from policies that promote technology adoption and diffusion. The chapter recommends SME owner-managers should focus their attention and efforts on establishing and maintaining cooperative networks with external knowledge sources. This is a critical source of knowledge for innovation in SMEs, might provide an impetus to the process of digitalization, which is turn, could provide synergistic effects on innovation performance.

The findings indicated that entrepreneurial marketing has a favourable and substantial impact on sustainable performance in times of uncertainty. Therefore, it may be inferred that entrepreneurial marketing is a reliable indicator of corporate performance. Hence, managers should enhance their skills and refine the execution of entrepreneurial marketing strategies to attain sustainable marketing performance. Therefore, SMEs managers in unstable environments must employ inventive strategies in order to meet the needs and desires of their clients. SME owner/managers need to allocate their resources strategically to attain marketing success amidst market volatility and uncertainties. Entrepreneurial marketing will help them optimises resource allocation for their businesses, ensuring maximum impact and efficiency.

Findings revealed that forming strategic partnerships has a substantial and positive influence on the sustained performance of SMEs in the manufacturing industry. The study has implications for SMEs. SMEs have the option to form strategic partnerships as a means of thriving in highly competitive situations. In addition, the collaborations between partners yield synergistic effects that assist in mitigating the adverse impacts of environmental change, and uncertainty, and achieving effective growth (Cacciolatti et al., 2020). The chapter recommends SMEs in Zimbabwe to acquire a greater amount of high-quality information through networks and partnerships. The information, experiences and knowledge need to be effectively and efficiently used to build entrepreneurial resilience capacity.

Finally, it was disclosed that BMI has a favourable and substantial impact on the long-term performance of SMEs in Zimbabwe. Therefore, the study determined that BMI plays a crucial role in maintaining consistent performance, particularly under unpredictable conditions. This conclusion strengthens the existing body of research that suggests a company's BMI has a positive effect on its capacity to endure and recover from adversities (Niemimaa et al., 2019). The discovery has significant managerial ramifications for various parties. The study suggests that directing resources towards new solutions, to provide customer value in a dynamic business environment could improve the ability of SMEs to withstand challenges. The study shows that BMI may have even more strategic importance during times of uncertain conditions. Moreover, institutional policies might additionally enhance the SME's ability to cultivate their company models.

LIMITATIONS AND AREAS OF FURTHER RESEARCH

The study on entrepreneurial strategies for sustainable performance of SMEs in unprecedented times is an interesting topic. While the chapter contributes to knowledge and theory development, we provide three limitations and areas for further study. Firstly, the chapter applied a cross-sectional design in which data were collected within a specific time frame. This could negatively impact the comprehensiveness of the findings. Future studies could consider a longitudinal approach to capture the dynamic nature of entrepreneurial strategies in unprecedented times. Secondly, the chapter was quantitative in nature. This may limit deeper understanding of the relationship between entrepreneurial strategies and sustainable performance. Future studies could consider mixed-method approaches or case studies to provide a more holistic view. Lastly, the study focused on a single region, Harare, Zimbabwe only. This potentially limit the comparison of different entrepreneurial strategies. Further research could involve a comparative analysis across different regions or countries to identify best practices and potential differences in strategies.

REFERENCES

Achtenhagen, L., Melin, L., & Naldi, L. (2013). Dynamics of business models–strategizing, critical capabilities and activities for sustained value creation. *Long Range Planning*, 46(6), 427–442. 10.1016/j.lrp.2013.04.002

Adam, N. A., & Alarifi, G. (2021). Innovation practices for survival of small and medium enterprises (SMEs) in the COVID-19 times: The role of external support. *Journal of Innovation and Entrepreneurship*, 10(1), 15. 10.1186/s13731-021-00156-634075328

Ahi, P., & Searcy, C. (2015). An analysis of metrics used to measure performance in green and sustainable supply chains. *Journal of Cleaner Production*, 86, 360–377. 10.1016/j.jclepro.2014.08.005

Ahsan, M. (2020). Entrepreneurship and ethics in the sharing economy: A critical perspective. *Journal of Business Ethics*, 161(1), 19–33. 10.1007/s10551-018-3975-2

Al-Shaikh, M. E., & Hanaysha, J. R. (2023). A conceptual review on entrepreneurial marketing and business sustainability in small and medium enterprises. *World Development Sustainability*, 2, 100039. 10.1016/j.wds.2022.100039

Al-Weshah, G., Kakeesh, D., & Alhammad, F. (2022). Entrepreneurial marketing in Jordanian SMEs: Initiatives and challenges. Entrepreneurial rise in the Middle East and North Africa: The influence of quadruple helix on technological innovation, 67-91.

Al-Weshah, G. A. (2019). The current status of customer relationship management: Experience of small businesses in the Jordanian food industry. *International Journal of Electronic Customer Relationship Management*, 12(1), 1–20. 10.1504/IJECRM.2019.098975

Albats, E., Podmetina, D., & Vanhaverbeke, W. (2023). Open innovation in SMEs: A process view towards business model innovation. *Journal of Small Business Management*, 61(6), 2519–2560. 10.1080/00472778.2021.1913595

Alqahtani, N., & Uslay, C. (2020). Entrepreneurial marketing and firm performance: Synthesis and conceptual development. *Journal of Business Research*, 113, 62–71. 10.1016/j.jbusres.2018.12.035

Amisano, D. C., & Anthony, P. (2017). Relationship between ethical leadership and sustainability in small businesses. *Journal of Leadership, Accountability and Ethics*, 14, 76–90.

Andrenelli, A. (2019). Micro-evidence on corporate relationships in global value chains: The role of trade, FDI and strategic partnerships. https://www.wita.org/wp-content/uploads/2019/05/OECD-micro.pdf

Audretsch, D. B., Belitski, M., Caiazza, R., & Phan, P. (2023). Collaboration strategies and SME innovation performance. *Journal of Business Research*, 164, 114018. 10.1016/j.jbusres.2023.114018

Barney, J. B. (1994). How a firm's capabilities affect boundary decisions. *MIT Sloan Management Review*.

Bashir, M., Alfalih, A., & Pradhan, S. (2023). Managerial ties, business model innovation & SME performance: Moderating role of environmental turbulence. *Journal of Innovation & Knowledge*, 8(1), 100329. 10.1016/j.jik.2023.100329

Bebbington, J., & Unerman, J. (2018). Achieving the United Nations Sustainable Development Goals: An enabling role for accounting research. *Accounting, Auditing & Accountability Journal*, 31(1), 2–24. 10.1108/AAAJ-05-2017-2929

Becherer, R. C., Helms, M. M., & McDonald, J. P. (2012). The effect of entrepreneurial marketing on outcome goals in SMEs. *New England Journal of Entrepreneurship*, 15(1/2), 1–7. 10.1108/NEJE-15-01-2012-B001

Bocken, N. M., & Short, S. W. (2021). Unsustainable business models–Recognising and resolving institutionalised social and environmental harm. *Journal of Cleaner Production*, 312, 127828. 10.1016/j.jclepro.2021.127828

Bodlaj, M., & Čater, B. (2019). The impact of environmental turbulence on the perceived importance of innovation and innovativeness in SMEs. *Journal of Small Business Management*, 57(sup2), 417–435. 10.1111/jsbm.12482

Bomani, M., Derera, E., & Mashingaidze, M. (2022). Urbanisation and SME growth in a developing economy: Implications for policy. *Corporate Governance and Organizational Behavior Review*, 6(2), 123–133. 10.22495/cgobrv6i2p12

Bomani, M., Fields, Z., & Derera, E. (2018). Historical overview of small and medium enterprise policies in Zimbabwe. *Journal of Social Sciences*, 45(2), 113–129. 10.1080/09718923.2015.11893493

Bomani, M., Fields, Z., & Derera, E. (2019). The role of higher education institutions in the development of SMEs in Zimbabwe. International. *Journal of Business and Management Studies*, 11(2), 1–15.

Bromiley, P., & Rau, D. (2014). Towards a practice-based view of strategy. *Strategic Management Journal*, 35(8), 1249–1256. 10.1002/smj.2238

Cacciolatti, L., Rosli, A., Ruiz-Alba, J. L., & Chang, J. (2020). Strategic alliances and firm performance in startups with a social mission. *Journal of Business Research*, 106, 106–117. 10.1016/j.jbusres.2019.08.047

Carrasco-Carvajal, O., Castillo-Vergara, M., & García-Pérez-de-Lema, D. (2023). Measuring open innovation in SMEs: An overview of current research. *Review of Managerial Science*, 17(2), 397–442. 10.1007/s11846-022-00533-9

Chen, L. H., Hung, P., & Ma, H. W. (2020). Integrating circular business models and development tools in the circular economy transition process: A firm-level framework. *Business Strategy and the Environment*, 29(5), 1887–1898. 10.1002/bse.2477

Chopra, M., Singh, S. K., Gupta, A., Aggarwal, K., Gupta, B. B., & Colace, F. (2022). Analysis & prognosis of sustainable development goals using big data-based approach during COVID-19 pandemic. *Sustainable Technology and Entrepreneurship*, 1(2), 100012. 10.1016/j.stae.2022.100012

Cucculelli, M., & Bettinelli, C. (2015). Business models, intangibles and firm performance: Evidence on corporate entrepreneurship from Italian manufacturing SMEs. *Small Business Economics*, 45(2), 329–350. 10.1007/s11187-015-9631-7

Damoah, O. B. O. (2020). Strategic factors predicting the likelihood of youth entrepreneurship in Ghana: A logistic regression analysis. *World Journal of Entrepreneurship, Management and Sustainable Development*, 16(4), 389–401. 10.1108/WJEMSD-06-2018-0057

Dana, L. P., Salamzadeh, A., Hadizadeh, M., Heydari, G., & Shamsoddin, S. (2022). Urban entrepreneurship and sustainable businesses in smart cities: Exploring the role of digital technologies. *Sustainable Technology and Entrepreneurship*, 1(2), 100016. 10.1016/j.stae.2022.100016

Delery, J. E., & Roumpi, D. (2017). Strategic human resource management, human capital and competitive advantage: Is the field going in circles? *Human Resource Management Journal*, 27(1), 1–21. 10.1111/1748-8583.12137

Dess, G. G., & Lumpkin, G. T. (2005). The role of entrepreneurial orientation in stimulating effective corporate entrepreneurship. *The Academy of Management Perspectives*, 19(1), 147–156. 10.5465/ame.2005.15841975

Eggers, F., Hansen, D. J., & Davis, A. E. (2012). Examining the relationship between customer and entrepreneurial orientation on nascent firms' marketing strategy. *The International Entrepreneurship and Management Journal*, 8(2), 203–222. 10.1007/s11365-011-0173-4

Ferreira, J. J., Fernandes, C. I., & Ferreira, F. A. (2019). To be or not to be digital, that is the question: Firm innovation and performance. *Journal of Business Research*, 101, 583–590. 10.1016/j.jbusres.2018.11.013

Foss, N. J., & Saebi, T. (2017). Fifteen years of research on business model innovation: How far have we come, and where should we go? *Journal of Management*, 43(1), 200–227. 10.1177/0149206316675927

Galván-Martínez, D., Espejel, I., Arredondo-García, M. C., Delgado-Ramírez, C., Vázquez-León, C., Hernández, A., & Gutiérrez, C. (2020). Sustainability assessment in indigenous communities: A tool for future participatory decision making. *Stewardship of Future Drylands and Climate Change in the Global South: Challenges and Opportunities for the Agenda*, 2030, 197–214. 10.1007/978-3-030-22464-6_12

Gandy, D. L. (2015). Small business strategies for company profitability and sustainability. Academic Press.

Garbie, I. (2016). *Sustainability in manufacturing enterprises: Concepts, analyses and assessments for industry 4.0*. Springer. 10.1007/978-3-319-29306-6

Gerhart, B., & Feng, J. (2021). The resource-based view of the firm, human resources, and human capital: Progress and prospects. *Journal of Management*, 47(7), 1796–1819. 10.1177/0149206320978799

Ghauri, S., Mazzarol, T., & Soutar, G. N. (2023). Networking benefits for SME members of co-operatives. *Journal of Co-operative Organization and Management*, 11(2), 100213. 10.1016/j.jcom.2023.100213

Gherghina, S. C., Botezatu, M. A., Hosszu, A., & Simionescu, L. N. (2020). Small and medium-sized enterprises (SMEs): The engine of economic growth through investments and innovation. *Sustainability (Basel)*, 12(1), 347. 10.3390/su12010347

Gilchrist, S., Sim, J. W., & Zakrajšek, E. (2014). *Uncertainty, financial frictions, and investment dynamics (No. w20038)*. National Bureau of Economic Research. 10.3386/w20038

Gilmore, A. (2011). Entrepreneurial and SME marketing. *Journal of Research in Marketing and Entrepreneurship*, 13(2), 137–145. 10.1108/14715201111176426

Giotopoulos, I., Kontolaimou, A., & Tsakanikas, A. (2022). Digital responses of SMEs to the COVID-19 crisis. *International Journal of Entrepreneurial Behaviour & Research*, 28(7), 1751–1772. 10.1108/IJEBR-11-2021-0924

Gonzalez-Dıaz, R. R., Guanilo-Gomez, S. L., Acevedo-Duque, A. E., Campos, J. S., & Cachicatari Vargas, E. (2021). Intrinsic alignment with strategy as a source of business sustainability in SMEs. *Entrepreneurship and Sustainability Issues*, 8(4), 377–388. 10.9770/jesi.2021.8.4(22)

Govindan, K., Shankar, K. M., & Kannan, D. (2020). Achieving sustainable development goals through identifying and analyzing barriers to industrial sharing economy: A framework development. *International Journal of Production Economics*, 227, 107575. 10.1016/j.ijpe.2019.107575

Haddoud, M. Y., Kock, N., Onjewu, A. K. E., Jafari-Sadeghi, V., & Jones, P. (2023). Technology, innovation and SMEs' export intensity: Evidence from Morocco. *Technological Forecasting and Social Change*, 191, 122475. 10.1016/j.techfore.2023.122475

Hakala, H. (2011). Strategic orientations in management literature: Three approaches to understanding the interaction between market, technology, entrepreneurial and learning orientations. *International Journal of Management Reviews*, 13(2), 199–217. 10.1111/j.1468-2370.2010.00292.x

Hambrick, D. C. (1983). Some tests of the effectiveness and functional attributes of Miles and Snow's strategic types. *Academy of Management Journal*, 26(1), 5–26. 10.2307/25613210299037

Haudi, H., Rahadjeng, E., Santamoko, R., Putra, R., Purwoko, D., Nurjannah, D., Koho, I. R., Wijoyo, H., Siagian, A. O., Cahyono, Y., & Purwanto, A. (2022). The role of e-marketing and e-CRM on e-loyalty of Indonesian companies during Covid pandemic and digital era. *Uncertain Supply Chain Management*, 10(1), 217–224. 10.5267/j.uscm.2021.9.006

Helmers, C., & Rogers, M. (2010). Innovation and the survival of new firms in the UK. *Review of Industrial Organization*, 36(3), 227–248. 10.1007/s11151-010-9247-7

Hendijani Fard, M., & Seyyed Amiri, N. (2018). The effect of entrepreneurial marketing on halal food SMEs performance. *Journal of Islamic Marketing*, 9(3), 598–620. 10.1108/JIMA-12-2016-0097

Islam, D. M. Z. (2020). COVID-19 and Financial Performance of SMEs: Examining the nexus of entrepreneurial self-efficacy, entrepreneurial resilience and innovative work behavior. *Revista Argentina de Clínica Psicológica*, 29(3), 587.

Jachi, M., & Muchongwe, N. (2019). Economic sustainability of small to medium enterprises (SMEs) in Zimbabwe: The impact of fiscal incentives and entrepreneur work engagement. *Public Policy and Administration Research*, 9(12), 17–32.

Jiang, K., & Messersmith, J. (2018). On the shoulders of giants: A meta-review of strategic human resource management. *International Journal of Human Resource Management*, 29(1), 6–33. 10.1080/09585192.2017.1384930

Kakeesh, D. F., Al-Weshah, G. A., & Alalwan, A. A. (2024). Entrepreneurial marketing and business performance in SMEs: the mediating role of competitive aggressiveness. *Journal of Marketing Analytics*, 1-24.

Kaplan, S. (2008). Framing contests: Strategy making under uncertainty. *Organization Science*, 19(5), 729–752. 10.1287/orsc.1070.0340

Kaufman, B. E. (2015). Evolution of strategic HRM as seen through two founding books: A 30th anniversary perspective on development of the field. *Human Resource Management*, 54(3), 389–407. 10.1002/hrm.21720

Ketchen, D. J., Jr., Crook, T. R., Todd, S. Y., Combs, J. G., & Woehr, D. J. (2017). Managing human capital. *The Oxford Handbook of Strategy Implementation*, 283-311.

Khan, N. U., Wu, W., Saufi, R. B. A., Sabri, N. A. A., & Shah, A. A. (2021). Antecedents of sustainable performance in manufacturing organizations: A structural equation modeling approach. *Sustainability (Basel)*, 13(2), 897. 10.3390/su13020897

Kim, S. K., & Min, S. (2015). Business model innovation performance: When does adding a new business model benefit an incumbent? *Strategic Entrepreneurship Journal*, 9(1), 34–57. 10.1002/sej.1193

Kiprotich, S., Kimosop, J., Chepkwony, P. K., & Kemboi, A. (2015). Moderating effect of social networking on the relationship between entrepreneurial orientation and performance of small and medium enterprise in Nakuru County. Academic Press.

Krejcie, R. V., & Morgan, D. W. (1970). Determining sample size for research activities. *Educational and Psychological Measurement*, 30(3), 607–610. 10.1177/001316447003000308

Laidoune, A., Zid, C., & Sahraoui, N. (2022). Innovate and overcome resistance to change to improve the resilience of systems and organizations. *Journal of the Knowledge Economy*, 13(4), 1–16. 10.1007/s13132-021-00840-8

Lew, Y. K., Zahoor, N., Donbesuur, F., & Khan, H. (2023). Entrepreneurial alertness and business model innovation in dynamic markets: International performance implications for SMEs. *R & D Management*, 53(2), 224–243. 10.1111/radm.12558

Mabenge, B. K., Ngorora-Madzimure, G. P. K., & Makanyeza, C. (2020). Dimensions of innovation and their effects on the performance of small and medium enterprises: The moderating role of firm's age and size. *Journal of Small Business and Entrepreneurship*, 0(0), 1–25. 10.1080/08276331.2020.1725727

Mabenge, B. K., Ngorora-Madzimure, G. P. K., & Makanyeza, C. (2022). Dimensions of innovation and their effects on the performance of small and medium enterprises: The moderating role of firm's age and size. *Journal of Small Business and Entrepreneurship*, 34(6), 684–708. 10.1080/08276331.2020.1725727

Madison, K., Moore, C. B., Daspit, J. J., & Nabisaalu, J. K. (2022). The influence of women on SME innovation in emerging markets. *Strategic Entrepreneurship Journal*, 16(2), 281–313. 10.1002/sej.1422

Makanyeza, C., & Dzvuke, G. (2015). The influence of innovation on the performance of small and medium enterprises in Zimbabwe. *Journal of African Business*, 16(1-2), 198–214. 10.1080/15228916.2015.1061406

Makanyeza, C., Mabenge, B. K., & Ngorora-Madzimure, G. P. K. (2023). Factors influencing small and medium enterprises' innovativeness: Evidence from manufacturing companies in Harare, Zimbabwe. *Global Business and Organizational Excellence*, 42(3), 10–23. 10.1002/joe.22180

Malesios, C., Skouloudis, A., Dey, P. K., Abdelaziz, F. B., Kantartzis, A., & Evangelinos, K. (2018). Impact of small-and medium-sized enterprises sustainability practices and performance on economic growth from a managerial perspective: Modeling considerations and empirical analysis results. *Business Strategy and the Environment*, 27(7), 960–972. 10.1002/bse.2045

Mashingaidze, M., Bomani, M., & Derera, E. (2021). Entrepreneurial Orientation and Business Growth: COVID-19 Implications for SMEs in Zimbabwe. In *Handbook of Research on Strategies and Interventions to Mitigate COVID-19 Impact on SMEs* (pp. 226–244). IGI Global. 10.4018/978-1-7998-7436-2.ch011

Mashingaidze, M., Phiri, M. A., & Bomani, M. (2021). Strategy formulation amongst small and medium manufacturing enterprises: An emerging market case study. *Journal of Governance and Regulation*, 10(1).

Massa, L., Tucci, C. L., & Afuah, A. (2017). A critical assessment of business model research. *The Academy of Management Annals*, 11(1), 73–104. 10.5465/annals.2014.0072

McDowell, W. C., Peake, W. O., Coder, L., & Harris, M. L. (2018). Building small firm performance through intellectual capital development: Exploring innovation as the "black box". *Journal of Business Research*, 88, 321–327. 10.1016/j.jbusres.2018.01.025

Minhas, J., & Sindakis, S. (2021). Implications of social cohesion in entrepreneurial collaboration: A systematic literature review. *Journal of the Knowledge Economy*, 1–32.

Mion, G., & Loza Adaui, C. R. (2020). Understanding the purpose of benefit corporations: An empirical study on the Italian case. *International Journal of Corporate Social Responsibility*, 5(1), 4. 10.1186/s40991-020-00050-6

Moore, S. B., & Manring, S. L. (2009). Strategy development in small and medium sized enterprises for sustainability and increased value creation. *Journal of Cleaner Production*, 17(2), 276–282. 10.1016/j.jclepro.2008.06.004

Morrish, S. C., Miles, M. P., & Deacon, J. H. (2010). Entrepreneurial marketing: Acknowledging the entrepreneur and customer-centric interrelationship. *Journal of Strategic Marketing*, 18(4), 303–316. 10.1080/09652541003768087

Muharam, H., Andria, F., & Tosida, E. T. (2020). Effect of Process Innovation and Market Innovation on Financial Performance with Moderating Role of Disruptive Technology. *Systematic Reviews in Pharmacy*, 11(1).

Musabayana, G. T., & Mutambara, E. (2020). Zimbabwe's Indigenous SME policy Framework, a tool for black empowerment. Academic Press.

Musabayana, G. T., Mutambara, E., & Ngwenya, T. (2022). An empirical assessment of how the government policies influenced the performance of the SMEs in Zimbabwe. *Journal of Innovation and Entrepreneurship*, 11(1), 40. 10.1186/s13731-021-00192-2

Niemimaa, M., Järveläinen, J., Heikkilä, M., & Heikkilä, J. (2019). Business continuity of business models: Evaluating the resilience of business models for contingencies. *International Journal of Information Management*, 49, 208–216. 10.1016/j.ijinfomgt.2019.04.010

Nilsson, A., Magnusson, J., & Enquist, H. (2003). SME network practice: A qualitative study of network management practice and design implications for ICT-support. *Global Journal of Emerging Market Economies*, 12(2), 199-216.

O'Regan, N., Ghobadian, A., & Gallear, D. (2006). In search of the drivers of high growth in manufacturing SMEs. *Technovation*, 26(1), 30–41. 10.1016/j.technovation.2005.05.004

OECD. (2019). *OECD SME and Entrepreneurship Outlook 2019*. OECD Publishing., 10.1787/34907e9c-

OECD. (2021). *OECD SME and Entrepreneurship Outlook 2021*. OECD Publishing.

OECD. (2022). *Financing Growth and Turning Data into Business: Helping SMEs Scale Up, OECD Studies on SMEs and Entrepreneurship*. OECD Publishing. 10.1787/81c738f0-

Onoshakpor, C., Etuknwa, A., & Karamalla-Gaiballa, N. (2020). Strategic Flexibility and Organizational Resilience of Women Entrepreneurs' in Africa During The Covid-19 Pandemic. *Research Journal of Business and Management*, 7(4), 277–287. 10.17261/Pressacademia.2020.1324

Oppong, N. B. (2022). Sustainable development goals and small and medium enterprises: A comparative study of emerging economies and Sub-Saharan Africa. *Global Business Review*, 09721509221087848. 10.1177/09721509221087848

Ordonez-Ponce, E., & Weber, O. (2022). Multinational financial corporations and the sustainable development goals in developing countries. *Journal of Environmental Planning and Management*, 65(6), 975–1000. 10.1080/09640568.2022.2030684

Parrilli, M. D., Balavac-Orlić, M., & Radicic, D. (2023). Environmental innovation across SMEs in Europe. *Technovation*, 119, 102541. 10.1016/j.technovation.2022.102541

Prabhudesai, R., & Prasad, C. V. (2017). Antecedents of SME alliance performance: A multilevel review. *Management Research Review*, 40(12), 1261–1279. 10.1108/MRR-12-2016-0286

Radicic, D., & Petković, S. (2023). Impact of digitalization on technological innovations in small and medium-sized enterprises (SMEs). *Technological Forecasting and Social Change*, 191, 122474. 10.1016/j.techfore.2023.122474

Rezaee, Z. (2016). Business sustainability research: A theoretical and integrated perspective. *Journal of Accounting Literature*, 36(1), 48–64. 10.1016/j.acclit.2016.05.003

Rezvani, M., & Fathollahzadeh, Z. (2020). The impact of entrepreneurial marketing on innovative marketing performance in small-and medium-sized companies. *Journal of Strategic Marketing*, 28(2), 136–148. 10.1080/0965254X.2018.1488762

Sadiku-Dushi, N., Dana, L. P., & Ramadani, V. (2019). Entrepreneurial marketing dimensions and SMEs performance. *Journal of Business Research*, 100, 86–99. 10.1016/j.jbusres.2019.03.025

Salfore, N., Ensermu, M., & Kinde, Z. (2023). Business model innovation and firm performance: Evidence from manufacturing SMEs. *Heliyon*, 9(6), e16384. 10.1016/j.heliyon.2023.e1638437251443

Sartal, A., Bellas, R., Mejías, A. M., & García-Collado, A. (2020). The sustainable manufacturing concept, evolution and opportunities within Industry 4.0: A literature review. *Advances in Mechanical Engineering*, 12(5). 10.1177/1687814020925232

Schumpeter, J. A. (1942). *Socialism, capitalism and democracy*. Harper and Brothers.

Schwab, K., Samans, R., Zahidi, S., Leopold, T. A., Ratcheva, V., Hausmann, R., & Tyson, L. D. (2017, November). The global gender gap report 2017. *World Economic Forum*.

Shao, J., Aneye, C., Kharitonova, A., & Fang, W. (2023). Essential innovation capability of producer-service enterprises towards circular business model: Motivators and barriers. *Business Strategy and the Environment*, 32(7), 4548–4567. 10.1002/bse.3380

Shuaib, M., Seevers, D., Zhang, X., Badurdeen, F., Rouch, K. E., & Jawahir, I. S. (2014). Product sustainability index (ProdSI) a metrics-based framework to evaluate the total life cycle sustainability of manufactured products. *Journal of Industrial Ecology*, 18(4), 491–507. 10.1111/jiec.12179

Sia, S. K., Soh, C., & Weill, P. (2016). How DBS bank pursued a digital business strategy. *MIS Quarterly Executive*, 15(2).

Smith, H., Discetti, R., Bellucci, M., & Acuti, D. (2022). SMEs engagement with the Sustainable Development Goals: A power perspective. *Journal of Business Research*, 149, 112–122. 10.1016/j.jbusres.2022.05.021

Solow, R. M. (1994). Perspectives on growth theory. *The Journal of Economic Perspectives*, 8(1), 45–54. 10.1257/jep.8.1.45

Stoian, M. C., Rialp, J., & Dimitratos, P. (2017). SME networks and international performance: Unveiling the significance of foreign market entry mode. *Journal of Small Business Management*, 55(1), 128–148. 10.1111/jsbm.12241

Storey, D. J. (2016). *Understanding the small business sector*. Routledge. 10.4324/9781315544335

Suchek, N., & Franco, M. (2023). Inter-organisational cooperation oriented towards sustainability involving SMEs: A systematic literature review. *Journal of the Knowledge Economy*, 1–21. 10.1007/s13132-023-01196-x

Sun, H., Mohsin, M., Alharthi, M., & Abbas, Q. (2020). Measuring environmental sustainability performance of South Asia. *Journal of Cleaner Production*, 251, 119519. 10.1016/j.jclepro.2019.119519

Thorgren, S., & Williams, T. A. (2020). Staying alive during an unfolding crisis: How SMEs ward off impending disaster. *Journal of Business Venturing Insights*, 14, e00187. 10.1016/j.jbvi.2020.e00187

Valdez-Juárez, L. E., García-Pérez de Lema, D., & Maldonado-Guzmán, G. (2016). Management of knowledge, innovation and performance in SMEs. Interdisciplinary. *Journal of Information, Knowledge, and Management*, 11(4), 141–176.

Wang, Y. (2016). What are the biggest obstacles to growth of SMEs in developing countries?– An empirical evidence from an enterprise survey. *Borsa Istanbul Review*, 16(3), 167–176. 10.1016/j.bir.2016.06.001

Whalen, P., Uslay, C., Pascal, V. J., Omura, G., McAuley, A., Kasouf, C. J., & Gilmore, A. (2016). Anatomy of competitive advantage: Towards a contingency theory of entrepreneurial marketing. *Journal of Strategic Marketing*, 24(1), 5–19. 10.1080/0965254X.2015.1035036

Whalen, P. S., & Akaka, M. A. (2016). A dynamic market conceptualization for entrepreneurial marketing: The co-creation of opportunities. *Journal of Strategic Marketing*, 24(1), 61–75. 10.1080/0965254X.2015.1035040

Widjajanti, K., Sugiyanto, E. K., Widyaevan, D. A., & Sari, A. R. (2023). Strategic Choice Development Using SWOT Analysis: Diversification Strategy of Batik Creative Industry in Blora, *Indonesia. The Journal of Economic Education*, 12(1), 198–212.

Wikaningrum, T., Ghozali, I., Nurcholis, L., & Nugroho, M. (2020). Strategic partnership: How important for reputation of small and medium enterprise. *Quality - Access to Success*, 21(174), 35–39.

Wiklund, J., & Shepherd, D. (2003). Knowledge-based resources, entrepreneurial orientation, and the performance of small and medium-sized businesses. *Strategic Management Journal*, 24(13), 1307–1314. 10.1002/smj.360

Willemse, L. (2012). A critical analysis of the barriers to entry for small business owners imposed by Sections 12E (4)(a)(iii) and (d) and paragraph 3 (b) of the Sixth Schedule Of The Income Tax Act, No. 58 of 1962. *Journal of Economic and Financial Sciences*, 5(2), 527–545. 10.4102/jef.v5i2.298

World Commission on Environment and Development. (1987). *Our common future*. Oxford University Press.

Xu, Y., Wang, J., Chen, Z., & Liang, C. (2021). Economic policy uncertainty and stock market returns: New evidence. *The North American Journal of Economics and Finance*, 58, 101525. 10.1016/j.najef.2021.101525

Youssef, A. B., Boubaker, S., & Omri, A. (2018). Entrepreneurship and sustainability: The need for innovative and institutional solutions. *Technological Forecasting and Social Change*, 129, 232–241. 10.1016/j.techfore.2017.11.003

Zahara, Z., Ikhsan, , Santi, I. N., & Farid, . (2023). Entrepreneurial marketing and marketing performance through digital marketing capabilities of SMEs in post-pandemic recovery. *Cogent Business & Management*, 10(2), 2204592. 10.1080/23311975.2023.2204592

Chapter 9
Factors Affecting Green Purchase Behaviors for Small and Medium Enterprises (SMEs) in Uganda

Wasswa Shafik
 http://orcid.org/0000-0002-9320-3186
School of Digital Science, Universiti Brunei Darussalam, Gadong, Brunei & Dig Connectivity Research Laboratory, Kampala, Uganda

ABSTRACT

This study examines the environmentally conscious purchasing patterns of small and medium-sized enterprises (SMEs) in Uganda through several approaches. This research offers a critical analysis of the definition and significance of the term, emphasizing the worldwide importance and relevance of environmentally conscious consumption to small and medium-sized enterprises in Uganda. This study examines the viability of Uganda's SMEs in terms of sustainability. The study found that economic, environmental, regulatory, and customer variables influence small and medium-sized enterprises' green purchasing. This study employs the ideas of planned behavior and the diffusion of innovation to predict these acts. The study acknowledges the limitations in its sample size and data-gathering methods despite conducting a thorough examination. Finally, considering the limitations imposed by SME constraints, the study suggests conducting further research on green procurement and learning from the experiences and insights gained.

DOI: 10.4018/979-8-3693-3518-5.ch009

INTRODUCTION TO GREEN PURCHASE BEHAVIOR

In Uganda[1], effectively overseeing Small and Medium-sized Enterprises[2] (SMEs) and startups is a vital element of the country's economic progress for the other 100 SMEs in the country (Turyakira et al., 2012). Explores Uganda's distinct viewpoints, emphasizing the present patterns, difficulties, possibilities, and unresolved research inquiries that are influencing the SMEs and startup environment. Uganda is currently experiencing a notable increase in SMEs and startups, which are playing a vital role in generating employment opportunities and fostering economic growth (Okello-Obura et al., 2008a). Amidst the worldwide digital transformation, the use of technology in corporate operations is becoming a significant trend. Ugandan SMEs are progressively utilizing digital tools, such as mobile payment solutions like MTN and Airtel mobile money and e-commerce platforms, to improve efficiency and expand their market presence (Turyahebwa et al., 2013).

Nevertheless, this shift to digital platforms is not without obstacles. Limited financial resources frequently hinder the implementation of state-of-the-art technologies, creating an obstacle for several SMEs. The acquisition of talent poses a significant problem, given the strong demand for competent people both domestically and internationally (Okello-Obura et al., 2008b). To successfully address these difficulties, it is necessary to employ creative ideas and adopt strategic management methods that are in line with the prevailing global trends. Ugandan SMEs and startups have abundant prospects thanks to an expanding customer base and improved entry to global markets (Mugisha et al., 2022). Collaboration and collaborations, whether on a local or global scale, provide opportunities for sharing resources and expanding into new markets. Furthermore, the government's dedication to bolstering entrepreneurship through grants and initiatives instills a sense of hope for the future of the sector (Muhire & Olyanga, 2022).

As the landscape of SMEs in Uganda changes, new research topics arise. It is necessary to investigate the elements of success that are peculiar to Uganda, considering the country's distinctive socio-economic and cultural characteristics. The effects of artificial intelligence and automation on SMEs in Uganda are becoming increasingly problematic and intriguing (Qudrat-Ullah et al., 2021). Furthermore, exploring the ways in which SMEs can enhance long-term sustainability and optimize risk management in the business landscape of Uganda is a promising field for research. The management of SMEs and startups in Uganda is being significantly influenced by the widespread use of digital technologies, which aligns with global patterns (Turyahebwa et al., 2013).

Mobile payment options, such as those offered by various companies, have become widely accepted and are making it easier for both businesses and consumers to conduct financial transactions (Bagorogoza & Nakasule, 2022). In addition, e-commerce platforms are developing as efficient instruments for expanding markets, allowing even tiny enterprises to access a wider customer base. Although there are clear patterns, the financial limitations pose a significant obstacle for respective SMEs in Uganda that aim to adopt digital transformation (Onyinyi & Kaberuka, 2019). The lack of sufficient money and capital hinders the widespread adoption of state-of-the-art technology, resulting in a disparity between businesses that have the financial means to innovate and others that are constrained by financial limitations.

Figure 1. Uganda's Tax Structure Representation

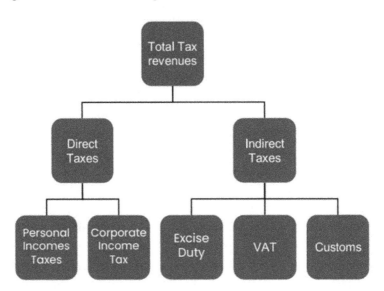

Another important challenge in Uganda's SME arena is talent acquisition due to different tax revenues, as demonstrated in Figure 1. There is a high demand for skilled workers both domestically and internationally, so there is always competition to hire talent (Hussein et al., 2022). SMEs have great difficulty attracting and retaining qualified professionals, which could harm their ability to use digital advancements fully or at least innovate in the way they do business. Uganda's growing consumer population and its opening to the world are creating growth opportunities (Shafik, 2023c). Local SMEs and startups are looking for collaborations and partnerships to get the benefit of these opportunities. For instance, a tech startup in Uganda that partners with an overseas company will gain access to new markets and resources that are supportive of mutual growth (Sendawula et al., 2020).

Support provided by the government also adds more opportunities for SMEs in Uganda. The initiatives include financial support through grants and programs aimed to encourage entrepreneurship (S. Mayanja et al., 2023). For example, a government-enforced program to help agricultural startups can be a game changer for the success and viability of ventures in this field. Research questions are multidimensional in the Ugandan setting. It is important to investigate the success factors peculiar to Uganda's socio-economic and cultural environment (S. Mayanja, Ntayi, Munene, Kagaari, et al., 2019). For instance, the ability to understand how businesses deal with cultural subtleties in marketing and customer relations might give additional information that often reflects the food export percentage to the gross domestic product (GDP), as in Figure 2 showing some selected East African Communities in relation to Indonesia, South Africa, and China.

Figure 2. Percentage of Food Exports to Total GDP (Source: World Bank, World Development Indicators)

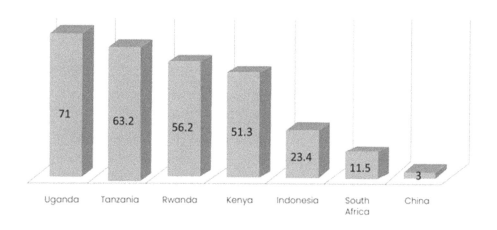

According to a survey by the World Economic Forum[3], 67% of SMEs have challenges in sustaining and expanding their businesses due to the combination of narrow profit margins and difficulties in scaling up (S. Mayanja et al., 2023). A further 48% of organizations face difficulties in both recruiting and maintaining skilled employees, and they also lack the necessary resources to enhance their skills and provide training for their workforce. SMEs have significant obstacles, such as limited access to financial resources and capital (24%) as well as technological advancements and innovation (25%) (Shafik, 2023c).

The rising impact of artificial intelligence[4] (AI) and automation[5] on SMEs in Uganda has become the focus area. Researching methodologies that support the wise implementation of these technologies to facilitate increased operational efficacy while protecting jobs is a crucial research direction (S. S. Mayanja et al., 2019). Additionally, the urgency of AI to conduct research and develop productive risk management strategies designed for individual peculiarities of the Ugandan business sphere is accentuated. Figure 3 shows the top 10 African countries with young populations that developed their economies. Such research initiatives are critical for strengthening the resilience of SMEs, which in turn allows them to approach uncertainties with strategic foresight and adaptability that ultimately support sustainable growth amid an ever-changing technological environment (Abaho et al., 2016).

Figure 3. Top 10 African Countries with Young Population (Share of the population under 18 years) (Source: UN World Population)

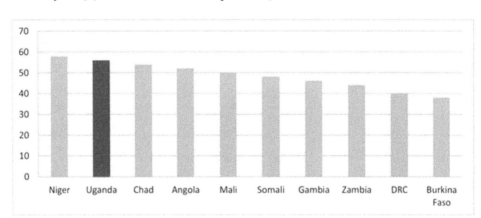

Chapter Contribution

This chapter presents the following contributions.

- This text aims to present a comprehensive analysis of the SME sector in Uganda and its significance in the economy. Our focus is on identifying the obstacles that SMEs have when adopting environmentally friendly purchasing practices, as well as the possible advantages that can be gained.
- This chapter highlights the increasing importance of environmentally responsible buying on a worldwide level, as well as its relevance to SMEs in Uganda.

- Real-world case studies or examples that show the use of these theoretical frameworks inside Ugandan SMEs are being incorporated into this process.
- It is putting forward recommendations for topics that could be subjected to additional research or studies, which could broaden the scope of the existing research and possibly investigate various sectors or regions within Uganda.
- Finally, it suggests potential areas for additional research or studies that could build upon the existing study, including examining different industries or regions within Uganda, future research, and some summarized lessons learned.

Chapter Organization

Section 2 examines Ugandan SMEs' green procurement motivations and decisions. Section 3 examines how economic and regulatory issues affect green procurement decisions. Section 4 discusses frameworks and theoretical viewpoints to analyze these behaviors. Section 5 identifies developing trends and opportunities for further research on Ugandan SMEs' sustainable business practices. Section 6 presents future research directions, summarizes lessons learned, and emphasizes the necessity of green purchase behaviors in responsible business management for Ugandan SMEs.

Understanding Green Purchase Behaviors in SMEs

Investigating green purchasing patterns in SMEs in Uganda is a complex endeavor that entails deciphering the numerous motivations and decision-making processes that drive environmentally conscious choices within this corporate environment (Hussein et al., 2022). The primary factor to contemplate is the paramount significance of sustainable business practices, given that SMEs hold a crucial position in Uganda's economic framework. With the growing urgency of global environmental issues, SMEs in Uganda are more motivated to evaluate and embrace environmentally friendly purchasing practices (Shafik, 2024a). This inquiry requires a more detailed analysis of the reasons that drive SMEs to make environmentally responsible decisions.

Examining the complexities of green purchasing patterns in Ugandan SMEs uncovers several elements that impact these choices. Economic factors, such as the efficiency and cost-effectiveness of sustainable practices, become crucial motivators (Sendawula et al., 2020). The decisions of SMEs to embrace environmentally sustainable products or services are greatly influenced by consumer preferences and market demands. The decision-making process for SMEs is influenced by regulatory frameworks and compliance requirements, which pertain to sustainable business practices and the accompanying legal landscape (Turyakira et al., 2012). An additional crucial aspect in comprehending green purchasing habits in Ugandan

SMEs is evaluating the obstacles and prospects encountered by organizations in embracing eco-friendly practices.

Potential obstacles may encompass budgetary limitations, lack of knowledge, or the apparent intricacy of incorporating sustainability into current activities. Concurrently, the implementation of green initiatives presents chances for cost savings, improved brand reputation, and market differentiation (Okello-Obura et al., 2008a). Comprehending green purchasing patterns necessitates a detailed analysis of how SMEs in Uganda manage the convergence of corporate principles and sustainability objectives. This entails examining how organizations integrate their mission and vision with ecologically sustainable decisions, counting both immediate benefits and long-term effects on the firm and the environment (Turyahebwa et al., 2013). Analyzing the unity of values unveils the genuineness and profoundness of small and medium enterprises' dedication to environmentally friendly activities.

Figure 4. Average annual Labour cost for an unskilled production operative (Source: FDI Benchmark, Financial Times)

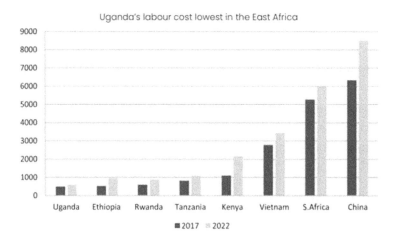

It is essential to examine the impact of consumer knowledge and education on influencing green purchasing patterns in this investigation based on the average annual labor costs, as Figure 4 demonstrates. Assessing customer knowledge and willingness to support environmentally responsible firms can offer valuable insights into the potential market demand for sustainable products and services (Okello-Obura et al., 2008b). When developing and executing green initiatives, SMEs in Uganda should consider consumer perceptions and attitudes. The utilization of metrics, reporting methods, and communication tactics by SMEs to demonstrate their dedication to sustainability plays a significant role in fostering consumer trust and engaging stakeholders (Turyakira et al., 2012). Transparently conveying the environmental consequences of eco-friendly choices improves the trustworthiness of SMEs in the perception of consumers and stakeholders.

To gain a deeper understanding of green purchasing behaviors in SMEs in Uganda, it is necessary to analyze the tactics implemented by businesses to include sustainability in their supply chain and production operations. This involves evaluating the implementation of environmentally sustainable materials, energy-conserving technology, and waste minimization strategies (Hussein et al., 2022). SMEs that are transitioning to more environmentally friendly supply chains must regard factors such as the availability of resources, the financial ramifications, and the compatibility of sustainable practices with their current operating frameworks (Shafik, 2024b). Examining these tactics offers a detailed comprehension of how Ugandan small and medium-sized enterprises integrate environmental factors into their daily economic activities.

An essential factor in understanding green consumer habits is analyzing the impact of partnerships and collaborations in promoting sustainable practices among SMEs in Uganda. Interacting with suppliers, industry associations, and other stakeholders can enhance the sharing of knowledge, resources, and best practices (Okello-Obura et al., 2008a). Collaborative endeavors may encompass cooperative endeavors for waste management, collective sustainability certifications, or consolidated resources for investing in renewable energy solutions (Turyahebwa et al., 2013). An assessment of the dynamics of these alliances provides insights into how SMEs use collective action to improve their environmental performance and overcome constraints caused by their limited individual capabilities (Mugisha et al., 2022). To illustrate this, the annual growth of the labor force in selected economies for 2018-2022 as per Benchmark from Financial Times Limited based on the ILOSTAT Database is presented in Figure 5.

Figure 5. Annual growth of labor force in selected economies for 2018-2022 (Source: fDi Benchmark from Financial Times Limited based on ILOSTAT Database)

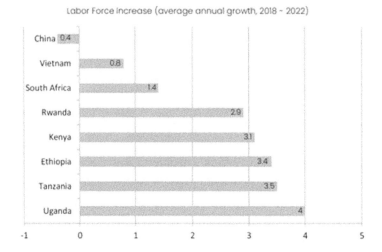

Governments frequently exert substantial influence on the corporate environment through the implementation of legislation, the provision of incentives, and the promotion of sustainable practices (Muhire & Olyanga, 2022). Probing the Ugandan policy landscape enables SMEs to understand the external influences that impact their efforts to maintain sustainability. Measures such as tax incentives for environmentally friendly activities, financial support for green initiatives, or regulations that prioritize the purchase of green products can greatly impact the decision-making processes of SMEs, creating a favorable environment for the adoption of environmentally conscious purchasing behaviors (Abubakar et al., 2019). This enables informed decision-making and the promotion of sustainable business practices in the region.

Factors Influencing Green Purchase Behaviors

A combination of factors influences the green purchase behaviors of SMEs and startups in Uganda. These factors include financial considerations, consumer demand, regulatory compliance, supply chain sustainability, corporate values, and technological innovation, as illustrated below.

Cost Considerations

Cost concerns play a crucial role in influencing the green purchasing behaviors of SMEs and startups in Uganda. Businesses, especially those with limited resources, need to thoroughly assess the financial consequences of implementing sustainable practices (Qudrat-Ullah et al., 2021). A nearby startup that intends to integrate environmentally friendly packaging materials may first encounter elevated expenses in contrast to conventional alternatives. Although there may be initial costs involved, investing in sustainable alternatives can ultimately result in long-term financial benefits by increasing efficiency, minimizing waste, and bolstering brand reputation (Turyahebwa et al., 2013). This strategy approach not only enhances the business's financial performance but also fosters sustainable conservation by mitigating the overall environmental footprint.

Consumer Demand and Preferences

The comprehension and reaction to consumer desire for environmentally friendly products have a substantial impact on the purchasing habits of SMEs and newly established businesses in Uganda. To remain competitive, businesses must ensure that their offers are in line with the changing desires of consumers (Bagorogoza & Nakasule, 2022). For instance, a nearby textile venture may integrate organic and ethically obtained materials to fulfill the increasing need for ecologically friendly fashion. Aligning with consumer preferences can lead to higher market share, more customer loyalty, and a favorable brand image (Onyinyi & Kaberuka, 2019). This customer-focused strategy not only advantages the company but also supports long-term preservation by encouraging the manufacturing and use of eco-friendly goods. Some identified note drives of SME growth and productivity are provided in Figure 6.

Regulatory Compliance

Compliance with environmental legislation and standards has a crucial role in influencing the green purchasing habits of SMEs and startups in Uganda. Businesses must adeptly negotiate and adhere to current regulations to evade legal ramifications (J. Mayanja & Perks, 2017). One instance involves a diminutive manufacturing enterprise implementing environmentally conscious production methods to adhere to governmental regulations about emissions. Adhering to regulatory compliance improves the standing of businesses, cultivates confidence among stakeholders, and guarantees enduring viability (Shafik, 2023b; Uwonda & Okello, 2015). Regulatory compliance ensures that firms function within environmentally acceptable frameworks, hence lowering their ecological imprint from a conservation standpoint.

Figure 6. Key Drive of SME Growth and Productivity

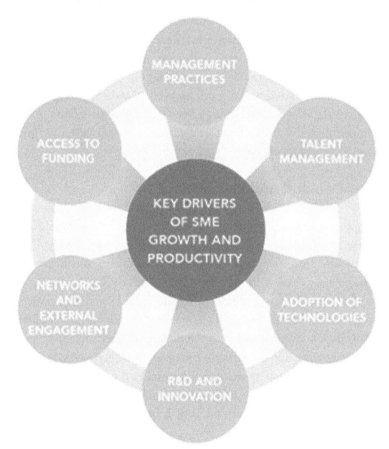

Supply Chain Sustainability

The sustainability of the supply chain is a crucial determinant affecting the green purchasing behaviors of SMEs in Uganda. Businesses must assess and choose suppliers who have a shared dedication to ecologically sustainable operations (Mugisha et al., 2022). A food processing firm in Uganda might opt to obtain ingredients from local farmers who employ organic farming techniques. Developing a sustainable supply chain improves the ability to recover from challenges, minimizes harm to the environment, and promotes the growth of local communities (Muhire & Olyanga, 2022). From a conservation perspective, a sustainable supply chain plays a crucial role in preserving biodiversity, reducing environmental harm, and bolstering local economies.

Corporate Values and Ethics

The correlation between the congruence of corporate values and ethical considerations with sustainable practices significantly impacts the adoption of environmentally friendly purchasing behaviors among startups in Uganda (Shafik, 2023a). Businesses must incorporate sustainability as a fundamental aspect of their core principles. One instance is an information technology startup in Uganda that advocates for energy-efficient solutions and appropriate ways for disposing of electronic waste. Integrating sustainability into company values improves brand credibility, draws environmentally conscientious customers, and cultivates a positive workplace culture (Turyahebwa et al., 2013). This alignment not only enhances the profitability of the firm but also promotes sustainable conservation by fostering responsible and naturally open activities.

Technological Innovation

The presence and acceptance of cutting-edge technologies are vital determinants influencing environmentally conscious buying habits for SMEs and newly established businesses in Uganda. Enterprises investigate and exploit emerging technology to develop sustainable solutions (Bagorogoza & Nakasule, 2022). For instance, a digital entrepreneur based in Uganda may create an application that enables businesses to access and utilize environmentally sustainable transportation alternatives easily. Adopting technological advancements can improve operational efficiency, minimize environmental footprint, and establish a competitive advantage in the market (Turyahebwa et al., 2013). Technological advancements play a crucial role in promoting the growth and acceptance of environmentally friendly solutions, hence facilitating the establishment of a more sustainable business environment from a conservation standpoint.

Employee Engagement and Awareness

The engagement and awareness of employees within SMEs and startups in Uganda are influential factors in shaping green purchase behaviors. Establishing a culture of sustainability and providing employees with education on eco-friendly practices can impact their purchasing decisions (Okello-Obura et al., 2008b). For instance, a small tech startup may implement initiatives like recycling programs or energy-saving campaigns, fostering a sense of collective responsibility. Engaged employees contribute to the overall success of sustainable initiatives, leading to increased efficiency and lower environmental impact (Qudrat-Ullah et al., 2021). This employee-centric approach not only benefits the internal culture of the business but also contributes to sustainable conservation by instilling eco-conscious behaviors.

Collaborations and East African Community Industry Networks

Engaging in partnerships with other companies and actively participating in industry networks have a substantial impact on shaping the environmentally conscious buying habits of SMEs and startups in Uganda (Mugisha et al., 2021). Partnerships facilitate the exchange of knowledge, resources, and optimal methods. SMEs in the manufacturing sector could partner with a sustainability-oriented industry network to share knowledge on ecologically responsive suppliers or eco-conscious technologies. Collaborative endeavors can lead to joint initiatives for waste reduction, shared certifications for sustainability, or combined resources for investments in renewable energy solutions (Ahimbisibwe et al., 2023). Engaging in industrial networks not only advantages individual enterprises but also promotes sustainable conservation by cultivating a community-oriented approach to environmental responsibility.

Frameworks and Theoretical Perspectives

An in-depth comprehension of frameworks and theoretical views is essential to fully grasping green purchasing habits in SMEs and startups in Uganda.

Discussion on Framework Relevance

These frameworks enhance our comprehension of how SMEs function and prosper in different business settings by analyzing internal capabilities, external impacts, entrepreneurial behaviors, and broader ecosystem dynamics.

Resource-Based View

This is a fundamental concept used to analyze the competitive advantage of SMEs. This theory suggests that the success of a company depends on its distinct resources and competencies. Within the realm of SMEs, this framework facilitates the recognition and utilization of internal advantages, such as specialized expertise or exclusive technology, which enhance their ability to compete and endure over time (Mugisha et al., 2021). The Resource-Based view framework assists SMEs in effectively using their resources to maximize their unique strengths and achieve a competitive advantage in the market. This approach promotes resilience and long-term success.

Institutional Theory

The use of Institutional Theory is crucial for comprehending how external influences influence the behavior of SMEs. This study explores the impact of societal norms, legislation, and industry standards on the decision-making processes of SMEs (Kikawa et al., 2022). This viewpoint aids in understanding the influence of both official and informal institutions on the actions of SMEs, providing insight into whether they adhere to or diverge from existing standards. Through an examination of the institutional framework, SMEs can effectively traverse regulatory frameworks, proactively anticipate changes in social expectations, and strategically position themselves within the wider institutional landscape (Shafik & Kalinaki, 2023).

Transaction Cost Economics

Transaction Cost Economics offers a valuable understanding of the governance structures and decision-making processes of SMEs, specifically in their dealings with stakeholders. This paradigm examines the strategies employed by SMEs to reduce transaction costs, handle relationships, and make strategic decisions about governance structures (Kobugabe & Rwakihembo, 2022). SMEs need to have a clear grasp of transaction costs to effectively allocate resources, handle relationships with suppliers and customers, and strategically position themselves in the market. Through the implementation of TCE, SMEs improve their decision-making procedures, minimize inefficiencies, and effectively manage the intricacies of transactions in diverse business settings (Muhammad et al., 2024).

Dynamic Capabilities Framework

The Dynamic Capabilities Framework centers on a company's capacity to adjust, create, and reorganize its assets in reaction to evolving circumstances. For SMEs, this viewpoint emphasizes the significance of being adaptable, acquiring knowledge, and strategically adjusting to navigate through unpredictable markets, technological progress, and changing customer expectations (Mugisha et al., 2020). SMEs can enhance their ability to adapt to external changes, seize emerging opportunities, and promote a culture of ongoing innovation by developing dynamic skills (Kobugabe & Rwakihembo, 2022). This framework enables SMEs to maintain their strength and adaptability in rapidly changing business environments, thereby promoting their capacity to prosper and achieve long-term success.

Entrepreneurial Orientation

Entrepreneurial Orientation is a viewpoint that analyzes the entrepreneurial traits and actions of SMEs. The focus is on characteristics like initiative, creativity, willingness to take risks, and a strong will to compete. SMEs that have a strong entrepreneurial mindset are more likely to recognize and actively pursue possibilities, which in turn promotes growth and enhances competitiveness (Shafik, 2024c). SMEs can effectively negotiate uncertainty, find market gaps, and take advantage of new trends by adopting an entrepreneurial attitude. This framework promotes the development of a proactive and innovative organizational culture in SMEs, which is crucial for attaining continuous growth and success in dynamic business settings (Kamukama, 2020).

Open Innovation

The Open Innovation approach promotes the idea of SMEs expanding their horizons beyond their internal research and development capabilities and actively participating in collaborative endeavors with external partners (Mugisha et al., 2020). This encompasses suppliers, customers, and research institutions. SMEs can improve their competitiveness and expedite the introduction of new products or services to the market by accessing external sources of knowledge and innovation (Abanis et al., 2022). Open Innovation promotes a culture of collaboration and knowledge exchange, allowing SMEs to utilize external skills and resources. This technique not only speeds up the invention process but also improves the overall abilities and flexibility of SMEs in response to changing market circumstances (Shafik, 2024d).

Ecosystem Perspective

The ecosystem perspective regards SMEs as essential components of larger business ecosystems, recognizing their interdependent connections with suppliers, customers, competitors, and regulatory entities (Mugisha et al., 2020). Comprehending the intricacies of these ecosystems enables SMEs to see prospects for cooperation, adapt to shifts in the sector, and strategically establish their place within the broader business environment. This viewpoint underscores the significance of relationships and interactions within the ecosystem, emphasizing the potential advantages of co-operative endeavors and strategic partnerships (Abanis et al., 2022; Shafik, 2024e). SMEs can enhance their performance and success in the ever-changing and linked business environment by embracing an ecosystem perspective. This approach allows them to utilize the combined capabilities of various stakeholders, overcome obstacles, and flourish.

Triple Bottom Line

The Triple Bottom Line[6] (TBL) framework broadens the scope of small and medium-sized enterprises (SMEs) to encompass not only financial performance but also social and environmental factors (J. Mayanja & Perks, 2017). It promotes the idea of SMEs evaluating their performance based not just on financial gains but also on their social influence and commitment to environmental sustainability. The concept of TBL corresponds with the increasing focus on corporate social responsibility, which encourages SMEs to embrace a comprehensive and accountable approach to conducting business (Mugisha et al., 2020). SMEs may bolster their reputation, appeal to socially conscious clients, and make a beneficial impact on the communities and surroundings they operate in by incorporating social and environmental objectives into their business plans (Mugisha et al., 2021). The concept of TBL highlights the interdependence of economic, social, and environmental factors when assessing the performance and influence of SMEs.

Theoretical Perspective

The combination of these theoretical views enhances our comprehension of SMEs in Uganda, providing frameworks to examine their reactions to institutional pressures.

Technology Adoption Framework

Due to the growing significance of technology in the business sector, SMEs in Uganda must have a Technology Adoption Framework. This perspective examines the ways in which SMEs adopt and use technological advancements in their business practices (Okumu & Buyinza, 2020). Gaining insights into the determinants of technology adoption enables SMEs in Uganda to effectively utilize digital tools to enhance efficiency, expand their market reach, and enhance their competitive advantage (Kato & Tsoka, 2020).

Community-Based Entrepreneurship

Community-based entrepreneurship is a theoretical paradigm that examines the function of SMEs within the context of Ugandan communities. The importance of the interdependence of enterprises and the social context in which they operate is emphasized (Tukamuhabwa et al., 2023). SMEs, which are frequently deeply ingrained in the areas in which they operate, play an essential part in the development of communities (Ntay et al., 2011). Within the unique context of Uganda, this viewpoint throws light on the ways in which SMEs can contribute to sustainable development, the creation of jobs, and social well-being.

Cultural Perspectives on Entrepreneurship

An analysis of cultural perspectives on entrepreneurship in Uganda sheds light on the impact of cultural values and traditions on the entrepreneurial activities of SMEs. This perspective examines how cultural influences influence business practices, decision-making, and relationships in Uganda's entrepreneurial environment (Mugisha et al., 2021). To maintain a competitive edge in Uganda's ever-changing markets and economic landscape, it is crucial to comprehend how SMEs develop their ability to adapt, learn from past experiences, and reorganize their resources.

Future Research Directions of SMEs in Uganda

Future study areas for SMEs in Uganda should include economic, cultural, policy, technological, supply chain, consumer, global market, and collaborative aspects as demonstrated.

Economic Perspective

Further investigation could examine the economic ramifications of implementing sustainable practices for SMEs in Uganda and many African countries. Examining the cost-benefit analysis of green initiatives, comprehending the financial motivations for adopting eco-friendly measures, and assessing the influence on overall economic performance would yield significant information (Abanis et al., 2022). By adopting this economic perspective, SMEs would have access to practical information that would help them match their sustainability initiatives with their financial objectives (Okumu & Buyinza, 2020). This approach would promote a harmonious relationship between profitability and environmental stewardship.

Cultural and Societal Context

An analysis from a cultural and societal standpoint could explore the impact of cultural norms and societal values on the green purchasing behaviors of SMEs. Gaining insight into the cultural factors that influence consumer choices and company practices would facilitate the development of more customized sustainable initiatives (Mugisha et al., 2020). SMEs may amplify their effect on both corporate and societal levels by harmonizing green activities with local values, hence fostering greater acceptance and engagement.

Policy and Regulatory Landscape

It is of the utmost importance to conduct research into the policy and regulatory framework that pertains to environmentally friendly SMEs in Uganda. Future studies need to investigate the ways in which existing policies affect decision-making, as well as the potential impact of specific restrictions or incentives (Kato & Tsoka, 2020). SMEs would benefit from a comprehensive study since it would offer them a more effective roadmap for navigating the regulatory landscape, ensuring that compliance is streamlined, and effectively encouraging sustainable practices (S. Mayanja, Ntayi, Munene, Balunywa, et al., 2019).

Technological Adoption and Innovation

Opportunities for SMEs and start-ups in Uganda and many African countries like Kenya and Tanzania may be uncovered by research that investigates the adoption and innovation of technology in the context of environmentally conscious purchasing patterns (Shafik, 2024f). SMEs would benefit from a strategic roadmap if they investigated how emerging technologies may improve environmentally friendly processes, lessen their influence on the environment, and encourage creativity in product development (S. Mayanja et al., 2022). This viewpoint has the potential to help SMEs discover creative methods to incorporate technology into their sustainability activities, thus enhancing both their operational efficiency and their environmental stewardship.

Supply Chain Dynamics

The dynamics of green supply chains within the SME sector in Uganda could be the object of future research. Comprehensive insights could be gained by gaining an understanding of how SMEs engage with their suppliers, the difficulties encountered in acquiring sustainable materials, and the influence on the overall resilience of the supply chain (Okello-Obura et al., 2009). With this point of view, SMEs would be able to optimize their supply chains for environmental sustainability while simultaneously assuring their robustness and agility in the face of shifting market dynamics (S. Mayanja, Ntayi, Munene, Kagaari, et al., 2019).

Consumer Behavior and Education

It would be helpful to analyze consumer behavior and education in Uganda in relation to environmentally friendly products and services for the sake of future research. This would cover the topic of environmental consciousness. Research into the ways in which consumer knowledge, preferences, and educational programs influence the green purchasing behaviors of SMEs is of the utmost importance (S. Mayanja et al., 2023). Suppose SMEs have a better understanding of the factors that influence consumer choices and the role that education plays in building eco-conscious attitudes. In that case, they will be able to modify their strategies to meet the expectations of consumers and to promote sustainable consumption patterns (Muhammad et al., 2024). This will allow them to meet the expectations of consumers and promote sustainable consumption patterns.

Collaborative Initiatives

It would be advantageous to study the ways in which SMEs could work together on initiatives related to sustainability, pool resources, and engage in partnership formation. Within the community of SMEs, it would be beneficial to investigate the influence that collaborative initiatives have on lowering costs, enhancing access to environmentally friendly technologies, and cultivating a culture of shared environmental accountability and responsibility (Okello-Obura et al., 2008a). This would be beneficial to the creation of effective strategies for collective sustainable action within the SME community (Kobugabe & Rwakihembo, 2022). Addressing these qualities would not only improve our understanding of environmentally conscious purchasing behaviors but also provide SMEs with information that they could put into action to assist them in navigating the shifting landscape of sustainability in Uganda (Okello-Obura et al., 2008a).

Lessons Learned and Conclusion

To achieve sustainable success, actively engage in collaboration, adjust to local circumstances, prioritize education, strategically incorporate technology, promote the ability to adapt, emphasize long-term value, and establish ongoing monitoring and assessment processes.

- An important lesson is understanding the interdependence of several factors that impact green purchasing choices. Businesses must adopt a comprehensive approach because of the interconnected nature of economic factors, consumer preferences, legal requirements, and cultural influences. A comprehensive comprehension of these interrelated elements is crucial for efficient decision-making and the triumphant implementation of sustainable practices.
- The exploration emphasizes the importance of engaging in partnership with stakeholders, such as suppliers, consumers, and industry partners. Collaborative endeavors enhance the availability of common resources, facilitate the sharing

of knowledge, and promote collaborative action, cultivating a more sustainable ecology. The necessity of establishing robust partnerships to tackle problems and capitalize on collective strengths in encouraging naturally friendly purchasing patterns is underscored by the lessons learned.
- Local settings, including cultural values, legislative frameworks, and economic realities significantly influence green purchase behaviors. The lessons gleaned underscore the significance of customizing sustainable solutions to harmonize with the particular intricacies of the local ecosystem. By adapting to local circumstances, projects can effectively connect with stakeholders and increase the likelihood of long-term acceptance and sustainability.
- The exploration highlights the significant impact of education in promoting environmentally conscious purchasing habits. Consumer knowledge and comprehension of the advantages of sustainable choices are essential. The lessons learned highlight the importance of businesses actively participating in educational activities to cultivate an informed consumer base that actively advocates for and seeks out ecologically sustainable products and services.
- Technology integration plays a crucial role in facilitating sustainable practices. The lessons acquired emphasize the significance of technology advancements in improving operational efficiency, minimizing environmental harm, and establishing competitive advantages. SMEs and startups should strategically utilize technology to further their environmentally friendly initiatives, acknowledging its capacity for beneficial transformation.
- The ever-changing nature of markets and external factors requires an understanding of the significance of being flexible and having the ability to adjust. Businesses must possess the ability to adapt quickly and effectively to shifts in consumer preferences, regulatory environments, and technological progress. The need to develop dynamic capacities to handle uncertainty and take advantage of emerging opportunities is highlighted by the lessons learned.
- The lessons learned highlight the need to emphasize enduring value over immediate profits. Although there may be upfront expenses involved in implementing environmentally friendly practices, the long-lasting advantages, such as improved brand image, customer retention, and ability to withstand environmental obstacles, highlight the strategic importance of investing in sustainability for SMEs and startups.
- Finally, the exploration emphasizes the significance of ongoing monitoring and evaluation of sustainability programs. The lessons learned highlight the importance for organizations to set strong measurements, consistently evaluate the effectiveness of their environmentally friendly tactics, and adjust their approaches based on performance data. This iterative method guarantees

that firms maintain alignment with their sustainability objectives and remain adaptable to changing market circumstances.

CONCLUSION

Conclusively, the investigation into green purchasing patterns in SMEs and startups uncovers an intricate and interrelated environment influenced by economic, cultural, legal, and technological elements. The significance of comprehensive strategies, cooperation among stakeholders, adjustment to specific circumstances, educational programs, deliberate incorporation of technology, adaptability, emphasis on lasting benefits, and ongoing evaluation for enduring achievements is underscored by the lessons learned. These insights offer guidance for SMEs and startups as they traverse the obstacles and opportunities of implementing environmentally responsible practices, enabling them to make informed decisions and engage in strategic planning. Adopting sustainability practices not only supports worldwide environmental objectives but also prepares organizations to succeed in a changing market where ethical consumerism and responsible corporate conduct are increasingly crucial for achieving success.

REFERENCES

Abaho, E., Aarakit, S., Ntayi, J., & Kisubi, M. (2016). Firm Capabilities, Entrepreneurial Competency and Performance of Ugandan SMEs. *Business Management Review, 19*(2). http://hdl.handle.net/11159/3229

Abanis, T., Eliab Mpora, B., Sunday, A., & Eton, M. (2022). Capital Structure, Investment Decision and Financial Performance of SMEs in Uganda. *International Journal of Scientific Research and Management*, 10(07), 3679–3688. Advance online publication. 10.18535/ijsrm/v10i7.em03

Abubakar, Y. A., Hand, C., Smallbone, D., & Saridakis, G. (2019). What specific modes of internationalization influence SME innovation in Sub-Saharan least developed countries (LDCs)? *Technovation*, 79, 56–70. Advance online publication. 10.1016/j.technovation.2018.05.004

Ahimbisibwe, G. M., Ngoma, M., Nabatanzi-Muyimba, A. K., & Kabagambe, L. B. (2023). Entrepreneurial mindset and SME internationalization in Uganda: The mediating role of international networking. *Review of International Business and Strategy*, 33(4), 669–690. Advance online publication. 10.1108/RIBS-11-2021-0149

Bagorogoza, J. K., & Nakasule, I. (2022). The mediating effect of knowledge management on talent management and firm performance in small and medium enterprise in Uganda. *Journal of Management Development*, 41(6), 349–366. Advance online publication. 10.1108/JMD-10-2021-0290

Hussein, K., Kassim, M., & Ali, M. (2022). Cloud Computing Acceptance in Small and Medium Enterprises (SMEs) in Uganda. *Saudian Review of Financial Technology and Management Studies*, 2(1). Advance online publication. 10.12691/srftms-2-1-1

Kamukama, N. (2020). Social Competence and Access to Finance in Financial Institutions: An Empirical Study Of Small And Medium Enterprises In Uganda. *American Journal of Finance*, 5(1), 54–70. Advance online publication. 10.47672/ajf.594

Kato, A. I., & Tsoka, G. E. (2020). Impact of venture capital financing on small-and medium-sized enterprises' performance in Uganda. *Southern African Journal of Entrepreneurship and Small Business Management*, 12(1). Advance online publication. 10.4102/sajesbm.v12i1.320

Kikawa, C. R., Kiconco, C., Agaba, M., Ntirampeba, D., Ssematimba, A., & Kalema, B. M. (2022). Social Media Marketing for Small and Medium Enterprise Performance in Uganda: A Structural Equation Model. *Sustainability (Basel)*, 14(21), 14391. Advance online publication. 10.3390/su142114391

Kobugabe, C., & Rwakihembo, J. (2022). Financial Literacy and Financial Inclusion: A positivist view of Proprietors of Small and Medium Enterprises in Fort Portal City, Western Uganda. *American Journal of Finance*, 7(2), 1–12. Advance online publication. 10.47672/ajf.1014

Mayanja, J., & Perks, S. (2017). Business practices influencing ethical conduct of small and medium-sized enterprises in Uganda. *African Journal of Business Ethics*, 11(1). Advance online publication. 10.15249/11-1-130

Mayanja, S., Ntayi, J. M., Munene, J. C., Balunywa, W., Sserwanga, A., & Kagaari, J. R. K. (2019). Informational differences and entrepreneurial networking among small and medium enterprises in Kampala, Uganda: The mediating role of ecologies of innovation. *Cogent Business and Management*, 6(1), 1617020. Advance online publication. 10.1080/23311975.2019.1617020

Mayanja, S., Ntayi, J. M., Munene, J. C., Kagaari, J. R. K., & Waswa, B. (2019). Ecologies of innovation among small and medium enterprises in Uganda as a mediator of entrepreneurial networking and opportunity exploitation. *Cogent Business and Management*, 6(1), 1641256. Advance online publication. 10.1080/23311975.2019.1641256

Mayanja, S., Ntayi, J. M., Munene, J. C., Wasswa, B., & Kagaari, J. R. K. (2023). Ecologies of innovation as a mediator between nexus of generative influence and entrepreneurial networking among small and medium enterprises in Uganda. *Journal of Small Business and Entrepreneurship*, 35(2), 236–262. Advance online publication. 10.1080/08276331.2020.1764731

Mayanja, S., Ntayi, J. M., Omeke, M., Kibirango, M. M., & Mutebi, H. (2022). Symbiotic Resonance, Nexus of Generative Influence, Ecologies of Innovation and Opportunity Exploitation among Small and Medium Enterprises. *Journal of African Business*, 23(4), 1009–1028. Advance online publication. 10.1080/15228916.2021.1977563

Mayanja, S. S., Ntayi, J. M., Munene, J. C., Kagaari, J. R. K., Balunywa, W., & Orobia, L. (2019). Positive deviance, ecologies of innovation and entrepreneurial networking. *World Journal of Entrepreneurship, Management and Sustainable Development*, 15(4), 308–324. Advance online publication. 10.1108/WJEMSD-12-2018-0110

Mugisha, H., Omagwa, J., & Kilika, J. (2020). Short-Term Debt and Financial Performance of Small and Medium Scale Enterprises in Buganda Region, Uganda. *International Journal of Finance & Banking Studies, 9*(4). 10.20525/ijfbs.v9i4.910

Mugisha, H., Omagwa, J., & Kilika, J. (2021). Capital structure, market conditions and financial performance of small and medium enterprises in Buganda Region, Uganda. *International Journal of Research in Business and Social Science, 10*(3). 10.20525/ijrbs.v10i3.1153

Mugisha, H., Omagwa, J., & Kilika, J. (2022). Capital Structure, Financial Capacity and Financial Performance of Small and Medium Enterprises in the Buganda Region, Uganda. Finance. *Markets and Valuation*, 2(2), 37–57. Advance online publication. 10.46503/GTOS1775

Muhammad, K., Salawu, R. O., Masibo, S., & Sikuku, I. (2024). The Government's Role in Nurturing Management for Sustainability Practices among Small and Medium Enterprises in Uganda. *TWIST, 19*(1), 409-416. https://twistjournal.net/twist/article/view/213

Muhire, F., & Olyanga, A. (2022). Credit and Sustainability of SMEs in Uganda: A Case of SMEs in Nakawa Division Kampala. Journal of Economics. *Finance and Accounting Studies*, 4(4), 145–158. Advance online publication. 10.32996/jefas.2022.4.4.17

Ntay, J. M., Eyaa, S., & Kalubanga, M. (2011). Ethical Culture of SMEs and Perceived Contract Enforcement in Ugandan Buyer-Supplier Contractual Arrangements. *Eastern Africa Social Science Research Review*, 27(2), 51–90. Advance online publication. 10.1353/eas.2011.0007

Okello-Obura, C., Minishi-Majanja, M. K., Cloete, L., & Ikoja-Odongo, J. R. (2008a). Business activities and information needs of SMEs in northern Uganda Prerequisites for an information system. *Library Management*, 29(4–5), 367–391. Advance online publication. 10.1108/01435120810869138

Okello-Obura, C., Minishi-Majanja, M. K., Cloete, L., & Ikoja-Odongo, J. R. (2008b). Sources of business information and means of access used by SMEs in Uganda: The case of Northern Uganda. *Libres*, 18(1). Advance online publication. 10.32655/LIBRES.2008.1.5

Okello-Obura, C., Minishi-Majanja, M. K., Cloete, L., & Ikoja-Odongo, J. R. (2009). Proposed business information system design (BISD) for small and medium enterprises (SMEs) in northern Uganda. *Libri*, 59(1). Advance online publication. 10.1515/libr.2009.004

Okumu, I. M., & Buyinza, F. (2020). Performance of Small and Medium-sized Enterprises in Uganda: the Role of Innovation. *African Economic Research Consortium*. http://localhost:80/xmlui/handle/123456789/496

Onyinyi, B., & Kaberuka, W. (2019). ICT fusion on the relationship between resource transformation capabilities and quality management practices among SMEs in Uganda. *Cogent Business and Management*, 6(1), 1586063. Advance online publication. 10.1080/23311975.2019.1586063

Qudrat-Ullah, H., Kayal, A., & Mugumya, A. (2021). Cost-effective energy billing mechanisms for small and medium-scale industrial customers in Uganda. *Energy*, 227, 120488. Advance online publication. 10.1016/j.energy.2021.120488

Sendawula, K., Bagire, V., Mbidde, C. I., & Turyakira, P. (2020). Environmental commitment and environmental sustainability practices of manufacturing small and medium enterprises in Uganda. *Journal of Enterprising Communities*, 15(4), 588–607. Advance online publication. 10.1108/JEC-07-2020-0132

Shafik, W. (2023a). A Comprehensive Cybersecurity Framework for Present and Future Global Information Technology Organizations. In *Effective Cybersecurity Operations for Enterprise-Wide Systems* (pp. 56–79). IGI Global. 10.4018/978-1-6684-9018-1.ch002

Shafik, W. (2023b). Cyber security perspectives in public spaces: Drone case study. In *Handbook of Research on Cybersecurity Risk in Contemporary Business Systems*. 10.4018/978-1-6684-7207-1.ch004

Shafik, W. (2023c). Making Cities Smarter: IoT and SDN Applications, Challenges, and Future Trends. In *Opportunities and Challenges of Industrial IoT in 5G and 6G Networks*. 10.4018/978-1-7998-9266-3.ch004

Shafik, W. (2024a). *Blockchain-Based Internet of Things (B-IoT): Challenges, Solutions, Opportunities, Open Research Questions, and Future Trends. Blockchain-based Internet of Things*. Chapman and Hall/CRC. 10.1201/9781003407096-3

Shafik, W. (2024b). Data-Driven Future Trends and Innovation in Telemedicine. In *Improving Security, Privacy, and Connectivity Among Telemedicine Platforms* (pp. 93-118). IGI Global. 10.4018/979-8-3693-2141-6.ch005

Shafik, W. (2024c). Introduction to ChatGPT. In *Advanced Applications of Generative AI and Natural Language Processing Models* (pp. 1–25). IGI Global. 10.4018/979-8-3693-0502-7.ch001

Shafik, W. (2024c). Navigating Emerging Challenges in Robotics and Artificial Intelligence in Africa. In *Examining the Rapid Advance of Digital Technology in Africa* (pp. 124-144). IGI Global. 10.4018/978-1-6684-9962-7.ch007

Shafik, W. (2024d). Predicting Future Cybercrime Trends in the Metaverse Era. In *Forecasting Cyber Crimes in the Age of the Metaverse* (pp. 78-113). IGI Global. 10.4018/979-8-3693-0220-0.ch005

Shafik, W. (2024e). Toward a More Ethical Future of Artificial Intelligence and Data Science. In *The Ethical Frontier of AI and Data Analysis* (pp. 362–388). IGI Global. 10.4018/979-8-3693-2964-1.ch022

Shafik, W. (2024f). *Wearable Medical Electronics in Artificial Intelligence of Medical Things. Handbook of Security and Privacy of AI-Enabled Healthcare Systems and Internet of Medical Things.* CRC Press. 10.1201/9781003370321-2

Shafik, W., & Kalinaki, K. (2023). Smart City Ecosystem: An Exploration of Requirements, Architecture, Applications, Security, and Emerging Motivations. In *Handbook of Research on Network-Enabled IoT Applications for Smart City Services* (pp. 75-98). IGI Global. 10.4018/979-8-3693-0744-1.ch005

Tukamuhabwa, B., Mutebi, H., & Kyomuhendo, R. (2023). Competitive advantage in SMEs: Effect of supply chain management practices, logistics capabilities and logistics integration in a developing country. *Journal of Business and Socio-Economic Development*, 3(4), 353–371. Advance online publication. 10.1108/JBSED-04-2021-0051

Turyahebwa, A., Sunday, A., & Ssekajugo, D. (2013). Financial management practices and business performance of small and medium enterprises in western Uganda. *African Journal of Business Management*, 7(38). Advance online publication. 10.5897/AJBM2013.6899

Turyakira, P., Smith, E., & Venter, E. (2012). Corporate social responsibility for SMEs: A proposed hypothesised model. *African Journal of Business Ethics*, 6(2), 106. Advance online publication. 10.4103/1817-7417.111015

Uwonda, G., & Okello, N. (2015). Cash Flow Management and Sustainability of Small Medium Enterprises (SMEs) in Northern Uganda. *International Journal of Social Science and Economics Invention*, 1(03). Advance online publication. 10.23958/ijssei/vol01-i03/02

ENDNOTES

[1] https://www.britannica.com/place/Uganda
[2] https://www.ugandainvest.go.ug/sme/
[3] https://www.weforum.org/agenda/2022/12/future-readiness-here-s-why-smaller-businesses-success-matters/

4. https://www.sas.com/en_us/insights/analytics/what-is-artificial-intelligence.html
5. https://industrialautomationindia.in/articleitm/2837/The-Importance-of-SME-Automation/articles
6. https://www.ibm.com/topics/triple-bottom-line

Chapter 10
Evaluating the Impact of Crowdfunding on Emerging Markets:
Legal Frameworks, Investment Potential, and Financial Reporting within IFRS in the Entrepreneurial Ecosystem

Betül Açikgöz
http://orcid.org/0000-0003-0140-3461
Yozgat Bozok University, Turkey

ABSTRACT

The study examines the impact of crowdfunding on E7 countries, highlighting its ongoing legal construction and potential for new investments and economic growth. Traditional financial institutions are hesitant to invest in innovative ventures due to risk perception. Crowdfunding, a non-conventional financial tool, has gained popularity in US and Europe, but its adoption in emerging markets is relatively recent. Study also discusses the financial reporting mechanism of crowdfunding activities, which are explained within the framework of IFRS. Crowdfunding transactions' accounting treatment depends on the campaign's nature and financial reporting requirements. Entities must determine appropriate treatment for funds received, such as revenue, liability, or equity. Equity crowdfunding may involve recognizing financial instruments like IFRS 9, while revenue recognition principles under IFRS 15 may apply for campaigns in exchange for goods or services. Disclosures about crowdfunding activities, contingent liabilities, and fair value measurement may be required in accordance with IFRS 13.

DOI: 10.4018/979-8-3693-3518-5.ch010

1. INTRODUCTION

Business historians believe that the early stages of commercial activities have been present since the beginning of civilizations. Entrepreneurs begin their ventures with a concept and need financial resources to execute it, which may be acquired through equity or financing from creditors. Financial sources at this stage have been limited, but alternative investments like venture capital, angel investment, private debt and, private equity are becoming more common among startup companies (Cumming and Zhang, 2016). Crowdfunding is an online marketplace where entrepreneurs solicit financing for their creative ideas from a multitude of individuals who contribute a little sum apiece (Mollick, 2014). Crowdfunding has been a rising alternative investment method in the recent years. It was emerged after the economic crisis which affected mainly the US and European economies in 2008. Since the investments to the new project ideas seemed more risky, the financial challenges were faced due to the high cost funds. Belleflamme et. al. (2014) describe the crowdfunding as community benefits to increase their utility. Before collecting funds to finance the bright and innovative business ideas, the earliest crowdfunding campaigns were held to support the artists by financially assisting them to release their music albums. In the cyber world, Artistshare.com is known as the first crowdfunding platform to fund art projects by bringing the artists and their fans together. It is not only the first crowdfunding activity but also the first business model by proposing a funding opportunity for the artists by the general public, which was established in 2001. The JOBS Act, passed in 2012 by the US Congress, legalized crowdfunding activities in the US to ease securities regulations for small businesses and stimulate economic growth after the 2008 crisis. The act aimed to provide a reliable investment environment for investors and prevent fraud and scams. Meanwhile, the European Union established the European Crowdfunding Network in 2012 to promote crowdfunding activities, boost entrepreneurship, and stimulate economic growth in the EU. Both acts aim to provide a reliable investment environment for small and medium-sized enterprises (SMEs).

The crowdfunding market is anticipated to expand significantly, reaching $17.87 billion in 2024 at a CAGR (compound annual growth rate) of 15.9%. This growth is attributed to factors such as funding needs for startups and small businesses, improved access to global capital markets, support for creative projects, and the regulatory environment governing crowdfunding for social causes (Crowdfunding Global Market Report 2024).

Figure 1. Global Crowdfunding Market

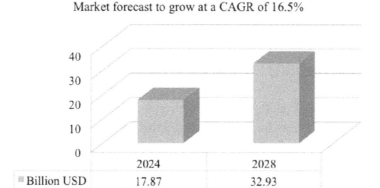

Source: Crowdfunding Global Market Report 2024 by Research and Markets The World's Largest Market Research Store (https://www.researchandmarkets.com/report/crowdfunding#tag-pos-1)

Crowdfunding is a method where a project is funded by public, who then decide which project to support financially. The process involves setting a budget, creating a website, and providing information about the project to potential investors. Backers then evaluate the alternatives and decide which project to support. Access to internet services and the legal environment of capital markets also contribute to the achievements of crowdfunding initiatives. This flow is summarized on the Figure 2 below.

Figure 2. The Flow of Crowdfunding Process

Source: Acikgoz, et. al. (2019)

This study evaluates the nature of the crowdfunding and its applications in the emerging economies. In the following chapter, the types of crowdfunding are explained. The literature is reviewed in the third chapter. The crowdfunding practices and the regulations in the emerging markets are discussed in the following chapter. Financial reporting mechanism of the crowdfunding activities and the accounting regulations of the E7 countries are discussed in the penultimate chapter. The paper concludes with an evaluation of the crowdfunding applications, the legal environment, and regulations at the capital boards and the current financial reporting standards in the emerging markets.

2. CROWDFUNDING MODELS

The entrepreneurs could apply to different crowdfunding alternatives in accordance with the targeted budget for the project and the legal environment of the country where they do business. Crowdfunding types include donation-based, rewards-based, equity-based, and debt-based crowdfunding, each offering different incentives and financial structures for fundraisers and contributors. It is also possible to classify debt-based and rewards-based crowdfunding models as non-capital-intensive and, debt-based and equity-based types as capital-intensive.

2.1. Donation and Rewards Based Crowdfunding Models

Donation-based crowdfunding initiatives are very common especially to accomplish a social responsibility movement to support the ideas for community benefits, for example recovering the damages after the natural disasters or financing art projects such as publishing a book, releasing an audio album records. They usually do not seek for-profit purposes. The roots of this kind of financing are based on philanthropy.

Crowdfunding involves entrepreneurs launching new product ideas through open call announcements on platforms. These projects raise funds by offering rewards such as products, services, pre-sale orders, discounts, or other incentives. Entrepreneurs provide brief product information and explain specifications in a short video before launching the product to the market. They also market the product, offer pre-order options, and provide price privileges to collect funds for production launch (Belleflamme et al., 2014).

2.2. Debt-Based Crowdfunding Model

It is a financing approach known as peer-to-peer (P2P) lending where individuals or enterprises borrow funds from creditors and repay the loans with interest over time. This method eliminates transaction fees for financial institutions like banks. This kind of crowdfunding model could be in the form of micro credits or larger amounts. Kiva.org, a social entrepreneurship initiative, provides an environment for individuals to receive micro credits for their financial needs. Lenders support borrowers without considering for-profit purposes, and after achieving financial sources, individuals repay the debt. This model is based on voluntary community mutualization.

On the other hand, the platforms such as Lending Club and Prosper Marketplace provide a more commercial atmosphere for the creditors and borrowers. The borrowers who need funds to finance the projects or pay their financial obligation apply to the platform. The business strategy of the model relies on little amounts of debt from a variety of creditors. The platform estimates the potential risks and assigns a credit score for the borrower then issues debt notes. Yet, the creditors choose the project in which they lend and buy the notes in return for the amount. The platform facilitates the process for both parties in return for getting small amount of fees in transactions.

2.3. Equity-Based Crowdfunding Model

Investors make financial contributions in return for ownership or shares in the business. This business model enables investors to become shareholders and engage in the achievement of the firms. Equity crowdfunding is an alternative model instead of business angels, risk capital and joint ventures where the entrepreneurs seek shareholders before offering their shares in public. It is very common especially among startups and rising entities that need external funds to implement their ideas in return for profit sharing after the project gets success at the market.

3. CROWDFUNDING PRACTICES IN THE EMERGING MARKETS

Institutions such as IMF, S&P, Dow Jones and, FTSE have characterized emerging markets for years. The economies are diversified in terms of the parameters that the institutions have assigned like GDP, growth rate and other socio-economic indicators. The "E7 economies" are a group of seven emerging economies with significant potential for growth and global impact. These include Brazil, India, China, Mexico, Turkey, Russia, and, Indonesia known for their large populations, robust economic growth, and growing influence in global politics.

Crowdfunding revolutionized conventional fundraising tools by enabling people, businesses, and organizations to use online platforms to connect with a worldwide audience. Crowdfunding campaigns can promptly gather momentum and attract support from an extensive network of backers by utilizing the power of social networks. Entrepreneurs who need small amount of financial sources to carry out their projects usually apply reward type crowdfunding. On the other hand, to finance the bigger amounts of funds, entrepreneurs prefer equity crowdfunding instead which enables profit sharing (Belleflamme et al., 2014). Ahmed and Rashid (2019) discussed about the potential benefits of crowdfunding campaigns for the SMEs in Nigeria and propose a conceptual framework. They mention that although the share of SMEs in total economy achieves 90%, the contribution to the economic development and the GDP is below 10% and they believe that crowdfunding will improve the economic growth by funding the SMEs.

The key component in the prevalence of the crowdfunding is accessibility to the internet. As it is demonstrated on the Figure 3, the proportion of the population residing in emerging markets and the World indicates the individuals using the internet. Although the internet usage levels are incrementally rising up by years on the list, two markets namely Indonesia and, India are still below the World average. Web 2.0 and the internet have boosted the use of crowdfunding financing globally, particularly in developing countries. This innovative investment and financing model offers useful marketing instruments. Although developed countries have made advances, the implementation of this technology remains limited in developing countries (Debbabi & Kaplan, 2022).

Figure 3. Individuals using the Internet (% of Population)

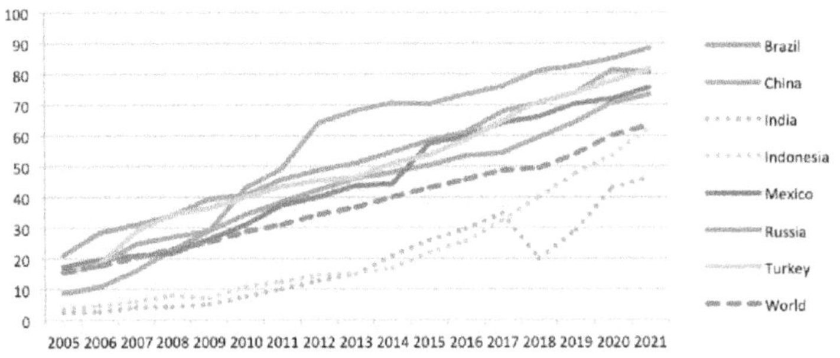

Source: https://data.worldbank.org

The crowdfunding market in E7 countries continues to grow rapidly, driven by factors such as increasing internet penetration, rising entrepreneurial activity, and growing investor interest in alternative investment opportunities.

Table 1. Comparison of Crowdfunding Activities in E7 Countries

	Types of Crowdfunding	Popular Platforms	Regulatory Body	Market Size is projected to reach in 2024 (USD)*
BRAZIL	Donation-Based, Rewards-Based, Debt-Based, Equity-Based, Real estate crowdfunding.	Kickante, Catarse, Benfeitoria, StartMeUp, Vakinha.	Securities Commission (Comissão de Valores Mobiliários - CVM)	US$5.84m
CHINA	Donation-Based, Rewards-Based, Debt-Based, Equity-Based, Property-based crowdfunding.	Taobao Crowdfunding, JD Crowdfunding, Zhongchou.	China Securities Regulatory Commission (CSRC) and the People's Bank of China (PBOC)	US$35.4m
INDIA	Donation-Based, Rewards-Based, Debt-Based, Equity-Based.	Ketto, Wishberry, Fueladream.	Securities and Exchange Board of India (SEBI)	US$5.77m
INDONESIA	Donation-Based, Rewards-Based, Debt-Based, Real estate crowdfunding.	Kitabisa, Bizhare, Crowde, Tanifund, Gandengtangan	Financial Services Authority (OJK)	US$7.0m
MEXICO	Donation-Based, Rewards-Based, Debt-Based, Equity-Based.	Fondeadora, Donadora, playbusiness.mx	National Banking and Securities Commission (CNBV)	US$2.6m
RUSSIA	Donation-Based, Rewards-Based, Debt-Based, Equity-Based.	Planeta.ru, Boomstarter, CrowdRepublic.	Central Bank of the Russian Federation (CBR) and the Federal Service for Financial Markets	US$11.9m
TURKEY	Donation-Based, Rewards-Based, Equity-Based.	Fongogo, Fonbulucu, Fonlabuyusun, Fonangels, Narfon, Bulusum.biz	Capital Markets Board of Turkey (SPK)	US$16.6m

* https://www.statista.com/outlook/fmo/capital-raising/digital-capital-raising

Creek et. al. (2023) investigated the impact of opinions regarding market orientation and unfamiliarity among crowdfunding backers on the impact of crowdfunding on emerging economies. They discovered that fundraising levels are positively correlated with behavioral market orientation signals, whereas decision criteria signals negatively effect it. Hapsari and Sulung (2021) ascertain how social capital and reward considerations have a big part in making crowdfunding campaigns successful in emerging economies from January 2017 to February 2019. Their study utilizes Ordinary Least Square data analysis for hypothesis testing, utilizing cross-sectional and secondary data from Kickstarter.com that represents campaigns from Russia, Brazil, South Africa, China, and India. Results show that internal social capital and customized rewards significantly influence fundraising success. External social capital and ego and community rewards have no influence. Project features, such as target amount and duration, also play a role (Hapsari and Sulung 2021). Nania and Sulung (2019) analyzed the influence of the reputation of the entrepreneur, the level of activity of backers, and the impact of entrepreneurial activity on the fundraising efficacy of crowdfunding initiatives from 2011 to 2018 in developing countries. The research uses data from three BRICS crowdfunding platforms. Results show that backer's activeness positively influences fundraising performance by providing constructive comments, reducing risk from asymmetric information, and demonstrating credibility through previous project success. The potential of crowdfunding in emerging countries where SMEs are most in need has not been fully realized. Erasmus et. al. (2023) analyzed the commercial potential of crowdfunding practices as a capital for SMEs in these countries. Results suggest that increasing public awareness of crowdfunding is crucial, as it exhibits empathy towards emerging enterprises and eagerness to assist and promote startup ventures. The motivations behind crowdfunding participation are not necessarily financial, but rather emotional.

3.1. Brazil

Brazil's crowdfunding scene has grown significantly due to its regulatory environment and the development of platforms. The market started in 2011 with Catarse and Kickante, offering flexible financing options for entrepreneurs, startups, and creative projects. StartMeUp focuses on equity crowdfunding, connecting investors with startups, while Benfeitoria specializes in creative and cultural projects. Brazil's Securities and Exchange Commission (CVM) introduced regulations for equity crowdfunding, allowing SMEs to raise capital through online platforms. CVM Resolution No. 588, enacted in 2017, establishes the legal framework, outlining platform rules, rights and obligations, and disclosure requirements for investor transparency.

Mourão et al. (2018) analyze the success of crowdfunding campaigns on the Kickante platform in Brazil. The researchers discovered a positive correlation between the number of backers, the lowest amount of money spent on rewards, and specific types of promoters or entities, and the total value of each project. The study suggests that a project's success depends on the right promoters and the use of convenient rewards for minimum investment. Mendes-Da-Silva et al. (2015) analyze 1835 pledges made to ten music production campaigns that are hosted on Catarse, the biggest platform in Brazil. The researchers assess the correlation between the duration of fundraising campaigns, the geographical distance between the backer and the project holder, and the backer's propensity to support projects. The study reveals a negative correlation between distance and capital pledged to projects, indicating that entrepreneurs' network may be crucial in funding. It also contradicts the idea that crowdfunding reduces donor-entrepreneur distance. Long project exposure leads to higher pledge values. Martins and Medeiros (2018) analyzed 43 tourism projects funded through Brazilian crowdfunding platforms, focusing on their scope, monetary goals, success, and geographic distribution. The study found that factors like social and environmental relevance, as well as rewards, contributes to campaign success. Felipe (2015) explores the concept of generating common value in Brazil's crowdfunding industry, focusing on the social elements and the creation of value in businesses developed through crowdfunding platforms. It aims to answer two central questions: what aspects of the shared value creation theory are present in crowdfunding and how it manifests itself in businesses founded on crowdfunding platforms. The study finds that reciprocity is perceived when the relationship between entrepreneur and investor is not simply localized, and sustainability is evident when the relationship is not intermediated by a financial agent, avoiding interest payments and administrative fees.

Amedomar and Spers (2018) explore into the reasons behind the preference of Brazilian Technology-Based Companies (TBCs) for rewards-based crowdfunding as a financing source. Four TBCs from various industries were included in a multiple-case study together with a crowdfunding platform. Five companies were selected: three successful campaigns, one unsuccessful but significant-funded campaign, and a pioneer crowdfunding platform, Catarse.me. The study found that TBCs choose rewards-based crowdfunding model because they are in the beginning stages of development, seeking funds for specific projects, and for motivations that do not directly involve fundraising. Lima and Araújo (2019) examine the impact of technological segments on crowdfunding platforms' operations in Brazil. A qualitative and exploratory approach was used, with a panel of experts conducting semi-structured interviews. The findings suggest that internet access is a key factor in scalability and the use of analytics for developing markets. The cultural feature also plays a role in platform access. The study highlights the importance of regulations and the socio-cultural segment in fostering co-creation and scaling crowdfunding operations. Analytics and marketing initiatives can significantly impact crowdfunding adoption, especially in developed economies with widespread internet connectivity and high-quality access. Another research by Bronzeri and Cunha (2021) analyzed the main objectives of crowdfunding campaigns for technological innovation in Brazil, using case studies and surveys. Qualitative content analysis identified financial, marketing, and product financing objectives. The findings revealed that crowdfunding provides an alternative funding source for innovation, contributing to market concerns, fostering entrepreneurship, and assisting in the economy's recovery post-Covid-19. Crowdfunding can also help to overcome the recession and promote economic revival.

Equity crowdfunding is a popular financing method for startups in Brazil, offering efficient financing. A study held by Mourão et. al. (2019) examining the factors determining the success of these campaigns found that venture profile characteristics can determine the success. 99 startup fundraising campaigns between 2014 and 2017 were examined in the study using logistic regression and survival models. The findings can help formulate strategies for estimating success and ensuring appropriate financial resource allocation.

Crowdfunding is a popular method for raising funds for political campaigns, allowing individuals to contribute to a cause and diversifying funding sources. Secchi et al. (2022) examined the use of crowdfunding in the Brazilian Congress election campaign in the 2018 general elections. Logistic regression is used in the study to examine the influence of socioeconomic and demographic profiles on candidates' decisions to adopt crowdfunding. The results suggest that white, young, well educated candidates from Brazil's Southern area, as well as candidates from newly formed and larger parties, used crowdfunding more frequently. The econometric model predicts an average rise of 5.55 percentage points in electoral success.

3.2. China

The Chinese crowdfunding industry, which gained popularity since 2011, faces slow diffusion due to its complexity. From the viewpoint of startups, Yang and Lee (2019) looked at the factors that encourage and discourage crowdfunding adoption intention using two-factor theory, status quo bias theory, and innovation diffusion theory. The results will fill the gap in empirical research in innovation resistance, shed light on entrepreneurs' motivations to avoid crowdfunding as a financing course, and provide strategic recommendations for crowdfunding managers and policymakers. Xie et al (2019) conducted a simulation study on crowdfunding success factors using a large sample of 5208 from Taobao.com, a leading Chinese platform. The study evaluated project positioning and funding decisions in a massive market, considering factors like project number, investor per project, entrepreneurs' moral risk, and community over financial benefits ratio. The results revealed complex crowdfunding market dynamics.

According to Funk (2019) China's crowdfunding market is unique compared to the West, with features such as donation-based crowdfunding and e-commerce crowdfunding being tailored to China's specific needs. The market is dominated by established players and start-up CFPs with substantial capitalization, influenced by the country's history of informal finance and advanced internet sectors like mobile internet, e-commerce, and payments. Cultural factors, as well as distinctive Chinese customs and values, further contribute to the hybrid character of crowdfunding in China. Based on social capital theory, Zheng et al. (2014) discovered that an entrepreneur's social network, commitments to support other entrepreneurs, and shared meaning of the crowdfunding project all have a substantial impact on crowdfunding performance in China and the United States. These factors were more predictive in China than in the United States, and obligation had a higher impact in China. Konhäusner et. al. (2021) studied the marketing mix adaptability of online crowdfunding platforms in Germany and China, focusing on campaign efficiency and company strategy. They analyzed the 4E marketing mix benefits, focusing on experience, value exchange, and marketing scales. The study found that the 4E adaptation is suitable for crowdfunding needs, enabling managers and project owners to better attract their target audience.

Crowdfunding is a popular tool for supporting micro, small, and medium-sized enterprises (MSMEs) by financing activities and facilitating risk-sharing. However, it faces challenges like information asymmetry between fundraisers and potential backers. A study conducted by Usman et al. (2020) discovered that signals such as goal setting, project comments, and updates can help alleviate this problem. In the UK, setting greater goals is strongly correlated with project success, whereas in China, good project comments are strongly linked to success. Hou and Philips (2021) analyzed successful reward-model campaigns in the UK and China, revealing similarities but also some differences. Chinese founders hired click farmers, used culturally significant colors in their pitches, and suggested heavily discounted pre-orders to attract risk-averse crowds.

Shahab et al. (2021) investigated the impact of online comments on the success or failure of alternative startup fundraising campaigns on crowdfunding platforms. Drawing on regulatory focus theory, the researchers discovered that online product or service feedback has a major impact on entrepreneurial enterprises. The findings, based on a dataset of 620 projects from the well-known Chinese crowdfunding portal "Demohour," imply that aspiring entrepreneurs must pay special attention to online criticism in order for their unique ventures to succeed in fundraising. Li et. al. (2022) examined how social capital, social recommendation, and other signals affect the performance of charity crowdfunding. It collected 4,780 pieces of project information from Sina MicroBlog's crowdfunding site. The study discovered that both external and internal social capital have a substantial impact on enhancing fundraising performance. Projects that have a higher number of social endorsements are more certain to acquire financial assistance. Wang et al. (2019) suggested a research model that predicts individuals' intents to donate through crowdfunding using self-determination theory (SDT) and contextual characteristics. Data from China is evaluated using structural equation modeling. The results show that self-identification and social identity mitigate the influence of self-worth, face concern, moral duty, perceived donor efficacy, social contact, and referent network size on donation intention. However, no evidence supports the idea that moral duty and self-identity are linked.

Equity crowdfunding is a novel form of obtaining financing for entrepreneurs that has minimal entry barriers, low fees, and a fast turnaround time. However, issues remain in China's equity crowdfunding practice. Blockchain technology, a decentralized and distributed ledger, has enormous potential in the financial industry because to its data security, transparency, and integrity. Zhu and Zhou (2016) investigated the practical applications of blockchain in Chinese equity crowdfunding, emphasizing its potential for secure, efficient, and low-cost solutions for stock registration, peer-to-peer transactions, regulatory compliance, backer voting systems, and market regulation and investor management.

3.3. India

India is a vibrant commercial location for startups, with a growing competitive sphere in the B2B technology sector, particularly in e-commerce, healthtech, and FinTech (Tripathy, 2018). Understanding the ecosystem requires identifying the actors involved and their influence. Sajjan (2017) seeks to analyze the factors that influence the progress of India's crowdfunding ecosystem and to create a crowdfunding promotion model. The study identified cultural, social, technological, and legislative issues as critical in creating an effective crowdfunding framework in India. Crowdfunding is a rapidly growing investment avenue in the financial services field, with many platforms evolving in the country. Some popular crowdfunding platforms operating in India include Ketto, Milaap, Wishberry, Impact Guru, and Fueladream. Technology has spurred India's startup movement by providing speed, effectiveness, and a varied range of financing alternatives. The government's initiatives to promote and nurture the startup environment could help create a sustainable environment for startups. Crowdfunding has become an essential platform for raising pre-seed capital in India. Kundu et al. (2023) investigated demographic variables, digital usage, and crowdfunding as a feasible alternative for generating pre-seed money and discovered that entrepreneurs' comprehension of utilizing social media platforms for business varies greatly depending on their age, gender, and educational background. Kedia and Mishra (2022) sought to grasp the notion of the proper crowd for crowdfunding, identify variables impacting its selection, and investigate the state of crowdfunding in India. Data was gathered from 191 respondents and processed with SPSS and AMOS software. The study found five variables: technological knowledge, perceived trust, perceived risk, peer influence, and crowdfunding experience. The findings confirmed the five factors of the scale, indicating that crowdfunding platforms can be a valuable tool for entrepreneurs seeking to raise funds. Gedar and Lodha (2024) explored the awareness and challenges of using crowdfunding as a source of finance in India. A survey was conducted with 75 respondents, focusing on demographic profile, awareness, challenges, and popular projects for investment. The results show that people are aware of crowdfunding, but there is a substantial variation in viewpoints depending on educational qualifications. The major challenges faced include lack of information on crowdfunding and the risk of failure and losing money. Baber (2019) investigated the influence of subjective norms on crowdfunding intention. Data from 155 crowdfunding campaign participants was analyzed using statistical tools. Results showed that family and friends significantly influence crowdfunding intentions, with high motivation to comply. Other reference groups like supervisors, teachers, neighbors, and social network friends had no impact.

Banerjee (2021) studied the role of the use of digital crowdfunding platforms in India for nonprofit fundraising, focusing on their complex partnerships with NGOs. It uses data from platforms GlobalGiving and Impact Guru to highlight the problematic nature of marketised fundraising models. The article argues that platforms' focus on profit generation limits their intention to create inclusive fundraising spaces for NGOs, as they constantly adjust and innovate their fundraising strategies. Khurana (2021) examined donor behavior and motivations on donation-based crowdfunding platforms, using data from Ketto.org, India's largest platform. It reveals that non-profit organizations with tax-deduction-qualified causes receive higher funding. Unregistered non-profit organizations and individuals follow. The study suggests that using subtle cues like "with tax-benefit" can motivate donors to provide more funding to unregistered non-profit organizations and individuals.

Fanea-Ivanovici and Baber (2023) compared donation intentions in the US and India using a civic voluntarism model. The study uses 529 questionnaires from the US and 374 from India, analyzing political participation and online community engagement. Results show a positive influence of political participation and political efficacy regarding the act of contributing funds to political crowdfunding campaigns. The differences are based on political participation (Fanea-Ivanovici and Baber, 2023).

3.4. Indonesia

In recent years, the crowdfunding sector is gaining traction in Indonesia and has the ability to make significant strides forward owing to a young, innovative population and a tradition of cooperating as a community. There are crowdfunding platforms namely Bizhare, DANAdidik, Kitabisa, Tanifund, GandengTangan providing medium for funders and fund-seekers. Also there is a broad literature related to the crowdfunding regulations and applications. To fulfill the financial needs of the entrepreneurs, Indonesian government put regulatory measures (Chang, 2018;

Yeon and Putri, 2022; Pratama, 2022). Ibrahim and Verliyantina (2012) suggested a business plan for financing micro-businesses that includes the support of donors and funders, volunteers, field partners, coaches, and non-profit organizations that collaborate in the process of screening, managing, and supervising the use of funds. Once this effective model for SMEs is established, it's not improbable that the platform will be used for other charitable endeavors like sponsoring public health initiatives and educational sponsorship. Arifah and Dalimunthe (2020) research into how financial literacy varies among Indonesian funders and non-funders of non-donation-based crowdfunding and how it affects the country's choice to invest through this type of crowdfunding. The study's major finding demonstrates that financial knowledge makes a significant difference in an Indonesian's tendency to invest through non-donation crowdfunding. Despite Indonesians' generally low financial literacy, the group of investors (funders) showed higher financial knowledge than the non-funders.

Since Indonesia is of the largest Muslim population in the world, Sharia rules apply. Crowdfunding is also performed under these laws and called as Islamic crowdfunding. Three organizations, including Bank Indonesia, the Indonesian Services Authority (OJK), and the National Islamic Board, are in charge of developing and regulating Islamic crowdfunding in Indonesia. Islamic crowdfunding has an effect on SMEs in terms of making access to funding easier, enhancing their welfare, and long-term economic prosperity for the country. The study by Mustafida et al. (2021) use a literature review to explain how Islamic crowdfunding evolves and how it impacts SMEs in Indonesia. The outcome demonstrates that Islamic crowdfunding may assist SMEs in gaining access to funds, boosting welfare, and stimulating economic progress. In similar vein, by using a website platform for new businesses, Hendratmi et al. (2019) aim to develop an Islamic crowdfunding model. This study was intended to provide important insights into the successful creation of an Islamic crowdfunding online platform integrated with startup businesses, investors, and a Sharia committee. The purpose of the study made by Roro et. al (2019) is to advance knowledge of the proportionality principle as it applies to Islamic crowdfunding in Indonesia, particularly as it relates to finance contracts for this new type of business innovation. This essay aims to further objectivity and achieve legal parity between Indonesian and Islamic law. They suggest that in order to keep the parties' relationships harmonious and fair, the proportionality concept ought to be used in Islamic crowdfunding. Through online charity donation-based crowdfunding, Kasri and Indriani (2021) examine the factors impacting Indonesian Muslims' giving behavior. The principal conclusions point to empathy and perceived credibility as the most important factors influencing donors' intentions to donate in charitable crowdfunding. Abdullah and Susamto (2019) examined the growth of the Islamic crowdfunding industry in Indonesia as well as the elements that influence the success of fundraising campaigns for these services. Using a quantitative method, they found that a minimum investment has a negative impact on campaign performance whereas financing objective, campaign duration, payback periods, and rate of return have favorable benefits. Finally, SWOT analysis was done to determine the opportunities and obstacles for the halal industry in using such Islamic crowdfunding service. Crowdfunding is also benefited for the purpose of reducing poverty in Indonesia; Manara et al. (2018) describe an appropriate strategic framework for boosting the potential of through Crowdfunding-Zakat System. With the use of the crowdfunding-zakat system, it is now more convenient to collect zakat money from the larger community in accordance with numerous Indonesian regions that have already demonstrated the potential and beneficial effects on income distribution.

3.5. Mexico

In Mexico, crowdfunding is now a widely used method of generating capital for startups, artists, and other projects. Businesses and individuals can generate money for a project by rewarding backers on websites like Fondeadora, Indiegogo, GoFundMe, Kickstarter and MuckRock. A few examples of these are special events, early access to merchandise, and additional rewards. Investments can be rewarded with a share in a firm through equity crowdfunding platforms like Play Business. Through the sale of shares or stock to several investors, this approach enables firms to raise funds. Peer-to-peer lending is made possible by crowdfunding platforms such as Prestadero, which link borrowers who are personally or professionally qualified with individual lenders. For the purpose of allowing this new financing option, Mexico's crowdfunding regulations have been changing. Crowdfunding operations in Mexico are governed and overseen by the National Banking and Securities Commission (CNBV). Through the Ley de Inversion y Finanzas Pblicas (LIFP), the Mexican government offers a framework for crowdfunding initiatives. This law lays forth the rules and specifications for conducting crowdfunding campaigns.

Gonzâlez et. al. (2021) studied a covariance analysis (Ancova) on a sample of businesses who secured funding through the collective fundraising site Pitchbull in order to ascertain the elements that impact the success financing of SMEs that engage in crowdfunding. The findings demonstrate that risk has a major role in financing success and that the following variables are also important: the amount financed, the interest rate paid, and the number of funders. The length of the loan, on the other hand, is not a significant covariate. The rate of return emerges as the primary motivator for funding enterprises based on the examination of funding performance and its correlation with risk.

Research conducted by García et al. (2021) focuses on assessing how people make decisions about investments and whether they follow herd behavior or not. Based on the gathered statistical data, 57% of the respondents who had backed a crowdfunding project said that they did so because of the project's popularity on the platform. This percentage is significant with a 90% confidence level. As a result, it may be deduced that the study sample's members exhibit statistical support for the prevalence of herd behavior.

Approximately 400,000 small and micro businesses in Mexico were forced to close during the Covid-19-related health contingency lockdown. The purpose of the study made by Segura-Mojica (2021) was to monitor micro-investor attitudes and the variables that might influence their inclination to support the rescue of micro-enterprises and employment in the case of an economic crisis. The study was quantitative, descriptive, and cross-sectional. For the analysis, the Actor-Network Theory (ANT) was utilized. Researchers discovered that, in the event of an economic downturn linked to health risks, roughly 23% of those in the workforce have excess income that could be pooled for group funding. Additionally, micro-investors' enthusiasm for initiatives that either generate new jobs or support the retention of current ones has been strengthened.

3.6. Russia

Similar to Kickstarter and IndieGoGo in the US, Planeta.ru is a crowdfunding website. Every project on Planeta.ru is subject to a 5% commission fee. Equity crowdfunding, on the other hand, is becoming more common in Russia. An online information and trading platform called IPOboard, a division of the Moscow Stock Exchange, assists cutting-edge, small- and medium-sized businesses in obtaining cash. It gives qualified investors the option to buy equity in promising new startups. The Russian crowdfunding market has had substantial volatility, but it is currently exhibiting consistent development. However, the number of successfully supported initiatives is limited. To improve the issue, it is vital to identify which crowdfunding projects potential backers are most likely to support. Ilenkov and Kapustina (2018) conduct a quantitative study of available data on 9179 projects from Russia's two main non-equity crowdfunding platforms, demonstrating that many Russians have similar preferences for backing initiatives with distinctive characteristics.

Russia has been experimenting with crowdfunding platforms like Kickstarter and Indiegogo, aiming to replicate their success. Between 2010 and 2013, there was a development of local platforms for raising funds online. However, the performance of these platforms is determined by the features of the national market as well as competition from foreign platforms. Torkanovskiy (2016) investigated the economics of Russian crowdfunding and its link with the worldwide community, providing a framework for speculating on its national and local development circumstances.

Tsvirko (2020) examines crowdfunding in Russia using a PEST analysis method. It identifies several drivers for its development, including new legislation, the need for financial resources for small and medium enterprises, and the demand for investment opportunities under lowered interest rates. However, the study also highlights the constraints of crowdfunding in Russia, including unresolved regulatory issues, poor investor protection, potential fraud, low real income and savings, and low profitability of many businesses.

The article by Garmashev et. al (2021) analyzes the legal regulations of crowdfunding and investment platforms in Germany, Russia, the USA, and France. It identifies risks and problems associated with using these platforms. The US, France, Germany, and Russia have specific crowdfunding legislation, which helps interested parties navigate the environment. However, Russia's legislation does not directly mention crowdfunding, leading to legal conflicts and limiting individual citizens' rights to attract investments. Mironova (2018) conducts a comparative analysis of two crowdfunding sites, namely Planeta.ru in Russia and Makeachamp in Canada, with a specific emphasis on sports crowdfunding. The analysis evaluates the benefits and drawbacks of each platform. Planeta.ru is the most extensive Russian platform for sports initiatives, whereas Makeachamp provides superior conditions for fundraising and aids to the successful completion of projects. The results show that both platforms have successfully developed and completed projects.

Kovshova and Nair (2017) aim to understand the reasons behind backers' participation in crowdfunding in Russia. The study categorizes users of the Russian crowdfunding portal Planeta.ru into two primary groups: external and internal, based on either project characteristics or user personality, as determined through in-depth interviews. The results show that the emotional, non-pecuniary nature of reasons among Russian respondents can be attributed to the novelty of crowdfunding as an alternative financing method, the 'supportive' logic of funders, and the current nature of projects on the platform. This shift in motivation towards charity projects is at the intrinsic end of the motivation continuum. Ilenkov (2019) analyzes the factors contributing to technology project success in crowdfunding using correlation and cluster analysis on 832 projects on two popular Russian crowdfunding platforms. The findings indicate that there is a negative correlation between an increase in project budget targets and the likelihood and magnitude of success. This implies that crowdfunding might be crucial in providing financial support for a select few Russian technology firms, given the typical amounts of investment received are insufficient for the majority of startups.

The Covid-19 pandemic did not directly impact the crowdfunding sector, according to a research that examined 7,024 rewards-based crowdfunding campaigns on two prominent Russian platforms. The study applied digital methodologies and conducted multiple regression analysis to examine the dynamics of demand and supply. It found that the sector remained resilient to the pandemic, unlike other investment classes. The study also revealed that sponsors' readiness to finance projects was highly seasonal, with more backers willing to invest in projects near year-end (Torkanovskiy and Voinov (2022)).

3.7. Turkey

In Turkey, the crowdfunding activities are steadily evolving, reflecting the growing entrepreneurial culture, increasing internet usage, and supportive regulatory infrastructure. There have been initiatives, which assist to collect funds to realize social responsibility projects, independent art and cultural activities. Online crowdfunding portals crowdfon.com, fongogo.com, and fonbulucu.com have all staged donation and crowdfunding events. Turkish Capital Markets Board regulates crowdfunding, with the first act defining it as collecting funds from the public through online platforms. The second regulation, drafted in early 2019 and promulgated in 2021, focuses on legal arrangements for Debt-based and equity crowdfunding campaigns, online platforms, and emerging startups for fund collection. Both acts aim to ensure fair and transparent crowdfunding practices in Turkey.

Crowdfunding, an innovative approach to entrepreneurship in the era of digitization, has gained popularity in Turkey and abroad due to increased user interest. Kilinc et. al. (2022) analyzed 1635 crowdfunding projects on various platforms, revealing a 23.18% success rate in projects. The most successful category was film-video-photo, with 34.36% success rate. The study suggests that while there have been more projects and users on crowdfunding platforms, the success rate has dropped.

Debbabi and Kaplan (2022) explore the genesis of crowdfunding and its foundations, as well as its marketing bases and benefits. Turkey has favorable conditions for crowdfunding development, but cultural, technical, economical, and political factors still hinder its growth. Strategic improvements are needed to overcome these challenges and enhance accessibility. It is the responsibility of financial and governmental organizations to establish a secure environment for entrepreneurship, improve laws, monitor platforms, and reinforce security systems. Public awareness campaigns and successful campaigns should be popularized.

Crowdfunding platforms have become a global platform for showcasing innovative approaches and products. However, awareness of crowdfunding is still low in Turkey. Turkish entrepreneurs have been motivated by the achievements of worldwide crowdfunding platforms like as Kickstarter and Indiegogo to establish their own local crowdfunding websites such as Fongogo, Crowdfon, Fonlabeni. However, these local platforms struggled due to usability issues. The research by Kayhan (2017) aims to identify the issues and evaluate the efficiency, effectiveness, and satisfaction of Fongogo, the most widely used Turkish crowdfunding website. A quantitative usability test was conducted on 14 Turkish users aged 20-40 and over 40, along with interviews with project owners and previous users. The findings suggest that usability problems negatively affect funding campaigns and suggest improvements for both backers and project owners. Sırma et. al. (2019) concluded a significant positive correlation between innovativeness and crowdfunding intention. Innovative individuals are eager to support projects on crowdfunding platforms in Turkey. This strong relationship could lead policymakers to emphasize innovativeness in the crowdfunding field, as it would encourage more people to support projects offered on these platforms. Demiray and Burnaz (2019) sought to ascertain the optimal positioning of crowdfunding platforms within Turkish burgeoning crowdfunding market. The analysis presents a positioning map of crowdfunding platforms, which is determined by two primary factors: the degree of complexity associated with regulatory procedures and the amount of competence in different project categories. The positioning map provides a comprehensive perspective for existing and prospective participants in the crowdfunding business, including platform managers, project creators, and funders. The first dimension is strongly related to crowdfunding models, providing insights into motivational factors, funding mechanisms, risk perception, enterprise life cycle phases, and required money. Platforms with low complexity levels are suitable for early-stage projects, while platforms with high complexity levels target funders with high risk and high return expectancy. Platforms operating at a multi-category level may have more volume compared to those operating as less or single category platforms. In their study, Gür and Özdoğan (2021) investigated the components of the technology acceptance model in the specific setting of scientific crowdfunding. They discovered that performance expectation has a favorable impact on the behavioral intention to use science crowdfunding, while social influence had the most significant effect.

4. FINANCIAL REPORTING STANDARDS AND ACCOUNTING REGULATIONS IN THE E7 COUNTRIES

Brazil has made significant progress in converging its accounting standards with IFRS. Since 2010, Brazilian publicly traded companies and large private entities have been mandated to follow IFRS while preparing their consolidated financial accounts. China has been gradually converging its accounting standards with IFRS since 2006. Listed companies in China are required to announce their financial

Evaluating the Impact of Crowdfunding on Emerging Markets

reports using Chinese Accounting Standards (CAS), which are mostly aligned with IFRS. Indian Accounting Standards (Ind AS) govern financial reporting in India, which is largely converged with IFRS, promoting global comparability and transparency. The Indonesian Financial Accounting Standards Board (IFASB), which establishes the standards in compliance with IFRS, is principally responsible for overseeing financial reporting standards in Indonesia. Mexico has achieved complete convergence of its accounting standards for publicly traded companies with IFRS since 2012. The convergence of the Mexican Financial Reporting Standards (NIFs) with IFRS ensures comparability and consistency with global standards. Russia has been striving to align its accounting standards with the IFRS. Although there are differences between Russian Accounting Standards (RAS) and IFRS, there have been gradual efforts to bring them into alignment. Turkey has adopted IFRS as the foundation for the guidelines for financial reporting for listed companies since 2005. Turkish Financial Reporting Standards (TFRS), which are largely converged with IFRS, are applicable to listed companies and certain other entities in Turkey.

Table 2. Comparison of Financial Reporting Standards and Accounting Regulations in E7 Countries

	IFRS Accounting Standards are required for domestic public companies	IFRS Accounting Standards are required or permitted for listings by foreign companies	The IFRS for SMEs Accounting Standard is required or permitted	The IFRS for SMEs Accounting Standard is under consideration
BRAZIL	Required.	Required.	Required.	
CHINA	China's national standards are closely aligned with IFRS Standards, and it has committed to adopting IFRS Standards for domestic companies, with over 30% of the market capitalisation producing IFRS-compliant financial statements.	Foreign companies do not trade currently in Chinese securities markets. Therefore, there is no relevant regulation on whether those companies would be permitted to use IFRS Standards.	No.	No.
INDIA	Indian Accounting Standards (Ind AS) are largely aligned with IFRS Standards, but India has not yet officially adopted IFRS Standards for domestic company reporting and has not committed to doing so.	No.	No.	No.

continued on following page

Table 2. Continued

	IFRS Accounting Standards are required for domestic public companies	IFRS Accounting Standards are required or permitted for listings by foreign companies	The IFRS for SMEs Accounting Standard is required or permitted	The IFRS for SMEs Accounting Standard is under consideration
INDONESIA	Indonesia is converting its national standards towards IFRS Standards without a comprehensive plan for full adoption of IFRS Standards for domestic company reporting.	No. All foreign companies whose securities trade in a public market are required to use Indonesian national accounting standards.	No.	No.
MEXICO	All listed companies must follow IFRS Standards except for financial institutions and insurance companies, which must follow national standards.	Foreign company may use either IFRS Standards or US GAAP.	No. No particular accounting framework is required for SMEs. Mexican national standards are used by most SMEs.	No.
RUSSIA	IFRS Standards required for listed companies, financial institutions and some government-owned companies.	Required for some, permitted for others.	No.	Yes.
TURKEY	IFRS Standards adopted as Turkish Accounting Standards are required for listed companies, financial institutions, and other public interest entities.	Required.	No.	No.

Source: https://www.ifrs.org/use-around-the-world/use-of-ifrs-standards-by-jurisdiction/

5. FINANCIAL REPORTING AND TAXATION MECHANISM OF CROWDFUNDING PRACTICES IN COMPLIANCE WITH IFRS

IFRS do not have specific guidelines for crowdfunding activities, but they focus on accounting and financial reporting for businesses and organizations. The accounting treatment of crowdfunding transactions may depend on the specific nature of the campaign and the financial reporting requirements of the entity involved. Entities must determine the appropriate accounting treatment for funds received, such as revenue, liability, or equity, depending on the terms and conditions of the campaign. Equity crowdfunding campaigns may involve the recognition of financial instruments, such as IFRS 9, which deals with financial instruments. Revenue recognition principles under IFRS 15 may be applicable for crowdfunding campaigns where funds are received in exchange for goods or services. Entities may also need to provide specific disclosures in their financial statements about the nature and terms of crowdfunding activities, including any contingent liabilities or obligations. Fair value measurement may be necessary, depending on the nature of crowdfunding, in accordance with relevant IFRS 13 standards. Donovan (2021) examined the implications of financial reporting and accounting on entrepreneurial finance, focusing on equity crowdfunding. The study reveals a positive correlation between financial reporting and capital raised, suggesting accounting reduces information asymmetry with investors. The importance of financial reporting varies across different sectors, with greater capital raised observed during longer historical operations, higher macroeconomic uncertainty, and detailed shareholder agreements. Financial reporting indirectly enhances post-performance by increasing capital raising likelihood. Axelton and Chandna (2023) suggest that issuers with quality financial reporting and disclosure practices are more likely to succeed in regulatory crowdfunding, as they meet all regulatory agencies' requirements, enhance financial statement credibility, and reduce asymmetry. The study by Narklor (2020) uses a mixed-method approach to examine the use of accounting and non-accounting information in the Thai equity crowdfunding setting. The study reveals that business model, estimated revenue, cost, and cash flow are crucial for investors, while non-accounting information like product/service characteristics and market potential also plays a significant role. Investors with mixed-type information are more likely to invest in equity crowdfunding campaigns. However, cognitive errors and emotional bias negatively influence investment decisions, suggesting that investment education could help reduce unfavorable outcomes resulting from investor bias.

Crowdfunding activities are subject to various tax regulations across different countries, influenced by the specific type of crowdfunding campaigns and the present regulatory structure. Rewards-based crowdfunding, where contributions are considered gifts, may be exempt from income tax for the campaign creator. Donation-based crowdfunding, where funds are collected for philanthropic causes, may qualify for tax deductions for donors in certain countries. Personal fundraising, where funds are received as personal gifts, may be exempt from income tax for the recipient. Equity crowdfunding involves equity investment taxation, where individuals who contribute financially to a company receive ownership stakes or shares as a result of their investments. Investors who earn dividends or realize capital gains from their equity crowdfunding investments may be obligated to comply with specific tax regulations pertaining to investment income. Peer-to-peer lending interest rates also involve interest income taxation. The precise tax implications of crowdfunding activities depend on factors such as the fundraising amount, campaign's objective, and the legal framework of the campaign creator (e.g., individual, business, non-profit organization). The 2016 US security-based crowdfunding regulations allow startups to raise funds via digital platforms. However, there's limited guidance on optimal methods for presenting financial information and providing a comprehensive account of disclosures.

6. CONCLUSION

Entrepreneurship is the primary catalyst of economic progress at the most fundamental level of society. Nowadays, entrepreneurship serves as the cornerstone of socioeconomic development and is heavily encouraged by national policies in emerging economies. The entrepreneurial revolution has propelled the endeavor to merge human aspects and digitization in order to achieve commercial growth and economic development. Crowdfunding is an emerging alternative to traditional equity markets for raising capital. Comparing to the developed countries' economies, the adoption of crowdfunding in emerging markets is still in early period. These emerging economies are required to reduce the unemployment rates, poverty and also improve the living standards to sustain economic growth by supporting their startups. The construction of legal and technical structure is made thoroughly to avoid malfeasance. In most of the emerging markets, the legal structure is still under process in comparison with the developed countries' economies. To avoid the fraud and protect the investment ecosystem, the authorities act more prudently. On the other hand, the contribution of crowdfunding type of investment on economic development is significant. Russia and Turkey has caught the nascent entrepreneurship climate and taken significant legal steps to contribute to the economic development.

In summary, the customized financial reporting standards for crowdfunding activities have not been regulated yet. IFRS do not include particular requirements for crowdfunding operations, although they do address accounting and financial reporting for corporations and organizations. The accounting treatment of crowdfunding transactions may vary according on the nature of the campaign and the entity's financial reporting needs. Depending on the terms and conditions of the campaign, entities must determine whether amounts received should be recorded as income, liability, or equity. Equity crowdfunding campaigns may require the reporting of financial instruments, such as IFRS 9, but revenue recognition procedures under IFRS 15 may apply to campaigns in which money are received in return for products or services. Entities may also be required to make particular disclosures in their financial statements concerning the nature and conditions of crowdfunding operations, such as any contingent liabilities or commitments. Fair value measurement may be required in line with applicable IFRS 13 requirements. Crowdfunding activities are subject to different tax regulations across countries, depending on the crowdfunding models and the existing regulatory framework. Rewards-based crowdfunding may be exempt from income tax for campaign creators, while donation-based crowdfunding may qualify for tax deductions for donors. Personal fundraising may also be exempt from income tax for recipients. Equity crowdfunding involves equity investment taxation, where individuals receive ownership stakes or shares as a result of their investments. Investors who earn dividends or realize capital gains from their equity crowdfunding investments may be obligated to comply with specific tax regulations. Peer-to-peer lending interest rates also involve interest income taxation.

REFERENCES

Abdullah, Z., & Susamto, A. A. (2019). The Role of Investment-Based Islamic Crowdfunding for Halal MSMEs: Evidence from Indonesia. *Al-Iqtishad: Jurnal Ilmu Ekonomi Syariah*, 11(2), 289–302.

Açıkgöz, B., Mutlu, M. D., & Kesebir, M. (2019). BANKACILIK SEKTÖRÜNDE DÜZEN BOZUCU INOVASYON: KİTLESEL FONLAMA. In İşletme ve Yönetim Araştırmaları II (pp. 15–32). Akademisyen Yayınevi, Türkiye.

Ahmed, M., & Rashid, A. (2019). Crowdfunding as Financial Option for Small and Medium Enterprises (SMEs) in Nigeria. *Pertanika J. Sch. Res. Rev.*, 4, 89–96.

Amedomar, A., & Spers, R. (2018). Reward-based crowdfunding: A study of the entrepreneurs' motivations when choosing the model as a venture capital alternative in Brazil. *International Journal of Innovation*, 6(2), 147–163. 10.5585/iji.v6i2.283

Arifah, J. N., & Dalimunthe, Z. (2020). The impact of financial literacy on the investment decision of non-donation-based crowdfunding in Indonesia. *International Journal of Business and Society*, 21(3), 1045–1057. 10.33736/ijbs.3310.2020

Axelton, Z., & Chandna, V. (2023). A practical guide to SEC financial reporting and disclosures for successful regulatory crowdfunding. *Business Horizons*, 66(6), 709–719. 10.1016/j.bushor.2023.02.006

Baber, H. (2019). Subjective norms and intention-A study of crowdfunding in India. *Research in World Economy*.

Banerjee, S. A. (2021). Digital philanthropy for the masses: Crowdfunding platforms marketising NGO partnerships for individual giving in India. *Development in Practice*, 31(7), 896–908. 10.1080/09614524.2021.1938515

Belleflamme, P., Lambert, T., & Schwienbacher, A. (2014). Crowdfunding: Tapping the right crowd. *Journal of Business Venturing*, 29(5), 585–609. 10.1016/j.jbusvent.2013.07.003

Chang, S. E. (2018). Regulation of crowdfunding in Indonesia. *Law Review*, 18(1), 41–71. 10.19166/lr.v0i1.1159

Creek, S. A., Maurer, J. D., & Kent, J. K. (2023). Perceptions of market orientation in emerging economy entrepreneurship: evidence from crowdfunding. *International Journal of Emerging Markets*.

Cumming, D., & Zhang, Y. (2016). Alternative investments in emerging markets: A review and new trends. *Emerging Markets Review*, 29, 1–23. 10.1016/j.ememar.2016.08.022

Debbabi, R., & Kaplan, B. (2022). Why crowdfunding? Understanding crowdfunding and the marketing roots of this fundraising model in Turkey. *Business & Management Studies: An International Journal*, 10(1), 429–446. 10.15295/bmij.v10i1.1996

Demiray, M., & Burnaz, S. (2019). Positioning of crowdfunding platforms: Turkey as an emerging market case. *Journal of Management Marketing and Logistics*, 6(2), 84–94. 10.17261/Pressacademia.2019.1036

Donovan, J. (2021). Financial reporting and entrepreneurial finance: Evidence from equity crowdfunding. *Management Science*, 67(11), 7214–7237. 10.1287/mnsc.2020.3810

Erasmus, A. C., Tocknell, G., & Schutte, F. (2023). The potential of crowdfunding to promote business in the context of an emerging economy. *Journal of Financial Services Marketing*, 28(3), 558–569. 10.1057/s41264-022-00165-w

Fanea-Ivanovici, M., & Baber, H. (2023). Using the civic voluntarism model to compare the donation intentions in US and India political crowdfunding. *International Journal of Electronic Governance*, 15(2), 188–201. 10.1504/IJEG.2023.132366

Felipe, I. J. D. S. (2015). Shared value creation and crowdfunding in Brazil. *Journal of Financial Innovation*, 1(3), 213–230.

Funk, A. S. (2019). Crowdfunding in China. In *Crowdfunding in China. Contributions to Management Science*. Springer. 10.1007/978-3-319-97253-4_5

García, D. A. R., Mata, L. M., & Mora, J. A. N. (2021). Herd Behavior Analysis in Crowdfunding Platforms in Mexico. *Entrepreneurship and Regional Development: Analyzing Growth Models in Emerging Markets*, 67-90.

Garmashev, M. A., Sakhno, J. A., Peremyshlennikova, I. N., Sedova, N. A., & Staroselzeva, M. M. (2021). Legal regulation of crowdfunding and investment platforms: The experience of the United States, Russia and Europe. *Linguistics and Culture Review*, 5(S3), 958–966. 10.21744/lingcure.v5nS3.1695

Gedar, B. L., & Lodha, S. (2024). Crowdfunding as a Source of Finance in India: An Empirical Study. *IUP Journal of Applied Finance, 30*(1).

González, J. D. J., Valdés Medina, F. E., & Saavedra García, M. L. (2021). Success factors in financing for SMEs through crowdfunding in Mexico. *Revista Mexicana de Economía y Finanzas*, 16(2).

Gür, U., & Özdoğan, B. (2021). Scientists' technology acceptance of crowdfunding in Turkey: The moderating effect of individual entrepreneurial orientation. *Journal of Entrepreneurship and Innovation Management*, 10(1), 53–80.

Hapsari, N. S., & Sulung, L. A. K. (2021, May). The Role of Social Capital and Reward Factor in the Success of Crowdfunding Project Fundraising: Case Study of Emerging Market Countries. In *Asia-Pacific Research in Social Sciences and Humanities Universitas Indonesia Conference (APRISH 2019)* (pp. 591-599). Atlantis Press.

Hendratmi, A., Ryandono, M. N. H., & Sukmaningrum, P. S. (2019). Developing Islamic crowdfunding website platform for startup companies in Indonesia. *Journal of Islamic Marketing*, 11(5), 1041–1053. 10.1108/JIMA-02-2019-0022

Ibrahim, N., & Verliyantina, V. (2012). The model of crowdfunding to support small and micro businesses in Indonesia through a web-based platform. *Procedia Economics and Finance*, 4, 390–397. 10.1016/S2212-5671(12)00353-X

Ilenkov, D. (2019). Technology Crowdfunding in Russia: Alternative Finance for Start-ups. [IJEBA]. *International Journal of Economics & Business Administration*, 7(2), 3–11. 10.35808/ijeba/210

Ilenkov, D., & Kapustina, V. (2018). Crowdfunding in Russia: An empirical study. *European Research Studies*, 21(2), 401–410. 10.35808/ersj/1010

Kasri, R. A., & Indriani, E. (2022). Empathy or perceived credibility? An empirical study of Muslim donating behaviour through online charitable crowdfunding in Indonesia. *International Journal of Islamic and Middle Eastern Finance and Management*, 15(5), 829–846. 10.1108/IMEFM-09-2020-0468

Kayhan, S. (2017). Fongogo: A case study on the usability of the local crowdfunding and fundraising websites in Turkey. *HUMANITAS-Uluslararası Sosyal Bilimler Dergisi*, 5(09), 95–105. 10.20304/humanitas.318510

Kedia, P., & Mishra, L. (2022). Factors Underlying Selection of the Right Crowd for Crowdfunding in India. *IUP Journal of Accounting Research & Audit Practices*, 21(3), 133–149.

Khurana, I. (2021). Legitimacy and reciprocal altruism in donation-based crowdfunding: Evidence from India. *Journal of Risk and Financial Management*, 14(5), 194. 10.3390/jrfm14050194

Kilinc, M., Aydin, C., & Tarhan, C. (2022). Türkiye'de sosyal ve dijital girişimcilik: Veri kazıma teknikleriyle kitle fonlaması platformlarının içerik analizi. *Acta Infologica*, 6(1), 83–97.

Konhäusner, P., Shang, B., & Dabija, D. C. (2021). Application of the 4Es in online crowdfunding platforms: A comparative perspective of Germany and China. *Journal of Risk and Financial Management*, 14(2), 49. 10.3390/jrfm14020049

Kovshova, L., & Nair, P. B. (2017). Crowdfunding in Russia: A thematic analysis of funder motives. *Global Business and Economics Review*, 19(3), 256–275. 10.1504/GBER.2017.083963

Kundu, S. G., & Jose, S. K. (2023, April). Dynamics of Demographic Factors, Digital Usage and Choice of Crowdfunding In India. In *Academy of Marketing Studies* (Vol. 27, No. 1). Academic Press.

Lima, A., & Araújo, F. F. M. (2019). Technology environment and crowdfunding platforms in Brazil. *Revista de Gestão*, 26(4), 352–368. 10.1108/REGE-12-2018-0119

Manara, A. S., Permata, A. R. E., & Pranjoto, R. G. H. (2018). Strategy model for increasing the potential of zakat through the crowdfunding-zakat system to overcome poverty in Indonesia. *International Journal of Zakat*, 3(4), 17–31. 10.37706/ijaz.v3i4.104

Martins, L., & Medeiros, M. D. L. (2018). Crowdfunding of tourism in Brazil. *Cultur: Revista de Cultura e Turismo*, 12(1), 59–79.

Mendes-Da-Silva, W., Rossoni, L., Conte, B. S., Gattaz, C. C., & Francisco, E. R. (2016). The impacts of fundraising periods and geographic distance on financing music production via crowdfunding in Brazil. *Journal of Cultural Economics*, 40(1), 75–99. 10.1007/s10824-015-9248-3

Mironova, E. (2018). Comparison of economic indicators of crowdfunding platforms Planeta. ru (Russia) and MAKEACHAMP (Canada). *Tsentr innovatsionnykh tekhnologii i sotsial'noi ekspertizy. Ekonomicheskie nauki*, (4), 17.

Mollick, E. (2014). The dynamics of crowdfunding: An exploratory study. *Journal of Business Venturing*, 29(1), 1–16. 10.1016/j.jbusvent.2013.06.005

Mourao, P., Silveira, M. A. P., & De Melo, R. S. (2018). Many are never too many: An analysis of crowdfunding projects in Brazil. *International Journal of Financial Studies*, 6(4), 95. 10.3390/ijfs6040095

Mourão, P. J. R., da Silveira, M. A. P., & de Melo, R. S. (2019). Determinants of the Well-Succeeded Crowdfunding Projects in Brazil: A Study of the Platform Kickante. In *Innovation, Engineering and Entrepreneurship* (pp. 856-862). Springer International Publishing. 10.1007/978-3-319-91334-6_117

Mustafida, R., Fauziah, N. N., & Kurnia, Z. N. (2021). The development of islamic crowdfunding in Indonesia and its impact towards SMEs. *Hasanuddin Economics and Business Review*, 4(3), 20–29. 10.26487/hebr.v4i3.2547

Nania, R. M., & Sulung, L. A. K. (2019). The management of reputation and activeness of crowdfunding players in emerging market countries. *Polish Journal of Management Studies*, 19(2), 298–308. 10.17512/pjms.2019.19.2.25

Narklor, A. (2020). The use and analysis of accounting and non-accounting information in equity-based crowdfunding. *Chulalongkorn University Theses and Dissertations (Chula ETD)*, 53. https://digital.car.chula.ac.th/chulaetd/53

Nisar, T. M., Prabhakar, G., & Torchia, M. (2020). Crowdfunding innovations in emerging economies: Risk and credit control in peer-to-peer lending network platforms. *Strategic Change*, 29(3), 355–361. 10.1002/jsc.2334

Pratama, K. J. (2022). Regulatory challenges in digital foreign investment through securities crowdfunding in Indonesia. *Indonesian Law Journal*, 15(2), 12–24.

Roro, F. S. R., Hernoko, A. Y., & Anand, G. (2019). The Characteristics Of Proportionality Principle In Islamic Crowdfunding In Indonesia. *Jurnal Hukum dan Pembangunan, 49*(2), 455-470.

Sajjan, R. (2017). Crowdfunding ecosystem in India. *International Journal of Scientific Research*, 6(12), 1230–1232.

Secchi, L., Wink, M. V.Jr, & Moraes, C. J. D. (2022). Crowdfunding and electoral performance in Brazil: Statistical analysis of the elections for federal deputy in 2018. *Revista de Administração Pública*, 55, 1191–1214. 10.1590/0034-761220200876

Segura-Mojica, F. J. (2021). Crowdfunding for the rescue of micro-businesses. Factors and perceptions of potential investors in Mexico. *RETOS.Revista de Ciencias de la Administración y Economía*, 11(21), 71–91.

Shahab, Y., Riaz, Y., Ntim, C. G., Ye, Z., Zhang, Q., & Feng, R. (2021). Online feedback and crowdfunding finance in China. *International Journal of Finance & Economics*, 26(3), 4634–4652. 10.1002/ijfe.2034

Sırma, İ., Ekici, O., & Aytürk, Y. (2019). Crowdfunding awareness in Turkey. *Procedia Computer Science*, 158, 490–497. 10.1016/j.procs.2019.09.080

Souza Bronzeri, M., & Cunha, J. C. (2021). Crowdfunding for Technological Innovation of Micro & Small Enterprises in Brazil. *International Journal of Developmental Research*, 11(06), 47650–47656.

Torkanovskiy, E. (2016). Non-equity crowdfunding as a National Phenomenon in a global industry: The case of Russia. *Crowdfunding in Europe: State of the Art in Theory and Practice*, 115-123.

Torkanovskiy, E., & Voinov, A. (2022). Covid-19 for Crowdfunding: Catalyst or Deterrent? Evidence from Russia. *The Indonesian Capital Market Review*, 14(2), 3. 10.21002/icmr.v14i2.1151

Tripathy, A. (2018). Crowdfunding in India: A Misnomer? *Business Law Review*, 39(5).

Tsvirko, S. (2021). Crowdfunding as a source of financing in Russia: PEST analysis. In *Integrated Science in Digital Age 2020* (pp. 154–163). Springer International Publishing. 10.1007/978-3-030-49264-9_14

Usman, S. M., Bukhari, F. A. S., You, H., Badulescu, D., & Gavrilut, D. (2020). The effect and impact of signals on investing decisions in reward-based crowdfunding: A comparative study of China and the United Kingdom. *Journal of Risk and Financial Management*, 13(12), 325. 10.3390/jrfm13120325

Wang, T., Li, Y., Kang, M., & Zheng, H. (2019). Exploring individuals' behavioral intentions toward donation crowdfunding: Evidence from China. *Industrial Management & Data Systems*, 119(7), 1515–1534. 10.1108/IMDS-10-2018-0451

Xie, K., Liu, Z., Chen, L., Zhang, W., Liu, S., & Chaudhry, S. S. (2019). Success factors and complex dynamics of crowdfunding: An empirical research on Taobao platform in China. *Electronic Markets*, 29(2), 187–199. 10.1007/s12525-018-0305-6

Yang, Q., & Lee, Y. C. (2019). An investigation of enablers and inhibitors of crowdfunding adoption: Empirical evidence from startups in China. *Human Factors and Ergonomics in Manufacturing*, 29(1), 5–21. 10.1002/hfm.20782

Yeon, A. L., & Putri, U. T. (2022). Equity crowdfunding industry regulations in Malaysia and Indonesia: Prospects and challenges during the Covid-19 pandemic. *Journal of International Students*, 18, 31–62.

Zheng, H., Li, D., Wu, J., & Xu, Y. (2014). The role of multidimensional social capital in crowdfunding: A comparative study in China and US. *Information & Management*, 51(4), 488–496. 10.1016/j.im.2014.03.003

Zhu, H., & Zhou, Z. Z. (2016). Analysis and outlook of applications of blockchain technology to equity crowdfunding in China. *Financial Innovation*, 2(1), 1–11. 10.1186/s40854-016-0044-7

Chapter 11
How Does Rural Entrepreneurship Contribute to the Resilience and Sustainability of Rural Communities?

Onan Marakali Siregar
Faculty of Social and Political Sciences, Universitas Sumatera Utara, Indonesia

Hatta Ridho
Faculty of Social and Political Sciences, Universitas Sumatera Utara, Indonesia

Muhammad Arifin Nasution
Faculty of Social and Political Sciences, Universitas Sumatera Utara, Indonesia

Muhammad Dharma Tuah Putra Nasution
https://orcid.org/0000-0002-4671-0230
Universitas Pembangunan Panca Budi, Indonesia

ABSTRACT

Research on rural entrepreneurship is essential for fostering economic advancement, generating employment opportunities, and reducing poverty in rural areas. This chapter explores the unique characteristics and challenges of rural entrepreneurship compared to urban settings, highlighting the need for tailored policies and support systems. Additionally, it examines how rural entrepreneurship contributes to the

DOI: 10.4018/979-8-3693-3518-5.ch011

resilience and sustainability of rural communities through innovative business models and economic diversification. Despite its significance, several issues remain unaddressed, prompting this study to investigate the role of rural entrepreneurship in driving economic growth, overcoming challenges, and fostering innovation for sustainable development.

INTRODUCTION

Research on entrepreneurship in rural areas holds paramount importance for several compelling reasons. Firstly, rural entrepreneurship serves as a cornerstone for the economic upliftment of rural regions, pivotal in generating employment opportunities, facilitating income generation, and mitigating poverty (Naminse & Zhuang, 2018). Scholars meticulously examine rural entrepreneurship to pinpoint challenges, formulate effective strategies, and propel economic growth and development within rural communities (Pangriya, 2022).

Secondly, such research yields valuable insights into the distinctive characteristics and intricate dynamics of rural entrepreneurship, distinguished by resource constraints, geographical remoteness, and nuanced cultural and social contexts (Barber et al., 2021). Grasping these nuances is imperative for crafting tailored policies and support systems that cater to the unique needs of rural entrepreneurs (Puie, 2019).

Moreover, investigations into entrepreneurship in rural areas contribute significantly to the resilience and sustainability of rural communities by delving into innovative and sustainable business models. This exploration uncovers avenues for diversification, thereby reducing reliance on traditional sectors like agriculture, while nurturing the emergence of novel industries and services that resonate with local contexts (Puie, 2019; Dhewanto et al., 2020).

Research on rural entrepreneurship is crucial for enhancing the economic, social, and environmental resilience of rural communities. However, several overlooked issues persist:

- To what extent can rural entrepreneurship drive economic growth in rural communities, particularly in terms of job creation and income enhancement?
- What are the primary challenges faced by rural entrepreneurs, such as resource limitations, geographic isolation, and specific cultural and social factors?
- How can innovative business models be effectively implemented in rural entrepreneurship to reduce dependence on the agricultural sector and foster economic diversification?

Therefore, this study aims to investigate the role of rural entrepreneurship in accelerating economic growth, with a specific focus on job creation and income enhancement in rural communities. Additionally, the research will delve deeper into the primary challenges faced by rural entrepreneurs, encompassing resource limitations, geographic isolation, and specific cultural and social factors. Further efforts will be dedicated to developing innovative business models applicable to rural entrepreneurship.

Research Methodology

Research on rural entrepreneurship is crucial for enhancing the economic, social, and environmental resilience of rural communities. However, there are several overlooked issues that persist in this field. To address these issues, our research methodology will utilize content analysis to examine existing literature on rural entrepreneurship. This will involve analyzing academic articles, reports, and other relevant sources to identify key themes and trends in the field. Our research will focus on three main areas: the economic impact of rural entrepreneurship, the challenges faced by rural entrepreneurs, and the implementation of innovative business models to reduce dependence on the agricultural sector and foster economic diversification. By conducting a thorough analysis of the literature, we aim to provide insights into these issues and contribute to the ongoing discourse on rural entrepreneurship

Result and Discussion

Table 1 presents key insights on rural entrepreneurship and its profound impact on economic development. Rural areas, often characterized by limited access to resources and opportunities, have witnessed significant transformations due to the emergence of rural entrepreneurship. This table synthesizes findings from various scholarly sources, highlighting the multifaceted role of rural entrepreneurship in driving economic growth, reducing unemployment, and fostering sustainable development.

Table 1. Key Insights on Rural Entrepreneurship and Economic Development

Key Points	Author(s)
Role of Rural Entrepreneurship in Economic Development	
Rural entrepreneurship drives economic growth by creating job opportunities and enhancing income levels in rural communities.	Dhewanto et al. (2020)

continued on following page

Table 1. Continued

Key Points	Author(s)
Farmer entrepreneurship significantly contributes to reducing rural poverty through job creation and economic empowerment.	Naminse & Zhuang (2018)
Rural entrepreneurs play a crucial role in generating jobs and wealth within rural communities, fostering economic development.	Betancourt et al. (2021)
Women's rural entrepreneurship is a significant contributor to economic growth, providing essential services and enhancing rural viability.	Kabagerayo (2022)
Rural entrepreneurship promotes diversified development of rural industries and aids in eliminating rural poverty, contributing to economic growth.	Yao et al. (2022)
Understanding different types of rural entrepreneurship and their engagement with place and space is crucial for leveraging their potential for economic growth.	Korsgaard et al. (2015)
Social capital and financial literacy mediate the effect of rural household entrepreneurship, highlighting the multifaceted nature of rural entrepreneurship.	Zhao & Tian-cheng (2021)
Women's rural entrepreneurship represents untapped potential for economic development, contributing to business creation and regional prosperity.	Tillmar et al. (2022)
Rural entrepreneurship fosters business creation and growth, contributing to regional and national prosperity by stimulating economic activities.	Sulistyorini & Santoso (2021)
Entrepreneurship training is instrumental in fostering the growth of new ventures and job creation, positively impacting economic growth in rural areas.	Mwatsika (2016)
Role of Rural Entrepreneurship in Reducing Unemployment	
Rural entrepreneurship reduces unemployment rates by generating job opportunities and fostering entrepreneurial activities in rural regions.	Boghean & State (2020)
Financial literacy plays a pivotal role in promoting rural entrepreneurship, elevating rural households out of poverty and reducing unemployment.	Zhao & Tian-cheng (2021)
Rural entrepreneurship effectively addresses unemployment challenges, serving as a solution to poverty, economic disparities, and migration in rural areas.	Supekar & Dhage (2022)
Combining entrepreneurship with innovation impacts unemployment rates in both rural and urban settings, contributing to job creation and economic growth.	Padi & Musah (2022)
Local economic development through well-coordinated entrepreneurship can address underdevelopment, poverty, and food insecurity, leading to reduced unemployment.	Madzivhandila & Musara (2020)
Social entrepreneurship drives community development, especially in economies with high unemployment rates, inspiring social change and economic empowerment.	Yiu et al. (2014)
Rural social entrepreneurship contributes to addressing unemployment and boosting rural economies by leveraging social capital and place-based initiatives.	Lang & Fink (2019)
Entrepreneurship development in agricultural sectors creates new jobs and employment opportunities in rural areas, reducing unemployment rates.	Saghaian et al. (2022)
Self-employed entrepreneurial activities lead to the employment of workers, resulting in decreased unemployment rates and enhanced economic development.	Feki & Mnif (2019)
Entrepreneurship positively impacts unemployment by reducing it through business start-ups, contributing to economic growth and development.	Beynon et al. (2019)

continued on following page

How Does Rural Entrepreneurship Contribute?

Table 1. Continued

Key Points	Author(s)
Encouraging entrepreneurship effectively reduces unemployment rates and stimulates rural economies, fostering sustainable development in rural areas.	Malebana & Swanepoel (2019)
Rural migrants exhibit higher entrepreneurship rates, contributing actively to the urban business landscape and employment generation.	Liu et al., 2018)
Economic Impact of Micro and Macro Entrepreneurship in Rural Areas	
Green entrepreneurship enhances national competitiveness and contributes to sustainable economic growth in rural communities.	Drăgoi et al. (2017)
Examines both micro-level entrepreneurial traits and macro-level growth and institutional frameworks to understand their impact on rural economies.	Nulleshi & Tillmar (2022)
Interactions between small entrepreneurs and rural communities have a significant impact on local economies, advocating for increased academic attention to rural areas.	Zhu et al. (2019)
Informal micro-entrepreneurship supports subsistence livelihoods in rural settings, providing a source of income for rural populations.	Asiedu et al. (2019)
Regional social capital influences entrepreneurial intention in rural areas, shaping the entrepreneurial landscape and economic activities.	Ali & Yousuf (2019)
Rising empirical studies on rural entrepreneurship in less developed countries indicate its global relevance and economic impact at the micro and macro levels.	Pato & Teixeira (2014)
Social capital contributes to sustainable micro-entrepreneurship among rural women, empowering them economically and fostering community development.	Mahato et al. (2022)
Disparities in entrepreneurial activity levels between rural and urban areas highlight the need for targeted interventions to support rural entrepreneurship.	Vaillant & Lafuente (2007)
Barriers to entrepreneurship in rural Pakistan include religious, socioeconomic, and structural factors, influencing entrepreneurial activities and economic growth.	Muhammad et al. (2017)
Rural Entrepreneurship and Sustainable Economic Growth	
Rural entrepreneurship fosters sustainable economic growth by connecting local communities to global markets and leveraging local resources for development.	Pato & Teixeira (2018)
Integration into the global economy through rural entrepreneurship contributes to increasing local incomes and wealth, promoting sustainable economic growth.	Nguyen et al. (2014)
Understanding rural-proof entrepreneurship ensures alignment with the unique dimensions of rurality, fostering sustainable development in rural areas.	Nulleshi & Tillmar (2022)
Adapting to challenges from market globalization, competition, and technological advancements is crucial for rural entrepreneurship to ensure sustainable growth.	Jovović et al. (2017)
Adaptability enables rural entrepreneurs to maintain a global perspective while navigating global markets, promoting sustainable economic growth.	Tallman et al. (2017)

Table 2 provides a detailed examination of the challenges and strategies inherent in rural entrepreneurship, shedding light on the complexities faced by entrepreneurs in rural areas. Rural entrepreneurship, while holding great potential for economic development, encounters various hurdles ranging from limited access to resources to socio-cultural barriers. Understanding these challenges is crucial for formulating effective support measures and strategies that bolster rural economic growth and sustainability.

Table 2. Challenges and Strategies in Rural Entrepreneurship

Key Points	Author(s)
Challenges of Rural Entrepreneurship	
Limited access to investment capital, resources, and state financial support for rural women entrepreneurs.	Ghouse et al. (2021)
Skill-related barriers, including lack of training, education, expertise, and knowledge gaps, especially for women entrepreneurs.	Rahman et al. (2022)
Transportation costs, scarcity of skilled labor, financial constraints, and inadequate access to resources due to geographic remoteness.	Pangriya (2022); Freiling et al. (2022)
Lack of educational qualifications, skills, capital, and management expertise among rural entrepreneurs.	Das & Pal (2022); Pathak & Varshney (2017)
Impact of the Covid-19 pandemic on exacerbating challenges for women entrepreneurs in rural areas.	Nso (2022)
Diverse networks with varying levels and types of social capital, influencing rural entrepreneurs' ventures.	Ring et al. (2010)
Gender roles posing significant challenges for female entrepreneurs, affecting their participation in entrepreneurial activities.	Tüzün & Takay (2017)
Socio-cultural barriers faced by immigrant entrepreneurs in rural areas, impacting their ventures.	Hack-Polay et al. (2020)
Financing challenges, including public and private barriers affecting access to funding for rural entrepreneurs.	Sadeghloo et al. (2018)
Support Measures for Rural Entrepreneurs	
Inadequate access to suppliers, skilled labor, infrastructure, and financial resources and markets for rural entrepreneurs.	Pathak & Varshney (2017); Pangriya (2022)
Scarcity and high costs of raw materials, unreliable communication and transport services, and lack of technical and business skills.	Mugobo & Ukpere (2012)
Essential role of training programs, educational initiatives, and government aid for rural entrepreneurs.	Patil & Bhurke (2019)
Need for holistic strategies by policymakers to support and sustain rural entrepreneurs, fostering regional socio-economic development.	Ghouse et al. (2021)
Infrastructure development and efforts to broaden access to essential amenities crucial for rural planning and development strategies.	Tuah et al. (2022)
Provision of entrepreneurial support enhances business performance, including access to vital goods and services.	Zin & Ibrahim (2020); Bello et al. (2021)
Significance of micro-credit programs in fostering the development of rural women entrepreneurship.	Nawaz (2009)
Cultural and Social Factors in Business Sustainability	
Success of rural enterprises relies on fostering a shared vision among local stakeholders and developing innovative business solutions for sustainability.	Galardi et al. (2022)

continued on following page

Table 2. Continued

Key Points	Author(s)
Economic constraints and unconventional approaches to sustainability in rural tourism development.	Wilson et al. (2001)
Interconnection of agritourism sustainability with economic, social, and cultural fabric of rural communities.	Ciolac et al. (2019)
Influence of regional and national policies, individual motivations, and cultural acceptance on sustainable development in rural areas.	Aleffi et al. (2020)
Proposed paradigm model for enhancing resilience of rural entrepreneurial businesses during crises.	Mohammadifar et al. (2022)

Table 3 provides an insightful overview of innovative business models in rural entrepreneurship, elucidating the diverse strategies and approaches adopted to foster economic diversification, integrate technology, and navigate regulatory landscapes. Rural entrepreneurship, often characterized by unique challenges and opportunities, plays a pivotal role in driving economic growth and sustainability in rural areas. Through innovative business models, entrepreneurs can leverage local resources, embrace digital technologies, and navigate regulatory frameworks to create lasting impact and foster community development.

Table 3. Innovative Business Models in Rural Entrepreneurship

Key Points	Scholar(s)
Economic Diversification	
Growth of agriculture and services correlates with poverty declines, indicating potential for rural economic diversification.	Loayza & Raddatz (2010)
Rural entrepreneurship and innovative business models create new opportunities and directly impact regional economic performance.	Rotaru & Dumitrache (2022)
Studying entrepreneurship in local food context enhances understanding of rural enterprise dynamics and industry development.	Rytkönen & Oghazi (2021)
Conceptual framework for rural business models aims to understand evolution and impact on community development.	Puie (2019)
While reducing dependence on agriculture is important, it remains vital for sustainable resource use and rural economic diversification.	Miteva & Doitchinova (2022)
Policies fostering innovative entrepreneurship create tourist attractions, contributing to economic diversification.	Aryaningsih et al. (2021)
Public expenditures and agricultural policies play a role in reducing rural poverty, promoting economic diversification.	Quintana et al. (2017)
Technology Integration	
Integration of digital technologies stimulates new social and institutional practices, creating opportunities for rural business representatives.	Dyba et al. (2020)

continued on following page

Table 3. Continued

Key Points	Scholar(s)
Introduction of new technology encourages business model innovation, especially in rural areas.	Lee et al. (2019); Huang et al. (2023)
Adoption of digital technologies moderates competitiveness and innovativeness of rural business entities.	Mukti et al. (2021)
SMEs in rural areas are more likely to use open innovation frameworks for technology acquisition and application.	Kmecová & Vokoun (2020)
Development of digital innovative hubs in rural areas presents challenges and opportunities, necessitating innovative digital policies.	Shcerbakova et al. (2019)
Financing of rural electrification in Sub-Saharan Africa requires new innovative business models, highlighting crucial role of technology.	Kyriakarakos et al. (2020)
Digital technologies offer opportunities but pose challenges for rural leaders in integrating technology into schools and classrooms.	Kotok & Kryst (2017)
Technological innovation contributes to business model innovation and company performance, indicating potential for technology-driven innovation in rural areas.	Smajlović et al. (2019)
Regulatory Support	
Regulatory environments influence innovation assimilation, particularly in developing countries, fostering innovation in rural business models.	Zhu et al. (2006)
Creation of shared vision among local actors clears barriers and creates innovative business solutions linked to sustainability in rural areas.	Galardi et al. (2022)
Integration of rural cooking techniques into innovative business strategies boosts rural economies, requiring regulatory support for infrastructure and sustainability.	Lee et al. (2021)
Lack of comprehensive framework for appraising rural business models necessitates development of tailored evaluation frameworks.	Zhang et al. (2018)
Importance of research in proposing sustainable business models, indicating need for specific evaluation frameworks tailored to rural contexts.	Nosratabadi et al. (2019)

CONCLUSION

Rural entrepreneurship serves as a critical driver of economic growth in rural areas, fostering the creation of new economic activities, job opportunities, and increased income levels. Through innovative business models, rural entrepreneurs diversify local industries, reduce unemployment, and alleviate poverty. Farmer entrepreneurship, in particular, has been instrumental in addressing rural poverty and facilitating wealth generation.

Beyond economic benefits, rural entrepreneurship also enhances social cohesion, environmental sustainability, and regional prosperity. Leveraging local resources, adopting technological advancements, and overcoming challenges such as resource limitations and geographic isolation are ways rural entrepreneurs boost productivity, competitiveness, and resilience. To amplify these impacts, policymakers and stakeholders must support rural entrepreneurs through customized initiatives, regulatory frameworks, and capacity-building programs.

However, rural entrepreneurs face numerous challenges, including resource limitations, geographic isolation, and specific cultural and social barriers. Limited access to investment capital, resources, and state financial support hinders the sustainability of rural businesses. Targeted interventions providing essential resources, training facilities, and entrepreneurial expertise are necessary to address these issues.

Skill-related barriers, particularly for women, such as inadequate training facilities, education, and supply chain management knowledge, further exacerbate the challenges faced by rural entrepreneurs. Bridging these gaps through capacity-building and mentorship programs is essential for empowering entrepreneurs.

High transportation costs, unreliable communication and transport services, and inadequate infrastructure further impede rural entrepreneurship. Investing in infrastructure development, improving transportation networks, and enhancing access to essential services are crucial steps to support rural business growth.

The Covid-19 pandemic has added layers of difficulty, especially for women entrepreneurs, emphasizing the need for targeted support and resilience-building measures. Additionally, diverse social capital networks and gender roles present challenges that necessitate gender-inclusive strategies, enhanced social networks, and cultural barrier mitigation.

Innovative business models are essential for reducing dependence on agriculture and promoting economic diversification. By expanding into new products, services, and value chains, rural entrepreneurs enhance economic resilience, reduce market vulnerability, and foster sustainable growth. These models enable better resource utilization, integration into broader economic networks, and adaptation to global market opportunities.

To support the transition from agricultural dependence, policymakers and stakeholders should implement supportive policies, provide financial resources, and offer capacity-building programs. Creating an enabling environment for entrepreneurship, promoting knowledge exchange, and fostering stakeholder collaboration are pivotal for unlocking the potential of innovative business models. This approach will drive economic diversification, resilience, and prosperity in rural communities.

REFERENCES

Aleffi, C., Tomasi, S., Ferrara, C., Santini, C., Paviotti, G., Federica, B., & Cavicchi, A. (2020). Universities and wineries: Supporting sustainable development in disadvantaged rural areas. *Agriculture*, 10(9), 378. 10.3390/agriculture10090378

Ali, A., & Yousuf, S. (2019). Social capital and entrepreneurial intention: Empirical evidence from rural community of Pakistan. *Journal of Global Entrepreneurship Research*, 9(1), 64. Advance online publication. 10.1186/s40497-019-0193-z

Aryaningsih, N. N., Suari, P. R. W., Darmayasa, N., & Utthavi, W. H. (2021, April). Management Model of Rural-Owned Enterprises Based on Entrepreneurship Innovation as a Tourist Attraction. In *International Conference on Applied Science and Technology on Social Science (ICAST-SS 2020)* (pp. 121-125). Atlantis Press. 10.2991/assehr.k.210424.024

Asiedu, E., Shortland, S., Nawar, Y., Jackson, P., & Baker, L. (2019). Supporting Ghanaian micro-entrepreneurships: The role of mobile technology. *Journal of Entrepreneurship in Emerging Economies*, 11(3), 306–327. 10.1108/JEEE-05-2018-0046

Barber, D.III, Harris, M., & Jones, J. (2021). An overview of rural entrepreneurship and future directions. *Journal of Small Business Strategy*, 31(4). Advance online publication. 10.53703/001c.29468

Bello, U., Marques, C., Sacramento, O., & Galvão, A. (2021). Neo-rural small entrepreneurs' motivations and challenges in Portugal's low-density regions. *Journal of Enterprising Communities People and Places in the Global Economy*, 16(6), 900–923. 10.1108/JEC-04-2021-0047

Betancourt, I., Téllez, M., Sánchez, P., Castro, L., & Carrasco, J. (2021). Entrepreneurship as a mechanism to strengthen rural communities. *European Journal of Business Management and Research*, 6(2), 107–110. 10.24018/ejbmr.2021.6.2.800

Beynon, M., Jones, P., & Pickernell, D. (2019). The role of entrepreneurship, innovation, and urbanity-diversity on growth, unemployment, and income: US state-level evidence and an fsqca elucidation. *Journal of Business Research*, 101, 675–687. 10.1016/j.jbusres.2019.01.074

Ciolac, R., Adamov, T., Iancu, T., Popescu, G., Lile, R., Rujescu, C., & Marin, D. (2019). Agritourism-a sustainable development factor for improving the 'health' of rural settlements. Case study Apuseni Mountains area. *Sustainability (Basel)*, 11(5), 1467. 10.3390/su11051467

Das, A., & Pal, B. (2022). Status of rural entrepreneurs in the post-pandemic situation: A study in selected blocks in Nadia district of West Bengal, India. *South Asian Journal of Social Studies and Economics*, 9-15. 10.9734/sajsse/2022/v15i330406

Dhewanto, W., Ratnaningtyas, S., Permatasari, A., Anggadwita, G., & Prasetio, E. (2020). Rural entrepreneurship: Towards collaborative participative models for economic sustainability. *Journal of Entrepreneurship and Sustainability Issues*, 8(1), 705–724. 10.9770/jesi.2020.8.1(48)

Drăgoi, M., Iamandi, I., Munteanu, S., Ciobanu, R., ar avulea, R., & Ladaru, R. (2017). Incentives for developing resilient agritourism entrepreneurship in rural communities in Romania in a European context. *Sustainability*, 9(12), 2205. 10.3390/su9122205

Dyba, M., Гернего, Ю., Dyba, O., & Oliynyk, A. (2020). Financial support and development of digital rural hubs in Europe. *Management Theory and Studies for Rural Business and Infrastructure Development*, 41(4), 51–59. 10.15544/mts.2020.06

Feki, C., & Mnif, S. (2019). Self-employment and unemployment in Tunisia: Application of the ARDL approach. *International Journal of Academic Research in Business & Social Sciences*, 9(7). Advance online publication. 10.6007/IJARBSS/v9-i7/6217

Freiling, J., Marquardt, L., & Reit, T. (2022). Virtual business incubators: A support for entrepreneurship in rural areas? In *Advances in Human Factors and Ergonomics* (pp. 65-88). https://doi.org/10.1007/978-3-031-04063-4_4

Galardi, M., Moruzzo, R., Riccioli, F., Granai, G., & Iacovo, F. (2022). Small rural enterprises and innovative business models: A case study of the Turin area. *Sustainability (Basel)*, 14(3), 1265. 10.3390/su14031265

Ghouse, S., Durrah, O., & McElwee, G. (2021). Rural women entrepreneurs in Oman: Problems and opportunities. *International Journal of Entrepreneurial Behaviour & Research*, 27(7), 1674–1695. 10.1108/IJEBR-03-2021-0209

Guo, Y., Zhu, L., & Yu-zong, Z. (2022). Tourism entrepreneurship in rural destinations: Measuring the effects of capital configurations using the fsQCA approach. *Tourism Review*, 78(3), 834–848. 10.1108/TR-07-2022-0333

Hack-Polay, D., Ogbaburu, J., Rahman, M., & Mahmoud, A. (2020). Immigrant entrepreneurs in rural England – An examination of the socio-cultural barriers facing migrant small businesses in Lincolnshire. *Local Economy*, 35(7), 676–694. 10.1177/0269094220988852

Huang, C., Rui, L., & Zhu, Y. (2023). Research on digital construction of characteristic towns in China under the background of digital economy—Taking the field investigation in 6 provinces and 6 towns in China as an example. In *Advances in Ergonomics and Human Factors* (pp. 139-150). https://doi.org/10.2991/978-94-6463-042-8_22

Jovović, R., Drašković, M., Delibasic, M., & Jovovic, M. (2017). The concept of sustainable regional development – Institutional aspects, policies, and prospects. *Journal of International Students*, 10(1), 255–266. 10.14254/2071-8330.2017/10-1/18

Kabagerayo, J., Mwambusa, F. E., Uyambaje, M. T., Olive, Z. B., Hamenyimana, L., Dusabe, P., Mwayuma, P. M., Joseph, M. E., & Mbafumoja, E. T. (2022). Impact of rural female entrepreneurs on social and economic inclusion: Case of Giharo district. *Modern Economy*, 13(06), 885–900. 10.4236/me.2022.136048

Kmecová, I., & Vokoun, M. (2020). Innovation activities of Czech businesses: Differences between urban and rural businesses. *SHS Web of Conferences, 73*, 02002. 10.1051/shsconf/20207302002

Korsgaard, S., Müller, S., & Tanvig, H. (2015). Rural entrepreneurship or entrepreneurship in the rural – Between place and space. *International Journal of Entrepreneurial Behaviour & Research*, 21(1), 5–26. 10.1108/IJEBR-11-2013-0205

Kotok, S., & Kryst, E. (2017). Digital technology: A double-edged sword for a school principal in rural Pennsylvania. *Journal of Cases in Educational Leadership*, 20(4), 3–16. 10.1177/1555458916685748

Kyriakarakos, G., Balafoutis, A., & Bochtis, D. (2020). Proposing a paradigm shift in rural electrification investments in sub-Saharan Africa through agriculture. *Sustainability (Basel)*, 12(8), 3096. 10.3390/su12083096

Lang, R., & Fink, M. (2019). Rural social entrepreneurship: The role of social capital within and across institutional levels. *Journal of Rural Studies*, 70, 155–168. 10.1016/j.jrurstud.2018.03.012

Lee, C., Chen, Y., Tsui, P., Che, C., & Chiang, M. (2021). Application of fuzzy Delphi technique approach in sustainable inheritance of rural cooking techniques and innovative business strategies modeling. *Agriculture*, 11(10), 924. 10.3390/agriculture11100924

Lee, J., Suh, T., Roy, D., & Baucus, M. (2019). Emerging technology and business model innovation: The case of artificial intelligence. *Journal of Open Innovation*, 5(3), 44. 10.3390/joitmc5030044

Lekhanya, L., & Mason, R. (2014). Selected key external factors influencing the success of rural small and medium enterprises in South Africa. *Journal of Enterprising Culture*, 22(03), 331–348. 10.1142/S0218495814500149

Lin, S., Laeeq, K., Malik, A., Varela, D., Rhee, J., Pillsbury, H., & Bhatti, N. (2013). Otolaryngology training programs: Resident and faculty perception of the mentorship experience. *The Laryngoscope*, 123(8), 1876–1883. 10.1002/lary.2404323483538

Liu, C., Ye, L., & Feng, B. (2018). Migrant entrepreneurship in China: Entrepreneurial transition and firm performance. *Small Business Economics*, 52(3), 681–696. 10.1007/s11187-017-9979-y

Loayza, N., & Raddatz, C. (2010). The composition of growth matters for poverty alleviation. *Journal of Development Economics*, 93(1), 137–151. 10.1016/j.jdeveco.2009.03.008

Madzivhandila, T., & Musara, M. (2020). Taking responsibility for entrepreneurship development in South Africa: The role of local municipalities. *Local Economy*, 35(3), 257–268. 10.1177/0269094220922820

Mahato, J., Jha, M., & Verma, S. (2022). The role of social capital in developing sustainable micro-entrepreneurship among rural women in India: A theoretical framework. *International Journal of Innovation*, 10(3), 504–526. 10.5585/iji.v10i3.21771

Malebana, M., & Swanepoel, E. (2019). The relationship between exposure to entrepreneurship education and entrepreneurial self-efficacy. *Southern African Business Review*, 18(1), 1–26. 10.25159/1998-8125/5630

Merenkova, I., Agibalov, A., Zakupnev, S., & Vorobyev, S. (2020, July). Modelling of Diversified Development of Rural Areas. In *International Conference on Policies and Economics Measures for Agricultural Development (AgroDevEco 2020)* (pp. 248-252). Atlantis Press. https://doi.org/10.2991/aebmr.k.200729.048

Miteva, A., & Doitchinova, J. (2022). Agriculture in the southwestern region of Bulgaria and its impact on rural development. *Ekonomika Poljoprivrede*, 69(4), 1003–1016. 10.5937/ekoPolj2204003M

Modrego, F., & Foster, W. (2021). Innovative rural entrepreneurship in Chile. *International Journal of Applied Nanotechnology Research*, 48(3), 149–170. 10.7764/ijanr.v48i3.2324

Mohammadifar, Y., Naderi, N., Khosravi, E., & Karamian, F. (2022). Developing a paradigm model for resilience of rural entrepreneurial businesses in dealing with the COVID-19 crisis; Application of grounded theory in western of Iran. *Frontiers in Public Health*, 10, 833909. Advance online publication. 10.3389/fpubh.2022.83390935284375

Moqadas, R. (2018). The role of rural tourism in sustainable rural development: A case study of Shandiz rural region, Khorasan Razavi province, Iran. *Journal of Sustainable Rural Development*. 10.32598/JSRD.01.03.280

Mugobo, V., & Ukpere, W. (2012). Rural entrepreneurship in the Western Cape: Challenges and opportunities. *African Journal of Business Management*, 6(3). Advance online publication. 10.5897/AJBM11.895

Muhammad, N., McElwee, G., & Dana, L. (2017). Barriers to the development and progress of entrepreneurship in rural Pakistan. *International Journal of Entrepreneurial Behaviour & Research*, 23(2), 279–295. 10.1108/IJEBR-08-2016-0246

Mukti, I., Iacob, M., Aldea, A., Govindaraju, R., & Hillegersberg, J. (2021). Defining rural smartness and its impact: A systematic literature review. *Journal of the Knowledge Economy*, 13(2), 956–1007. 10.1007/s13132-021-00736-7

Mwatsika, C. (2016). Measuring the number of jobs created through entrepreneurship training. *International Journal of Academic Research in Business & Social Sciences*, 6(7). Advance online publication. 10.6007/IJARBSS/v6-i7/2243

Naminse, E., & Zhuang, J. (2018). Does farmer entrepreneurship alleviate rural poverty in China? Evidence from Guangxi province. *PLoS One*, 13(3), e0194912. 10.1371/journal.pone.019491229596517

Nawaz, F. (2009). Critical factors of women entrepreneurship development in rural Bangladesh. SSRN *Electronic Journal*. 10.2139/ssrn.1403411

Nguyen, C., Frederick, H., & Nguyen, H. (2014). Female entrepreneurship in rural Vietnam: An exploratory study. *International Journal of Gender and Entrepreneurship*, 6(1), 50–67. 10.1108/IJGE-04-2013-0034

Nosratabadi, S., Mosavi, A., Shamshirband, S., Zavadskas, E., Rakotonirainy, A., & Chau, K. (2019). Sustainable business models: A review. *Sustainability (Basel)*, 11(6), 1663. 10.3390/su11061663

Nso, M. (2022). An assessment of the challenges and opportunities in financing rural women entrepreneurship in the micro, small and medium enterprises sector in Cameroon. *Journal of Management and Science*, 12(4), 33–38. 10.26524/jms.12.60

Nulleshi, S., & Tillmar, M. (2022). Rural proofing entrepreneurship in two fields of research. *International Journal of Entrepreneurial Behaviour & Research*, 28(9), 332–356. 10.1108/IJEBR-05-2021-0323

Padi, A., & Musah, A. (2022). Entrepreneurship as a potential solution to high unemployment: A systematic review of growing research and lessons for Ghana. *International Journal of Entrepreneurship and Business Innovation*, 5(2), 26–41. 10.52589/IJEBI-NNERQQRP

Pangriya, R. (2022). An explorative study on problems and challenges of rural entrepreneurs in hilly rural areas. *Asia-Pacific Journal of Management Research and Innovation*, 18(3-4), 163–168. 10.1177/2319510X231155235

Pathak, A., & Varshney, S. (2017). Challenges faced by women entrepreneurs in rural India. *International Journal of Entrepreneurship and Innovation*, 18(1), 65–72. 10.1177/1465750316686245

Patil, R., & Bhurke, V. (2019). Impact of rural entrepreneurship on migration: A case study of Dahanu (Maharashtra), India. *Indian Journal of Agricultural Research*, (of). Advance online publication. 10.18805/IJARe.A-5014

Pato, M., & Teixeira, A. (2014). Twenty years of rural entrepreneurship: A bibliometric survey. *Sociologia Ruralis*, 56(1), 3–28. 10.1111/soru.12058

Pato, M., & Teixeira, A. (2018). Rural entrepreneurship: The tale of a rare event. *Journal of Place Management and Development*, 11(1), 46–59. 10.1108/JPMD-08-2017-0085

Pociovalisteanu, D., Novo-Corti, I., Aceleanu, M., erban, A., & Grecu, E. (2015). Employment policies for a green economy at the European Union level. *Sustainability (Basel)*, 7(7), 9231–9250. 10.3390/su7079231

Podgorskaya, S. (2021). Methodological aspects of rural economy diversification in the context of modern civilizational transformations. *E3s Web of Conferences, 273*, 08041. 10.1051/e3sconf/202127308041

Puie, F. (2019). Conceptual framework for rural business models. *Proceedings of the International Conference on Business Excellence, 13*(1), 1130-1139. 10.2478/picbe-2019-0099

Quintana, S., Díaz, A., Monagas, M., & García, E. (2017). Agricultural policies and their impact on poverty reduction in developing countries: Lessons learned from three water basins in Cape Verde. *Sustainability (Basel)*, 9(10), 1841. 10.3390/su9101841

Rahman, M., Dana, L., Moral, I., Anjum, N., & Rahaman, M. (2022). Challenges of rural women entrepreneurs in Bangladesh to survive their family entrepreneurship: A narrative inquiry through storytelling. *Journal of Family Business Management*, 13(3), 645–664. 10.1108/JFBM-04-2022-0054

Ring, J., Peredo, A., & Chrisman, J. (2010). Business networks and economic development in rural communities in the United States. *Entrepreneurship Theory and Practice*, 34(1), 171–195. 10.1111/j.1540-6520.2009.00307.x

Rosa, M., McElwee, G., & Smith, R. (2019). Farm diversification strategies in response to rural policy: A case from rural Italy. *Land Use Policy*, 81, 291–301. 10.1016/j.landusepol.2018.11.006

Rotaru, C., & Dumitrache, V. (2022). Can entrepreneurship be a strategic option for the development of the rural space in Romania? 10.24818/CAFEE/2020/9/07

Rytkönen, P., & Oghazi, P. (2021). Bringing innovation back in–strategies and driving forces behind entrepreneurial responses in small-scale rural industries in Sweden. *British Food Journal*, 124(8), 2550–2565. 10.1108/BFJ-05-2021-0587

Sadeghloo, T., Qeidari, H., Salehi, M., & Jalali, A. (2018). Obstacles and methods of financing for the development of local entrepreneurship in Iran. *International Journal of Development Issues*, 17(1), 114–138. 10.1108/IJDI-05-2017-0046

Saghaian, S., Mohammadi, H., & Mohammadi, M. (2022). Factors affecting success of entrepreneurship in agribusinesses: Evidence from the city of Mashhad, Iran. *Sustainability (Basel)*, 14(13), 7700. 10.3390/su14137700

Shcerbakova, L., Evdokimova, E., & Savintseva, S. (2019, June). Impact of the complimentary nature of the digital resource on the accelerating dynamics of the agricultural sector. In *International Scientific and Practical Conference "Digital agriculture-development strategy" (ISPC 2019)* (pp. 69-75). Atlantis Press. 10.2991/ispc-19.2019.16

Smajlović, S., Umihanić, B., & Turulja, L. (2019). The interplay of technological innovation and business model innovation toward company performance. *Management*, 24(2), 63–79. 10.30924/mjcmi.24.2.5

Sulistyorini, Y., & Santoso, B. (2021). Entrepreneurial knowledge on entrepreneurial intention: The mediating of perceived desirability and perceived feasibility. *Baskara Journal of Business and Entrepreneurship*, 3(2), 39. 10.24853/baskara.3.2.39-47

Supekar, S., & Dhage, S. (2022). Rural entrepreneurship through khadi and village industries. *Sedme (Small Enterprises Development Management & Extension Journal) a Worldwide Window on MSME Studies*, 49(3), 219-226. 10.1177/09708464221111220

Tallman, S., Luo, Y., & Buckley, P. (2017). Business models in global competition. *Global Strategy Journal*, 8(4), 517–535. 10.1002/gsj.1165

Tillmar, M., Sköld, B., Ahl, H., Berglund, K., & Pettersson, K. (2022). Women's rural businesses: For economic viability or gender equality? – A database study from the Swedish context. *International Journal of Gender and Entrepreneurship*, 14(3), 323–351. 10.1108/IJGE-06-2021-0091

Tuah, M., Tedong, P., & Dali, M. (2022). The challenges in rural infrastructure planning governance in Sarawak. *Planning Malaysia*, 20. Advance online publication. 10.21837/pm.v20i24.1214

Tüzün, İ., & Takay, B. (2017). Patterns of female entrepreneurial activities in Turkey. *Gender in Management*, 32(3), 166–182. 10.1108/GM-05-2016-0102

Vaillant, Y., & Lafuente, E. (2007). Do different institutional frameworks condition the influence of local fear of failure and entrepreneurial examples over entrepreneurial activity? *Entrepreneurship and Regional Development*, 19(4), 313–337. 10.1080/08985620701440007

Vik, J., & McElwee, G. (2011). Diversification and the entrepreneurial motivations of farmers in Norway. *Journal of Small Business Management*, 49(3), 390–410. 10.1111/j.1540-627X.2011.00327.x

Wang, S., Lin, X., Xiao, H., Bu, N., & Li, Y. (2022). Empirical study on human capital, economic growth and sustainable development: Taking Shandong province as an example. *Sustainability (Basel)*, 14(12), 7221. 10.3390/su14127221

Wilson, S., Fesenmaier, D., Fesenmaier, J., & Es, J. (2001). Factors for success in rural tourism development. *Journal of Travel Research*, 40(2), 132–138. 10.1177/004728750104000203

Yao, J., Li, H., Xu, X., Qiu, S., & Shang, D. (2022). Path of exploring opportunities in a migrant workers returning to home entrepreneurial ecosystem. *Ciência Rural*, 52(11), e20210493. Advance online publication. 10.1590/0103-8478cr20210493

Yiu, D., Wan, W., Ng, F., Chen, X., & Su, J. (2014). Sentimental drivers of social entrepreneurship: A study of China's guangcai (glorious) program. *Management and Organization Review*, 10(1), 55–80. 10.1111/more.12043

Zhang, X., Hu, L., Salimath, M., & Kuo, C. (2018). Developing evaluation frameworks for business models in China's rural markets. *Sustainability (Basel)*, 11(1), 118. 10.3390/su11010118

Zhao, J., & Tian-cheng, L. (2021). Social capital, financial literacy, and rural household entrepreneurship: A mediating effect analysis. *Frontiers in Psychology*, 12, 724605. Advance online publication. 10.3389/fpsyg.2021.72460534512479

Zhu, H., Chen, Y., & Chen, K. (2019). Vitalizing rural communities: China's rural entrepreneurial activities from the perspective of mixed embeddedness. *Sustainability (Basel)*, 11(6), 1609. 10.3390/su11061609

Zhu, K., Kraemer, K., & Xu, S. (2006). The process of innovation assimilation by firms in different countries: A technology diffusion perspective on e-business. *Management Science*, 52(10), 1557–1576. 10.1287/mnsc.1050.0487

Zin, L., & Ibrahim, H. (2020). The influence of entrepreneurial supports on business performance among rural entrepreneurs. *Annals of Contemporary Developments in Management & HR*, 2(1), 31–41. 10.33166/ACDMHR.2020.01.004

Chapter 12
Innovation Dynamics in Family Firms:
A Content Analysis Study

Muhammad Dharma Tuah Putra Nasution
https://orcid.org/0000-0002-4671-0230
Universitas Pembangunan Panca Budi, Indonesia

Muhammad Chaerul Rizky
Universitas Pembangunan Panca Budi, Indonesia

Maya Macia
Universitas Pembangunan Panca Budi, Indonesia

Noni Ardian
Universitas Pembangunan Panca Budi, Indonesia

Suwarno Suwarno
Universitas Pembangunan Panca Budi, Indonesia

Husni Muharram Ritonga
Universitas Pembangunan Panca Budi, Indonesia

ABSTRACT

This chapter explores the significance of incremental innovation in family-owned businesses, examining their engagement, the factors shaping their innovation behavior, and the practical implications for stakeholders. Content analysis delves into various facets of entrepreneurial activities within these businesses, offering insights into their innovation processes and challenges. The findings highlight the pivotal role of existing and new knowledge in driving incremental innovation. Despite challenges such as risk aversion and succession planning, family firms leverage their unique resources to maintain a competitive edge. This chapter contributes to understanding how family-owned businesses engage in incremental innovation and its implications for long-term success and sustainability. Future research could

DOI: 10.4018/979-8-3693-3518-5.ch012

explore wealth creation dynamics and the influence of organizational culture on innovation within these firms.

INTRODUCTION

Family-owned businesses, marked by active family involvement in both ownership and management, play vital roles in the global economy. They constitute a significant portion of businesses worldwide and make substantial contributions to job creation and economic growth (Durán et al., 2016). However, these firms often exhibit hesitancy toward embracing innovation, typically preferring incremental changes over radical ones (Massis et al., 2013). Understanding the intricacies of incremental innovation within family firms is imperative for several reasons:

Firstly, incremental innovation is foundational for securing the long-term success and sustainability of family businesses. Unlike radical innovation, which entails significant changes, incremental innovation allows these firms to systematically enhance their products, processes, and services, thereby maintaining and strengthening their competitive edge (Asaba & Wada, 2019). Family firms typically prioritize long-term goals and the preservation of socioemotional wealth, such as maintaining family control, identity, and values (Massis et al., 2016). Incremental innovation aligns with these objectives, enabling family firms to adapt and evolve gradually while safeguarding their core principles and identity.

Secondly, a thorough exploration of incremental innovation within family-owned businesses offers valuable insights into their unique characteristics and complex challenges. Operating within a distinctive context shaped by the intricate interplay of family dynamics, ownership structures, and management paradigms, family firms encounter challenges in decision-making, resource allocation, and risk-taking (Comin et al., 2022). By carefully examining how family firms engage in incremental innovation, researchers can gain a deep understanding of the factors influencing innovation within these entities, guiding the development of strategies and interventions to enhance innovation capabilities.

Thirdly, scholarly investigation of incremental innovation within family firms contributes significantly to the broader field of knowledge in innovation and entrepreneurship. Family firms, with their unique organizational structure blending family and business systems, exhibit distinct behaviors and outcomes (Massis et al., 2015). Through rigorous examination of the innovation behavior of family firms, scholars can contribute to the formulation of theories and frameworks that differentiate family firms from non-family ones in terms of innovation (Massis et al., 2012). This knowledge provides valuable insights for policymakers and practitioners in devising and implementing strategies to promote innovation within family-owned businesses.

Understanding the factors influencing incremental innovation within family firms has practical implications for family business owners and managers. Such insights enable them to identify and implement strategies that foster an innovative culture, streamline innovation processes, and leverage their unique resources and capabilities to promote incremental innovation (Zainal, 2020). Embracing incremental innovation positions family firms to enhance competitiveness, adapt to evolving market conditions, and ensure enduring sustainability in their business endeavors.

Incremental innovation, characterized by the gradual enhancement of existing products, services, or processes, aims to optimize efficiency, reduce costs, or improve performance (Leminen et al., 2016). It builds upon existing knowledge and capabilities and poses lower risks and disruptions compared to radical innovation, allowing organizations to strengthen their capabilities and maintain a competitive edge in the market (Nieto et al., 2013).

In contrast, radical innovation involves a transformative approach that entails developing entirely new products, services, or processes, significantly disrupting existing markets or industries (Leminen et al., 2016). This approach demands organizations to adopt new technical and commercial skills alongside innovative problem-solving approaches (Nieto et al., 2013), often accompanied by high levels of uncertainty and risk (Gurtner & Reinhardt, 2016). Motivated by the identification of new needs or opportunities, radical innovation aims to create breakthrough possibilities (Gurtner & Reinhardt, 2016).

While there exists a continuum of innovation types between incremental and radical innovation (Martínez-Ros & Orfila-Sintes, 2009), organizations often adopt a blend of both, known as ambidextrous innovation. This approach balances the exploitation of existing capabilities with the exploration of new opportunities (Lin et al., 2013), enabling organizations to sustain their operations while pursuing new avenues for growth (Ndlovu et al., 2022).

The primary objective of this chapter is to elucidate the importance of incremental innovation within the context of family-owned businesses, considering their unique challenges and characteristics. Furthermore, it aims to outline practical implications for family business owners and managers, offering a comprehensive perspective on how incremental innovation contributes to the long-term success and sustainability of family firms within the broader landscape of innovation and entrepreneurship.

Research Methodology

Content analysis serves as a pivotal research methodology, facilitating the systematic exploration of various facets concerning entrepreneurial activities. Through a meticulous examination of literature and data content, researchers can glean valuable insights into entrepreneurial marketing strategies, behaviors, and outcomes. Breit

(2023) emphasizes the critical role of thematic analysis in entrepreneurial marketing research, highlighting the necessity of comprehending diverse perspectives within the broader context of entrepreneurial marketing. This approach not only unveils significant research opportunities but also contributes to the advancement of knowledge in the field.

Furthermore, Kansheba and Wald (2020) delve into how content analysis can illuminate the roles of different actors and the outcomes of entrepreneurial ecosystems, providing a holistic understanding of the underlying dynamics. Rauch et al. (2009) underscore the importance of content analysis in assessing prior research and charting future directions in entrepreneurial orientation and business performance. By amalgamating these perspectives through content analysis, researchers can yield theoretical, methodological, and empirical insights that enrich our comprehension of entrepreneurial marketing practices and their implications for business performance.

Results and Discussion

Incremental and Radical Innovation

The table 1 below provides a comparison between incremental and radical innovation across various aspects. Incremental innovation involves making gradual improvements to existing products, processes, or services, while radical innovation focuses on the development of new and disruptive technologies, products, or business models. The key characteristics of each type of innovation, along with their associated concepts and roles, are outlined. Additionally, examples from different industries illustrate how these types of innovation manifest in practice.

Table 1. Comparison of Incremental and Radical Innovation

Aspect	Incremental Innovation	Radical Innovation
Definition	Gradual improvements to existing products, processes, or services (Nieto et al., 2013)	Development of new and disruptive technologies, products, or business models (Subramaniam & Youndt, 2005)
Key Characteristics	Builds upon existing knowledge and capabilities (Nieto et al., 2013)	Requires organizations to chart a new course and acquire new skills (Subramaniam & Youndt, 2005)
Key Concept	Exploitation (Andriopoulos & Lewis, 2009)	Exploration (Andriopoulos & Lewis, 2009)
Role	Refining and extending current knowledge to improve efficiency (Andriopoulos & Lewis, 2009)	Seeking new knowledge and capabilities to achieve radical innovation (Andriopoulos & Lewis, 2009)
Industry Examples	Hotel industry (Zain et al., 2018)	Technology or pharmaceuticals (Taghizadeh et al., 2019)

Innovation Dynamics in Family Firms

Theoretical Frameworks for Incremental Innovation

The table below outlines several key theoretical frameworks that contribute to our understanding of incremental innovation. Each framework is accompanied by its main concepts and the authors who have developed and advanced these ideas. These theoretical perspectives offer insights into different aspects of incremental innovation, including leveraging existing knowledge, the role of external knowledge search and network embeddedness, the importance of open innovation practices, and considerations regarding weak appropriability and its implications for innovation strategies.

Table 2. Theoretical Frameworks for Incremental Innovation

Theoretical Framework	Main Concepts	Authors
Knowledge-Based View of the Firm	Emphasizes leveraging existing knowledge for incremental improvements.	Keupp et al., 2011
	Highlights knowledge stock and flow for enhancing incremental innovation.	Rupietta & Backes-Gellner, 2019
External Knowledge Search and	Combines social network theory and technological proximity for insights.	Shi et al., 2020
Network Embeddedness	Emphasizes the importance of network embeddedness for innovation.	
Open Innovation	Focuses on collaboration and knowledge sharing with external partners.	Han et al., 2020
	Highlights the role of partnerships and open search strategies.	Chiang & Hung, 2010
Weak Appropriability	Addresses limited benefits due to weak intellectual property rights.	Malen & Marcus, 2017
	Encourages firms to prioritize exploratory innovation strategies.	

Table 3 provides a summary of notable studies focusing on incremental innovation within family-owned businesses. These studies shed light on the preference for incremental improvements over radical innovation among family firms, highlighting various factors influencing this tendency. From prioritizing efficiency and gradual enhancements to exploring the impact of family management involvement and top management team diversity, these findings offer valuable insights into the innovation dynamics within family firms.

Table 3. Studies on Incremental Innovation in Family Firms

Authors	Key Findings
Durán et al., 2016	Family firms prioritize incremental over radical innovation, focusing on efficiency and gradual improvements.
Massis et al., 2013	Family firms prioritize incremental innovation due to perceiving technological innovation as less critical, potentially leading to slower growth.
Asaba & Wada, 2019	Family firms in pharmaceuticals primarily pursue incremental innovations in R&D efforts.
Nieto et al., 2013	Family firms generally prefer incremental innovation, consistent across various industries.
Massis et al., 2015	Family-driven innovation could resolve innovation paradox in family firms, emphasizing readiness for innovation.
Hu and Hughes, 2020	Majority of family firm innovation is incremental rather than radical.
Fredyna et al., 2019	Explores how family management involvement moderates the link between entrepreneurial orientation and product innovation.
Röd, 2019	Investigates how top management team diversity influences innovation in family firms.

Characteristics of Family Firms

Table 4 provides a comprehensive overview of the dynamics and characteristics influencing innovation within family-owned businesses. It outlines key aspects such as the definition of family firms, their strategic direction, sustainability priorities, unique resources and capabilities stemming from family involvement, and their distinctive behaviors and values. Additionally, the table explores how family firms approach innovation, highlighting factors such as risk aversion, long-term orientation, and the role of customer knowledge. Furthermore, it discusses the unique resources available to family firms for innovation, including their agility, commitment to customer relationships, and alignment with family values. Lastly, the table addresses challenges such as risk aversion and succession planning, which can impact the innovation trajectory of family-owned businesses.

Table 4. Dynamics and Characteristics of Innovation in Family Firms

Aspect	Description	Sources
Definition	Family firms are characterized by significant ownership and managerial positions held by family members. They typically involve family influence in decision-making and control.	Massis et al., 2013; Chrisman et al., 2005

continued on following page

Table 4. Continued

Aspect	Description	Sources
Strategic Direction	Family involvement in decision-making and control influences the strategic direction of the firm.	Chrisman et al., 2005
Sustainability	Family firms prioritize long-term sustainability and continuity, reflecting in their strategic decisions.	Chrisman et al., 2005; Williams et al., 2013
Resources and Capabilities	Family involvement fosters unique resources and capabilities, such as trust, loyalty, and commitment, contributing to the firm's competitive advantage.	Chrisman et al., 2005; Felício & Galindo-Villardón, 2015
Transgenerational Succession	Family firms focus on transferring management within the family across generations, distinguishing them from non-family firms.	Williams et al., 2013
Behaviors and Values	Family dynamics influence decision-making processes and priorities, with an emphasis on non-financial goals like family unity and legacy preservation.	Xu & Hitt, 2018; Nieto et al., 2013
Innovation Behavior	Family firms may exhibit a more risk-averse and conservative approach to innovation, prioritizing incremental improvements over radical breakthroughs.	Nieto et al., 2013
Unique Resources for Innovation	Family firms possess unique resources such as robust social bonds within the family, contributing significantly to their innovation efforts.	Casprini et al., 2017; Kallmuenzer, 2018
Long-term Orientation and Identity Preservation	Their long-term orientation and commitment to preserving their identity provide a stable foundation for innovation efforts.	Massis et al., 2016
Agility and Decision-making Flexibility	Family firms can make nimble decisions without bureaucratic hurdles, enabling rapid responses to market shifts and technological advancements.	Broekaert et al., 2016
Culture of Commitment and Loyalty	Strong commitment and loyalty foster a culture conducive to innovation and risk-taking within family firms.	Nieto et al., 2013
Customer Knowledge	Deep understanding of customer needs cultivated through long-term relationships provides valuable insights for innovative product development.	Migliori et al., 2020
Collaboration and Knowledge Exchange with External Partners	Prioritization of relationship cultivation facilitates collaboration and knowledge exchange with external partners, enhancing innovation capabilities.	Casprini et al., 2017
Alignment with Family Values	Family firms align innovation efforts with family values and objectives, aiming to create a lasting legacy and contribute to future generations' success.	Rondi et al., 2019; Doluca et al., 2017

continued on following page

Table 4. Continued

Aspect	Description	Sources
Reputation and Credibility	Leveraging family reputation and history enhances trust and credibility in the marketplace, facilitating the adoption and diffusion of innovative products and services.	Doluca et al., 2017
Risk Aversion	Higher risk aversion may hinder investment in risky innovation projects, impacting the firm's willingness to pursue uncertain ventures.	Massis et al., 2016; Carnes & Ireland, 2013
Succession Planning	Challenges related to succession planning and knowledge transfer affect the firm's ability to sustain innovation over the long term.	Akram et al., 2022

Table 5 provides an overview of key studies in business literature that explore the dynamics and characteristics of family firms. These studies offer insights into various aspects, such as how family firms generate competitive advantage, leverage distinctive resources, and address challenges like succession planning. Additionally, they examine the role of organizational culture, entrepreneurship, and family networks in shaping family business dynamics. Each study contributes unique perspectives, ranging from resource-based analyses to explorations of multigenerational transitions and the impact of entrepreneurship on family dynamics. Together, they offer valuable insights into the complex and dynamic nature of family-owned businesses.

Table 5. Example of Studies on Dynamics and Characteristics of Family Firms in Business Literature

Key Authors	Main Focus and Findings
Liao et al., 2021	Explores how family firms generate dynamics and dynamic capabilities to achieve competitive advantage, emphasizing the importance of understanding unique family dynamics.
Hoffman et al., 2006	Discusses how family firms leverage distinctive resources and family dynamics to gain sustained competitive advantage, providing examples of unique resources contributing to their success.
Habbershon & Pistrui, 2002	Points out the lack of wealth-creation topics in family business literature, highlighting the need for further research on entrepreneurial orientation, high-growth companies, and strategic experimentation.
Zahra et al., 2004	Offers a resource-based analysis of how organizational culture influences entrepreneurship in family versus non-family firms, emphasizing the role of culture in shaping family business dynamics.
Chirico & Nordqvist, 2010	Examines the role of organizational culture in dynamic capabilities and transgenerational value creation in family firms, highlighting the significance of culture in shaping family business dynamics.
Andersson et al., 2002	Presents case studies and cross-case analysis of family business goals in the tourism and hospitality sector, offering insights into specific dynamics and goals of family firms in this industry.

continued on following page

Table 5. Continued

Key Authors	Main Focus and Findings
Mcquaid & Seaman, 2021	Discusses how family firms integrate family, friendship, and business networks, exploring the unique characteristics of family networks and their impact on family business dynamics.
Lambrecht, 2005	Provides an explanatory model for multigenerational transition in family firms, drawing on literature and case studies to illustrate experiences and complexities involved in transitioning across generations.
Wang, 2016	Explores the relationship between environmental dynamism, trust, and dynamic capabilities in family firms, highlighting the need for more research on dynamic capabilities specific to family-controlled firms.
Melin & Nordqvist, 2007	Investigates the reflexive dynamics of institutionalization in family firms, illustrating how influential actors shape family business practices and the importance of reflexivity in managing family business dynamics.
Brockhaus, 2004	Suggests future research directions for family business succession, emphasizing the practical value of research on succession planning and management in addressing the specific challenges of family firms.
Jennings et al., 2013	Explores the impact of entrepreneurship on families involved in family firms, focusing on gendered roles and experiences of next-generation members, and highlighting the complex dynamics and challenges faced.

Drivers of Incremental Innovation in Family Firms

Table 6 presents a summary of studies focusing on the drivers of incremental innovation in family firms. These studies shed light on various factors influencing the inclination of family firms towards incremental innovation and the strategies they employ to foster such innovation. Key findings highlight the idiosyncrasies of family firms, their reliance on tradition and internal searches, readiness for innovation, innovation behavior from an outcome perspective, the role of top management team diversity, paradoxical approaches to innovation, and the significance of organizational flexibility. Understanding these drivers is essential for comprehending how family firms navigate innovation processes and adapt to changing market dynamics.

Table 6. Drivers of Incremental Innovation in Family Firms

Study	Authors	Main Findings
Idiosyncrasies of Family Firms	Durán et al., 2016	Family firms' unique traits, such as long-term orientation and strong social capital, influence incremental innovation drivers. While they may invest less in innovation input, their conversion rate from input to output is higher, resulting in greater innovation output.

continued on following page

Table 6. Continued

Study	Authors	Main Findings
Tradition and Internal Searches	Asaba & Wada, 2019	Family firms rely on tradition and narrow internal searches for incremental innovation, leveraging existing knowledge and resources. This strategy preserves the firm's unique identity and socio-emotional wealth while making gradual improvements.
Readiness for Innovation and Socio-emotional Wealth	Massis et al., 2015	Family firms inclined toward innovation readiness and possessing a strong socio-emotional wealth orientation are more likely to invest in incremental innovation efforts. They recognize innovation's importance for long-term success and are willing to take calculated risks to adapt and evolve.
Innovation Behavior from Outcome Perspective	Nieto et al., 2013	Understanding family firms' innovation behavior through innovation outcomes is crucial for identifying drivers of incremental innovation. Analyzing innovation results provides insights into factors contributing to successful incremental innovation in family firms.
Top Management Team Diversity	Röd, 2019	Top management team (TMT) diversity in family firms drives both radical and incremental innovation by enabling innovation ambidexterity. Diverse perspectives within the TMT facilitate a balance between exploratory and exploitative innovation efforts, crucial for long-term success.
Paradoxical Approach to Innovation	Massis et al., 2016	Family firms exhibit a paradoxical approach to innovation, possessing resources and capabilities but facing hindrances due to the family's desire for control and identity preservation. Overcoming this paradox requires balancing family values with innovation for growth and adaptation.
Organizational Flexibility	Broekaert et al., 2016	Organizational flexibility is a key driver of innovation in family firms. Greater flexibility in structures and processes enables family firms to adapt to market changes and technological advancements, facilitating the effective implementation of incremental innovations.

Factors Influencing Incremental Innovation in Family Firms

Table 7 presents a summary of the factors influencing innovation in family firms, based on insights from diverse studies in the field. These factors cover various aspects such as market conditions, competition, social capital, industry trends, family involvement, risk aversion, resource constraints, family dynamics, heterogeneity, and strategy and leadership. A comprehensive understanding of these influences is essential for family firms to formulate effective innovation strategies, overcome challenges, and sustain competitiveness in dynamic business environments.

Table 7. Factors Influencing Innovation in Family Firms

Factor	Key Authors	Main Findings
Market Conditions	Durán et al., 2016	Family firms efficiently convert innovation input into output, indicating adeptness in navigating market conditions for innovation.
Market Competition	Yin et al., 2022	Market competition can either inhibit or facilitate innovation in family firms. Understanding its influence is crucial for shaping innovation strategies.
Social Capital and External Knowledge	Massis et al., 2012	Family firms' social capital influences their reliance on external knowledge sources for innovation. Collaboration and partnerships are common strategies for acquiring innovation resources.
Industry Trends	Groote et al., 2020	Family firms may react differently to disruptive versus sustaining innovation based on industry trends. Understanding industry dynamics is essential for shaping innovation strategies.
Industry Life-cycle	Cucculelli & Peruzzi, 2020	Family firms' innovation behavior may vary depending on the stage of the industry life-cycle. Adaptation of innovation strategies based on industry conditions is necessary for sustained innovation success.
Type of Family Involvement	Magistretti et al., 2019	The nature of family involvement influences practices in managing relationships with external designers in innovation processes. Understanding these dynamics is crucial for effective innovation management.
Risk Aversion	Dangelico et al., 2019	Risk aversion in family firms hinders innovation despite their flexibility and long-term perspective. Overcoming this challenge requires strategies to balance risk management with innovation initiatives.
Resource Constraints	Dangelico et al., 2019	Limited resources and knowledge hinder family firms' ability to drive innovation, particularly in radical innovation. Seeking external collaborations and investments can alleviate resource constraints and foster innovation.
Family Dynamics	Nieto et al., 2013	Family dynamics and multiple family members' involvement in decision-making can create challenges in maintaining focus on innovation and making strategic decisions. Clear governance structures and strategic alignment are essential for effective innovation management.
Heterogeneity	Cesaroni et al., 2021	Family firms exhibit heterogeneity in their innovation orientation. Understanding the factors driving this heterogeneity is crucial for addressing specific challenges and tailoring innovation strategies to different family firm contexts.
Strategy and Leadership	Carnes & Ireland, 2013	Developing effective innovation processes, fostering a culture of innovation, and aligning top management support are essential for overcoming innovation challenges in family firms and maintaining competitiveness.

Family Dynamics and Innovation in Family-Owned Enterprises

Table 8 offers insights from studies investigating how family dynamics affect innovation in family firms. These studies explore topics like innovation input and output, the balance between continuity and innovation, the influence of family management, the role of family governance, and the impact of socioemotional wealth. Understanding these dynamics is vital for grasping the intricate relationship between family dynamics and innovation results in family-owned enterprises.

Table 8. Studies on Family Dynamics and Innovation in Family Firms

Study	Key Authors	Main Findings
Innovation Input and Output	Durán et al., 2016	Family firms exhibit lower levels of innovation input but achieve higher conversion rates of input into output, resulting in overall higher levels of innovation output.
Priority of Continuity over Innovation	Singh & Kota, 2017	Family firms often prioritize continuity across generations and succession issues over innovation, which may lead to a lack of emphasis on innovative efforts.
Positive Influence of Family Management	Matzler et al., 2014	Family management in family firms positively influences innovation output due to the shared vision and commitment to innovation fostered by the close-knit nature of family firms.
Impact of Family Governance	Yin et al., 2022	Internal governance structures within family-owned firms affect their innovation efforts, with firms having higher family involvement in management being more likely to engage in innovative activities.
Influence of Socioemotional Wealth	Ng et al., 2021	Socioemotional wealth factors in family firms, such as family influence and control, can both positively and negatively affect innovation, shaping the risk-taking behavior and innovation propensity of non-family managers.

Family Firms Face Unique Challenges

Table 9 outlines strategies for addressing challenges commonly faced by family firms. These strategies encompass leveraging technological innovation, building resilience, engaging in portfolio strategies, succession planning, building strong social networks, and aligning strategies with nonfinancial goals. By understanding and implementing these approaches, family firms can navigate obstacles effectively and ensure long-term success while preserving their unique identity and values.

Table 9. Strategies for Overcoming Challenges in Family Firms

Strategy	Description	Key Authors
Leveraging Technological Innovation	Invest in research and development to develop new products and services, staying ahead of the curve and embracing innovation to maintain relevance and continue growth.	Massis et al., 2013
Building Resilience	Implement strategies such as diversifying offerings, adopting new business models, and implementing cost-cutting measures to survive economic downturns, demonstrating resilience and adaptability.	Piramanayagam et al., 2022
Engaging in Portfolio Strategies	Expand into new markets or industries to reduce dependence on a single business and mitigate risks, leveraging existing resources and knowledge to explore new opportunities.	Zellweger et al., 2012
Succession Planning	Develop clear succession plans, identifying and grooming potential successors, providing necessary training and support, and establishing governance structures for smooth leadership transitions.	Suárez et al., 2001
Building Strong Social Networks	Utilize social networks to access resources, knowledge, and opportunities for internationalization, establishing partnerships and gaining valuable insights for informed strategies.	Kryeziu et al., 2021
Aligning Strategies with Nonfinancial Goals	Focus on preserving family legacy, maintaining family harmony, and contributing to the community, creating a sense of purpose and identity that guides strategic decisions.	Zellweger et al., 2013

CONCLUSION

The examination of innovation within family firms uncovers various significant perspectives and research findings. The knowledge-based view of the firm underscores the pivotal role of existing knowledge and the acquisition of new knowledge in driving incremental innovation. Additionally, concepts such as external knowledge search, network embeddedness, and open innovation emphasize the importance of robust external networks and collaboration with external partners in fostering incremental innovation capabilities. Despite the tendency of family firms to prioritize incremental innovations due to their focus on stability and efficiency, research suggests the need for a nuanced understanding of innovation in these firms.

Family firms are characterized by their unique features, including family influence on strategic decisions, a commitment to long-term sustainability, and a focus on transgenerational succession. These distinctive traits, shaped by family dynamics, influence the strategic direction, resource base, and approach to innovation within family firms. While family firms possess strengths such as strong social bonds, a long-term orientation, and alignment with family values, they also face challenges such as risk aversion and succession planning, which can impact their innovation potential.

Case examples in the literature illustrate the diverse dynamics within family firms and highlight how they can leverage their unique resources and dynamics to gain a competitive edge. However, there are still areas for future research to explore. One avenue could involve further investigation into wealth creation dynamics in family firms, delving deeper into how family capital contributes to sustained competitive advantage. Additionally, research could focus on understanding the impact of organizational culture on innovation within family firms and exploring strategies to overcome challenges such as risk aversion and succession planning.

In essence, understanding the dynamics and challenges within family firms is crucial for both scholars and practitioners in the field of family business. By addressing these challenges and exploring future research avenues, family firms can continue to thrive and innovate in today's dynamic business landscape.

REFERENCES

Akram, M. U., Ghosh, K., & Sharma, D. (2022). A systematic review of innovation in family firms and future research agenda. *International Journal of Emerging Markets*, 17(7), 1759–1792. 10.1108/IJOEM-06-2021-0936

Andersson, T., Carlsen, J., & Getz, D. (2002). Family business goals in the tourism and hospitality sector: Case studies and cross-case analysis from Australia, Canada, and Sweden. *Family Business Review*, 15(2), 89–106. 10.1111/j.1741-6248.2002.00089.x

Andriopoulos, C., & Lewis, M. W. (2009). Exploitation-exploration tensions and organizational ambidexterity: Managing paradoxes of innovation. *Organization Science*, 20(4), 696–717. 10.1287/orsc.1080.0406

Asaba, S., & Wada, T. (2019). The contact-hitting R&D strategy of family firms in the Japanese pharmaceutical industry. *Family Business Review*, 32(3), 277–295. 10.1177/0894486519852449

Breit, L., & Volkmann, C. K. (2023). Recent developments in entrepreneurial marketing: Systematic literature review, thematic analysis and research agenda. *Journal of Research in Marketing and Entrepreneurship*, 26(2), 228–256. 10.1108/JRME-11-2022-0136

Brockhaus, R. H. (2004). Family business succession: Suggestions for future research. *Family Business Review*, 17(2), 165–177. 10.1111/j.1741-6248.2004.00011.x

Broekaert, W., Andries, P., & Debackere, K. (2016). Innovation processes in family firms: The relevance of organizational flexibility. *Small Business Economics*, 47(3), 771–785. 10.1007/s11187-016-9760-7

Carnes, C. M., & Ireland, R. D. (2013). Familiness and innovation: Resource bundling as the missing link. *Entrepreneurship Theory and Practice*, 37(6), 1399–1419. 10.1111/etap.12073

Casprini, E., De Massis, A., Di Minin, A., Frattini, F., & Piccaluga, A. (2017). How family firms execute open innovation strategies: The Loccioni case. *Journal of Knowledge Management*, 21(6), 1459–1485. 10.1108/JKM-11-2016-0515

Cesaroni, F. M., Chamochumbi Diaz, G. D., & Sentuti, A. (2021). Family firms and innovation from founder to successor. *Administrative Sciences*, 11(2), 54. 10.3390/admsci11020054

Chiang, Y. H., & Hung, K. P. (2010). Exploring open search strategies and perceived innovation performance from the perspective of inter-organizational knowledge flows. *Research Management*, 40(3), 292–299.

Chirico, F., & Nordqvist, M. (2010). Dynamic capabilities and trans-generational value creation in family firms: The role of organizational culture. *International Small Business Journal*, 28(5), 487–504. 10.1177/0266242610370402

Chrisman, J. J., Chua, J. H., & Sharma, P. (2005). Trends and directions in the development of a strategic management theory of the family firm. *Entrepreneurship Theory and Practice*, 29(5), 555–575. 10.1111/j.1540-6520.2005.00098.x

Comin, L. C., Oro, I. M., & Carvalho, C. E. (2022). Family involvement and innovation: a proposition for studies. *Revista Brasileira de Inovação, 21*.

Cucculelli, M., & Peruzzi, V. (2020). Innovation over the industry life-cycle. Does ownership matter? *Research Policy*, 49(1), 103878. 10.1016/j.respol.2019.103878

Dangelico, R. M., Nastasi, A., & Pisa, S. (2019). A comparison of family and nonfamily small firms in their approach to green innovation: A study of Italian companies in the agri-food industry. *Business Strategy and the Environment*, 28(7), 1434–1448. 10.1002/bse.2324

De Groote, J. K., Conrad, W., & Hack, A. (2021). How can family businesses survive disruptive industry changes? Insights from the traditional mail order industry. *Review of Managerial Science*, 15(8), 2239–2273. 10.1007/s11846-020-00424-x

De Massis, A., Di Minin, A., & Frattini, F. (2015). Family-driven innovation: Resolving the paradox in family firms. *California Management Review*, 58(1), 5–19. 10.1525/cmr.2015.58.1.5

De Massis, A., Frattini, F., Kotlar, J., Petruzzelli, A. M., & Wright, M. (2016). Innovation through tradition: Lessons from innovative family businesses and directions for future research. *The Academy of Management Perspectives*, 30(1), 93–116. 10.5465/amp.2015.0017

De Massis, A., Frattini, F., & Lichtenthaler, U. (2013). Research on technological innovation in family firms: Present debates and future directions. *Family Business Review*, 26(1), 10–31. 10.1177/0894486512466258

De Massis, A., Frattini, F., Pizzurno, E., & Cassia, L. (2015). Product innovation in family versus nonfamily firms: An exploratory analysis. *Journal of Small Business Management*, 53(1), 1–36. 10.1111/jsbm.12068

Doluca, H., Wagner, M., & Block, J. (2018). Sustainability and environmental behaviour in family firms: A longitudinal analysis of environment-related activities, innovation and performance. *Business Strategy and the Environment*, 27(1), 152–172. 10.1002/bse.1998

Duran, P., Kammerlander, N., Van Essen, M., & Zellweger, T. (2016). Doing more with less: Innovation input and output in family firms. *Academy of Management Journal*, 59(4), 1224–1264. 10.5465/amj.2014.0424

Felício, J. A., & Galindo Villardón, M. P. (2015). Family characteristics and governance of small and medium-sized family firms. *Journal of Business Economics and Management*, 16(6), 1069–1084. 10.3846/16111699.2012.747446

Fredyna, T., Ruíz-Palomo, D., & Diéguez-Soto, J. (2019). Entrepreneurial orientation and product innovation. The moderating role of family involvement in management. *European Journal of Family Business*, 9(2), 128–145. 10.24310/ejfbejfb.v9i2.5392

Gurtner, S., & Reinhardt, R. (2016). Ambidextrous idea generation—Antecedents and outcomes. *Journal of Product Innovation Management*, 33(S1), 34–54. 10.1111/jpim.12353

Habbershon, T. G., & Pistrui, J. (2002). Enterprising families domain: Family-influenced ownership groups in pursuit of transgenerational wealth. *Family Business Review*, 15(3), 223–237. 10.1111/j.1741-6248.2002.00223.x

Han, S., Lyu, Y., Ji, R., Zhu, Y., Su, J., & Bao, L. (2020). Open innovation, network embeddedness and incremental innovation capability. *Management Decision*, 58(12), 2655–2680. 10.1108/MD-08-2019-1038

Hoffman, J., Hoelscher, M., & Sorenson, R. (2006). Achieving sustained competitive advantage: A family capital theory. *Family Business Review*, 19(2), 135–145. 10.1111/j.1741-6248.2006.00065.x

Hu, Q., & Hughes, M. (2020). Radical innovation in family firms: A systematic analysis and research agenda. *International Journal of Entrepreneurial Behaviour & Research*, 26(6), 1199–1234. 10.1108/IJEBR-11-2019-0658

Jennings, J. E., Breitkreuz, R. S., & James, A. E. (2013). When family members are also business owners: Is entrepreneurship good for families? *Family Relations*, 62(3), 472–489. 10.1111/fare.12013

Kallmuenzer, A. (2018). Exploring drivers of innovation in hospitality family firms. *International Journal of Contemporary Hospitality Management*, 30(3), 1978–1995. 10.1108/IJCHM-04-2017-0242

Kansheba, J., & Wald, A. (2020). Entrepreneurial ecosystems: A systematic literature review and research agenda. *Journal of Small Business and Enterprise Development*, 27(6), 943–964. 10.1108/JSBED-11-2019-0364

Keupp, M. M., Palmié, M., & Gassmann, O. (2012). The strategic management of innovation: A systematic review and paths for future research. *International Journal of Management Reviews*, 14(4), 367–390. 10.1111/j.1468-2370.2011.00321.x

Kryeziu, L., Coşkun, R., & Krasniqi, B. (2022). Social networks and family firm internationalisation: Cases from a transition economy. *Review of International Business and Strategy*, 32(2), 284–304. 10.1108/RIBS-03-2021-0052

Lambrecht, J. (2005). Multigenerational transition in family businesses: A new explanatory model. *Family Business Review*, 18(4), 267–282. 10.1111/j.1741-6248.2005.00048.x

Leminen, S., Nyström, A. G., Westerlund, M., & Kortelainen, M. J. (2016). The effect of network structure on radical innovation in living labs. *Journal of Business and Industrial Marketing*, 31(6), 743–757. 10.1108/JBIM-10-2012-0179

Liao, T. S., Pham, T. T. D., & Lu, J. C. (2021). The Dynamic Model of Intellectual Capital Creation in Family Business: The Dynamic Capabilities Perspective. *Journal of Business Administration Research*, 4(2). Advance online publication. 10.30564/jbar.v4i2.2635

Lin, H. E., McDonough, E. F.III, Lin, S. J., & Lin, C. Y. Y. (2013). Managing the exploitation/exploration paradox: The role of a learning capability and innovation ambidexterity. *Journal of Product Innovation Management*, 30(2), 262–278. 10.1111/j.1540-5885.2012.00998.x

Magistretti, S., Dell'Era, C., De Massis, A., & Frattini, F. (2019). Exploring the relationship between types of family involvement and collaborative innovation in design-intensive firms: Insights from two leading players in the furniture industry. *Industry and Innovation*, 26(10), 1121–1151. 10.1080/13662716.2019.1623762

Martínez-Ros, E., & Orfila-Sintes, F. (2009). Innovation activity in the hotel industry. *Technovation*, 29(9), 632–641. 10.1016/j.technovation.2009.02.004

Matzler, K., Veider, V., Hautz, J., & Stadler, C. (2015). The impact of family ownership, management, and governance on innovation. *Journal of Product Innovation Management*, 32(3), 319–333. 10.1111/jpim.12202

McQuaid, R., & Seaman, C. (2022). Integrating family, friendship and business networks in family firms. *Journal of Family Business Management*, 12(4), 799–815.

Melin, L., & Nordqvist, M. (2007). The reflexive dynamics of institutionalization: The case of the family business. *Strategic Organization*, 5(3), 321–333. 10.1177/1476127007079959

Migliori, S., De Massis, A., Maturo, F., & Paolone, F. (2020). How does family management affect innovation investment propensity? The key role of innovation impulses. *Journal of Business Research*, 113, 243–256. 10.1016/j.jbusres.2020.01.039

Ndlovu, N., Ochara, N. M., & Martin, R. (2023). Influence of digital government innovation on transformational government in resource-constrained contexts. *Journal of Science and Technology Policy Management*, 14(5), 960–981. 10.1108/JSTPM-11-2021-0173

Ng, P. Y., Dayan, M., & Makri, M. (2022). Influence of socioemotional wealth on non-family managers' risk taking and product innovation in family businesses. *Cross Cultural & Strategic Management*, 29(2), 297–319. 10.1108/CCSM-03-2021-0058

Nieto, M. J., Santamaria, L., & Fernandez, Z. (2015). Understanding the innovation behavior of family firms. *Journal of Small Business Management*, 53(2), 382–399. 10.1111/jsbm.12075

Piramanayagam, S., Dixit, S. K., & Seal, P. P. (2022). We are in survival mode: How family-owned small foodservice firms in India responded to the Covid-19 pandemic. *Journal of Family Business Management*, 12(3), 436–449. 10.1108/JFBM-10-2021-0130

Rauch, A., Wiklund, J., Lumpkin, G., & Fresé, M. (2009). Entrepreneurial orientation and business performance: An assessment of past research and suggestions for the future. *Entrepreneurship Theory and Practice*, 33(3), 761–787. 10.1111/j.1540-6520.2009.00308.x

Röd, I. (2019). TMT diversity and innovation ambidexterity in family firms: The mediating role of open innovation breadth. *Journal of Family Business Management*, 9(4), 377–392. 10.1108/JFBM-09-2018-0031

Rondi, E., De Massis, A., & Kotlar, J. (2019). Unlocking innovation potential: A typology of family business innovation postures and the critical role of the family system. *Journal of Family Business Strategy, 10*(4), 100236.

Rupietta, C., & Backes-Gellner, U. (2019). Combining knowledge stock and knowledge flow to generate superior incremental innovation performance—Evidence from Swiss manufacturing. *Journal of Business Research*, 94, 209–222. 10.1016/j.jbusres.2017.04.003

Shi, X., Zheng, Z., Zhang, Q., & Liang, H. (2020). External knowledge search and firms' incremental innovation capability: The joint moderating effect of technological proximity and network embeddedness. *Management Decision*, 58(9), 2049–2072. 10.1108/MD-08-2019-1078

Singh, R., & Kota, H. B. (2017). A resource dependency framework for innovation and internationalization of family businesses: Evidence from India. *Journal of Entrepreneurship in Emerging Economies*, 9(2), 207–231. 10.1108/JEEE-04-2016-0013

Subramaniam, M., & Youndt, M. A. (2005). The influence of intellectual capital on the types of innovative capabilities. *Academy of Management Journal*, 48(3), 450–463. 10.5465/amj.2005.17407911

Taghizadeh, S. K., Rahman, S. A., Hossain, M. M., & Haque, M. M. (2020). Characteristics of organizational culture in stimulating service innovation and performance. *Marketing Intelligence & Planning*, 38(2), 224–238. 10.1108/MIP-12-2018-0561

Wang, Y. (2016). Environmental dynamism, trust and dynamic capabilities of family businesses. *International Journal of Entrepreneurial Behaviour & Research*, 22(5), 643–670. 10.1108/IJEBR-11-2015-0234

Williams, D. W., Zorn, M. L., Russell Crook, T., & Combs, J. G. (2013). Passing the torch: Factors influencing transgenerational intent in family firms. *Family Relations*, 62(3), 415–428. 10.1111/fare.12016

Xu, K., & Hitt, M. A. (2020). The international expansion of family firms: The moderating role of internal financial slack and external capital availability. *Asia Pacific Journal of Management*, 37(1), 127–153. 10.1007/s10490-018-9593-9

Yin, Y., Crowley, F., Doran, J., Du, J., & O'Connor, M. (2023). Research and innovation and the role of competition in family owned and managed firms. *International Journal of Entrepreneurial Behaviour & Research*, 29(1), 166–194. 10.1108/IJEBR-12-2021-1031

Zahra, S. A., Hayton, J. C., & Salvato, C. (2004). Entrepreneurship in family vs. non–family firms: A resource–based analysis of the effect of organizational culture. *Entrepreneurship Theory and Practice*, 28(4), 363–381. 10.1111/j.1540-6520.2004.00051.x

Zainal, M. (2022). Innovation orientation and performance of Kuwaiti family businesses: Evidence from the initial period of COVID-19 pandemic. *Journal of Family Business Management*, 12(2), 251–265. 10.1108/JFBM-09-2020-0086

Zellweger, T. M., Nason, R. S., & Nordqvist, M. (2012). From longevity of firms to transgenerational entrepreneurship of families: Introducing family entrepreneurial orientation. *Family Business Review*, 25(2), 136–155. 10.1177/0894486511423531

Zellweger, T. M., Nason, R. S., Nordqvist, M., & Brush, C. G. (2013). Why do family firms strive for nonfinancial goals? An organizational identity perspective. *Entrepreneurship Theory and Practice*, 37(2), 229–248. 10.1111/j.1540-6520.2011.00466.x

Chapter 13
Internationalisation of Family SMEs:
A Bibliometric Analysis of Recent Trends and Future Research Direction

Maulidar Agustina
http://orcid.org/0000-0002-7319-5318
Universitas Syiah Kuala, Indonesia

M. Shabri Abd. Majid
http://orcid.org/0000-0003-3558-8783
Universitas Syiah Kuala, Indonesia

Hafasnuddin Hafasnuddin
Universitas Syiah Kuala, Indonesia

Yahya Yahya
Sekolah Tinggi Ilmu Ekonomi Sabang, Indonesia

ABSTRACT

The global business landscape is undergoing a transformative shift, with small and medium-sized enterprises (SMEs) gaining prominence. Among them, family-owned SMEs uniquely blend familial ties with entrepreneurship, playing a pivotal role in the international market. This study conducts a bibliometric analysis of 1,355 scholarly articles within the Scopus database, revealing nine thematic clusters related to the internationalization of family SMEs. Key areas include SMEs, family business, family firms, small and medium sized enterprises, and innovation. The analysis highlights a growing scholarly interest in this field, with the Family Business

DOI: 10.4018/979-8-3693-3518-5.ch013

Review originating from the United States, indexed Q1, emerging as a significant contributor. The insights not only contribute to academic discourse but also offer guidance for practitioners and policymakers aiming to support the sustainable growth and competitiveness of family SMEs globally. This study lays a foundation for future research, directing scholars towards unexplored areas in the dynamic realm of family SME internationalization.

1. INTRODUCTION

Amidst the dynamic and constantly evolving landscape of global business, the internationalisation of small and medium-sized enterprises (SMEs) has emerged as a critical driver of economic growth, innovation, and competitiveness. Internationalisation refers to the process of expanding involvement in foreign markets, which is widely acknowledged as a crucial strategy for business growth and expansion (Metsola et al., 2020). Within this context, family-owned SMEs constitute a substantial proportion of businesses globally, contributing significantly to employment generation, economic growth, and wealth creation in many economies (Chrisman et al., 2015). These enterprises are characterized by the intertwining of family relationships, business operations, and ownership interests, which can both facilitate and complicate their internationalization efforts (Chung & Zhu, 2021). While family ownership can confer distinct advantages such as long-term orientation, commitment to community, and shared values among family members, it also introduces complexities related to succession planning, decision-making processes, and intergenerational dynamics (Eddleston et al., 2019).

Moreover, family-owned SMEs often face resource constraints, limited access to external financing, and a reluctance to relinquish control, which can impede their ability to compete effectively in foreign markets (De Massis & Foss, 2018). Despite these challenges, family enterprises exhibit resilience and adaptability, leveraging their familial ties, reputation, and distinctive capabilities to carve out niches in global markets (Conz et al., 2023; Liew & Loo, 2024).

To navigate the complexities of internationalization, family-owned SMEs must adopt tailored strategies that balance the imperatives of business growth with the preservation of family values and identity (Miller & Le Breton-Miller, 2021; Salmon & Allman, 2020). This requires careful consideration of factors such as succession planning, family governance structures, and the alignment of family and business goals (González-Cruz et al., 2021; Naldi et al., 2015). Additionally, family enterprises must cultivate a global mindset, embrace innovation, and build strategic partnerships to compete effectively on the international stage (Amaechi, 2021; Zapata-Cantu et al., 2023).

Scholarly discussions surrounding internationalisation of family SMEs have seen a notable rise in recent times, indicating a heightened interest in understanding the intricate and evolving dynamics of this crucial field. For example, Shi et al. (2019) examined how intergenerational succession impacts the internationalization strategies of Chinese family firms, identifying three distinct succession patterns that influence the commitment and resources for internationalization of the next generation. Braga et al. (2017) found a significant association between innovation and internationalization processes within family businesses, emphasizing their critical role in ensuring success and continuity. Olivares et al. (2020) explored the internationalization of SMEs in Spain's Valencian region, noting a substantial increase in their presence in Latin American markets since 1990, reflecting a shift towards diversified markets and tailored strategies for each country. Heydari et al. (2023) investigated how personality traits of managers, founders, and owners of family firms impact business internationalization, highlighting the inclination of individuals with certain traits towards expanding their businesses internationally. Kampouri and Hajidimitriou (2023) examined how family SMEs' emphasis on family goals can hinder the development of international partnerships, based on a case study of Greek family SMEs in the food and beverages sector. Additionally, recent studies by Alayo et al. (2022), Basly and Saunier (2020), Fernández-Olmos and Malorgio (2020), Torkkeli et al. (2021), and Del Bosco and Bettinelli (2020) further contribute to understanding the complexities of internationalization in family SMEs by exploring factors such as innovation activities, socio-emotional goals, institutional networking, strategic orientations, foreign market entry modes, and the role of social capital in different contexts. These studies collectively enhance understanding of the challenges and opportunities faced by family SMEs in their internationalization endeavors and provide valuable insights for practitioners and policymakers.

Based on the synthesis of previous studies, this study aims to address several notable research gaps within the field. Firstly, it seeks to provide a holistic analysis of recent trends in internationalization among family-owned SMEs, integrating various dimensions such as ownership structures, succession planning, and socio-emotional goals. By conducting a comprehensive bibliometric analysis, the article intends to systematically identify emerging themes and areas that require further investigation. Furthermore, it also aims to fill the gap in identifying specific knowledge gaps within the literature, guiding future research efforts and priorities. Additionally, the article seeks to offer insights into future research directions for the broader field, synthesizing existing knowledge and proposing a roadmap for further exploration. Finally, by integrating bibliometric analysis techniques, the research intends to provide novel insights into the research landscape of internationalization in family SMEs, including patterns of publication, citation networks, and collaboration trends among researchers, thereby enriching our understanding of the field as a whole.

Subsequently, this article is organized into several sections: review of previous related studies, research methods, results and discussion, future research directions, and conclusion. Each section serves a distinct purpose, providing context, discussing prior studies, outlining the methodology, presenting findings, offering concluding remarks, and suggesting potential avenues for future research.

2. PREVIOUS STUDIES

Previous studies have explored various facets of the relationship between family firms and internationalization strategies. For instance, Shi et al. (2019) delve into how intergenerational succession shapes the internationalization strategies of Chinese family firms. Their qualitative analysis of eleven firms transitioning across generations reveals three distinct succession patterns, influencing the commitment and resources for internationalization in the next generation. This highlights the intricate dynamics between incumbents and successors in driving internationalization decisions. Braga et al. (2017) uncover a significant link between innovation and internationalization processes within family businesses, emphasizing their pivotal role in ensuring sustained success. Olivares et al. (2020) shed light on the internationalization journey of SMEs in Spain's Valencian region, particularly focusing on their expansion into Latin American markets. Through case studies spanning various sectors, they observe a notable surge in the presence of Valencian SMEs in Latin America since 1990, reflecting a strategic shift towards diversified markets with tailored approaches for each country. Heydari et al. (2023) explore how the personality traits of managers, founders, and owners influence the internationalization decisions of family firms, noting that individuals characterized by extroversion, openness, and low neuroticism tend to pursue international expansion strategically. Additionally, Kampouri & Hajidimitriou (2023) investigate how family SMEs' emphasis on family goals may impede the formation of international partnerships, drawing insights from a case study of Greek family SMEs in the food and beverages sector.

Alayo et al. (2022) emphasized the pivotal role of innovation activities in driving the internationalization of family SMEs, highlighting the significance of family involvement in this process. Their study reveals how factors such as the generation leading the business and family participation in the top management team influence the relationship between innovation and international expansion. Basly and Saunier (2020) delve into the impact of socio-emotional goals of owning families on export levels in family SMEs, alongside the influence of family business essence. Through an analysis of 46 French family SMEs, they uncover the nuanced effects of socio-emotional goals on export intensity and identify the positive relationship between familiness components and family business essence, enriching our understanding of family SMEs' internationalization dynamics. Fernández-Olmos and Malorgio (2020) explore the role of institutional networking in the internationalization of family SMEs in the DOC Rioja wine industry, focusing on the impact of family involvement in the Top Management Team (TMT). Their findings highlight the significant influence of institutional networking on internationalization speed, particularly when fewer family members are part of the TMT, offering practical insights for effective internationalization strategies. Torkkeli et al. (2021) address gaps in research on foreign market entry and success for family-controlled SMEs, emphasizing strategic orientations in international entrepreneurship. Through an analysis of 169 Finnish family SMEs, they uncover the impact of international growth orientation on internationalization propensity and degree, providing valuable insights into the role of innovation and entrepreneurial orientation in international operations. Del Bosco and Bettinelli (2020) examine the decision-making process of family-owned SMEs in choosing between wholly owned subsidiaries and joint ventures for foreign investments. Their analysis of 1,475 foreign subsidiaries owned by 701 family SMEs reveals how cultural, geographic, and institutional distance influence ownership mode, moderated by family control, offering valuable insights into family leaders' preferences and variations under different conditions. Furthermore, Torkkeli et al. (2021) underscore the importance of strong linking for internationalization among family SMEs in Mexico, highlighting the role of social capital and advising exporters to manage connections abroad. Their research addresses a gap in understanding internationalization among Mexican family businesses and emphasizes the need for further research in emerging economies. Rexhepi et al. (2017) recommends that family businesses in developing and transition countries use the new Uppsala model for internationalization due to its comprehensive nature and emphasis on networking. The export strategy is identified as the most effective entry method, and its combination with the new Uppsala model is considered optimal. The study proposes a three-step conceptual framework: understanding the domestic and target foreign markets, selecting an internationalization model (new Uppsala, network theory, or international entrepreneurship), and choosing a market entry strategy aligned with the model and market understanding. This structured approach aims to guide family businesses through successful internationalization. Lahiri (2020) reviews the internationalization of small and medium-sized family enterprises (family SMEs) through a strategy tripod framework, identifying key resource-based, institution-based, and industry-based factors. The study highlights how home-host country institutional and industry contingencies can impact these factors and emphasizes the importance of behavioral orientations in understanding family SME internationalization strategies. Rochayatun (2022) examines the internationalization of SMEs in East Java, Indonesia, highlighting their significant economic contributions despite numerous obstacles. These challenges include limited market knowledge, trade regulations, communication barriers, financing, and inadequate transportation infrastructure. The study underscores the importance of a networking strategy as a primary mode of entry for SMEs to independently navigate internationalization. This research provides both theoretical and practical insights into the entry strategies for SME internationalization. Urban et al. (2023) examines SME internationalization in seven countries, identifying operations, outbound logistics, and marketing and sales as key areas. The study finds that while marketing and sales are typical for internationalization, SMEs frequently engage in other value chain areas. Key barriers include knowledge, experience, and competition, with cultural differences and strong competition impacting advanced internationalization. Knowledge-related and financial barriers are significant in medium-income countries during early stages. The study underscores the value chain framework's importance for future research and policy to support SME internationalization despite its limited sample size.

3. RESEARCH METHODS

This study delves into a thorough investigation of the intricate dynamics within the realm of internationalisation of family SMEs through an extensive bibliometric analysis. The primary aim is to carefully examine the multifaceted developments, prevailing trends, and potential research avenues within this crucial field. Beyond merely providing valuable insights, the research endeavors to make significant contributions to informed decision-making, aid in policy formulation, and precisely pinpoint directions for future research endeavors. Through the bibliometric exploration, the study not only conducts a retrospective examination of the scholarly landscape but also lays the groundwork for understanding the current state of internationalisation of family SMEs research and envisioning its potential trajectories. This, in turn, fosters a deeper comprehension of the challenges and opportunities inherent in this vital domain (Mejia et al., 2021).

In order to ensure the reliability and comprehensiveness of our findings, we meticulously gathered data from the Scopus database. The selection of Scopus, recognized as the largest multidisciplinary database encompassing social science literature, was motivated by its commitment to maintaining the highest standards of peer-reviewed articles (Baas et al., 2020). The data collection process adhered to rigorous accuracy through the implementation of precise search strings and keywords. Specifically targeting "internationalisation of family SMEs" in titles, keywords, and abstracts, we obtained a substantial dataset consisting of 1355 relevant documents. Subsequent analysis of this dataset was conducted using Vosviewer, a robust tool for visualizing and interpreting bibliometric data (Agustina et al., 2021; Murkhana et al.,

2023). Through these meticulous steps, our research aims to provide comprehensive and valuable insights into the evolving landscape of internationalisation of family SMEs research, thereby benefiting stakeholders in academia, policy, and practice.

4. FINDING AND DISCUSSION

4.1 Document by Year

Figure 1 provides a visual representation of the distribution of 1,355 documents, categorized based on their respective years of publication spanning from 1990 to January 2024. The graph displays a discernible fluctuation in the number of publications related to internationalisation of family SMEs over this period. From 1990 to 2007, there was a steady rise in the number of articles published in this field, indicating an increasing interest or emphasis on the subject matter. However, there was a downward trend observed starting in 2008, followed by a gradual increase from 2009 to 2016. Subsequently, there was another decline in 2017, but the trend reversed with an uptick in the following year. A notable spike was witnessed in 2019 to 2023, indicating a potential surge in research attention and activity within the field of Internationalization of family SMEs during this period. This spike may signify an enhanced recognition of the importance of Internationalization of family SMEs. The data illustrates a significant acceleration in scholarly contributions, possibly reflecting heightened awareness and interest in addressing the challenges associated with Internationalization of family SMEs. Notably, publications on this topic are already evident as early as 2024, indicating a sustained scholarly focus. The early presence of these articles suggests the likelihood of a continued increase in publications by the end of 2024, reaffirming the enduring prominence and growing interest in Internationalization of family SMEs among the academic community.

Figure 1. Number of Internationalisation of Family SMEs Documents by Year

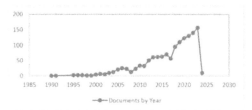

Source: Data processed (2024).

4.2 Most Productive Authors, Organizations, and Countries

In the field of internationalisation of family SMEs, the diversity among authors is notable, with no significant difference in the number of documents produced by each. Table 1 and Figure 2 highlight the most productive authors in this area. Ferrari (2023) emerges at the top of the list with 8 publications, although the total citations for their work remain relatively low at 37. In contrast, Kontinen and Ojala (2012) collectively authored 6 publications, which received a substantially higher number of citations, totaling 646. Authors Iborra et al. (2020) contributed to 3 publications, yet these works have not garnered any citations to date. Cristiano (2020) produced 3 publications, with a modest citation count of 13, while Ince (2022), also with 3 publications, received only 2 citations for their contributions.

Table 1. Most Productive Authors

No.	Author Name	Number of Publications	Number of Citations
1.	Ferrari (2023)	8	37
2.	Kontinen and Ojala (2012)	6	646
3.	Iborra et al. (2020)	3	0
4.	Cristiano (2020)	3	13
5.	Ince (2022)	3	2

Source: Data processed, Vosviewer (2024)

Figure 2. Density Visualization of the Most Productive

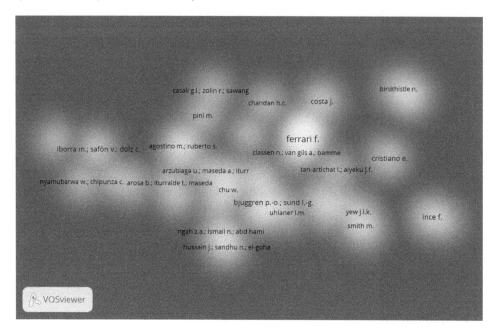

Furthermore, the most active organizations in the field of internationalisation of family SMEs can be observed in Table 2 and Figure 3. The University of Valencia in Spain leads the list as the most productive organization, having generated 6 publications. However, despite this high productivity, these publications have not received any citations. Nevertheless, the university boasts a notably high total link strength of 4,119, indicative of robust collaborative efforts within the academic community. In contrast, the Free University of Bozen-Bolzano in Italy produced slightly fewer publications, with a total of 5. Despite this lower output, these publications have garnered a significant number of citations, totaling 1,355. Impressively, the university also boasts a substantial total link strength of 7,597, reflecting a strong presence in collaborative research networks. Similarly, both Lancaster University and its Management School in the United Kingdom have produced 5 publications each. However, they diverge significantly in terms of their impact and collaborative efforts. While Lancaster University's publications have received a modest number of citations (28), its total link strength stands at a considerable 5,802. On the other hand, Lancaster University Management School's publications have received a higher number of citations (270), suggesting a greater impact, although its total link strength is comparatively lower at 2415. Lastly, Jönköping International Business School in Sweden also produced 5 publications. While the number of citations for these publications is higher at 294, its total link strength is relatively moderate at

2,162. This indicates a solid level of impact and collaboration but perhaps not as extensive as some of the other institutions listed.

Table 2. Most Productive Organizations

No.	Organization Name	Number of Publications	Number of Citations	Total Link Strength
1.	University of Valencia, Spain	6	0	4,119
2.	Free University of Bozen-Bolzano, Italy	5	1,355	7,597
3.	Lancaster University, United Kingdom	5	28	5,802
4.	Lancaster University Management School, United Kingdom	5	270	2,415
5.	Jönköping International Business School, Sweden	5	294	2,162

Source: Data processed, Vosviewer (2024)

Figure 3. Network Visualization of the Most Productive Organizations

Finally, Table 3 and Figure 4 provide insights into the leading contributors in the realm of internationalisation of family SMEs, with each country's productivity and impact delineated. The United Kingdom emerges as the most active participant, with a notable contribution of 163 documents. Impressively, these publications have garnered 4,506 citations, reflecting the significant impact of the research originating from the UK. Moreover, the Total Link Strength, a measure of collaborative efforts and networking, stands impressively high at 43,558, underscoring the robust engagement of UK researchers in this field. Following closely behind is Italy, matching the UK's output with 163 documents. While its citation count is slightly lower at 4,295, Italy still maintains a considerable presence in terms of research impact. The Total Link Strength for Italy is noteworthy at 39418, indicating a strong collaborative network within the Italian research community focused on internationalisation of family SMEs. Spain occupies the third position, demonstrating a commendable contribution of 138 documents. Despite a similar citation count to Italy at 4,259, Spain's research output is notable, reflecting its active engagement in exploring the internationalization dynamics of family SMEs. Moreover, the Total Link Strength for Spain mirrors that of Italy, suggesting a comparable level of collaboration and networking within the Spanish research landscape. The United States secures the fourth spot, with 110 documents contributing to the discourse on internationalisation of family SMEs. Although its citation count surpasses that of the UK and Italy at 5,686, indicating a strong impact, the Total Link Strength is relatively lower at 27,375. Nevertheless, the US remains a significant player in this field, leveraging its research output to influence scholarly conversations globally. Finally, Malaysia ranks fifth with 74 documents. While its citation count is modest at 713, Malaysia demonstrates an active involvement in researching the internationalization endeavors of family SMEs. The Total Link Strength, although lower compared to other leading nations, still showcases Malaysia's collaborative efforts within the research community focused on this subject matter.

Table 3. Most Productive Countries

No.	Country	Number of Publications	Number of Citations	Total Link Strength
1.	United Kingdom	163	4,506	43,558
2.	Italy	163	4,295	57,073
3.	Spain	138	4,259	39,418
4.	United States	110	5,686	27,375
5.	Malaysia	74	713	10,349

Source: Data processed, Vosviewer (2024)

Figure 4. Network Visualization of the Most Productive Counties

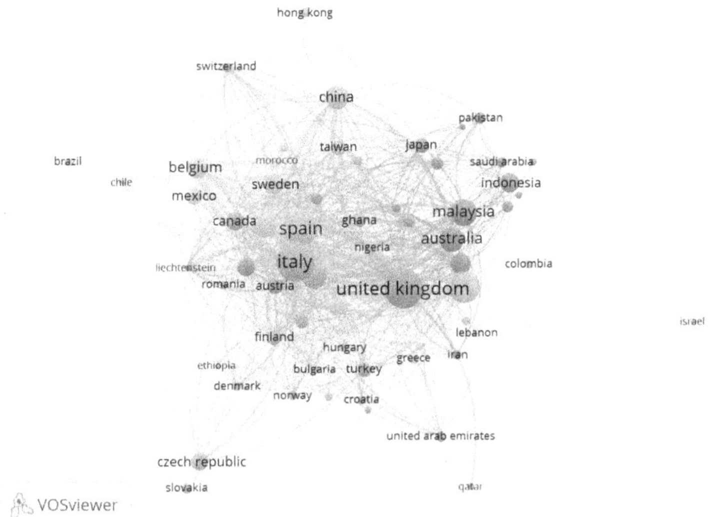

4.3 Bibliographic Coupling

Bibliographic coupling, a methodological approach in scholarly analysis, unveils a significant facet of academic research wherein two or more articles within a specific field reference the same source. This analysis serves as a valuable tool in identifying prevalent and impactful research activities, providing insights into the key themes and contributions within the academic domain under study. In the context of Family SMEs research, Table 4 and Figure 5 offer a comprehensive overview of the top five papers most frequently cited, determined by the total number of citations resulting from bibliographic coupling analysis. These papers represent seminal works that have consistently influenced and shaped scholarly discussions in the field.

At the forefront is the paper authored by Naldi et al. (2015), titled "Entrepreneurial orientation, risk taking, and performance in family firms." Published in the esteemed Journal Family Business Review, this paper has garnered an impressive 821 citations, underlining its profound impact on the understanding of entrepreneurial dynamics and performance outcomes within family-owned enterprises. Similarly, the works of Fernández and Nieto (2005) on the internationalization strategies of small and medium-sized family businesses have emerged as significant contributions, with two separate papers ranking second and third in terms of citations. These studies delve into the influential factors driving internationalization decisions, offering valuable insights into the complexities and challenges faced by family SMEs venturing into global markets. Further down the list, the study by Ayyagari et al. (2011) on firm innovation in emerging markets, published in the Journal of Financial and Quantitative Analysis, stands out with 441 citations. This paper sheds light on the critical role of finance, governance, and competition in fostering innovation within family-owned enterprises operating in emerging economies. Additionally, the work of Romano et al. (2001) on capital structure decision-making for family businesses, featured in the Journal of Business Venturing, has garnered 405 citations. This paper presents a comprehensive model for understanding the complexities involved in determining the optimal capital structure for family SMEs, providing valuable guidance for practitioners and scholars alike. In sum, these top-cited papers exemplify the depth and breadth of research efforts in the field of Family SMEs, covering a range of topics from entrepreneurial orientation and internationalization strategies to firm innovation and capital structure decision-making. The high number of citations and total link strength associated with these papers underscore their enduring significance and influence within the academic discourse, reaffirming their status as seminal contributions in advancing knowledge and understanding in the realm of Family SMEs research.

Table 4. Bibliographic Coupling

No.	Authors	Title	Source and SJR Quartile	Number of Citations	Total Link Strength
1.	Naldi et al. (2015)	Entrepreneurial orientation, risk taking, and performance in family firms	Family Business Review (Q1).	821	221
2.	Fernández and Nieto (2005)	Internationalization strategy of small and medium-sized family businesses: Some influential factors	Family Business Review (Q1).	456	333
3.	Ayyagari et al. (2011)	Firm innovation in emerging markets: The role of finance, governance, and competition	Journal of Financial and Quantitative Analysis (Q1)	441	39
4.	Romano et al. (2001)	Capital structure decision making: A model for family business	Journal of Business Venturing (Q1)	405	96

Source: Data processed, Vosviewer (2024)

Figure 5. Network Visualization of Bibliographic Coupling

4.4 Co-Word Analysis

Co-word analysis involves amalgamating keywords that commonly co-occur in a given field, sourced from an extensive collection of articles. This analysis elucidates prevalent research themes and reveals relationships within related sub-fields, shedding light on the underlying structure of scholarly discourse and thematic trends. This methodological approach enables a deeper understanding of the underlying structure and thematic focus of research endeavors within the field of interest (Narong & Hallinger, 2023). The analysis identified 511 keywords distributed across 9 clusters, representing the most frequently occurring terms among a total of 4,432 keywords in the literature. The top 5 keywords from the co-word analysis are presented in Table 5 and Figure 6. Notably, "SMEs" emerged as the most recurrent keyword, appearing 209 times in past studies, followed by "Family Business" with 198 occurrences, "Family Firms" with 164 occurrences, "Small and medium sized enterprise" with 129 occurrences, and "innovation" with 84 occurrences.

continued on following page

Table 5. Continued
Table 5. Co-Occurrences of Keyword

No	Keyword	Occurrences	Total Link Strength
1	SMEs	209	698
2	Family Business	198	633
3	Family Firms	164	591
4	Small and medium sized enterprise	129	864
5	Innovation	84	400

Source: Data processed, Vosviewer (2024)

Figure 6. Network Visualization of Co-Occurrences of Keyword

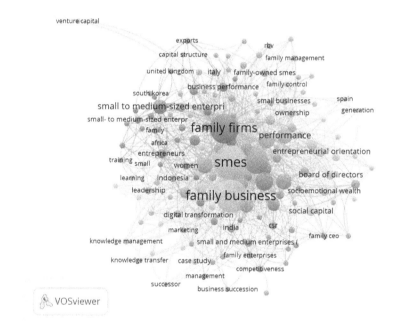

5. FUTURE RESEARCH DIRECTIONS

Moving forward, the bibliometric analysis conducted in this study offers valuable insights that can guide future research directions in the field of internationalization of family-owned SMEs. To advance the scholarly discourse, researchers are encouraged to explore emerging markets in greater depth, investigating how family enterprises navigate cultural, regulatory, and market complexities. Moreover, there is a pressing need to examine the role of digital transformation in facilitating internationalization efforts, alongside exploring sustainability practices, succession planning strategies, and cross-cultural management dynamics. Additionally, studies focusing on resilience, crisis management, and the formation of collaborative networks and partnerships can provide practical insights for family-owned SMEs operating in global markets. Longitudinal research tracking the performance and growth trajectories of these enterprises over time can also contribute to a deeper understanding of their internationalization journey. By addressing these future research directions, scholars can not only enhance theoretical knowledge but also offer actionable recommendations for practitioners and policymakers aiming to support the sustainable growth and competitiveness of family-owned SMEs on the global stage.

6. CONCLUSION

The comprehensive bibliometric analysis of internationalisation of family SMEs dynamics from 1990 to January 2024 reveals notable trends and significant contributions. Spanning from 1990 to 2024, dynamic fluctuations in scholarly output indicate a burgeoning interest in this field, with a pronounced spike in publications from 2019 to 2023 suggesting heightened attention to the challenges and opportunities faced by family-owned enterprises in global markets. Prolific authors, diverse organizations, and active countries have all played pivotal roles in advancing knowledge in this domain. The most cited papers underscore critical themes such as entrepreneurial orientation and internationalization strategies, offering valuable insights for practitioners and policymakers.

This study carries significant implications for various stakeholders. Firstly, it enriches the existing knowledge base by offering a comprehensive overview of the current landscape of internationalisation of family SMEs research. Through meticulous bibliometric analysis, the research elucidates key contributors, prolific authors, and thematic clusters, shedding light on the interconnectedness of various sub-disciplines within this field. This holistic understanding aids in recognizing influential journals and discerning prevailing trends, thereby fostering a deeper insight into the evolving nature of research in this domain. Secondly, the study aims to identify key research directions and provide valuable insights for policymakers, researchers, and practitioners involved in shaping the future of sustainable internationalisation of family SMEs. By examining citation patterns and collaboration networks, the research facilitates the identification of research prospects and gaps in the existing literature. This comprehensive approach underscores the study's focus on not only comprehending current developments and trends but also charting a course for future research avenues. Thirdly, the integration of bibliometric analysis enhances the depth and scholarly rigor of the discourse, contributing to a more nuanced understanding of internationalisation of family SMEs dynamics. This is particularly crucial in a rapidly evolving global landscape where agricultural sustainability and productivity are paramount. The insights gleaned from the study can inform evidence-based decision-making, policy formulation, and strategic planning in the agricultural sector, thereby potentially shaping the trajectory of sustainable development in this domain.

Based on the findings, managers can take several specific actionable steps to enhance their international ventures. Firstly, fostering an entrepreneurial orientation is crucial; this involves promoting a culture that values innovation, proactiveness, and risk-taking by investing in continuous training programs, establishing dedicated innovation teams, and implementing structured risk management practices. Developing robust internationalization strategies tailored to the unique strengths and challenges of family SMEs is essential; this includes conducting thorough market research, evaluating appropriate market entry modes, and adapting products and marketing strategies to meet the cultural and regulatory requirements of target markets. Leveraging collaboration networks with other organizations, research institutions, and industry bodies can significantly aid internationalization efforts; managers should forge strategic partnerships, join industry associations, and collaborate with academic institutions to stay updated on the latest research and technological advancements. Engaging with policymakers and advocacy groups is also critical for influencing policies that support the internationalization of family SMEs; this can be achieved by participating in policy dialogues, engaging in public-private partnerships, and ensuring compliance with regulatory changes in target markets. Utilizing insights from bibliometric analysis to inform strategic planning and evidence-based decision-making is highly beneficial; managers should monitor publication trends, benchmark against best practices, and establish a knowledge management system to capture and disseminate research insights within the organization. Additionally, incorporating sustainability principles into internationalization strategies, particularly for family SMEs in the agricultural sector, can enhance productivity and environmental stewardship; this involves adopting sustainable practices, obtaining relevant certifications, and engaging stakeholders to communicate the firm's commitment to sustainability. Finally, investing in capacity building for family members and employees to handle the complexities of internationalization is vital; implementing leadership development programs, providing training in cultural competence, and encouraging the adoption of advanced technologies can prepare the next generation of family leaders for global challenges, ensure effective communication in diverse markets, and enhance global reach and operational efficiency. By implementing these actionable recommendations, managers of family SMEs can better navigate the

Internationalisation of Family SMEs

complexities of internationalization, leverage emerging opportunities, and contribute to the sustainable growth and development of their enterprises in the global market.

REFERENCES

Agustina, M., Majid, M. S. A., & Hafasnuddin, H. (2021). Islamic bank amid the 2008 Global financial crisis: A bibliometric analysis. *Library Philosophy and Practice*, 1–26. https://digitalcommons.unl.edu/libphilprac

Alayo, M., Iturralde, T., & Maseda, A. (2022). Innovation and internationalization in family SMEs: Analyzing the role of family involvement. *European Journal of Innovation Management*, 25(2), 454–478. 10.1108/EJIM-07-2020-0302

Amaechi, E. (2021). Understanding culture and success in global business: developing cultural and innovative intrapreneurs in small businesses. In Thakkar, B. S. (Ed.), *Culture in Global Businesses: Addressing National and Organizational Challenges* (pp. 205–224). Springer International Publishing. 10.1007/978-3-030-60296-3_9

Ayyagari, M., Demirgüç-Kunt, A., & Maksimovic, V. (2011). Firm innovation in emerging markets: The role of finance, governance, and competition. *Journal of Financial and Quantitative Analysis*, 46(6), 1545–1580. 10.1017/S0022109011000378

Baas, J., Schotten, M., Plume, A., Côté, G., & Karimi, R. (2020). Scopus as a curated, high-quality bibliometric data source for academic research in quantitative science studies. *Quantitative Science Studies*, 1(1), 377–386. 10.1162/qss_a_00019

Basly, S., & Saunier, P. L. (2020). Familiness, socio-emotional goals and the internationalization of French family SMEs. *Journal of International Entrepreneurship*, 18(3), 270–311. 10.1007/s10843-019-00265-0

Braga, V., Correia, A., Braga, A., & Lemos, S. (2017). The innovation and internationalisation processes of family businesses. *Review of International Business and Strategy*, 27(2), 231–247. 10.1108/RIBS-01-2017-0005

Chrisman, J. J., Chua, J. H., De Massis, A., Frattini, F., & Wright, M. (2015). The ability and willingness paradox in family firm innovation. *Journal of Product Innovation Management*, 32(3), 310–318. 10.1111/jpim.12207

Chung, C. N., & Zhu, H. (2021). Corporate governance dynamics of political tie formation in emerging economies: Business group affiliation, family ownership, and institutional transition. *Corporate Governance*, 29(4), 381–401. 10.1111/corg.12367

Conz, E., Denicolai, S., & De Massis, A. (2023). Preserving the longevity of long-lasting family businesses: A multilevel model. *The Journal of Management and Governance*, 1–38. 10.1007/s10997-023-09670-z

Cristiano, E. (2020). The growth of family businesses: The path to internationalization. *Management Controlling and Governance of Family Businesses: Theoretical Insights and Empirical Evidence from Italy*, 75-95.

De Massis, A., & Foss, N. J. (2018). Advancing family business research: The promise of microfoundations. In *Family Business Review* (Vol. 31, Issue 4, pp. 386–396). SAGE Publications Inc. 10.1177/0894486518803422

Del Bosco, B., & Bettinelli, C. (2020). How do family SMEs control their investments abroad? The role of distance and family control. *MIR. Management International Review*, 60(1), 1–35. 10.1007/s11575-019-00406-6

Eddleston, K. A., Kellermanns, F. W., & Collier, G. (2019). Research on family firm innovation: What do family firms actually think and do? *Journal of Family Business Strategy*, 10(4), 1–7. 10.1016/j.jfbs.2019.100308

Fernández, Z., & Nieto, M. J. (2005). Internationalization strategy of small and medium-sized family businesses: Some influential factors. *Family Business Review*, 18(1), 77–89. 10.1111/j.1741-6248.2005.00031.x

Fernández-Olmos, M., & Malorgio, G. (2020). The speed of the internationalisation process and the institutional networks of family SMEs in the DOC Rioja Wine Industry. *Wine Economics and Policy*, 9(1), 43–50. www.fupress.com/wep. 10.36253/web-8371

Ferrari, F. (2023). The postponed succession: An investigation of the obstacles hindering business transmission planning in family firms. *Journal of Family Business Management*, 13(2), 412–431. 10.1108/JFBM-09-2020-0088

González-Cruz, T., Clemente-Almendros, J. A., & Puig-Denia, A. (2021). Family governance systems: The complementary role of constitutions and councils. *Ekonomska Istrazivanja*, 34(1), 3139–3165. 10.1080/1331677X.2020.1867603

Heydari, E., Rezaei, M., Pironti, M., & Chmet, F. (2023). How does owners' personality impacts business internationalisation in family SMEs? In Jafari-Sadeghi, V., & Amoozad Mahdiraji, H. (Eds.), *Decision-Making in International Entrepreneurship: Unveiling Cognitive Implications Towards Entrepreneurial Internationalisation* (pp. 331–347). Emerald Publishing Limited. 10.1108/978-1-80382-233-420231016

Iborra, M., Safón, V., & Dolz, C. (2020). The role of family ownership in survival and bouncing back: Good and bad news? In *Competitiveness, Organizational Management, and Governance in Family Firms* (pp. 261-282). IGI Global.

Ince, F. (2022). Leadership and sustainability: From the first to the second generation of SMEs ownership. In *Research Anthology on Strategies for Maintaining Successful Family Firms* (pp. 639–660). IGI Global. 10.4018/978-1-6684-3550-2.ch029

Kampouri, K., & Hajidimitriou, Y. (2023). International partnership failures in the context of family small and medium enterprises internationalisation. *European Journal of Family Business*, 13(1), 56–70. 10.24310/ejfbejfb.vi.15154

Kontinen, T., & Ojala, A. (2012). Social capital in the international operations of family SMEs. *Journal of Small Business and Enterprise Development*, 19(1), 39–55. 10.1108/14626001211196398

Lahiri, S., Mukherjee, D., & Peng, M. W. (2020). Behind the internationalization of family SMEs: A strategy tripod synthesis. *Global Strategy Journal*, 10(4), 813–838. 10.1002/gsj.1376

Liew, M. X., & Loo, Y. M. (2024). Harnessing the power of generations through participative strategy: A study on Malaysia Small Family Firms. *Journal of Small Business and Entrepreneurship*, 1–23. 10.1080/08276331.2024.2311947

Metsola, J., Leppäaho, T., Paavilainen-Mäntymäki, E., & Plakoyiannaki, E. (2020). Process in family business internationalisation: The state of the art and ways forward. *International Business Review*, 29(2), 1–14. 10.1016/j.ibusrev.2020.101665

Miller, D., & Le Breton-Miller, I. (2021). Family firms: A breed of extremes? *Entrepreneurship Theory and Practice*, 45(4), 663–681. 10.1177/1042258720964186

Murkhana, M., Idris, S., Majid, M. S. A., Agustina, M., Sakir, A., & Hafasnuddin, H. (2023). How important is workload affect occupational frustration? A bibliometrics analysis. *2023 International Conference on Decision Aid Sciences and Applications (DASA)*, 530–535. 10.1109/DASA59624.2023.10286791

Naldi, L., Chirico, F., Kellermanns, F. W., & Campopiano, G. (2015). All in the Family? An Exploratory Study of Family Member Advisors and Firm Performance. *Family Business Review*, 28(3), 227–242. 10.1177/0894486515581951

Narong, D. K., & Hallinger, P. (2023). A keyword co-occurrence analysis of research on service learning: Conceptual foci and emerging research trends. In *Education Sciences* (Vol. 13, Issue 4). MDPI. 10.3390/educsci13040339

Olivares, J. V., Saiz, C., Torró, L., & Zabalza, J. (2020). The internationalisation of family SMEs in the Valencian region: The growing role played by Latin America, 1980-2018. *Journal of Evolutionary Studies in Business*, 5(2), 115–149. 10.1344/jesb2020.2.j078

Rexhepi, G., Ramadani, V., Rahdari, A., & Anggadwita, G. (2017). Models and strategies of family businesses internationalization: A conceptual framework and future research directions. *Review of International Business and Strategy*, 27(2), 248–260. 10.1108/RIBS-12-2016-0081

Rochayatun, S. S., & Bidin, R. (2022). Mode of Entry Strategy on SMEs Internationalization in East Java: A Review of Literature. *Asian Journal of Economics. Business and Accounting*, 22(15), 20–32. 10.9734/ajeba/2022/v22i1530626

Romano, C. A., Tanewski, G. A., & Smyrnios, K. X. (2001). Capital structure decision making: A model for family business. *Journal of Business Venturing*, 16(3), 285–310. 10.1016/S0883-9026(99)00053-1

Salmon, U., & Allman, K. (2020). Innovation in family firms: An empirical taxonomy of owners using a mixed methods approach. *Journal of Family Business Management*, 10(1), 20–39. 10.1108/JFBM-05-2019-0037

Shi, H. X., Graves, C., & Barbera, F. (2019). Intergenerational succession and internationalisation strategy of family SMEs: Evidence from China. *Long Range Planning*, 52(4), 1–18. 10.1016/j.lrp.2018.05.004

Torkkeli, L., Uzhegova, M., Kuivalainen, O., Saarenketo, S., & Puumalainen, K. (2021). Internationalisation of family enterprises: The role of entrepreneurial orientation and international growth orientation. *International Journal of Business and Globalisation*, 29(3), 354–375. 10.1504/IJBG.2021.118681

Urban, W., Krot, K., & Tomaszuk, A. (2023). A cross-national study of internationalisation barriers with reference to SME value chain. Equilibrium. *Quarterly Journal of Economics and Economic Policy*, 18(2), 523–549. 10.24136/eq.2023.016

Zapata-Cantu, L., Sanguino, R., Barroso, A., & Nicola-Gavrilă, L. (2023). Family business adapting a new digital-based economy: Opportunities and challenges for future research. *Journal of the Knowledge Economy*, 14(1), 408–425. 10.1007/s13132-021-00871-1

Chapter 14
Internationalization Strategies:
A Complementary Perspective Using the Resource Dependency Theory

António Carrizo Moreira
 http://orcid.org/0000-0002-6613-8796
University of Aveiro, Portugal

Adriana Simões
University of Aveiro, Portugal

Ana Sofia Sousa
University of Aveiro, Portugal

João Gonçalo Martins
University of Aveiro, Portugal

ABSTRACT

This chapter explores the internationalization path of ALPHA, a family-owned, medium-sized Portuguese company. The analysis reveals a two-stage process. Initially, ALPHA's gradual market entry aligns with the Uppsala model, prioritizing geographically close markets and leveraging accumulated experience. However, later stages demonstrate network-based theory influences. While lacking formal networks, ALPHA prioritizes strong B2B relationships with large international clients, mirroring network bridges for market access. The case highlights the importance of trust-based B2B relationships for success. ALPHA leverages these partnerships to gain market knowledge and access new opportunities. Exporting plays a vital role,

DOI: 10.4018/979-8-3693-3518-5.ch014

Internationalization Strategies

keeping ALPHA updated on technological trends and fostering innovation through diverse client projects. The company prioritizes a pragmatic approach focused on strong client relationships and win-win partnerships, emphasizing trust as a key resource. While the RBV perspective highlights investment in internal resources, reliance on intermediaries introduces limitations.

INTRODUCTION

Small and medium-sized enterprises (SMEs) have extensively employed internationalization strategies to expand their operations overseas. This approach enables them to participate more actively in international markets (Ribau et al., 2015, 2018).

Several theoretical frameworks and models elucidate the internationalization process and the modes of entry typically adopted by firms. Amongst the most prominent are the Uppsala model and the network-based view of the firm (Bell, McNaughton, & Young, 2001; Ribau et al., 2015). The Uppsala model posits a gradual and sequential progression of international involvement (Ribau et al., 2015), while the network-based view emphasizes the role of relationships between market actors in firm internationalization (Hakansson & Snehota, 2006).

Despite the evolving nature of globalization and its impact on the economy, many firms, particularly those operating in a business-to-business (B2B) environment, continue to adhere to traditional internationalization approaches. Moreover, although the literature review on SMEs internationalization is abundant (Maciejewski & Wach, 2019; Luostarinen & Gabrielsson, 2006; Ribau et al., 2018), there are opportunities, especially in relation to resource-constrained SMEs. This chapter aims to examine the historical context of the internationalization process and critically discuss the nuances of the two main internationalization theories, namely the Uppsala model and the network-based view of the firm. The purpose is to compare and contrast these theories in light of the specific characteristics of a Portuguese technology-based firm, codenamed ALPHA for confidentiality reasons, which achieves nearly 50% of its sales volume through international channels. The analysis focuses specifically on the firm's dependence on the B2B channel, which contributes to its seemingly passive internationalization approach. As such, based on a case study of a technology-based SME, this chapter aims to address the following research question: Can a resource-constrained SME with strong technology mastery and international experience brake away of dependent relationships with downstream intermediaries? While case studies are subject to criticism due to limitations in generalizability, they undeniably contribute to knowledge acquisition and development (Ghauri, 2004; Vissak & Francioni, 2013). This case study, therefore, seeks to explore, understand,

and analyze ALPHA's strategic formulation and internationalization process, offering a framework for classroom discussions.

The chapter is structured into six sections. Following this introductory section, the second section presents a concise literature review to establish the key concepts and theories necessary for a comprehensive interpretation of the case study analysis. Subsequently, the third section details the research methodology, specifically the qualitative component employing an interview conducted with the company's Finance Director. The fourth section presents the key findings gleaned from the interview. The fifth section provides a discussion that integrates these findings with the established literature. Finally, the concluding section summarizes the study's key takeaways and acknowledges its limitations.

THEORETICAL BACKGROUND

Internationalization

In the contemporary globalized marketplace, fostering collaboration and seeking optimal solutions is crucial for businesses to differentiate their products or services and, consequently, gain a competitive edge (Brown & Bell, 2001). Globalization inherently entails increasing complexity and diversity, impacting strategic decision-making when entering international markets (Bayfield et al., 2009; Ribau et al., 2015). Networks, encompassing both formal and informal relationships, have emerged as key facilitators of the internationalization process (Coviello & Martin, 1999; Ribau et al., 2019).

The rapid evolution towards globalized businesses, industries, and markets has been extensively documented. Scholars have continuously refined and contextualized concepts of internationalization to reflect this changing landscape. As a result, the field of business internationalization now encompasses a diverse array of theoretical perspectives and analytical frameworks (Ietto-Gillies, 2012; Ribau et al., 2015). While various definitions exist, internationalization can be broadly understood as any business activity conducted across national borders (Olejnik & Swoboda, 2012). However, it is increasingly recognized as a significant form of innovative activity. Its scope encompasses a range of phenomena, including spot and continuous export activities, cross-border collaboration, alliances, greenfield investments, and the establishment of subsidiaries, branches, and joint ventures (Chetty & Campbell-Hunt, 2003).

Jones (2001) posits that international activity can begin with even minimal connections between countries, as long as these connections generate efficiency and synergies. Over time, as the business becomes more internationalized, management develops higher expectations and implements new, more comprehensive, and rational policies and procedures for governing international operations (Cavusgil, 1984). Export potential, export intensity, interest in international opportunities, and the need for external support are among the key variables utilized to assess a firm's level of internationalization (Jones, 2001).

Small and medium-sized enterprises (SMEs) often face significant disadvantages when entering international markets due to limited resources and technical capabilities (Reuber & Fischer, 1997). These disadvantages tend to be more pronounced for capital-intensive industries, where large corporations hold a distinct advantage (Erramilli & D'Souza, 1993; Ribau et al., 2018). Nevertheless, despite the challenges, internationalization is increasingly crucial for SMEs, as they require strategies to navigate the intensifying competition within global markets. For SMEs in smaller countries with limited domestic markets, internationalization can even be considered essential for survival (Brown & Bell, 2001). Notably, Reuber and Fischer (1997) argue that the determining factor for success in international ventures is often the international experience of the involved teams, rather than the company's size or age.

Modes of Entry

The intensifying competitiveness of the global marketplace has spurred a growing number of companies to seek opportunities in international markets to achieve their objectives and safeguard their market positions (Larimo, 2015). SME internationalization decisions encompass two key aspects: selecting target markets and determining the structure of their operations within those markets (Carazo & Lumiste, 2010; Lee & Lieberman, 2010).

Swoboda et al. (2015) highlight the significant influence of both external environments and internationalization knowledge on the relationship between preferred entry modes and subsequent internationalization choices. Internationalization encompasses diverse entry modes, including the establishment of international subsidiaries and joint ventures, licensing agreements, and exporting activities (Johanson & Vahlne, 1990).

SMEs often exhibit a preference for markets with cultural or economic similarities to their home country, as this strategy minimizes risk exposure (Erramilli & D'Souza, 1993). Additionally, SMEs tend to favor entry modes requiring minimal investment and risk initially, potentially transitioning to modes involving greater commitment as they exploit the full market potential (Johanson & Vahlne, 1977; Vahlne & Johanson, 2013). Coviello and Martin (1999) emphasize the pivotal role of network relationships in the selection of initial markets and corresponding entry modes.

Exporting remains the most prevalent mode of foreign operation for SMEs (Larimo, 2015). Compared to other options, exporting generally necessitates fewer financial, human, and other resources, entails lower financial risk, and offers greater structural and strategic flexibility within the foreign market (Young et al., 1989). However, although exporting requires resources, it is precisely undertaken to acquire them, requiring firms to identify, commit to, direct, coordinate, and evaluate external resources in support of exporting activities (Christensen, 2006). By exporting goods and/or services, firms not only expand their markets but also gain valuable knowledge and techniques, leading to enhanced productivity (Harris & Li, 2007).

The "learning-through-exporting" hypothesis posits that entering foreign markets fosters increased productivity, improved product/service quality, and enhanced process efficiency due to the knowledge gained through buyer-seller relationships. This hypothesis further suggests that increased competition from foreign producers and exposure to foreign consumers stimulates firm innovation performance (Damijan et al., 2010; De Loecker, 2013; Greenaway & Kneller, 2007).

Exporting, as a foreign market entry mode, manifests itself in three primary forms: direct export, indirect export, and own export (De Loecker, 2013). Direct exporting involves selling to an importer in the foreign country, typically mediated by agents or distributors abroad (Simões et al., 2013). Importers independently purchase and market the products at their own risk. Agents or distributors, while acting on behalf of the exporting company by contacting customers, collecting orders, and managing collections, do not assume ownership of the products and may or may not operate on an exclusive basis (Simões et al., 2013).

Direct exporting can potentially enhance a firm's likelihood of introducing product and/or service innovations in transitional economies due to the knowledge obtained (Liu & Buck, 2007) from customers and suppliers. This knowledge pertains to technical and product development, as well as the broader global market, ultimately contributing to the firm's own innovation performance (Salomon & Shaver, 2005).

Indirect exports involve the utilization of intermediaries (import-export agents, trading companies, subcontractors, central purchasing offices of large distribution chains, etc.) located in the company's home country (Simões et al., 2013). As the company relinquishes control over export operations in this scenario, the primary motivation for employing intermediaries often stems from cost reduction (Di Cintio et al., 2020).

While intermediaries offer smaller firms access to foreign trade without incurring substantial exporting costs, indirect exporters experience lower variable profits due to the intermediary's share of the gains (Bai et al., 2017). Furthermore, engaging with intermediaries can hinder an exporter's ability to acquire knowledge and, consequently, limit its innovation potential (Di Cintio et al., 2020). This stems from reduced direct contact with foreign buyers, which can lead to diminished knowledge transfer compared to direct exporting (Bai et al., 2017). Additionally, there is a potential risk that intermediaries may strategically withhold relevant information or even provide inaccurate data for their own (Salomon, 2006).

Own exports consist of selling directly to the final customers in the destination country (Simões et al., 2013). In this sense, companies are solely responsible for the marketing and then distribution of their products and/or services, with no intervention of any intermediary.

Resource-Based Theory

The Resource-Based View (RBV) of the firm, rooted in strategic management literature, posits that firms achieve competitive advantage through "unique" business resources that offer value, rarity, inimitability, and non-substitutability (Barney, 1991; Schulze, 1992). This framework emphasizes a firm's distinctive competencies through established strategic concepts and further explores intriguing propositions regarding diversification strategies (Andersen & Kheamb, 1998). Therefore, the RBV supports the notion that a firm's specific resources serve as a driving force for its diversification strategy, viewed as a response to indivisibilities and market failures (Mahoney & Pandian, 1992; Teece, 1982).

Unlike physical and financial resources, defining the concept of intangible resources presents challenges and fosters disagreement among scholars (Anderson & Kheamb, 1998). While Grant (1991) identifies human resources, technological resources, organizational assets, and reputation as key intangibles, Berg and Friedman (1981) and Duncan (1982) focus on experiences, reputation, and goodwill.

Amit and Schoemaker (1993) differentiate between resources and capabilities. Resources encompass all internal factors that contribute to a firm's final product, including tangible and intangible assets, financial resources, and human resources. Conversely, capabilities refer to how a firm, through its human capital, manages and utilizes various forms of information for its benefit, encompassing implemented processes and the interconnectedness among available resources. Thus, defining a business based on its capabilities, or what it can do, might offer a more sustainable foundation for strategy than defining it solely based on the needs it aims to fulfill (Grant, 2001).

An analysis of small and medium-sized enterprises (SMEs) reveals the presence of strategic resources and capabilities that can create competitive advantages. Customer trust and perceptions of quality are common characteristics of many SMEs. Additionally, such firms often possess unique ways of doing business, including specialized technology or business know-how that sets them apart from competitors. These rare, valuable, invisible, and imperfectly imitable resources and capabilities empower SMEs to develop, choose, and implement strategies that their counterparts lacking such assets cannot replicate (Cabrera-Suárez, 2001).

The core objective of resource-based strategic formulation lies in comprehending the relationship between resources, capabilities, competitive advantage, and ultimately, profitability. Specifically, it involves understanding the mechanisms that enable firms to sustain their competitive advantage over time. This necessitates creating strategies that fully exploit the unique characteristics of each individual firm (Grant, 2001).

Resource Dependency Theory

Pfeffer and Salancik (2003) proposed the Resource Dependence Theory (RDT) to explain the managerial role in mitigating external dependencies and acquiring control over crucial resources (Hillman et al., 2009). This theory acknowledges the influence of external factors on a firm's behavior, prompting the formulation of strategies to reduce resource dependence and enhance power (Hafiz et al., 2022). Nicholson and Kiel (2007) highlight the absence of a universally accepted definition of "important resources" within RDT, as it draws from diverse fields like sociology and management (Jackling & Johl, 2009).

RDT emphasizes the inherent dependence of organizations on external resources, such as raw materials, labor, or partners, for their operation (Hafiz et al., 2022; Schnack et al., 2022). This dependence intensifies for "critical resources," indispensable for organizational functioning (Pfeffer & Salancik, 2003). Such dependence creates uncertainty, prompting organizations to manage their resource environment to mitigate it (Nienhüser, 2008).

Collaborative environments, where organizations mutually support each other through resource sharing and information exchange for mutual benefit, naturally lead to reduced uncertainty (Pfeffer & Salancik, 2003). Recognizing the high level of uncertainty inherent in dynamic and complex environments (Yeager et al., 2014), Davis and Cobb (2010), building upon RDT, argue that organizations are not passive actors at the mercy of their environments. Additionally, Christensen and Bower (1996) suggest that external observation can help identify patterns in new ventures where firms leverage their resources. To address associated risks, organizations adopt various strategies, including adapting to or avoiding environmental influences, pursuing cooperation, engaging in growth, or exerting political influence (Niehuser, 2008).

Acs et al. (1994) argue that SMEs are particularly susceptible to environmental dependence. Hessels and Terjesen (2010) note that SMEs, with limited fixed resources compared to multinationals, are expected to be highly dependent on resources available in their home country. This dependence can render them vulnerable to the national economic context, particularly concerning access to financial, technological,

Internationalization Strategies

and production resources (raw materials) necessary for export (Hessels & Terjesen, 2010). Conversely, abundant domestic resources can benefit SMEs.

While the RBV emphasizes the significance of partners' resources and assets, RDT highlights that the partners' level of control and power over the SME determines the nature and formation of the partnership (Street & Cameron, 2007).

Uppsala Model

The Uppsala model is based on inductive studies of Swedish multinationals that begin their internationalization by focusing on markets close to their domestic market, especially in terms of psychic distance, opting for gradual entry into more distant markets (Johanson & Vahlne, 1977; Vahlne & Johanson, 2013). The Uppsala model is particularly important especially in activities involving the commercialization of complex and knowledge-intensive products (Vahlne & Johanson, 2013).

The Uppsala Internationalization Model rests upon four fundamental concepts: market knowledge, market commitment, commitment decisions, and current activities (Johanson & Vahlne, 1990; Forsgren, 2002). The model posits that a firm's level of market knowledge and market commitment at a given time influences its commitment decisions and subsequent activities, which in turn shape its future market knowledge and commitment. Based on these core concepts, the Uppsala model predicts two key patterns in firm internationalization:

- **Incremental Internationalization:** Firms tend to initiate and maintain investments in a single or a few neighboring countries, rather than venturing into multiple markets simultaneously (Johanson & Vahlne, 1990).
- **Sequential Learning-Based Expansion:** Investments in a specific market unfold cautiously, with a sequential progression and concurrent learning by the firm's personnel operating within that market (Johanson & Vahlne, 1990). This necessitates entering new markets with progressively increasing psychic distance, with market investments following the so-called "establishment chain" (Johanson & Vahlne, 1990).

Family businesses often exemplify the Uppsala model. They typically commence their internationalization journey with export activities in geographically and culturally close nations. As they accumulate knowledge and resources, they incrementally expand into more distant markets (Kontinen & Ojala, 2010; Pukall & Calabro, 2014).

In 2009, Vahlne and Johanson (2009) further developed their core argument by incorporating research on entrepreneurial networks. They propose a two-stage model:

- **Networks as Market Structures:** The model asserts that markets function as networks of relationships, wherein firms are interconnected in intricate and largely invisible ways. Consequently, "insidership" in relevant networks becomes crucial for successful internationalization, while "outsidership" presents a challenge (Vahlne & Johanson, 2009).
- **Networks for Learning and Trust Building:** The second stage emphasizes that relationships offer opportunities for learning and establishing trust and commitment, both of which are essential prerequisites for internationalization success (Vahlne & Johanson, 2009).

Network-Based Theory

Emerging as an extension of the Uppsala Internationalization Model, network internationalization theory analyzes the industrial markets of SMEs as networks of firms. This theory builds upon the foundation of the RDT, which posits that actors (firms) rely on resources controlled by other entities (Ribau et al., 2015).

Networks are increasingly recognized as crucial elements in a firm's internationalization journey. In contrast to the firm-specific advantage approach, network internationalization theory emphasizes that a firm's ability and extent of successful internationalization hinge on its network of relationships (Coviello & McAuley, 1999). According to Johanson and Mattsson's (1988) model, internationalization is initiated through the development of relationships with other firms within a foreign country's network. These cross-border firm relationships act as bridges to new markets (Johanson & Vahlne, 1990). The core objective of network theory lies in leveraging acquired information to gain insight into the target market and the firm's resource mobility capabilities (Rexhepi et al., 2017).

While the network-based theory does not explicitly address the impact of geographical or psychic distance on market entry or the influence of network relationships on entry mode selection (Johanson & Mattsson, 1988; Johanson & Vahlne, 2003), numerous studies on the internationalization of knowledge-intensive SMEs (Coviello & Martin, 1999; Ojala, 2009; Sharma & Blomstermo, 2003; Zain & Ng, 2006) highlight the significant influence of networks on both market selection and entry mode choices. However, even without direct communication channels, firms may be influenced by the internationalization decisions of others, exhibiting a "bandwagon Effect" in strategic outcomes (Bonaccorsi, 1992; Hadley & Wilson, 2003). This tendency arises from decision-makers using "reference points" to guide their choices, especially in high-risk scenarios.

Relationships with customers and suppliers are pivotal and develop over time through interactions. These interactions foster mutual understanding of one another's needs, capabilities, and strategies, ultimately leading to trust. However, a potential downside is adapting to each other's practices, which could hinder the resources needed to nurture the relationship. The interconnectedness of businesses extends beyond immediate dyadic relationships, encompassing customer's customers, supplier's suppliers, consultants, competitors, additional suppliers, intermediaries, and public or semi-public agencies. This interconnectedness underscores the crucial role of networks in shaping the relative stability of markets (Forsgren, 2002).

METHODOLOGY

This chapter is based on a case study of an SME firm—ALPHA—whose core business is on the metallurgic industry with headquarters in Vale de Cambra, Portugal. The chapter involves a qualitative analysis based on both an interview carried out with ALPHA's CEO and previous knowledge of the firm, gained from public presentations and recognition. The choice of ALPHA was based on its commitment and success both at national and international level. Moreover, taking into account the company's 69 years of existence, it was thought to be interesting to understand the company's entire relational strategy that allows it to be an international success story.

Qualitative research is particularly useful when aiming to understand complex phenomena, like firm internationalization, which involves a multifaceted interplay of factors (Durão & Moreira, 2019; Vissak & Francioni, 2013; Silva & Moreira, 2019). Moreocer, the case study method is recognized by enabling the analysis of particular situations. Although quantitative studies tend to support "what" happened (e.g., sales figures increase after entering a new market), qualitative studies, through interviews and observations, help uncover the "why" behind the numbers (Durão & Moreira, 2019; Yin, 2008). They can reveal the decision-making processes, cultural considerations, and unforeseen challenges encountered during internationalization.

Qualitative studies provide rich, detailed data. Case studies can offer a deep dive into a specific firm's experience, supporting previously unknown factors that might influence internationalization success. Moreover, qualitative research allows to explore the context surrounding a firm's internationalization efforts. Through case studies, it is possible to examine the interplay between a firm's internal particularities, external pressures, and the specific market dynamics that influence its strategies (Eisenhardt, 1989; Ribau et al., 2019; Yin, 2008).

Other important factor that supported the decision to use a qualitative study is that case studies allow for a comprehensive examination of an unique firm's internationalization process, in which it is possible to explore and understand the firm's strategic choices, operational challenges, and adaptations, providing a holistic understanding of the situation, showcasing real-world experiences. Although not statistically generalizable to a whole population, insights from a well-chosen case study can be applied to similar contexts, offering valuable lessons for firms in analogous situations (Eisenhardt, 1989; Yin, 2008).

As such, it was selected to analyze ALPHA, in order to address the main theories that could explain specific situations under analysis. ALPHA was selected based on three important requirements for this research (Patton, 2015): (a) it is involved in international business activities; (b) it has a core activity applied serving different market segments; and (c) half of its sales activities serve international markets. Typical of a qualitative methodology, a semi-structured interview was arranged with ALPHA's chief financial officer (CFO) to collect primary data. Secondary information was sought after to complement primary data from the interview. Some public sources—such as the firm's website, marketing information from industrial associations and previous public presentation—were consulted to ensure the validity and reliability of data (Ghauri, 2004). The interview was complemented by a visit to ALPHA's premises to get a deeper understanding of their operations. The interview was helpful in understanding the B2B market strategies and underpinned the understanding of the internationalization activities testing the different theoretical perspectives covered in the literature review section.

PRESENTATION OF ALPHA

The Metallurgic and Metalworking Sector

The Portuguese metallurgical and metalworking sector comprises 15,000 companies and 250,000 workers (OBSERVADOR, 2022). Thise companies specialize in various subsectors, including production technologies, technical parts, automotive and aeronautical components, metal tableware and cutlery, and metallic structures.

A recent news report by Agência de Notícias de Portugal, S.A. (ECO SAPO, 2022), titled is "Metallurgy and metalworking hits record exports in March", highlights the positive performance of the Portuguese metallurgy and metalworking industry. The report reveals that the sector achieves its year "best record in history" in March 2022 with exports reaching a staggering €1.983 billion euros. This figure surpasses the previous record set in March 2020 by 5% (ECO SAPO, 2022).

The Associação dos Industriais Metalúrgicos, Metalomecânicos e Afins de Portugal (AIMMAP) credits the export growth to a surge in demand from European Union countries. The first quarter of 2022 saw a 10.9% increase in exports to the EU, with Spain (7.3%), France (15.4%), and Germany (18.1%) leading the charge. AIMMAP also emphasizes the accelerating rise in exports to the US, with year-on-year growth jumping from 70% (February, accumulated over two months) to 100% (March, accumulated over three months).

AIMMAP's vice president acknowledges the "very difficult" economic climate companies face due to the pandemic and the war in Ukraine. However, he emphasizes the "remarkable" performance of Portuguese metal companies, highlighting their "positive performance and the assertive way they work." He further emphasizes that the sector has consistently been the biggest contributor to Portugal's Gross Domestic Product (GDP) between 2011 and 2021.

Rafael Campos Pereira underscores the sector's remarkable resilience. Despite the enormous constraints caused by the COVID-19 pandemic, including restrictions, workforce shortages, raw material price hikes, rising energy and fuel costs, and logistical challenges, companies were able to "reinvent themselves and adapt to the market." This adaptability, Pereira concludes, reinforces the position of the metallurgy and metalworking industry as "the most dynamic in the country."

History and Values

By 1958, they had secured their own facilities and expanded into new markets, specifically food processing for dairy products, wines, beers, soft drinks, and water. Over the years, ALPHA has prioritized continuous growth, investing in production capacity, facility expansion, and technological modernization.

A significant achievement came in 1992 when this family-owned SME earned quality certification according to NP EN ISO 9002 standards. This certification fueled their pursuit of national and international business consolidation.

Nowadays, ALPHA is a global leader, exporting to over 90 countries. They specialize in designing and manufacturing engineered solutions across various sectors, including dairy products and beverages, oenology (winemaking), chemicals and petrochemicals, automation, and baby food. Their offerings encompass stainless steel equipment, turnkey engineering projects, and control software for equipment automation.

Beyond its core business, ALPHA is committed to sustainability and social impact. As an eco-friendly company, they actively integrate environmental, social, and economic best practices. They continuously strive to minimize the environmental footprint of their operations.

ALPHA operates under a well-defined code of conduct grounded in a core set of ethical principles. These values include:
(1) Innovation—adding value in their core business areas;
(2) Rigor—high technical, productive, and commercial standards;
(3) Trust—exceeding the expectations of customers, partners, and suppliers;

(4) Passion—delivering complete dedication to projects;
(5) Social responsibility—sustainable economic, social and environmental development;
(6) Talent development—encountering and promoting knowledge and skill growth within the company;
(7) Market-orientation—prioritizing customer needs and market trends.

RESULTS

Established in 1953, ALPHA is a family-owned, third-generation managed, medium-sized company with around 150 employees and a €12 million annual turnover. Approximately 45-50% of the turnover originates from external markets.

The CFO prioritizes profitability over increased turnover, aiming to reduce debt while focusing on market penetration within the expanding Spanish pharmaceutical industry. This sector, characterized by high-quality standards, aligns with ALPHA's capabilities, making it a strategic target market. While expressing no aversion to neighboring markets, ALPHA's global export reach is attributed to accumulated experience.

Employees adhere to core principles of hard work, meticulousness, and maximized quality and efficiency instilled at the company's foundation. These principles are instrumental in building long-term trust essential in B2B markets.

ALPHA prioritizes close collaboration with clients who provide unique project specifications. Each project involves technical uniqueness, customization, and bespoke technical solutions. This approach caters to demanding clients like Danone and Tetra Pak, who, in turn, drive ALPHA's continuous development and excellence, facilitating network expansion and attracting new clients.

Despite acknowledging the importance of marketing for positioning and differentiation, ALPHA currently invests minimally in this area. The CFO emphasizes the absence of a deliberate strategy to increase market share.

The industry faced significant challenges due to the London Metal Exchange suspensions and subsequent metal price surges. These disruptions, coupled with the last years' logistical difficulties (transportation issues, overloaded ports, and rising raw material costs), have impacted ongoing projects. To mitigate potential setbacks and meet deadlines, ALPHA maintains a significant margin of maneuverability throughout its manufacturing process, from raw material procurement to final finishing.

Internationalization was not initially an objective but developed organically due to ALPHA's success. Initial forays into international markets, mirroring a common path for Portuguese companies, began with Spain. ALPHA utilizes a single-entry mode for international expansion. Export share fluctuations across different continents over the past five years are depicted in Table 1.

Table 1. Exports Percentage by Continent

	2017	2018	2019	2020	2021
Africa	34.2%	23.8%	10.4%	12.4%	4.3%
America	13.1%	14.0%	16.1%	11.9%	3.1%
Europe	52.1%	57.7%	66.9%	63.4%	89.1%
Asia	0.6%	4.5%	6.7%	12.3%	3.5%

A notable surge in exports to Europe is evident during the COVID-19 pandemic (2020-2021), despite border closures and disrupted international relations. Although exports spanned several continents, Asian markets experienced growth (excluding 2021), while African and American markets witnessed relatively consistent declines.

The CFO confirms the diverse export destinations, reaching all continents and approximately 90 countries. Key markets in 2021 included Algeria, Egypt, Libya, Nigeria, Senegal, USA, Argentina, Chile, Panama, Belgium, Denmark, Spain, France, Ireland, Switzerland, Sweden, and the United Arab Emirates. While ALPHA has previously exported to Korea, Japan, Canada, and Russia, these markets are currently inactive.

ALPHA acknowledges past concerns regarding Portuguese companies' technical capabilities in delivering high-quality products and services. However, the company has established its international reputation for quality standards. Another acknowledged challenge, prevalent globally, is meeting delivery deadlines. The interviewee attributes this partly to the broader Portuguese culture, but emphasizes that unforeseen circumstances beyond their control can also contribute to delays. Recent delays primarily stem from logistical issues, material shortages, and skilled labor gaps. To mitigate delays, ALPHA incorporates safety margins into production schedules. The CFO acknowledges that delays can damage company image and potentially incur financial penalties depending on contract terms.

ALPHA identifies excellence in technical capacity, pursuit of quality and rigor, and customer request flexibility as key success factors. While acknowledging intercultural differences, they prioritize concerns about working in countries with higher economic and financial risks, particularly in Africa. Financial policies in some countries create payment barriers. Despite cultural and communication differences, ALPHA reports building strong relationships with Algeria, Egypt, Libya, Nigeria, Senegal, and the United Arab Emirates in recent years.

Regarding cultural adaptation, the CFO emphasizes ALPHA's extensive experience in international markets, largely attributed to employee longevity. Accumulated knowledge facilitates international interactions. However, the interviewee acknowledges the difficulty or impossibility of transferring soft skills, suggesting they are acquired individually.

The CFO highlights the significant influence of internationalization on product quality improvement. Constant exposure to market trends and technical details from diverse international projects necessitates continuous learning and innovation to remain competitive. Currently, their involvement in an industrial project with American and German technicians fosters a stimulating environment for continuous improvement. The CFO expresses pride in his team's ability to address international colleagues' queries, emphasizing the importance of exporting to leverage the company's capabilities.

ALPHA prioritizes customer guidance over independent selection of international markets, ensuring profitability regardless of export type. They choose not to explore alternative entry modes due to the perceived lack of additional benefits.

ALPHA adapts product/service offerings according to customer demand, tailoring technical specifications to specific needs. This requires employee training investments, particularly in welding, radiography certification, and microcrack detection, ultimately leading to improved quality, productivity, and technical capabilities. Having closed Lisbon offices 15-20 years ago, all current operations are centralized at the Vale de Cambra headquarters.

ALPHA prioritizes close collaboration with major long-standing customers like Tetra Pak, Danone, and Nestlé. They also leverage intermediary engineering companies, which will be called AGENT, which handle extensive customer accounts and manage product design and development. However, this collaboration necessitates profit margin concessions in exchange for security and stability. As such, ALPHA is in a dependent position *vis-à-vis* AGENT, since ALPHA clearly dominates the technical dossiers, but is far away from the market relationships that are so important for leveraging direct relations with final clients. As a result, ALPHA hardly has direct access to relationships with end clients and is therefore dependent on AGENT to leverage its market position. On the other hand, AGENT does not give up its commercial relationship with clients, positioning itself as a technological intermediary, maintaining its upstream relationship with ALPHA and its relationship with the end clients. Finally, building win-win relationships with suppliers is also fundamental, emphasizing the importance of fulfilling responsibilities within all stakeholder relationships.

DISCUSSION

ALPHA, established for over half a century, possesses maturity and industry knowledge. However, its growth trajectory was not linear. Initially a micro-enterprise, it progressively scaled into a small and then a medium-sized company with a substantial export volume. The CFO's mention of a "natural and gradual" foreign market entry aligns with the Uppsala model by Johanson and Vahlne (1977).

The focus on the Spanish pharmaceutical industry indicates an interest in establishing and maintaining relationships with geographically and culturally close markets, a common practice among family-owned businesses that prioritize minimizing risk and familiarity (Fonte). Although the interviewee referred to numerous export destinations, most of them are from the European Union, further supporting the preference for proximity.

Despite continuous improvement efforts, ALPHA prioritizes the market and customers over competitor analysis, emphasizing service improvement. This cultural emphasis fosters healthy network relationships. During the interview, long-standing international customers like Danone, Tetra Pak, and Nestlé were highlighted. These renowned companies prioritize excellence in both products and values, particularly relevant in the food industry.

While not explicitly mentioned, ALPHA's network likely developed through the intrinsic primacy it enjoys, leveraging word-of-mouth recommendations from major clients like those mentioned above to potential customers. This aligns with Johanson and Mattson's (1988) model which emphasizes the role of "relationship bridges" to new markets. As these networks mature, they foster higher ambitions and differentiation, further aligning with network-based theories in ALPHA's strategy. ALPHA values close, long-term relationships with stakeholders, considering them 'partners' and 'allies' within its overall business strategy. Building trust and cooperation is crucial, ensuring fulfillment of mutual responsibilities, a natural characteristic of B2B markets. These relationships can become both business and personal, especially in long-standing partnerships where trust transcends other factors, becoming a valuable intangible asset built over time. They facilitate access to new international opportunities and foster mutual learning through a win-win approach, ensuring survival in a competitive and dynamic environment.

The interview corroborates the literature review regarding the lack of technical capacity as a significant internationalization barrier. However, the reasons differ. While the literature highlights size-related difficulties faced by SMEs due to limited resources compared to larger corporations, the interviewee emphasizes the lack of a proven market track record, linked to Portugal's negative technological image in international markets. This has been naturally overcome through continuous improvement and sustained growth over the years.

International experience, particularly for key decision-makers, is crucial for international success. However, it is a gradual process acquired through participation in various company endeavors. As Cavusgil (1984) suggests, increasing international experience fosters higher expectations, stricter processes, and a greater ease of adapting to diverse international cultures. Combining the interviewee's emphasis on international experience with their focus on technical capacity and continuous quality improvement further aligns ALPHA's strategy with the Uppsala model. According to Johanson and Vahlne (1990) and Forsgren (2002), this model emphasizes knowledge and commitment to the market, commitment decisions, and current activities as its four central pillars.

As mentioned in the literature review, exporting plays a critical role in boosting productivity through internalizing new knowledge and work methods. This aligns with the CFO's explanation of how exporting influences the company's problem-solving approach by staying updated on market trends through participation in diverse projects across various markets. Furthermore, it serves as a source of pride and motivation for personal and professional development for all employees. While acknowledging the importance of customer-derived know-how from a RBV perspective, the interviewee suggests that executed projects can fulfill goals, but competitive advantage is only achieved through fostering trust-based B2B relationships built over time.

Companies like ALPHA prioritize acquiring new technologies and employee training, ensuring skilled human capital and aligning with the RBV perspective. Essentially, they fulfill market and customer expectations while consistently striving for excellence. Trust built in customer relationships reinforces the importance of intangible resources that foster commitment, which reemphasize trust-based relationships, essential in B2B markets.

Regarding the RDT, ALPHA exhibits limitations and dependencies typical of an SME. While intermediary relationships offer advantages, as is the case of the relationship with AGENT, they can also constrain profit margins when accessing international markets. Reliance on companies like AGENT, responsible for relationships with large companies from product development to supply partner selection, relegates ALPHA to a passive role. Furthermore, it would be difficult for ALPHA to have privileged access to AGENT's clients, otherwise it could lose the trust it has gained in the meantime and the relationship it has with AGENT. As such, it seems that ALPHA would continue to have a relationship of dependence with AGENT.

A sound product strategy, while not guaranteeing success, increases the probability of achieving it. ALPHA prioritizes producing according to customer demand. Although standardization has undeniable advantages, differentiation plays a key role in catering to customer needs and maximizing resource utilization. Table 2 presents the relationship between the results and the literature review.

Internationalization Strategies

Table 2. Relationships Between Findings and Theoretical Background

Results	Literature support
• ALPHA's case contributes to understanding the limitations and dependencies faced by SMEs in international R&D activities, often relying on intermediaries like AGENT. This is typical among SMEs.	Resource Dependence Theory
• Tangible and intangible resources (successfully-based relationships) are important competitive advantages. • Generational know-how • Relational capital to deal with clients on win-win relationships. • ALPHA utilizes customer-derived knowledge and employee training to build human capital and achieve a competitive advantage.	Resource-based Theory
• ALPHA's internationalization path aligns with the Uppsala model's stages, particularly gradually expanding to geographically close markets, through exports, based on a relational perspective. • The focus on the Spanish pharmaceutical industry and the preference for European markets, reflects a typical risk aversion and cultural proximity.	*Uppsala Model*
• ALPHA seeks to leverage relationships with major clients like Danone and Tetra Pack, to access new markets, which is aligned with the network-based theory. • The growth of the contact networks fosters internalization knowledge, continuous improvement, product quality and efficiency.	Network-based Theory
• trust-based relationships with clients and suppliers are important success drivers in B2B markets. Successful B2B relationships facilitate access to new opportunities, knowledge sharing strategies, and trust building among parties involved.	B2B relationships

CONCLUSION AND LIMITATIONS

An analysis of ALPHA, informed by the interview with the CFO, suggests a two-stage explanation for its internationalization journey. Early on, ALPHA's gradual and close geographically market entry aligns with the Uppsala model of internationalization (Johanson & Vahlne, 1977). This is further supported by the emphasis placed on "natural and gradual" growth and the importance of international experience as a success factor.

However, the company's later internationalization efforts demonstrate elements of network-based theory. While ALPHA does not actively pursue membership in formal international networks, its focus on maintaining strong B2B relationships with key clients and suppliers mirrors the importance of network bridges highlighted by Johanson and Mattson (1988). These relationships play a crucial role in facilitating access to diverse international markets.

The case study emphasizes the significance of trust-based relationships for success in B2B markets. ALPHA leverages its long-standing partnerships with major customers (such as Danone and Tetra Pak) to gain access to new opportunities and market knowledge. Additionally, strong supplier relationships ensure reliable access to resources needed to fulfill customer demands.

The case study suggests that exporting plays a vital role in keeping ALPHA at the forefront of technological trends and market developments. Exposure to diverse client projects across various international markets fosters continuous learning and innovation. This emphasis on market responsiveness aligns with the Resource-Based View (RBV) perspective, where knowledge gained through exporting strengthens the company's internal resources.

ALPHA's production strategy exemplifies its high degree of market responsiveness. By initiating product development upon customer order, the company can tailor its offerings to specific needs. This approach enables ALPHA to adapt to a constantly changing market environment, increasing its probability of long-term success.

The case study acknowledges that ALPHA's success is influenced by external factors like national and international economic conditions, project allocation by clients, and technological advancements. Additionally, the scarcity of skilled labor presents a persistent challenge. Nevertheless, ALPHA's established reputation, built over several decades, serves as a valuable asset in overcoming such challenges.

Despite its success in international markets, ALPHA's internationalization process primarily aligns with the traditional Uppsala model and network-based theory. While the company might lack a strong strategic focus on expanding market share, it demonstrates a pragmatic and efficient approach. This is reflected in the CFO's adherence to the "if it ain't broke, don't fix it" philosophy. However, the case study underscores the importance of continuous improvement within existing processes and adapting to maintain strong client relationships. The focus remains on establishing win-win partnerships where trust is a key resource.

While the RBV perspective highlights the importance of ALPHA's investment in internal resources, its reliance on intermediaries like AGENT for relationships with large international companies introduces limitations, despite all the advantages it brings to ALPHA, as ALPHA will certainly find it difficult to move away of the dependent position it has in this relationship. This dependence places ALPHA's success with major accounts at the mercy of the intermediary's relational resources.

A primary limitation of this case study lies in its reliance on a single interview. Conducting additional interviews with other company personnel could provide a more comprehensive picture. Furthermore, comparative research with companies in the same industry, particularly those with a higher degree of internationalization, or even national companies from different sectors but similar size, would offer valuable insights. Such comparisons could shed light on the contrasting approaches companies take and their underlying rationales for internationalization.

REFERENCES

Acs, Z. J., Audretsch, D. B., & Feldman, M. P. (1994). R & D spillovers and recipient firm size. *The Review of Economics and Statistics*, 76(2), 336–340. 10.2307/2109888

Andersson, S., Evers, N., & Griot, C. (2013). Local and international networks in small firm internationalization: Cases from the Rhône-Alpes medical technology regional cluster. *Entrepreneurship and Regional Development*, 25(9/10), 867–888. 10.1080/08985626.2013.847975

Bai, X., Krishna, K., & Ma, H. (2017). How you export matters: Export mode, learning and productivity in China. *Journal of International Economics*, 104, 122–137. 10.1016/j.jinteco.2016.10.009

Bayfield, R., Dana, L. P., & Stewart, S. (2009). Firm characteristics and internationalisation strategies: An empirical investigation of New Zealand exporters. *International Journal of Globalisation and Small Business*, 3(3), 275–287. 10.1504/IJGSB.2009.024571

Bonaccorsi, A. (1992). On the relationship between firm size and export intensity. *Journal of International Business Studies*, 23(4), 605–635. 10.1057/palgrave.jibs.8490280

Brown, P., & Bell, J. (2001). Industrial clusters and small firm internationalisation (Best paper). In *Multinationals in a New Era*. Palgrave Macmillan. 10.1057/9781403907622_2

Carazo, P. C. M., & Lumiste, R. (2010). Foreign entry modes of Colombian small and medium enterprises. *International Journal of Business and Economics Perspectives*, 5(1), 16–41.

Cavusgil, S. T. (1984). Differences among exporting firms based on their degree of internationalization. *Journal of Business Research*, 12(2), 195–208. 10.1016/0148-2963(84)90006-7

Chetty, S., & Campbell-Hunt, C. (2003). Paths to internationalisation among small to medium-sized firms: A global versus regional approach. *European Journal of Marketing*, 37(5/6), 796–820. 10.1108/03090560310465152

Christensen, C. M., & Bower, J. L. (1996). Customer power, strategic investment, and the failure of leading firms. *Strategic Management Journal*, 17(3), 197–218. 10.1002/(SICI)1097-0266(199603)17:3<197::AID-SMJ804>3.0.CO;2-U

Christensen, R. (2006). The small and medium sized exporters squeeze: Empirical evidence and model reflections. *Entrepreneurship and Regional Development*, 3(1), 49–65. 10.1080/08985629100000004

Coviello, N. E., & Martin, K. A. (1999). Internationalization of Service SMEs: An Integrated Perspective from the Engineering Consulting Sector. *Journal of International Marketing*, 7(4), 42–66. 10.1177/1069031X9900700404

Damijan, J. P., Kostevc, Č., & Polanec, S. (2010). From innovation to exporting or vice versa? *World Economy*, 33(3), 374–398. 10.1111/j.1467-9701.2010.01260.x

Davis, G. F., & Cobb, J. A. (2010). Resource Dependence Theory: Past and Future. In *Stanford's Organization Theory Renaissance, 1970–2000 (Research in the Sociology of Organizations*, Vol. 28), Emerald. 10.1108/S0733-558X(2010)0000028006

De Loecker, J. (2013). Detecting learning by exporting. *American Economic Journal. Microeconomics*, 5(3), 1–21. 10.1257/mic.5.3.1

Di Cintio, M., Ghosh, S., & Grassi, E. (2020). Direct or indirect exports: What matters for firms' innovation activities? *Applied Economics Letters*, 27(2), 93–103. 10.1080/13504851.2019.1610693

Durão, V., & Moreira, A. C. (2019). Critical and inhibiting success factors in inter-organizational networks: A case study. In Teixeira, S., & Ferreira, J. (Eds.), *Multilevel Approach to Competitiveness in the Global Tourism Industry* (pp. 63–86). IGI Global. 10.4018/978-1-7998-0365-2.ch005

ECO SAPO. (2022). Metalurgia e metalomecânica bate recorde de exportações em março. https://eco.sapo.pt/2022/05/18/metalurgia-e-metalomecanica-bate-recorde-de-exportacoes-em-marco/

Eisenhardt, K. M. (1989). Building theories from case study research. *Academy of Management Review*, 14(4), 532–550. 10.2307/258557

Erramilli, M. K., & D'Souza, D. E. (1993). Venturing into foreign markets: The case of the small service firm. *Entrepreneurship Theory and Practice*, 17(4), 29–41. 10.1177/104225879301700403

Forsgren, M. (2002). The concept of learning in the Uppsala internationalization process model: A critical review. *International Business Review*, 11(3), 257–277. 10.1016/S0969-5931(01)00060-9

Ghauri, P. (2004). Designing and conducting case studies in international business research. In Marschan-Piekkari, R., & Welch, C. (Eds.), *Handbook of Qualitative Research Methods for International Business* (pp. 109–124). Edward Elgar. 10.4337/9781781954331.00019

Greenaway, D., & Kneller, R. (2007). Firm heterogeneity, exporting and foreign direct investment. *Economic Journal (London)*, 117(517), F134–F161. 10.1111/j.1468-0297.2007.02018.x

Hadley, R. D., & Wilson, H. I. (2003). The network model of internationalisation and experiential knowledge. *International Business Review*, 12(6), 697–717. 10.1016/j.ibusrev.2003.01.001

Hafiz, N., Latiff, A. S. A., Islam, M. A., Saif, A. N., & Wahab, S. A. (2022). Towards the underlying theories of small firm growth: A literature review. *FIIB Business Review*, 11(1), 36–51. 10.1177/23197145211049627

Harris, R., & Li, Q. C. (2007). Learning-by-exporting? Firm-level evidence for UK manufacturing and services sectors. *Department of Economics Discussion Paper, 22.*

Hessels, J., & Terjesen, S. (2010). Resource dependency and institutional theory perspectives on direct and indirect export choices. *Small Business Economics*, 34(2), 203–220. 10.1007/s11187-008-9156-4

Hillman, A., Withers, M., & Collins, B. (2009). Resource dependence theory: A review. *Journal of Management*, 35(6), 1404–1427. 10.1177/0149206309343469

Ietto-Gillies, G. (2012). *Transnational Corporations: Fragmentation Amidst Integration*. Routeldge.

Jackling, B., & Johl, S. (2009). Board structure and firm performance: Evidence from India's top companies. *Corporate Governance*, 17(4), 492–509. 10.1111/j.1467-8683.2009.00760.x

Johanson, J., & Mattsson, L.-G. (1988) Internationalization in industrial systems: a network approach. In *Strategies in Global Competition: Selected Papers from the Prince Bertil Symposium at the Institute of International Business.* Stockholm School of Economics.

Johanson, J., & Vahlne, J. E. (1977). The internationalization process of the firm—A model of knowledge development and increasing foreign market commitments. *Journal of International Business Studies*, 8(1), 23–32. 10.1057/palgrave.jibs.8490676

Johanson, J., & Vahlne, J. E. (1990). The mechanism of internationalisation. *International Marketing Review*, 7(4). Advance online publication. 10.1108/02651339010137414

Johanson, J., & Vahlne, J. E. (2003). Business relationship learning and commitment in the internationalization process. *Journal of International Entrepreneurship*, 1(1), 83–101. 10.1023/A:1023219207042

Johanson, J., & Vahlne, J. E. (2009). The Uppsala internationalization process model revisited: From liability of foreignness to liability of outsidership. *Journal of International Business Studies*, 40(9), 1411–1431. 10.1057/jibs.2009.24

Jones, M. V. (2001). First steps in internationalization: Concepts and evidence from a sample of small high-technology firms. *Journal of International Management*, 7(3), 191–210. 10.1016/S1075-4253(01)00044-8

Kontinen, T., & Ojala, A. (2010). The internationalization of family businesses: A review of extant research. *Journal of Family Business Strategy*, 1(2), 97–107. 10.1016/j.jfbs.2010.04.001

Larimo, J. (2015). Different Types of Exporting SMEs: Similarities and Differences in Export Performance. In *International Marketing Research* (*Advances in International Marketing, Vol. 17*). Emerald, Leeds. 10.1016/S1474-7979(06)17001-5

Lee, G. K., & Liebermann, M. B. (2010). Acquisition vs. internal development as modes of market entry. *Strategic Management Journal*, 31(2), 140–158. 10.1002/smj.804

Liu, X., & Buck, T. (2007). Innovation Performance and Channels for International Technology Spillovers: Evidence from Chinese High-Tech Industries. *Research Policy*, 36(3), 355–366. 10.1016/j.respol.2006.12.003

Moreira, A. C., Ribau, C. P., & Borges, M. (2024). Internationalisation of SMEs: A comparative perspective between Africa and Latin America. *International Journal of Entrepreneurship and Small Business*, 51(4), 513–541. 10.1504/IJESB.2024.136944

Mota, J. H., & Moreira, A. C. (2017). Determinants of the capital structure of Portuguese firms with investments in Angola. *South African Journal of Economic and Management Sciences*, 20(1), a885. 10.4102/sajems.v20i1.885

Nicholson, G. J., & Kiel, G. C. (2007). Can directors impact performance? A case-based test of three theories of corporate governance. *Corporate Governance*, 15(4), 585–608. 10.1111/j.1467-8683.2007.00590.x

OBSERVADOR. (2022). Exportações de metalurgia e metalomecânica batem recorde em 2021 para quase 20 mil milhões de euros. https://observador.pt/2022/02/10/exportacoes-de-metalurgia-e-metalomecanica-batem-recorde-em-2021-para-quase-20-mil-milhoes-de-euros/

Ojala, A. (2009). Internationalization of knowledge-intensive SMEs: The role of network relationships in the entry to a psychically distant market. *International Business Review*, 18(1), 50–59. 10.1016/j.ibusrev.2008.10.002

Olejnik, E., & Swoboda, B. (2012). SMEs' internationalisation patterns: Descriptives, dynamics and determinants. *International Marketing Review*, 29(5), 466–495. 10.1108/02651331211260340

Pfeffer, J., & Salanick, G. R. (2003). *The External Control of Organizations: A Resource Dependence Perspective*. Stanford University Press.

Pukall, T. J., & Calabro, A. (2014). The internationalization of family firms: A critical review and integrative model. *Family Business Review*, 27(2), 103–125. 10.1177/0894486513491423

Reuber, A. R., & Fischer, E. (1997). The influence of the management team's international experience on the internationalization behaviors of SMEs. *Journal of International Business Studies*, 28(4), 807–825. 10.1057/palgrave.jibs.8490120

Ribau, C. P., Moreira, A. C., & Raposo, M. (2015). Internationalisation of the firm theories: A schematic synthesis. *International Journal of Business and Globalisation*, 15(4), 528–554. 10.1504/IJBG.2015.072535

Ribau, C. P., Moreira, A. C., & Raposo, M. (2017). Export performance and the internationalisation of SMEs. *International Journal of Entrepreneurship and Small Business*, 30(2), 214–240. 10.1504/IJESB.2017.081438

Ribau, C. P., Moreira, A. C., & Raposo, M. (2018). SME internationalization research: Mapping the state of the art. *Canadian Journal of Administrative Sciences*, 35(2), 280–303. 10.1002/cjas.1419

Ribau, C. P., Moreira, A. C., & Raposo, M. (2018). Categorising the internationalisation of SMEs with social network analysis. *International Journal of Entrepreneurship and Small Business*, 35(1), 57–80. 10.1504/IJESB.2018.094264

Ribau, C. P., Moreira, A. C., & Raposo, M. (2019). Multidyadic Relationships: A multi-stage perspective. *Global Business and Economics Review*, 21(6), 732–755. 10.1504/GBER.2019.102553

Salomon, R. (2006). *Learning from Exporting: New Insights, New Perspectives.* Edward Elgar Publishing. 10.4337/9781781953006

Salomon, R. M., & Shaver, J. M. (2005). Learning by exporting: New insights from examining firm innovation. *Journal of Economics & Management Strategy*, 14(2), 431–460. 10.1111/j.1530-9134.2005.00047.x

Schnack, H., Uthoff, S. A., & Ansmann, L. (2022). The perceived impact of physician shortages on human resource strategies in German hospitals–a resource dependency perspective. *Journal of Health Organization and Management*, 36(9), 196–211. 10.1108/JHOM-05-2021-020336098505

Sharma, D. D., & Blomstermo, A. (2003). The internationalization process of born globals: A network view. *International Business Review*, 12(6), 739–753. 10.1016/j.ibusrev.2003.05.002

Silva, P., & Moreira, A. C. (2019). Subsidiary survival: A case study from the Portuguese electronics industry. *Review of International Business and Strategy*, 29(3), 226–252. 10.1108/RIBS-10-2018-0094

Simões, C., Esperança, J., & Simões, V. (2013). *Horizonte Internacionalizar.* http://www.portugalglobal.pt/PT/Internacionalizar/Documents/HorizonteInternacionalizarGuiaparaPME.pdf

Street, C. T., & Cameron, A. F. (2007). External relationships and the small business: A review of small business alliance and network research. *Journal of Small Business Management*, 45(2), 239–266. 10.1111/j.1540-627X.2007.00211.x

Swoboda, B., Elsner, S., & Olejnik, E. (2015). How do past mode choices influences subsequent entry? A study on the boundary conditions of preferred entry modes of retail firms. *International Business Review*, 24(3), 506–517. 10.1016/j.ibusrev.2014.10.008

Vahlne, J.-E., & Johanson, J. (2013). The Uppsala model on evolution of the multinational business enterprise – from internalization to coordination of networks. *International Marketing Review*, 30(3), 189–210. 10.1108/02651331311321963

Vissak, T., & Francioni, B. (2013). Serial nonlinear internationalization in practice: A case study. *International Business Review*, 22(6), 951–962. 10.1016/j.ibusrev.2013.01.010

Wind, J., & Rangaswamy, A. (2001). Customization: The next revolution in mass customization. *Journal of Interactive Marketing*, 15(1), 13–32. 10.1002/1520-6653(200124)15:1<13::AID-DIR1001>3.0.CO;2-#

Yeager, V. A., Menachemi, N., Savage, G. T., Ginter, P. M., Sen, B. P., & Beitsch, L. M. (2014). Using resource dependency theory to measure the environment in health care organizational studies. *Health Care Management Review*, 39(1), 50–65. 10.1097/HMR.0b013e318282662423358132

Yin, R. (2008). Case Study Research: Design and Methods. *Sage (Atlanta, Ga.)*.

Young, S., Hamill, J., Wheeler, S., & Davies, J. R. (1989). *International Market Entry and Development*. Prentice-Hall.

KEY TERMS AND DEFINITIONS

Case Study: A case study is a qualitative research methodology commonly employed in the social sciences. It aims to interpret a specific phenomenon or situation through a chosen lens. This approach is particularly suited for addressing questions focused on "how" and "why" phenomena unfold. Case studies are often used within a constructivist research framework, which emphasizes the subjective nature of knowledge and the importance of understanding lived experiences.

Globalization: Globalization refers to the multifaceted process of increasing interconnectedness across the globe, encompassing economic, financial, trade, and communication spheres. This phenomenon often manifests as a reduction in trade barriers between nations, facilitated by free trade agreements. Globalization entails a shift from local and nationalistic perspectives to a broader understanding of an interdependent world. This interconnectedness fosters the free flow of capital, goods, and services across national borders, potentially leading to increased investment opportunities.

Internationalization Process: The internationalization process describes a company's trajectory as it transitions from a domestic market to engage in foreign markets. This process typically involves various entry modes, such as exporting, foreign direct investment (FDI), or franchising. The chosen entry mode plays a critical role in shaping the company's subsequent internationalization path and associated costs. Two prominent theories that illuminate the internationalization process include the Uppsala model and the network-based approach, which will be discussed further (see below).

Uppsala Model: The Uppsala model is a dynamic theory that has garnered significant attention within the field of International Business Studies, particularly within the Nordic School of thought. It seeks to explain the gradual process by which firms internationalize. This theory posits that companies learn and adapt as they navigate international expansion. The Uppsala model emphasizes the staged nature of this process, suggesting that firms progress from limited international exposure, such as non-regular exports, to establishing a more robust foreign presence through subsidiaries.

Chapter 15
Synergizing Fashion Design and Entrepreneurship Education:
Pathways and Implications

Zhang Xiaohan
Shandong Vocational College of Science and Technology, China

Rohana Zur
College of Creative Arts, University Technology MARA, Malaysia

ABSTRACT

This chapter examines the integration of fashion design education with innovative entrepreneurship education in response to the contemporary socio-economic demands of the global fashion industry. By interweaving different theories, it articulates a theoretical foundation for a cohesive approach that aims to enhance the entrepreneurial capacities of fashion design students. The first section introduces the evolving landscape of the fashion industry, marked by technological advancements, shifting market dynamics, and sustainable practices. Subsequent analysis reveals the impact of an integrated curriculum on cultivating entrepreneurial intentions, as evidenced by a longitudinal study in Shandong. Strategies for implementing this integrated approach emphasize the creation of a curriculum that mirrors the symbiotic relationship of a DNA double helix, with fashion design and entrepreneurship education as inseparable strands. The innovative educational model is posited as essential for developing the multifaceted skill set required for aspiring fashion entrepreneurs to thrive in industry.

DOI: 10.4018/979-8-3693-3518-5.ch015

1. INTRODUCTION

1.1 Background of the Study

In the evolving landscape of global fashion, integrating fashion design education with innovative entrepreneurship education is crucial for meeting contemporary socio-economic demands. The fashion industry's role in global GDP highlights the importance of equipping students with relevant skills and an entrepreneurial mindset. Recent studies like Rahayu (2024) emphasize the entrepreneurial behavior of bachelor students in fashion education, underlining the significance of entrepreneurship in fashion programs.

Recent data suggest that the fashion industry contributes approximately 2% to the global GDP, with fashion education playing a critical role in sustaining this economic powerhouse by equipping students with relevant skills and an entrepreneurial mindset (Roy, 2019). Integrating entrepreneurial principles into fashion education responds to industry demands, with 73% of fashion executives identifying the need for teams that possess a blend of creative and analytical talents (Gazzola et al., 2020).

The trends in innovative entrepreneurship education are characterized by a robust emphasis on digital literacy, with 68% of fashion programs now incorporating digital marketing strategies into their curricula (Sharma et al., 2023). Similarly, sustainability has emerged as a core component of entrepreneurship education, reflecting a 30% increase in courses dedicated to ethical practices within the last five years (García-Morales et al., 2020).

The convergence of these educational domains facilitates a learning environment where students are not only design-savvy but also adept in navigating the complex business landscape. This is exemplified by the adoption of interdisciplinary approaches in 80% of fashion design programs, bridging technology, design, and business education (Trivers, 2017).

This study concludes with strategic recommendations for policy and curriculum development, emphasizing the need for an adaptable and synergistic educational framework. Such a framework is essential for cultivating a new generation of fashion professionals who are innovative, adaptable, and culturally informed, capable of contributing to the industry's sustainable and ethical development.

1.2 The Significance of Fashion Design in Modern Educational Systems

In contemporary educational systems, the role of fashion design transcends mere aesthetic concerns, emerging as a multidimensional discipline with profound implications across cultural, economic, and technological domains. González-Pérez

& Ramírez-Montoya (2022) emphasized the significance of fashion design as a vital medium for cultural and artistic expression, facilitating individual and communal articulation of heritage and identity while fostering a culture of innovation and creativity. This artistic engagement is not only an avenue for self-expression but also a catalyst for personal development, enhancing self-esteem and interpersonal skills.

From an economic perspective, as highlighted by Ratten & Usmanij (2021), the integration of fashion design into educational curricula equips students with skills pertinent to the global fashion industry, which brings a significant economic impact. This integration often includes entrepreneurial elements, preparing students for future business ventures and contributing to economic development. Concurrently, fashion design education is characterized by its interdisciplinary nature, merging art, culture, technology, and business, thereby promoting a multifaceted learning experience that encompasses critical thinking and decision-making skills, essential in various life and work scenarios (Ratten & Jones, 2021).

Magd and Khan (2022) provide a strategic framework for entrepreneurship education to promote social entrepreneurship in GCC countries during and post-COVID-19, demonstrating the evolving landscape of entrepreneurship education in response to global challenges. This is complemented by Magd, Khan, and Bhuyan (2022), who investigate social entrepreneurship intentions among business students in Oman, shedding light on the growing interest in social entrepreneurship within the business education community.

Furthermore, the field of fashion design education is at the forefront of addressing contemporary challenges such as sustainability and social responsibility. Camacho (2022) highlighted the discipline's commitment to sustainable design practices and ethical fashion, educating students on environmental concerns and inclusive design. The technological evolution of the fashion industry, encompassing 3D printing and digital fabrication, also plays a crucial role in shaping modern fashion design education, as underscored by Song (2021). This technological integration not only prepares students for the changing landscape of the fashion industry but also fosters digital literacy vital for success in their careers.

Moreover, fashion design education plays a pivotal role in cultivating global perspectives and cross-cultural understanding, as it exposes students to global trends and cultures, thereby enhancing global awareness (Clarke, 2020). This exposure is crucial in an increasingly interconnected world, where understanding diverse cultural dynamics is key to fostering global harmony and cooperation.

In summary, fashion design within modern educational systems is a comprehensive discipline that significantly contributes to cultural richness, economic development, personal growth, and social responsibility. It nurtures a generation of individuals who are not only creatively and technically proficient but also socially conscious and globally aware, equipped to navigate and contribute positively to the contemporary world.

1.3 The Trends in Innovative Entrepreneurship Education

Innovative entrepreneurship education is facing transformative trends that are reshaping its role and significance in academic curricula, reflecting the dynamic and evolving nature of entrepreneurship as a pivotal area of educational focus. One of the key trends observed is the increasing emphasis on digital literacy and technology integration, a response to the digitalization of the marketplace. Hsu & Wu (2023) asserted that entrepreneurship programs are incorporating digital tools and platforms more extensively to simulate real-world business scenarios, thereby equipping students with essential skills to navigate the digital business landscape effectively.

Concurrently, there is a growing focus on sustainability and social responsibility within entrepreneurship education. This shift, as noted by Chandler (2022), includes integrating concepts of sustainable development and ethical practices into courses, mirroring the global movement towards responsible and sustainable business models and reflecting modern societal expectations of enterprises.

Moreover, contemporary entrepreneurship education is placing significant importance on experiential learning and real-world application. Oliveira & Cardoso (2021) emphasized the value of practical experiences, such as internships and project-based learning, in the development of entrepreneurial skills. This hands-on approach facilitates the application of theoretical knowledge in real-world contexts, thereby enhancing students' understanding and readiness for entrepreneurial ventures.

Additionally, there is a growing acknowledgment of the importance of an interdisciplinary approach in entrepreneurship education. Eltanahy et al. (2020) argued for the integration of various disciplines, such as technology, design, and business, to provide a more comprehensive understanding of entrepreneurship, which prepares students to address complex challenges in their entrepreneurial endeavors.

Furthermore, the development of an entrepreneurial mindset and soft skills, including creativity, problem-solving, and resilience, is receiving increased attention. Dumitru & Halpern (2020) highlighted that these skills are critical for entrepreneurial success and have become integral components of entrepreneurship education programs.

Lastly, incorporating a global perspective and developing cross-cultural understanding has become essential in entrepreneurship education, recognizing the global nature of modern business. Clarke (2020) stressed the importance of understanding different cultural and market dynamics, which is indispensable for entrepreneurs operating in a globalized economy.

In summary, the trends in innovative entrepreneurship education signal a shift towards an approach that is more integrated, experiential, and socially responsible, reflecting the changing dynamics of the business world and underscoring the need for entrepreneurial education to continuously adapt and evolve in response to these changes.

1.4 Significance of the Study

Emphasizing the Theoretical and Practical Importance of the Study

The significance of this study is two-fold, providing both a rich theoretical framework and practical pathways for integrating fashion design education with innovative entrepreneurship education. Its implications extend beyond immediate educational outcomes, projecting potential long-term impacts on the fashion industry at large.

Theoretical Contributions

a. Enhancing Educational Paradigms: The study's in-depth analysis contributes to the academic literature by delineating a pathway for the integration of entrepreneurial skills within the context of fashion design, thereby expanding upon the foundational work of Dumitru and Halpern (2023).
b. Interdisciplinary Approach: This research substantiates the call for interdisciplinary education made by Eltanahy et al. (2020), adding to the discourse on the benefits and challenges of such approaches within higher education.

Practical Implications

1. Curriculum Development: With digital literacy becoming an indispensable component in education, the study proposes strategic methods for its incorporation into fashion design courses, aligning with the practical recommendations of Oliveira & Cardoso (2021).
2. Industry and Academia Collaboration: By emphasizing the need for a partnership between academia and the industry, as Perkmann et al. (2021) advocated, the study underscores the value of relevant skills in student training.
3. Fostering Entrepreneurial Mindsets: The study reinforces the necessity of instilling an entrepreneurial mindset in students, as suggested by Clarke (2020), to enhance their competitiveness and ensure their success in the ever-changing fashion industry.

4. Promoting Sustainable and Ethical Practices: According to the research results of Murzyn-Kupisz & Hołuj (2021), the study presents strategies for integrating sustainable and ethical principles into fashion education, helping students to be leaders who are honest and conscientious in fashion industry.

In conclusion, this study synthesizes theoretical insights with actionable strategies, providing a well-supported framework for educators, policymakers, and industry stakeholders. By fostering a curriculum that is responsive to evolving industry needs, the study suggests that the long-term impact on the fashion industry will be marked by the emergence of professionals who are not only creatively and technically proficient but also equipped with a strong entrepreneurial ethos, ready to lead with innovation, sustainability, and ethical responsibility.

1.5 Key Concepts

Clarifying Interrelations and Setting Stages for Integration

In of this study, three key concepts that are pivotal to the integration of fashion design and innovative entrepreneurship education are proposed: Fashion Design, Innovative Entrepreneurship Education, and Integration. These three concepts are not only individually defined but are also intrinsically connected, collectively forming the bedrock of a synthesized educational approach.

Fashion Design: As a multifaceted discipline, fashion design is the amalgamation of creative artistry and practical functionality, producing clothing and accessories that reflect both personal identity and broader cultural currents (Qwelane, 2022). It is this combination of aesthetic expression and utilitarian design that provides a fertile ground for the generation of entrepreneurial thinking.

Innovative Entrepreneurship Education: This educational approach extends beyond traditional business training, incorporating a spirit of innovation that encourages students to develop groundbreaking ideas and adaptable business models (Perkmann et al., 2021). The proactive and innovative mindset fostered through this education complements the creative prowess cultivated in fashion design.

Integration: Defined as the harmonious unification of fashion design with innovative entrepreneurship education, integration is the central theme of this study. Eltanahy et al. (2020) described it as a blend of artistic creativity with strategic business acumen, resulting in a holistic educational experience. This synergy of disciplines is essential for preparing students to navigate the complex interplay between design innovation and market viability.

The interrelation of these key concepts forms the cornerstone of this research. Fashion design's inherent creativity, when interwoven with the dynamic strategies from entrepreneurship education, lays the foundation for an integrated educational model. This model is posited to effectively enhance the entrepreneurial capacities of students majoring in fashion design, equipping them with a skill set that is increasingly demanded by the modern fashion industry.

2. LITERATURE REVIEW

2.1 Reflecting Current Trends in Fashion Design and Entrepreneurship Education

This literature review methodically investigates the most current and pertinent research in fashion design and entrepreneurship education, elucidating the contemporary developments within relevant fields.

2.2 Advancements in Fashion Design Education

Technological Integration: The integration of cutting-edge technologies in fashion design education is pivotal in keeping pace with industry progression. The recent work of Attaran et al. (2024) proposes the adoption of virtual reality and artificial intelligence in design processes, showing the digital trend in the fashion industry.

Cultural and Artistic Influences: The research of Amatullo et al. (2021) remains relevant, while newer studies advocate for the inclusion of global cultural narratives, recognizing the impact of cultural diversity on fashion innovation and design.

2.3 Trends in Entrepreneurship Education

Shift Towards Innovation: The innovation-centric approach in entrepreneurship education, highlighted by Perkmann et al. (2021), continues to gain traction, with recent literature focusing on the integration of entrepreneurial thinking from the onset of design education.

Sustainability and Ethics: Murzyn-Kupisz & Hołuj (2021) initially noted the trend towards sustainability, which has since burgeoned into a central tenet of entrepreneurship education, with new studies emphasizing the role of ethical leadership in fashion.

2.4 Integrating Fashion Design With Entrepreneurship

Interdisciplinary Approach: Eltanahy et al. (2020) promoted an interdisciplinary curriculum, which has been further validated by contemporary research indicating that interdisciplinary competencies are crucial for professional success in the modern fashion landscape.

Industry-Academia Collaboration: Recent literature has corroborated the view of Oliveira & Cardoso (2021) on the benefits of industry-academia collaborations, particularly in light of the pandemic, which has necessitated more robust and real-time industry linkages.

2.5 Challenges and Opportunities

Balancing Creativity with Business Acumen: Dumitru & Halpern (2023) proposed that it is necessary to balance design creativity with business skills, and advocated for modular and flexible curriculums.

Global and Cultural Sensitivities: Clarke (2020) emphasis on global perspectives has been further expanded upon, with recent studies calling for an immersive educational experience that exposes students to multiple cultural contexts.

2.6 Conclusion of Literature Review

Through literature review, it is found that there is a dynamic interaction between fashion design and entrepreneurship education, with an ever-increasing focus on technological prowess, sustainable and ethical practices, and interdisciplinary learning. Therefore, educational institutions should develop a curriculum that is not only current but also anticipatory of future industry requirements.

3. THEORETICAL FOUNDATION

3.1 Educational Theories and Integration

Ecological Theory in Education

The ecological theory in education, primarily derived from Bronfenbrenner's ecological systems theory, provides a comprehensive framework for understanding the complex interplay between an individual and the environment in the learning process. This theory, when applied to fashion design education, offers valuable insights into how different environmental factors influence learning outcomes.

1. Bronfenbrenner's Ecological Systems Theory: Bronfenbrenner (1979) proposed that an individual's development is affected by their environment, which he categorized into several layers: microsystem, mesosystem, exosystem, and macrosystem. In the context of fashion design education, these systems can be interpreted as follows:
   a. Microsystem: This layer represents the immediate environment in which students learn, such as the classroom, peers, and instructors. According to Amatullo et al. (2021), the interaction in this system, including hands-on experiences with fabrics and designs, directly impacts students' learning and creativity in fashion design.
   b. Mesosystem: The mesosystem involves the interrelation between different microsystems. For students majoring in fashion design, this might include the interaction between their academic studies and internships, as highlighted by Oliveira & Cardoso (2021).
   c. Exosystem: This layer consists of external environmental settings that indirectly influence the student's development. For example, fashion industry trends and technological advancements shape the curriculum and teaching methodologies in fashion design, as discussed by Attaran et al. (2024).
   d. Macrosystem: The outermost layer encompasses the broader cultural and societal values. In fashion design education, this relates to the wider cultural, economic, and social influences that shape fashion trends and industry demands, as noted by Clarke (2020).
2. Application in Fashion Design Education: The ecological theory underscores the importance of a holistic educational approach. It suggests that effective fashion design education should not only focus on technical skills and creativity but also consider the broader environmental factors that influence this field. This approach aligns with Dumitru & Halpern (2023) viewpoint that understanding the ecological context can enhance students' ability to adapt and innovate in the dynamic field of fashion design.
3. Implications for Curriculum Development: The ecological theory provides a framework for developing a comprehensive fashion design curriculum that incorporates a range of influences from the immediate learning environment to broader societal trends. This involves integrating practical skills with insights into the fashion industry's socio-economic dimensions, ensuring that students are well-prepared for tackling challenges in the fashion world.

The ecological theory in education offers a valuable lens through which to view fashion design education, emphasizing the importance of a multifaceted and adaptive learning environment that responds to both internal and external influences.

3.2 Application in Fashion Design Education

The application of ecological theory in fashion design education underscores the significance of various environmental influences in shaping the educational experience. It also provides a nuanced understanding of how different ecological systems contribute to the development of skills, creativity, and knowledge of students majoring in fashion design.

1. Incorporating Multiple Learning Environments: According to Amatullo et al. (2021), the microsystem in fashion design education involves direct interaction with faculty, peers, and industry professionals. This layer emphasizes the importance of hands-on learning experiences, such as studio work, workshops, and design collaborations. These interactions are pivotal in developing students' technical skills and artistic vision.
2. Interconnection of Academic and Professional Realms: The mesosystem, involving the interplay between various microsystems, reflects the connection between academic learning and professional practice. As highlighted by Oliveira & Cardoso (2021), integrating internship and industry project within the curriculum bridges the gap between classroom learning and real-world applications. This integration is crucial for students to understand the practical aspects of fashion design and market dynamics.
3. External Influences on Curriculum Design: The exosystem in fashion design education includes factors like emerging fashion trends, technological advancements, and market demands. Attaran et al. (2024) suggested that contemporary design technologies and market-oriented projects should be added into the curriculum to help students meet the demands of the fashion industry.
4. Cultural and Societal Contexts: The macrosystem, which represents broader cultural and societal influences, plays a significant role in shaping the ethos of fashion design education. Clarke (2020) emphasized the need for curricula to reflect diverse cultural aesthetics and ethical considerations, including sustainable and ethical fashion practices. This broad perspective helps students develop designs that are not only innovative but also culturally sensitive and socially responsible.
5. Holistic Educational Approach: The application of ecological theory in fashion design education calls for a holistic approach that considers these multiple layers of influence. Dumitru & Halpern (2023) argued that such an approach equips students with a well-rounded education, enabling them to become not just skilled designers but also insightful contributors to the fashion industry.

The application of ecological theory in fashion design education highlights the importance of a multi-dimensional learning environment. It underscores the need to balance technical skill development with an understanding of the broader cultural,

3.3 Competency-Based Theory

Competency-Based Theory in Fashion Design and Entrepreneurship Education
Competency-Based Theory, a pivotal educational framework, emphasizes the development of specific skills and knowledge that are directly relevant to the demands of a particular profession. In the context of fashion design and entrepreneurship education, this theory plays a crucial role in structuring curricula that align with industry requirements and market expectations.

1. Skill Development in Fashion Design: Competency-Based Theory in fashion design education focuses on the development of essential skills such as technical proficiency in design, understanding of materials, and mastery of new technologies. As proposed by Attaran et al. (2024), this involves not just the acquisition of knowledge but the ability to apply this knowledge in practical settings. The theory underlines the importance of hands-on experiences in studios and workshops, ensuring that students develop the competencies required for the development of fashion industry.
2. Entrepreneurial Skills in Fashion Design Education: Competency-Based Theory advocates for the development of business acumen, market analysis skills, and entrepreneurial strategies. Dumitru & Halpern (2023) highlighted that such education should encompass more than traditional business skills, extending to areas like innovative problem-solving, leadership, and digital marketing, which are increasingly relevant in today's digitalized market landscape.
3. Integration of Competencies: The integration of competencies in both fashion design and entrepreneurship is crucial for preparing students to navigate the complexities of the fashion industry. According to Oliveira & Cardoso (2021), this integration ensures that students are not only creatively proficient but also capable of strategically positioning their designs in the market, understanding consumer trends, and managing business operations.
4. Outcome-Oriented Approach: It is an outcome-oriented approach in education. As Amatullo et al. (2021) suggested, such an approach in fashion design and entrepreneurship education involves setting clear skill and knowledge goals and structuring the learning experience to achieve desired outcomes. This approach ensures that graduates possess the competencies necessary to succeed in their careers.

5. Adaptability to Industry Changes: In line with Competency-Based Theory, fashion design and entrepreneurship education must be adaptable to changes in the industry. Clarke (2020) argued for the continuous update of curricula to reflect evolving industry standards, technological advancements, and shifting market dynamics, ensuring that the competencies taught remain relevant and forward-looking.

Competency-Based Theory in fashion design and entrepreneurship education highlights the importance of a skill-focused, outcome-oriented educational approach. It underscores the need for an adaptable and integrated curriculum that equips students with both creative and business competencies, preparing them for tackling challenges in the fashion industry.

3.4 Guiding Innovative Entrepreneurship Education

The trends in innovative entrepreneurship education emphasize the necessity of adapting to the digital marketplace and incorporating sustainability. Dana et al. (2024) explores the intersection of fashion, environmental sustainability, entrepreneurship, innovation, and technology, highlighting the critical role of entrepreneurship in driving sustainable fashion. Furthermore, Khan et al. (2019) and Saxena et al. (2023) delve into the role of attitude and entrepreneurship education in fostering entrepreneurial orientation among business students, emphasizing the need for comprehensive education models that support entrepreneurial development.

1. Developing an Innovative Mindset: Central to innovative entrepreneurship education is the development of an innovative mindset. Dumitru & Halpern (2023) emphasized that this involves encouraging students to think beyond conventional boundaries and develop unique, creative solutions to problems. This mindset is particularly crucial in fashion design, where innovation drives both aesthetic and functional aspects of the field.
2. Integration of Technological Advances: As noted by Attaran et al. (2024), the incorporation of the latest technological advancements is a key aspect of fostering innovation in entrepreneurship education. This includes teaching students how to leverage digital tools and platforms not only for design purposes but also for business operations, marketing, and market research.
3. Developing Business and Entrepreneurial Skills: According to Oliveira & Cardoso (2021), innovative entrepreneurship education in fashion design should focus on developing business skills. This involves understanding market dynamics, financial management, branding, and customer relations. It also includes fostering skills in areas like sustainable business practices and ethical entrepreneurship, as highlighted by Murzyn-Kupisz & Hołuj (2021).

4. Project-Based and Experiential Learning: Perkmann et al. (2021) argued for the effectiveness of project-based and experiential learning approaches in entrepreneurship education. In fashion design, this can involve real-world projects such as designing collections, developing business plans, and collaborating with industry professionals, providing students with practical experience and a deeper understanding of the industry.
5. Adapting to Market Needs: Clarke (2020) emphasized the importance of adapting entrepreneurship education to the ever-changing needs of the market. This requires keeping the curriculum dynamic and responsive, ensuring that students learn skills that are relevant and in demand in the fashion industry.

Guiding innovative entrepreneurship education in fashion design involves a multifaceted approach that combines fostering an innovative mindset with the development of practical business and technological skills. It requires an adaptive and responsive curriculum that prepares students for the challenges and opportunities in the evolving world of fashion design and business.

3.5 Synergy Theory in Fashion Design and Entrepreneurship Education

Synergy Theory, an important concept in educational discourse, posits that the interaction of different elements in an educational system can produce an outcome greater than the sum of its parts. In the context of fashion design and entrepreneurship education, this theory underscores the potential of integrating creative design with business acumen to produce comprehensive educational outcomes.

1. Interdisciplinary Integration: The core of Synergy Theory in education is the interdisciplinary integration, where diverse knowledge domains intersect to enrich learning experiences. Eltanahy et al. (2020) highlighted this as essential in modern education, particularly in fields like fashion design where artistic creativity meets market and business strategies. This integration forms a more holistic understanding among students, who can appreciate and apply both design principles and entrepreneurial strategies.
2. Collaborative Learning Environments: Synergy Theory also emphasizes the importance of a collaborative learning environment. As discussed by Amatullo et al. (2021), in fashion design education, it can mean collaborations between design students and business students, or partnerships with industry professionals. Such collaborations not only enhance learning through practical experience but also encourage the sharing of diverse perspectives.
3. Enhancing Creativity and Innovation: Oliveira & Cardoso (2021) argued that synergy in education, particularly when applied to fields like fashion design, enhances creativity and innovation. By combining creative design education

with entrepreneurial education, students are encouraged to think innovatively, not only about design aesthetics but also about how these designs can be viably marketed and sold.
4. Application in Curriculum Development: The application of Synergy Theory in curriculum development involves creating courses that bridge fashion design and entrepreneurship. According to Dumitru, & Halpern (2023), this includes incorporating elements of business planning, marketing strategies, and consumer behavior into design courses, ensuring that students can see and understand the real-world applications of their design work.
5. Preparing for Industry Challenges: The synergy between fashion design and entrepreneurship education is particularly significant in preparing students for the multifaceted challenges of the fashion industry. Attaran et al. (2024) noted that this educational approach equips students with a versatile skill set, enabling them to navigate the complexities of the modern fashion landscape effectively.

3.6 Conclusion

From the perspective of fashion design and entrepreneurship education, Synergy Theory highlights the importance of an integrated, interdisciplinary approach. This theory guides the development of educational programs that effectively combine creativity with business acumen, preparing students to meet the demands and challenges of the fashion industry with innovative and comprehensive skill sets.

3.6.1 Role in Integrating Professional and Entrepreneurial Education

The role of Synergy Theory in integrating professional and entrepreneurial education, especially within the context of fashion design, is pivotal in creating a cohesive and effective educational framework. This integration is essential for cultivating professionals who are not only adept in design but also proficient in the business aspects of the fashion industry.

1. Creating a Composite Curriculum: The primary role of synergy in integrating professional and entrepreneurial education lies in the development of a composite curriculum. As noted by Dumitru & Halpern (2023), such a curriculum seamlessly combines the artistic aspects of fashion design with core entrepreneurial skills like market analysis, financial management, and strategic planning. This integrated approach ensures that students acquire a balanced set of skills that are crucial for success in the modern fashion industry.
2. Enhancing Employability and Market Relevance: The integration facilitated by Synergy Theory significantly enhances the employability of graduates. Attaran et al. (2024) emphasized that students who receive an education that marries design

proficiency with entrepreneurial skills are more adaptable and market-relevant. They are equipped to not only find opportunities within established companies but also to create their ventures in the fashion industry.
3. Promoting Innovation and Competitive Advantage: According to Eltanahy et al. (2020), the synergy between professional and entrepreneurial education helps to build an environment of innovation. In this environment, students are encouraged to develop unique design concepts to provide viable products or services.
4. Facilitating Industry and Academic Collaboration: The role of synergy in this integration also extends to fostering collaborations between academia and the fashion industry. Oliveira and Cardoso (2021) highlight that such collaborations are crucial for providing students with real-world exposure and insights, thereby enhancing the practical aspect of education.
5. Addressing Contemporary Challenges: In the context of rapidly changing market dynamics and consumer preferences, the integrated approach advocated by Synergy Theory is instrumental in preparing students to address contemporary challenges. Amatullo et al. (2021) argued that this approach equips students with the ability to adapt to shifts in fashion trends, sustainability concerns, and digital transformation in the industry.

The integration of professional and entrepreneurial education through Synergy Theory plays a crucial role in fashion design education. It helps to create a comprehensive learning experience that equips students with the necessary skills to succeed as professionals and entrepreneurs in the fashion industry, fostering innovation, adaptability, and competitiveness.

3.7 Conclusion of Theoretical Foundation

In conclusion, this chapter has delved into the crucial role of Ecological Theory, Competency-Based Theory, and Synergy Theory in sculpting a contemporary educational paradigm for fashion design and entrepreneurship. Each theory brings unique perspectives and methodologies that, when integrated, create a dynamic and holistic educational experience. This integration is paramount in preparing students for tackling challenges in the fashion industry, equipping them with the necessary creative, technical, and business competencies. The convergence of these theories not only enhances the quality and relevance of education but also helps to develop a generation of professionals who are innovative, adaptable, and ready to make significant contributions to the world of fashion and entrepreneurship.

This chapter underscores the significance of a nuanced and synergistic approach to education, highlighting the need for curricula that are responsive to both the requirements of fashion design and the complexities of the business world.

4. METHODOLOGY

This study aims to synergize fashion design and entrepreneurship education, focusing on exploring the integration pathways and their implications. The research employs a quantitative approach, utilizing questionnaire to gather data.

4.1 Survey Analysis

Survey Design: A structured questionnaire was developed to gather data from students and graduates of Shandong Technology Vocational College's Fashion Design program. The survey included both closed and open-ended questions designed to assess the level of integration between fashion design and entrepreneurship education and its impact on students' entrepreneurial intentions.

4.2 Population and Sample

The research targets students from Shandong Vocational College of Science and Technology: fashion design. Due to the uncertainty of the total population size, the sample size was determined using the Lemeshow formula, accounting for a 5% margin of error and a 50% outcome prevalence. The final sample consisted of 385 students, selected through purposive and snowball sampling techniques, focusing only on students with entrepreneurial intentions. The data collection was conducted via Google Forms from November 2022 to February 2023. Out of the targeted 385 responses, 376 were returned and deemed suitable for analysis, indicating a data collection success rate of 97.66%.

The survey targeted a sample of 376 students and graduates from 2017 to 2023. The sampling method was purposive, focusing on individuals who had direct experience with the curriculum. Data were collected through online platforms to ensure a wide reach and a great convenience for respondents.

4.3 Measurement

Part A: Personal Information and Education Experience

Part A gathers personal information that includes basic individual data along with details about the respondent's educational background. It comprises three items catering to information regarding gender, grade, and the entrepreneurial background of the family (Table 1).

Table 1. Demographic and Family Entrepreneurial Background Information

Number	Item
A1	Gender
A2	Grade
A3	Whether your family member has started a business?

Source: Questionnaire on Students majoring in fashion design' Willingness to Start a Business

Part B: Education Experience and Extracurricular Involvement

In Part B, the questionnaire delves into the respondents' educational experiences. It investigates whether they have engaged in entrepreneurial competitions, participated in extracurricular club activities, and their evaluation of internship experiences, providing insights into their exposure to practical scenarios and competitive environments (Table 2).

Table 2. Student Participation in Entrepreneurship Competitions and Club Activities

Number	Item
B1	I often participate in entrepreneurship competitions.
B2	I often participate in various club activities.

Source: Questionnaire on Students majoring in fashion design' Willingness to Start a Business

Part C: Satisfaction Towards Entrepreneurship Education

Part C assesses the degree of satisfaction among students concerning the entrepreneurship education provided by their educational institutions. Adopting a five-point Likert Scale, informed by the advice of academic experts and scholars, this section measures students' satisfaction towards entrepreneurship education of their schools through ten items (C1-C10). The items have been carefully crafted to elicit the students' perceptions of the relevance and impact of entrepreneurship education within the sphere of fashion design major (Table 3).

Table 3. Student Perceptions on the Impact and Relevance of Entrepreneurship Education in Fashion Design Major

Number	Item
C1	I think there is a close connection between professional courses and entrepreneurship courses.
C2	The entrepreneurship education courses provided by the school are very helpful for my professional development.

continued on following page

Table 3. Continued

Number	Item
C3	The entrepreneurship education courses at my school can help me improve my entrepreneurial abilities.
C4	The entrepreneurship guidance and resources provided by the school are very helpful for my business plans.
C5	I believe the school's entrepreneurship education can help me understand the market demand in the fashion industry.
C6	The entrepreneurship courses provided by the school are highly relevant to my major.
C7	During my time at school, I feel that my teachers and classmates have provided enough support and help for my business plans.
C8	The school provides us with many practice opportunities to better understand the entrepreneurial environment.
C9	The teaching methods and content of entrepreneurship education at my school meet my expectations.
C10	I believe that the entrepreneurship education at my school will have a positive impact on my future career development.

Source: Questionnaire on Fashion Design Students' Willingness to Start a Business

Part D: Career-Exploring Willingness

Part D is designed, drawing inspiration from the measurement scale proposed by Macro van Gelderen et al. (2006), with the aim to delve into the respondents' willingness to forge a career in the relevant field. The framework for this section is chiefly constructed based on the research carried out by Xu Shuying (2002), endorsing the perspective that subjective evaluations carry a considerable weightage and can contribute meaningful insights.

Table 4. Assessment of Entrepreneurial Intent and Feasibility among Students Majoring in Fashion Design

Number	Item
D1	Considering my current situation and various constraints (e.g., lack of funds), I would still choose to start my own business.
D2	What do you think is the possibility of you starting a business in the next 5 years?

Source: Questionnaire on Fashion Design Students' Willingness to Start a Business

4.4 Data Analysis

The quantitative data from the survey were analyzed by Statistical Package for the Social Sciences (SPSS). Descriptive statistics provided an overview of the trends, while inferential statistics, including regression analysis, were used to determine the relationship between the level of integration in education and students' entrepreneurial intentions.

Synergizing Fashion Design and Entrepreneurship Education

4.4.1 Data Analysis and Results

This chapter presents an analysis of the current integration of fashion design and innovative entrepreneurship education, informed by a comprehensive survey conducted at Shandong Technology Vocational College. The survey targeted 376 students and graduates from the Fashion Design program spanning seven years (2017-2023), focusing on the extent of integration between students' professional education and entrepreneurship training and its impact on their entrepreneurial intentions.

4.4.2 Status Quo Analysis

The survey results reveal varying levels of entrepreneurial intention among different cohorts. Notably, the 2017 cohort displayed the lowest entrepreneurial intention, with a slight increase observed in the 2018 cohort. A significant increase of nearly 5% in entrepreneurial intention was noted in the 2019 cohort, attributed to factors such as the students' socioeconomic background, including a higher proportion coming from affluent regions of China and having family members who are entrepreneurs.

The 2020 cohort maintained similar levels of entrepreneurial intention as the 2019 cohort, despite less favorable family entrepreneurial backgrounds. However, this cohort benefited from the college's increased emphasis on innovation and entrepreneurship competitions, including dedicated guidance courses for these competitions. This shift highlights the positive impact of targeted entrepreneurship courses on students' entrepreneurial intentions.

4.4.3 SPSS Analysis and Graphical Representation

Satisfaction in Entrepreneurship Education

The Symbiotic Relationship Theory guided the analysis of satisfaction levels within entrepreneurship education. Findings indicate a strong link between course content satisfaction and entrepreneurial skill development, emphasizing the importance of integrating practical experiences into the curriculum.

Unveiling Complex Interplays: An Exhaustive Correlation Analysis of Satisfaction Dimensions within Entrepreneurship Education in Part C

This section hinges on the robust statistical results showcased in Table 4.6. The table encapsulates an intensive Pearson correlation analysis, scrutinizing variables $C1$ through $C5$ and elucidating the relationships they share with the parameters $E1$ and $E2$.

The defined variables are as follows:

C1: Integration of Professional and Entrepreneurship Education
C2: Entrepreneurship Education's Role in Professional Growth
C3: Boosting Entrepreneurial Skills through Education
C4: School Support in Entrepreneurial Endeavors
C5: Market Insights via Entrepreneurship Education
C6: Major-Relevant Entrepreneurship Education
C7: Academic Support for Business Ventures
C8: Practical Insights into Entrepreneurial Environment
C9: Matching Expectations in Entrepreneurship Education
C10: Career Benefits from Entrepreneurship Education.

The Pearson correlation coefficient, renowned for its efficacy in capturing the strength and direction of linear relationships between variables, serves as the key instrument for this analysis.

Upon examining the data in Table 4.6, it is manifest that a significant correlation exists between each pair of variables — C1 through C10 with E1 and E2. The double asterisks following the coefficient values denote a significance level of less than 0.01, solidifying the statistical validity of these findings.

Table 5. Pearson Correlation on C1, C2, C3, C4, C5 - Standard Format

C1	C2	C3	C4	C5
0.707**	0.718**	0.718**	0.713**	0.721**
0.834**	0.844**	0.846**	0.836**	0.853**

Note: * $p<0.05$ ** $p<0.01$
C1: Integration of Professional and Entrepreneurship Education
C2: Entrepreneurship Education's Role in Professional Growth
C3: Boosting Entrepreneurial Skills through Education
C4: School Support in Entrepreneurial Endeavors
C5: Market Insights via Entrepreneurship Education
Source: The data was obtained by using SPSS.

Examining these relationships at a more nuanced level reveals that all variables from C1 to C10 exhibit a potent positive correlation with both D1 and D2. The magnitude of these correlations is captured through the coefficient values, all of which are comfortably above the 0.7 mark. This implies strong positive correlations, signifying that improvements in the areas denoted by C1 through C10 are associated with favorable shifts in both D1 and D2. For a visually concise rendition of these significant interrelationships between D1, D2, and C1-C10, readers may refer to Figure 1.

Figure 1. Significance Between D1, D2, C1-C10

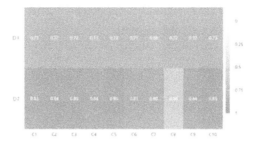

This thorough correlation analysis unravels the intricate interdependencies that exist among these satisfaction components within entrepreneurship education. It does not merely demystify the complex relationships, but significantly elevates the depth of understanding of the underlying dynamics. The insights garnered herein are invaluable, providing academia and industry practitioners with a refined comprehension of the multifaceted nature of satisfaction within entrepreneurship education. This study, therefore, represents a significant stride in enriching the existing literature and paves the way for further investigations in this realm.

Figure 2. Trends in Entrepreneurial Intentions

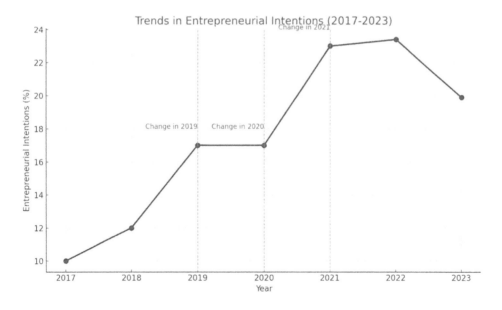

The figure 2 above visually represents the trends in entrepreneurial intentions among students majoring in fashion design at Shandong Technology Vocational College from 2017 to 2023. This trend is marked by significant changes in students' entrepreneurial intentions over these years.

4.5 Key Observations

A steady increase in entrepreneurial intentions is observed from 2017, with a notable rise in 2019.

In 2019, a nearly 5% increase in entrepreneurial intentions corresponds to students from more affluent backgrounds and with family influences.

The years 2020 and 2021 show a stabilization and then a significant rise in entrepreneurial intentions. This aligns with the introduction of specialized entrepreneurship courses and an increased emphasis on innovation and entrepreneurship competitions.

The slight increase in 2022 and the subsequent decline in 2023 are indicative of the external economic environment's impact, suggesting a need for curricula that adapt to market conditions and build entrepreneurial confidence.

4.6 Results

The survey underscores the strengths of integrating specific entrepreneurship courses, such as "Market Marketing" and "Beauty Store Management and Operation," into the fashion design curriculum. The 2021 cohort exhibited an 11% increase in entrepreneurial intention compared to the 2017-2018 cohorts and a 6% increase compared to the 2019-2020 cohorts. This rise is primarily attributed to the introduction of professional entrepreneurship courses, effectively blending entrepreneurship training with fashion design education.

The 2022 cohort showed a marginal increase of 0.4% in entrepreneurial intention over the 2021 cohort, indicating a stabilization of the trend. However, the 2023 cohort experienced a 3.5% decrease in entrepreneurial intention, attributed to a lack of market confidence influenced by the economic environment in China. This finding suggests the need for integrating modules in the curriculum that build entrepreneurial confidence, keeping pace with market demands and external economic factors.

4.7 Conclusion

This analysis of the integration of fashion design and entrepreneurship education at Shandong Technology Vocational College highlights the critical role of specialized entrepreneurship courses in enhancing students' entrepreneurial intentions. The findings demonstrate the need for curricula that not only equip students with the requisite professional skills in fashion design but also enhance entrepreneurial capabilities and confidence, adapting to both internal educational demands and external economic conditions. The evolution of this integration over time, as evidenced by the survey data, provides valuable insights for future curriculum development in fashion design education.

5. DISCUSSION, LIMITATIONS, AND FUTURE RESEARCH

5.1 Discussion

This research has explored the strategic pathways and frameworks necessary for integrating professional and entrepreneurial education in fashion design, underpinned by theories such as Ecological Theory and Competency-Based Theory and corroborated by empirical findings. The proposed synergistic curriculum design, inspired by the symbiosis concept and the DNA double helix structure, aims to intertwine professional and entrepreneurial courses effectively. This approach, according to Eltanahy et al. (2020), is expected to enrich the learning experience by ensuring that both sets of courses are mutually enhancing. The incorporation of practical skills with business acumen, while being adaptable to various socio-economic backgrounds and external economic environments, is pivotal.

The integration of fashion design with innovative entrepreneurship education necessitates a framework that not only fosters creativity and technical proficiency but also instills a robust entrepreneurial ethos among students. The references by Rahayu (2024), Dana et al. (2024), and others underscore the importance of a curriculum that embraces the complexities of the modern fashion industry, highlighting the role of environmental sustainability, social responsibility, and digital innovation.

The implementation framework further delineates course settings and content, teaching methodologies, student assessment, and the necessity for a continuously evolving curriculum. The integration of theory and practice, as well as the continuous adaptation of the curriculum in response to changing market needs and entrepreneurial intentions, are essential components of this educational model.

In the present discourse, the depiction of the double helix model, serving as a pivotal illustration of the intricate amalgamation of innovation and entrepreneurship education with disciplinary education, is derived from the seminal work by Yin Guojun, Lu Song, and Chen Jinsong. Their scholarly investigation and application of the double helix paradigm at Zhejiang University elucidates the essential interplay between these domains of educational pursuit. This conceptual framework and its illustrative representation are extensively elaborated upon in their article,

'Exploration and Practice of the Double Helix Model for the Deep Integration of Innovation and Entrepreneurship Education with Professional Education: A Case Study of Zhejiang University,' available in the Contemporary Educational Forum.

Figure 3. Implementation Framework

(Source: Yin, G., Lu, S., & Chen, J. (2024)

5.2 Limitations and Future Research

While this study provides a comprehensive overview and insightful recommendations, it is not without limitations. The primary constraint lies in its scope, being confined to a single educational institution, which may impact the generalizability of the findings. Future research should expand the scope to study diverse educational settings in different geographic locations, enhancing the validity and applicability of the results.

The rapidly evolving nature of the fashion industry, coupled with continuous technological advancements, necessitates ongoing research in this field. Future studies should focus on the impact of specific educational interventions on entrepreneurial success post-graduation and explore how digital advancements can be integrated to enhance educational outcomes further. Such research would contribute significantly to the dynamic field of fashion design and entrepreneurship education.

5.3 Conclusion

In conclusion, this study underscores the critical importance of integrating fashion design with innovative entrepreneurship education. The findings and recommendations propose a cohesive framework designed to equip students with essential skills and knowledge, preparing them for the complexities of the modern fashion industry. The study highlights the need for educational models to evolve in tandem with industry developments, thereby preparing a generation of fashion professionals who are adept, innovative, and responsive to the dynamic nature of their field. The integration of these educational domains is not just a theoretical ideal but a practical necessity to develop a generation of skilled, creative, and adaptable professionals in the ever-evolving fashion industry.

Author Note

The authors of this publication declare there are no competing interests. This research received no specific grant from any funding agency in the public, commercial, or not-for-profit sectors. Funding for this research was covered by the author(s) of the article.

Data Availability Statement

The data supporting the findings of this study are openly available in the article and its supplementary materials. For further inquiries or requests regarding the data, readers are encouraged to contact the corresponding author(s).

Author Contributions

This research was collaboratively designed and conceptualized by two authors, they were primarily responsible for conducting a review of the relevant literature and developing the conceptual model integral to the study, and undertook the statistical analysis and spearheaded the writing of the initial manuscript draft. All authors actively participated in revising the manuscript, ensuring thorough reading and approval of the final version before submission. This collective effort underscores the multidisciplinary nature of the research and the diverse contributions of each author to the study's successful completion.

REFERENCES

Amatullo, M., Boyer, B., May, J., & Shea, A. (Eds.). (2021). *Design for social innovation: Case studies from around the world*. Routledge. 10.4324/9781003021360

Attaran, S., Attaran, M., & Celik, B. G. (2024). Digital Twins and Industrial Internet of Things: Uncovering operational intelligence in industry 4.0. *Decision Analytics Journal*, 100398.

Bronfenbrenner, U. (1979). *The ecology of human development: Experiments by nature and design*. Harvard University Press. 10.4159/9780674028845

Camacho, G. (2022). Sustainable fashion: The case of a Mexican BCorp. In *Fashion Marketing in Emerging Economies Volume I: Brand, Consumer and Sustainability Perspectives* (pp. 237-263). Cham: Springer International Publishing.

Ceyhan, P., Haklıdır, E. A., & Tellez, F. A. (2022). Rethinking the design studio curriculum through adaptive and transformative strategies and acts: Cross-cultural reflections. *Journal of Design. Business & Society*, 9(1), 79–101.

Chandler, D. (2022). *Strategic corporate social responsibility: Sustainable value creation*. Sage Publications.

Clarke, L. W. (2020). Walk a day in my shoes: Cultivating cross-cultural understanding through digital literacy. *The Reading Teacher*, 73(5), 662–665. 10.1002/trtr.1890

Dana, L. P., Boardman, R., Salamzadeh, A., Pereira, V., & Brandstrup, M. (2024). *Fashion and environmental sustainability: Entrepreneurship, innovation, and technology*. De Gruyter.

Dumitru, D., & Halpern, D. F. (2023). Critical Thinking: Creating Job-Proof Skills for the Future of Work. *Journal of Intelligence*, 11(10), 194. 10.3390/jintelligence11100019437888426

Eltanahy, M., Forawi, S., & Mansour, N. (2020). Incorporating entrepreneurial practices into STEM education: Development of interdisciplinary E-STEM model in high school in the United Arab Emirates. *Thinking Skills and Creativity*, 37, 100697. 10.1016/j.tsc.2020.100697

García-Morales, V. J., Martín-Rojas, R., & Garde-Sánchez, R. (2020). How to encourage social entrepreneurship action? Using Web 2.0 technologies in higher education institutions. *Journal of Business Ethics*, 161(2), 329–350. 10.1007/s10551-019-04216-6

Gazzola, P., Pavione, E., Pezzetti, R., & Grechi, D. (2020). Trends in the fashion industry. The perception of sustainability and circular economy: A gender/generation quantitative approach. *Sustainability (Basel)*, 12(7), 2809. 10.3390/su12072809

González-Pérez, L. I., & Ramírez-Montoya, M. S. (2022). Components of Education 4.0 in 21st century skills frameworks: Systematic review. *Sustainability (Basel)*, 14(3), 1493. 10.3390/su14031493

Hsu, C. Y., & Wu, T. T. (2023). Application of Business Simulation Games in Flipped Classrooms to Facilitate Student Engagement and Higher-Order Thinking Skills for Sustainable Learning Practices. *Sustainability (Basel)*, 15(24), 16867. 10.3390/su152416867

Khan, S. A., Sharma, P. P., & Thoudam, P. (2019). Role of attitude and entrepreneurship education towards entrepreneurial orientation among business students of Bhutan. *International Journal of Recent Technology and Engineering*, 8(2), 335–342. 10.35940/ijrte.C1072.1083S19

Magd, H., & Khan, S. A. (2022). Strategic framework for entrepreneurship education in promoting social entrepreneurship in GCC countries during and post COVID-19. In Magd, H., Singh, D., Syed, R., & Spicer, D. (Eds.), *International perspectives on value creation and sustainability through social entrepreneurship* (pp. 61–75). IGI Global. 10.4018/978-1-6684-4666-9.ch004

Magd, H., Khan, S. A., & Bhuyan, U. (2022). Social entrepreneurship intentions among business students in Oman. In Magd, H., Singh, D., Syed, R., & Spicer, D. (Eds.), *International perspectives on value creation and sustainability through social entrepreneurship* (pp. 76–93). IGI Global. 10.4018/978-1-6684-4666-9.ch005

Murzyn-Kupisz, M., & Hołuj, D. (2021). Fashion design education and sustainability: Towards an equilibrium between craftsmanship and artistic and business skills? *Education Sciences*, 11(9), 531. 10.3390/educsci11090531

Oliveira, L., & Cardoso, E. L. (2021). A project-based learning approach to promote innovation and academic entrepreneurship in a master's degree in food engineering. *Journal of Food Science Education*, 20(4), 120–129. 10.1111/1541-4329.12230

Peng, F., & Kueh, C. (2022). Integration of design thinking with cultural intelligence in higher education for a socially complex environment. *International Journal of Art & Design Education*, 41(2), 341–354. 10.1111/jade.12402

Perkmann, M., Salandra, R., Tartari, V., McKelvey, M., & Hughes, A. (2021). Academic engagement: A review of the literature 2011-2019. *Research Policy*, 50(1), 104114. 10.1016/j.respol.2020.104114

Qwelane, M. J. (2022). *An investigation of how contemporary South African fashion designers communicate creative brand storytelling and brand aesthetics* (Doctoral dissertation, The IIE).

Rahayu, I. (2024, February). Entrepreneurial behavior of bachelor students in fashion education, Surabaya State University. In *5th Vocational Education International Conference (VEIC-5 2023)* (pp. 904-909). Atlantis Press.

Ratten, V., & Jones, P. (2021). Entrepreneurship and management education: Exploring trends and gaps. *International Journal of Management Education*, 19(1), 100431. 10.1016/j.ijme.2020.100431

Ratten, V., & Usmanij, P. (2021). Entrepreneurship education: Time for a change in research direction? *International Journal of Management Education*, 19(1), 100367. 10.1016/j.ijme.2020.100367

Roy, M. (2019). Elevating services: Services trade policy, WTO commitments, and their role in economic development and trade integration. *Journal of World Trade*, 53(6).

Saxena, C., Khatri, B., & Khan, S. A. (2023). Factors hindering women entrepreneurs' access to institutional finance: An empirical study from the banker perspective. In Gupta, V. (Ed.), *Fostering global entrepreneurship through business model innovation* (pp. 101–114). IGI Global. 10.4018/978-1-6684-6975-0.ch004

Sharma, Y., Suri, A., Sijariya, R., & Jindal, L. (2023). Role of education 4.0 in innovative curriculum practices and digital literacy–A bibliometric approach. *E-Learning and Digital Media*. 10.1177/20427530231221073

Short, K. G. (2023). A curriculum that is intercultural. In *Teaching Globally* (pp. 3–24). Routledge. 10.4324/9781032682693-2

Song, M. J. (2021). Teacher professional development in integrating digital fabrication technologies into teaching and learning. *Educational Media International*, 58(4), 317–334. 10.1080/09523987.2021.1989766

Trivers, I. R. (2017). *Mobilizing the High Line* (Doctoral dissertation, University of Michigan).

Yin, G., Lu, S., & Chen, J. (2024). Exploration and Practice of the Double Helix Model for the Deep Integration of Innovation and Entrepreneurship Education with Professional Education: A Case Study of Zhejiang University. Contemporary Educational Forum. 10.13694/j.cnki.ddjylt.20240008.001

Chapter 16
The Impact of Value Co-Creation of the NAIFEST Exhibition on the Perceived Value of INDOBUILDTECH 2022 Exhibitors:
The Dynamic Interaction of DART Model on Value Co-Creation Towards Customer Perceived Value

Sakanti Sasri
https://orcid.org/0000-0003-4481-8587
University of Indonesia, Indonesia

Retno Kusumastuti
University of Indonesia, Indonesia

ABSTRACT

This research study discusses the impact of NAIFEST exhibition co-creation value on the perceived value of IndoBuildTech 2022 exhibitors. Co-creation is a strategy made to provide easy access for IndoBuildTech exhibitors to meet and interact with SME architects who are one of the main targets of IndoBuildTech expo visitors. Authors use the concept of the DART framework (dialogue, access, risk assessment,

DOI: 10.4018/979-8-3693-3518-5.ch016

and transparency) as a dimension of value co-creation to determine the factors that affect the perceived value of IndoBuildTech 2022 exhibitors with price and quality dimensions. The findings in this study prove that there is an impact of the DART dimension that affects the value of the co-creation of the NAIFEST exhibition on the perceived quality of IndoBuildTech 2022 exhibitors. Meanwhile, the risk assessment dimension consistently does not affect the co-creation value of the NAIFEST exhibition on the perceived price and quality of IndoBuildTech 2022 exhibitors.

1. INTRODUCTION

The global market has experienced significant growth in the past decade, leading to increased competition among businesses in various industries. In the MICE industry, this growth has had a profound impact on the dynamics between businesses (Samiee, 2008). As businesses compete for a larger share of the market, they are compelled to constantly innovate and improve their offerings to stay ahead of their competitors. This has resulted in a greater emphasis on the use of technology and digital platforms to reach a wider audience, improve customer relationships, and retain existing customers. In addition, the growing competition has created a need for destination management organizations in the MICE industry to invest in innovation (Liew-Tsonis & Cheuk, 2012). Unless they can secure a competitive advantage through innovative approaches in terms of their destinations or the products they offer, these organizations will face uncertainty and instability. Furthermore, the MICE industry must also be proactive in anticipating changes in the global tourism market to maintain their market share. Failure to adapt and embrace globalisation can result in a loss of competitiveness and market share. The increasing global competition has also influenced the relationships between small and medium-sized tourism enterprises and large companies in the MICE industry (Samiee, 2008). Smaller businesses may fear the dominance and influence of larger companies, while larger companies must also adapt to meet consumer demands for universal appeal and adaptability to succeed in the global marketplace. Moreover, with the rapid digitization and globalization across industries, small and medium-sized enterprises in the MICE industry have turned to social media applications to expand their reach and engage with a larger audience. They utilize these platforms to improve their relationship with potential customers and retain existing ones. Moreover, the rapid growth of global business activities and the emergence of new competitors have intensified global competition in the MICE industry. This heightened competition has led to a greater focus on the use of electronic distribution channels, such as the Internet, to represent developing countries and new markets on an equal footing in the global market (Ibarnia et al., 2020). In today's highly competitive global market, the MICE industry must constantly innovate and adapt to changes in order to maintain their market share. In addition, the evolution of information and communication technology has disrupted the traditional tourism distribution channel, leading to new processes such as reintermediation, disintermediation, and hypermediation. Thus, intermediary companies in the MICE industry have invested in innovative processes and products to achieve revenue growth and improve profitability. They understand that innovation is costly and time-consuming, but also necessary for maintaining their competitive edge.

As a result of the phenomenon that occurs in conditions of increasingly rapid and tight global competition, it influences the growth and development of the MICE (Meeting, Incentive, Conference & Exhibition) business industry both globally and in Indonesia. The MICE industry is a type of tourism that consists of a large group, usually carefully planned, and for a specific purpose. MICE service providers are inextricably linked to the tourist industry's supply chain as well as other industry sectors. Numerous companies, industries, and parties are constantly involved in the planning of MICE events; as a result, there is a multiplier effect that affects numerous parties and increases the ensuing economic impact (Kesrul, 2004). Indonesia's exhibition industry is expanding quickly as well. The growing number of professional exhibition organizing businesses (PEO) in Indonesia serves as evidence of this.

Figure 1. Chart of Members of the Indonesian Exhibition Entrepreneurs Association

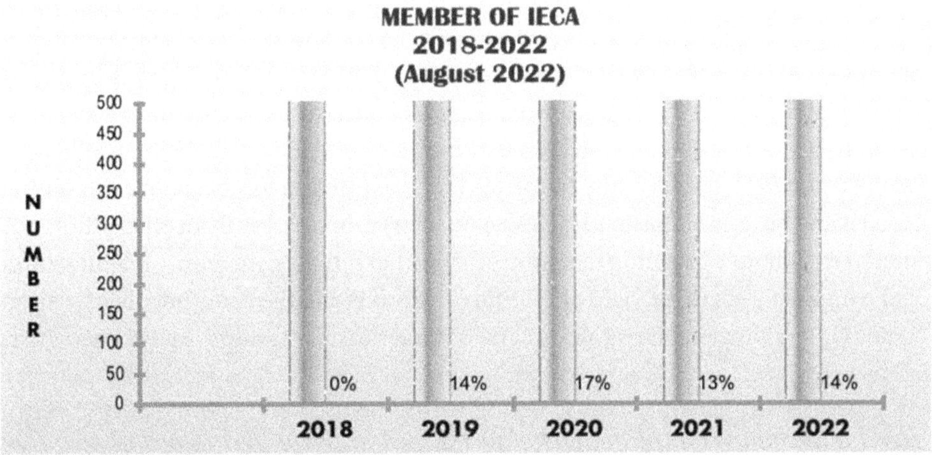

Source: ASPERAPI August 2022 Statistical Data

Based on the data in Figure 1.1 above, every year ASPERAPI (Indonesian Exhibition Entrepreneurs Association) experiences an increase in the number of registered members. In 2019 the number of MICE service entrepreneurs increased by 14% from the previous year, and even in 2020, which was during the pandemic, ASPERAPI members increased by 17%. In 2021 it will increase 13% and in 2022 it will be 14%. This shows that every year ASPERAPI receives applications for new members from MICE service entrepreneurs. So, from this data it is identified that every year there is a growth of MICE companies in Indonesia which continues to grow. Along with this growth, MICE service entrepreneurs, especially PEOs, are competing to create and organize exhibition activities in accordance with business sector targets that are considered to have opportunities. The impact of this phenomenon resulted in the emergence of similar or similar exhibition activities which then created competition between PEO actors. The impact of this competition is that PEO actors compete from the aspect of exhibitors and exhibition visitors. These two things are two essential aspects that influence the success of an exhibition. In essence, in organizing an exhibition, the success or success achieved must be felt by all parties involved, namely: success for Exhibition Visitors (Visitors), success for Exhibitors (Participants), success for Organizers (Organizer) and success for Executors (Technical Organizers) (Nasution & Propertiu, 2014).

PT Debindo International Trade Exhibition (Debindo-ITE) as organizer of the Indonesia Building Technology (IndoBuildTech) exhibition. This exhibition has been held annually since 2002. To date, the IndoBuildTech exhibition can be said to be the largest and most comprehensive exhibition specifically in the field of architecture, building materials and interiors in Indonesia. This exhibition has an area of ± 50,000 square meters and more than 250 brands participated in this exhibition and were able to attract more than 50,000 visitors during the 5 days of the exhibition. With the IndoBuildTech exhibition's good reputation and excellence in competition for 2 decades, the IndoBuildTech exhibition has been able to continue to exist and be held consistently. However, many competitors from other PEOs hold similar exhibitions targeting the same profile of exhibitors, including manufacturers and manufacturers in the field of building materials and the same profile of visitors, including architects, interior designers, contractors, distributors and homeowners.

Table 1. Asperapi Data for Building Materials, Architectural & Interior Exhibitions

No.	Events	Product Profile	Organizer
1.	Kitchen + Bathroom Indonesia	Kitchen and Bathroom products and accessories	Wahana Kemalaniaga Makmur

continued on following page

Table 1. Continued

No.	Events	Product Profile	Organizer
2.	ARCH:ID	Architectural, Building Materials Conference & Exhibition	CIS Exhibition
3.	Megabuild 2022	Building Material, Architectural & Interior	Panorama Media
4.	Electric & Power Indonesia, Building Systems & Automation	Energy, Electric, Power, Distribution, Renewable Energy, Energy Efficiency, Electrical Equipment, Building Systems Automation, Facility Management	Pamerindo Indonesia
5.	Construction Indonesia	Construction Structure, Building Technology, Engineering, Procurement & Equipment	The Ministry of Public Works and Public Housing
6.	Refrigeration & HVAC Indonesia (RHVAC) in conjunction with Door Window Façade (DWF) and Solar & Energy Storage Indonesia (SESI)	Refrigeration, Heating, Ventilation, Air Conditioning and Energy Efficient Technology.	Pelita Promo Internusa (PPI)
7.	Pasific Coating Show Indonesia (PCS)	Paintings, Coatings, Adhesives, Sealants and Chemicals	Nurnberg Messe & PT. Pelita Promo Internusa (PPI)
8.	INDOBUILDTECH Expo (Indonesia Building Technology Expo) – IBT	Building Material, Architectural & Interior	Debindo-ITE
9	HOMEDEC	Home Interior, Furniture, Electronics, Appliances, Decoration	CIS Exhibition

Source: ASPERAPI Data Exhibition 2022

Based on the table data above, it can be seen that there are 10 companies PEO which organizes building materials, architectural and interior exhibitions and become part of the IndoBuildTech exhibition competitors. This is also the case giving rise to competition between PEO actors as exhibition organizers in their efforts seize the targeted market to achieve quality exhibition activities and according to expectations. According to Esti & Suryani (2008) in the journal Mulyana & Sutapa (2015) currently The global market requires a competitive basis that does not only refer to competition in price and quality, but also in terms of innovation, technology, creativity and imagination (Mulyana & Sutapa, 2015). The goal of this effort is to improve the quality and quality of the products and services offered, so that they can provide offering greater value for products to consumers as the last chain of a product or service offered. Factors considered important for creating a successful advantage or good competitive advantage is necessary innovation in products, markets and services.

Competitive advantage shows a company acting to be superior to its competitors the same business industry (Hasan, 2009). A good competitive advantage can be achieved produce good business performance as well (Russell & Millar, 2014). Therefore, every PEO needs to have a competitive advantage in order to be able to compete within presenting high quality exhibition products. To become a company that is dynamic in competition, PEO needs expertise in reading opportunities and opportunities. By understanding the opportunities and advantages they have can make it easier to innovate. Innovation that occurs within a company requires investment in meeting quality new services and products in order to achieve competitive advantage (Najafi-Tavani et al., 2018). The current era of globalization is an era that presents continuity and synergy through connectivity (João Leitão & Ken Riopelle, 2018). Therefore, collaborative choice is the most ideal idea to utilize the connectivity. Collaboration between teams internally creates efforts innovation and also collaboration between external networks or external parties able to contribute to the development of the company. Collaboration is possible placing stakeholder positions more precisely (Saleh & Hanafi, 2020). Therefore, every MICE service business, especially in the exhibition sector, is very important in building collaboration or cooperation involving many stakeholders. Debindo-ITE realizes the importance of collaboration in quality improvement efforts and the quality of the IndoBuildTech exhibition. To realize competitive advantage IndoBuildTech exhibition is able to compete with similar exhibitions, something is needed innovation that can optimize the two important aspects of the exhibition, namely participants and exhibition visitors.

Center of Innovation and Collaboration (CIC) PPM Management in the 5th period this past year conducted research that showed that most changes experienced by companies in Indonesia through innovation. These innovations include product, organizational, marketing and innovation process. The CIC PPM Coordinator explained the results of the survey and research conducted As much as 80% of the purpose of innovation is to increase competitiveness in global market (Saksono, 2019). Debindo-ITE chose to collaborate in efforts to produce innovation new products through a co-creation process. New product innovation created requires resources that are competent enough according to their field, so they are capable create adequate co-creation . The concept of co-creation is a form cooperation or collaboration between companies (organizations) and internal consumers produce new values or advantages (Prahalad & Ramaswamy, 2004). Industry exhibitions, as a service system, have great potential in realizing profits of shared value creation according to its business network structure (Jin et al.,2012). By utilizing co-creation from external parties, especially consumers can create new product innovations. Expectations from the co-creation concept. This construction can strengthen the synergy of the two aspects so that they are interdependent and creating cross benefit value. In general, exhibition activities can be focused based on the target market visitors, namely B2B (Business to Business), B2C (Business to Consumer), and B2G (Business to Government).

The Impact of Value Co-Creation of the NAIFEST Exhibition

Based on post-show report data from the IndoBuildTech exhibition recently reported that there were 13,405 people who had the profession of architect of the total visitors, namely 56,829. This is followed by people who own it interior designer profession as many as 10,233 people, 7,649 people with contractor profession, and 4,710 for general visitors visiting the exhibition IndoBuildTech. So, it can be concluded from this data that visitors IndoBuildTech is dominated by architects, namely belonging to the B2B market.

This is the reason Debindo-ITE focuses on strengthening cooperation network through collaboration with SME architects through the Host program Partner Program or HPP. HPP is a form of collaborative program that was built along with architects as one of the main targets for exhibition visitors IndoBuildTech. This can also be said to be the strategy carried out by Debindo-ITE as the organizer with the aim of mutual symbiosis, in which each party benefit from this collaboration program. HPP or Host Partner Program created to enrich the quality of visitors to the IndoBuildTech exhibition where SME architects are one of the main targets for visitors to the expo. Debindo-ITE as the organizer hopes that architects will not play a role as a visitor who attends the exhibition only, but also becomes part of it IndoBuildTech exhibition activity partner. Debindo-ITE realizes by involving SME architects who are one of the main targets for exhibition visitors as partners can realize synergy and strengthen the chain network of exhibition activities IndoBuildTech.

Relationship between co-creation produced between the organizer, Debindo-ITE and the SME architect as profiles of IndoBuildTech exhibition visitors espoused to collaborate. This new product innovation is a co-creation which has the main goal of providing value creation towards exhibitors as the main consumers of the IndoBuildTech exhibition. Basically co-creation has the creation of value that can be felt back consumers (Prahalad & Ramaswamy, 2004). In this study the main consumers are referred to are IndoBuildTech exhibitors, not general visitors to the exhibition other. Other general visitors are also consumers of the exhibition IndoBuildTech, but no commercial value or price perception is created with other general visitors. This is due to exhibition visitors IndoBuildTech is free of charge when attending the IndoBuildTech exhibition. Meanwhile, IndoBuildTech exhibitors are companies from the building materials sector, interior products, and architecture. IndoBuildTech exhibitors are main consumers who have commercial value because every company that joining and registering as an exhibitor at the IndoBuildTech exhibition is subject with a fee participation. Co-creation has value or value obtained from activities and interwoven experiences. Collaborative activities and creativity created by companies and consumers to produce a new innovation is form of value co-creation (Prahalad & Ramaswamy, 2004).

Value co-creation is the result of a process created from co-creation (Prahalad & Ramaswamy, 2004). In this research case study, one of the product innovations was produced in co-creation process through HPP, namely the National Architecture Installation Festival (NAIFEST). The following is a counter-performance of the agreement between architect with Debindo-ITE as organizer with a co-creation approach:

Table 2. HPP Proposals – Value Contrast of Architect & Organizer Collaboration

Host Partner Program Architect	PEO Benefits

1. Benefits will be given a time slot in our business program to carry out activities in the form of discussions as mentioned above. Host Partners can choose any topic they want to discuss with the audience. We are willing to help facilitate Host Partner needs related to your business program.
2. At IndoBuildTech Expo 2022, our team will also hold several programs. Host Partners can choose any program they want to participate in as one of the speakers or panelists. We will encourage Host Partners to become part of the IndoBuildTech business program so that audiences can meet and discuss directly with experts.
3. Opportunity to follow IndoBuildTech Awards to strengthen networking between valuable stakeholders and among participating companies, which is of course, it can have a positive impact on the progress of industrial development in the future.
4. Host Partner Card:
   - Access to get an exclusive registration path (fast track).
   - Access to the Architect's Lounge.
   - Free show catalogue
   - Free admission to all business programs
	1. Build Architecture Installation as the part of National Architecture Installation Festival in the space provided with design and content as entertaining and interactive as possible to attract visitors and gain exposures.
	2. Post these following promo campaign materials:
	• Email containing IndoBuildTech poster to be blasted to Host Partner's email database.
	• IndoBuildTech's Pre-Show and Post-Show Video to be posted on Host Partner's social media.
	• Posters and captions (subject to be edited) mentioning IndoBuildTech and Debindo ITE to be posted on Host Partner's social media.
	• Record Host Partner's activities during the expo such as via instagram story, facebook live, etc.
	• Create instagram highlights with stories containing the activities at IndoBuildTech Expo 2024.
	3. Give testimonies regarding IndoBuildTech Expo 2024 and the technologies used in architecture industry.
	4. Conduct a design consultation for the visitors in need and not forgetting to post this activity as well.
	5. Share your insights and knowledge in one or more IndoBuildTech's business programs as forum participant or panelists.
	6. Invite friends, colleagues and other talented professionals with interests in building, architecture, construction, interior design and technology to IndoBuildTech Expo 2024.

Source: HPP Proposal – Debindo-ITE

Based on the agreement or counter-performance table above, every SME architect who is a member of HPP has benefits and opportunities to participate in the National Architectural Installation Festival (NAIFEST) installation exhibition. NAIFEST is part of a series of activities at the IndoBuildTech exhibition and forms

the result of product innovation from collaboration between exhibition organizers IndoBuildTech, namely Debindo-ITE with SME architects who are members of HPP. Exhibition NAIFEST was held simultaneously and coincided with the IndoBuildTech exhibition which contains the installation works of architects, some of whom collaborated with product brands from IndoBuildTech 2022 exhibitors. The NAIFEST exhibition was created as supporting content as well as attractions in organizing the IndoBuildTech expo 2022. IndoBuildTech expo 2022 is a trade show that is being held with the use of hall area 5 to hall 10 area at the ICE BSD City venue, Tangerang. Meanwhile, the NAIFEST exhibition was held using part of the area hall 10 at the IndoBuildTech exhibition. SME Architects included in the exhibition NAIFEST no longer act as regular visitor to the exhibition, but also as exhibitors at the NAIFEST exhibition. The NAIFEST exhibition is inside IndoBuildTech exhibition, therefore both IndoBuildTech exhibition exhibitors and also architects who are participants of the NAIFEST exhibition can have the opportunity greater opportunity to interact and communicate. The benefits of the NAIFEST exhibition are not only good for the exhibition IndoBuildTech as attraction content for all other general visitors but also for IndoBuildTech exhibitors. For the organizers, the NAIFEST exhibition is a strategy carried out to make the architect's role as a visitor IndoBuildTech exhibition become more than just ordinary visitors. This too shows that there is a relationship between the role of co-evolution for architects as Ordinary visitors turn into strategic partners capable of bringing value benefits for the perception of IndoBuildTech exhibitors. Hence, concept collaboration carried out by Debindo-ITE with architects as the main target exhibition visitors through the value co-creation approach are expected to fulfil expectations and hopes for IndoBuildTech exhibition participants. Value co-creation in the NAIFEST exhibition will be able to provide Perception of value towards IndoBuildTech exhibitors. Based on understanding regarding value co-creation recommended by Prahalad & Ramaswamny (2004) that variables can be measured through the DART model, which consists of dialogue, access, risk assessment and transparency. Exhibitors are the actors who are important in the exhibition activities that they are parties who have an interest in showcase their products. Generally, exhibition participants are charged a registration fee join in the exhibition. For obviously, the registration fee includes the exhibition participants have an expectation of reciprocity that can be obtained from participating in the exhibition activities. Trade fairs aim to provide opportunities for exhibitors to introduce products to a large number of people, get potential new customers, and gain company publicity (Herbig, et al., 1998, Rizana, et al., 2017). Apart from that, by participating in trade shows can obtain information about competitors' or competitors' products and improve their image brand of the company (Kerin Kron, 1987., Rizana, et al., 2017). Trade shows are activities carried out face to face with consumers, So it is hoped that there will be a possibility of communication between visitors with companies, introducing products and encouraging visitors to make purchases (Tanner Jr, 2002., Rizana, et al., 2017). IndoBuildTech exhibitors takes part in the IndoBuildTech exhibition with the aim of being able to introduce their products to visitors and also gain business opportunities new. IndoBuildTech exhibitors have expectations while investing participation fees at the IndoBuildTech exhibition can earn sales through as many potential new projects as possible. Remind of the IndoBuildTech exhibitors are mostly building material manufacture company, by and large of development projects often coming from professionals such as architects, contractors, interior designers, consultants, and developers. This is in line with the most B2B visitors on the IndoBuildTech exhibition is from architects. Therefore collaborate with SME architects are expected to provide opportunities for exhibitors IndoBuildTech gains new business and project possibilities. For this reason, Debindo- ITE as PEO to meet the needs expected by exhibitors IndoBuildTech is by creating a forum for co-creation with architects so that IndoBuildTech exhibitors can easily have access to interact directly during the IndoBuildTech exhibition.

The co-creation forum is through the NAIFEST exhibition. With the participation of IndoBuildTech exhibition participants, there will definitely be a perception expected profit value. Perception of value or perceived value is a perspective customer regarding the quality of service and price of a product offering (Setiawan, 2021). Customer perception of value is a form of profit value between benefits perceived and perceived effort from the value of positive and negative consequences (Payne & Holt, 2001., Rahab, 2015). The expected benefits of perceived value are a combination of a number of attribute elements, namely physical, service and technical support obtained from using the product. Efforts to perceived value consist of all costs incurred in purchasing the products or services used (Setiawan, 2015). Exhibitors' perceptions of value can be defined by two things, namely first in terms of the price they have spent in participating in IndoBuildTech 2022 exhibition.

Then secondly, the quality of service obtained from the NAIFEST exhibition where this exhibition is part of the content of the exhibition IndoBuildTech and held in one IndoBuildTech 2022 exhibition arena. Apart from that, NAIFEST exhibition is still part of the facilities that can be obtained from the exhibition IndoBuildTech which can be experienced by IndoBuildTech exhibitors. Therefore, the perceived value of IndoBuildTech 2022 exhibitors is focused on space price scope of exhibition participation fees and quality of exhibition services NAIFEST.

Based on this background, this research tries to analyze the impact that influences value co-creation in organizing an exhibition. Researchers use the implications of the DART framework model theory with case studies NAIFEST exhibition as a result of co-creation that is and part of IndoBuildTech exhibition. The DART model functions as a tool for knowing improving organizational knowledge processes in value co-creation (Prahalad & Rawasmamy, 2004). The DART framework describes key blocks. The building blocks needed for value creation are: dialogue, access, risk assessment and transparency. On instruments the dialogue will focus the exhibitors' viewpoints and experiences. IndoBuildTech in conducting dialogue and interaction with architects at exhibitions NAIFEST. The access instrument will examine more about easy access visit and obtain information about architects at the NAIFEST exhibition. The risk assessment instrument is the same as for IndoBuildTech exhibitors receive information regarding the benefits and risks that will occur or arise from the presence of the NAIFEST exhibition. Lastly, the instrument of transparency or openness will be examine the openness of information presented by organizers regarding architects NAIFEST exhibition to IndoBuildTech 2022 exhibition participants. Through the framework DART researchers want to know what factors influence and provide impact on value co-creation of the NAIFEST exhibition on perceived value consisting of aspects of price and quality perceptions of IndoBuildTech 2022 exhibitors. The benefits of this research are so that in the future we can find out what the concept of value co-creation has an influence on the profit or perceived value for exhibitors as an important aspect in organizing exhibition. Research related to value co-creation in the tourism sector, especially the sector The MICE industry is still relatively under-researched and still needs development as well as comparisons of different case study objects. This research is still ongoing has relevance to the scientific elements of innovation administration and intrapreneurship. Value co-creation can be said to be a strategy carried out by PEOs creating a new product innovation with the aim of providing superior value for customers (exhibitors). The research object used is content exhibition of architectural installation work at trade shows. Co-creation results from a form of collaboration between the PEO and the SME architect as the chosen strategic partner most visitor profiles at the IndoBuildTech exhibition.

2. MAIN ISSUE

There are many exhibition entrepreneurs (PEOs) who create and organize them similar exhibition activities give rise to increasingly fierce competition from all aspects. Primarily the sales aspect to exhibitors from the profile the same industry and the same visitor aspects, so there is mutual attraction attract stakeholders to support and participate in each exhibition offered. To maintain its position as an exhibition continuous improvement is needed in the quality and quality of services in activities the exhibition. Every PEO needs to have competitive advantage value against exhibitions that are held to be able to compete with similar exhibitions or similar. One effort so that PEO has competitive advantage value is needed innovation in organizing exhibition activities. One of the innovations that can be what PEO does to utilize related parties to cooperate and collaborate to create new innovative service products.

Responding to the many similar exhibitions such as the IndoBuildTech exhibition, Debindo-ITE as the organizer is trying to continue to maintain it IndoBuildTech exhibition that survives in the building materials, architectural and design interior. The strategic efforts carried out by Debindo-ITE are: co-creation approach . The co-creation carried out by Debindo-ITE is through collaboration with SME architects who are one of IndoBuildTech's target visitors the most. The form of implementation of this co-creation is an installation exhibition architect NAIFEST (National Architect Installation Festival) the fruit of the agreement through the Host Partner Program (HPP). NAIFEST exhibition as a form of co-creation.

NAIFEST Exhibition held at the same time and place as the exhibition IndoBuildTech. This is also an attractive content for general visitors and also a participant in the IndoBuildTech exhibition. Both general visitors and exhibitors IndoBuildTech can visit, enjoy and get information about architects who joined the NAIFEST exhibition. General visitors other than architects visiting the NAIFEST exhibition at the IndoBuildTech exhibition is a target for architects who joined the NAIFEST exhibition so they could show off their work and portfolios as well their credibility. Meanwhile, IndoBuildTech exhibitors visited the area The NAIFEST exhibition is an opportunity for IndoBuildTech exhibitors to obtain potential new projects that can be collaborated with architects. From the value co-creation carried out by Debindo-ITE through exhibitions NAIFEST with SME architects is of course still dynamic. Of course, the initial goal of co-creation of the NAIFEST exhibition was created to provide hope within meet the needs of perceived value for IndoBuildTech's exhibitors. Therefore, further research references are needed discusses the impact of value co-creation on the perceived value of consumer.

In this study, researchers will discuss the impact of value co-creation exhibitions NAIFEST on the perceived value of IndoBuildTech 2022 exhibition participants. Focus The research will analyze the impact of factors that influence the value given through the presence of the NAIFEST exhibition as a form of co-creation to IndoBuildTech exhibitors through the DART (dialogue, access, risk) instrument assessment, and transparency). The dialogue instrument will analyze the angle views and experiences of IndoBuildTech exhibitors through interaction activities and their communication with the architects at the NAIFEST exhibition. Access will analyze the ease of experience of visiting IndoBuildTech exhibitors NAIFEST exhibition and obtain information regarding architects who are members of the NAIFEST exhibition. Risk assessment will focus on assessing benefits and risks which is understood and accepted by IndoBuildTech exhibitors NAIFEST exhibition at the IndoBuildTech exhibition. Lastly, transparency is openness to all NAIFEST exhibition information that you wish to obtain IndoBuildTech exhibitor. Of the four DART instruments, researchers will analyze the factors that have the most impact or influence on perception value of IndoBuildTech exhibitors. Instruments used to support the results of the profit value from the perceived value of IndoBuildTech exhibitors are through aspects of price and quality perception.

2.1 Co-Creation

The business environment is rapidly changing and increasingly competitive future collaborative innovation practices. This can be explained by the fact that the process innovation increasingly relies on external knowledge sources and levels of collaboration higher among diverse teams (Ollila et al., 2016). The nature of dynamic innovation and messy collaboration is very resource consuming and often painful, making it more challenging to manage more multi-actors difficult to engage, coordinate, and support in knowledge creation them (Ollila & Yström, 2016). Co-creation is an active, creative and social process, based on collaboration between producers and users, initiated by companies to generate value for customers (Coates, 2009; Patricio et al.,2020). Co-creation emerges from interactions between customers and service providers create added value. The impact of co-creation has encouraged companies to rethink their focus on services and products by engaging customers in the creation of experiences, rather than seeing consumers as just that objects for sale (Harkison, 2018). Co-creation refers to an interactive process involves some form of collaboration between at least two mutual actors profitable and results in value creation for these actors (Frow et al.,2015). Co-creation is a process based on the concept of Service Dominant Logic (SDL), where consumers are not considered strategic targets, but are sources potential power that needs to be involved in the value creation process (Vargo & Lusch, 2004; Kurniawan et al., nd). Consumers can partner with companies to supporting innovative products and services that influence the creation of experiences unforgettable (Chathoth et al., 2016). Co-creation activities begin with changing the consumer's perspective from product-centric to oriented towards experience centric (Ramaswamy & Ozcan, 2018). Therefore, business organizations must reconsider the role consumers to design experiences that meet their satisfaction and expectations both (Chathoth et al., 2016).

2.2 Value Co-Creation

Value co-creation as an emerging paradigm proposes a change from enterprise-centric view to demand-centric processes and interactive involving participants who integrate resources for mutually beneficial collaboration (Frow & Payne, 2011). Value co- paradigm creation seeks mutual value propositions among its stakeholders (Ballantyne & Varey, 2006; Ramaswamy & Ozcan, 2018). Companies can creating value in collaboration with or influenced by others (Jaakkola, et al., 2015). The paradigm characterizes shifting boundaries, where consumers perform a simultaneous role in providing value to the company within form of co-creation activity and in the form of their purchasing activity (O'Hern & Rindfleisch, 2010).

Co-creation of value is defined, as follows: Consumer and company closely engaged in jointly creating unique value for consumption individual. Interaction between consumers and companies is becoming a new locus of co-creation value (Prahalad & Ramaswamy, 2004). Understanding of value co- activities creation carried out by customers is very important, because it is a customer value activity co-creation will influence customer satisfaction and dissatisfaction (Wong & Lai, 2019). From a company perspective, creating value for customers starts with understanding of the customer value creation process (Frow et al., 2015). Therefore that is, understanding the value co-creation activities carried out by customers very important, because customer value co-creation activities will influence customer satisfaction and dissatisfaction (Wong & Lai, 2019).

Exhibitions are the main form of MICE events (meetings, incentives, conferences, and exhibitions), and is one of the main components of the tourism industry (Whitfield et al., 2014). In the exhibition, value co-creation activities between exhibition organizers and exhibitors can improve exhibition performance and increase exhibitor satisfaction. The results of this research provide several suggestions for exhibition organizers in the process of value co-creation activities (Wong & Lai, 2019).

3. IMPLICATIONS OF DART MODEL IN NAIFEST

The DART model was introduced by (Prahalad & Ramaswamy, 2004) as a roadmap for companies to engage customers in value co-creation. It consists of four dimensions: dialog, access, risk, and transparency (DART), which can be interchanged in several ways for optimal results. The DART model is used to test whether customer perceptions of price and quality are influenced by value co-creation. Value co-creation requires democratizing procedures for all stakeholders (Ramaswamy & Ozcan, 2018), and the consumer perspective on the DART model will provide valuable insights into its effectiveness as a value co-creation tool. Value co-creation relies on a four-element interaction between a company and its consumers (Prahalad & Ramaswamy, 2004).

3.1 Conceptual DART Framework

The DART (Dialogue, Access, Risk-assessment, and Transparency) model is a model that clearly describes the foundation or basic principles necessary and must be had in implementing shared value creation (Anwar, 2021). Availability of access to information and dialogue capabilities through consumer communities changing consumer experience in the business system (Anwar, 2021). Future competition relies on a new approach to value co-creation that refers to the individual with customers and also companies (Prahalad & Ramaswamy, 2004). DART models introduced by (Prahalad & Ramaswamy, 2004) as a road map for companies to involve customers in value co-creation. It consists of four dimensions: dialogue, access, risk and transparency (DART), which can be interchanged in several ways for optimal results. The DART model is used to test whether customer perceptions of price and quality are influenced by value co-creation. Despite the fact that it is an enterprise-oriented model, the DART model will be explored from the customer perspective due to the four building blocks concept interactions are equally applicable to all actors involved (Prahalad & Ramaswamy, 2004).

Value co-creation requires democratization procedures for all stakeholders interests (Ramaswamy & Ozcan, 2018), and consumer viewpoints on the model DART will provide valuable insight into its effectiveness as a value tool co-creation. Value co-creation depends on the interaction of four elements between companies and their consumers (Prahalad & Ramaswamy, 2004). This interaction defined in Table 3.1:

Table 3. Definitions of Dart

Definition of DART		
D	Dialogue	Requires interaction, deep commitment, the ability and willingness to act on both sides.
A	Access	This refers to providing complete information to company customers.
R	Risk Assessment	Relates to some of the risks associated with products or services offered by the company.
T	Transparency	Manage the flow of information between the company and customers transparently.

Source: Prahalad & Ramaswamy (2004)

The value co-creation paradigm shows that if customers play a role proactively in the value co-creation process, then they will be inclined provide an assessment of positive experiences and feelings related to offering of a product (Prahalad &

Ramaswamy, 2004). Therefore, it becomes important to assess the validity of this idea and the extent of co-creation influence customer perceived value. This study adopted the DART framework as a representative of the value co-creation process and two characteristics of perceived value customers, namely perceived price and perceived quality to test this relationship.

3.2 Perceived Value (Profit Value)

According to Sirdeshmukh, Singh and Sabol (2002), perceived customer value shows the customer's behavioural intentions towards loyalty to the service provider if relational exchange has added value (Gunarto, 2018). Perceived value is become one of the most misused concepts in the world social science literature, especially in services marketing (Khalifah, 2004; Boksberger & Melsen, 2011).

Figure 2. Components of Product Value Perceived by Customers

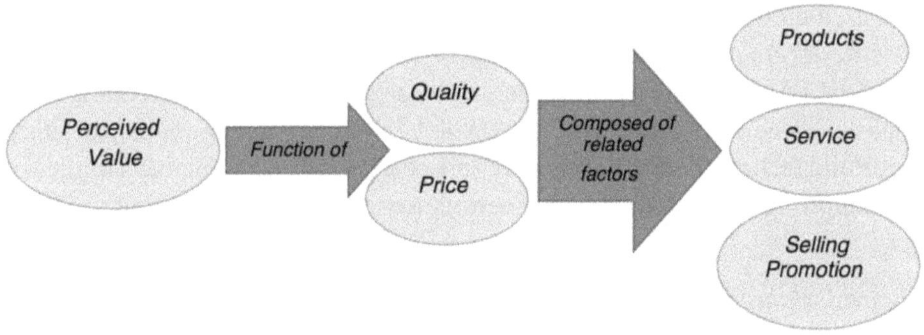

Source: JM Spiteri, PA Dion (2004)

In exhibitions, perceived performance is widely used to evaluate whether an exhibition is successful or not (Severt et al., 2007). A success exhibitions can be measured by their objectives - sales, customer relations, research marketing, brand building, channel support and media relations. (EEAA, 2016). In this study, perceived value refers to the overall assessment made by exhibitors regarding exhibition performance. perceived value influence exhibitor satisfaction and behavioral intentions. A similar study concluded that perceived value has a significant impact on satisfaction and exhibitor loyalty.

Perceived value refers to the customer's perspective or opinion towards a product or service that is often influenced by how goods and services it meets customer needs and expectations (Gordon, 2022). The value perceived otherwise is called customer perceived value, that is how customers evaluate or judge a product or service when compared with other similar products. Driven out of the customer's perception of an product, perceived value is important to marketing professionals because it helps they know the right strategy in marketing their products and services.

Thus, it becomes important to understand the relationship between value co-creation and perceived value, as well as exploring other possible competitive opportunities inherent in this relationship. Therefore, the reader appeal of this article is realized in two ways. First, this study describes two characteristics of perceived value, namely quality and price, as a source of competitive strategy and trying to determine the influence of the application of value co-creation on strategic resources and the intensity of its influence. Second, the business implications of reaping the benefits. The potential for co-creation requires organizations to realign resources power between the functions that make customer promises and those that deliver promises customers (Frow et al., 2015).

3.3 Research Hypothesis

Based on the theory explained above, the next step is for researchers develop hypotheses in analyzing the relationships between existing variables stated previously. Comprehensively, researchers will carry out analysis and looking for the impact of value co-creation in the context of the NAIFEST exhibition on participants IndoBuildTech exhibition. This research uses the DART model approach framework. The following is the conceptual framework for the research framework used:

Figure 3. Conceptual Research Framework

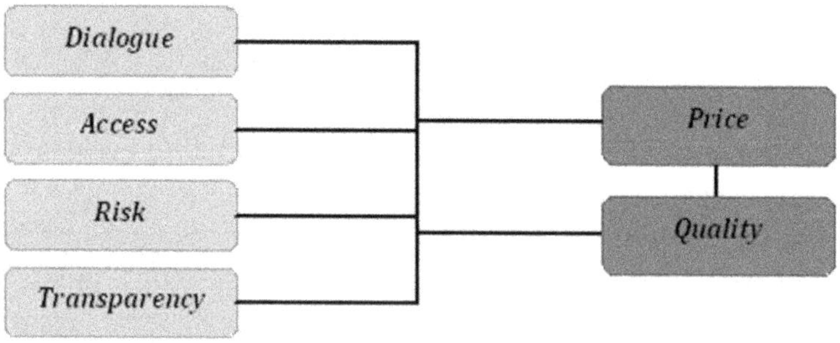

Source: Researcher Analysis Results (2022)

3.3.1 The Influence of Dialogue on Perceived Value: Price and Quality

As a building block of interaction, dialogue is the only way to interact and share knowledge (Ballantyne & Varey, 2006; Grönroos, 2004; Prahalad & Ramaswamy, 2004). Dialogue as a meaningful learning process that the actors involved have the opportunity to gain knowledge and creating new knowledge (Gronroos, 2004). In service logic perspective- dominant (SDL), marketing is a structure of relationships, meetings, and dialogue (Payne et al., 2008). Interactive dialogue, that is, deep involvement and inter-tendency both sides. Dialogue can create and maintain a strong community loyal (Anwar, 2021). This means that the NAIFEST exhibition wants to provide experience and an opportunity for dialogue between architects and exhibitors. Such dialogue must happen as the function of the NAIFEST exhibition is as a channel communication which includes synchronous-asynchronous communication between exhibitors IndoBuildTech with architects. Even though it has many communication channels it doesn't immediately there will be an active dialogue, but more and more channels the more opportunities to communicate, the greater the opportunity to start a dialogue active (Ballantyne, 2004). The better the quality of the dialogue, the more valuable the experience co-created (Binkhorst & Dekker, 2009; Solakis et al., 2017). Its creation dialogue in building networking according to important attributes exhibition, meaning this aspect has the power to influence customer perceptions about the prices and quality of services of the exhibition itself.

H1a: NAIFEST exhibition dialogue has an impact on IBT exhibition prices. H1b: NAIFEST exhibition dialogue has an impact on exhibition quality IBT.

3.3.2 Effect of Access on Perceived Value: Price and Quality

The company provides access to tools and information for customers to together creating value experiences (Prahalad & Ramaswamy, 2004). Access starting with the provision of information and equipment, companies can provide access data regarding designs and processes to consumers. This access is intended as value chain to create and transfer ownership of products to consumers (Anwar, 2021). The main purpose of this co-creation is to provide access as added value for customers. This is an important element in co-creation which aims to provide access for customers. NAIFEST Exhibition offers access for exhibitors to meet directly with the target their consumers, namely architects. The presence of architects who are also involved in IndoBuildTech exhibition through an architectural installation exhibition. NAIFEST Exhibition provide networking access in accordance with the important attribute points in exhibition. Apart from that, the NAIFEST exhibition provides access to information related to architects involved with IndoBuildTech exhibitors.

Sharma (2017) notes that providing information that is relevant, interesting, or personal to customers can increase customer attention and improve their loyalty (Solakis et al., 2017). In this way, it becomes possible to hypothesize that by providing relevant and information about visitors exhibition to exhibitors, organizers can influence perceptions customers about the quality and price of their services.

H2a: NAIFEST exhibition access has an impact on IBT exhibition prices.
H2b: Access to the NAIFEST exhibition has an impact on the quality of the IBT exhibition.

3.3.3 Effect of Risk Assessment on Perceived Value: Price and Quality

Although, the NAIFEST exhibition provides access to information and dialogue opportunities, the co-creation process can pose risks for all actors involved. Risk assessment of co-creation results must be carried out by all actors involved value co-creation (Prahalad & Ramaswamy, 2004). Companies must communicate not only the benefits, but also the potential risks of their proposal to help their customers make informed decisions and improve trust between them (Prahalad & Ramaswamy, 2004). In other words, Risk assessment refers to the risks that a person is likely to face companies and customers during the value co-creation process are built. Baqer (2006) found that customers were willing to purchase co-produced services when they realize the risks involved in producing shared services (Christian, 2019). When consumers and companies become co-creators of value, requests for information regarding potential risks will increase, they may also increase predict future risks. Risk here refers to probability endanger consumers (Anwar, 2021).

Risk has a dominant influence on the perceived value of ownership the relative intensity is higher or negative. In this case, there is a risk in the situation certain conditions lowers the perceived value of consumers in that context (Christian, 2019). Therefore, researchers expect the ability of exhibitors to assess the risks that will arise in the process of creating co-creation. This is in fact can significantly influence their perception of the value of benefits in following IndoBuildTech exhibition. If the NAIFEST exhibition is unable to provide adequate information and access required for exhibitors to meet with the architect, then there is a possibility risk of failure. In other words, the value of the co-creation created can be risks not satisfying the expected perceptions of exhibition participants.

H3a: Risk Assessment of the NAIFEST exhibition has an impact on prices IndoBuildTech exhibition.

H3b: Risk Assessment of the NAIFEST exhibition has an impact on quality IndoBuildTech exhibition.

3.3.4 Effect of Transparency on Perceived Value: Price and Quality

Transparency is the fourth element of the value co-creation assessment method . Transparency is essential for genuine, active dialogue between equal partners (Solakis et al., 2017). Corporate openness facilitates trust, equality, and discussions, leading to improved customer experience (Solakis et al., 2017). Transparency of information is necessary to develop trust between companies and customers. Additionally, transparency is necessary for building close relationship between customer and company and thus enabling the creation of shared value (Neghina et al., 2015). Information regarding products, business systems become more accessible, thereby creating a new level of transparency that increases consumer demand (Anwar, 2021). By providing open dialogue and transparency builds trust and increasing customer commitment to the company (Terho et al., 2012). Thus, researchers hypothesize that transparency can function in fulfilling perceptions of IndoBuildTech exhibitors regarding the value of co-creation being built through the NAIFEST exhibition.

H4a: NAIFEST exhibition transparency has an impact on exhibition prices IBT.
H4b: NAIFEST exhibition transparency has an impact on quality IBT exhibition.

3.3.5 Value of Price Advantages Over Quality (Perceived Value: Price and Quality)

Perceived Price (PP) and Perceived Quality (PQ) are often used together alternate. A high price can be an indicator of high quality, and quality high ones can indicate high prices (Solakis et al., 2022). Quality and price always correlates with customer experience. Implementation on time customers gain experience, then at that time a learning process occurs, so this is an indication of connected customer perceptions (Solakis et al., 2022). This research focuses on the use of the DART framework model concept on customer perceptions regarding price and quality, is therefore very important the concept of customer value to be studied. Customer value is the ratio of value received consumers with the costs incurred in providing certain products/services to customers (Dovaliene et al., 2015). Without both factors quality and price do not may maintain the foundation of price marketing strategies

(Solakis et al., 2022). The higher the quality, the higher the price, and this is related to strategy premium pricing. Premium pricing is used to inform customers that a particular hotel offers superior quality (Solakis et al., 2022). In this study, the customer perception is that exhibitors are the main consumers who have rented a location to participate in the IndoBuildTech exhibition. As an exhibitor, of course you have to pay a fee to participate IndoBuildTech exhibition cuts quite expensive costs. Of the costs that have been issued, of course there are expectations and expectations that the exhibitor wants to obtain. This is the perception of quality that exhibitors want to expect. So, in this context, perceived quality also has a relationship with perceived price exhibitor.

H5: The quality of the NAIFEST exhibition has an impact on the price of the exhibition IndoBuildTech.

4. ANALYSIS MODEL

This research model was created with the aim of analyzing the impact of value co- creation of the NAIFEST exhibition on the perceived value of IndoBuildTech exhibitors. Researchers will look for factors that influence the assessment of NAIFEST exhibition regarding the perceptions of IndoBuildTech exhibitors. As in

The previous explanation was that the NAIFEST exhibition was created as a result of an initiation organizers in collaboration with architects. It is known that architect is the main target of visitors to the IndoBuildTech exhibition. In other words, architects is the main target of visitors who are expected to attend the IndoBuildTech exhibition for IndoBuildTech exhibitors. In connection with this analysis, researchers using the value co-creation concept of the NAIFEST exhibition as an independent variable or independent (X) and perceived value of IndoBuildTech exhibitors as variables bound or dependent (Y).

Based on the results of the literature review, researchers obtained tools to measure value-co-creation as a research reference. Tools use the framework concept DART model, namely dialogue, access, risk assessment, and transparency. So, for the independent variable the researcher elaborates; X1: Dialogue; X2: Access; X3: Risk Assessment; and X4: Transparency. Meanwhile for the dependent variable (Y), based on the literature review obtained, there are two main factors of perceived value Customers consist of Price and Quality. So, the researcher elaborated on variable Y, become; Y1: Price; and Y2: Quality. The two variables used are intended to obtain comprehensive results regarding the value co-creation created through the exhibition form NAIFEST has an impact on expectations through perception value of IndoBuildTech exhibitors. Overall based on nine hypothesis that has been described in the research hypothesis section, then formulate the model analysis of this research, as follows:

Figure 4. Research Analysis Model

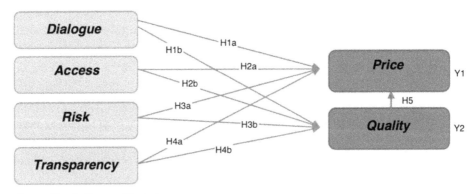

Source: Results Processed by Author

Basically the value co-creation framework shows an analysis of customer's value co-creation behavior (Yi & Gong, 2013). In the journal Solakis (2017) identified the value co-creation dimension was developed to measure customer behavior based on the customer's point of view (Solakis, et.al., 2017). Building block model on DART which consists of dialogue, access, risk assessment, and transparency is an element or indicator that is ready to be measured from the concept of value co-creation (Prahalad & Ramaswamy, 2004). Indicator measuring tool for each block variable DART buildings are associated with the value co-creation dimension which is based on perspective of the experiences of IndoBuildTech exhibitors in the context of the exhibition NAIFEST.

5. METHODS

In this study, researchers will focus on measuring value co-creation using the DART framework model. Then, researchers conducted a survey on the perceived value of exhibitors, namely based on price & quality assessments. The data collection technique is quantitative, namely primary data collection. Sampling for research if the subject is less than 100 people should be taken all, if the subject is large or more than 100 people can be taken 10-15% or 20-25% or more (Suharsimi Arikunto, 2012). This study has a population quota of 170 exhibitors, determined based on Quota Sampling, namely 100 exhibitor respondents or more than 50% of the population sample taken. If calculated using the Slovin formula, **n = N / (1 + (N x e²))**, then the result is 170 / (1 + (170)0.05²) = 119.29. From these results the researcher made a rounding quota, namely 100. Therefore, the sample determined for this study was 100 respondents from the total exhibitor population.

The collected data was analyzed using SPSS to produce the required information. The validity and reliability of the constructs were tested after a pilot study by conducting PLS (Partial Least Square) analysis using structural equation modeling (SEM) techniques to evaluate the research hypotheses. The reason for using this technique is because the SEM-PLS model has its own advantages in working both with unobserved conceptual variables (latent components) and with components consisting of a large number of indicators (observable variables) (Lowry & Gaskin, 2014). By using the Smart PLS software, this study was able to predict and explain the construction of latent variables from testing a theory in a small number of samples. Then, the instrument was tested on a sample of 100 respondents for internal consistency. Various items will be developed for each research model configuration.

5.1. Characteristic of Respondent

The characteristics of respondents identified that the facts of respondents have different backgrounds. This feature aims to see the background of the respondent. The respondent was one in charged representative of the company participating in the IndoBuildTech 2022 exhibition. In this study, the respondent's background is focused on gender, age range, province of origin, job title, and company category products. The following are the results obtained:

Table 5. Respondent Characteristics

No.	Respondent Characteristic	Result of The Most	Percentage
1.	Gender	Male	75%
2.	Age	38-48	51%
3.	Occupation	Director/GM/VP	44%
4.	Company Domicile	DKI Jakarta	65%
5.	Product Category	Building Materials Construction	48%

Source: Tabulation of Research Questionnaire Recap

Gender characteristics of respondents from 100 respondents, 75% were male and the remaining 25% were female. This shows that the average respondent of IBT Expo 2022 exhibitors is represented by men. Based on the respondent data in Table 2.1, obtained from the research results, the highest age group who answered this questionnaire was 38-48 years old which reached 51%. Followed by the number of the group with the age vulnerability of 27-37 years at 35%. While the number of groups with vulnerable ages 26 years and under is 5%, 49-59 years is 9%, and above 60 years is none or 0%. Testing the characteristics of respondents based on the position of respondents at the exhibitor company. The highest number obtained 44% which is the level of director/general manager/vice president. The second is associate/manager/supervisor level respondents with a percentage of 33%. Followed by executive/staff/secretary/admin level respondents who obtained 16% and finally respondents with the position of company owner (owner)/CEO/CTO/COO/President Director at 7%. Of the 100 respondents representing companies participating in the IBT 2022 exhibition, 65% were dominated by companies from DKI Jakarta. Second followed by companies domiciled in Banten at 17% and third from East Java reaching 12%. Next is 4% from West Java and the same figure of 1% from Central Java and DI. Yogyakarta. Based on the data obtained, there are no companies from outside Java. Of the five product categories of IBT 2022 exhibitors that have been classified by PT Debindo-ITE, the acquisition of the most respondents of IBT 2022 exhibitors is the building material construction product category by reaching 48% of the 100 respondents. Second is the company respondents who belong to the building interior & finishes category products which reached 32%. As for the intelligent building & digital architecture category products 8%, HVACR & Solar Technologies 7%, and Ceramic & Marbles at 5%.

6. RESULTS AND DISCUSSION

In this study, there are 2 variables, namely the independent variable and the dependent variable. The independent variable expressed by variable X shows 4 indicators of value co-creation measurement with the DART model approach, namely X1-dialogue, X2-access, X3-risk assessment, and X4-transparency. Meanwhile, the dependent variable is expressed by variable Y which shows the measurement of perceived value through 2 indicators Y1-price and Y2-quality.

Table 6. Questionnaire Distribution and Respondents' Answers

No	Questionnaires	Statistics Result				
		Mean	Outer Loadings	Cronbach's Alpha	Composite Reliability (rho_a)	Average Variance Extracted (AVE)
	X1: Dialogue			0,807	0,949	0,723
1	Exhibitors had an active dialog interaction with architects at the NAIFEST exhibition.	3.910	0,959			
2	At NAIFEST exhibitors can share information with architects.	3.920	0,954			
3	The NAIFEST exhibition provides a new experience for exhibitors through architects' installation works.	4.310	0,581			
	X2: Access			0,849	0,849	0,768
1	The NAIFEST exhibition provides access to opportunities to collaborate with architects through installation works.	3.320	0,865			
2	Easy access to NAIFEST exhibition for exhibitors.	4.220	0,859			
3	The NAIFEST exhibition provides access to possible business relationships between exhibitors and architects.	3.790	0,904			
	X3: Risk Assessment			0,881	0,883	0,808
1	The presence of the NAIFEST exhibition at IndoBuildTech provides both benefits and risks for exhibitors.	4.080	0,921			
2	Exhibitors were informed about the risk factors involved in the NAIFEST exhibition.	3.620	0,881			
3	Exhibitors are committed to creating value even though NAIFEST exhibitions can be risky.	4.070	0,895			
	X4: Transparency			0,898	0,899	0,831
1	Open and clear information about the NAIFEST exhibition.	4.230	0,939			
2	Open and clear information about participating architects at the NAIFEST exhibition.	4.080	0,917			

continued on following page

The Impact of Value Co-Creation of the NAIFEST Exhibition

Table 6. Continued

No	Questionnaires	Statistics Result				
		Mean	Outer Loadings	Cronbach's Alpha	Composite Reliability (rho_a)	Average Variance Extracted (AVE)
X1: Dialogue				0,807	0,949	0,723
3	The NAIFEST exhibition provides an inspirational platform for exhibitors through the installation works of architects.	4.330	0,878			
Y1: Price				0,901	0,909	0,771
1	Dialogue's experience at the NAIFEST exhibition matched the price expectations of the IndoBuildTech exhibition.	4.090	0,900			
2	Access' experience at the NAIFEST exhibition matched the price expectations of the IndoBuildTech exhibition.	4.210	0,840			
3	Risk Assessment experience at NAIFEST exhibition in line with IndoBuildTech exhibition price expectations.	3.930	0,886			
4	Transparency's experience at the NAIFEST exhibition matched IndoBuildTech exhibition pricing expectations.	3.980	0,885			
Y2: Quality				0,956	0,958	0,849
1	Dialogue's experience at the NAIFEST exhibition lived up to expectations of the quality of the IndoBuildTech exhibition.	4.110	0,932			
2	Access' experience at the NAIFEST show matched expectations of IndoBuildTech show quality.	4.180	0,922			
3	Risk Assessment experience at NAIFEST exhibition meets IndoBuildTech exhibition quality expectations.	4.040	0,902			
4	Transparency's experience at the NAIFEST exhibition matched the quality expectations of the IndoBuildTech exhibition.	4.080	0,936			

continued on following page

Table 6. Continued

No	Questionnaires	Statistics Result				
		Mean	Outer Loadings	Cronbach's Alpha	Composite Reliability (rho_a)	Average Variance Extracted (AVE)
X1: Dialogue				0,807	0,949	0,723
5	The quality and benefits of the NAIFEST exhibition have been worth the price of the IndoBuildTech exhibition participation fee.	4.140	0,915			

Source: Tabulation of Research Questionnaire Recap

The acquisition of questionnaire data recapitulation is statistically processed with SEM or structure equation modelling techniques using SmartPLS 4 software. The PLS-SEM model serves to test the predictive relationship between variables (Hair, et al., 2018). In this study, testing the reliability and validity of a variable serves to determine whether all variables that have been determined are appropriate as tools for hypothesis testing or not. To understand the feasibility of variable construction, it is shown in Table 3.1, the index value of Cronbach's alpha, composite reliability, and average variance extracted (AVE). The requirements for the index value of Cronbach's alpha, composite reliability and AVE are not less than the minimum value, which is 0.6 (Hair, et.al., 2019). Based on Table 3.1 above, all variables obtained a composite reliability value above 0.6 or more than 60%. This shows that all variables are declared feasible both in terms of reliability and validity. Then, from the results obtained from the measurement of outer loadings which is the loading factor also obtained a value above 0.6. The loading factor value must be greater than 0.6 so it is said to be valid and the results obtained show the magnitude of the correlation with the latent variable (Hair, et.al., 2019). It's just that in variable X1. Dialogue point 3 with the statement NAIFEST Exhibition provides a new experience for exhibitors through the architect's installation work, obtained a value of 0.581 which indicates that <0.6. In fact, this variable is considered invalid, but the results of the reliability and validity tests still show a positive value. In addition, the mean was 4.31 on a Likert scale, which means that respondents responded 'strongly agree'. Overall, the values obtained in statistical data Table 3.2 for dialogue, access, risk assessment, and transparency towards price and quality show quite positive results based on the experience felt by IndoBuildTech 2022 exhibitors with the presence of the NAIFEST exhibition as a form of co-creation.

7. CONCLUSION

This study finds factors that influence or have an impact value co-creation of the NAIFEST exhibition on the perceived value of exhibitors IndoBuildTech. This research found several unique implications for organizers find out the impact of value co-creation through the NAIFEST exhibition on customers who are IndoBuildTech exhibitors. Value co-creation paradigm shows that when customers take a proactive role in the value process co-creation, then assess the experience and tend to have positive feelings about product offerings (Prahalad & Ramaswamy, 2004). With thus, it becomes imperative to assess the validity of this idea and the extent to which co-creation influences customers' perceived value (Solakis, 2022). Value co-creation is something new for the existing exhibition business requires exploration and knowledge regarding this in the future.

In measuring value co-creation indicators using the DART approach framework model consisting of dialogue, access, risk assessment and dimensions transparency. The DART model framework is considered capable of providing recommendations that customers can see aspects of dialogue, access, risk assessment and transparency from the level of openness the company shares information about service offerings and price (Prahalad & Ramaswamy, 2004). The use of this model can be revealing the strengths and weaknesses of the dimensions of the DART framework are primarily due to this model focused on the customer perspective. Lastly, using this model can be helpful managers to increase understanding of value co-creation and design rework services as well as appropriate co-creation operations. Hence the assessment perspective a customer is based on perceived value indicators through the perceived price dimension and perceived quality. The findings of this research indicate that there are several factors NAIFEST exhibition value co-creation indicators which have an influence on perceived value of IndoBuildTech exhibitors and also non-dimensional indicators have influence or correlation. Of the four indicators of the DART framework, dialogue, access, and transparency have an impact on perceived quality. Risk indicators assessment consistently has no impact on perceived quality and perceived price. This makes it possible that the explanation related to risk assessment is shallow communication so as not to reach important understandings value co-creation. For risk assessment effects that are not significant are present the NAIFEST exhibition at the IndoBuildTech exhibition can provide benefits and risk. Information related to the risk assessment of NAIFEST exhibitions at the exhibition IndoBuildTech which may not have been conveyed well to participants IndoBuildTech exhibition. IndoBuildTech exhibitors who are reluctant to do so risk-benefit trade-off at the NAIFEST exhibition. When compared with previous research, namely in the first journal compiled by Solakis (2022) entitled, "Value co-creation and perceived value: A customer perspective in the hospitality context.", from the results of this research which has proactive and contradictory. Contradictory to the results of research by Solakis (2022) which in his research suggests risk influences customer perceptions regarding price and quality. Apart from that, access only determines quality, not price. Meanwhile, in this study it was found that risk does not have factors that can impact on price and quality. Then, there is the dialogue consistently has no influence on either price or quality, contradictory in this research which states that dialogue has an influence on quality. On this research, only risk assessment has no influence on prices and quality. From a proactive perspective, Solakis' (2022) research states that the results support the idea that perceived quality influences price felt, this is in line with this case study research. In addition, access points too. The same has factors that only determine quality. Then, instruments perceived price is not influenced by the four DART factors, meaning dialogue indicators, access, risk assessment and transparency have no correlation to price perception for IndoBuildTech exhibitors. Although the dimensions of the DART are not a factor which influences the perceived price of exhibitors, but this also coincides with positively perceived price the factor is most influenced by perception quality. The intermediary role of perceived quality implies the existence of a quality-price inference, meaning consumers can measure the price of services based on perceived quality of the three those dimensions.

The DART model framework is considered capable of providing recommendations that customers can see aspects of dialog, access, risk assessment and transparency from the level of openness of companies sharing information about service offerings and prices (Prahalad & Ramaswamy, 2004). The use of this model can reveal the strengths and weaknesses of the dimensions of the DART framework especially since this model is focused on the customer perspective. The use of this model can help managers to improve understanding of value co-creation and redesign services and co-creation operations accordingly. Therefore, the perspective of a customer's assessment is based on perceived value indicators through the dimensions of perceived price and perceived quality.

This study found some unique implications for organizers to know the effect of value co-creation through NAIFEST exhibition to customers who are IBT exhibitors. The value co-creation paradigm suggests that when customers take a proactive role in the value co-creation process, then they value the experience and tend to have positive feelings about the product offering (Prahalad & Ramaswamy, 2004). Thus, it becomes imperative to assess the validity of this notion and the extent to which co-creation affects customers' perceived value (Solakis, 2022). Value co-creation is new to the exhibition business and requires future exploration and knowledge in this area. Organizers need to be aware of the importance of perceived quality of the four DART dimensions that can validly influence value co-creation, including dialogue, access, risk assessment and transparency. Research on value co-creation

The Impact of Value Co-Creation of the NAIFEST Exhibition

and perceived value in the tourism sector, especially in the MICE sector, is still not much and is very dynamic. Organizers need to be motivated and aware of the importance of the 4 aspects of the DART dimension, namely dialogue, access, risk assessment, and transparency that drive value co-creation benefits to exhibitors' perceived value. The better the value co-creation provided, the more positive the perceived value by exhibitors.

ACKNOWLEDGMENT

This publication is supported by the grant from Faculty of Administrative Sciences, Universitas Indonesia under the agreement number NKB 083/UN2.RST/HKP.05.00/2022

REFERENCES

Boksberger, P. E., & Melsen, L. (2011). Perceived value: A critical examination of definitions, concepts and measures for the service industry. In Journal of Services Marketing (Vol. 25, Issue 3, pp. 229-240). 10.1108/08876041111129209

Camisón, C., & Villar-López, A. (2014). Organizational innovation as an enabler of technological innovation capabilities and firm performance. *Journal of Business Research*, 67(1), 2891–2902. 10.1016/j.jbusres.2012.06.004

Chathoth, P. K., Ungson, G. R., Harrington, R. J., & Chan, E. S. W. (2016). Co-creation and higher order customer engagement in hospitality and tourism services: A critical review. *International Journal of Contemporary Hospitality Management*, 28(2), 222–245. 10.1108/IJCHM-10-2014-0526

Christian, O. O. (2019). Using The Dart Model Of Value Co-Creation To Predict Customer Loyalty In Pension Fund Administration In Nigeria. British Journal Of Management and Marketing Studies, 2(3), 13-26. https://www.researchgate.net/publication/338570525

Curatman, A., Soesanty, R., Mastur, M., & Ikhsani, M. (2016). Analysis of Factors Influencing Product Innovation that Impacts on the Competitive Advantage of Food and Beverage SMEs in the Harjamukti Region of Cirebon City. Journal of Logic, 18(3). www.jurnal.unswagati.ac.id

Dovaliene, A., Masiulyte, A., & Piligrimiene, Z. (2015). The Relations between Customer Engagement, Perceivedd Value and Satisfaction: The Case of Mobile Applications. *Procedia: Social and Behavioral Sciences*, 213, 659–664. 10.1016/j.sbspro.2015.11.469

Ellitan, L. (2006). Innovation Strategy and Performance of Manufacturing Companies in Indonesia: A Simultaneous and Sequential Model Approach. *Journal of Management*, 6(1).

Frow, P., Nenonen, S., Payne, A., & Storbacka, K. (2015). Managing Co-creation Design: A Strategic Approach to Innovation. *British Journal of Management*, 26(3), 463–483. 10.1111/1467-8551.12087

Frow, P., & Payne, A. (2011). A stakeholder perspective of the value proposition concept. *European Journal of Marketing*, 45(1), 223–240. 10.1108/03090561111095676

Ghozali, I., & Latan, H. (2015). *Partial Least Square Concepts, Techniques, and Applications Using the SmartPLS 3.0 Program*. Diponegoro University Publishing Agency.

Gunarto, M. (2018). *The Co-Creation Model and its Implications for Student Loyalty at Private Universities*. Study at PTS in South Sumatra Province.

Hair, J. F., Sarstedt, M., Ringle, C. M., & Gudergan, S. P. (2018). *Advanced issues in partial least squares structural equation modeling (PLS-SEM)*. Sage.

Hair, Black, Babin, & Anderson. (2019). Multivariate Data Analysis. 8th Edition. Annabel Ainscow.

Harkison, T. (2018). The use of co-creation within the luxury accommodation experience - myth or reality? *International Journal of Hospitality Management*, 71, 11–18. 10.1016/j.ijhm.2017.11.006

Haryanti, S. S. (2016). Building Marketing Performance Based on Product Innovation and Competitive Advantage (Empirical Study on Gitardi Crafts Sukoharjo Regency). *ACTUAL*, 2, 1–19.

Henseler, J., Ringle, C. M., & Sarstedt, M. (2015). A New Criterion for Assessing. Discriminant Validity in Variance-based Structural Equation Modeling. *Journal of the Academy of Marketing Science*, 43(1), 115–135. 10.1007/s11747-014-0403-8

Jaakkola, E., Helkkula, A., & Aarikka-Stenroos, L. (2015). Service experience co-creation: Conceptualization, implications, and future research directions. *Journal of Service Management*, 26(2), 182–205. 10.1108/JOSM-12-2014-0323

Jin, X., Weber, K., & Bauer, T. (2012). Relationship quality between exhibitors and organizers: A perspective from Mainland China's exhibition industry. *International Journal of Hospitality Management*, 31(4), 1222–1234. 10.1016/j.ijhm.2012.02.012

João Leitão, F. G., & Ken Riopelle, J. G. P. G. (2018). Collaborative Innovation Networks Building Adaptive and Resilient Organizations. https://www.springer.com/series/15330

Kotler, P., & Keller, K. L. (2016). Marketing Management (Stephanie Wall, Ed.; 15th ed.). Pearson Education Limited.

Kurniawan, C. N., Kusumawati, A., & Iqbal, M. (n.d.). Analysis of Experience Co-Creation and Its Impact in the Tourism Context. https://profit.ub.ac.id

Lai, E. R. (2011). Collaboration: A Literature Review Research Report. https://www.pearsonassessments.com/research

Lowry, P. B., & Gaskin, J. (2014). Partial least squares (PLS) structural equation modeling (SEM) for building and testing behavioral causal theory: When to choose it and how to use it. *IEEE Transactions on Professional Communication*, 57(2), 123–146. 10.1109/TPC.2014.2312452

Mulyana & Sutapa (2015). The Role of Quadruple Helix in Improving Creativity and Innovation Capability (Study on Creative Industries in Fashion Sector). UNISSULA, 2, 111.

Najafi-Tavani, S., Najafi-Tavani, Z., Naudé, P., Oghazi, P., & Zeynaloo, E. (2018). How collaborative innovation networks affect new product performance: Product innovation capability, process innovation capability, and absorptive capacity. *Industrial Marketing Management*, 73, 193–205. 10.1016/j.indmarman.2018.02.009

Neghina, C., Caniëls, M. C. J., Bloemer, J. M. M., & van Birgelen, M. J. H. (2015). Value cocreation in service interactions: Dimensions and antecedents. *Marketing Theory*, 15(2), 221–242. 10.1177/1470593114552580

Neuman, W. L. (2015). Social research methods: qualitative and quantitative approaches (7th ed.). Pearson Education Limited.

O'Hern, M. S., & Rindfleisch, A. (2010). Customer co-creation: A typology and research agenda. *Review of Marketing Research*, 6, 84–106. 10.1108/S1548-6435(2009)0000006008

Ollila, S., & Yström, A. (2016). Exploring Design Principles of Organizing for Collaborative Innovation: The Case of an Open Innovation Initiative. *Creativity and Innovation Management*, 25(3), 363–377. 10.1111/caim.12177

Ollila, S., Yström, A., & Elmquist, M. (2016). Beyond intermediation: The open innovation arena as an actor enabling joint knowledge creation. *International Journal of Technology Management*, 72(4), 273. 10.1504/IJTM.2016.081573

Patricio, R., Moreira, A., Zurlo, F., & Melazzini, M. (2020). Co-creation of new solutions through gamification: A collaborative innovation practice. *Creativity and Innovation Management*, 29(1), 146–160. Advance online publication. 10.1111/caim.12356

Prahalad, C. K., & Ramaswamy, V. (2004). Co-creation experiences: The next practice in value creation. *Journal of Interactive Marketing*, 18(3), 5–14. 10.1002/dir.20015

Ramaswamy, V., & Ozcan, K. (2018). What is co-creation? An interactional creation framework and its implications for value creation. *Journal of Business Research*, 84, 196205. 10.1016/j.jbusres.2017.11.027

Russell, S. N., & Millar, H. H. (2014). Exploring the Relationships among Sustainable Manufacturing Practices, Business Performance and Competitive Advantage: Perspectives from a Developing Economy. *Journal of Management and Sustainability*, 4(3). Advance online publication. 10.5539/jms.v4n3p37

Saleh, C., & Hanafi, I. (2020). Government Collaboration (Vol. 1). Academic Press.

Severt, D., Wang, Y., Chen, P. J., & Breiter, D. (2007). Examining the motivation, perceivedd performance, and behavioral intentions of convention attendees: Evidence from a regional conference. *Tourism Management*, 28(2), 399–408. 10.1016/j.tourman.2006.04.003

Solakis, K., Peña-Vinces, J., & Lopez-Bonilla, J. M. (2022). Value co-creation and perceivedd value: A customer perspective in the hospitality context. *European Research on Management and Business Economics*, 28(1), 100175. Advance online publication. 10.1016/j.iedeen.2021.100175

Solakis, K., Pena-Vinces, J. C., & Lopex-Bonilla, J. M. (2017). DART model from a customer's perspective: An exploratory study in the hospitality industry of Greece. *Business Perspectives, 15*(2). www.businessperspectives.org

Terho, H., Haas, A., Eggert, A., & Ulaga, W. (2012). 'It's almost like taking the sales out of selling'-Towards a conceptualization of value-based selling in business markets. *Industrial Marketing Management*, 41(1), 174–185. 10.1016/j.indmarman.2011.11.011

Whitfield, J., Dioko, L. D. A. N., Webber, D., & Zhang, L. (2014). Attracting convention and exhibition attendance to complex MICE venues: Emerging data from Macao. *International Journal of Tourism Research*, 16(2), 169–179. 10.1002/jtr.1911

Wong, J. W. C., & Lai, I. K. W. (2019). The effects of value co-creation activities on the perceivedd performance of exhibitions: A service science perspective. *Journal of Hospitality and Tourism Management*, 39, 97–109. 10.1016/j.jhtm.2019.03.003

Wong, K. K. (2013). Partial Least Squares Structural Equation Modeling (PLS-SEM) Techniques Using SmartPLS. *Marketing Bulletin*.

Chapter 17
Modeling Service Quality and Religiosity Towards the Implementation of the Principles of Trust and Customer Satisfaction

Nilam Sari
State Islamic University of Ar-Raniry, Indonesia

Winny Dian Winny Safitri
 https://orcid.org/0000-0003-1104-524X
State Islamic University of Ar-Raniry, Indonesia

Riski Rinaldi
State Islamic University of Ar-Raniry, Indonesia

Nevi Hasnita
State Islamic University of Ar-Raniry, Indonesia

Maisya Auliandhana
State Islamic University of Ar-Raniry, Indonesia

ABSTRACT

Satisfaction is a feeling that arises, happy or disappointed, after seeing the results of a product that meets expectations. Basically, consumers will choose goods that are

DOI: 10.4018/979-8-3693-3518-5.ch017

cheap and of good quality. Then there are other things that influence this, namely service quality and religiosity. In the practice of buying and selling, the principle of trust is also applied. When carrying out the practice of buying and selling, both traders and consumers must have the same nature of trust. This research aims to analyze the influence of service quality and religiosity on the application of the principles of trust and customer satisfaction with a case study at the electronic store using probability sampling techniques. The analytical method in this research uses structural equation modeling (SEM) PLS. The customer satisfaction model shows that the service variable influences the implementation of trust and satisfaction, while the trust variable influences customer satisfaction.

INTRODUCTION

Human activity basically cannot be separated from economic activity. The objectives of economic activity include the achievement of human desires such as the fulfillment of the necessities of life, to the realization of a prosperous and happy life, but this will be impossible if there is no good financial condition.

Along with the continuous development and unlimited human wants and needs following the times, a problem will inevitably arise. When problems arise and when humans fail to realize their needs and desires, that's when an organization is needed that can realize these human needs and desires. In line with this, in the business world, it is demanded to be able to develop rapidly along with the development of the era of globalization, the high business competition that marks this both in marketing its products to consumers and offering its services. In order to meet the needs and desires of consumers, of course, business people will compete with each other in offering their products and providing satisfaction to consumers.

Customer satisfaction is a feeling that arises, happy or disappointed after seeing the results of a product based on expectations (Kotler, 2007). On the other hand, customer satisfaction according to Bachtiar (2011) is a good impression from customers related to products/services while using or after using the service or product.

Basically consumers will choose goods that are cheap and of good quality, then there are other things that affect this, namely the quality of service and religiosity. If a company cannot meet the expectations of consumers such as the need for an item, the desire for certain goods, the tastes of consumers will ultimately affect the final consumer purchasing decision.

Then there is the factor of religiosity that affects consumer satisfaction, religiosity is the attitude and response of those based on individual beliefs or beliefs in a religion. Religious views are a condition in individuals that make them act according to their level of obedience to religion. Religiosity can be realized from various aspects which are not only measured from religious rituals but can be from other activities such as economics.

Islamic economic thought itself comes from the Qur'an and the Prophet's Hadith. All matters relating to Islamic economics cannot be separated from the provisions contained in these two sources. There are many universal values in Islamic economics as a basis for economic development and are used as guidelines for economic rules among Muslims which are taken from and adhere to these two things.

In the practice of Islamic economics, there is one principle that must be implemented, namely the principle of trust. Trustworthy has the meaning of giving back the rights that are truly owned by the owner, not reaping anything beyond their rights and not taking the rights of others, even if it is wages or prices.

In the practice of buying and selling, the principle of trust is also implemented. When carrying out the practice of buying and selling, both traders and consumers must have the same trustworthiness. This mandate applies to all types of buying and selling, such as fish traders, cloth sellers, and even electronic trading businesses.

This research is expected to increase scientific insight about the effect of service quality and religiosity on the application of the principle of trust and customer satisfaction. The formulation of the research problem is 1) Does the quality of service affect consumer satisfaction at the electronic store? 2) Does religiosity affect consumer satisfaction at the electronic store? 3) Does the principle of trust affect consumer satisfaction at the electronic store? 4) Does the quality of service affect the principle of trust in the electronic store? 5) Does religiosity affect the principle of trust in the electronic store?.

LITERATURE REVIEW

Consumer Satisfaction

Satisfaction is a feeling of joy when someone succeeds in getting what they hoped for (Kotler, 2007). A consumer feels satisfied as indicated by the conditions obtained according to what is needed (Tjiptono, 2012). Meanwhile, Bachtiar (2011) defines that consumer satisfaction can be realized from the consumer's positive feelings regarding the product/service when using or after using the service or product.

There are three measures to measure customer satisfaction, including those related to products, services and purchases (Marwa, 2018). In general, customer satisfaction includes that the service obtained does not exceed expectations.

The Principle of Trustworthy

Trustworthy is the basic foundation in human social relations, the definition of trust is very broad in scope. Trustworthy covers all matters relating to interpersonal relationships among human beings and relationships with the Creator, namely Allah. Katsir (2013) mandates all religious obligations or responsibilities which include issues of the world and the hereafter, all of which are aimed at humans.

Trustworthy is a trust given to someone to fulfill the right to Amirin (2007). A trustworthy person is a person who is able to carry out the given obligations. Trustworthy in the perspective of Islam has a broad meaning and content, where all of these meanings and contents lead to one understanding, namely that everyone feels that Allah swt is always with him in every business that is burdened with him, and everyone understands with full confidence that one day he will be asked for. responsibility for this matter.

There are several indicators in the mandate, among others: obeying the law, being responsible for tasks (both in the context of worship and to muamalah), loyalty and commitment, being firm in keeping promises, being honest with yourself, maintaining friendly relations, and protecting nature.

The Service Quality

Service quality is very important to increase consumer satisfaction. If the quality is good then consumers will feel satisfied. Quality defines the quality of a good or service. Service quality is very important. Service quality is a necessity that must be carried out by companies in order to survive and continue to gain the trust of customers. Service quality can be assessed from something consumed or a person's lifestyle. Service quality is the main key to the success of a company. If the service received or felt is as expected, then the quality of the service is perceived as good and satisfactory. The importance of quality can be explained from two points of view, namely from the perspective of operational management and marketing management. Viewed from an operational perspective, product quality is an important policy in increasing product competitiveness which must satisfy consumers more than or at least the same as the quality of competitors' products. important to increase consumer satisfaction. If the quality is good then consumers will feel satisfied.

Religiosity

Religiosity can be interpreted as a close bond that unites people. Religiosity is demonstrated by daily activities that are regulated by Islamic teachings and applicable norms. Religiosity is a rule in living daily life that is related to a person's spirituality.

In contemporary religion, it is explained that religion is no longer what the ancients understood, that is, it is only related to issues of divinity or faith. Religiosity can be manifested in various aspects of life. Religiosity can not only be done through religious rituals, but can be done through economic activities such as buying and selling and banking.The high and low level of a person's religiosity can be seen from his religious expression, namely a person's ability to recognize or understand religious values which lie in his noble values and make the values in attitude and behavior a hallmark of his religious maturity. Religious maturity can be seen from a person's ability to understand, appreciate and apply the noble values of the religion he adheres to in everyday life.

METHODOLOGY

The approach used in this paper is quantitative (Sugiyono, 2012). The purpose of quantitative research is to determine the relationship between variables in a population. In this study, the variables are service quality, religiosity, the principle of trust and customer satisfaction.

Sources of data used in this study are primary data. Primary data is a data source that directly provides data to data collectors Sugiyono (2016). Primary data sources were obtained through interviews with research subjects and by direct observation or observance in the field. In this study the primary data is in the form of notes from interviews and direct observations in the field obtained through interviews with consumers at the electronic store in Syiah Kuala, Banda Aceh.

The technique of collecting data in this research is by distributing questionnaires either directly or via *Google Form*. This research questionnaire was distributed to respondents who are consumers of electronic store.

The population in this study were all consumers of the electronic store in 2020 as many as 5,069 people. In this study, the authors use the method, *probability sampling, namely simple random sampling,* to select a sample of respondents who are consumers of the Lestari Elektronik store at the time of data collection through questionnaires. With regard to the determination of the number of respondents to be sampled, as many as 90 consumers were obtained from the results of calculations using *software raosoft sampling size* with a *margin of error of* 10%.

In this study using *Structural Equation Modeling* (SEM) analysis is a method used to cover the weaknesses contained in the regression method. SEM in this study uses the approach *Partial Least Square* (PLS) with the method *bootstrapping* or random doubling, in this method the assumption of normality is not a problem for PLS. The purpose of using PLS is to make provisional conjectures or hypotheses.

RESULT AND DISCUSSION

In the results that will be seen from the test of the reliability indicator value that meets if *the loading factor (λ) < 0.6*. This shows that the selected indicator can already describe the variable. The results of the *loading factor (λ)* obtained from the initial model are as follows:

Figure 1. Loading Factors

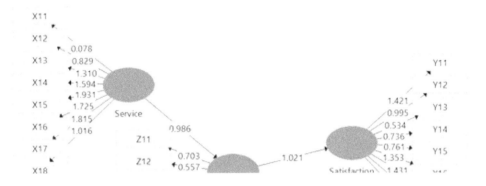

The *output* of the Smart-PLS application can be seen in the image above, there are several indicators that have a loading factor value (λ) < 0.6. Therefore, indicators that do not meet these must be eliminated (removed) from the model, those indicators are X12, X22, X23, X25, Y15, Y18, Y19 while for latent variables that do not meet the criteria, they will be modified into a revised model as follows.

Figure 2. Modified Models

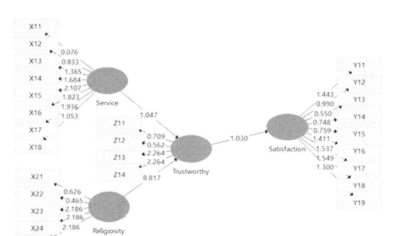

The results of the *loading factor* in the figure show that indicators that have value *loading factor* of more than 0.6 can be interpreted that more than 67% of the variants of each X11, X13, X14, X15, X16, X17, X18 can be explained by the service latent variable. . The latent variable of religiosity can explain the variance of the X21 and X24 indicators, each of which is more than 72%. Each of the variants of Z11, Z12, Z13, Z14 can be explained by the trustworthiness latent variable above 75%, the satisfaction variable is able to explain the variance of the indicators Y11, Y12, Y13, Y14, Y16 each more than 61%.

Table 1. Significant Variable

Variable	T statistic	P-value	Status
Trustworthy → Satisfaction	4.287	0.000	Significant
Service → Trustworthy	5.063	0.000	Significant
Service → Satisfaction	15.105	0.000	Significant
Religiosity → Trustworthy	0.140	0.889	Insignificant
Religiosity → Satisfaction	0.327	0.744	Insignificant

From the table above, not all variables have a significant effect on each other, firstly, trust has a significant effect on satisfaction, secondly, the quality of service has a significant effect on trust, the third quality of service has a significant effect on consumer satisfaction, the fourth religiosity has no significant effect on the principle of trust, and the fifth religiosity insignificant effect on consumer satisfaction.

The Effect of Service Quality on Consumer Satisfaction

The results of this study indicate that the effect of service quality on consumer satisfaction at the electronic store shows a significant effect from the comparison of the significance value (0.000) which is smaller than the value of $= 0.05$. This means that the service provided by the electronic store is very good, seen from the ability of the service variable to explain satisfaction of more than 67%, while the hypothesis has a significant influence between service quality and customer satisfaction is accepted (H_1 is accepted, H_0 is rejected).

From the findings above, it can be concluded that respondents consider the quality of service provided by the electronic store to provide satisfaction for consumers who shop at the store.

The Influence of Religiosity on Consumer Satisfaction

Religiosity according to (Ma'zumi, 2017) is the attitude of a person's diversity or activities related to religion. Religiosity does not significantly affect the level of consumer satisfaction physically. However, elements of the trading system must have an element of religiosity. This can be seen from the results of research on electronic store visitors: more than 72% religiosity can describe the level of satisfaction. Significance value of 0.744 is greater than the value of $\alpha = 0.05$, so the hypothesis of a significant effect between religiosity and customer satisfaction declined (H_1 rejected, H_0 is accepted). Religiosity is not significantly related to consumer satisfaction because those who have high religious values, namely regularly praying, diligently reading the Qur'an and considering Islam as the source of all laws do not necessarily understand consumer satisfaction in an Islamic perspective.

The Effect of Trust Principles on Consumer Satisfaction

Consumer satisfaction is influenced by many factors, including the level of trust contained in the principle of trust given by producers to consumers. The principle of trust is all religious obligations or responsibilities which include issues of the world and the hereafter, all of which are aimed at humans. The results of this study indicate that the principle of trust has a significant effect on consumer satisfaction at the electronic store. (H_1 accepted, $H_{0\,is}$ rejected).

The Influence of Service Quality on the Principles of Trustworthiness

Service quality is the expected level of excellence and control over the level of excellence to meet customer desires. Service quality consists of several elements including appearance, punctuality and promise, willingness to serve, knowledge and expertise, courtesy and hospitality, honesty and trust, simplicity. This study shows that service quality has a significant effect on the principle of trust in the electronic store. That influence can be seen in the significant value of 0.000 is less than 0.05 the hypothesis systemically significant influence between the quality of service to the principle of trustworthiness (H_1 accepted, $H_{0\,is}$ rejected).

The Effect of Religiosity on the Principles of Trustworthiness

The diversity of characteristics of consumers who visit the electronic store shows the various levels of education. Most of the consumers are dominated by students. Given the location of the store is in a strategic location around a large campus in Aceh. This diversity of characteristics prioritizes things that support the level of consumer confidence in the electronic store. The level of trust contained in the principle of trust will be well proven, such as giving good goods, explaining the function of goods honestly, and so on. However, in simple terms, the real element that affects the principle of trust is the correct attitude given by the service from the electronic store. Of the 90 consumers who were interviewed in this study, it showed that religiosity did not significantly affect the principle of trust at the electronic store, it can be seen from the significance value of this variable of 0.889 which is greater than 0.05 so that the hypothesis of a significant influence between religiosity with the principle of trust is rejected ($H_{1\,is}$ rejected, $H_{0\,is}$ accepted).

CONCLUSION

From this study, it can be concluded several things, namely the existence of a significant relationship between the trustworthy variable and the satisfaction variable at a significant level of 5%, then there is a significant influence between the service variable and the trust variable at a 5% significance level. Then the path parameter coefficient obtained from the influence between the service variable and satisfaction states that there is a significant influence between the service variable and the satisfaction variable at a significant level of 5%, the path parameter coefficient obtained from the influence between the religiosity and trust variables states that there is no significant effect. The significant difference between the religiosity

Modeling Service Quality and Religiosity

variable on the trust variable at the 5% significance level, and the path parameter coefficient obtained from the influence between the religiosity and satisfaction variables stated that there was no significant effect between the religiosity variable on the satisfaction variable at the 5% significance level. This study shows that there is a significant influence between service quality and customer satisfaction, so the advice that can be given is that the electronic store must improve service quality standards that make the achievement of customer satisfaction, of course it will provide good benefits on the turnover of the store.

REFERENCES

Amirin. (2007). Kepemimpinan Yang Amanah. Jurnal Dinamika Pendidikan, 1.

Bachtiar. (2011). Analisis yang Mempengaruhi Kepuasan Mahasiswa dalam Politeknik Sawunggalih Aji Purworejo. Jurnal Dinamika Sosial Ekonomi, 7(1).

Depdiknas, K. B. B. I. P. B. (2013). *Cet.Kelima*. PT Gramedia Pustaka Utama.

Katsir, I., & Katsir, T. I. (2013). Jakarta: Pustaka Imam Syafii.

Kotler, M. P. (2007). Indeks. Academic Press.

Ma'zumi. (2017). Pengaruh Religiusitas Terhadap Perilaku Ekonomi Masyarakat Pasar Tradisional (Studi Empris Pada Masyarakat Pasar Tradisional di Kota Serang Provinsi Banten). Jurnal Universitas Sultan Ageng Tirtayasa, 34(2).

Marwa. (2018). Kualitas Pelanggan Terhadap Kepuasan Pelanggan. Jurnal Ecodomica, 2(2).

Sugiyono, M. P. K. (2012). Bandung: Alfabeta.

Sugiyono, M. P. K. (2016). *Kualitatif dan R&D*. PT Alfabeta.

Sugiyono. (2007). Metode Penelitian Kuantitatif Kualitatif dan R&D. Alfabeta.

Tjiptono, F., & Pemasaran, S. (Eds.). (2012). Yogyakarta: Andi.

Compilation of References

Abaho, E., Aarakit, S., Ntayi, J., & Kisubi, M. (2016). Firm Capabilities, Entrepreneurial Competency and Performance of Ugandan SMEs. *Business Management Review, 19*(2). http://hdl.handle.net/11159/3229

Abanis, T., Eliab Mpora, B., Sunday, A., & Eton, M. (2022). Capital Structure, Investment Decision and Financial Performance of SMEs in Uganda. *International Journal of Scientific Research and Management*, 10(07), 3679–3688. Advance online publication. 10.18535/ijsrm/v10i7.em03

Abdullah, Z., & Susamto, A. A. (2019). The Role of Investment-Based Islamic Crowdfunding for Halal MSMEs: Evidence from Indonesia. *Al-Iqtishad: Jurnal Ilmu Ekonomi Syariah*, 11(2), 289–302.

Abubakar, Y. A., Hand, C., Smallbone, D., & Saridakis, G. (2019). What specific modes of internationalization influence SME innovation in Sub-Saharan least developed countries (LDCs)? *Technovation*, 79, 56–70. Advance online publication. 10.1016/j.technovation.2018.05.004

Achtenhagen, L., Melin, L., & Naldi, L. (2013). Dynamics of business models–strategizing, critical capabilities and activities for sustained value creation. *Long Range Planning*, 46(6), 427–442. 10.1016/j.lrp.2013.04.002

Açıkgöz, B., Mutlu, M. D., & Kesebir, M. (2019). BANKACILIK SEKTÖRÜNDE DÜZEN BOZUCU INOVASYON: KİTLESEL FONLAMA. In İşletme ve Yönetim Araştırmaları II (pp. 15–32). Akademisyen Yayınevi, Türkiye.

Acs, Z. J., Audretsch, D. B., & Feldman, M. P. (1994). R & D spillovers and recipient firm size. *The Review of Economics and Statistics*, 76(2), 336–340. 10.2307/2109888

Adam, A. I. (2020). Impact of Visual Merchandising on Customer Impulse buying behavior in retail stores in Sudan. *Asian Journal of Management*, 11(1), 29. 10.5958/2321-5763.2020.00006.2

Adam, N. A., & Alarifi, G. (2021). Innovation practices for survival of small and medium enterprises (SMEs) in the COVID-19 times: The role of external support. *Journal of Innovation and Entrepreneurship*, 10(1), 15. 10.1186/s13731-021-00156-634075328

Advincula, R. C., Dizon, J. R. C., Caldona, E. B., Viers, R. A., Siacor, F. D. C., Maalihan, R. D., & Espera, A. H.Jr. (2021). On the progress of 3D-printed hydrogels for tissue engineering. *MRS Communications*, 11(5), 539–553. 10.1557/s43579-021-00069-134367725

Aghazadeh, H., Zandi, F., Amoozad Mahdiraji, H. & Sadraei, R. (2023). Digital transformation and SME internationalisation: unravelling the moderated-mediation role of digital capabilities, digital resilience and digital maturity. *Journal of Enterprise Information Management*. 10.1108/JEIM-02-2023-0092

Agustina, M., Majid, M. S. A., & Hafasnuddin, H. (2021). Islamic bank amid the 2008 Global financial crisis: A bibliometric analysis. *Library Philosophy and Practice*, 1–26. https://digitalcommons.unl.edu/libphilprac

Ahadi, S., & Kasraie, S. (2020). Contextual factors of entrepreneurship intention in manufacturing SMEs: The case study of Iran. *Journal of Small Business and Enterprise Development*, 27(4), 633–657. 10.1108/JSBED-02-2019-0074

Ahimbisibwe, G. M., Ngoma, M., Nabatanzi-Muyimba, A. K., & Kabagambe, L. B. (2023). Entrepreneurial mindset and SME internationalization in Uganda: The mediating role of international networking. *Review of International Business and Strategy*, 33(4), 669–690. Advance online publication. 10.1108/RIBS-11-2021-0149

Ahi, P., & Searcy, C. (2015). An analysis of metrics used to measure performance in green and sustainable supply chains. *Journal of Cleaner Production*, 86, 360–377. 10.1016/j.jclepro.2014.08.005

Ahmad, N. H., Ismail, H., & Wok, S. (2019). High-performance work practices, human capital and performance of SMEs in Malaysia. *Journal of Small Business and Enterprise Development*, 26(2), 298–315.

Ahmad, N., Ng, S. I., Basha, N. K., & Aziz, Y. A. (2021). How do the dynamic capabilities of Malaysian service small and medium-sized enterprises (SMEs) translate into international performance? Uncovering the mechanism and conditional factors. *International Journal of Business Science and Applied Management*, 16(1), 1–27.

Ahmad, N., Ng, S. I., Basha, N. K., & Aziz, Y. A. (2022). Why knowledge-based human resource management matters for business service SMEs? *International Journal of Management Practice*, 15(5), 549–585. 10.1504/IJMP.2022.125470

Ahmad, N., Ng, S. I., Kamal Basha, N., & Abdul Aziz, Y. (2023). Exploring The Driving Factors of International Performance: Evidence from Business Service SMEs in Malaysia. *Journal of International Students*, 19(2), 119–159. 10.32890/jis2023.19.2.5

Ahmed, M., & Rashid, A. (2019). Crowdfunding as Financial Option for Small and Medium Enterprises (SMEs) in Nigeria. *Pertanika J. Sch. Res. Rev.*, 4, 89–96.

Ahsan, M. (2020). Entrepreneurship and ethics in the sharing economy: A critical perspective. *Journal of Business Ethics*, 161(1), 19–33. 10.1007/s10551-018-3975-2

Compilation of References

Ainin, S., Parveen, F., Moghavvemi, S., Jaafar, N. I., & Mohd Shuib, N. L. (2015). Factors influencing the use of social media by SMEs and its performance outcomes. *Industrial Management & Data Systems*, 115(3), 570–588. 10.1108/IMDS-07-2014-0205

Ajzen, I. (1991). The theory of planned behavior. *Organizational Behavior and Human Decision Processes*, 50(2), 179–211. 10.1016/0749-5978(91)90020-T

Akçura, M. T. (2010). Affiliated marketing. *Information Systems and e-Business Management*, 8(4), 379–394. 10.1007/s10257-009-0118-4

Akpan, I. J., Effiom, L., & Akpanobong, A. C. (2023). Towards developing a knowledge base for small business survival techniques during COVID-19 and sustainable growth strategies for the post-pandemic era. *Journal of Small Business and Entrepreneurship*, 1–23. 10.1080/08276331.2023.2232649

Akram, M. U., Ghosh, K., & Sharma, D. (2022). A systematic review of innovation in family firms and future research agenda. *International Journal of Emerging Markets*, 17(7), 1759–1792. 10.1108/IJOEM-06-2021-0936

Aksoy, C. (2023). Digital Innovation Management: Frameworks, Strategies, and Future Perspectives. *Uluslararası İşletme Bilimi ve Uygulamaları Dergisi*, 3(2), 1–19.

Alalwan, A. A. (2018). Investigating the impact of social media advertising features on customer purchase intention. *International Journal of Information Management*, 42, 65–77. 10.1016/j.ijinfomgt.2018.06.001

Alayo, M., Iturralde, T., & Maseda, A. (2022). Innovation and internationalization in family SMEs: Analyzing the role of family involvement. *European Journal of Innovation Management*, 25(2), 454–478. 10.1108/EJIM-07-2020-0302

Albats, E., Podmetina, D., & Vanhaverbeke, W. (2023). Open innovation in SMEs: A process view towards business model innovation. *Journal of Small Business Management*, 61(6), 2519–2560. 10.1080/00472778.2021.1913595

Aleffi, C., Tomasi, S., Ferrara, C., Santini, C., Paviotti, G., Federica, B., & Cavicchi, A. (2020). Universities and wineries: Supporting sustainable development in disadvantaged rural areas. *Agriculture*, 10(9), 378. 10.3390/agriculture10090378

Alford, P., & Page, S. J. (2015). Marketing technology for adoption by small business. *Service Industries Journal*, 35(11–12), 655–669. 10.1080/02642069.2015.1062884

Ali, A., & Yousuf, S. (2019). Social capital and entrepreneurial intention: Empirical evidence from rural community of Pakistan. *Journal of Global Entrepreneurship Research*, 9(1), 64. Advance online publication. 10.1186/s40497-019-0193-z

Alimian, M., Ghezavati, V., & Reza, T.-M. (2020). New integration of preventive maintenance and production planning with cell formation and group scheduling for dynamic cellular manufacturing systems. *Journal of Manufacturing Systems*, 56, 341–358. Advance online publication. 10.1016/j.jmsy.2020.06.011

Aljuboori, Z. M., Singh, H., Haddad, H., Al-Ramahi, N. M., & Ali, M. A. (2021). Intellectual capital and firm performance correlation: The mediation role of innovation capability in Malaysian manufacturing SMEs perspective. *Sustainability (Basel)*, 14(1), 154. 10.3390/su14010154

Alqahtani, N., & Uslay, C. (2020). Entrepreneurial marketing and firm performance: Synthesis and conceptual development. *Journal of Business Research*, 113, 62–71. 10.1016/j.jbusres.2018.12.035

AlQershi, N. A., Saufi, R. B. A., Mokhtar, S. S. M., Muhammad, N. M. N., & Yusoff, M. N. H. B. (2022). Is strategic orientation always beneficial? A meta-analysis of the relationship between innovation and business sustainability: A dynamic capabilities perspective from Malaysian insurance companies. *Sustainable Futures : An Applied Journal of Technology, Environment and Society*, 4, 100075. 10.1016/j.sftr.2022.100075

Al-Shaikh, M. E., & Hanaysha, J. R. (2023). A conceptual review on entrepreneurial marketing and business sustainability in small and medium enterprises. *World Development Sustainability*, 2, 100039. 10.1016/j.wds.2022.100039

Al-Weshah, G., Kakeesh, D., & Alhammad, F. (2022). Entrepreneurial marketing in Jordanian SMEs: Initiatives and challenges. Entrepreneurial rise in the Middle East and North Africa: The influence of quadruple helix on technological innovation, 67-91.

Al-Weshah, G. A. (2019). The current status of customer relationship management: Experience of small businesses in the Jordanian food industry. *International Journal of Electronic Customer Relationship Management*, 12(1), 1–20. 10.1504/IJECRM.2019.098975

Amaechi, E. (2021). Understanding culture and success in global business: developing cultural and innovative intrapreneurs in small businesses. In Thakkar, B. S. (Ed.), *Culture in Global Businesses: Addressing National and Organizational Challenges* (pp. 205–224). Springer International Publishing. 10.1007/978-3-030-60296-3_9

Amatullo, M., Boyer, B., May, J., & Shea, A. (Eds.). (2021). *Design for social innovation: Case studies from around the world.* Routledge. 10.4324/9781003021360

Amedomar, A., & Spers, R. (2018). Reward-based crowdfunding: A study of the entrepreneurs' motivations when choosing the model as a venture capital alternative in Brazil. *International Journal of Innovation*, 6(2), 147–163. 10.5585/iji.v6i2.283

Amisano, D. C., & Anthony, P. (2017). Relationship between ethical leadership and sustainability in small businesses. *Journal of Leadership, Accountability and Ethics*, 14, 76–90.

Amos, C., Holmes, G., & Strutton, D. (2008). Exploring the relationship between celebrity endorser effects and advertising effectiveness: A quantitative synthesis of effect size. *International Journal of Advertising*, 27(2), 209–234. 10.1080/02650487.2008.11073052

Andersson, S., Evers, N., & Griot, C. (2013). Local and international networks in small firm internationalization: Cases from the Rhône-Alpes medical technology regional cluster. *Entrepreneurship and Regional Development*, 25(9/10), 867–888. 10.1080/08985626.2013.847975

Compilation of References

Andersson, T., Carlsen, J., & Getz, D. (2002). Family business goals in the tourism and hospitality sector: Case studies and cross-case analysis from Australia, Canada, and Sweden. *Family Business Review*, 15(2), 89–106. 10.1111/j.1741-6248.2002.00089.x

Andreas, I. (2022). Three-dimensional bioprinting in medical surgery, 3D Printing: Applications in Medicine and Surgery. https://science.sciencemag.org/content/338/6109/921

Andrenelli, A. (2019). Micro-evidence on corporate relationships in global value chains: The role of trade, FDI and strategic partnerships. https://www.wita.org/wp-content/uploads/2019/05/OECD-micro.pdf

Andres, B., Poler, R., & Guzman, E. (2022). The influence of collaboration on enterprises internationalization process. *Sustainability (Basel)*, 14(5), 2843. 10.3390/su14052843

Andriopoulos, C., & Lewis, M. W. (2009). Exploitation-exploration tensions and organizational ambidexterity: Managing paradoxes of innovation. *Organization Science*, 20(4), 696–717. 10.1287/orsc.1080.0406

Anjana, S. S. (2018). A study on factors influencing cosmetic buying behavior of consumers. *International Journal of Pure and Applied Mathematics*, 118(9), 453–459.

Annamalah, S., Paraman, P., Ahmed, S., Pertheban, T. R., Marimuthu, A., Venkatachalam, K. R., & Ramayah, T. (2023). Exploitation, exploration and ambidextrous strategies of SMES in accelerating organisational effectiveness. *Journal of Global Operations and Strategic Sourcing*.

Anwar, M., Clauss, T., & Issah, W. B. (2022). Entrepreneurial orientation and new venture performance in emerging markets: The mediating role of opportunity recognition. *Review of Managerial Science*, 16(3), 769–796. 10.1007/s11846-021-00457-w

Aral, S., Dellarocas, C., & Godes, D. (2013). Introduction to the Special Issue —Social Media and Business Transformation: A Framework for Research. *Information Systems Research*, 24(1), 3–13. 10.1287/isre.1120.0470

Arifah, J. N., & Dalimunthe, Z. (2020). The impact of financial literacy on the investment decision of non-donation-based crowdfunding in Indonesia. *International Journal of Business and Society*, 21(3), 1045–1057. 10.33736/ijbs.3310.2020

Arora, T., Kumar, A., & Agarwal, B. (2020). Impact of social media advertising on millennials buying behaviour. *International Journal of Intelligent Enterprise*, 7(4), 481–500. 10.1504/IJIE.2020.110795

Arslan, K. (2002). Üniversiteli Gençlerde Mesleki Tercihler ve Girişimcilik Eğitimleri. *Doğuş Üniversitesi Dergisi*, 6, 1–11.

Aryaningsih, N. N., Suari, P. R. W., Darmayasa, N., & Utthavi, W. H. (2021, April). Management Model of Rural-Owned Enterprises Based on Entrepreneurship Innovation as a Tourist Attraction. In *International Conference on Applied Science and Technology on Social Science (ICAST-SS 2020)* (pp. 121-125). Atlantis Press. 10.2991/assehr.k.210424.024

Asaba, S., & Wada, T. (2019). The contact-hitting R&D strategy of family firms in the Japanese pharmaceutical industry. *Family Business Review*, 32(3), 277–295. 10.1177/0894486519852449

Ashraf, M. G., Rizwan, M., Iqbal, A., & Khan, M. A. (2014). The promotional tools and situational factors' impact on consumer buying behaviour and sales promotion. *Journal of Public Administration and Governance*, 4(2), 179. 10.5296/jpag.v4i2.5844

Asian Development Bank. (2022). Asian Development Outlook 2022 Update: Entrepreneurship in the Digital Age. Author.

Asiedu, E., Shortland, S., Nawar, Y., Jackson, P., & Baker, L. (2019). Supporting Ghanaian micro-entrepreneurships: The role of mobile technology. *Journal of Entrepreneurship in Emerging Economies*, 11(3), 306–327. 10.1108/JEEE-05-2018-0046

Atkinson, A., & Messy, F. (2012). Measuring financial literacy: Results of the OECD/international network on financial education (INFE) pilot study. In OECD working Papers on finance, Insurance and private pensions, No. 15. OECD Publishing. https://www.oecd-ilibrary.org/finance-and-investment/measuring-financial-literacy_5k9csfs90fr4-en

Atkinson, A., McKay, S., Collard, S., & Kempson, E. (2007). Levels of financial capability in the UK. *Public Money & Management*, 27(1), 29–36. 10.1111/j.1467-9302.2007.00552.x

Attaran, S., Attaran, M., & Celik, B. G. (2024). Digital Twins and Industrial Internet of Things: Uncovering operational intelligence in industry 4.0. *Decision Analytics Journal*, 100398.

Audretsch, D. B., Belitski, M., Caiazza, R., & Phan, P. (2023). Collaboration strategies and SME innovation performance. *Journal of Business Research*, 164, 114018. 10.1016/j.jbusres.2023.114018

Audrezet, A., de Kerviler, G., & Guidry Moulard, J. (2020). Authenticity under threat: When social media influencers need to go beyond self-presentation. *Journal of Business Research*, 117, 557–569. 10.1016/j.jbusres.2018.07.008

Axelton, Z., & Chandna, V. (2023). A practical guide to SEC financial reporting and disclosures for successful regulatory crowdfunding. *Business Horizons*, 66(6), 709–719. 10.1016/j.bushor.2023.02.006

Ayyagari, M., Demirgüç-Kunt, A., & Maksimovic, V. (2011). Firm innovation in emerging markets: The role of finance, governance, and competition. *Journal of Financial and Quantitative Analysis*, 46(6), 1545–1580. 10.1017/S0022109011000378

Ayyaswamy, K. (2024b). Enhancing Digital Technology Planning, Leadership, and Management to Transform Education. In Bhatia, M., & Mushtaq, M. T. (Eds.), *Navigating Innovative Technologies and Intelligent Systems in Modern Education* (pp. 1–9). IGI Global. 10.4018/979-8-3693-5370-7.ch001

Baas, J., Schotten, M., Plume, A., Côté, G., & Karimi, R. (2020). Scopus as a curated, high-quality bibliometric data source for academic research in quantitative science studies. *Quantitative Science Studies*, 1(1), 377–386. 10.1162/qss_a_00019

Compilation of References

Baber, H. (2019). Subjective norms and intention-A study of crowdfunding in India. *Research in World Economy*.

Baethge, C., Klier, J., & Klier, M. (2016). Social commerce—State-of-the-art and future research directions. *Electronic Markets*, 26(3), 269–290. 10.1007/s12525-016-0225-2

Bagorogoza, J. K., & Nakasule, I. (2022). The mediating effect of knowledge management on talent management and firm performance in small and medium enterprise in Uganda. *Journal of Management Development*, 41(6), 349–366. Advance online publication. 10.1108/JMD-10-2021-0290

Bai, X., Krishna, K., & Ma, H. (2017). How you export matters: Export mode, learning and productivity in China. *Journal of International Economics*, 104, 122–137. 10.1016/j.jinteco.2016.10.009

Balaban, D., & Muștătea, M. (2019). Users' perspective on the credibility of social media influencers in Romania and Germany. *Romanian Journal of Communication and Public Relations*, 21(1), 31–46. 10.21018/rjcpr.2019.1.269

Baláž, V., Jeck, T., & Balog, M. (2023). Firm performance over innovation cycle: Evidence from a small European economy. *Journal of Innovation and Entrepreneurship*, 12(40).

Banerjee, S. A. (2021). Digital philanthropy for the masses: Crowdfunding platforms marketising NGO partnerships for individual giving in India. *Development in Practice*, 31(7), 896–908. 10.1080/09614524.2021.1938515

Bansal, S., Bruno, P., Denecker, O., Goparaju, M., & Niederkorn, M. (2018). Global payments 2018: A dynamic industry continues to break new ground. McKinsey Global Banking Report. https://www.mckinsey.com/~/media/McKinsey/Industries/Financial%20Services/Our%20Insights/Global%20payments%20Expansive%20growth%20targeted%20opportunities/Global-payments-map-2018.ashx

Barber, D. III, Harris, M., & Jones, J. (2021). An overview of rural entrepreneurship and future directions. *Journal of Small Business Strategy*, 31(4). Advance online publication. 10.53703/001c.29468

Barney, J. B. (1994). How a firm's capabilities affect boundary decisions. *MIT Sloan Management Review*.

Barron, J. A., Wu, P., Ladouceur, H. D., & Ringeisen, B. R. (2004). Biological laser printing: a novel technique for creating heterogeneous 3-dimensional cell patterns. Biomed Microdevices. https://pubmed.ncbi.nlm.nih.gov/15320636/

Bashir, M., Alfalih, A., & Pradhan, S. (2023). Managerial ties, business model innovation & SME performance: Moderating role of environmental turbulence. *Journal of Innovation & Knowledge*, 8(1), 100329. 10.1016/j.jik.2023.100329

Basly, S., & Saunier, P. L. (2020). Familiness, socio-emotional goals and the internationalization of French family SMEs. *Journal of International Entrepreneurship*, 18(3), 270–311. 10.1007/s10843-019-00265-0

Basuki, C., Pratiwi, C. P., & Rahmatika, R. A. (2023). Implementation Search Engine Optimization (SEO) to Improve Marketing F&B Industry. *Bit-Tech: Binary Digital - Technology, 6*(1), 87–94. 10.32877/bt.v6i1.904

Bayfield, R., Dana, L. P., & Stewart, S. (2009). Firm characteristics and internationalisation strategies: An empirical investigation of New Zealand exporters. *International Journal of Globalisation and Small Business, 3*(3), 275–287. 10.1504/IJGSB.2009.024571

Bebbington, J., & Unerman, J. (2018). Achieving the United Nations Sustainable Development Goals: An enabling role for accounting research. *Accounting, Auditing & Accountability Journal, 31*(1), 2–24. 10.1108/AAAJ-05-2017-2929

Becherer, R. C., Helms, M. M., & McDonald, J. P. (2012). The effect of entrepreneurial marketing on outcome goals in SMEs. *New England Journal of Entrepreneurship, 15*(1/2), 1–7. 10.1108/NEJE-15-01-2012-B001

Belanche, D., Casaló, L. V., Flavián, M., & Ibáñez-Sánchez, S. (2021). Building influencers' credibility on Instagram: Effects on followers' attitudes and behavioral responses toward the influencer. *Journal of Retailing and Consumer Services, 61*, 102585. Advance online publication. 10.1016/j.jretconser.2021.102585

Beliaeva, T., Ferasso, M., Kraus, S., & Damke, E. J. (2020). Dynamics of digital entrepreneurship and the innovation ecosystem: A multilevel perspective. *International Journal of Entrepreneurial Behaviour & Research, 26*(2), 266–284. 10.1108/IJEBR-06-2019-0397

Belleflamme, P., Lambert, T., & Schwienbacher, A. (2014). Crowdfunding: Tapping the right crowd. *Journal of Business Venturing, 29*(5), 585–609. 10.1016/j.jbusvent.2013.07.003

Bellefleur, D., Murad, Z., & Tangkau, P. (2012). *and Micro, Small, and Medium Sized Enterprise Development*. United States Agency International Development From The American People.

Bello, U., Marques, C., Sacramento, O., & Galvão, A. (2021). Neo-rural small entrepreneurs' motivations and challenges in Portugal's low-density regions. *Journal of Enterprising Communities People and Places in the Global Economy, 16*(6), 900–923. 10.1108/JEC-04-2021-0047

Ben Oumlil, A., & Balloun, J. L. (2020). Millennials' attitude toward advertising: An international exploratory study. *Young Consumers, 21*(1), 17–34. 10.1108/YC-10-2018-0865

Berger, E. S., Von Briel, F., Davidsson, P., & Kuckertz, A. (2021). Digital or not–The future of entrepreneurship and innovation: Introduction to the special issue. *Journal of Business Research, 125*, 436–442. 10.1016/j.jbusres.2019.12.020

Betancourt, I., Téllez, M., Sánchez, P., Castro, L., & Carrasco, J. (2021). Entrepreneurship as a mechanism to strengthen rural communities. *European Journal of Business Management and Research, 6*(2), 107–110. 10.24018/ejbmr.2021.6.2.800

Beynon, M., Jones, P., & Pickernell, D. (2019). The role of entrepreneurship, innovation, and urbanity-diversity on growth, unemployment, and income: US state-level evidence and an fsqca elucidation. *Journal of Business Research, 101*, 675–687. 10.1016/j.jbusres.2019.01.074

Compilation of References

Bharadwaj, A., El Sawy, O. A., Pavlou, P. A., & Venkatraman, N. (2013). Digital business strategy: Toward a next generation of insights. MIS Quarterly: Management. *Information Systems*, 37(2), 471–482.

Bocken, N. M., & Short, S. W. (2021). Unsustainable business models–Recognising and resolving institutionalised social and environmental harm. *Journal of Cleaner Production*, 312, 127828. 10.1016/j.jclepro.2021.127828

Bodlaj, M., & Čater, B. (2019). The impact of environmental turbulence on the perceived importance of innovation and innovativeness in SMEs. *Journal of Small Business Management*, 57(sup2), 417–435. 10.1111/jsbm.12482

Boksberger, P. E., & Melsen, L. (2011). Perceived value: A critical examination of definitions, concepts and measures for the service industry. In Journal of Services Marketing (Vol. 25, Issue 3, pp. 229-240). 10.1108/08876041111129209

Bomani, M., Derera, E., & Mashingaidze, M. (2022). Urbanisation and SME growth in a developing economy: Implications for policy. *Corporate Governance and Organizational Behavior Review*, 6(2), 123–133. 10.22495/cgobrv6i2p12

Bomani, M., Fields, Z., & Derera, E. (2018). Historical overview of small and medium enterprise policies in Zimbabwe. *Journal of Social Sciences*, 45(2), 113–129. 10.1080/09718923.2015.11893493

Bomani, M., Fields, Z., & Derera, E. (2019). The role of higher education institutions in the development of SMEs in Zimbabwe. International. *Journal of Business and Management Studies*, 11(2), 1–15.

Bonaccorsi, A. (1992). On the relationship between firm size and export intensity. *Journal of International Business Studies*, 23(4), 605–635. 10.1057/palgrave.jibs.8490280

Braga, V., Correia, A., Braga, A., & Lemos, S. (2017). The innovation and internationalisation processes of family businesses. *Review of International Business and Strategy*, 27(2), 231–247. 10.1108/RIBS-01-2017-0005

Breit, L., & Volkmann, C. K. (2023). Recent developments in entrepreneurial marketing: Systematic literature review, thematic analysis and research agenda. *Journal of Research in Marketing and Entrepreneurship*, 26(2), 228–256. 10.1108/JRME-11-2022-0136

Brockhaus, R. H. (2004). Family business succession: Suggestions for future research. *Family Business Review*, 17(2), 165–177. 10.1111/j.1741-6248.2004.00011.x

Broekaert, W., Andries, P., & Debackere, K. (2016). Innovation processes in family firms: The relevance of organizational flexibility. *Small Business Economics*, 47(3), 771–785. 10.1007/s11187-016-9760-7

Bromiley, P., & Rau, D. (2014). Towards a practice-based view of strategy. *Strategic Management Journal*, 35(8), 1249–1256. 10.1002/smj.2238

Bronfenbrenner, U. (1979). *The ecology of human development: Experiments by nature and design*. Harvard University Press. 10.4159/9780674028845

Brown, P., & Bell, J. (2001). Industrial clusters and small firm internationalisation (Best paper). In *Multinationals in a New Era*. Palgrave Macmillan. 10.1057/9781403907622_2

Business, N. S. T. (2023, February 10). *Malaysian MSMEs post higher revenue in 2022*. New Straits Times. https://www.nst.com.my/business/2023/02/878451/malaysian-msmes-post-higher-revenue-2022

Cacciolatti, L., Rosli, A., Ruiz-Alba, J. L., & Chang, J. (2020). Strategic alliances and firm performance in startups with a social mission. *Journal of Business Research*, 106, 106–117. 10.1016/j.jbusres.2019.08.047

Calvino, F., & Criscuolo, C. (2019). Business dynamics and digitalisation. OECD STI Policy Papers, 62. https:// www. oecd- ilibrary. org/ scien ce- and- techn ology/ busin ess- dynam ics- and- digit alisa tion_ 6e0b0 11a- en

Camacho, G. (2022). Sustainable fashion: The case of a Mexican BCorp. In *Fashion Marketing in Emerging Economies Volume I: Brand, Consumer and Sustainability Perspectives* (pp. 237-263). Cham: Springer International Publishing.

Camisón, C., & Villar-López, A. (2014). Organizational innovation as an enabler of technological innovation capabilities and firm performance. *Journal of Business Research*, 67(1), 2891–2902. 10.1016/j.jbusres.2012.06.004

Carazo, P. C. M., & Lumiste, R. (2010). Foreign entry modes of Colombian small and medium enterprises. *International Journal of Business and Economics Perspectives*, 5(1), 16–41.

Carnes, C. M., & Ireland, R. D. (2013). Familiness and innovation: Resource bundling as the missing link. *Entrepreneurship Theory and Practice*, 37(6), 1399–1419. 10.1111/etap.12073

Carrasco-Carvajal, O., Castillo-Vergara, M., & García-Pérez-de-Lema, D. (2023). Measuring open innovation in SMEs: An overview of current research. *Review of Managerial Science*, 17(2), 397–442. 10.1007/s11846-022-00533-9

Casprini, E., De Massis, A., Di Minin, A., Frattini, F., & Piccaluga, A. (2017). How family firms execute open innovation strategies: The Loccioni case. *Journal of Knowledge Management*, 21(6), 1459–1485. 10.1108/JKM-11-2016-0515

Cavusgil, S. T. (1984). Differences among exporting firms based on their degree of internationalization. *Journal of Business Research*, 12(2), 195–208. 10.1016/0148-2963(84)90006-7

Cesaroni, F. M., Chamochumbi Diaz, G. D., & Sentuti, A. (2021). Family firms and innovation from founder to successor. *Administrative Sciences*, 11(2), 54. 10.3390/admsci11020054

Ceyhan, P., Haklıdır, E. A., & Tellez, F. A. (2022). Rethinking the design studio curriculum through adaptive and transformative strategies and acts: Cross-cultural reflections. *Journal of Design. Business & Society*, 9(1), 79–101.

Compilation of References

Chae, B. (2019). A general framework for studying the evolution of the digital innovation ecosystem: The case of big data. *International Journal of Information Management*, 45, 83–94. 10.1016/j.ijinfomgt.2018.10.023

Chandler, D. (2022). *Strategic corporate social responsibility: Sustainable value creation*. Sage Publications.

Chang, S. E. (2018). Regulation of crowdfunding in Indonesia. *Law Review*, 18(1), 41–71. 10.19166/lr.v0i1.1159

Chathoth, P. K., Ungson, G. R., Harrington, R. J., & Chan, E. S. W. (2016). Co-creation and higher order customer engagement in hospitality and tourism services: A critical review. *International Journal of Contemporary Hospitality Management*, 28(2), 222–245. 10.1108/IJCHM-10-2014-0526

Chatterjee, S., & Kumar Kar, A. (2020). Why do small and medium enterprises use social media marketing and what is the impact: Empirical insights from India. *International Journal of Information Management*, 53, 102103. 10.1016/j.ijinfomgt.2020.102103

Chen, L. (2016). From Fintech to Finlife: The case of Fintech Development in China. *China Economic Journal*, 9(3), 225–239. 10.1080/17538963.2016.1215057

Chen, L. H., Hung, P., & Ma, H. W. (2020). Integrating circular business models and development tools in the circular economy transition process: A firm-level framework. *Business Strategy and the Environment*, 29(5), 1887–1898. 10.1002/bse.2477

Chetioui, Y., Benlafqih, H., & Lebdaoui, H. (2020). How fashion influencers contribute to consumers' purchase intention. *Journal of Fashion Marketing and Management*, 24(3), 361–380. 10.1108/JFMM-08-2019-0157

Chetty, S., & Campbell-Hunt, C. (2003). Paths to internationalisation among small to medium-sized firms: A global versus regional approach. *European Journal of Marketing*, 37(5/6), 796–820. 10.1108/03090560310465152

Chiang, Y. H., & Hung, K. P. (2010). Exploring open search strategies and perceived innovation performance from the perspective of inter-organizational knowledge flows. *Research Management*, 40(3), 292–299.

Chirico, F., & Nordqvist, M. (2010). Dynamic capabilities and trans-generational value creation in family firms: The role of organizational culture. *International Small Business Journal*, 28(5), 487–504. 10.1177/0266242610370402

Choi, W., & Lee, Y. (2019). Effects of fashion vlogger attributes on product attitude and content sharing. *Fashion and Textiles*, 6(1), 6. Advance online publication. 10.1186/s40691-018-0161-1

Chopra, M., Singh, S. K., Gupta, A., Aggarwal, K., Gupta, B. B., & Colace, F. (2022). Analysis & prognosis of sustainable development goals using big data-based approach during COVID-19 pandemic. *Sustainable Technology and Entrepreneurship*, 1(2), 100012. 10.1016/j.stae.2022.100012

Chrisman, J. J., Chua, J. H., De Massis, A., Frattini, F., & Wright, M. (2015). The ability and willingness paradox in family firm innovation. *Journal of Product Innovation Management*, 32(3), 310–318. 10.1111/jpim.12207

Chrisman, J. J., Chua, J. H., & Sharma, P. (2005). Trends and directions in the development of a strategic management theory of the family firm. *Entrepreneurship Theory and Practice*, 29(5), 555–575. 10.1111/j.1540-6520.2005.00098.x

Christensen, C. M., & Bower, J. L. (1996). Customer power, strategic investment, and the failure of leading firms. *Strategic Management Journal*, 17(3), 197–218. 10.1002/(SICI)1097-0266(199603)17:3<197::AID-SMJ804>3.0.CO;2-U

Christensen, R. (2006). The small and medium sized exporters squeeze: Empirical evidence and model reflections. *Entrepreneurship and Regional Development*, 3(1), 49–65. 10.1080/08985629100000004

Christian, O. O. (2019). Using The Dart Model Of Value Co-Creation To Predict Customer Loyalty In Pension Fund Administration In Nigeria. British Journal Of Management and Marketing Studies, 2(3), 13-26. https://www.researchgate.net/publication/338570525

Christodoulides, G., Jevons, C., & Blackshaw, P. (2011). The Voice of the Consumer Speaks Forcefully in Brand Identity. *Journal of Advertising Research, 51*(1), 101–111. 10.2501/JAR-51-1-101-111

Chung, J. J., Im, H., Kim, S. H., Park, J. W., & Jung, Y. (2020). Toward Biomimetic Scaffolds for Tissue Engineering: 3D Printing Techniques in Regenerative Medicine. Front. Bioeng. Biotechnol. https://www.frontiersin.org/articles/10.3389/fbioe.2020.586406/full

Chung, C. N., & Zhu, H. (2021). Corporate governance dynamics of political tie formation in emerging economies: Business group affiliation, family ownership, and institutional transition. *Corporate Governance*, 29(4), 381–401. 10.1111/corg.12367

Ciolac, R., Adamov, T., Iancu, T., Popescu, G., Lile, R., Rujescu, C., & Marin, D. (2019). Agritourism-a sustainable development factor for improving the 'health' of rural settlements. Case study Apuseni Mountains area. *Sustainability (Basel)*, 11(5), 1467. 10.3390/su11051467

Clarke, L. W. (2020). Walk a day in my shoes: Cultivating cross-cultural understanding through digital literacy. *The Reading Teacher*, 73(5), 662–665. 10.1002/trtr.1890

Cohen, J. (1992). Statistical power analysis. *Current Directions in Psychological Science*, 1(3), 98–101. 10.1111/1467-8721.ep10768783

Comin, L. C., Oro, I. M., & Carvalho, C. E. (2022). Family involvement and innovation: a proposition for studies. *Revista Brasileira de Inovação, 21*.

Conz, E., Denicolai, S., & De Massis, A. (2023). Preserving the longevity of long-lasting family businesses: A multilevel model. *The Journal of Management and Governance*, 1–38. 10.1007/s10997-023-09670-z

Compilation of References

Coviello, N. E., & Martin, K. A. (1999). Internationalization of Service SMEs: An Integrated Perspective from the Engineering Consulting Sector. *Journal of International Marketing*, 7(4), 42–66. 10.1177/1069031X9900700404

Creek, S. A., Maurer, J. D., & Kent, J. K. (2023). Perceptions of market orientation in emerging economy entrepreneurship: evidence from crowdfunding. *International Journal of Emerging Markets*.

Cristiano, E. (2020). The growth of family businesses: The path to internationalization. *Management Controlling and Governance of Family Businesses: Theoretical Insights and Empirical Evidence from Italy*, 75-95.

Cucculelli, M., & Bettinelli, C. (2015). Business models, intangibles and firm performance: Evidence on corporate entrepreneurship from Italian manufacturing SMEs. *Small Business Economics*, 45(2), 329–350. 10.1007/s11187-015-9631-7

Cucculelli, M., & Peruzzi, V. (2020). Innovation over the industry life-cycle. Does ownership matter? *Research Policy*, 49(1), 103878. 10.1016/j.respol.2019.103878

Cui, T. H., Ghose, A., Halaburda, H., Iyengar, R., Pauwels, K., Sriram, S., Tucker, C., & Venkataraman, S. (2021). Informational Challenges in Omnichannel Marketing: Remedies and Future Research. *Journal of Marketing, 85*(1), 103-120. 10.1177/0022242920968810

Cumming, D., & Zhang, Y. (2016). Alternative investments in emerging markets: A review and new trends. *Emerging Markets Review*, 29, 1–23. 10.1016/j.ememar.2016.08.022

Cumurovic, A., & Hyll, W. (2019). Financial literacy and self-employment. *The Journal of Consumer Affairs*, 53(2), 455–487. 10.1111/joca.12198

Cunningham, J. A., Damij, N., Modic, D., & Olan, F. (2023). MSME technology adoption, entrepreneurial mindset and value creation: A configurational approach. *The Journal of Technology Transfer*, 48(5), 1574–1598. 10.1007/s10961-023-10022-0

Cunningham, P., Cunningham, M., & Ekenberg, L. (2015). Assessment of potential ICT-related collaboration and innovation capacity in east Africa [Paper presentation]. *2015 IEEE Global Humanitarian Technology Conference (GHTC)*, Seattle, WA, USA. 10.1109/GHTC.2015.7343961

Curatman, A., Soesanty, R., Mastur, M., & Ikhsani, M. (2016). Analysis of Factors Influencing Product Innovation that Impacts on the Competitive Advantage of Food and Beverage SMEs in the Harjamukti Region of Cirebon City. Journal of Logic, 18(3). www.jurnal.unswagati.ac.id

Cyrus, W. (2021). A fluid-supported 3D hydrogel bioprinting method. *Biomaterials*, 276, 121034. Advance online publication. 10.1016/j.biomaterials.2021.121034

Damijan, J. P., Kostevc, Č., & Polanec, S. (2010). From innovation to exporting or vice versa? *World Economy*, 33(3), 374–398. 10.1111/j.1467-9701.2010.01260.x

Damoah, O. B. O. (2020). Strategic factors predicting the likelihood of youth entrepreneurship in Ghana: A logistic regression analysis. *World Journal of Entrepreneurship, Management and Sustainable Development*, 16(4), 389–401. 10.1108/WJEMSD-06-2018-0057

Dana, L. P., Boardman, R., Salamzadeh, A., Pereira, V., & Brandstrup, M. (2024). *Fashion and environmental sustainability: Entrepreneurship, innovation, and technology*. De Gruyter.

Dana, L. P., Salamzadeh, A., Hadizadeh, M., Heydari, G., & Shamsoddin, S. (2022). Urban entrepreneurship and sustainable businesses in smart cities: Exploring the role of digital technologies. *Sustainable Technology and Entrepreneurship*, 1(2), 100016. 10.1016/j.stae.2022.100016

Dangelico, R. M., Nastasi, A., & Pisa, S. (2019). A comparison of family and nonfamily small firms in their approach to green innovation: A study of Italian companies in the agri-food industry. *Business Strategy and the Environment*, 28(7), 1434–1448. 10.1002/bse.2324

Dangi, N., Gupta, S. K., & Narula, S. A. (2020). Consumer buying behaviour and purchase intention of organic food: A conceptual framework. *Management of Environmental Quality*, 31(6), 1515–1530. 10.1108/MEQ-01-2020-0014

Das, A., & Pal, B. (2022). Status of rural entrepreneurs in the post-pandemic situation: A study in selected blocks in Nadia district of West Bengal, India. *South Asian Journal of Social Studies and Economics*, 9-15. 10.9734/sajsse/2022/v15i330406

Daugherty, T., & Hoffman, E. (2014). eWOM and the importance of capturing consumer attention within social media. *Journal of Marketing Communications*, 20(1–2), 82–102. 10.1080/13527266.2013.797764

Dávila, M. A. M., Pantaleón, A. J. S., Caro, O. C., Bueloth, M. R., & Rios, I. D. M. (2023). Innovation and Entrepreneurship Skills in University Students, Amazonas, Peru, 2023. *Migration Letters : An International Journal of Migration Studies*, 20(7), 557–575.

Davis, G. F., & Cobb, J. A. (2010). Resource Dependence Theory: Past and Future. In *Stanford's Organization Theory Renaissance, 1970–2000* (*Research in the Sociology of Organizations*, Vol. 28), Emerald. 10.1108/S0733-558X(2010)0000028006

De Groote, J. K., Conrad, W., & Hack, A. (2021). How can family businesses survive disruptive industry changes? Insights from the traditional mail order industry. *Review of Managerial Science*, 15(8), 2239–2273. 10.1007/s11846-020-00424-x

De Loecker, J. (2013). Detecting learning by exporting. *American Economic Journal. Microeconomics*, 5(3), 1–21. 10.1257/mic.5.3.1

De Massis, A., & Foss, N. J. (2018). Advancing family business research: The promise of microfoundations. In *Family Business Review* (Vol. 31, Issue 4, pp. 386–396). SAGE Publications Inc. 10.1177/0894486518803422

De Massis, A., Di Minin, A., & Frattini, F. (2015). Family-driven innovation: Resolving the paradox in family firms. *California Management Review*, 58(1), 5–19. 10.1525/cmr.2015.58.1.5

De Massis, A., Frattini, F., Kotlar, J., Petruzzelli, A. M., & Wright, M. (2016). Innovation through tradition: Lessons from innovative family businesses and directions for future research. *The Academy of Management Perspectives*, 30(1), 93–116. 10.5465/amp.2015.0017

Compilation of References

De Massis, A., Frattini, F., & Lichtenthaler, U. (2013). Research on technological innovation in family firms: Present debates and future directions. *Family Business Review*, 26(1), 10–31. 10.1177/0894486512466258

De Massis, A., Frattini, F., Pizzurno, E., & Cassia, L. (2015). Product innovation in family versus nonfamily firms: An exploratory analysis. *Journal of Small Business Management*, 53(1), 1–36. 10.1111/jsbm.12068

De Veirman, M., & Hudders, L. (2020). Disclosing sponsored Instagram posts: The role of material connection with the brand and message-sidedness when disclosing covert advertising. *International Journal of Advertising*, 39(1), 94–130. 10.1080/02650487.2019.1575108

Debbabi, R., & Kaplan, B. (2022). Why crowdfunding? Understanding crowdfunding and the marketing roots of this fundraising model in Turkey. *Business & Management Studies: An International Journal*, 10(1), 429–446. 10.15295/bmij.v10i1.1996

Del Bosco, B., & Bettinelli, C. (2020). How do family SMEs control their investments abroad? The role of distance and family control. *MIR. Management International Review*, 60(1), 1–35. 10.1007/s11575-019-00406-6

Delery, J. E., & Roumpi, D. (2017). Strategic human resource management, human capital and competitive advantage: Is the field going in circles? *Human Resource Management Journal*, 27(1), 1–21. 10.1111/1748-8583.12137

Demiray, M., & Burnaz, S. (2019). Positioning of crowdfunding platforms: Turkey as an emerging market case. *Journal of Management Marketing and Logistics*, 6(2), 84–94. 10.17261/Pressacademia.2019.1036

Deng, X., Hui, S. K., & Hutchinson, J. W. (2010). Consumer preferences for color combinations: An empirical analysis of similarity-based color relationships. *Journal of Consumer Psychology*, 20(4), 476–484. 10.1016/j.jcps.2010.07.005

Denli, İ. (2023). Girişimci Adaylarının Girişimcilik Profillerinin Belirlenmesi: Üniversite Öğrencileri Örneği. *Girişimcilik ve Kalkınma Dergisi*, 18(1), 49–63.

Dess, G. G., & Lumpkin, G. T. (2005). The role of entrepreneurial orientation in stimulating effective corporate entrepreneurship. *The Academy of Management Perspectives*, 19(1), 147–156. 10.5465/ame.2005.15841975

Dhewanto, W., Ratnaningtyas, S., Permatasari, A., Anggadwita, G., & Prasetio, E. (2020). Rural entrepreneurship: Towards collaborative participative models for economic sustainability. *Journal of Entrepreneurship and Sustainability Issues*, 8(1), 705–724. 10.9770/jesi.2020.8.1(48)

Di Cintio, M., Ghosh, S., & Grassi, E. (2020). Direct or indirect exports: What matters for firms' innovation activities? *Applied Economics Letters*, 27(2), 93–103. 10.1080/13504851.2019.1610693

Doğrusöz, L. A., & Uluçay, A. P. (2023). Kültürün Girişimcilik Niyeti Üzerindeki Etkisinde Algılanan İsteğin Moderatör Rolü: İstanbul Örneği. *İşletme Araştırmaları Dergisi*, 15(1), 147-161.

Doluca, H., Wagner, M., & Block, J. (2018). Sustainability and environmental behaviour in family firms: A longitudinal analysis of environment-related activities, innovation and performance. *Business Strategy and the Environment*, 27(1), 152–172. 10.1002/bse.1998

Donovan, J. (2021). Financial reporting and entrepreneurial finance: Evidence from equity crowdfunding. *Management Science*, 67(11), 7214–7237. 10.1287/mnsc.2020.3810

Dovaliene, A., Masiulyte, A., & Piligrimiene, Z. (2015). The Relations between Customer Engagement, Perceivedd Value and Satisfaction: The Case of Mobile Applications. *Procedia: Social and Behavioral Sciences*, 213, 659–664. 10.1016/j.sbspro.2015.11.469

Drăgoi, M., Iamandi, I., Munteanu, S., Ciobanu, R., ar avulea, R., & Ladaru, R. (2017). Incentives for developing resilient agritourism entrepreneurship in rural communities in Romania in a European context. *Sustainability*, 9(12), 2205. 10.3390/su9122205

Drucker, P. F. (2006). *Innovation and entre-preneurship: practice and principles*. HarperCollins Publishers.

Drucker, P., & Maciariello, J. (2014). *Innovation and entrepreneurship*. Routledge. 10.4324/9781315747453

Duffy, D. L. (2005). Affiliate marketing and its impact on e-commerce. *Journal of Consumer Marketing*, 22(3), 161–163. 10.1108/07363760510595986

Duh, H. I., & Thabethe, T. (2021). Attributes of Instagram influencers impacting consumer brand engagement. *International Journal of Internet Marketing and Advertising*, 15(5), 1. 10.1504/IJIMA.2021.118261

Dumitru, D., & Halpern, D. F. (2023). Critical Thinking: Creating Job-Proof Skills for the Future of Work. *Journal of Intelligence*, 11(10), 194. 10.3390/jintelligence1110019437888426

Duran, P., Kammerlander, N., Van Essen, M., & Zellweger, T. (2016). Doing more with less: Innovation input and output in family firms. *Academy of Management Journal*, 59(4), 1224–1264. 10.5465/amj.2014.0424

Durão, V., & Moreira, A. C. (2019). Critical and inhibiting success factors in inter-organizational networks: A case study. In Teixeira, S., & Ferreira, J. (Eds.), *Multilevel Approach to Competitiveness in the Global Tourism Industry* (pp. 63–86). IGI Global. 10.4018/978-1-7998-0365-2.ch005

Durkin, M., McGowan, P., & McKeown, N. (2013). Exploring social media adoption in small to medium-sized enterprises in Ireland. *Journal of Small Business and Enterprise Development*, 20(4), 716–734. 10.1108/JSBED-08-2012-0094

Dyba, M., Гернего, Ю., Dyba, O., & Oliynyk, A. (2020). Financial support and development of digital rural hubs in Europe. *Management Theory and Studies for Rural Business and Infrastructure Development*, 41(4), 51–59. 10.15544/mts.2020.06

Earnest, P. (2021). 3D Bioprinting of Vascularized Tissues for in vitro and in vivo Applications. Front Bioeng Biotechnol. https://www.ncbi.nlm.nih.gov/pmc/articles/PMC8158943/

Compilation of References

Ebrahim, R. S. (2020). The Role of Trust in Understanding the Impact of Social Media Marketing on Brand Equity and Brand Loyalty. *Journal of Relationship Marketing*, 19(4), 287–308. 10.1080/15332667.2019.1705742

ECO SAPO. (2022). Metalurgia e metalomecânica bate recorde de exportações em março. https://eco.sapo.pt/2022/05/18/metalurgia-e-metalomecanica-bate-recorde-de-exportacoes-em-marco/

Eddleston, K. A., Kellermanns, F. W., & Collier, G. (2019). Research on family firm innovation: What do family firms actually think and do? *Journal of Family Business Strategy*, 10(4), 1–7. 10.1016/j.jfbs.2019.100308

Eggers, F., Hansen, D. J., & Davis, A. E. (2012). Examining the relationship between customer and entrepreneurial orientation on nascent firms' marketing strategy. *The International Entrepreneurship and Management Journal*, 8(2), 203–222. 10.1007/s11365-011-0173-4

Eid, R., & El-Gohary, H. (2013). The impact of E-marketing use on small business enterprises' marketing success. *Service Industries Journal*, 33(1), 31–50. 10.1080/02642069.2011.594878

Eisenhardt, K. M. (1989). Building theories from case study research. *Academy of Management Review*, 14(4), 532–550. 10.2307/258557

Ellitan, L. (2006). Innovation Strategy and Performance of Manufacturing Companies in Indonesia: A Simultaneous and Sequential Model Approach. *Journal of Management*, 6(1).

Eltanahy, M., Forawi, S., & Mansour, N. (2020). Incorporating entrepreneurial practices into STEM education: Development of interdisciplinary E-STEM model in high school in the United Arab Emirates. *Thinking Skills and Creativity*, 37, 100697. 10.1016/j.tsc.2020.100697

Ensari, M. Ş., & Karabay, M. E. (2014). What helps to make SMEs successful in global markets? *Procedia: Social and Behavioral Sciences*, 150, 192–201. 10.1016/j.sbspro.2014.09.030

Erasmus, A. C., Tocknell, G., & Schutte, F. (2023). The potential of crowdfunding to promote business in the context of an emerging economy. *Journal of Financial Services Marketing*, 28(3), 558–569. 10.1057/s41264-022-00165-w

Erramilli, M. K., & D'Souza, D. E. (1993). Venturing into foreign markets: The case of the small service firm. *Entrepreneurship Theory and Practice*, 17(4), 29–41. 10.1177/104225879301700403

Fahim, T. (2020). *A Study on Consumer Attitude towards Affiliate Marketing for E-Business*. Academic Press.

Falahat, M., Lee, Y. Y., Soto-Acosta, P., & Ramayah, T. (2021). Entrepreneurial, market, learning and networking orientations as determinants of business capability and international performance: The contingent role of government support. *The International Entrepreneurship and Management Journal*, 17(4), 1–22. 10.1007/s11365-020-00738-y

Falahat, M., Soto-Acosta, P., & Ramayah, T. (2022). Analysing the importance of international knowledge, orientation, networking and commitment as entrepreneurial culture and market orientation in gaining competitive advantage and international performance. *International Marketing Review*, 39(3), 463–481. 10.1108/IMR-02-2021-0053

Fanea-Ivanovici, M., & Baber, H. (2023). Using the civic voluntarism model to compare the donation intentions in US and India political crowdfunding. *International Journal of Electronic Governance*, 15(2), 188–201. 10.1504/IJEG.2023.132366

Fan, F., Chan, K., Wang, Y., Li, Y., & Prieler, M. (2023). How influencers' social media posts have an influence on audience engagement among young consumers. *Young Consumers*, 24(4), 427–444. 10.1108/YC-08-2022-1588

Fang, Guo, Liu, Xu, Mao, Mo, Zhang, Ouyang, Xiong, & Sun. (2022). Advances in 3D Bioprinting. *Chinese Journal of Mechanical Engineering: Additive Manufacturing Frontiers*. 10.1016/j.cjmeam.2022.100011

Faul, F., Erdfelder, E., Buchner, A., & Lang, A. G. (2009). Statistical power analyses using G* Power 3.1: Tests for correlation and regression analyses. *Behavior Research Methods*, 41(4), 1149–1160. 10.3758/BRM.41.4.114919897823

Feki, C., & Mnif, S. (2019). Self-employment and unemployment in Tunisia: Application of the ARDL approach. *International Journal of Academic Research in Business & Social Sciences*, 9(7). Advance online publication. 10.6007/IJARBSS/v9-i7/6217

Felício, J. A., & Galindo Villardón, M. P. (2015). Family characteristics and governance of small and medium-sized family firms. *Journal of Business Economics and Management*, 16(6), 1069–1084. 10.3846/16111699.2012.747446

Felipe, I. J. D. S. (2015). Shared value creation and crowdfunding in Brazil. *Journal of Financial Innovation*, 1(3), 213–230.

Fernández-Olmos, M., & Malorgio, G. (2020). The speed of the internationalisation process and the institutional networks of family SMEs in the DOC Rioja Wine Industry. *Wine Economics and Policy*, 9(1), 43–50. www.fupress.com/wep. 10.36253/web-8371

Fernández, Z., & Nieto, M. J. (2005). Internationalization strategy of small and medium-sized family businesses: Some influential factors. *Family Business Review*, 18(1), 77–89. 10.1111/j.1741-6248.2005.00031.x

Ferrari, F. (2023). The postponed succession: An investigation of the obstacles hindering business transmission planning in family firms. *Journal of Family Business Management*, 13(2), 412–431. 10.1108/JFBM-09-2020-0088

Ferreira, J. J., Fernandes, C. I., & Ferreira, F. A. (2019). To be or not to be digital, that is the question: Firm innovation and performance. *Journal of Business Research*, 101, 583–590. 10.1016/j.jbusres.2018.11.013

Compilation of References

Forsgren, M. (2002). The concept of learning in the Uppsala internationalization process model: A critical review. *International Business Review*, 11(3), 257–277. 10.1016/S0969-5931(01)00060-9

Foss, N. J., & Saebi, T. (2017). Fifteen years of research on business model innovation: How far have we come, and where should we go? *Journal of Management*, 43(1), 200–227. 10.1177/0149206316675927

Fox, P. B., & Wareham, J. D. (2012). Governance mechanisms in internet-based affiliate marketing programs in Spain. In *Transformations in E-Business Technologies and Commerce: Emerging Impacts* (pp. 222-239). IGI Global. 10.4018/978-1-61350-462-8.ch014

Fox, P., & Wareham, J. (2007). Controlling your brand: Contractual restrictions placed by Internet retailers on affiliate marketing activities in Spain. *20th Bled EConference - EMergence: Merging and Emerging Technologies, Processes, and Institutions - Conference Proceedings*, 125–142.

Franke, G., & Sarstedt, M. (2019). Heuristics versus statistics in discriminant validity testing: A comparison of four procedures. *Internet Research*, 29(3), 430–447. 10.1108/IntR-12-2017-0515

Frank, H., Kessler, A., Mitterer, G., & Weismeier-Sammer, D. (2012). Learning orientation of SMEs and its impact on firm performance. *Journal of Marketing Development and Competitiveness*, 6(3), 29–41.

Fredyna, T., Ruíz-Palomo, D., & Diéguez-Soto, J. (2019). Entrepreneurial orientation and product innovation. The moderating role of family involvement in management. *European Journal of Family Business*, 9(2), 128–145. 10.24310/ejfbejfb.v9i2.5392

Freiling, J., Marquardt, L., & Reit, T. (2022). Virtual business incubators: A support for entrepreneurship in rural areas? In *Advances in Human Factors and Ergonomics* (pp. 65-88). https://doi.org/10.1007/978-3-031-04063-4_4

Frow, P., Nenonen, S., Payne, A., & Storbacka, K. (2015). Managing Co-creation Design: A Strategic Approach to Innovation. *British Journal of Management*, 26(3), 463–483. 10.1111/1467-8551.12087

Frow, P., & Payne, A. (2011). A stakeholder perspective of the value proposition concept. *European Journal of Marketing*, 45(1), 223–240. 10.1108/03090561111095676

Funk, A. S. (2019). Crowdfunding in China. In *Crowdfunding in China. Contributions to Management Science*. Springer. 10.1007/978-3-319-97253-4_5

Gaber, H. R., Wright, L. T., & Kooli, K. (2019). Consumer attitudes towards Instagram advertisements in Egypt: The role of the perceived advertising value and personalization. *Cogent Business and Management*, 6(1), 1618431. Advance online publication. 10.1080/23311975.2019.1618431

Galardi, M., Moruzzo, R., Riccioli, F., Granai, G., & Iacovo, F. (2022). Small rural enterprises and innovative business models: A case study of the Turin area. *Sustainability (Basel)*, 14(3), 1265. 10.3390/su14031265

Galindo-Martín, M., Castaño-Martinez, M. S., & Méndez-Picazo, M. T. (2019). Digital transformation, digital dividends and entrepreneurship: A quantitative analysis. *Journal of Business Research*, 101, 522–527. 10.1016/j.jbusres.2018.12.014

Galván-Martínez, D., Espejel, I., Arredondo-García, M. C., Delgado-Ramírez, C., Vázquez-León, C., Hernández, A., & Gutiérrez, C. (2020). Sustainability assessment in indigenous communities: A tool for future participatory decision making. *Stewardship of Future Drylands and Climate Change in the Global South: Challenges and Opportunities for the Agenda*, 2030, 197–214. 10.1007/978-3-030-22464-6_12

Gamage, S. K. N., Ekanayake, E. M. S., Abeyrathne, G. A. K. N. J., Prasanna, R. P. I. R., Jayasundara, J. M. S. B., & Rajapakshe, P. S. K. (2020). A review of global challenges and survival strategies of small and medium enterprises (SMEs). *Economies*, 8(4), 79. 10.3390/economies8040079

Gandy, D. L. (2015). Small business strategies for company profitability and sustainability. Academic Press.

Gao, Q., Liu, Z., Lin, Z., Qiu, J., Liu, Y., Liu, A., Wang, Y., Xiang, M., Chen, B., Fu, J., & He, Y. (2017). 3D Bioprinting of Vessel-like Structures with Multilevel Fluidic. *ACS Biomaterials Science & Engineering*, 3(3), 399–408. Advance online publication. 10.1021/acsbiomaterials.6b0064333465937

Garbie, I. (2016). *Sustainability in manufacturing enterprises: Concepts, analyses and assessments for industry 4.0*. Springer. 10.1007/978-3-319-29306-6

García, D. A. R., Mata, L. M., & Mora, J. A. N. (2021). Herd Behavior Analysis in Crowdfunding Platforms in Mexico. *Entrepreneurship and Regional Development: Analyzing Growth Models in Emerging Markets*, 67-90.

García-Morales, V. J., Martín-Rojas, R., & Garde-Sánchez, R. (2020). How to encourage social entrepreneurship action? Using Web 2.0 technologies in higher education institutions. *Journal of Business Ethics*, 161(2), 329–350. 10.1007/s10551-019-04216-6

Garmashev, M. A., Sakhno, J. A., Peremyshlennikova, I. N., Sedova, N. A., & Staroselzeva, M. M. (2021). Legal regulation of crowdfunding and investment platforms: The experience of the United States, Russia and Europe. *Linguistics and Culture Review*, 5(S3), 958–966. 10.21744/lingcure.v5nS3.1695

Gaweł, A., Mroczek-Dąbrowska, K., & Pietrzykowski, M. (2022). Digitalization and Its Impact on the Internationalization Models of SMEs. doi:10.1007/978-3-031-11371-0_210.1007/978-3-031-11371-0_2

Gazzola, P., Pavione, E., Pezzetti, R., & Grechi, D. (2020). Trends in the fashion industry. The perception of sustainability and circular economy: A gender/generation quantitative approach. *Sustainability (Basel)*, 12(7), 2809. 10.3390/su12072809

Gedar, B. L., & Lodha, S. (2024). Crowdfunding as a Source of Finance in India: An Empirical Study. *IUP Journal of Applied Finance, 30*(1).

Compilation of References

George, B. A. (2011). Entrepreneurial orientation: A theoretical and empirical examination of the consequences of differing construct representations. *Journal of Management Studies*, 48(6), 1291–1313. 10.1111/j.1467-6486.2010.01004.x

George, G., Merrill, R. K., & Schillebeeckx, S. J. (2021). Digital sustainability and entrepreneurship: How digital innovations are helping tackle climate change and sustainable development. *Entrepreneurship Theory and Practice*, 45(5), 999–1027. 10.1177/1042258719899425

George, J. M., & Jones, G. R. (2012). *Understanding and managing organizational behavior* (6th ed.). Pearson Prentice Hall.

Gerhart, B., & Feng, J. (2021). The resource-based view of the firm, human resources, and human capital: Progress and prospects. *Journal of Management*, 47(7), 1796–1819. 10.1177/0149206320978799

Geyser, W. (2023). *36 Vital TikTok Stats to Inform Your Marketing Strategy*. https://influencermarketinghub.com/tiktok-stats/#toc-2

Ghauri, P. (2004). Designing and conducting case studies in international business research. In Marschan-Piekkari, R., & Welch, C. (Eds.), *Handbook of Qualitative Research Methods for International Business* (pp. 109–124). Edward Elgar. 10.4337/9781781954331.00019

Ghauri, S., Mazzarol, T., & Soutar, G. N. (2023). Networking benefits for SME members of co-operatives. *Journal of Co-operative Organization and Management*, 11(2), 100213. 10.1016/j.jcom.2023.100213

Gherghina, . C., Botezatu, M. A., Hosszu, A., & Simionescu, L. N. (2020). Small and medium-sized enterprises (SMEs): The engine of economic growth through investments and innovation. *Sustainability (Basel)*, 12(1), 347. 10.3390/su12010347

Ghosal, I., Prasad, B., & Behera, M. (2020). Impact of Affiliate Marketing on E-Buying Behavior of Millennial – A TAM Based Approach With Text Analysis. SSRN *Electronic Journal*. 10.2139/ssrn.3638929

Ghouse, S., Durrah, O., & McElwee, G. (2021). Rural women entrepreneurs in Oman: Problems and opportunities. *International Journal of Entrepreneurial Behaviour & Research*, 27(7), 1674–1695. 10.1108/IJEBR-03-2021-0209

Ghozali, I., & Latan, H. (2015). *Partial Least Square Concepts, Techniques, and Applications Using the SmartPLS 3.0 Program*. Diponegoro University Publishing Agency.

Gilchrist, S., Sim, J. W., & Zakrajšek, E. (2014). *Uncertainty, financial frictions, and investment dynamics (No. w20038)*. National Bureau of Economic Research. 10.3386/w20038

Gilmore, A. (2011). Entrepreneurial and SME marketing. *Journal of Research in Marketing and Entrepreneurship*, 13(2), 137–145. 10.1108/14715201111176426

Giotopoulos, I., Kontolaimou, A., & Tsakanikas, A. (2022). Digital responses of SMEs to the COVID-19 crisis. *International Journal of Entrepreneurial Behaviour & Research*, 28(7), 1751–1772. 10.1108/IJEBR-11-2021-0924

Gjellerup, P. (2000). SME support services in the face of globalisation. Concerted action seminar, Opening address. In *Conference Proceedings, Danish Agency for Trade and Industry, Copenhagen* (pp. 16-28). Academic Press.

Gobinath, V. M., Kathirvel, A., Rajesh Kanna, S. K., & Annamalai, K. (2024). Chapter 5: Smart Technology in Management Industries: A Useful Perspective. Artificial Intelligence Applied to Industry 4.0. Wiley Publisher. https://www.wiley.com/en-us/Topics+in+Artificial+Intelligence+Applied+to+Industry+4+0-p-978139421611610.1002/9781394216147.ch5

Gobinath, V., Ayyaswamy, K., & Kathirvel, N. (2024). Information Communication Technology and Intelligent Manufacturing Industries Perspective: An Insight. *Asian Science Bulletin*, 2(1), 36–45. 10.3923/asb.2024.36.45

Gomes, M. A., Marques, S., & Dias, Á. (2022). The impact of digital influencers' characteristics on purchase intention of fashion products. *Journal of Global Fashion Marketing*, 13(3), 187–204. 10.1080/20932685.2022.2039263

González-Cruz, T., Clemente-Almendros, J. A., & Puig-Denia, A. (2021). Family governance systems: The complementary role of constitutions and councils. *Ekonomska Istrazivanja*, 34(1), 3139–3165. 10.1080/1331677X.2020.1867603

Gonzalez-Dıaz, R. R., Guanilo-Gomez, S. L., Acevedo-Duque, A. E., Campos, J. S., & Cachicatari Vargas, E. (2021). Intrinsic alignment with strategy as a source of business sustainability in SMEs. *Entrepreneurship and Sustainability Issues*, 8(4), 377–388. 10.9770/jesi.2021.8.4(22)

González, J. D. J., Valdés Medina, F. E., & Saavedra García, M. L. (2021). Success factors in financing for SMEs through crowdfunding in Mexico. *Revista Mexicana de Economía y Finanzas*, 16(2).

González-Pérez, L. I., & Ramírez-Montoya, M. S. (2022). Components of Education 4.0 in 21st century skills frameworks: Systematic review. *Sustainability (Basel)*, 14(3), 1493. 10.3390/su14031493

Govindan, K., Shankar, K. M., & Kannan, D. (2020). Achieving sustainable development goals through identifying and analyzing barriers to industrial sharing economy: A framework development. *International Journal of Production Economics*, 227, 107575. 10.1016/j.ijpe.2019.107575

Greenaway, D., & Kneller, R. (2007). Firm heterogeneity, exporting and foreign direct investment. *Economic Journal (London)*, 117(517), F134–F161. 10.1111/j.1468-0297.2007.02018.x

Guarda, T., Balseca, J., García, K., González, J., Yagual, F., & Castillo-Beltran, H. (2021, March). Digital transformation trends and innovation. *IOP Conference Series. Materials Science and Engineering*, 1099(1), 012062. 10.1088/1757-899X/1099/1/012062

Gunarto, M. (2018). *The Co-Creation Model and its Implications for Student Loyalty at Private Universities*. Study at PTS in South Sumatra Province.

Compilation of References

Guo, Y., Zhu, L., & Yu-zong, Z. (2022). Tourism entrepreneurship in rural destinations: Measuring the effects of capital configurations using the fsQCA approach. *Tourism Review*, 78(3), 834–848. 10.1108/TR-07-2022-0333

Gurtner, S., & Reinhardt, R. (2016). Ambidextrous idea generation—Antecedents and outcomes. *Journal of Product Innovation Management*, 33(S1), 34–54. 10.1111/jpim.12353

Gür, U., & Özdoğan, B. (2021). Scientists' technology acceptance of crowdfunding in Turkey: The moderating effect of individual entrepreneurial orientation. *Journal of Entrepreneurship and Innovation Management*, 10(1), 53–80.

Habbershon, T. G., & Pistrui, J. (2002). Enterprising families domain: Family-influenced ownership groups in pursuit of transgenerational wealth. *Family Business Review*, 15(3), 223–237. 10.1111/j.1741-6248.2002.00223.x

Hack-Polay, D., Ogbaburu, J., Rahman, M., & Mahmoud, A. (2020). Immigrant entrepreneurs in rural England – An examination of the socio-cultural barriers facing migrant small businesses in Lincolnshire. *Local Economy*, 35(7), 676–694. 10.1177/0269094220988852

Haddoud, M. Y., Kock, N., Onjewu, A. K. E., Jafari-Sadeghi, V., & Jones, P. (2023). Technology, innovation and SMEs' export intensity: Evidence from Morocco. *Technological Forecasting and Social Change*, 191, 122475. 10.1016/j.techfore.2023.122475

Hadley, R. D., & Wilson, H. I. (2003). The network model of internationalisation and experiential knowledge. *International Business Review*, 12(6), 697–717. 10.1016/j.ibusrev.2003.01.001

Hafiz, N., Latiff, A. S. A., Islam, M. A., Saif, A. N., & Wahab, S. A. (2022). Towards the underlying theories of small firm growth: A literature review. *FIIB Business Review*, 11(1), 36–51. 10.1177/23197145211049627

Hahn, E. D., & Ang, S. H. (2017). From the editors: New directions in the reporting of statistical results in the Journal of World Business. In *Journal of World Business* (Vol. 52, Issue 2, pp. 125–126). Elsevier.

Haikal, E. K., Freihat, S. M., Homsi, D., Joudeh, J. M. M., & Hashem, T. N. (2020). The role of supply chain strategy and affiliate marketing in increasing the demand for ecommerce-Social media POV. *International Journal of Supply Chain Management*, 9(1), 832–844.

Hair, Black, Babin, & Anderson. (2019). Multivariate Data Analysis. 8th Edition. Annabel Ainscow.

Hair, J. F.Jr, Howard, M. C., & Nitzl, C. (2020). Assessing measurement model quality in PLS-SEM using confirmatory composite analysis. *Journal of Business Research*, 109, 101–110. 10.1016/j.jbusres.2019.11.069

Hair, J. F., Risher, J. J., Sarstedt, M., & Ringle, C. M. (2019). When to use and how to report the results of PLS-SEM. *European Business Review*, 31(1), 2–24. 10.1108/EBR-11-2018-0203

Hair, J. F., Sarstedt, M., Ringle, C. M., & Gudergan, S. P. (2018). *Advanced issues in partial least squares structural equation modeling (PLS-SEM)*. Sage.

Hajli, M. N. (2014). A study of the impact of social media on consumers. *International Journal of Market Research*, 56(3), 387–404. 10.2501/IJMR-2014-025

Hakala, H. (2011). Strategic orientations in management literature: Three approaches to understanding the interaction between market, technology, entrepreneurial and learning orientations. *International Journal of Management Reviews*, 13(2), 199–217. 10.1111/j.1468-2370.2010.00292.x

Halder, D., Pradhan, D., & Roy Chaudhuri, H. (2021). Forty-five years of celebrity credibility and endorsement literature: Review and learnings. In *Journal of Business Research* (Vol. 125, pp. 397–415). Elsevier Inc. 10.1016/j.jbusres.2020.12.031

Hambrick, D. C. (1983). Some tests of the effectiveness and functional attributes of Miles and Snow's strategic types. *Academy of Management Journal*, 26(1), 5–26. 10.2307/25613210299037

Hamburg, I. (2019). Implementation of a digital workplace strategy to drive behaviour change and 19 improve competencies. In *Strategy and Behaviors in the Digital Economy*. IntechOpen.

Hamidi, F., Shams Gharneh, N., & Khajeheian, D. (2019). A Conceptual Framework for Value Co-Creation in Service Enterprises (Case of Tourism Agencies). *Sustainability (Basel)*, 12(1), 213. 10.3390/su12010213

Han, S., Lyu, Y., Ji, R., Zhu, Y., Su, J., & Bao, L. (2020). Open innovation, network embeddedness and incremental innovation capability. *Management Decision*, 58(12), 2655–2680. 10.1108/MD-08-2019-1038

Hapsari, N. S., & Sulung, L. A. K. (2021, May). The Role of Social Capital and Reward Factor in the Success of Crowdfunding Project Fundraising: Case Study of Emerging Market Countries. In *Asia-Pacific Research in Social Sciences and Humanities Universitas Indonesia Conference (APRISH 2019)* (pp. 591-599). Atlantis Press.

Harkison, T. (2018). The use of co-creation within the luxury accommodation experience - myth or reality? *International Journal of Hospitality Management*, 71, 11–18. 10.1016/j.ijhm.2017.11.006

Harris, R., & Li, Q. C. (2007). Learning-by-exporting? Firm-level evidence for UK manufacturing and services sectors. *Department of Economics Discussion Paper, 22*.

Haryanti, S. S. (2016). Building Marketing Performance Based on Product Innovation and Competitive Advantage (Empirical Study on Gitardi Crafts Sukoharjo Regency). *ACTUAL*, 2, 1–19.

Haslam, S. A., & Ellemers, N. (2005). Social identity in industrial and organizational psychology: Concepts, controversies and contributions. *International Review of Industrial and Organizational Psychology*, 2005(20), 39–118. 10.1002/0470029307.ch2

Hatala, J. P. (2005). Identifying barriers to self-employment: The development and validation of the barriers to entrepreneurship success tool. *Performance Improvement Quarterly, 18*(4), 50-70.

Compilation of References

Haudi, H., Rahadjeng, E., Santamoko, R., Putra, R., Purwoko, D., Nurjannah, D., Koho, I. R., Wijoyo, H., Siagian, A. O., Cahyono, Y., & Purwanto, A. (2022). The role of e-marketing and e-CRM on e-loyalty of Indonesian companies during Covid pandemic and digital era. *Uncertain Supply Chain Management*, 10(1), 217–224. 10.5267/j.uscm.2021.9.006

Havinal, V. (2009). *Management and Entrepreneurship*. New Age International.

Helmers, C., & Rogers, M. (2010). Innovation and the survival of new firms in the UK. *Review of Industrial Organization*, 36(3), 227–248. 10.1007/s11151-010-9247-7

Hendijani Fard, M., & Seyyed Amiri, N. (2018). The effect of entrepreneurial marketing on halal food SMEs performance. *Journal of Islamic Marketing*, 9(3), 598–620. 10.1108/JIMA-12-2016-0097

Hendratmi, A., Ryandono, M. N. H., & Sukmaningrum, P. S. (2019). Developing Islamic crowdfunding website platform for startup companies in Indonesia. *Journal of Islamic Marketing*, 11(5), 1041–1053. 10.1108/JIMA-02-2019-0022

Henseler, J., Ringle, C. M., & Sarstedt, M. (2015). A new criterion for assessing discriminant validity in variance-based structural equation modeling. *Journal of the Academy of Marketing Science*, 43(1), 115–135. 10.1007/s11747-014-0403-8

Herrando, C., & Martín-De Hoyos, M. J. (2022). Influencer endorsement posts and their effects on advertising attitudes and purchase intentions. *International Journal of Consumer Studies*, 46(6), 2288–2299. 10.1111/ijcs.12785

Hervé, A., Schmitt, C., & Baldegger, R. (2020). Internationalization and Digitalization: Applying digital technologies to the internationalization process of small and medium-sized enterprises. *Technology Innovation Management Review, 10*(7), 29-41. doi:10.22215/timreview/137310.22215/timreview/1373

Hessels, J., & Terjesen, S. (2010). Resource dependency and institutional theory perspectives on direct and indirect export choices. *Small Business Economics*, 34(2), 203–220. 10.1007/s11187-008-9156-4

Heydari, E., Rezaei, M., Pironti, M., & Chmet, F. (2023). How does owners' personality impacts business internationalisation in family SMEs? In Jafari-Sadeghi, V., & Amoozad Mahdiraji, H. (Eds.), *Decision-Making in International Entrepreneurship: Unveiling Cognitive Implications Towards Entrepreneurial Internationalisation* (pp. 331–347). Emerald Publishing Limited. 10.1108/978-1-80382-233-420231016

Hillman, A., Withers, M., & Collins, B. (2009). Resource dependence theory: A review. *Journal of Management*, 35(6), 1404–1427. 10.1177/0149206309343469

Hoffman, J., Hoelscher, M., & Sorenson, R. (2006). Achieving sustained competitive advantage: A family capital theory. *Family Business Review*, 19(2), 135–145. 10.1111/j.1741-6248.2006.00065.x

Hogg, M. A., & Abrams, D. (1988). Social identifications: A social psychology of intergroup relations and group processes. In *Social identifications: A social psychology of intergroup relations and group processes*. Taylor & Frances/Routledge.

Holmström, J. (2018). Recombination in digital innovation: Challenges, opportunities, and the importance of a theoretical framework. *Information and Organization*, 28(2), 107–110. 10.1016/j.infoandorg.2018.04.002

Hovland, C. I., Janis, I. L., & Kelley, H. H. (1953). Communication and persuasion. In *Communication and persuasion*. Yale University Press.

Hovland, C. I., & Weiss, W. (1951). The influence of source credibility on communication effectiveness. *Public Opinion Quarterly*, 15(4), 635–650. 10.1086/266350

Hsu, C. Y., & Wu, T. T. (2023). Application of Business Simulation Games in Flipped Classrooms to Facilitate Student Engagement and Higher-Order Thinking Skills for Sustainable Learning Practices. *Sustainability (Basel)*, 15(24), 16867. 10.3390/su152416867

Hu, M. K., & Kee, D. M. H. (2022). Fostering sustainability: reinventing SME strategy in the new normal. *Foresight*, 24(3/4), 301-318.

Huang, C., Rui, L., & Zhu, Y. (2023). Research on digital construction of characteristic towns in China under the background of digital economy—Taking the field investigation in 6 provinces and 6 towns in China as an example. In *Advances in Ergonomics and Human Factors* (pp. 139-150). https://doi.org/10.2991/978-94-6463-042-8_22

Hudders, L., De Jans, S., & De Veirman, M. (2021). The commercialization of social media stars: A literature review and conceptual framework on the strategic use of social media influencers. *International Journal of Advertising*, 40(3), 327–375. 10.1080/02650487.2020.1836925

Hughes, C., Swaminathan, V., & Brooks, G. (2019). Driving Brand Engagement Through Online Social Influencers: An Empirical Investigation of Sponsored Blogging Campaigns. *Journal of Marketing*, 83(5), 78–96. 10.1177/0022242919854374

Hu, Q., & Hughes, M. (2020). Radical innovation in family firms: A systematic analysis and research agenda. *International Journal of Entrepreneurial Behaviour & Research*, 26(6), 1199–1234. 10.1108/IJEBR-11-2019-0658

Hussein, K., Kassim, M., & Ali, M. (2022). Cloud Computing Acceptance in Small and Medium Enterprises (SMEs) in Uganda. *Saudian Review of Financial Technology and Management Studies*, 2(1). Advance online publication. 10.12691/srftms-2-1-1

Iankova, S., Davies, I., Archer-Brown, C., Marder, B., & Yau, A. (2019). A comparison of social media marketing between B2B, B2C and mixed business models. *Industrial Marketing Management*, 81, 169–179. 10.1016/j.indmarman.2018.01.001

Iborra, M., Safón, V., & Dolz, C. (2020). The role of family ownership in survival and bouncing back: Good and bad news? In *Competitiveness, Organizational Management, and Governance in Family Firms* (pp. 261-282). IGI Global.

Ibrahim & Hospodiuk. (2015). Current advances and future perspectives in extrusion-based bioprinting. 10.1016/j.biomaterials.2015.10.076

Compilation of References

Ibrahim, N., & Verliyantina, V. (2012). The model of crowdfunding to support small and micro businesses in Indonesia through a web-based platform. *Procedia Economics and Finance*, 4, 390–397. 10.1016/S2212-5671(12)00353-X

Ietto-Gillies, G. (2012). *Transnational Corporations: Fragmentation Amidst Integration*. Routeldge.

Ilenkov, D. (2019). Technology Crowdfunding in Russia: Alternative Finance for Start-ups. [IJEBA]. *International Journal of Economics & Business Administration*, 7(2), 3–11. 10.35808/ijeba/210

Ilenkov, D., & Kapustina, V. (2018). Crowdfunding in Russia: An empirical study. *European Research Studies*, 21(2), 401–410. 10.35808/ersj/1010

Ince, F. (2022). Leadership and sustainability: From the first to the second generation of SMEs ownership. In *Research Anthology on Strategies for Maintaining Successful Family Firms* (pp. 639–660). IGI Global. 10.4018/978-1-6684-3550-2.ch029

Ing, G. P., & Ming, T. (2018). Antecedents of consumer attitude towards blogger recommendations and its impact on purchase intention. *Asian Journal of Business and Accounting*, 11(1), 293–323.

Islam, D. M. Z. (2020). COVID-19 and Financial Performance of SMEs: Examining the nexus of entrepreneurial self-efficacy, entrepreneurial resilience and innovative work behavior. *Revista Argentina de Clínica Psicológica*, 29(3), 587.

Ismagilova, E., Slade, E., Rana, N. P., & Dwivedi, Y. K. (2020). The effect of characteristics of source credibility on consumer behaviour: A meta-analysis. *Journal of Retailing and Consumer Services*, 53, 101736. Advance online publication. 10.1016/j.jretconser.2019.01.005

Ismail, M., Mohamad, N., & Ahamat, A. (2023). Learning Orientation as Mediator between International Entrepreneurial Orientation and International Firm Performance in Global Halal Industry. Academic Press.

Ismail, A., Majid, A. H. A., Rahman, M. A., Jamaluddin, N. A., Susantiy, A. I., & Setiawati, C. I. (2021). Aligning Malaysian SMEs with the megatrends: The roles of HPWPs and employee creativity in enhancing Malaysian SME performance. *Global Business Review*, 22(2), 364–380. 10.1177/0972150918811236

Ismail, M., Mohamad, N., & Ahamat, A. (2023). Managerial Capabilities, Learning Orientation And Performance Of International Halal Industry Using Upper Echelon Theory. *International Journal of Business and Society*, 24(1), 119–140. 10.33736/ijbs.5608.2023

Iwashita, M., & Tanimoto, S. (2016). Highly secure transaction system for affiliate marketing. *2016 IEEE 5th Global Conference on Consumer Electronics, GCCE 2016*, 1–3. 10.1109/GCCE.2016.7800492

Iwashita, M., Tanimoto, S., & Tsuchiya, K. (2018). Framework of highly secure transaction management for affiliate Services of video advertising. *Procedia Computer Science*, 126, 1802–1809. 10.1016/j.procs.2018.08.097

Iwueke, E. L., Anyarum, G. O., Fagorite, V. I., Okeke, O. C., & Ehujuo, N. N. (2019). Entrepreneurship: Characteristics, practices and impacts on Nigeria economy in relation to geosciences. *IIARD Int J Econ Bus Manage*, 5, 48–63.

Jaakkola, E., Helkkula, A., & Aarikka-Stenroos, L. (2015). Service experience co-creation: Conceptualization, implications, and future research directions. *Journal of Service Management*, 26(2), 182–205. 10.1108/JOSM-12-2014-0323

Jachi, M., & Muchongwe, N. (2019). Economic sustainability of small to medium enterprises (SMEs) in Zimbabwe: The impact of fiscal incentives and entrepreneur work engagement. *Public Policy and Administration Research*, 9(12), 17–32.

Jackling, B., & Johl, S. (2009). Board structure and firm performance: Evidence from India's top companies. *Corporate Governance*, 17(4), 492–509. 10.1111/j.1467-8683.2009.00760.x

Jafari-Sadeghi, V., Garcia-Perez, A., Candelo, E., & Couturier, J. (2021). Exploring the impact of digital transformation on technology entrepreneurship and technological market expansion: The role of technology readiness, exploration and exploitation. *Journal of Business Research*, 124, 100–111. 10.1016/j.jbusres.2020.11.020

Janssen, D., & van Heck, E. (2007). How Will Online Affiliate Marketing Networks Impact Search Engine Rankings? *ERIM Report Series Reference No. ERS-2007-042-LIS*.

Jennings, J. E., Breitkreuz, R. S., & James, A. E. (2013). When family members are also business owners: Is entrepreneurship good for families? *Family Relations*, 62(3), 472–489. 10.1111/fare.12013

Jiang, K., & Messersmith, J. (2018). On the shoulders of giants: A meta-review of strategic human resource management. *International Journal of Human Resource Management*, 29(1), 6–33. 10.1080/09585192.2017.1384930

Jin, S. V., & Muqaddam, A. (2019). Product placement 2.0: "Do Brands Need Influencers, or Do Influencers Need Brands?" *Journal of Brand Management*, 26(5), 522–537. 10.1057/s41262-019-00151-z

Jin, X., Weber, K., & Bauer, T. (2012). Relationship quality between exhibitors and organizers: A perspective from Mainland China's exhibition industry. *International Journal of Hospitality Management*, 31(4), 1222–1234. 10.1016/j.ijhm.2012.02.012

João Leitão, F. G., & Ken Riopelle, J. G. P. G. (2018). Collaborative Innovation Networks Building Adaptive and Resilient Organizations. https://www.springer.com/series/15330

Johanson, J., & Mattsson, L.-G. (1988) Internationalization in industrial systems: a network approach. In *Strategies in Global Competition: Selected Papers from the Prince Bertil Symposium at the Institute of International Business*. Stockholm School of Economics.

Johanson, J., & Vahlne, J. E. (1977). The internationalization process of the firm—A model of knowledge development and increasing foreign market commitments. *Journal of International Business Studies*, 8(1), 23–32. 10.1057/palgrave.jibs.8490676

Compilation of References

Johanson, J., & Vahlne, J. E. (1990). The mechanism of internationalisation. *International Marketing Review*, 7(4). Advance online publication. 10.1108/02651339010137414

Johanson, J., & Vahlne, J. E. (2003). Business relationship learning and commitment in the internationalization process. *Journal of International Entrepreneurship*, 1(1), 83–101. 10.1023/A:1023219207042

Johanson, J., & Vahlne, J. E. (2009). The Uppsala internationalization process model revisited: From liability of foreignness to liability of outsidership. *Journal of International Business Studies*, 40(9), 1411–1431. 10.1057/jibs.2009.24

Johnson, E., & Sherraden, M. S. (2007). From financial literacy to financial capability among youth. *Journal of Sociology and Social Welfare*, 34(3), 119. 10.15453/0191-5096.3276

Johri, A., Asif, M., Tarkar, P., Khan, W., Rahisha, , & Wasiq, M. (2024). Digital financial inclusion in micro enterprises: Understanding the determinants and impact on ease of doing business from World Bank survey. *Humanities & Social Sciences Communications*, 11(1), 361. 10.1057/s41599-024-02856-2

Jones, M. V. (2001). First steps in internationalization: Concepts and evidence from a sample of small high-technology firms. *Journal of International Management*, 7(3), 191–210. 10.1016/S1075-4253(01)00044-8

Journal, I., & Movement, I. (2018). Affiliate Marketing : Meaning. *Working and Challenges.*, 2(X), 199–203.

Jovović, R., Drašković, M., Delibasic, M., & Jovovic, M. (2017). The concept of sustainable regional development – Institutional aspects, policies, and prospects. *Journal of International Students*, 10(1), 255–266. 10.14254/2071-8330.2017/10-1/18

Kabagerayo, J., Mwambusa, F. E., Uyambaje, M. T., Olive, Z. B., Hamenyimana, L., Dusabe, P., Mwayuma, P. M., Joseph, M. E., & Mbafumoja, E. T. (2022). Impact of rural female entrepreneurs on social and economic inclusion: Case of Giharo district. *Modern Economy*, 13(06), 885–900. 10.4236/me.2022.136048

Kakeesh, D. F., Al-Weshah, G. A., & Alalwan, A. A. (2024). Entrepreneurial marketing and business performance in SMEs: the mediating role of competitive aggressiveness. *Journal of Marketing Analytics*, 1-24.

Kallmuenzer, A. (2018). Exploring drivers of innovation in hospitality family firms. *International Journal of Contemporary Hospitality Management*, 30(3), 1978–1995. 10.1108/IJCHM-04-2017-0242

Kamal, S., Naim, A., Magd, H., Khan, S. A., & Khan, F. M. (2022). The Relationship Between E-Service Quality, Ease of Use, and E-CRM Performance Referred by Brand Image. In Naim, A., & Kautish, S. (Eds.), *Building a Brand Image Through Electronic Customer Relationship Management* (pp. 84–108). IGI Global. 10.4018/978-1-6684-5386-5.ch005

Kampouri, K., & Hajidimitriou, Y. (2023). International partnership failures in the context of family small and medium enterprises internationalisation. *European Journal of Family Business*, 13(1), 56–70. 10.24310/ejfbejfb.vi.15154

Kamukama, N. (2020). Social Competence and Access to Finance in Financial Institutions: An Empirical Study Of Small And Medium Enterprises In Uganda. *American Journal of Finance*, 5(1), 54–70. Advance online publication. 10.47672/ajf.594

Kang, H. W., Lee, S., Ko, I., Kengla, C., Yoo, J. J., & Atala, A. (2016). A 3D bioprinting system to produce human-scale tissue constructs with structural integrity. *Nature Biotechnology*, 34(3), 312–319. Advance online publication. 10.1038/nbt.341326878319

Kansheba, J., & Wald, A. (2020). Entrepreneurial ecosystems: A systematic literature review and research agenda. *Journal of Small Business and Enterprise Development*, 27(6), 943–964. 10.1108/JSBED-11-2019-0364

Kaplan, S. (2008). Framing contests: Strategy making under uncertainty. *Organization Science*, 19(5), 729–752. 10.1287/orsc.1070.0340

Karaçuha, E., & Güven, P. A. D. O. (2018). Dijital inovasyon stratejisi yönetimi. *Uluslararası Bilimsel Araştırmalar Dergisi*, 3(1), 118–130.

Karyamsetty, H. J., Khan, S. A., & Nayyar, A. (2023). Envisioning Towards Modernization of Society 5.0- A Prospective Glimpse on Status, Opportunities, and Challenges With XAI. In Al-Turjman, F., Nayyar, A., Naved, M., Singh, A. K., & Bilal, M. (Eds.), *XAI Based Intelligent Systems for Society 5.0* (pp. 223–267). Elsevier. 10.1016/B978-0-323-95315-3.00005-X

Kasri, R. A., & Indriani, E. (2022). Empathy or perceived credibility? An empirical study of Muslim donating behaviour through online charitable crowdfunding in Indonesia. *International Journal of Islamic and Middle Eastern Finance and Management*, 15(5), 829–846. 10.1108/IMEFM-09-2020-0468

Kathirvel, A., & Gobinath, V. M. (2024). Chapter 1: A Review on Additive Manufactuing in Industrial. *Modern Hybird Machince and Super Finishing Process: Technology and Application*. CRC Publiser/Chapman and Hall. https://books.google.co.in/books/about/Modern_Hybrid_Machining_and_Super_Finish.html?id=I_VW0AEACAAJ&source=kp_book_description&redir_esc=y

Kathirvel, A., & Maheswaran, C. P. (2023). Chapter 8: Enhanced AI-Based Intrusion Detection and Response System for WSN. Artificial Intelligence for Intrusion Detection Systems. CRC Publiser/Chapman and Hall. https://www.taylorfrancis.com/chapters/edit/10.1201/9781003346340-8/enhanced-ai-based-intrusion-detection-response-system-wsn-kathirvel-maheswaran10.1201/9781003346340-8

Kathirvel, A., Rithik, G., & Naren, A. K. (2024). Chapter 11: Automation of IOT Robotics. In *Predicting Natural Disasters with AI and Machine Learning*. IGI Global. 10.4018/979-8-3693-2280-2.ch011

Compilation of References

Kathirvel, A., Subramaniam, M., Navaneethan, S., & Sabarinath, C. (2021). Improved IDR Response System for Sensor Network. *Journal of Web Engineering*, 20(1), 53–88. 10.13052/jwe1540-9589.2013

Kathirvel, Maheswaran, Subramaniam, & Naren. (2023). Chapter 25: Quantum Computers Based on Distributed Computing Systems for the Next Generation: Overview and Applications. Quantum Computers Based on Distributed Computing Systems for the Next Generation, Handbook of Research on Quantum Computing for Smart Environments. IGI Global. 10.4018/978-1-6684-6697-1.ch025

Kathirvel, A. (2024a). Applications of Serverless Computing: Systematic Overview. In Aluvalu, R., & Maheswari, U. (Eds.), *Serverless Computing Concepts, Technology and Architecture* (Vol. 221-233). IGI Global. 10.4018/979-8-3693-1682-5.ch014

Kathirvel, A. (2024b). Innovation and Industry Application: IoT-Based Robotics Frontier of Automation in Industry Application. In Satishkumar, D., & Sivaraja, M. (Eds.), *Internet of Things and AI for Natural Disaster Management and Prediction* (pp. 83–105). IGI Global. 10.4018/979-8-3693-4284-8.ch004

Kathirvel, A., Gopinath, V. M., Naren, K., Nithyanand, D., & Nirmaladevi, K. (2024). Manufacturing Smart Industry Perspective an Overview. *American Journal of Engineering and Applied Sciences*, 17(1), 33–39. 10.3844/ajeassp.2024.33.39

Kathirvel, A., & Naren, A. K. (2024a). Critical Approaches to Data Engineering Systems Innovation and Industry Application Using IoT. In *Critical Approaches to Data Engineering Systems and Analysis*. IGI Global. 10.4018/979-8-3693-2260-4.ch005

Kathirvel, A., & Naren, A. K. (2024b). Diabetes and Pre-Diabetes Prediction by AI Using Tuned XGB Classifier. In Khang, A. (Ed.), *Medical Robotics and AI-Assisted Diagnostics for a High-Tech Healthcare Industry* (pp. 52–64). IGI Global., 10.4018/979-8-3693-2105-8.ch004

Kathirvel, A., Naren, K., Nithyanand, D., & Santhoshi, B. (2024). Overview of 5G Technology: Streamlined Virtual Event Experiences. *Advances of Robotic Technology*, 2(1), 1–8. 10.23880/art-16000109

Kathirvel, A., Sudha, D., Naveneethan, S., Subramaniam, M., Das, D., & Kirubakaran, S. (2022). AI Based Mobile Bill Payment System using Biometric Fingerprint. *American Journal of Engineering and Applied Sciences*, 15(1), 23–31. 10.3844/ajeassp.2022.23.31

Kato, A. I., & Tsoka, G. E. (2020). Impact of venture capital financing on small-and medium-sized enterprises' performance in Uganda. *Southern African Journal of Entrepreneurship and Small Business Management*, 12(1). Advance online publication. 10.4102/sajesbm.v12i1.320

Kaufman, B. E. (2015). Evolution of strategic HRM as seen through two founding books: A 30th anniversary perspective on development of the field. *Human Resource Management*, 54(3), 389–407. 10.1002/hrm.21720

Kaya, A., & Girgin, D. (2023). Sınıf Öğretmeni Adaylarının Girişimcilik Becerilerinin İncelenmesi: Bir Karma Yöntem Araştırması. *Pamukkale Üniversitesi Sosyal Bilimler Enstitüsü Dergisi*, (55), 21–42.

Kayhan, S. (2017). Fongogo: A case study on the usability of the local crowdfunding and fundraising websites in Turkey. *HUMANITAS-Uluslararası Sosyal Bilimler Dergisi*, 5(09), 95–105. 10.20304/humanitas.318510

Kedia, P., & Mishra, L. (2022). Factors Underlying Selection of the Right Crowd for Crowdfunding in India. *IUP Journal of Accounting Research & Audit Practices*, 21(3), 133–149.

Ketchen, D. J., Jr., Crook, T. R., Todd, S. Y., Combs, J. G., & Woehr, D. J. (2017). Managing human capital. *The Oxford Handbook of Strategy Implementation*, 283-311.

Keupp, M. M., Palmié, M., & Gassmann, O. (2012). The strategic management of innovation: A systematic review and paths for future research. *International Journal of Management Reviews*, 14(4), 367–390. 10.1111/j.1468-2370.2011.00321.x

Khalaf, A. T., Wei, Y., Wan, J., Zhu, J., Peng, Y., Abdul Kadir, S. Y., Zainol, J., Oglah, Z., Cheng, L., & Shi, Z. (2022). Bone Tissue Engineering through 3D Bioprinting of Bioceramic Scaffolds: A Review and Update. *Life (Chicago, Ill.)*, 12(6), 903. Advance online publication. 10.3390/life1206090335743934

Khan, S. A., Magd, H., Bhuyan, U., Jonathan, H., & Naim, A. (2024). Digital Marketing (DM): How are Small Business Enterprises (SBEs) of Bhutan and Sikkim (India) Responding to it? In *Digital Influence on Consumer Habits: Marketing Challenges and Opportunities* (pp. 135-145). Emerald Publishing Limited. 10.1108/978-1-80455-342-820241008

Khandwalla, P. N. (1977). Some top management styles, their context and performance. *Organization and Administrative Sciences, 7*(4), 21-51.

Khan, N. U., Wu, W., Saufi, R. B. A., Sabri, N. A. A., & Shah, A. A. (2021). Antecedents of sustainable performance in manufacturing organizations: A structural equation modeling approach. *Sustainability (Basel)*, 13(2), 897. 10.3390/su13020897

Khan, S. A. (2023). E-Marketing, E-Commerce, E-Business, and Internet of Things: An Overview of Terms in the Context of Small and Medium Enterprises (SMEs). In Naim, A., & Devi, V. (Eds.), *Global Applications of the Internet of Things in Digital Marketing* (pp. 332–348). IGI Global. 10.4018/978-1-6684-8166-0.ch017

Khan, S. A., & Magd, H. (2021). Empirical Examination of MS Teams in Conducting Webinar: Evidence from International Online Program conducted in Oman. *Journal of Content. Community and Communication*, 14(8), 159–175. 10.31620/JCCC.12.21/13

Khan, S. A., Magd, H., & Epoc, F. (2022). Application of Data Management System in Business to Business Electronic Commerce. In Naim, A., & Malik, P. K. (Eds.), *Competitive Trends and Technologies in Business Management* (pp. 109–124). Nova Science Publishers.

Compilation of References

Khan, S. A., Narula, S., Kansra, P., Naim, A., & Kalra, D. (2023b). Should Marketing and Public Relations be Part of the Institutional Accreditation Criterion of Business Schools? An Appraisal of Accreditation Criterion of Selected Accreditation Agencies. In Naim, A. (Ed.), *Accreditation Processes and Frameworks in Higher Education* (pp. 349–375). Nova Science Publishers. 10.52305/QUVJ6658

Khan, S. A., Sharma, P. P., & Thoudam, P. (2019). Role of attitude and entrepreneurship education towards entrepreneurial orientation among business students of Bhutan. *International Journal of Recent Technology and Engineering*, 8(2), 335–342. 10.35940/ijrte.C1072.1083S19

Khatri, B., Shrimali, H., Khan, S. A., & Naim, A. (2023). Role of HR Analytics in Ensuring Psychological Wellbeing and Job Security: Learnings From COVID-19. In Yadav, R., Sinha, M., & Kureethara, J. (Eds.), *HR Analytics in an Era of Rapid Automation* (pp. 36–53). IGI Global. 10.4018/978-1-6684-8942-0.ch003

Khatri, B., Singh, R. K., Arora, S., Khan, S. A., & Naim, A. (2024). Optimizing Supply Chain Management Indicators for Sustainable Supply Chain Integration and Customer Loyalty: Potential Role of Environmentally Responsible Practices. In Ramakrishna, Y., & Srivastava, B. (Eds.), *Strategies for Environmentally Responsible Supply Chain and Production Management* (pp. 156–181). IGI Global. 10.4018/979-8-3693-0669-7.ch008

Khurana, I. (2021). Legitimacy and reciprocal altruism in donation-based crowdfunding: Evidence from India. *Journal of Risk and Financial Management*, 14(5), 194. 10.3390/jrfm14050194

Kikawa, C. R., Kiconco, C., Agaba, M., Ntirampeba, D., Ssematimba, A., & Kalema, B. M. (2022). Social Media Marketing for Small and Medium Enterprise Performance in Uganda: A Structural Equation Model. *Sustainability (Basel)*, 14(21), 14391. Advance online publication. 10.3390/su142114391

Kilinc, M., Aydin, C., & Tarhan, C. (2022). Türkiye'de sosyal ve dijital girişimcilik: Veri kazıma teknikleriyle kitle fonlaması platformlarının içerik analizi. *Acta Infologica*, 6(1), 83–97.

Kim, S. K., & Min, S. (2015). Business model innovation performance: When does adding a new business model benefit an incumbent? *Strategic Entrepreneurship Journal*, 9(1), 34–57. 10.1002/sej.1193

Kiprotich, S., Kimosop, J., Chepkwony, P. K., & Kemboi, A. (2015). Moderating effect of social networking on the relationship between entrepreneurial orientation and performance of small and medium enterprise in Nakuru County. Academic Press.

Kirmani, A., & Campbell, M. C. (2009). Taking the target's perspective: The persuasion knowledge model. *Social Psychology of Consumer Behavior*, 297–316.

Klapper, L. (2006). Entrepreneurship: how much does the business environment matter? Viewpoint series. note 313. Financial and Private Sector Development Vice Presidency, World Bank Group.

Kmecová, I., & Vokoun, M. (2020). Innovation activities of Czech businesses: Differences between urban and rural businesses. *SHS Web of Conferences, 73*, 02002. 10.1051/shsconf/20207302002

Kobugabe, C., & Rwakihembo, J. (2022). Financial Literacy and Financial Inclusion: A positivist view of Proprietors of Small and Medium Enterprises in Fort Portal City, Western Uganda. *American Journal of Finance*, 7(2), 1–12. Advance online publication. 10.47672/ajf.1014

Kock, F., Berbekova, A., & Assaf, A. G. (2021). Understanding and managing the threat of common method bias: Detection, prevention and control. *Tourism Management*, 86, 104330. 10.1016/j.tourman.2021.104330

Kohli, R., & Melville, N. P. (2018). Digital innovation: A review and synthesis. *Information Systems Journal*, 29(1), 200–223. 10.1111/isj.12193

Kojo Oseifuah, E. (2010). Financial literacy and youth entrepreneurship in South Africa. *African Journal of Economic and Management Studies*, 1(2), 164–182. 10.1108/20400701011073473

Konhäusner, P., Shang, B., & Dabija, D. C. (2021). Application of the 4Es in online crowdfunding platforms: A comparative perspective of Germany and China. *Journal of Risk and Financial Management*, 14(2), 49. 10.3390/jrfm14020049

Kontinen, T., & Ojala, A. (2010). The internationalization of family businesses: A review of extant research. *Journal of Family Business Strategy*, 1(2), 97–107. 10.1016/j.jfbs.2010.04.001

Kontinen, T., & Ojala, A. (2012). Social capital in the international operations of family SMEs. *Journal of Small Business and Enterprise Development*, 19(1), 39–55. 10.1108/14626001211196398

Korsgaard, S., Müller, S., & Tanvig, H. (2015). Rural entrepreneurship or entrepreneurship in the rural – Between place and space. *International Journal of Entrepreneurial Behaviour & Research*, 21(1), 5–26. 10.1108/IJEBR-11-2013-0205

Kotler, P., & Keller, K. L. (2016). Marketing Management (Stephanie Wall, Ed.; 15th ed.). Pearson Education Limited.

Kotok, S., & Kryst, E. (2017). Digital technology: A double-edged sword for a school principal in rural Pennsylvania. *Journal of Cases in Educational Leadership*, 20(4), 3–16. 10.1177/1555458916685748

Kovshova, L., & Nair, P. B. (2017). Crowdfunding in Russia: A thematic analysis of funder motives. *Global Business and Economics Review*, 19(3), 256–275. 10.1504/GBER.2017.083963

Kraus, S., Palmer, C., Kailer, N., Kallinger, F. L., & Spitzer, J. (2019). Digital entrepreneurship. *International Journal of Entrepreneurial Behaviour & Research*. Advance online publication. 10.1108/IJEBR-06-2018-0425

Kreiterling, C. (2023). Digital innovation and entrepreneurship: A review of challenges in competitive markets. *Journal of Innovation and Entrepreneurship*, 12(1), 49. 10.1186/s13731-023-00320-0

Krejcie, R. V., & Morgan, D. W. (1970). Determining sample size for research activities. *Educational and Psychological Measurement*, 30(3), 607–610. 10.1177/001316447003000308

Compilation of References

Krishnamurthy, S., & Singh, N. (2005). The international e-marketing framework (IEMF). *International Marketing Review*, 22(6), 605–610. 10.1108/02651330510630230

Kryeziu, L., Coşkun, R., & Krasniqi, B. (2022). Social networks and family firm internationalisation: Cases from a transition economy. *Review of International Business and Strategy*, 32(2), 284–304. 10.1108/RIBS-03-2021-0052

Kumar, V., Hundal, B. S., & Kaur, K. (2019). Factors affecting consumer buying behaviour of solar water pumping system. *Smart and Sustainable Built Environment*, 8(4), 351–364. 10.1108/SASBE-10-2018-0052

Kundu, S. G., & Jose, S. K. (2023, April). Dynamics of Demographic Factors, Digital Usage and Choice of Crowdfunding In India. In *Academy of Marketing Studies* (Vol. 27, No. 1). Academic Press.

Kurniawan, C. N., Kusumawati, A., & Iqbal, M. (n.d.). Analysis of Experience Co-Creation and Its Impact in the Tourism Context. https://profit.ub.ac.id

Kwahk, K.-Y., & Kim, B. (2017). Effects of social media on consumers' purchase decisions: Evidence from Taobao. *Service Business*, 11(4), 803–829. 10.1007/s11628-016-0331-4

Kyriakarakos, G., Balafoutis, A., & Bochtis, D. (2020). Proposing a paradigm shift in rural electrification investments in sub-Saharan Africa through agriculture. *Sustainability (Basel)*, 12(8), 3096. 10.3390/su12083096

Lahiri, S., Mukherjee, D., & Peng, M. W. (2020). Behind the internationalization of family SMEs: A strategy tripod synthesis. *Global Strategy Journal*, 10(4), 813–838. 10.1002/gsj.1376

Lai, E. R. (2011). Collaboration: A Literature Review Research Report. https://www.pearsonassessments.com/research

Laidoune, A., Zid, C., & Sahraoui, N. (2022). Innovate and overcome resistance to change to improve the resilience of systems and organizations. *Journal of the Knowledge Economy*, 13(4), 1–16. 10.1007/s13132-021-00840-8

Lambing, P., & Kuehl, C. R. (2000). *Entrepreneurship*. Prentice Hall.

Lambrecht, J. (2005). Multigenerational transition in family businesses: A new explanatory model. *Family Business Review*, 18(4), 267–282. 10.1111/j.1741-6248.2005.00048.x

Lang, R., & Fink, M. (2019). Rural social entrepreneurship: The role of social capital within and across institutional levels. *Journal of Rural Studies*, 70, 155–168. 10.1016/j.jrurstud.2018.03.012

Larimo, J. (2015). Different Types of Exporting SMEs: Similarities and Differences in Export Performance. In *International Marketing Research* (*Advances in International Marketing, Vol. 17*). Emerald, Leeds. 10.1016/S1474-7979(06)17001-5

Latif, S., & Calicioglu, C. (2020). Impact of social media advertisement on consumer purchase intention with the intermediary effect of brand attitude. *International Journal of Innovation. Creativity and Change*, 11(12), 602–619.

Lazazzara, A., Nacamulli, R. C., Rossignoli, C., & Za, S. (2019). *Organizing for Digital Innovation*. Springer. 10.1007/978-3-319-90500-6

Lee, C. Y., & Park, S. (2020). The impact of digital technology on the internationalization of SMEs: Evidence from developing countries. *Journal of International Business Studies*, 51(6), 1005–1024.

Lee, C., Chen, Y., Tsui, P., Che, C., & Chiang, M. (2021). Application of fuzzy Delphi technique approach in sustainable inheritance of rural cooking techniques and innovative business strategies modeling. *Agriculture*, 11(10), 924. 10.3390/agriculture11100924

Lee, G. K., & Liebermann, M. B. (2010). Acquisition vs. internal development as modes of market entry. *Strategic Management Journal*, 31(2), 140–158. 10.1002/smj.804

Lee, G., Park, G., & Yoon, B. (2014). Open innovation in SMEs-An intermediated network model. *Research Policy*, 43(5), 865–874.

Lee, J., Suh, T., Roy, D., & Baucus, M. (2019). Emerging technology and business model innovation: The case of artificial intelligence. *Journal of Open Innovation*, 5(3), 44. 10.3390/joitmc5030044

Legner, C., Eymann, T., Hess, T., Matt, C., Böhmann, T., Drews, P., Mädche, A., Urbach, N., & Ahle-mann, F. (2017). Digitalization: Opportunity and Challenge for the Business and Information Systems Engineering Community. *Business & Information Systems Engineering*, 59(4), 301–308. 10.1007/s12599-017-0484-2

Lekhanya, L., & Mason, R. (2014). Selected key external factors influencing the success of rural small and medium enterprises in South Africa. *Journal of Enterprising Culture*, 22(03), 331–348. 10.1142/S0218495814500149

Le, L. H., & Hancer, M. (2021). Using social learning theory in examining YouTube viewers' desire to imitate travel vloggers. *Journal of Hospitality and Tourism Technology*, 12(3), 512–532. 10.1108/JHTT-08-2020-0200

Leminen, S., Nyström, A. G., Westerlund, M., & Kortelainen, M. J. (2016). The effect of network structure on radical innovation in living labs. *Journal of Business and Industrial Marketing*, 31(6), 743–757. 10.1108/JBIM-10-2012-0179

Lemon, K. N., & Verhoef, P. C. (2016). Understanding Customer Experience Throughout the Customer Journey. *Journal of Marketing, 80*(6), 69-96. doi:10.1509/jm.15.042010.1509/jm.15.0420

Lew, S., & Sulaiman, Z. (2014). Consumer Purchase Intention toward Products Made in Malaysia vs. Made in China: A Conceptual Paper. *Procedia: Social and Behavioral Sciences*, 130, 37–45. 10.1016/j.sbspro.2014.04.005

Compilation of References

Lew, Y. K., Zahoor, N., Donbesuur, F., & Khan, H. (2023). Entrepreneurial alertness and business model innovation in dynamic markets: International performance implications for SMEs. *R & D Management*, 53(2), 224–243. 10.1111/radm.12558

Liao, T. S., Pham, T. T. D., & Lu, J. C. (2021). The Dynamic Model of Intellectual Capital Creation in Family Business: The Dynamic Capabilities Perspective. *Journal of Business Administration Research*, 4(2). Advance online publication. 10.30564/jbar.v4i2.2635

Libai, B., Biyalogorsky, E., & Gerstner, E. (2003). Setting Referral Fees in Affiliate Marketing. *Journal of Service Research*, 5(4), 303–315. 10.1177/1094670503005004003

Liew, M. X., & Loo, Y. M. (2024). Harnessing the power of generations through participative strategy: A study on Malaysia Small Family Firms. *Journal of Small Business and Entrepreneurship*, 1–23. 10.1080/08276331.2024.2311947

Li, L., Su, F., Zhang, W., & Mao, J. Y. (2018). Digital transformation by SME entrepreneurs: A capability perspective. *Information Systems Journal*, 28(6), 1129–1157. 10.1111/isj.12153

Lima, A., & Araújo, F. F. M. (2019). Technology environment and crowdfunding platforms in Brazil. *Revista de Gestão*, 26(4), 352–368. 10.1108/REGE-12-2018-0119

Lin, H. E., McDonough, E. F.III, Lin, S. J., & Lin, C. Y. Y. (2013). Managing the exploitation/exploration paradox: The role of a learning capability and innovation ambidexterity. *Journal of Product Innovation Management*, 30(2), 262–278. 10.1111/j.1540-5885.2012.00998.x

Lin, S., Laeeq, K., Malik, A., Varela, D., Rhee, J., Pillsbury, H., & Bhatti, N. (2013). Otolaryngology training programs: Resident and faculty perception of the mentorship experience. *The Laryngoscope*, 123(8), 1876–1883. 10.1002/lary.2404323483538

Li, R., & Qian, Y. (2020). Entrepreneurial participation and performance: The role of financial literacy. *Management Decision*, 58(3), 583–599. 10.1108/MD-11-2018-1283

Liu, P., Zhao, R., Li, H., Zhu, T., Li, Y., Wang, H., & Zhang, X.-D. (2022). Near-infrared-II deep tissue fluorescence microscopy and application. Nano Research. https://www.ncbi.nlm.nih.gov/pmc/articles/PMC8126817/

Liu, C., Ye, L., & Feng, B. (2018). Migrant entrepreneurship in China: Entrepreneurial transition and firm performance. *Small Business Economics*, 52(3), 681–696. 10.1007/s11187-017-9979-y

Liu, X., & Buck, T. (2007). Innovation Performance and Channels for International Technology Spillovers: Evidence from Chinese High-Tech Industries. *Research Policy*, 36(3), 355–366. 10.1016/j.respol.2006.12.003

Li, Y., & Peng, Y. (2021). Influencer marketing: Purchase intention and its antecedents. *Marketing Intelligence & Planning*, 39(7), 960–978. 10.1108/MIP-04-2021-0104

Loayza, N., & Raddatz, C. (2010). The composition of growth matters for poverty alleviation. *Journal of Development Economics*, 93(1), 137–151. 10.1016/j.jdeveco.2009.03.008

Lou, C., & Yuan, S. (2019). Influencer Marketing: How Message Value and Credibility Affect Consumer Trust of Branded Content on Social Media. *Journal of Interactive Advertising*, 19(1), 58–73. 10.1080/15252019.2018.1533501

Lowry, P. B., & Gaskin, J. (2014). Partial least squares (PLS) structural equation modeling (SEM) for building and testing behavioral causal theory: When to choose it and how to use it. *IEEE Transactions on Professional Communication*, 57(2), 123–146. 10.1109/TPC.2014.2312452

Luo, Y., Peng, Y., & Zeng, L. (2021). Digital financial capability and entrepreneurial performance. International Review of Economics & Finance, 76, 55–74. https://doi.org/. 2021.05.01010.1016/j.iref

Lyons, A. C., Kass-Hanna, J., Liu, F., Greenlee, A. J., & Zeng, L. (2020). Building financial resilience through financial and digital literacy in South Asia and SubSaharan Africa. In *ADBI working paper 1098*. Asian Development Bank Institute.

Mabenge, B. K., Ngorora-Madzimure, G. P. K., & Makanyeza, C. (2020). Dimensions of innovation and their effects on the performance of small and medium enterprises: The moderating role of firm's age and size. *Journal of Small Business and Entrepreneurship*, 0(0), 1–25. 10.1080/08276331.2020.1725727

MacGregor, R., & Vrazalic, L. (2007). The Role of Small Business Strategic Alliances in the Adoption of E-Commerce in Small/Medium Enterprises (SMEs). In *Small Business Clustering Technologies* (pp. 242–280). IGI Global. 10.4018/978-1-59904-126-1.ch012

MacKenzie, S. B., Lutz, R. J., & Belch, G. E. (1986). The Role of Attitude toward the Ad as a Mediator of Advertising Effectiveness: A Test of Competing Explanations. *JMR, Journal of Marketing Research*, 23(2), 130–143. 10.1177/002224378602300205

Madison, K., Moore, C. B., Daspit, J. J., & Nabisaalu, J. K. (2022). The influence of women on SME innovation in emerging markets. *Strategic Entrepreneurship Journal*, 16(2), 281–313. 10.1002/sej.1422

Madzivhandila, T., & Musara, M. (2020). Taking responsibility for entrepreneurship development in South Africa: The role of local municipalities. *Local Economy*, 35(3), 257–268. 10.1177/0269094220922820

Magd, H., & Khan, S. A. (2022). Effectiveness of using online teaching platforms as communication tools in higher education institutions in Oman: Stakeholders perspectives. *Journal of Content. Community and Communication*, 16, 148–160. 10.31620/JCCC.12.22/13

Magd, H., & Khan, S. A. (2022). Strategic framework for entrepreneurship education in promoting social entrepreneurship in GCC countries during and post COVID-19. In Magd, H., Singh, D., Syed, R., & Spicer, D. (Eds.), *International perspectives on value creation and sustainability through social entrepreneurship* (pp. 61–75). IGI Global. 10.4018/978-1-6684-4666-9.ch004

Compilation of References

Magd, H., Khan, S. A., & Bhuyan, U. (2022). Social Entrepreneurship Intentions Among Business Students in Oman. In Magd, H., Singh, D., Syed, R., & Spicer, D. (Eds.), *International Perspectives on Value Creation and Sustainability Through Social Entrepreneurship* (pp. 76–93). IGI Global. 10.4018/978-1-6684-4666-9.ch005

Magistretti, S., Dell'Era, C., De Massis, A., & Frattini, F. (2019). Exploring the relationship between types of family involvement and collaborative innovation in design-intensive firms: Insights from two leading players in the furniture industry. *Industry and Innovation*, 26(10), 1121–1151. 10.1080/13662716.2019.1623762

Mahato, J., Jha, M., & Verma, S. (2022). The role of social capital in developing sustainable micro-entrepreneurship among rural women in India: A theoretical framework. *International Journal of Innovation*, 10(3), 504–526. 10.5585/iji.v10i3.21771

Mah, P. Y., Chuah, F., & Sahar, E. (2023). Corporate Sustainability Orientation, Sustainable Development Practices, and Firm Performance of MSMEs in Malaysia. *Asian Journal of Business Research*, 13(2), 107–127. 10.14707/ajbr.230152

Makanyeza, C., & Dzvuke, G. (2015). The influence of innovation on the performance of small and medium enterprises in Zimbabwe. *Journal of African Business*, 16(1-2), 198–214. 10.1080/15228916.2015.1061406

Makanyeza, C., Mabenge, B. K., & Ngorora-Madzimure, G. P. K. (2023). Factors influencing small and medium enterprises' innovativeness: Evidence from manufacturing companies in Harare, Zimbabwe. *Global Business and Organizational Excellence*, 42(3), 10–23. 10.1002/joe.22180

Maksimovic, M. (2018). *Greening the Future: Green Internet of Things (G-IoT) as a Key Technological Enabler of Sustainable Development*. 10.1007/978-3-319-60435-0_12

Malebana, M., & Swanepoel, E. (2019). The relationship between exposure to entrepreneurship education and entrepreneurial self-efficacy. *Southern African Business Review*, 18(1), 1–26. 10.25159/1998-8125/5630

Malesios, C., Skouloudis, A., Dey, P. K., Abdelaziz, F. B., Kantartzis, A., & Evangelinos, K. (2018). Impact of small-and medium-sized enterprises sustainability practices and performance on economic growth from a managerial perspective: Modeling considerations and empirical analysis results. *Business Strategy and the Environment*, 27(7), 960–972. 10.1002/bse.2045

Manara, A. S., Permata, A. R. E., & Pranjoto, R. G. H. (2018). Strategy model for increasing the potential of zakat through the crowdfunding-zakat system to overcome poverty in Indonesia. *International Journal of Zakat*, 3(4), 17–31. 10.37706/ijaz.v3i4.104

Manzoor, U., Baig, S. A., Hashim, M., & Sami, A. (2020). Impact of Social Media Marketing on Consumer's Purchase Intentions: The Mediating role of Customer Trust. *International Journal of Entrepreneurial Research*, 3(2), 41–48. 10.31580/ijer.v3i2.1386

Marga & Jakab. (2012). Toward engineering functional organ modules by additive manufacturing. 10.1088/1758-5082/4/2/022001

Mariussen, A. (2011). Rethinking marketing performance measurement: Justification and operationalisation of an alternative approach to affiliate marketing performance measurement in Tourism. *Ereview of Tourism Research*, 9(3), 65–87.

Mariussen, A., Bowie, D., & Paraskevas, A. (2010). Affiliate Marketing Optimisation in Hospitality and Tourism: A Multiple Stakeholder Perspective. *Service Industries Journal*, 30(10), 1707–1722. 10.1080/02642060903580714

Markard, J., Geels, F. W., & Raven, R. (2020). Challenges in the acceleration of sustainability transitions. *Environmental Research Letters*, 15(8), 081001. 10.1088/1748-9326/ab9468

Martínez-Peláez, R., Ochoa-Brust, A., Rivera, S., Félix, V. G., Ostos, R., Brito, H., Félix, R. A., & Mena, L. J. (2023). Role of Digital Transformation for Achieving Sustainability: Mediated Role of Stakeholders, Key Capabilities, and Technology. *Sustainability*, 15(14), 11221. doi:10.3390/su15141122110.3390/su151411221

Martins, L., & Medeiros, M. D. L. (2018). Crowdfunding of tourism in Brazil. *Cultur: Revista de Cultura e Turismo*, 12(1), 59–79.

Martínez-Ros, E., & Orfila-Sintes, F. (2009). Innovation activity in the hotel industry. *Technovation*, 29(9), 632–641. 10.1016/j.technovation.2009.02.004

Mashingaidze, M., Phiri, M. A., & Bomani, M. (2021). Strategy formulation amongst small and medium manufacturing enterprises: An emerging market case study. *Journal of Governance and Regulation*, 10(1).

Mashingaidze, M., Bomani, M., & Derera, E. (2021). Entrepreneurial Orientation and Business Growth: COVID-19 Implications for SMEs in Zimbabwe. In *Handbook of Research on Strategies and Interventions to Mitigate COVID-19 Impact on SMEs* (pp. 226–244). IGI Global. 10.4018/978-1-7998-7436-2.ch011

Masood, A., Hati, S. R. H., & Rahim, A. A. (2023). Halal cosmetics industry for sustainable development: A systematic literature review. In *International Journal of Business and Society* (Vol. 24, Issue 1, pp. 141–163). Universiti Malaysia Sarawak. 10.33736/ijbs.5609.2023

Masoom, K., Rastogi, A., & Khan, S. A. (2024). Impact of AI on Knowledge-based Marketing: A Study of B2B Markets. In Singh, N., Kansra, P., & Gupta, S. L. (Eds.), *Digital Influence on Consumer Habits: Marketing Challenges and Opportunities* (pp. 147–158). Emerald Publishing Limited. 10.1108/978-1-80455-342-820241009

Massa, L., Tucci, C. L., & Afuah, A. (2017). A critical assessment of business model research. *The Academy of Management Annals*, 11(1), 73–104. 10.5465/annals.2014.0072

Master, O., & Master, O. (2020). *Four Consumer Behavior Theories Every Marketer Should Know Theory of Reasoned Action Engel, Kollet, Blackwell (EKB) Model*. Academic Press.

Masuda, H., Han, S. H., & Lee, J. (2022). Impacts of influencer attributes on purchase intentions in social media influencer marketing: Mediating roles of characterizations. *Technological Forecasting and Social Change*, 174, 121246. Advance online publication. 10.1016/j.techfore.2021.121246

Compilation of References

Matzler, K., Veider, V., Hautz, J., & Stadler, C. (2015). The impact of family ownership, management, and governance on innovation. *Journal of Product Innovation Management*, 32(3), 319–333. 10.1111/jpim.12202

Mayanja, J., & Perks, S. (2017). Business practices influencing ethical conduct of small and medium-sized enterprises in Uganda. *African Journal of Business Ethics*, 11(1). Advance online publication. 10.15249/11-1-130

Mayanja, S. S., Ntayi, J. M., Munene, J. C., Kagaari, J. R. K., Balunywa, W., & Orobia, L. (2019). Positive deviance, ecologies of innovation and entrepreneurial networking. *World Journal of Entrepreneurship, Management and Sustainable Development*, 15(4), 308–324. Advance online publication. 10.1108/WJEMSD-12-2018-0110

Mayanja, S., Ntayi, J. M., Munene, J. C., Balunywa, W., Sserwanga, A., & Kagaari, J. R. K. (2019). Informational differences and entrepreneurial networking among small and medium enterprises in Kampala, Uganda: The mediating role of ecologies of innovation. *Cogent Business and Management*, 6(1), 1617020. Advance online publication. 10.1080/23311975.2019.1617020

Mayanja, S., Ntayi, J. M., Munene, J. C., Kagaari, J. R. K., & Waswa, B. (2019). Ecologies of innovation among small and medium enterprises in Uganda as a mediator of entrepreneurial networking and opportunity exploitation. *Cogent Business and Management*, 6(1), 1641256. Advance online publication. 10.1080/23311975.2019.1641256

Mayanja, S., Ntayi, J. M., Munene, J. C., Wasswa, B., & Kagaari, J. R. K. (2023). Ecologies of innovation as a mediator between nexus of generative influence and entrepreneurial networking among small and medium enterprises in Uganda. *Journal of Small Business and Entrepreneurship*, 35(2), 236–262. Advance online publication. 10.1080/08276331.2020.1764731

Mayanja, S., Ntayi, J. M., Omeke, M., Kibirango, M. M., & Mutebi, H. (2022). Symbiotic Resonance, Nexus of Generative Influence, Ecologies of Innovation and Opportunity Exploitation among Small and Medium Enterprises. *Journal of African Business*, 23(4), 1009–1028. Advance online publication. 10.1080/15228916.2021.1977563

Mazurek, G., & Kucia, M. (2011). Potential of affiliate marketing. *The 7th International Conference Management of Technological Changes – MTC 2011*, 1–4.

McCann, M., & Barlow, A. (2015). Use and measurement of social media for SMEs. *Journal of Small Business and Enterprise Development*, 22(2), 273–287. 10.1108/JSBED-08-2012-0096

McDowell, W. C., Peake, W. O., Coder, L., & Harris, M. L. (2018). Building small firm performance through intellectual capital development: Exploring innovation as the "black box". *Journal of Business Research*, 88, 321–327. 10.1016/j.jbusres.2018.01.025

McQuaid, R., & Seaman, C. (2022). Integrating family, friendship and business networks in family firms. *Journal of Family Business Management*, 12(4), 799–815.

Meitiana, M., Setiawan, M., Rohman, F., & Irawanto, D. W. (2019). Factors affecting souvenir purchase behavior: Valuable insight for tourism marketers and industry. *The Journal of Business and Retail Management Research*, 13(03), 248–255. 10.24052/JBRMR/V13IS03/ART-22

Melane-Lavado, A., Álvarez-Herranz, A., & González-González, I. (2018). Foreign direct investment as a way to guide the innovative process towards sustainability. *Journal of Cleaner Production*, 172, 3578–3590. 10.1016/j.jclepro.2017.03.131

Melin, L., & Nordqvist, M. (2007). The reflexive dynamics of institutionalization: The case of the family business. *Strategic Organization*, 5(3), 321–333. 10.1177/1476127007079959

Mendes-Da-Silva, W., Rossoni, L., Conte, B. S., Gattaz, C. C., & Francisco, E. R. (2016). The impacts of fundraising periods and geographic distance on financing music production via crowdfunding in Brazil. *Journal of Cultural Economics*, 40(1), 75–99. 10.1007/s10824-015-9248-3

Merenkova, I., Agibalov, A., Zakupnev, S., & Vorobyev, S. (2020, July). Modelling of Diversified Development of Rural Areas. In *International Conference on Policicies and Economics Measures for Agricultural Development (AgroDevEco 2020)* (pp. 248-252). Atlantis Press. https://doi.org/10.2991/aebmr.k.200729.048

Metsola, J., Leppäaho, T., Paavilainen-Mäntymäki, E., & Plakoyiannaki, E. (2020). Process in family business internationalisation: The state of the art and ways forward. *International Business Review*, 29(2), 1–14. 10.1016/j.ibusrev.2020.101665

Michael, Pramanik, Basak, Prakash, & Shankar. (2022). Progress and challenges on extrusion based three-dimensional (3D) printing of biomaterials. 10.1016/j.bprint.2022.e00223

Michna, A. (2009). The relationship between organizational learning and SME performance in Poland. *Journal of European Industrial Training*, 33(4), 356–370. 10.1108/03090590910959308

Migliori, S., De Massis, A., Maturo, F., & Paolone, F. (2020). How does family management affect innovation investment propensity? The key role of innovation impulses. *Journal of Business Research*, 113, 243–256. 10.1016/j.jbusres.2020.01.039

Miller, B. K., & Chiodo, B. (2008). Academic entitlement: Adapting the equity preference questionnaire for a university setting. *Southern Management Association Meeting*.

Miller, D. (1983). The correlates of entrepreneurship in three types of firms. *Management Science*, 29(7), 770–791. 10.1287/mnsc.29.7.770

Miller, D., & Le Breton-Miller, I. (2021). Family firms: A breed of extremes? *Entrepreneurship Theory and Practice*, 45(4), 663–681. 10.1177/1042258720964186

Minhas, J., & Sindakis, S. (2021). Implications of social cohesion in entrepreneurial collaboration: A systematic literature review. *Journal of the Knowledge Economy*, 1–32.

Mintzberg, H. (1973). Strategy-making in three modes. *California Management Review*, 16(2), 44–53. 10.2307/41164491

Compilation of References

Mion, G., & Loza Adaui, C. R. (2020). Understanding the purpose of benefit corporations: An empirical study on the Italian case. *International Journal of Corporate Social Responsibility*, 5(1), 4. 10.1186/s40991-020-00050-6

Miranda, S., Cunha, P., & Duarte, M. (2021). An integrated model of factors affecting consumer attitudes and intentions towards youtuber-generated product content. *Review of Managerial Science*, 15(1), 55–73. 10.1007/s11846-019-00370-3

Mironova, E. (2018). Comparison of economic indicators of crowdfunding platforms Planeta. ru (Russia) and MAKEACHAMP (Canada). *Tsentr innovatsionnykh tekhnologii i sotsial'noi ekspertizy. Ekonomicheskie nauki*, (4), 17.

Miteva, A., & Doitchinova, J. (2022). Agriculture in the southwestern region of Bulgaria and its impact on rural development. *Ekonomika Poljoprivrede*, 69(4), 1003–1016. 10.5937/ekoPolj2204003M

Modrego, F., & Foster, W. (2021). Innovative rural entrepreneurship in Chile. *International Journal of Applied Nanotechnology Research*, 48(3), 149–170. 10.7764/ijanr.v48i3.2324

Mohamad, A., Mohd Rizal, A., Kamarudin, S., & Sahimi, M. (2022). Exploring the Co-Creation of Small and Medium Enterprises, and Service Providers Enabled by Digital Interactive Platforms for Internationalization: A Case Study in Malaysia. *Sustainability (Basel)*, 14(23), 16119. 10.3390/su142316119

Mohammadifar, Y., Naderi, N., Khosravi, E., & Karamian, F. (2022). Developing a paradigm model for resilience of rural entrepreneurial businesses in dealing with the COVID-19 crisis; Application of grounded theory in western of Iran. *Frontiers in Public Health*, 10, 833909. Advance online publication. 10.3389/fpubh.2022.83390935284375

Mollick, E. (2014). The dynamics of crowdfunding: An exploratory study. *Journal of Business Venturing*, 29(1), 1–16. 10.1016/j.jbusvent.2013.06.005

Moore, S. B., & Manring, S. L. (2009). Strategy development in small and medium sized enterprises for sustainability and increased value creation. *Journal of Cleaner Production*, 17(2), 276–282. 10.1016/j.jclepro.2008.06.004

Moqadas, R. (2018). The role of rural tourism in sustainable rural development: A case study of Shandiz rural region, Khorasan Razavi province, Iran. *Journal of Sustainable Rural Development*. 10.32598/JSRD.01.03.280

Moreira, A. C., Ribau, C. P., & Borges, M. (2024). Internationalisation of SMEs: A comparative perspective between Africa and Latin America. *International Journal of Entrepreneurship and Small Business*, 51(4), 513–541. 10.1504/IJESB.2024.136944

Morgan, P. J., Huang, B., & Trinh, L. Q. (2019). The need to promote digital financial literacy for the digital age. In Realizing education for all in the digital age. T20 Report (pp. 40–46). https://www.adb.org/sites/default/files/publication/503706/adbi-realizing-education-all-digital-age.pdf#page=56

Morgan, N. A., Vorhies, D. W., & Mason, C. H. (2009). Market orientation, marketing capabilities, and firm performance. *Strategic Management Journal*, 30(8), 909–920. 10.1002/smj.764

Morrish, S. C., Miles, M. P., & Deacon, J. H. (2010). Entrepreneurial marketing: Acknowledging the entrepreneur and customer-centric interrelationship. *Journal of Strategic Marketing*, 18(4), 303–316. 10.1080/09652541003768087

Mota, J. H., & Moreira, A. C. (2017). Determinants of the capital structure of Portuguese firms with investments in Angola. *South African Journal of Economic and Management Sciences*, 20(1), a885. 10.4102/sajems.v20i1.885

Mourão, P. J. R., da Silveira, M. A. P., & de Melo, R. S. (2019). Determinants of the Well-Succeeded Crowdfunding Projects in Brazil: A Study of the Platform Kickante. In *Innovation, Engineering and Entrepreneurship* (pp. 856-862). Springer International Publishing. 10.1007/978-3-319-91334-6_117

Mourao, P., Silveira, M. A. P., & De Melo, R. S. (2018). Many are never too many: An analysis of crowdfunding projects in Brazil. *International Journal of Financial Studies*, 6(4), 95. 10.3390/ijfs6040095

Mubarik, M. S. (2015) Human Capital and Performance of Small & Medium Manufacturing Enterprises: A Study of Pakistan, University of Malaya, Malaysia, PhD thesis.

Muda, M. (2019). Examining the source credibility of user-generated beauty contents (UGBC) on youtube in influencing consumers' purchase intention. *Malaysian Journal of Consumer and Family Economics, 22*(2), 167–184. https://www.scopus.com/inward/record.uri?eid=2-s2.0-85074890363&partnerID=40&md5=d35167bbab9a46d50f11a80a7e15c7fa

Muda, M., & Hamzah, M. I. (2021). Should I suggest this YouTube clip? The impact of UGC source credibility on eWOM and purchase intention. *Journal of Research in Interactive Marketing*, 15(3), 441–459. 10.1108/JRIM-04-2020-0072

Mugisha, H., Omagwa, J., & Kilika, J. (2020). Short-Term Debt and Financial Performance of Small and Medium Scale Enterprises in Buganda Region, Uganda. *International Journal of Finance & Banking Studies, 9*(4). 10.20525/ijfbs.v9i4.910

Mugisha, H., Omagwa, J., & Kilika, J. (2021). Capital structure, market conditions and financial performance of small and medium enterprises in Buganda Region, Uganda. *International Journal of Research in Business and Social Science, 10*(3). 10.20525/ijrbs.v10i3.1153

Mugisha, H., Omagwa, J., & Kilika, J. (2022). Capital Structure, Financial Capacity and Financial Performance of Small and Medium Enterprises in the Buganda Region, Uganda. Finance. *Markets and Valuation*, 2(2), 37–57. Advance online publication. 10.46503/GTOS1775

Mugobo, V., & Ukpere, W. (2012). Rural entrepreneurship in the Western Cape: Challenges and opportunities. *African Journal of Business Management*, 6(3). Advance online publication. 10.5897/AJBM11.895

Compilation of References

Muhammad, K., Salawu, R. O., Masibo, S., & Sikuku, I. (2024). The Government's Role in Nurturing Management for Sustainability Practices among Small and Medium Enterprises in Uganda. *TWIST, 19*(1), 409-416. https://twistjournal.net/twist/article/view/213

Muhammad, N., McElwee, G., & Dana, L. (2017). Barriers to the development and progress of entrepreneurship in rural Pakistan. *International Journal of Entrepreneurial Behaviour & Research*, 23(2), 279–295. 10.1108/IJEBR-08-2016-0246

Muharam, H., Andria, F., & Tosida, E. T. (2020). Effect of Process Innovation and Market Innovation on Financial Performance with Moderating Role of Disruptive Technology. *Systematic Reviews in Pharmacy*, 11(1).

Muhire, F., & Olyanga, A. (2022). Credit and Sustainability of SMEs in Uganda: A Case of SMEs in Nakawa Division Kampala. Journal of Economics. *Finance and Accounting Studies*, 4(4), 145–158. Advance online publication. 10.32996/jefas.2022.4.4.17

Mukti, I., Iacob, M., Aldea, A., Govindaraju, R., & Hillegersberg, J. (2021). Defining rural smartness and its impact: A systematic literature review. *Journal of the Knowledge Economy*, 13(2), 956–1007. 10.1007/s13132-021-00736-7

Mulyana & Sutapa (2015). The Role of Quadruple Helix in Improving Creativity and Innovation Capability (Study on Creative Industries in Fashion Sector). UNISSULA, 2, 111.

Munnukka, J., Uusitalo, O., & Toivonen, H. (2016). Credibility of a peer endorser and advertising effectiveness. *Journal of Consumer Marketing*, 33(3), 182–192. 10.1108/JCM-11-2014-1221

Murkhana, M., Idris, S., Majid, M. S. A., Agustina, M., Sakir, A., & Hafasnuddin, H. (2023). How important is workload affect occupational frustration? A bibliometrics analysis. *2023 International Conference on Decision Aid Sciences and Applications (DASA)*, 530–535. 10.1109/DASA59624.2023.10286791

Murphy, S., & Atala, A. (2014). 3D bioprinting of tissues and organs. *Nature Biotechnology*, 32(8), 773–785. 10.1038/nbt.295825093879

Murzyn-Kupisz, M., & Hołuj, D. (2021). Fashion design education and sustainability: Towards an equilibrium between craftsmanship and artistic and business skills? *Education Sciences*, 11(9), 531. 10.3390/educsci11090531

Musabayana, G. T., & Mutambara, E. (2020). Zimbabwe's Indigenous SME policy Framework, a tool for black empowerment. Academic Press.

Musabayana, G. T., Mutambara, E., & Ngwenya, T. (2022). An empirical assessment of how the government policies influenced the performance of the SMEs in Zimbabwe. *Journal of Innovation and Entrepreneurship*, 11(1), 40. 10.1186/s13731-021-00192-2

Mustafida, R., Fauziah, N. N., & Kurnia, Z. N. (2021). The development of islamic crowdfunding in Indonesia and its impact towards SMEs. *Hasanuddin Economics and Business Review*, 4(3), 20–29. 10.26487/hebr.v4i3.2547

Mwatsika, C. (2016). Measuring the number of jobs created through entrepreneurship training. *International Journal of Academic Research in Business & Social Sciences*, 6(7). Advance online publication. 10.6007/IJARBSS/v6-i7/2243

Nafees, L., Cook, C. M., Nikolov, A. N., & Stoddard, J. E. (2021). Can social media influencer (SMI) power influence consumer brand attitudes? The mediating role of perceived SMI credibility. *Digital Business*, 1(2), 100008. Advance online publication. 10.1016/j.digbus.2021.100008

Naim, A., Khan, S. A., Malik, P. K., Hussain, M. R., & Dildar, M. S. (2023). Internet of things support for Marketing Sports and Fitness Products. *2023 3rd International Conference on Advancement in Electronics & Communication Engineering (AECE)*, 215-219. 10.1109/AECE59614.2023.10428323

Naim, A., Khan, S. A., Mohammed, A. B., & Malik, P. K. (2024a). Applications of High Performance Computing and AI in Green Digital Marketing. In Naim, A. (Ed.), *AI Applications for Business, Medical, and Agricultural Sustainability* (pp. 47–67). IGI Global. 10.4018/979-8-3693-5266-3.ch003

Najafi-Tavani, S., Najafi-Tavani, Z., Naudé, P., Oghazi, P., & Zeynaloo, E. (2018). How collaborative innovation networks affect new product performance: Product innovation capability, process innovation capability, and absorptive capacity. *Industrial Marketing Management*, 73, 193–205. 10.1016/j.indmarman.2018.02.009

Naldi, L., Chirico, F., Kellermanns, F. W., & Campopiano, G. (2015). All in the Family? An Exploratory Study of Family Member Advisors and Firm Performance. *Family Business Review*, 28(3), 227–242. 10.1177/0894486515581951

Nambisan, S., Lyytinen, K., Majchrzak, A., & Song, M. (2017). Digital innovation management. *Management Information Systems Quarterly*, 41(1), 223–238. 10.25300/MISQ/2017/41:1.03

Naminse, E., & Zhuang, J. (2018). Does farmer entrepreneurship alleviate rural poverty in China? Evidence from Guangxi province. *PLoS One*, 13(3), e0194912. 10.1371/journal.pone.019491229596517

Nania, R. M., & Sulung, L. A. K. (2019). The management of reputation and activeness of crowdfunding players in emerging market countries. *Polish Journal of Management Studies*, 19(2), 298–308. 10.17512/pjms.2019.19.2.25

Narklor, A. (2020). The use and analysis of accounting and non-accounting information in equity-based crowdfunding. *Chulalongkorn University Theses and Dissertations (Chula ETD)*, 53. https://digital.car.chula.ac.th/chulaetd/53

Narong, D. K., & Hallinger, P. (2023). A keyword co-occurrence analysis of research on service learning: Conceptual foci and emerging research trends. In *Education Sciences* (Vol. 13, Issue 4). MDPI. 10.3390/educsci13040339

Compilation of References

Naveneethan, Madhan, & Kathirvel. (2022). Identifying and Eliminating the Misbehavior Nodes in the Wireless Sensor Network. In Soft Computing and Signal Processing. ICSCSP 2021. Advances in Intelligent Systems and Computing, vol 1413. Springer International Publishing. 10.1007/978-981-16-7088-6_36

Nawaz, F. (2009). Critical factors of women entrepreneurship development in rural Bangladesh. SSRN *Electronic Journal*. 10.2139/ssrn.1403411

Ndlovu, N., Ochara, N. M., & Martin, R. (2023). Influence of digital government innovation on transformational government in resource-constrained contexts. *Journal of Science and Technology Policy Management*, 14(5), 960–981. 10.1108/JSTPM-11-2021-0173

Neghina, C., Caniëls, M. C. J., Bloemer, J. M. M., & van Birgelen, M. J. H. (2015). Value cocreation in service interactions: Dimensions and antecedents. *Marketing Theory*, 15(2), 221–242. 10.1177/1470593114552580

Neuman, W. L. (2015). Social research methods: qualitative and quantitative approaches (7th ed.). Pearson Education Limited.

Newton, S., & Ojo, M. (2018). *Driving Traffic and Customer Activity Through Affiliate Marketing*. 10.4018/978-1-5225-2656-8.ch007

Ng, P. Y., Dayan, M., & Makri, M. (2022). Influence of socioemotional wealth on non-family managers' risk taking and product innovation in family businesses. *Cross Cultural & Strategic Management*, 29(2), 297–319. 10.1108/CCSM-03-2021-0058

Nguyen, C., Frederick, H., & Nguyen, H. (2014). Female entrepreneurship in rural Vietnam: An exploratory study. *International Journal of Gender and Entrepreneurship*, 6(1), 50–67. 10.1108/IJGE-04-2013-0034

Nguyen, P. V., Huynh, H. T. N., Lam, L. N. H., Le, T. B., & Nguyen, N. H. X. (2021). The impact of entrepreneurial leadership on SMEs' performance: The mediating effects of organizational factors. *Heliyon*, 7(6), e07326. 10.1016/j.heliyon.2021.e0732634195431

Nicholson, G. J., & Kiel, G. C. (2007). Can directors impact performance? A case-based test of three theories of corporate governance. *Corporate Governance*, 15(4), 585–608. 10.1111/j.1467-8683.2007.00590.x

Niemimaa, M., Järveläinen, J., Heikkilä, M., & Heikkilä, J. (2019). Business continuity of business models: Evaluating the resilience of business models for contingencies. *International Journal of Information Management*, 49, 208–216. 10.1016/j.ijinfomgt.2019.04.010

Nieto, M. J., Santamaria, L., & Fernandez, Z. (2015). Understanding the innovation behavior of family firms. *Journal of Small Business Management*, 53(2), 382–399. 10.1111/jsbm.12075

Nilsson, A., Magnusson, J., & Enquist, H. (2003). SME network practice: A qualitative study of network management practice and design implications for ICT-support. *Global Journal of Emerging Market Economies*, 12(2), 199-216.

Nisar, T. M., Prabhakar, G., & Torchia, M. (2020). Crowdfunding innovations in emerging economies: Risk and credit control in peer-to-peer lending network platforms. *Strategic Change*, 29(3), 355–361. 10.1002/jsc.2334

Nithya, C. L., Dixit, S., & Khodhanpur, B. I. (2019). Prediction of breast cancer using Find-S and Candidate elimination algorithm. In *2019 4th International Conference on Computational Systems and Information Technology for Sustainable Solution (CSITSS)* (pp. 1-4). Bengaluru, India: IEEE. doi:10.1109/CSITSS47250.2019.903104610.1109/CSITSS47250.2019.9031046

Nosratabadi, S., Mosavi, A., Shamshirband, S., Zavadskas, E., Rakotonirainy, A., & Chau, K. (2019). Sustainable business models: A review. *Sustainability (Basel)*, 11(6), 1663. 10.3390/su11061663

Nowsin, N., Hossain, I., & Bala, T. (2020). *Impact of Social Media on Consumer Buying Behavior through Online Value Proposition: A Study on E-Commerce Business in Bangladesh*. Academic Press.

Nso, M. (2022). An assessment of the challenges and opportunities in financing rural women entrepreneurship in the micro, small and medium enterprises sector in Cameroon. *Journal of Management and Science*, 12(4), 33–38. 10.26524/jms.12.60

Ntay, J. M., Eyaa, S., & Kalubanga, M. (2011). Ethical Culture of SMEs and Perceived Contract Enforcement in Ugandan Buyer-Supplier Contractual Arrangements. *Eastern Africa Social Science Research Review*, 27(2), 51–90. Advance online publication. 10.1353/eas.2011.0007

Nulleshi, S., & Tillmar, M. (2022). Rural proofing entrepreneurship in two fields of research. *International Journal of Entrepreneurial Behaviour & Research*, 28(9), 332–356. 10.1108/IJEBR-05-2021-0323

O'Hern, M. S., & Rindfleisch, A. (2010). Customer co-creation: A typology and research agenda. *Review of Marketing Research*, 6, 84–106. 10.1108/S1548-6435(2009)0000006008

O'Regan, N., Ghobadian, A., & Gallear, D. (2006). In search of the drivers of high growth in manufacturing SMEs. *Technovation*, 26(1), 30–41. 10.1016/j.technovation.2005.05.004

OBSERVADOR. (2022). Exportações de metalurgia e metalomecânica batem recorde em 2021 para quase 20 mil milhões de euros. https://observador.pt/2022/02/10/exportacoes-de-metalurgia-e-metalomecanica-batem-recorde-em-2021-para-quase-20-mil-milhoes-de-euros/

OECD. (2017a). Financial education for micro, small and medium-sized enterprises in asia. https://www.oecd.org/finance/Financial-education-for-MSMEs-in-Asia.pdf

OECD. (2017b). G20/OECD INFE report on adult financial literacy in G20 countries. Paris: OECD. https://www.oecd.org/daf/fin/financial-education/G20-OECD-INFE

OECD. (2019). *OECD SME and Entrepreneurship Outlook 2019*. OECD Publishing., 10.1787/34907e9c-

OECD. (2021). *OECD SME and Entrepreneurship Outlook 2021*. OECD Publishing.

Compilation of References

OECD. (2021). *The Digital Transformation of SMEs*. OECD.

OECD. (2022). *Financing Growth and Turning Data into Business: Helping SMEs Scale Up, OECD Studies on SMEs and Entrepreneurship*. OECD Publishing. 10.1787/81c738f0-

Ohanian, R. (1990). Construction and validation of a scale to measure celebrity endorsers' perceived expertise, trustworthiness, and attractiveness. *Journal of Advertising*, 19(3), 39–52. 10.1080/00913367.1990.10673191

Ojala, A. (2009). Internationalization of knowledge-intensive SMEs: The role of network relationships in the entry to a psychically distant market. *International Business Review*, 18(1), 50–59. 10.1016/j.ibusrev.2008.10.002

Okello-Obura, C., Minishi-Majanja, M. K., Cloete, L., & Ikoja-Odongo, J. R. (2008a). Business activities and information needs of SMEs in northern Uganda Prerequisites for an information system. *Library Management*, 29(4–5), 367–391. Advance online publication. 10.1108/01435120810869138

Okello-Obura, C., Minishi-Majanja, M. K., Cloete, L., & Ikoja-Odongo, J. R. (2008b). Sources of business information and means of access used by SMEs in Uganda: The case of Northern Uganda. *Libres*, 18(1). Advance online publication. 10.32655/LIBRES.2008.1.5

Okello-Obura, C., Minishi-Majanja, M. K., Cloete, L., & Ikoja-Odongo, J. R. (2009). Proposed business information system design (BISD) for small and medium enterprises (SMEs) in northern Uganda. *Libri*, 59(1). Advance online publication. 10.1515/libr.2009.004

Okumu, I. M., & Buyinza, F. (2020). Performance of Small and Medium-sized Enterprises in Uganda: the Role of Innovation. *African Economic Research Consortium*. http://localhost:80/xmlui/handle/123456789/496

Olanrewaju, A. S. T., Hossain, M. A., Whiteside, N., & Mercieca, P. (2020). Social media and entrepreneurship research: A literature review. *International Journal of Information Management*, 50, 90–110. 10.1016/j.ijinfomgt.2019.05.011

Olbrich, R., Schultz, C. D., & Bormann, P. M. (2019). The effect of social media and advertising activities on affiliate marketing. *International Journal of Internet Marketing and Advertising*, 13(1), 47–72. 10.1504/IJIMA.2019.097896

Olejnik, E., & Swoboda, B. (2012). SMEs' internationalisation patterns: Descriptives, dynamics and determinants. *International Marketing Review*, 29(5), 466–495. 10.1108/02651331211260340

Olivares, J. V., Saiz, C., Torró, L., & Zabalza, J. (2020). The internationalisation of family SMEs in the Valencian region: The growing role played by Latin America, 1980-2018. *Journal of Evolutionary Studies in Business*, 5(2), 115–149. 10.1344/jesb2020.2.j078

Oliveira, L., & Cardoso, E. L. (2021). A project-based learning approach to promote innovation and academic entrepreneurship in a master's degree in food engineering. *Journal of Food Science Education*, 20(4), 120–129. 10.1111/1541-4329.12230

Ollila, S., & Yström, A. (2016). Exploring Design Principles of Organizing for Collaborative Innovation: The Case of an Open Innovation Initiative. *Creativity and Innovation Management*, 25(3), 363–377. 10.1111/caim.12177

Ollila, S., Yström, A., & Elmquist, M. (2016). Beyond intermediation: The open innovation arena as an actor enabling joint knowledge creation. *International Journal of Technology Management*, 72(4), 273. 10.1504/IJTM.2016.081573

Onoshakpor, C., Etuknwa, A., & Karamalla-Gaiballa, N. (2020). Strategic Flexibility and Organizational Resilience of Women Entrepreneurs' in Africa During The Covid-19 Pandemic. *Research Journal of Business and Management*, 7(4), 277–287. 10.17261/Pressacademia.2020.1324

Onyinyi, B., & Kaberuka, W. (2019). ICT fusion on the relationship between resource transformation capabilities and quality management practices among SMEs in Uganda. *Cogent Business and Management*, 6(1), 1586063. Advance online publication. 10.1080/23311975.2019.1586063

Oppong, N. B. (2022). Sustainable development goals and small and medium enterprises: A comparative study of emerging economies and Sub-Saharan Africa. *Global Business Review*, 09721509221087848. 10.1177/09721509221087848

Ordonez-Ponce, E., & Weber, O. (2022). Multinational financial corporations and the sustainable development goals in developing countries. *Journal of Environmental Planning and Management*, 65(6), 975–1000. 10.1080/09640568.2022.2030684

Osano, H. M. (2019). Global expansion of SMEs: Role of global market strategy for Kenyan SMEs. *Journal of Innovation and Entrepreneurship*, 8(1), 13. 10.1186/s13731-019-0109-8

Padi, A., & Musah, A. (2022). Entrepreneurship as a potential solution to high unemployment: A systematic review of growing research and lessons for Ghana. *International Journal of Entrepreneurship and Business Innovation*, 5(2), 26–41. 10.52589/IJEBI-NNERQQRP

Pangriya, R. (2022). An explorative study on problems and challenges of rural entrepreneurs in hilly rural areas. *Asia-Pacific Journal of Management Research and Innovation*, 18(3-4), 163–168. 10.1177/2319510X231155235

Parrilli, M. D., Balavac-Orlić, M., & Radicic, D. (2023). Environmental innovation across SMEs in Europe. *Technovation*, 119, 102541. 10.1016/j.technovation.2022.102541

Parveen, F., Jaafar, N. I., & Ainin, S. (2016). Social media's impact on organizational performance and entrepreneurial orientation in organizations. *Management Decision*, 54(9), 2208–2234. 10.1108/MD-08-2015-0336

Pathak, A., & Varshney, S. (2017). Challenges faced by women entrepreneurs in rural India. *International Journal of Entrepreneurship and Innovation*, 18(1), 65–72. 10.1177/1465750316686245

Patil, R., & Bhurke, V. (2019). Impact of rural entrepreneurship on migration: A case study of Dahanu (Maharashtra), India. *Indian Journal of Agricultural Research*, (of). Advance online publication. 10.18805/IJARe.A-5014

Compilation of References

Pato, M., & Teixeira, A. (2014). Twenty years of rural entrepreneurship: A bibliometric survey. *Sociologia Ruralis*, 56(1), 3–28. 10.1111/soru.12058

Pato, M., & Teixeira, A. (2018). Rural entrepreneurship: The tale of a rare event. *Journal of Place Management and Development*, 11(1), 46–59. 10.1108/JPMD-08-2017-0085

Patricio, R., Moreira, A., Zurlo, F., & Melazzini, M. (2020). Co-creation of new solutions through gamification: A collaborative innovation practice. *Creativity and Innovation Management*, 29(1), 146–160. Advance online publication. 10.1111/caim.12356

Patrick, Z., & Hee, O. C. (2019). Factors Influencing the Intention to Use Affiliate Marketing: A Conceptual Analysis. *International Journal of Academic Research in Business & Social Sciences*, 9(2), 701–710. 10.6007/IJARBSS/v9-i2/5608

Peng, F., & Kueh, C. (2022). Integration of design thinking with cultural intelligence in higher education for a socially complex environment. *International Journal of Art & Design Education*, 41(2), 341–354. 10.1111/jade.12402

Peng, M. W. (2018). *Global 4: global business*. Cengage Learning.

Pereira, C. S., Durão, N., Moreira, F., & Veloso, B. (2022). The Importance of Digital Transformation in International Business. *Sustainability, 14*(2), 834. doi:10.3390/su1402083410.3390/su14020834

Perkmann, M., Salandra, R., Tartari, V., McKelvey, M., & Hughes, A. (2021). Academic engagement: A review of the literature 2011-2019. *Research Policy*, 50(1), 104114. 10.1016/j.respol.2020.104114

Perotti, V., Zottel, S., Iarossi, G., & Bolaji-Adio, A. (2013). *Making sense of financial capability surveys around the world: A review of existing financial capability and literacy measurement instruments*. The World Bank.

Pertheban, T. R., Thurasamy, R., Marimuthu, A., Venkatachalam, K. R., Annamalah, S., Paraman, P., & Hoo, W. C. (2023). The Impact of Proactive Resilience Strategies on Organizational Performance: Role of Ambidextrous and Dynamic Capabilities of SMEs in Manufacturing Sector. *Sustainability (Basel)*, 15(16), 12665. 10.3390/su151612665

Pfeffer, J., & Salanick, G. R. (2003). *The External Control of Organizations: A Resource Dependence Perspective*. Stanford University Press.

Piramanayagam, S., Dixit, S. K., & Seal, P. P. (2022). We are in survival mode: How family-owned small foodservice firms in India responded to the Covid-19 pandemic. *Journal of Family Business Management*, 12(3), 436–449. 10.1108/JFBM-10-2021-0130

Pociovalisteanu, D., Novo-Corti, I., Aceleanu, M., erban, A., & Grecu, E. (2015). Employment policies for a green economy at the European Union level. *Sustainability (Basel)*, 7(7), 9231–9250. 10.3390/su7079231

Podgorskaya, S. (2021). Methodological aspects of rural economy diversification in the context of modern civilizational transformations. *E3s Web of Conferences, 273*, 08041. 10.1051/e3sconf/202127308041

Pornpitakpan, C. (2004). The Persuasiveness of Source Credibility: A Critical Review of Five Decades' Evidence. *Journal of Applied Social Psychology*, 34(2), 243–281. 10.1111/j.1559-1816.2004.tb02547.x

Prabhudesai, R., & Prasad, C. V. (2017). Antecedents of SME alliance performance: A multi-level review. *Management Research Review*, 40(12), 1261–1279. 10.1108/MRR-12-2016-0286

Prahalad, C. K., & Ramaswamy, V. (2004). Co-creation experiences: The next practice in value creation. *Journal of Interactive Marketing*, 18(3), 5–14. 10.1002/dir.20015

Pratama, K. J. (2022). Regulatory challenges in digital foreign investment through securities crowdfunding in Indonesia. *Indonesian Law Journal*, 15(2), 12–24.

Priester, J. R., & Petty, R. E. (2003). The Influence of Spokesperson Trustworthiness on Message Elaboration, Attitude Strength, and Advertising Effectiveness. *Journal of Consumer Psychology*, 13(4), 408–421. 10.1207/S15327663JCP1304_08

Puie, F. (2019). Conceptual framework for rural business models. *Proceedings of the International Conference on Business Excellence, 13*(1), 1130-1139. 10.2478/picbe-2019-0099

Pukall, T. J., & Calabro, A. (2014). The internationalization of family firms: A critical review and integrative model. *Family Business Review*, 27(2), 103–125. 10.1177/0894486513491423

Purbasari, R., Munajat, E., & Fauzan, F. (2023). Digital Innovation Ecosystem on Digital Entrepreneur: Social Network Analysis Approach. *International Journal of E-Entrepreneurship and Innovation*, 13(1), 1–21. 10.4018/IJEEI.319040

Qalati, S. A., Ostic, D., Sulaiman, M. A. B. A., Gopang, A. A., & Khan, A. (2022). Social media and SMEs' performance in developing countries: Effects of technological-organizational-environmental factors on the adoption of social media. *SAGE Open*, 12(2). 10.1177/21582440221094594

Qudrat-Ullah, H., Kayal, A., & Mugumya, A. (2021). Cost-effective energy billing mechanisms for small and medium-scale industrial customers in Uganda. *Energy*, 227, 120488. Advance online publication. 10.1016/j.energy.2021.120488

Queiroz, J., Leitão, P., Pontes, J., Chaves, A., Parra, J., & Perez-Pons, M. E. (2020). A quality innovation strategy for an inter-regional digital innovation hub. *ADCAIJ: Advances in Distributed Computing and Artificial Intelligence Journal*, 9(4), 31–45. 10.14201/ADCAIJ2020943145

Quintana, S., Díaz, A., Monagas, M., & García, E. (2017). Agricultural policies and their impact on poverty reduction in developing countries: Lessons learned from three water basins in Cape Verde. *Sustainability (Basel)*, 9(10), 1841. 10.3390/su9101841

Qwelane, M. J. (2022). *An investigation of how contemporary South African fashion designers communicate creative brand storytelling and brand aesthetics* (Doctoral dissertation, The IIE).

Compilation of References

Radicic, D., & Petković, S. (2023). Impact of digitalization on technological innovations in small and medium-sized enterprises (SMEs). *Technological Forecasting and Social Change*, 191, 122474. 10.1016/j.techfore.2023.122474

Rahayu, I. (2024, February). Entrepreneurial behavior of bachelor students in fashion education, Surabaya State University. In *5th Vocational Education International Conference (VEIC-5 2023)* (pp. 904-909). Atlantis Press.

Rahman, M., Akter, M., Odunukan, K., & Haque, S. E. (2020). Examining economic and technology-related barriers of small-and medium-sized enterprises internationalisation: An emerging economy context. *Business Strategy & Development*, 3(1), 16–27. 10.1002/bsd2.71

Rahman, M., Dana, L., Moral, I., Anjum, N., & Rahaman, M. (2022). Challenges of rural women entrepreneurs in Bangladesh to survive their family entrepreneurship: A narrative inquiry through storytelling. *Journal of Family Business Management*, 13(3), 645–664. 10.1108/JFBM-04-2022-0054

Rahman, M., Hack-Polay, D., Shafique, S., & Igwe, P. A. (2023). Dynamic capability of the firm: Analysis of the impact of internationalisation on SME performance in an emerging economy. *International Journal of Emerging Markets*, 18(9), 2383–2401. 10.1108/IJOEM-02-2021-0236

Ramanathan, R., Ramanathan, U., & Hsiao, H.-L. (2012). The impact of e-commerce on Taiwanese SMEs: Marketing and operations effects. *International Journal of Production Economics*, 140(2), 934–943. 10.1016/j.ijpe.2012.07.017

Ramaswamy, V., & Ozcan, K. (2018). What is co-creation? An interactional creation framework and its implications for value creation. *Journal of Business Research*, 84, 196205. 10.1016/j.jbusres.2017.11.027

Ramayah, T., Cheah, J., Chuah, F., Ting, H., & Memon, M. A. (2018). Partial least squares structural equation modeling (PLS-SEM) using smartPLS 3.0. *An Updated Guide and Practical Guide to Statistical Analysis*.

Ramilo, R. D. (2016). *Key Determinants and Barriers to Digital Innovation Adaptation Among Architectural Practices* (Doctoral dissertation, Universiti Teknologi Malaysia).

Rani, N. S. A., & Krishnan, K. S. D. (2018). Factors that influence Malay students in purchasing skincare products in Malaysia. *The Journal of Business and Retail Management Research*, 13(01). Advance online publication. 10.24052/JBRMR/V13IS01/ART-02

Rao, P., Kumar, S., Chavan, M., & Lim, W. M. (2023). A systematic literature review on SME financing: Trends and future directions. *Journal of Small Business Management*, 61(3), 1247–1277. 10.1080/00472778.2021.1955123

Ratten, V., & Jones, P. (2021). Entrepreneurship and management education: Exploring trends and gaps. *International Journal of Management Education*, 19(1), 100431. 10.1016/j.ijme.2020.100431

Ratten, V., & Usmanij, P. (2021). Entrepreneurship education: Time for a change in research direction? *International Journal of Management Education*, 19(1), 100367. 10.1016/j.ijme.2020.100367

Rauch, A., Wiklund, J., Lumpkin, G., & Fresé, M. (2009). Entrepreneurial orientation and business performance: An assessment of past research and suggestions for the future. *Entrepreneurship Theory and Practice*, 33(3), 761–787. 10.1111/j.1540-6520.2009.00308.x

Reim, W., Yli-Viitala, P., Arrasvuori, J., & Parida, V. (2022). Tackling business model challenges in SME internationalization through digitalization. *Journal of Innovation & Knowledge, 7*, 100199. doi:10.1016/j.jik.2022.10019910.1016/j.jik.2022.100199

Reuber, A. R., & Fischer, E. (1997). The influence of the management team's international experience on the internationalization behaviors of SMEs. *Journal of International Business Studies*, 28(4), 807–825. 10.1057/palgrave.jibs.8490120

Rexhepi, G., Ramadani, V., Rahdari, A., & Anggadwita, G. (2017). Models and strategies of family businesses internationalization: A conceptual framework and future research directions. *Review of International Business and Strategy*, 27(2), 248–260. 10.1108/RIBS-12-2016-0081

Reza, A., Sarraf, A., & Teshnizi, H. (2020). The Effect of Social Media Advertising Properties on Customer Buying Intention (Case Study: Consumers of Cosmetic Products). *International Journal of Research in Business Studies and Management*, 7(5), 10–17.

Rezaee, Z. (2016). Business sustainability research: A theoretical and integrated perspective. *Journal of Accounting Literature*, 36(1), 48–64. 10.1016/j.acclit.2016.05.003

Reza, S., Mubarik, M. S., Naghavi, N., & Nawaz, R. R. (2021). Internationalisation challenges of SMEs: Role of intellectual capital. *International Journal of Learning and Intellectual Capital*, 18(3), 252–277. 10.1504/IJLIC.2021.116468

Rezvani, M., & Fathollahzadeh, Z. (2020). The impact of entrepreneurial marketing on innovative marketing performance in small-and medium-sized companies. *Journal of Strategic Marketing*, 28(2), 136–148. 10.1080/0965254X.2018.1488762

Ribau, C. P., Moreira, A. C., & Raposo, M. (2015). Internationalisation of the firm theories: A schematic synthesis. *International Journal of Business and Globalisation*, 15(4), 528–554. 10.1504/IJBG.2015.072535

Ribau, C. P., Moreira, A. C., & Raposo, M. (2017). Export performance and the internationalisation of SMEs. *International Journal of Entrepreneurship and Small Business*, 30(2), 214–240. 10.1504/IJESB.2017.081438

Ribau, C. P., Moreira, A. C., & Raposo, M. (2018). Categorising the internationalisation of SMEs with social network analysis. *International Journal of Entrepreneurship and Small Business*, 35(1), 57–80. 10.1504/IJESB.2018.094264

Ribau, C. P., Moreira, A. C., & Raposo, M. (2018). SME internationalization research: Mapping the state of the art. *Canadian Journal of Administrative Sciences*, 35(2), 280–303. 10.1002/cjas.1419

Ribau, C. P., Moreira, A. C., & Raposo, M. (2019). Multidyadic Relationships: A multi-stage perspective. *Global Business and Economics Review*, 21(6), 732–755. 10.1504/GBER.2019.102553

Compilation of References

Ring, J., Peredo, A., & Chrisman, J. (2010). Business networks and economic development in rural communities in the United States. *Entrepreneurship Theory and Practice*, 34(1), 171–195. 10.1111/j.1540-6520.2009.00307.x

Ringle, C. M., Wende, S., & Becker, J.-M. (2022). SmartPLS 4. Oststeinbek: SmartPLS GmbH. *J. Appl. Struct. Equ. Model.*

Robbins, S. P., & Coulter, M. A. (2012). *Management* (11th ed.). Pearson Education.

Rochayatun, S. S., & Bidin, R. (2022). Mode of Entry Strategy on SMEs Internationalization in East Java: A Review of Literature. *Asian Journal of Economics. Business and Accounting*, 22(15), 20–32. 10.9734/ajeba/2022/v22i1530626

Röd, I. (2019). TMT diversity and innovation ambidexterity in family firms: The mediating role of open innovation breadth. *Journal of Family Business Management*, 9(4), 377–392. 10.1108/JFBM-09-2018-0031

Romano, C. A., Tanewski, G. A., & Smyrnios, K. X. (2001). Capital structure decision making: A model for family business. *Journal of Business Venturing*, 16(3), 285–310. 10.1016/S0883-9026(99)00053-1

Rondi, E., De Massis, A., & Kotlar, J. (2019). Unlocking innovation potential: A typology of family business innovation postures and the critical role of the family system. *Journal of Family Business Strategy, 10*(4), 100236.

Roro, F. S. R., Hernoko, A. Y., & Anand, G. (2019). The Characteristics Of Proportionality Principle In Islamic Crowdfunding In Indonesia. *Jurnal Hukum dan Pembangunan, 49*(2), 455-470.

Rosa, M., McElwee, G., & Smith, R. (2019). Farm diversification strategies in response to rural policy: A case from rural Italy. *Land Use Policy*, 81, 291–301. 10.1016/j.landusepol.2018.11.006

Rotaru, C., & Dumitrache, V. (2022). Can entrepreneurship be a strategic option for the development of the rural space in Romania? 10.24818/CAFEE/2020/9/07

Roy, M. (2019). Elevating services: Services trade policy, WTO commitments, and their role in economic development and trade integration. *Journal of World Trade*, 53(6).

Rozak, H. A., Adhiatma, A., Fachrunnisa, O., & Rahayu, T. (2023, November). Social Media Engagement, Organizational Agility and Digitalization Strategic Plan to Improve SMEs' Performance. *IEEE Transactions on Engineering Management*, 70(11), 3766–3775. 10.1109/TEM.2021.3085977

Rupietta, C., & Backes-Gellner, U. (2019). Combining knowledge stock and knowledge flow to generate superior incremental innovation performance—Evidence from Swiss manufacturing. *Journal of Business Research*, 94, 209–222. 10.1016/j.jbusres.2017.04.003

Russell, S. N., & Millar, H. H. (2014). Exploring the Relationships among Sustainable Manufacturing Practices, Business Performance and Competitive Advantage: Perspectives from a Developing Economy. *Journal of Management and Sustainability*, 4(3). Advance online publication. 10.5539/jms.v4n3p37

Ruzzier, M., Hisrich, R. D., & Antoncic, B. (2006). SME internationalization research: Past, present, and future. *Journal of Small Business and Enterprise Development*, 13(4), 476–497. 10.1108/14626000610705705

Rytkönen, P., & Oghazi, P. (2021). Bringing innovation back in–strategies and driving forces behind entrepreneurial responses in small-scale rural industries in Sweden. *British Food Journal*, 124(8), 2550–2565. 10.1108/BFJ-05-2021-0587

Sadeghloo, T., Qeidari, H., Salehi, M., & Jalali, A. (2018). Obstacles and methods of financing for the development of local entrepreneurship in Iran. *International Journal of Development Issues*, 17(1), 114–138. 10.1108/IJDI-05-2017-0046

Sadiku-Dushi, N., Dana, L. P., & Ramadani, V. (2019). Entrepreneurial marketing dimensions and SMEs performance. *Journal of Business Research*, 100, 86–99. 10.1016/j.jbusres.2019.03.025

Saghaian, S., Mohammadi, H., & Mohammadi, M. (2022). Factors affecting success of entrepreneurship in agribusinesses: Evidence from the city of Mashhad, Iran. *Sustainability (Basel)*, 14(13), 7700. 10.3390/su14137700

Sajjan, R. (2017). Crowdfunding ecosystem in India. *International Journal of Scientific Research*, 6(12), 1230–1232.

Saleh, C., & Hanafi, I. (2020). Government Collaboration (Vol. 1). Academic Press.

Salfore, N., Ensermu, M., & Kinde, Z. (2023). Business model innovation and firm performance: Evidence from manufacturing SMEs. *Heliyon*, 9(6), e16384. 10.1016/j.heliyon.2023.e1638437251443

Salmon, U., & Allman, K. (2020). Innovation in family firms: An empirical taxonomy of owners using a mixed methods approach. *Journal of Family Business Management*, 10(1), 20–39. 10.1108/JFBM-05-2019-0037

Salomon, R. (2006). *Learning from Exporting: New Insights, New Perspectives*. Edward Elgar Publishing. 10.4337/9781781953006

Salomon, R. M., & Shaver, J. M. (2005). Learning by exporting: New insights from examining firm innovation. *Journal of Economics & Management Strategy*, 14(2), 431–460. 10.1111/j.1530-9134.2005.00047.x

Santora, J. (2023). *17 Key Influencer Marketing Statistics to Fuel Your Strategy*. https://influencermarketinghub.com/influencer-marketing-statistics/

Compilation of References

Sartal, A., Bellas, R., Mejías, A. M., & García-Collado, A. (2020). The sustainable manufacturing concept, evolution and opportunities within Industry 4.0: A literature review. *Advances in Mechanical Engineering*, 12(5). 10.1177/1687814020925232

Satı, Z. (2023). Yeni Dijital Teknolojiler ve Dijital İnovasyon Yönetimi. Academic Press.

Saxena, C., Khatri, B., & Khan, S. A. (2023). Factors Hindering Women Entrepreneurs' Access to Institutional Finance: An Empirical Study From the Banker Perspective. In Gupta, V. (Ed.), *Fostering Global Entrepreneurship Through Business Model Innovation* (pp. 101–114). IGI Global. 10.4018/978-1-6684-6975-0.ch004

Schimmelpfennig, C., & Hunt, J. B. (2020). Fifty years of celebrity endorser research: Support for a comprehensive celebrity endorsement strategy framework. *Psychology and Marketing*, 37(3), 488–505. 10.1002/mar.21315

Schnack, H., Uthoff, S. A., & Ansmann, L. (2022). The perceived impact of physician shortages on human resource strategies in German hospitals–a resource dependency perspective. *Journal of Health Organization and Management*, 36(9), 196–211. 10.1108/JHOM-05-2021-020336098505

Schotten, M., Meester, W. J., Steiginga, S., & Ross, C. A. (2017). A brief history of Scopus: The world's largest abstract and citation database of scientific literature. In *Research analytics* (pp. 31–58). Auerbach Publications. 10.1201/9781315155890-3

Schouten, A. P., Janssen, L., & Verspaget, M. (2020). Celebrity vs. Influencer endorsements in advertising: The role of identification, credibility, and Product-Endorser fit. *International Journal of Advertising*, 39(2), 258–281. 10.1080/02650487.2019.1634898

Schumpeter, J. A. (1942). *Socialism, capitalism and democracy*. Harper and Brothers.

Schwab, K., Samans, R., Zahidi, S., Leopold, T. A., Ratcheva, V., Hausmann, R., & Tyson, L. D. (2017, November). The global gender gap report 2017. *World Economic Forum*.

Scott, J. E. (2007). An e-transformation study using the technology-organization-environment framework. *BLED 2007 Proceedings*, 55.

Secchi, L., Wink, M. V.Jr, & Moraes, C. J. D. (2022). Crowdfunding and electoral performance in Brazil: Statistical analysis of the elections for federal deputy in 2018. *Revista de Administração Pública*, 55, 1191–1214. 10.1590/0034-761220200876

Segura-Mojica, F. J. (2021). Crowdfunding for the rescue of micro-businesses. Factors and perceptions of potential investors in Mexico. *RETOS.Revista de Ciencias de la Administración y Economía*, 11(21), 71–91.

Sekabira, H., & Qaim, M. (2017). Can mobile phones improve gender equality and nutrition? Panel data evidence from farm households in Uganda. *Food Policy*, 73, 95–103. 10.1016/j.foodpol.2017.10.004

Sendawula, K., Bagire, V., Mbidde, C. I., & Turyakira, P. (2020). Environmental commitment and environmental sustainability practices of manufacturing small and medium enterprises in Uganda. *Journal of Enterprising Communities*, 15(4), 588–607. Advance online publication. 10.1108/JEC-07-2020-0132

Setia, S. (2018). Personality profile of successful entrepreneurs. Journal of Economics. *Business & Accountancy Ventura*, 21(1), 13–23. 10.14414/jebav.v21i1.1004

Severt, D., Wang, Y., Chen, P. J., & Breiter, D. (2007). Examining the motivation, perceivedd performance, and behavioral intentions of convention attendees: Evidence from a regional conference. *Tourism Management*, 28(2), 399–408. 10.1016/j.tourman.2006.04.003

Shafigullina, A. V., Akhmetshin, R. M., Martynova, O. V., Vorontsova, L. V., & Sergienko, E. S. (2020). Analysis of entrepreneurial activity and digital technologies in business. *Advances in Intelligent Systems and Computing*, 908, 183–188. 10.1007/978-3-030-11367-4_17

Shafik, W. (2023b). Cyber security perspectives in public spaces: Drone case study. In *Handbook of Research on Cybersecurity Risk in Contemporary Business Systems*. 10.4018/978-1-6684-7207-1.ch004

Shafik, W. (2023c). Making Cities Smarter: IoT and SDN Applications, Challenges, and Future Trends. In *Opportunities and Challenges of Industrial IoT in 5G and 6G Networks*. 10.4018/978-1-7998-9266-3.ch004

Shafik, W. (2024b). Data-Driven Future Trends and Innovation in Telemedicine. In *Improving Security, Privacy, and Connectivity Among Telemedicine Platforms* (pp. 93-118). IGI Global. 10.4018/979-8-3693-2141-6.ch005

Shafik, W. (2024c). Navigating Emerging Challenges in Robotics and Artificial Intelligence in Africa. In *Examining the Rapid Advance of Digital Technology in Africa* (pp. 124-144). IGI Global. 10.4018/978-1-6684-9962-7.ch007

Shafik, W. (2024d). Predicting Future Cybercrime Trends in the Metaverse Era. In *Forecasting Cyber Crimes in the Age of the Metaverse* (pp. 78-113). IGI Global. 10.4018/979-8-3693-0220-0.ch005

Shafik, W., & Kalinaki, K. (2023). Smart City Ecosystem: An Exploration of Requirements, Architecture, Applications, Security, and Emerging Motivations. In *Handbook of Research on Network-Enabled IoT Applications for Smart City Services* (pp. 75-98). IGI Global. 10.4018/979-8-3693-0744-1.ch005

Shafik, W. (2023a). A Comprehensive Cybersecurity Framework for Present and Future Global Information Technology Organizations. In *Effective Cybersecurity Operations for Enterprise-Wide Systems* (pp. 56–79). IGI Global. 10.4018/978-1-6684-9018-1.ch002

Shafik, W. (2024a). *Blockchain-Based Internet of Things (B-IoT): Challenges, Solutions, Opportunities, Open Research Questions, and Future Trends. Blockchain-based Internet of Things*. Chapman and Hall/CRC. 10.1201/9781003407096-3

Compilation of References

Shafik, W. (2024c). Introduction to ChatGPT. In *Advanced Applications of Generative AI and Natural Language Processing Models* (pp. 1–25). IGI Global. 10.4018/979-8-3693-0502-7.ch001

Shafik, W. (2024e). Toward a More Ethical Future of Artificial Intelligence and Data Science. In *The Ethical Frontier of AI and Data Analysis* (pp. 362–388). IGI Global. 10.4018/979-8-3693-2964-1.ch022

Shafik, W. (2024f). *Wearable Medical Electronics in Artificial Intelligence of Medical Things. Handbook of Security and Privacy of AI-Enabled Healthcare Systems and Internet of Medical Things*. CRC Press. 10.1201/9781003370321-2

Shahab, Y., Riaz, Y., Ntim, C. G., Ye, Z., Zhang, Q., & Feng, R. (2021). Online feedback and crowdfunding finance in China. *International Journal of Finance & Economics*, 26(3), 4634–4652. 10.1002/ijfe.2034

Shao, J., Aneye, C., Kharitonova, A., & Fang, W. (2023). Essential innovation capability of producer-service enterprises towards circular business model: Motivators and barriers. *Business Strategy and the Environment*, 32(7), 4548–4567. 10.1002/bse.3380

Sharfaei, S., Ong, J. W., & Ojo, A. O. (2023). The effects of dynamic capabilities on international SMEs' performance. *International Journal of Globalisation and Small Business*, 13(3), 247–267. 10.1504/IJGSB.2023.130321

Sharma, D. D., & Blomstermo, A. (2003). The internationalization process of born globals: A network view. *International Business Review*, 12(6), 739–753. 10.1016/j.ibusrev.2003.05.002

Sharma, N., Khatri, B., & Khan, S. A. (2023a). Do e-WOM Persuade Travelers Destination Visit Intentions? An investigation on how Travelers Adopt the Information from the Social Media Channels. *Journal of Content. Community and Communication*, 17(9), 147–161. 10.31620/JCCC.06.23/11

Sharma, N., Khatri, B., Khan, S. A., & Shamsi, M. S. (2023b). Extending the UTAUT Model to Examine the Influence of social media on Tourists' Destination Selection. *Indian Journal of Marketing*, 53(4), 47–64. 10.17010/ijom/2023/v53/i4/172689

Sharma, Y., Suri, A., Sijariya, R., & Jindal, L. (2023). Role of education 4.0 in innovative curriculum practices and digital literacy–A bibliometric approach. *E-Learning and Digital Media*. 10.1177/20427530231221073

Shcerbakova, L., Evdokimova, E., & Savintseva, S. (2019, June). Impact of the complimentary nature of the digital resource on the accelerating dynamics of the agricultural sector. In *International Scientific and Practical Conference "Digital agriculture-development strategy" (ISPC 2019)* (pp. 69-75). Atlantis Press. 10.2991/ispc-19.2019.16

Shi, H. X., Graves, C., & Barbera, F. (2019). Intergenerational succession and internationalisation strategy of family SMEs: Evidence from China. *Long Range Planning*, 52(4), 1–18. 10.1016/j.lrp.2018.05.004

Shinozaki, S. (2022). Informal Micro, Small, and Medium-Sized Enterprises and Digitalization: Evidence from Surveys in Indonesia. ADBI Working Paper 1310. Tokyo: Asian Development Bank Institute

Shi, X., Zheng, Z., Zhang, Q., & Liang, H. (2020). External knowledge search and firms' incremental innovation capability: The joint moderating effect of technological proximity and network embeddedness. *Management Decision*, 58(9), 2049–2072. 10.1108/MD-08-2019-1078

Short, K. G. (2023). A curriculum that is intercultural. In *Teaching Globally* (pp. 3–24). Routledge. 10.4324/9781032682693-2

Shoukat, M. H., Selem, K. M., & Asim Shah, S. (2023). How Does Social Media Influencer Credibility Blow the Promotional Horn? A Dual Mediation Model. *Journal of Relationship Marketing*, 22(3), 172–201. 10.1080/15332667.2023.2197767

Shuaib, M., Seevers, D., Zhang, X., Badurdeen, F., Rouch, K. E., & Jawahir, I. S. (2014). Product sustainability index (ProdSI) a metrics-based framework to evaluate the total life cycle sustainability of manufactured products. *Journal of Industrial Ecology*, 18(4), 491–507. 10.1111/jiec.12179

Shukla, A. K., Gao, G., & Kim, B. S. (2022). Applications of 3D Bioprinting Technology in Induced Pluripotent Stem Cells-Based Tissue Engineering. Micromachines. https://www.ncbi.nlm.nih.gov/pmc/articles/PMC8876961/

Sia, S. K., Soh, C., & Weill, P. (2016). How DBS bank pursued a digital business strategy. *MIS Quarterly Executive*, 15(2).

Silva, P., & Moreira, A. C. (2019). Subsidiary survival: A case study from the Portuguese electronics industry. *Review of International Business and Strategy*, 29(3), 226–252. 10.1108/RIBS-10-2018-0094

Simmering, M. J., Fuller, C. M., Richardson, H. A., Ocal, Y., & Atinc, G. M. (2015). Marker variable choice, reporting, and interpretation in the detection of common method variance: A review and demonstration. *Organizational Research Methods*, 18(3), 473–511. 10.1177/1094428114560023

Simões, C., Esperança, J., & Simões, V. (2013). *Horizonte Internacionalizar*. http://www.portugalglobal.pt/PT/Internacionalizar/Documents/HorizonteInternacionalizarGuiaparaPME.pdf

Simpson, M., & Docherty, A. J. (2004). E-commerce adoption support and advice for UK SMEs. *Journal of Small Business and Enterprise Development*, 11(3), 315–328. 10.1108/14626000410551573

Singh, A.K. (2022). A study on the growth and role of SMES in Indian economy. International journal of financial management and economics. 10.33545/26179210.2022.v5.i2.158

Singh, R., & Kota, H. B. (2017). A resource dependency framework for innovation and internationalization of family businesses: Evidence from India. *Journal of Entrepreneurship in Emerging Economies*, 9(2), 207–231. 10.1108/JEEE-04-2016-0013

Sırma, İ., Ekici, O., & Aytürk, Y. (2019). Crowdfunding awareness in Turkey. *Procedia Computer Science*, 158, 490–497. 10.1016/j.procs.2019.09.080

Compilation of References

Smajlović, S., Umihanić, B., & Turulja, L. (2019). The interplay of technological innovation and business model innovation toward company performance. *Management*, 24(2), 63–79. 10.30924/mjcmi.24.2.5

Smith, H., Discetti, R., Bellucci, M., & Acuti, D. (2022). SMEs engagement with the Sustainable Development Goals: A power perspective. *Journal of Business Research*, 149, 112–122. 10.1016/j.jbusres.2022.05.021

Sokolova, K., & Kefi, H. (2020). Instagram and YouTube bloggers promote it, why should I buy? How credibility and parasocial interaction influence purchase intentions. *Journal of Retailing and Consumer Services*, 53, 101742. Advance online publication. 10.1016/j.jretconser.2019.01.011

Solakis, K., Pena-Vinces, J. C., & Lopex-Bonilla, J. M. (2017). DART model from a customer's perspective: An exploratory study in the hospitality industry of Greece. *Business Perspectives*, 15(2). www.businessperspectives.org

Solakis, K., Peña-Vinces, J., & Lopez-Bonilla, J. M. (2022). Value co-creation and perceivedd value: A customer perspective in the hospitality context. *European Research on Management and Business Economics*, 28(1), 100175. Advance online publication. 10.1016/j.iedeen.2021.100175

Solow, R. M. (1994). Perspectives on growth theory. *The Journal of Economic Perspectives*, 8(1), 45–54. 10.1257/jep.8.1.45

Song, M. J. (2021). Teacher professional development in integrating digital fabrication technologies into teaching and learning. *Educational Media International*, 58(4), 317–334. 10.1080/09523987.2021.1989766

Souza Bronzeri, M., & Cunha, J. C. (2021). Crowdfunding for Technological Innovation of Micro & Small Enterprises in Brazil. *International Journal of Developmental Research*, 11(06), 47650–47656.

Sparkman, R. M.Jr, & Locander, W. B. (1980). Attribution Theory and Advertising Effectiveness. *The Journal of Consumer Research*, 7(3), 219. 10.1086/208810

Staake, T., Thiesse, F., & Fleisch, E. (2009). The emergence of counterfeit trade: A literature review. *European Journal of Marketing*, 43(3/4), 320–349. 10.1108/03090560910935451

Stam, E. (2008). Entrepreneurship and innovation. In Nooteboom, B., & Stam, E. (Eds.), *Micro-foundations for innovation policy*. Amsterdam University Press.

Statista. (2023a). *Beauty and personal care industry in Malaysia - statistics & facts*. https://www.statista.com/topics/11070/beauty-and-personal-care-industry-in-malaysia/#topicOverview

Statista. (2023b). *Effectiveness of influencers worldwide 2021*. https://www.statista.com/statistics/1275239/effectiveness-influencers-worldwide/

Statista. (2023c). *TikTok penetration in selected countries and territories 2023*. https://www.statista.com/statistics/1299829/tiktok-penetration-worldwide-by-country/

Steinhäuser, V. P. S., Paula, F. D. O., & de Macedo-Soares, T. D. L. V. A. (2021). Internationalization of SMEs: A systematic review of 20 years of research. *Journal of International Entrepreneurship*, 19(2), 164–195. 10.1007/s10843-020-00271-7

Stoian, M. C., Rialp, J., & Dimitratos, P. (2017). SME networks and international performance: Unveiling the significance of foreign market entry mode. *Journal of Small Business Management*, 55(1), 128–148. 10.1111/jsbm.12241

Storey, D. J. (2016). *Understanding the small business sector*. Routledge. 10.4324/9781315544335

Street, C. T., & Cameron, A. F. (2007). External relationships and the small business: A review of small business alliance and network research. *Journal of Small Business Management*, 45(2), 239–266. 10.1111/j.1540-627X.2007.00211.x

Subramaniam, M., Kathirvel, A., Sabitha, E., & Anwar Basha, H. (2021). Modified Firefly Algorithm and Fuzzy C-Mean Clustering Based Semantic Information Retrieval. Journal of Web Engineering, 20(1), 33–52. 10.13052/jwe1540-9589.2012

Subramaniam, M., & Youndt, M. A. (2005). The influence of intellectual capital on the types of innovative capabilities. *Academy of Management Journal*, 48(3), 450–463. 10.5465/amj.2005.17407911

Suchek, N., & Franco, M. (2023). Inter-organisational cooperation oriented towards sustainability involving SMEs: A systematic literature review. *Journal of the Knowledge Economy*, 1–21. 10.1007/s13132-023-01196-x

Sudha, D., & Kathirvel, A. (2022). An Intrusion Detection System to Detect and Mitigating Attacks Using Hidden Markov Model (HMM) Energy Monitoring Technique. Stochastic Modeling an Applications, 26(3), 467-476.

Sudha, D., & Kathirvel, A. (2023a). The performance enhancement of Aodv protocol using GETUS. International Journal of Early Childhood Special Education, 15(2), 115-125. DOI:10.48047/INTJECSE/V15I2.11

Sudha, D., & Kathirvel, A. (2023b). The effect of ETUS in various generic attacks in mobile ad hoc networks to improve the performance of Aodv protocol. International Journal of Humanities, Law, and Social Sciences, 9(1), 467-476.

Su, L. L., & Kong, R. (2019). Financial literacy, entrepreneurial training and farmers' entrepreneurial decision-making. *Journal of South China Agricultural University*, 18(03), 53–66.

Sulistyorini, Y., & Santoso, B. (2021). Entrepreneurial knowledge on entrepreneurial intention: The mediating of perceived desirability and perceived feasibility. *Baskara Journal of Business and Entrepreneurship*, 3(2), 39. 10.24853/baskara.3.2.39-47

Sun, H., Mohsin, M., Alharthi, M., & Abbas, Q. (2020). Measuring environmental sustainability performance of South Asia. *Journal of Cleaner Production*, 251, 119519. 10.1016/j.jclepro.2019.119519

Compilation of References

Sun, J., & Zhang, J. (2024). Digital Financial Inclusion and Innovation of MSMEs. *Sustainability (Basel)*, 16(4), 1404. 10.3390/su16041404

Supekar, S., & Dhage, S. (2022). Rural entrepreneurship through khadi and village industries. *Sedme (Small Enterprises Development Management & Extension Journal) a Worldwide Window on MSME Studies, 49*(3), 219-226. 10.1177/09708464221111220

Suresh Babu, C. V. (2023). *Artificial Intelligence and Expert Systems*. Anniyappa Publications.

Suresh Babu, C. V., Mahalashmi, J., Vidhya, A., Nila Devagi, S., & Bowshith, G. (2023). Save Soil Through Machine Learning. In Habib, M. (Ed.), *Global Perspectives on Robotics and Autonomous Systems: Development and Applications* (pp. 345–362). IGI Global. 10.4018/978-1-6684-7791-5.ch016

Suresh Babu, C. V., & Praveen, S. (2023). Swarm Intelligence and Evolutionary Machine Learning Algorithms for COVID-19: Pandemic and Epidemic Review. In Suresh Kumar, A., Kose, U., Sharma, S., & Jerald Nirmal Kumar, S. (Eds.), *Dynamics of Swarm Intelligence Health Analysis for the Next Generation* (pp. 83–103). IGI Global. 10.4018/978-1-6684-6894-4.ch005

Suresh Babu, C. V., & Rahul, A. (2024). Securing the Future: Unveiling Risks and Safeguarding Strategies in Machine Learning-Powered Cybersecurity. In Almaiah, M., Maleh, Y., & Alkhassawneh, A. (Eds.), *Risk Assessment and Countermeasures for Cybersecurity* (pp. 80–95). IGI Global. 10.4018/979-8-3693-2691-6.ch005

Suresh Babu, C. V., Swapna, A., Chowdary, D. S., Vardhan, B. S., & Imran, M. (2023). Leaf Disease Detection Using Machine Learning (ML). In Khang, A. (Ed.), *Handbook of Research on AI-Equipped IoT Applications in High-Tech Agriculture* (pp. 188–199). IGI Global. 10.4018/978-1-6684-9231-4.ch010

Suseno, Y., & Standing, C. (2017). The systems perspective of national innovation ecosystems. *Systems Research and Behavioral Science*, 35(3), 282–307. 10.1002/sres.2494

Swoboda, B., Elsner, S., & Olejnik, E. (2015). How do past mode choices influences subsequent entry? A study on the boundary conditions of preferred entry modes of retail firms. *International Business Review*, 24(3), 506–517. 10.1016/j.ibusrev.2014.10.008

Taghizadeh, S. K., Rahman, S. A., Hossain, M. M., & Haque, M. M. (2020). Characteristics of organizational culture in stimulating service innovation and performance. *Marketing Intelligence & Planning*, 38(2), 224–238. 10.1108/MIP-12-2018-0561

Tajfel, H. E. (1978). *Differentiation between social groups: Studies in the social psychology of intergroup relations*. Academic Press.

Tajudeen, F. P., Jaafar, N. I., & Ainin, S. (2018). Understanding the impact of social media usage among organizations. *Information & Management*, 55(3), 308–321. 10.1016/j.im.2017.08.004

Tallman, S., Luo, Y., & Buckley, P. (2017). Business models in global competition. *Global Strategy Journal*, 8(4), 517–535. 10.1002/gsj.1165

Tarhan, M. (2021). Girişimcilik becerisinin kazandırılması bağlamında girişimcilerin öz yaşam öykülerine yönelik bir değerlendirme. *Bolu Abant İzzet Baysal Üniversitesi Eğitim Fakültesi Dergisi*, 21(1), 74–86. 10.17240/aibuefd.2021.21.60703-815358

Terho, H., Haas, A., Eggert, A., & Ulaga, W. (2012). 'It's almost like taking the sales out of selling'-Towards a conceptualization of value-based selling in business markets. *Industrial Marketing Management*, 41(1), 174–185. 10.1016/j.indmarman.2011.11.011

Thorgren, S., & Williams, T. A. (2020). Staying alive during an unfolding crisis: How SMEs ward off impending disaster. *Journal of Business Venturing Insights*, 14, e00187. 10.1016/j.jbvi.2020.e00187

Tillmar, M., Sköld, B., Ahl, H., Berglund, K., & Pettersson, K. (2022). Women's rural businesses: For economic viability or gender equality? – A database study from the Swedish context. *International Journal of Gender and Entrepreneurship*, 14(3), 323–351. 10.1108/IJGE-06-2021-0091

Tiwari, A., Kumar, A., Kant, R., & Jaiswal, D. (2023). Impact of fashion influencers on consumers' purchase intentions: Theory of planned behaviour and mediation of attitude. *Journal of Fashion Marketing and Management*. Advance online publication. 10.1108/JFMM-11-2022-0253

Tiwari, S. (2022). Supply chain innovation in the era of industry 4.0. In *Handbook of Research on Supply Chain Resiliency, Efficiency, and Visibility in the Post-Pandemic Era* (pp. 40–60). IGI Global. 10.4018/978-1-7998-9506-0.ch003

Tomizawa, R., Dolan, K. A., & Englis, B. G. (2020). Digitalization and business model innovation: A review and synthesis. *Journal of Business Research*, 122, 860–869.

Torkanovskiy, E. (2016). Non-equity crowdfunding as a National Phenomenon in a global industry: The case of Russia. *Crowdfunding in Europe: State of the Art in Theory and Practice*, 115-123.

Torkanovskiy, E., & Voinov, A. (2022). Covid-19 for Crowdfunding: Catalyst or Deterrent? Evidence from Russia. *The Indonesian Capital Market Review*, 14(2), 3. 10.21002/icmr.v14i2.1151

Torkkeli, L., Uzhegova, M., Kuivalainen, O., Saarenketo, S., & Puumalainen, K. (2021). Internationalisation of family enterprises: The role of entrepreneurial orientation and international growth orientation. *International Journal of Business and Globalisation*, 29(3), 354–375. 10.1504/IJBG.2021.118681

Tranfield, D., Denyer, D., & Smart, P. (2003). Towards a methodology for developing evidence-informed management knowledge by means of systematic review. *British Journal of Management*, 14(3), 207–222. 10.1111/1467-8551.00375

Trepte, S., & Loy, L. S. (2017). Social identity theory and self-categorization theory. *The International Encyclopedia of Media Effects*, 1–13.

Trepte, S. (2013). Social Identity Theory. In *Psychology of Entertainment* (pp. 255–271). Routledge.

Tripathy, A. (2018). Crowdfunding in India: A Misnomer? *Business Law Review*, 39(5).

Compilation of References

Trivers, I. R. (2017). *Mobilizing the High Line* (Doctoral dissertation, University of Michigan).

Tsvirko, S. (2021). Crowdfunding as a source of financing in Russia: PEST analysis. In *Integrated Science in Digital Age 2020* (pp. 154–163). Springer International Publishing. 10.1007/978-3-030-49264-9_14

Tuah, M., Tedong, P., & Dali, M. (2022). The challenges in rural infrastructure planning governance in Sarawak. *Planning Malaysia*, 20. Advance online publication. 10.21837/pm.v20i24.1214

Tukamuhabwa, B., Mutebi, H., & Kyomuhendo, R. (2023). Competitive advantage in SMEs: Effect of supply chain management practices, logistics capabilities and logistics integration in a developing country. *Journal of Business and Socio-Economic Development*, 3(4), 353–371. Advance online publication. 10.1108/JBSED-04-2021-0051

Turyahebwa, A., Sunday, A., & Ssekajugo, D. (2013). Financial management practices and business performance of small and medium enterprises in western Uganda. *African Journal of Business Management*, 7(38). Advance online publication. 10.5897/AJBM2013.6899

Turyakira, P., Smith, E., & Venter, E. (2012). Corporate social responsibility for SMEs: A proposed hypothesised model. *African Journal of Business Ethics*, 6(2), 106. Advance online publication. 10.4103/1817-7417.111015

Tüzün, İ., & Takay, B. (2017). Patterns of female entrepreneurial activities in Turkey. *Gender in Management*, 32(3), 166–182. 10.1108/GM-05-2016-0102

Tze San, O., Latif, B., & Di Vaio, A. (2022). GEO and sustainable performance: The moderating role of GTD and environmental consciousness. *Journal of Intellectual Capital*, 23(7), 38–67. 10.1108/JIC-10-2021-0290

Urban, W., Krot, K., & Tomaszuk, A. (2023). A cross-national study of internationalisation barriers with reference to SME value chain. Equilibrium. *Quarterly Journal of Economics and Economic Policy*, 18(2), 523–549. 10.24136/eq.2023.016

Usman, S. M., Bukhari, F. A. S., You, H., Badulescu, D., & Gavrilut, D. (2020). The effect and impact of signals on investing decisions in reward-based crowdfunding: A comparative study of China and the United Kingdom. *Journal of Risk and Financial Management*, 13(12), 325. 10.3390/jrfm13120325

Uwonda, G., & Okello, N. (2015). Cash Flow Management and Sustainability of Small Medium Enterprises (SMEs) in Northern Uganda. *International Journal of Social Science and Economics Invention*, 1(03). Advance online publication. 10.23958/ijssei/vol01-i03/02

Uzoamaka, N. O. P., Ifeoma, A. R., & Nosike, C. J. (2020). Strategic orientation dimensions: A critical review. *Int J Res Innov Soc Sci*, 4(9), 609–612.

V, S., M, V. S., K, M., & Priya, A. R. S. (2018). A study on impact of an affiliate marketing in e-business for consumers' perspective. *International Journal of Engineering and Technology*, 10(2), 471–475. 10.21817/ijet/2018/v10i2/181002050

Vahlne, J.-E., & Johanson, J. (2013). The Uppsala model on evolution of the multinational business enterprise – from internalization to coordination of networks. *International Marketing Review*, 30(3), 189–210. 10.1108/02651331311321963

Vaillant, Y., & Lafuente, E. (2007). Do different institutional frameworks condition the influence of local fear of failure and entrepreneurial examples over entrepreneurial activity? *Entrepreneurship and Regional Development*, 19(4), 313–337. 10.1080/08985620701440007

Valdez-Juárez, L. E., García-Pérez de Lema, D., & Maldonado-Guzmán, G. (2016). Management of knowledge, innovation and performance in SMEs. Interdisciplinary. *Journal of Information, Knowledge, and Management*, 11(4), 141–176.

Veloso, E., da Silva, R. C., Trevisan, L., & Dutra, J. (2020). Technological innovations in the work environment and the career of the millennium generation. *Innovation & Management Review*, 17(4), 379–394. 10.1108/INMR-05-2019-0070

Verma, D., & Dewani, P. P. (2021). eWOM credibility: A comprehensive framework and literature review. *Online Information Review*, 45(3), 481–500. 10.1108/OIR-06-2020-0263

Vik, J., & McElwee, G. (2011). Diversification and the entrepreneurial motivations of farmers in Norway. *Journal of Small Business Management*, 49(3), 390–410. 10.1111/j.1540-627X.2011.00327.x

Vissak, T., & Francioni, B. (2013). Serial nonlinear internationalization in practice: A case study. *International Business Review*, 22(6), 951–962. 10.1016/j.ibusrev.2013.01.010

Vithayathil, J., Dadgar, M., & Osiri, J. K. (2020). Social media use and consumer shopping preferences. *International Journal of Information Management*, 54, 102117. 10.1016/j.ijinfomgt.2020.102117

Vivian, Real, & Palma. (2020). A new method for 3D printing drugs: melting solidification printing process. 10.2217/3dp-2020-0024

von Briel, F., Davidsson, P., & Recker, J. (2018). Digital technologies as external enablers of new venture creation in the IT hardware sector. *Entrepreneurship Theory and Practice*, 42(4), 553–576. 10.1177/1042258717732779

Vrontis, D., Makrides, A., Christofi, M., & Thrassou, A. (2021). Social media influencer marketing: A systematic review, integrative framework and future research agenda. *International Journal of Consumer Studies*, 45(4), 617–644. 10.1111/ijcs.12647

Wang, C., Zhang, L., Qin, T., Xi, Z., Sun, L., Wu, H., & Li, D. (2020). 3D printing in adult cardiovascular surgery and interventions: a systematic review. J Thorac Dis. https://www.ncbi.nlm.nih.gov/pmc/articles/PMC7330795/

Wang, K. (2021). Unified distributed robust regression and variable selection framework for massive data. *Expert Systems with Applications*, 186, 115701. Advance online publication. 10.1016/j.eswa.2021.115701

Compilation of References

Wang, S., Lin, X., Xiao, H., Bu, N., & Li, Y. (2022). Empirical study on human capital, economic growth and sustainable development: Taking Shandong province as an example. *Sustainability (Basel)*, 14(12), 7221. 10.3390/su14127221

Wang, T., Li, Y., Kang, M., & Zheng, H. (2019). Exploring individuals' behavioral intentions toward donation crowdfunding: Evidence from China. *Industrial Management & Data Systems*, 119(7), 1515–1534. 10.1108/IMDS-10-2018-0451

Wang, X., Lin, X., & Spencer, M. K. (2019). Exploring the effects of extrinsic motivation on consumer behaviors in social commerce: Revealing consumers' perceptions of social commerce benefits. *International Journal of Information Management*, 45, 163–175. 10.1016/j.ijinfomgt.2018.11.010

Wang, X.-W., Cao, Y.-M., & Park, C. (2019). The relationships among community experience, community commitment, brand attitude, and purchase intention in social media. *International Journal of Information Management*, 49, 475–488. 10.1016/j.ijinfomgt.2019.07.018

Wang, Y. (2016). Environmental dynamism, trust and dynamic capabilities of family businesses. *International Journal of Entrepreneurial Behaviour & Research*, 22(5), 643–670. 10.1108/IJEBR-11-2015-0234

Wang, Y. (2016). What are the biggest obstacles to growth of SMEs in developing countries?– An empirical evidence from an enterprise survey. *Borsa Istanbul Review*, 16(3), 167–176. 10.1016/j.bir.2016.06.001

Wang, Y., Deng, L., Zheng, L., & Robert, X. (2021). Temporal convolutional network with soft thresholding and attention mechanism for machinery prognostics. *Journal of Manufacturing Systems*, 60, 512–526. Advance online publication. 10.1016/j.jmsy.2021.07.008

Wang, Y., Xue, X., & Guo, H. (2022). The sustainability of market orientation from a dynamic perspective: The mediation of dynamic capability and the moderation of error management climate. *Sustainability (Basel)*, 14(7), 3763. 10.3390/su14073763

Waqas, A., Halim, H. A., & Ahmad, N. H. (2022). Design leadership and SMEs Sustainability; Role of Frugal Innovation and Technology Turbulence. *International Journal of Systematic Innovation*, 7(4), 1–17.

Whalen, P. S., & Akaka, M. A. (2016). A dynamic market conceptualization for entrepreneurial marketing: The co-creation of opportunities. *Journal of Strategic Marketing*, 24(1), 61–75. 10.1080/0965254X.2015.1035040

Whalen, P., Uslay, C., Pascal, V. J., Omura, G., McAuley, A., Kasouf, C. J., & Gilmore, A. (2016). Anatomy of competitive advantage: Towards a contingency theory of entrepreneurial marketing. *Journal of Strategic Marketing*, 24(1), 5–19. 10.1080/0965254X.2015.1035036

Whitfield, J., Dioko, L. D. A. N., Webber, D., & Zhang, L. (2014). Attracting convention and exhibition attendance to complex MICE venues: Emerging data from Macao. *International Journal of Tourism Research*, 16(2), 169–179. 10.1002/jtr.1911

Wibawa, B. M., Baihaqi, I., Nareswari, N., Mardhotillah, R. R., & Pramesti, F. (2022). Utilization of social media and its impact on marketing performance: A case study of SMEs in Indonesia. *International Journal of Business and Society*, 23(1), 19–34. 10.33736/ijbs.4596.2022

Widjajanti, K., Sugiyanto, E. K., Widyaevan, D. A., & Sari, A. R. (2023). Strategic Choice Development Using SWOT Analysis: Diversification Strategy of Batik Creative Industry in Blora, Indonesia.*The Journal of Economic Education*, 12(1), 198–212.

Wiedmann, K.-P., & von Mettenheim, W. (2020). Attractiveness, trustworthiness and expertise – social influencers' winning formula? *Journal of Product and Brand Management*, 30(5), 707–725. 10.1108/JPBM-06-2019-2442

Wikaningrum, T., Ghozali, I., Nurcholis, L., & Nugroho, M. (2020). Strategic partnership: How important for reputation of small and medium enterprise. *Quality - Access to Success*, 21(174), 35–39.

Wiklund, J., & Shepherd, D. (2003). Knowledge-based resources, entrepreneurial orientation, and the performance of small and medium-sized businesses. *Strategic Management Journal*, 24(13), 1307–1314. 10.1002/smj.360

Willemse, L. (2012). A critical analysis of the barriers to entry for small business owners imposed by Sections 12E (4)(a)(iii) and (d) and paragraph 3 (b) of the Sixth Schedule Of The Income Tax Act, No. 58 of 1962. *Journal of Economic and Financial Sciences*, 5(2), 527–545. 10.4102/jef.v5i2.298

Williams, D. W., Zorn, M. L., Russell Crook, T., & Combs, J. G. (2013). Passing the torch: Factors influencing transgenerational intent in family firms. *Family Relations*, 62(3), 415–428. 10.1111/fare.12016

Wilson, S., Fesenmaier, D., Fesenmaier, J., & Es, J. (2001). Factors for success in rural tourism development. *Journal of Travel Research*, 40(2), 132–138. 10.1177/004728750104000203

Wind, J., & Rangaswamy, A. (2001). Customization: The next revolution in mass customization. *Journal of Interactive Marketing*, 15(1), 13–32. 10.1002/1520-6653(200124)15:1<13::AID-DIR1001>3.0.CO;2-#

Wong, J. W. C., & Lai, I. K. W. (2019). The effects of value co-creation activities on the perceivedd performance of exhibitions: A service science perspective. *Journal of Hospitality and Tourism Management*, 39, 97–109. 10.1016/j.jhtm.2019.03.003

Wong, K. K. (2013). Partial Least Squares Structural Equation Modeling (PLS-SEM) Techniques Using SmartPLS. *Marketing Bulletin*.

Workie, B., Chane, M., Mohammed, M., & Birhanu, T. (2019). Enteepreneurship. Addis Ababa, Ethiopia: Ministry of Science and Higher Education.

World Bank. (2020). World Bank SME Finance. Author.

Compilation of References

World Commission on Environment and Development. (1987). *Our common future*. Oxford University Press.

Wu, G., Hashemi, M., & Srinivasa, C. (2022). PUMA: Performance Unchanged Model Augmentation for Training Data Removal. *Proceedings of the AAAI Conference on Artificial Intelligence*, 36(8), 8675–8682. 10.1609/aaai.v36i8.20846

Xiao, M., Wang, R., & Chan-Olmsted, S. (2018). Factors affecting YouTube influencer marketing credibility: A heuristic-systematic model. *Journal of Media Business Studies*, 15(3), 188–213. 10.1080/16522354.2018.1501146

Xie, K., Liu, Z., Chen, L., Zhang, W., Liu, S., & Chaudhry, S. S. (2019). Success factors and complex dynamics of crowdfunding: An empirical research on Taobao platform in China. *Electronic Markets*, 29(2), 187–199. 10.1007/s12525-018-0305-6

Xue, Z., Jin, T., Xu, S., Bai, K., He, Q., Zhang, F., Cheng, X., Ji, Z., Pang, W., Shen, Z., Song, H., Shuai, Y., & Zhang, Y. (2022). Assembly of complex 3D structures and electronics on curved surfaces. *Science Advances*, 8(32), 32. 10.1126/sciadv.abm692235947653

Xu, K., & Hitt, M. A. (2020). The international expansion of family firms: The moderating role of internal financial slack and external capital availability. *Asia Pacific Journal of Management*, 37(1), 127–153. 10.1007/s10490-018-9593-9

Xu, Q., Chen, W., Dang, B., & Shi, Y. (2024, February 28). (2024). Employee protection and innovation in small and medium-sized enterprises: The moderating effect of regional digitalization. *Journal of Small Business and Entrepreneurship*, 1–21. Advance online publication. 10.1080/08276331.2024.2315541

Xu, S., Jiang, M., Lu, Q., Gao, S., Feng, J., Wang, X., He, X., Chen, K., Li, Y., & Ouyang, P. (2020). Properties of Polyvinyl Alcohol Films Composited With Hemicellulose and Nanocellulose Extracted From Artemisia selengensis Straw. *Frontiers in Bioengineering and Biotechnology*, 8, 980. Advance online publication. 10.3389/fbioe.2020.0098032984277

Xu, Y., Wang, J., Chen, Z., & Liang, C. (2021). Economic policy uncertainty and stock market returns: New evidence. *The North American Journal of Economics and Finance*, 58, 101525. 10.1016/j.najef.2021.101525

Yadav, R., & Mahara, T. (2019). An Empirical Study of Consumers Intention to Purchase Wooden Handicraft Items Online: Using Extended Technology Acceptance Model. *Global Business Review*, 20(2), 479–497. 10.1177/0972150917713899

Yadav, U. S., Tripathi, R., Rena, R., Khan, S. A., & Ghosal, I. (2025). Use and Effect of Fintech Awareness in Women for Sustainable Development in Small Industry during COVID-19 Pandemic: An Empirical Analysis with UTUAT model. *International Journal of Electronic Finance*. Advance online publication. 10.1504/IJEF.2025.10062118

Yang, Q., & Lee, Y. C. (2019). An investigation of enablers and inhibitors of crowdfunding adoption: Empirical evidence from startups in China. *Human Factors and Ergonomics in Manufacturing*, 29(1), 5–21. 10.1002/hfm.20782

Yao, J., Li, H., Xu, X., Qiu, S., & Shang, D. (2022). Path of exploring opportunities in a migrant workers returning to home entrepreneurial ecosystem. *Ciência Rural*, 52(11), e20210493. Advance online publication. 10.1590/0103-8478cr20210493

Yeager, V. A., Menachemi, N., Savage, G. T., Ginter, P. M., Sen, B. P., & Beitsch, L. M. (2014). Using resource dependency theory to measure the environment in health care organizational studies. *Health Care Management Review*, 39(1), 50–65. 10.1097/HMR.0b013e318282662423358132

Ye, G., Hudders, L., De Jans, S., & De Veirman, M. (2021). The Value of Influencer Marketing for Business: A Bibliometric Analysis and Managerial Implications. *Journal of Advertising*, 50(2), 160–178. 10.1080/00913367.2020.1857888

Yeon, A. L., & Putri, U. T. (2022). Equity crowdfunding industry regulations in Malaysia and Indonesia: Prospects and challenges during the Covid-19 pandemic. *Journal of International Students*, 18, 31–62.

Yi, H., Meng, X., Linghu, Y., & Zhang, Z. (2023). Can financial capability improve entrepreneurial performance? Evidence from rural China, Economic Research-. *Ekonomska Istrazivanja*, 36(1), 1631–1650. 10.1080/1331677X.2022.2091631

Yin, G., Lu, S., & Chen, J. (2024). Exploration and Practice of the Double Helix Model for the Deep Integration of Innovation and Entrepreneurship Education with Professional Education: A Case Study of Zhejiang University. Contemporary Educational Forum. 10.13694/j.cnki.ddjylt.20240008.001

Yin, R. (2008). Case Study Research: Design and Methods. *Sage (Atlanta, Ga.)*.

Yin, Y., Crowley, F., Doran, J., Du, J., & O'Connor, M. (2023). Research and innovation and the role of competition in family owned and managed firms. *International Journal of Entrepreneurial Behaviour & Research*, 29(1), 166–194. 10.1108/IJEBR-12-2021-1031

Yin, Z., Gong, X., & Guo, P. (2019). The impact of mobile payment on entrepreneurship——micro evidence from China household finance survey. *China Industrial Economics*, (3), 119–137.

Yin, Z., Song, Q., Wu, Y., & Peng, C. (2015). Financial knowledge, entrepreneurial decision and motivation. *Guanli Shijie*, (1), 87–98.

Yiu, D., Wan, W., Ng, F., Chen, X., & Su, J. (2014). Sentimental drivers of social entrepreneurship: A study of China's guangcai (glorious) program. *Management and Organization Review*, 10(1), 55–80. 10.1111/more.12043

Yoo, Y., Henfridsson, O., & Lyytinen, K. (2010). Research commentary-the new organizing logic of digital innovation: An agenda for information systems research. *Information Systems Research*, 21(4), 724–735. 10.1287/isre.1100.0322

Compilation of References

Young, S., Hamill, J., Wheeler, S., & Davies, J. R. (1989). *International Market Entry and Development*. Prentice-Hall.

Youssef, A. B., Boubaker, S., & Omri, A. (2018). Entrepreneurship and sustainability: The need for innovative and institutional solutions. *Technological Forecasting and Social Change*, 129, 232–241. 10.1016/j.techfore.2017.11.003

Yu, C. (2020). A Perspective on Using Machine Learning in 3D Bioprinting. *International Journal of Bioprinting*, 253. https://www.ncbi.nlm.nih.gov/pmc/articles/PMC7415853/32782987

Yusuf, M., Surya, B., Menne, F., Ruslan, M., Suriani, S., & Iskandar, I. (2022). Business agility and competitive advantage of SMEs in Makassar City, Indonesia. *Sustainability (Basel)*, 15(1), 627. 10.3390/su15010627

Zahara, Z., Ikhsan, , Santi, I. N., & Farid, . (2023). Entrepreneurial marketing and marketing performance through digital marketing capabilities of SMEs in post-pandemic recovery. *Cogent Business & Management*, 10(2), 2204592. 10.1080/23311975.2023.2204592

Zahra, S. A., Hayton, J. C., & Salvato, C. (2004). Entrepreneurship in family vs. non–family firms: A resource–based analysis of the effect of organizational culture. *Entrepreneurship Theory and Practice*, 28(4), 363–381. 10.1111/j.1540-6520.2004.00051.x

Zainal, M. (2022). Innovation orientation and performance of Kuwaiti family businesses: Evidence from the initial period of COVID-19 pandemic. *Journal of Family Business Management*, 12(2), 251–265. 10.1108/JFBM-09-2020-0086

Zapata-Cantu, L., Sanguino, R., Barroso, A., & Nicola-Gavrilă, L. (2023). Family business adapting a new digital-based economy: Opportunities and challenges for future research. *Journal of the Knowledge Economy*, 14(1), 408–425. 10.1007/s13132-021-00871-1

Zellweger, T. M., Nason, R. S., & Nordqvist, M. (2012). From longevity of firms to transgenerational entrepreneurship of families: Introducing family entrepreneurial orientation. *Family Business Review*, 25(2), 136–155. 10.1177/0894486511423531

Zellweger, T. M., Nason, R. S., Nordqvist, M., & Brush, C. G. (2013). Why do family firms strive for nonfinancial goals? An organizational identity perspective. *Entrepreneurship Theory and Practice*, 37(2), 229–248. 10.1111/j.1540-6520.2011.00466.x

Zhang, X., Hu, L., Salimath, M., & Kuo, C. (2018). Developing evaluation frameworks for business models in China's rural markets. *Sustainability (Basel)*, 11(1), 118. 10.3390/su11010118

Zhao, F. (2006). Entrepreneurship and innovation in e-business: An integrative perspective. In Zhao, F. (Ed.), *Entrepreneurship and Innovations in EBusiness: An Integrative Perspective* (pp. 1–17). Igi Global.

Zhao, J., & Tian-cheng, L. (2021). Social capital, financial literacy, and rural household entrepreneurship: A mediating effect analysis. *Frontiers in Psychology*, 12, 724605. Advance online publication. 10.3389/fpsyg.2021.72460534512479

Zheng, H., Li, D., Wu, J., & Xu, Y. (2014). The role of multidimensional social capital in crowdfunding: A comparative study in China and US. *Information & Management*, 51(4), 488–496. 10.1016/j.im.2014.03.003

Zhou, W., Li, X., Duan, H., & Pengyu, L. (2021). Multi-Material Integrated Three-Dimensional Printing of Cylindrical Li-Ion Battery. Journal of Manufacturing Science and Engineering. https://www.sciencedirect.com/science/article/pii/S1226086X17301559

Zhu, H., Chen, Y., & Chen, K. (2019). Vitalizing rural communities: China's rural entrepreneurial activities from the perspective of mixed embeddedness. *Sustainability (Basel)*, 11(6), 1609. 10.3390/su11061609

Zhu, H., & Zhou, Z. Z. (2016). Analysis and outlook of applications of blockchain technology to equity crowdfunding in China. *Financial Innovation*, 2(1), 1–11. 10.1186/s40854-016-0044-7

Zhu, K., Kraemer, K., & Xu, S. (2006). The process of innovation assimilation by firms in different countries: A technology diffusion perspective on e-business. *Management Science*, 52(10), 1557–1576. 10.1287/mnsc.1050.0487

Zin, L., & Ibrahim, H. (2020). The influence of entrepreneurial supports on business performance among rural entrepreneurs. *Annals of Contemporary Developments in Management & HR*, 2(1), 31–41. 10.33166/ACDMHR.2020.01.004

Zulkiffli, N. A., & Padlee, F. (2021). Sustainable outsourcing decisions, competitive capabilities and business performance of Malaysian manufacturing SMEs: A confirmatory factor analysis approach. *Journal of Sustainability Science and Management*, 16(1), 158–173. 10.46754/jssm.2021.01.014

About the Contributors

Ahmad Rafiki is currently as an Associate Professor in the Faculty of Economics and Business of Universitas Medan Area, Indonesia. He awarded Doctor of Philosophy from Islamic Science University of Malaysia. He has published many chapters of books/authored books and articles related to Islamic management, entrepreneurship, SMEs, leadership and halal industry by International publishers such as IBA-MacMillan, IGI Global, Emerald Publishing, Springer, Routledge etc. He also became the editorial advisory board and reviewer in reputable publishers of Emerald and Elsevier. He just won as the Outstanding Reviewer of Literati Awards 2020 by Emerald Publishing.

Sylvia Nabila Azwa Ambad has been serving as a senior lecturer at UiTM Sabah Branch since 2014. She has supervised over 30 postgraduate students, with 12 PhD and Master students graduating under her guidance as the main supervisor. Her fervor for research is evident through her engagement in projects that have garnered research grants exceeding RM1 million. Moreover, she boasts a portfolio of over 80 published works. Complementing her academic endeavors, she actively participates in innovation competitions, having secured more than 20 innovation awards. She is also actively involved in international collaboration, serving as an invited speaker, editor, and steering committee member for various international conferences and seminars.

Nor Farradila Abdul Aziz is a Senior Lecturer at the Faculty of Business and Management, Universiti Teknologi MARA (Shah Alam) and graduated from La Trobe University, Melbourne for PhD Degree. Her research interest are corporate finance and financial markets, microstructure and information.

* * *

Betül Açıkgöz is currently employed as an Assistant Professor at the Faculty of Economics and Administrative Sciences of Yozgat Bozok University in Turkey. She has a PhD in Accounting from Rutgers, The State University of New Jersey, a Master of Science in Accountancy from the University of Illinois at Urbana-Champaign, and a Bachelor of Science in Business Administration from Gazi University in Ankara, Türkiye. Financial accounting, international accounting standards, and FinTech comprise her research interests. She has authored numerous papers in these areas. She aspires to make a significant contribution to the academic literature through her exceptional publications.

About the Contributors

Kathirvel Ayyaswamy acquired, B.E. (CSE), M.E. (CSE) from Crescent Engineering College affiliated to University of Madras and Ph. D (CSE.) from Anna University. He is currently working as Professor, Dept of Computer Science and Engineering, Karunya Institute of Technology and Sciences, Coimbatore. He is a studious researcher by himself, completed 18 sponsored research projects worth of Rs 103 lakhs and published more than 110 articles in journals and conferences. 4 research scholars have completed Ph. D and 3 under progress under his guidance. He is working as scientific and editorial board member of many journals. He has reviewed dozens of papers in many journals. He has author of 13 books. His research interests are protocol development for wireless ad hoc networks, security in ad hoc network, data communication and networks, mobile computing, wireless networks, WSN and DTN. He is a Life member of the ISTE (India), IACSIT (Singapore), Life Member IAENG (Hong Kong), Member ICST (Europe), IAES, etc. He has given a number of guest lecturers/expert talks and seminars, workshops and symposiums.

C. V. Suresh Babu is a pioneer in content development. A true entrepreneur, he founded Anniyappa Publications, a company that is highly active in publishing books related to Computer Science and Management. Dr. C.V. Suresh Babu has also ventured into SB Institute, a center for knowledge transfer. He holds a Ph.D. in Engineering Education from the National Institute of Technical Teachers Training & Research in Chennai, along with seven master's degrees in various disciplines such as Engineering, Computer Applications, Management, Commerce, Economics, Psychology, Law, and Education. Additionally, he has UGC-NET/SET qualifications in the fields of Computer Science, Management, Commerce, and Education. Currently, Dr. C.V. Suresh Babu is a Professor in the Department of Information Technology at the School of Computing Science, Hindustan Institute of Technology and Science (Hindustan University) in Padur, Chennai, Tamil Nadu, India. For more information, you can visit his personal blog at https://sites.google.com/view/cvsureshbabu/.

Tugba Erhan, PhD, is an assistant professor of business at Suleyman Demirel University. Tugba earned her BA in English Language from Uludag University and her PhD in business from Suleyman Demirel University. Her research interests focus on employee behaviors, approaches to work as calling, and decent work. Tugba loves spending time in nature, taking photos of nature and swimming. She lives with her husband Mustafa and their daughter in Isparta, Turkey.

Şerife Karagöz earned PhD degree management and organization from Süleyman Demirel University in Turkey. She earned her BA in Business from Akdeniz University and her master degree management and organization from Mehmet Akif Ersoy University. Her research interests are positive psychology, behavioral science and organizational behavior.

Shad Ahmad Khan is serving as Assistant Professor in College of Business, University of Buraimi in Sultanate of Oman. He is an active researcher who has a professional strength in the area of Business Management and Marketing. He has a vast experience of organizing international events like conferences and seminars. His area of interest is Data Sciences, green practices, entrepreneurship, administration sciences and marketing.

M. Shabri Abd. Majid, M.Ec, is a Professor in Islamic Economics at the Faculty of Economics and Business, Universitas Syiah Kuala, Indonesia. He received his Sarjana Ekonomi (SE) from Syiah Kuala University, Indonesia, in 1995. He completed his Master of Economics (M.Ec) and Ph.D. in Financial Economics from the International Islamic University Malaysia (IIUM) in 1998 and 2005. He has served Kulliyyah of Economics and Management Sciences (KENMS) IIUM as the Assistant Professor (2011-2008) and the Associate Professor for six years (2009-2011). He has been Currently, he is the Coordinator, the Ph.D. in Economics at the Universitas Syiah Kuala (USK), Indonesia. His research interests include financial economics, applied econometrics, Islamic economics, banking, and finance. He has published more than 100 articles in international journal.

João Gonçalo Martins is currently enrolled as a Master's degree student in Management, specializing in Corporate Finance at the University of Aveiro. He holds a Bachelor's degree in Business Management from Coimbra Business School. With practical experience in the consulting industry, he has been actively engaged in Global Compliance and Reporting projects, collaborating with a diverse range of international clients across various industries.

About the Contributors

Mazurina Mohd Ali is an Associate Professor at the Faculty of Accountancy, Universiti Teknologi MARA (UiTM), Selangor, Puncak Alam Campus. She obtained her PhD in accounting from the Royal Melbourne Institute of Technology (RMIT), Melbourne, Australia in 2013; Master of Accountancy from UiTM, Shah Alam in 2007 and Bachelor of Accountancy (Hons) from UiTM in 2002. She has been with UiTM since 2008. Dr Mazurina teaches undergraduate and postgraduate students in the accounting-related subjects including risk management and research methodology. Dr Mazurina also supervises master's and doctoral students in her area of expertise. Her main research interest area is financial accounting and reporting. She has published and presented papers in that area.

António C. Moreira obtained a Bachelor's degree in Electrical Engineering and a Master's degree in Management, both from the University of Porto, Portugal. He received his Ph.D. in Management from the University of Manchester, England. He has a solid international background in industry leveraged working for a multinational company in Germany as well as in Portugal. He has also been involved in consultancy projects and research activities. He is an Associate Professor at the Department of Economics, Management, Industrial Engineering, and Tourism, University of Aveiro, Portugal. He is a member of GOVCOPP research unit.

Cynthia Robert Dawayan is a staff member of the Faculty of Business and Management, Universiti Teknologi MARA (UiTM). She is currently attached to UiTM Sabah Branch, Kota Kinabalu Campus. Her passion in the tourism industry has led her to take up a Diploma in Tourism Management following the completion of high school. She then continued studying BSc. (Hons.) Tourism Management, after which she decided to join the industry to gain real life experience. After a while, Cynthia decided to further her knowledge and skills in the marketing field, by continuing her studies taking MBA (Marketing) in Universiti Malaysia Sabah (UMS) and finally landed herself a permanent lecturing job at UiTM Sabah Branch. While working, Cynthia pursued her Phd in Marketing in UMS, where she focused her studies in homestay marketing. She graduated in 2021, despite having to face lockdowns and the uncertainties of Covid-19 while writing her thesis. Over the years Cynthia has authored and co-authored several journals, newspaper articles as well as chapters in books.

Wasswa Shafik (Member, IEEE) received a Bachelor of Science degree in information technology engineering with a minor in mathematics from Ndejje University, Kampala, Uganda, a Master of Engineering degree in information technology engineering (MIT) from Yazd University, Iran, and a Ph.D. degree in computer science with the School of Digital Science, Universiti Brunei Darussalam, Brunei Darussalam. He is also the Founder and a Principal Investigator of the Dig Connectivity Research Laboratory (DCRLab) after serving as a Research Associate at Network Interconnectivity Research Laboratory, Yazd University. Prior to this, he worked as a Community Data Analyst at Population Services International (PSI-Uganda), Community Data Officer at Programme for Accessible Health Communication (PACE-Uganda), Research Assistant at the Socio-Economic Data Centre (SEDC-Uganda), Prime Minister's Office, Kampala, Uganda, an Assistant Data Officer at TechnoServe, Kampala, IT Support at Thurayya Islam Media, Uganda, and Asmaah Charity Organization. He has more than 60 publications in renowned journals and conferences. His research interests include Computer Vision, AI-enabled IoT/IoMTs, Smart Cities.

Nidhi Sharma is currently working as a research scholar at Chandigarh University, Mohali, India. Her research interest includes social media, destination marketing, travel and ecotourism. She has published several papers and book chapters in reputed journals and books.

Bernadine Adel Sitorus is currently enrolled as a graduate student pursuing her Master's of Science (Business Management) at Universiti Teknologi MARA Sabah Branch, Kota Kinabalu Campus. Her academic journey begins with the completion of a Bachelor's Degree in Business Administration with Honours in Marketing from UiTM Sabah in 2020. Driven by a profound interest in the dynamic realm of digital marketing, Bernadine had chosen to specialise in this field for her master's degree. She is particularly intrigued by the substantial impact of Social Media Influencers (SMIs) on consumer behaviour, leading her to dedicate her research endeavours to an exploration of this phenomenon.

About the Contributors

Hasan Huseyin Uzunbacak received his Master's degree and PhD in Business Administration Department in Suleyman Demirel University. He is working in Suleyman Demirel University, Turkey, since 2017. He studies on organizational behavior in his academic studies. Especially his interested topics consist of leadership, positive organizational behavior, HRM, employee empowerment and career planning.

Zhang Xiaohan is a distinguished academic in Artistic Design, holding a Ph.D. from Universiti Teknologi MARA with a specialization in Fashion Design. Her research, which has been published in reputable international databases including Scopus, explores the integration of cultural elements into contemporary fashion and their role in global cultural exchange. With a Master's degree in Drama and Film Studies from Shandong Art Institute, she has extensive practical experience in theatrical makeup and costume design. Currently, she is a faculty member at Shandong University of Science and Technology, where she develops and teaches courses integrating cultural aesthetics into modern design practices. Dr. Zhang is poised to lead advancements in immersive performance arts within the cultural and tourism sectors.

Rohana Zur is a prominent academic in the field of Fashion Design, renowned for her extensive research on sustainable fashion design and fashion entrepreneurship. She holds a doctoral degree and has made significant contributions to the academic community through her high-quality publications. Dr. Zur's work focuses on the integration of sustainability principles within the fashion industry, exploring innovative approaches to reduce environmental impact and promote ethical practices. Her research also delves into the dynamics of fashion entrepreneurship, examining strategies for success in the rapidly evolving fashion market. As a thought leader, Dr. Zur is committed to shaping the future of fashion with sustainability and innovation at its core.

Index

A

Accounting 50, 52, 96, 105, 179, 181, 187, 194, 221, 225, 227, 243, 244, 245, 246, 247, 251, 253, 315, 358
Affiliate Marketing 21, 22, 23, 24, 26, 27, 28, 29, 32, 33, 35, 36, 37, 40, 41, 42, 44, 45, 46, 47
Agriculture Field 157
Algorithmic Decision-Making 112, 114, 117, 123, 125, 132
Alternative Finance 251
Amanah 416

B

B2B Relationships 316, 332, 333
Bibliometric Analysis 44, 109, 294, 296, 299, 308, 309, 310, 312
Blockchain 10, 14, 67, 133, 137, 138, 139, 140, 141, 142, 143, 144, 145, 146, 147, 148, 155, 157, 162, 222, 236, 254
Business Model Innovation 20, 47, 164, 165, 172, 174, 175, 182, 183, 186, 187, 189, 191, 194, 262, 266, 270, 370

C

Candidate Elimination Algorithms 110, 111, 112, 113, 114, 115, 116, 117, 118, 119, 124, 125, 132, 133
Challenges 5, 6, 7, 9, 11, 13, 17, 18, 19, 42, 45, 49, 51, 52, 54, 57, 58, 59, 63, 65, 72, 74, 113, 116, 117, 134, 135, 149, 155, 161, 165, 166, 169, 185, 186, 189, 201, 208, 222, 226, 235, 237, 242, 253, 254, 255, 256, 257, 258, 259, 260, 261, 262, 263, 264, 268, 269, 270, 271, 273, 274, 275, 278, 280, 281, 282, 283, 284, 285, 286, 295, 296, 298, 299, 300, 305, 309, 310, 312, 315, 319, 321, 325, 326, 327, 328, 334, 345, 346, 347, 350, 351, 353, 354, 355, 356, 357

Consumer Buying Intention 21, 22, 23, 37
Content Analysis 77, 82, 233, 257, 273, 275, 276
Cosmetics 89, 91, 92, 95, 100, 106
Crowdfunding 225, 226, 227, 228, 229, 230, 231, 232, 233, 234, 235, 236, 237, 238, 239, 240, 241, 242, 243, 245, 246, 247, 248, 249, 250, 251, 252, 253, 254
Cryptocurrencies 137, 138, 140, 157, 162
Curriculum Development 344, 347, 351, 356, 365
Customer Satisfaction 79, 156, 385, 406, 407, 408, 410, 413, 415

D

DART Framework 371, 382, 386, 387, 391, 393, 399, 400
Digital Financial Capabilities 77, 80, 82, 83, 84, 85
Digital Innovation 1, 2, 3, 4, 6, 7, 8, 9, 11, 12, 13, 14, 15, 16, 17, 18, 19, 20, 365
Digitalization 2, 3, 8, 9, 10, 12, 13, 18, 20, 22, 26, 79, 80, 84, 87, 110, 111, 113, 114, 116, 119, 134, 135, 136, 184, 194, 346
Digital Literacy 57, 79, 81, 83, 84, 87, 344, 345, 346, 347, 368, 370
Digital Marketing Strategies 111, 169, 344

E

East African Community 210
Economic Growth 2, 3, 8, 50, 73, 79, 80, 165, 166, 189, 192, 199, 225, 226, 229, 230, 247, 256, 257, 258, 259, 260, 261, 262, 271, 274, 295
Emerging Markets 61, 72, 135, 192, 225, 227, 228, 229, 230, 247, 249, 250, 287, 306, 308, 312
Entrepreneurial Marketing 164, 169, 172, 173, 175, 177, 178, 180, 181, 184, 186, 187, 190, 191, 193, 194, 196, 197, 275, 276, 287
Entrepreneurial Marketing Strategy 164, 172
Entrepreneurial Performance 77, 79, 81,

82, 83, 84, 85, 87, 88
Entrepreneurial Strategies 137, 164, 165, 167, 168, 172, 174, 178, 183, 185, 353, 355
Entrepreneurship 1, 2, 3, 4, 5, 6, 7, 8, 9, 10, 11, 12, 13, 14, 15, 16, 17, 18, 19, 20, 28, 39, 44, 46, 47, 55, 56, 57, 66, 69, 71, 72, 73, 74, 75, 80, 81, 82, 86, 87, 88, 136, 155, 165, 169, 186, 187, 188, 189, 191, 192, 193, 194, 197, 199, 201, 213, 214, 219, 220, 226, 228, 233, 242, 247, 249, 250, 251, 252, 255, 256, 257, 258, 259, 260, 261, 262, 263, 264, 265, 266, 267, 268, 269, 270, 271, 272, 274, 275, 280, 281, 287, 288, 289, 291, 292, 293, 294, 298, 312, 313, 314, 335, 336, 338, 339, 343, 344, 345, 346, 347, 348, 349, 350, 353, 354, 355, 356, 357, 358, 359, 360, 361, 362, 363, 364, 365, 366, 367, 368, 369, 370
Exhibition 371, 372, 373, 374, 375, 376, 377, 380, 381, 382, 383, 384, 385, 387, 388, 389, 390, 391, 392, 393, 394, 395, 396, 397, 398, 399, 400, 403, 405
Experiential Learning 346, 355
Exports 4, 50, 320, 321, 326, 327, 329, 333, 336, 342

F

Family Business 270, 275, 280, 281, 286, 287, 288, 289, 290, 291, 292, 293, 294, 297, 305, 306, 307, 308, 313, 314, 315, 338, 339
Family-Owned Businesses 273, 274, 275, 277, 278, 280, 331
Family-Owned SMEs 294, 295, 296, 298, 308, 309
Fashion Design 343, 344, 345, 347, 348, 349, 350, 351, 352, 353, 354, 355, 356, 357, 358, 359, 360, 361, 364, 365, 366, 367, 369
Financial Reporting 225, 227, 228, 243, 244, 245, 246, 247, 249, 250
Future Directions 135, 264, 276, 288

G

Global Business Landscape 63, 294
Green Purchase Behaviors 198, 203, 206, 209, 217

H

Healthcare Sector 141, 157

I

IFRS 225, 243, 244, 245, 246, 247
Incremental Innovation 273, 274, 275, 276, 277, 278, 281, 282, 285, 289, 291, 292
Influencer Marketing 89, 90, 91, 93, 94, 100, 102, 106, 107, 109
Innovation 1, 2, 3, 4, 5, 6, 7, 8, 9, 10, 11, 12, 13, 14, 15, 16, 17, 18, 19, 20, 44, 47, 49, 50, 53, 55, 56, 57, 58, 60, 61, 66, 67, 68, 69, 71, 73, 74, 75, 79, 80, 82, 84, 85, 87, 134, 135, 136, 141, 157, 159, 160, 164, 165, 168, 169, 170, 172, 173, 174, 175, 177, 178, 179, 180, 181, 182, 183, 184, 186, 187, 188, 189, 190, 191, 192, 193, 194, 195, 196, 198, 201, 206, 209, 211, 212, 215, 219, 220, 221, 222, 233, 234, 238, 249, 250, 251, 252, 253, 254, 256, 258, 262, 264, 266, 267, 269, 270, 272, 273, 274, 275, 276, 277, 278, 279, 280, 281, 282, 283, 284, 285, 286, 287, 288, 289, 290, 291, 292, 294, 295, 296, 297, 298, 306, 307, 308, 310, 312, 313, 315, 317, 320, 327, 330, 334, 336, 338, 340, 345, 348, 349, 354, 355, 357, 361, 364, 365, 366, 368, 369, 370, 372, 373, 375, 376, 377, 380, 382, 383, 384, 402, 403, 404
Innovative Business 155, 226, 256, 257, 260, 261, 262, 263, 265, 266
Innovative Entrepreneurship Education 343, 344, 346, 347, 348, 354, 355, 361, 365, 367
Integration 7, 9, 35, 43, 51, 57, 67, 111, 115, 116, 119, 133, 145, 147, 158, 165, 169, 217, 223, 259, 261, 262, 263, 310, 337, 343, 345, 346, 347, 348, 349, 350, 352, 353, 354, 355,

356, 357, 358, 360, 361, 362, 364, 365, 366, 367, 369, 370

Internationalization 51, 54, 56, 67, 71, 73, 74, 75, 110, 111, 112, 113, 114, 116, 118, 123, 134, 135, 219, 285, 292, 294, 295, 296, 297, 298, 299, 300, 304, 305, 306, 308, 309, 310, 311, 312, 313, 314, 315, 316, 317, 318, 319, 323, 324, 325, 326, 328, 330, 331, 333, 334, 335, 336, 337, 338, 339, 340, 341

J

Job Creation 50, 79, 166, 256, 257, 258, 274

M

MICE 372, 373, 374, 376, 382, 385, 401, 405

MSMEs 53, 72, 73, 77, 78, 79, 80, 82, 83, 84, 85, 87, 235, 249

N

Network Theory 240, 277, 298, 324

P

Perceived Price 372, 387, 391, 392, 399, 400

Perceived Quality 33, 372, 387, 391, 392, 399, 400

Perceived Value 33, 371, 372, 374, 381, 382, 383, 384, 387, 388, 389, 390, 391, 392, 393, 395, 399, 400, 401, 402

R

Real-Time Marketing 111, 112, 113, 114, 115, 116, 118, 119, 124, 125, 132

Religiosity 406, 407, 408, 409, 410, 412, 413, 414, 415

Research Trends 314

Rural Entrepreneurship 255, 256, 257, 258, 259, 260, 261, 262, 263, 264, 265, 266, 267, 268, 269, 270

S

Service Quality 42, 320, 406, 407, 408, 409, 410, 413, 414, 415

Small and Medium Enterprises 21, 22, 40, 42, 52, 54, 56, 72, 74, 80, 114, 164, 166, 184, 186, 191, 192, 194, 198, 204, 219, 220, 221, 222, 223, 241, 249, 267, 268, 314, 335

SMEs 18, 21, 22, 23, 26, 27, 28, 29, 30, 35, 36, 37, 39, 42, 44, 45, 46, 47, 49, 50, 51, 52, 53, 54, 55, 56, 57, 58, 59, 60, 61, 62, 63, 64, 65, 66, 67, 68, 69, 71, 72, 73, 74, 75, 76, 78, 87, 89, 90, 101, 111, 112, 113, 114, 115, 117, 118, 119, 123, 124, 125, 132, 133, 134, 135, 136, 164, 165, 166, 167, 168, 169, 170, 171, 172, 173, 174, 175, 177, 179, 180, 181, 182, 183, 184, 185, 186, 187, 188, 189, 190, 191, 192, 193, 194, 195, 196, 197, 198, 199, 200, 201, 202, 203, 204, 205, 206, 207, 208, 209, 210, 211, 212, 213, 214, 215, 216, 217, 218, 219, 221, 222, 223, 226, 230, 232, 238, 239, 244, 245, 249, 250, 253, 262, 294, 295, 296, 297, 298, 299, 300, 301, 302, 303, 304, 305, 306, 307, 308, 309, 310, 312, 313, 314, 315, 317, 319, 320, 321, 322, 323, 324, 331, 333, 336, 338, 339, 402

Social Media 7, 10, 11, 21, 22, 23, 24, 25, 26, 27, 28, 29, 32, 33, 35, 36, 37, 39, 40, 41, 43, 44, 45, 46, 47, 48, 53, 58, 74, 80, 84, 90, 91, 92, 93, 100, 101, 102, 103, 104, 105, 106, 107, 108, 109, 111, 112, 113, 114, 116, 118, 119, 120, 123, 124, 125, 132, 135, 136, 140, 156, 219, 236, 372, 379

Source Credibility Model 91, 95, 101

Strategic Partnerships 164, 169, 170, 172, 173, 178, 182, 184, 186, 212, 295, 310

Sustainability 3, 6, 7, 8, 12, 13, 14, 17, 19, 33, 41, 44, 45, 46, 49, 53, 54, 56, 57, 58, 60, 61, 62, 64, 66, 68, 69, 71, 73, 74, 75, 76, 79, 80, 85, 87, 133, 134, 135, 165, 166, 167, 170, 171, 186, 189, 190, 191, 192, 193, 194, 195, 197,

198, 199, 204, 205, 206, 208, 209,
210, 213, 214, 215, 216, 217, 218,
219, 221, 222, 223, 233, 255, 256,
260, 261, 262, 263, 264, 265, 266,
268, 269, 270, 271, 272, 273, 274,
275, 278, 279, 285, 289, 309, 310,
314, 327, 344, 345, 346, 348, 349,
354, 357, 365, 368, 369, 405

Sustainable Performance 53, 61, 62, 75, 164, 165, 166, 171, 172, 173, 174, 175, 177, 178, 179, 180, 181, 182, 183, 184, 185, 191

Symbiotic Relationship 27, 343, 361

T

Taxation 231, 245, 246, 248
Technological Innovation 141, 164, 172, 177, 178, 180, 186, 206, 209, 233, 253, 262, 270, 278, 284, 285, 288, 402

TikTok 89, 90, 91, 92, 93, 95, 96, 100, 101, 102, 104, 108

U

Uganda 87, 167, 198, 199, 200, 201, 202, 203, 204, 205, 206, 207, 208, 209, 210, 213, 214, 215, 216, 219, 220, 221, 222, 223

Uppsala 298, 316, 317, 323, 324, 331, 332, 333, 334, 336, 338, 340, 341, 342

V

Value Co-Creation 41, 371, 372, 377, 378, 380, 382, 383, 385, 386, 387, 388, 390, 391, 392, 393, 395, 399, 400, 401, 402, 405

Vocational College 343, 358, 361, 364
VOSviewer 299, 301, 303, 304, 306, 308

Publishing Tomorrow's Research Today

Uncover Current Insights and Future Trends in
Business & Management
with IGI Global's Cutting-Edge Recommended Books

Print Only, E-Book Only, or Print + E-Book.
Order direct through IGI Global's Online Bookstore at www.igi-global.com or through your preferred provider.

ISBN: 9798369306444
© 2023; 436 pp.
List Price: US$ 230

ISBN: 9798369300084
© 2023; 358 pp.
List Price: US$ 250

ISBN: 9781668458594
© 2023; 366 pp.
List Price: US$ 240

ISBN: 9781668486344
© 2023; 256 pp.
List Price: US$ 280

ISBN: 9781668493243
© 2024; 318 pp.
List Price: US$ 250

ISBN: 9798369304181
© 2023; 415 pp.
List Price: US$ 250

Do you want to stay current on the latest research trends, product announcements, news, and special offers?
Join IGI Global's mailing list to receive customized recommendations, exclusive discounts, and more.
Sign up at: www.igi-global.com/newsletters.

Scan the QR Code here to view more related titles in Business & Management.

www.igi-global.com | Sign up at www.igi-global.com/newsletters | facebook.com/igiglobal | twitter.com/igiglobal | linkedin.com/igiglobal

Ensure Quality Research is Introduced to the Academic Community

Become a Reviewer for IGI Global Authored Book Projects

  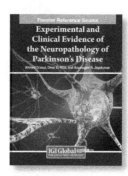 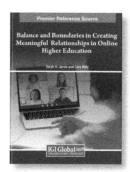

The overall success of an authored book project is dependent on quality and timely manuscript evaluations.

Applications and Inquiries may be sent to:
development@igi-global.com

Applicants must have a doctorate (or equivalent degree) as well as publishing, research, and reviewing experience. Authored Book Evaluators are appointed for one-year terms and are expected to complete at least three evaluations per term. Upon successful completion of this term, evaluators can be considered for an additional term.

If you have a colleague that may be interested in this opportunity, we encourage you to share this information with them.

IGI Global's Open Access Journal Program
Publishing Tomorrow's Research Today

Including Nearly 200 Peer-Reviewed, Gold (Full) Open Access Journals across IGI Global's Three Academic Subject Areas: Business & Management; Scientific, Technical, and Medical (STM); and Education

Consider Submitting Your Manuscript to One of These Nearly 200 Open Access Journals for to Increase Their Discoverability & Citation Impact

Web of Science Impact Factor 6.5	Web of Science Impact Factor 4.7	Web of Science Impact Factor 3.2	Web of Science Impact Factor 2.6
JOURNAL OF **Organizational and End User Computing**	JOURNAL OF **Global Information Management**	INTERNATIONAL JOURNAL ON **Semantic Web and Information Systems**	JOURNAL OF **Database Management**

Choosing IGI Global's Open Access Journal Program Can Greatly Increase the Reach of Your Research

Higher Usage — Open access papers are 2-3 times more likely to be read than non-open access papers.

Higher Download Rates — Open access papers benefit from 89% higher download rates than non-open access papers.

Higher Citation Rates — Open access papers are 47% more likely to be cited than non-open access papers.

Submitting an article to a journal offers an invaluable opportunity for you to share your work with the broader academic community, fostering knowledge dissemination and constructive feedback.

Submit an Article and Browse the IGI Global Call for Papers Pages

We can work with you to find the journal most well-suited for your next research manuscript.
For open access publishing support, contact: journaleditor@igi-global.com

Publishing Tomorrow's Research Today
IGI Global
e-Book Collection

Including Essential Reference Books Within Three Fundamental Academic Areas

Business & Management
Scientific, Technical, & Medical (STM)
Education

- Acquisition options include Perpetual, Subscription, and Read & Publish
- No Additional Charge for Multi-User Licensing
- No Maintenance, Hosting, or Archiving Fees
- Continually Enhanced Accessibility Compliance Features (WCAG)

| Over **150,000+** Chapters | Contributions From **200,000+** Scholars Worldwide | More Than **1,000,000+** Citations | Majority of e-Books Indexed in Web of Science & Scopus | Consists of Tomorrow's Research Available Today! |

Recommended Titles from our e-Book Collection

Innovation Capabilities and Entrepreneurial Opportunities of Smart Working
ISBN: 9781799887973

Advanced Applications of Generative AI and Natural Language Processing Models
ISBN: 9798369305027

Using Influencer Marketing as a Digital Business Strategy
ISBN: 9798369305515

Human-Centered Approaches in Industry 5.0
ISBN: 9798369326473

Modeling and Monitoring Extreme Hydrometeorological Events
ISBN: 9781668487716

Data-Driven Intelligent Business Sustainability
ISBN: 9798369300497

Information Logistics for Organizational Empowerment and Effective Supply Chain Management
ISBN: 9798369301593

Data Envelopment Analysis (DEA) Methods for Maximizing Efficiency
ISBN: 9798369302552

Request More Information, or Recommend the IGI Global e-Book Collection to Your Institution's Librarian

For More Information or to Request a Free Trial, Contact IGI Global's e-Collections Team: eresources@igi-global.com | 1-866-342-6657 ext. 100 | 717-533-8845 ext. 100

Are You Ready to Publish Your Research?

IGI Global — Publishing Tomorrow's Research Today

IGI Global offers book authorship and editorship opportunities across three major subject areas, including Business, STM, and Education.

Benefits of Publishing with IGI Global:

- Free one-on-one editorial and promotional support.
- Expedited publishing timelines that can take your book from start to finish in less than one (1) year.
- Choose from a variety of formats, including Edited and Authored References, Handbooks of Research, Encyclopedias, and Research Insights.
- Utilize IGI Global's eEditorial Discovery® submission system in support of conducting the submission and double-blind peer review process.
- IGI Global maintains a strict adherence to ethical practices due in part to our full membership with the Committee on Publication Ethics (COPE).
- Indexing potential in prestigious indices such as Scopus®, Web of Science™, PsycINFO®, and ERIC – Education Resources Information Center.
- Ability to connect your ORCID iD to your IGI Global publications.
- Earn honorariums and royalties on your full book publications as well as complimentary content and exclusive discounts.

Join Your Colleagues from Prestigious Institutions, Including:

Australian National University
Massachusetts Institute of Technology
Johns Hopkins University
Harvard University
Columbia University in the City of New York

Learn More at: www.igi-global.com/publish
or by Contacting the Acquisitions Department at: acquisition@igi-global.com

Individual Article & Chapter Downloads
US$ 37.50/each

Easily Identify, Acquire, and Utilize Published Peer-Reviewed Findings in Support of Your Current Research

- Browse Over **170,000+ Articles & Chapters**
- **Accurate & Advanced** Search
- Affordably Acquire **International Research**
- **Instantly Access** Your Content
- Benefit from the **InfoSci® Platform Features**

It really provides an excellent entry into the research literature of the field. It presents a manageable number of highly relevant sources on topics of interest to a wide range of researchers. The sources are scholarly, but also accessible to 'practitioners'.

- Ms. Lisa Stimatz, MLS, University of North Carolina at Chapel Hill, USA

Milton Keynes UK
Ingram Content Group UK Ltd.
UKHW010227300724
446304UK00005B/93